Real Estate Decisions

DONALD R. EPLEY
WASHINGTON STATE UNIVERSITY

JOSEPH S. RABIANSKI
GEORGIA STATE UNIVERSITY

RICHARD L. HANEY, JR.
TEXAS A & M UNIVERSITY

SOUTH-WESTERN
THOMSON LEARNING™

Australia · Canada · Mexico · Singapore · Spain · United Kingdom · United States

Real Estate Decisions by Donald R. Epley, Joseph S. Rabianski, Richard L. Haney, Jr.

Executive Publisher: Dave Shaut
Senior Acquisitions Editor: Scott Person
Marketing Manager: Dennis Capraro
Production Editor: Tamborah Moore
Manufacturing Coordinator: Charlene Taylor
Internal Design: Aerocraft Charter Art Service
Production House: Holcomb Hathaway
Compositor: Aerocraft Charter Art Service
Printer: Courier Westford, Inc.

ISBN 0-324-14361-3

Printed in the United States of America
    3 4 5 04

For more information contact South-Western, 5191 Natorp Blvd., Mason, Ohio, 45040. Or you can visit our Internet site at http://www.swcollege.com

For permission to use material from this text or product contact us by

• telephone: 1-800-730-2214
• fax: 1-800-730-2215
• web: http://www.thomsonrights.com

Library of Congress Cataloging-in-Publication Data

Epley, Donald R.
    Real estate decisions / Donald R. Epley, Joseph S. Rabianski, Richard L. Haney, Jr.
        p. cm.
    Includes index.
    ISBN 0-324-14361-3
    1. Real estate business.   2. Real estate business—Decision making.   I. Rabianski, Joseph.
II. Haney, Richard L.   III. Title.

    HD1375 .E643 2002
    333.33—dc21   2001018521

Contents

Part II

Part III

Part VI

THE DECISION TO MANAGE THE PROPERTY AND SEEK INFORMATION ABOUT THE LEASE

Part VII

THE DECISION TO ACQUIRE OR TRANSFER THE PROPERTY

Preface

This text makes four unique contributions. First, the material is presented in the "need to know" order that a prospective buyer or seller requires for real estate decision making. This book is organized around *decisions* and the flow of the decision-making process. Thus, the information is arranged in the order required by the typical consumer for decision making in a typical real estate transaction.

The viewpoint is that of the *consumer* who is the prospective buyer, seller, or real estate agent. The underlying question addressed is: What does the consumer need to know to make decisions in various steps of the typical real estate transaction? We suggest that prospective real estate agents or sales associates and brokers need to know the same information as consumers to represent adequately the needs of their clients.

The second contribution of the book is that legal concepts are integrated into the subject matter rather than studied as a separate topic. We view real estate law only as a tool to assist in the successful completion of a transaction. We have included a description of many detailed points within the sales contract and the lease because we view them as "decision" documents. Many of the clauses within both documents can be adapted to the needs and wishes of the parties involved. Deeds are discussed to provide the consumer with the information necessary to ascertain whether the deed is the one requested in the sales contract. The deed is not in the same class of decision documents because its components are typically predetermined and not negotiable. Consequently, the reader of this book is given only enough information to protect his or her interests instead of a detailed description of the deed's clauses and their ramifications.

Concerns regarding legal documents and questions about legal issues should rightfully be referred to an attorney for an opinion. We intend the legal material in this book to be used for educational purposes only. We define some terminology as we have encountered it in our activities; thus, this applied usage may not coincide exactly with the standard legal literature. We emphasize that this material is supplementary to and not a substitute for legal advice.

The book's third contribution is the way in which its theoretical concepts are oriented toward decision making rather than presented in a descriptive manner only. For example, students are shown in Part II, The Decision to Estimate Market Value, how the theory of value can be applied to their benefit and why they need to know it. They are also shown how the appraiser uses the three appraisal techniques.

The fourth contribution is an attempt to achieve an appropriate balance between theoretical concepts and applied material. Our hope is that a student who finishes this text will understand why a concept exists, how it works, when it should be applied in the decision process, and what the motives of the participants in the market and the transaction are.

This text is designed for a one-semester or a one-quarter course in the Principles of Real Estate. We do not presume that students have completed any prerequisites.

Each chapter is a separate entity containing the information needed to make the decision at hand. Certain material is reiterated among sections as needed.

Each chapter contains helpful teaching aids. Learning objectives are listed to guide the reader. A list of important terminology identifies key terms and concepts, which are also highlighted in the text discussion. Review questions are provided at the end of each chapter to test the student's reading comprehension. Discussion questions that give the instructor a starting point for open-end class discussion follow the review questions.

Finally, we have introduced the Internet into the fabric of the text; a website has been established for this text at **http://epley.swcollege.com**.

Any new entrant into the textbook market must pass four tests to be successful; it must be **well organized, easily teachable, pedagogically sound,** and **incorporate current technology.** We think that our text meets all these requirements. Our intention is to offer the marketplace a good alternative, and we feel we have accomplished that objective.

Acknowledgments

We would like to thank the following individuals, who reviewed this text in earlier stages and offered suggestions for its improvement: Terrence M. Clauretie, *University of Nevada, Las Vegas;* Joseph Goeters, *Houston Community College;* Larry Cowart, *Morehead State University, KY*; Theron Nelson, *University of North Dakota;* and Glenn Crellin, *Washington State University.* The book is better as a result of their efforts.

Pullman, Washington   D.R.E.
Atlanta, Georgia   J.S.R.
College Station, Texas   R.L.H

Introduction

What Is the Nature and Purpose of the Text?

Most real estate texts are topic-oriented. Typically, each chapter covers one topic in detail without much discussion of the reasons for studying one topic before or after another. For example, why are deeds examined prior to settlement statements? Why are property taxes examined after a discussion of estimating the market value of a parcel? Why are license laws examined in the first chapter of the book?

This text presents topics on a need-to-know basis; that is, topics are presented and discussed in the order in which a typical consumer encounters the need to use this information in a real estate transaction. In addition, information is presented in a decision-making framework that the reader can use to make intelligent decisions.

The consumer may be a buyer, a seller, an interested citizen, a potential agent, or an actual agent. The typical transaction is basically the same for all. The same questions arise and must be answered in approximately the same order. Exceptions may exist in the order of the topics encountered for a particular transaction, but the steps remain essentially the same for the majority of transactions.

What Are Typical Steps in the Real Estate Transaction?

A summary of the typical steps in a normal real estate transaction appears in the Contents as Parts I through VIII. The following paragraphs preview and expand upon these steps.

Step 1. The Decision to Acquire Knowledge about Real Estate

The consumer must understand the nature of real estate by first examining both the definition of real estate and the meaning of real estate as a commodity. What characteristics does it have? What restrictions are placed upon its use? In addition, the consumer must decide whether any benefits are to be gained from asking for help from one or several of the many individuals and firms that provide services. What services are provided? Who provides them? What are the advantages and disadvantages of asking for help, and should I ask? What is the role of the government in land-use development, and what are the tools commonly used? How do land-use controls influence business development and metropolitan growth?

Step 2. The Decision to Estimate Market Value

A question that the typical consumer asks very early is: What is my property worth? Immediately he or she is expected to interpret local housing trends and understand the mechanics and concepts of income-property appraisal and residential appraisal. If this task is too time-consuming, the consumer may use the services of an appraiser.

Step 3. The Decision to Finance the Transaction

All of the earlier decisions assume the buyer is able to raise the necessary cash to pay the negotiated purchase price. Later material covers the residential and commercial loan application processes and presents the types of information that the consumer will need to know to evaluate a loan application process and the contracts used in residential financing.

Step 4. The Decision to Invest in the Property

The typical consumer will inquire early about the chance of receiving a capital gain and will ask whether the property is a good buy. In addition, the typical consumer may be interested in investment real estate in order to receive a tax shelter or a capital gain from either price appreciation or mortgage reduction.

Step 5. The Decision to Buy or Sell the Property

If an agent is involved, the typical buyer or seller needs to know the economic motivations behind the agent's actions in order to evaluate the circumstances.

Step 6. The Decision to Manage the Property and Seek Information About the Lease

This step covers the principles of real estate management and includes the components of a typical lease.

Step 7. The Decision to Acquire or Transfer the Property

This step covers preparation for the closing, when the title is transferred. This chapter offers a settlement statement, and its goal is that each party to a transaction should be able to verify the accuracy of the settlement statement. The discussion also includes the types of required insurance and the deed.

Step 8. The Decision to Develop the Property

Finally, the process of converting vacant land into usable property ready for occupancy or sale is discussed.

In sum, every chapter contains the information that we believe typical buyers, sellers, and agents need to know about that step of a real estate transaction. In addition, the steps follow a central theme of "need-to-know" that presents information to the consumer as he or she would encounter it in a real transaction. The topics and their presentation in the text should allow consumers to make informed decisions about each particular set of circumstances in a particular transaction.

## PART I

The Decision to Acquire Knowledge About Real Estate

## CHAPTER 1

The Real Estate Commodity in a Legal Environment

1. What is real estate?

2. What is the nature of the real estate business?

3. What is the relationship among participants in the real estate business?

4. What do the participants in the real estate business offer a potential buyer or seller?

When finished with this chapter, the student should be able to:

1. Explain the nature of real estate by analyzing its physical and ownership components.

2. Identify the economic characteristics of real estate.

3. Describe the various services an agent can offer a client.

4. Explain the differences among an agent, a REALTOR®, a REALTOR®-ASSOCIATE, and an agent who holds a designation in a specialty.

5. Explain the differences among the Real Estate Commission, the National Association of REALTORS®, the State Association of REALTORS®, and the local board.

6. Identify the other professionals who contribute to the real estate business and explain the services that each offers to a prospective buyer or seller.

7. Identify the current trends of the real estate business.

air rights

appraiser

bundle of rights

community property

curtesy

dower

equity funds

escrow agent

estate for years

estate from year to year

estate in expectancy

estate in possession

estate *pur autre vie*

fee simple estate

fixture

freehold estate

general agent

general contractor

holdover tenant

improvements

joint tenancy

land

leasehold

less-than-freehold estate

life estate

mineral rights

multiplier effect

National Association of REALTORS®

property manager

real estate

real estate agent

real estate attorney

real estate business

real estate commission

real estate commissioner

real estate counselor

real estate developer

real estate lender

real property

REALTOR®

REALTOR®-ASSOCIATE

realty

remainder

reversion

rights of ownership

situs

special agency

tenancy at will

tenancy by sufferance

tenancy by the entirety

tenancy in common

title company

unity of interest

unity of possession

unity of time

unity of title

waste

INTRODUCTION

The reader is about to embark on a fascinating journey into the world of real estate. As indicated in the introduction, this world is discussed in the order that a typical consumer will discover it and ask questions. The material should provide a good understanding of the *physical* side with terms, concepts, calculations, and legal documents that are important to the transaction. Also, it includes a periodic discussion of the *people*—the professionals who make a living by satisfying the needs of the public to either rent or own the land and the improvements.

What Is the Real Estate Commodity?

Real estate is a commodity in the same sense that an automobile and a television set are commodities. Each of these items is useful to an individual, and each one is bought and sold in its own specialized market. Moreover, each product is complex. Automobiles can be classified by their obviously different external characteristics, such as luxury versus compact, new versus used, four-door sedan versus sports car, domestic versus foreign, red versus blue. Less obvious but also important are such components as an eight-cylinder versus a four-cylinder engine, automatic versus standard transmission, and disc versus drum brakes. An analysis of television sets would reveal that they also could be categorized by external characteristics and on the basis of major components.

To understand the nature of a complex commodity, the consumer must identify and closely examine its components. Before buying an automobile, the consumer must know about the engine, the transmission, the brake system, and so on. These components are just as important as the external features of the commodity. The greater the consumer's knowledge about the component parts, the greater will be the consumer's understanding of the nature and the functions of the product.

This section presents a discussion of the commodity known as **real estate.** The real estate commodity has two major physical components—the land and the improvements—and a legal dimension consisting of a bundle of legal rights. The consumer must analyze each of the components and the legal aspects in detail in order to understand the nature and function of the commodity as a whole.

THE COMPONENTS OF REAL ESTATE

Legal Concept of Land

When the term *land* is used, it typically refers to the solid surface of the earth. It is the ground upon which individuals live and build things. It is the dirt in which vegetation grows. An examination of any dictionary definition of the term reveals that this concept underlies the major part of the meaning of the word *land* in the sense of its being a physical entity or commodity.

The legal concept of **land,** however, includes more than just the visible solid surface of the earth. The legal definition of land contains two additional, less visible components. When the consumer buys a parcel of land, that person legally buys whatever is below ground, the mineral rights, and whatever is above ground, the air rights. The term *rights* is used in this sense to identify the claim or the interest to which the owner is justly entitled under law or custom. The term **mineral rights** denotes the owner's claim of land to the minerals under the surface. The term **air rights** denotes the owner's claim in the space above the surface area of the property.

Mineral rights apply to a legally specified, three-dimensional, subterranean space. The surface area of the parcel forms the base of the three-dimensional figure. For simplicity, assume that the land area is a square. In this case, the three-dimensional figure is an inverted pyramid with a square base and a depth that is the distance from the surface to the center of the earth—roughly 4,000 miles.

Under the legal concept of land, the owner has an automatic claim to all minerals enclosed within the geometric shape formed by the surface area and the center of the earth. The minerals belong to the owner unless the owner and the seller agreed that mineral rights did not transfer when the property sold. Even though the legal extent of the mineral rights reaches to the center of the earth, the current state of technology establishes a practical limit to the extent of these mineral rights. Mine shafts and oil wells can reach a depth of several miles; they do not descend for tens or hundreds of miles. The technology of the extractive industry determines the feasible quantity of mineral rights, and the law defines the full extent of these rights within the U. S. system of laws and customs.

Air rights also apply to a legally defined, three-dimensional space. In this case, the surface area or shape of the parcel defines the air space. If the three-dimensional figure used to define the mineral rights were to be extended above the surface of the land parcel, the base and the sides of the air rights space could be outlined. The height of this space, or the upward extent of the air rights, must still be defined. Typically, the height dimension is expressed as extending "to the sky" or "to the heavens."

These statements could lead to an esoteric debate about the exact location of the sky and whether celestial bodies belong to the owners of land parcels. However, two considerations eliminate the need for such discussion: (1) The state of construction technology limits the feasible height of the landowner's air rights. Currently, the height of most commercial structures does not exceed 1,400 feet above the surface. The tallest buildings are only slightly higher than 1,400 feet. (2) The federal government limits the height of air rights by establishing the airways above a stated height as public property for use by aircraft. Local governments also limit the upward extent of air rights by enacting building-height restrictions.

Due to the technological and governmental restrictions, the space in which a person has air and mineral rights, for all practical purposes, extends no more than 20,000 feet below the ground and no more than 1,500 feet above the ground, and the boundaries are established by the size and shape of the land parcel.

Exhibit 1.1 shows the legal concept of land. Notice the distinction between legal dimensions and the feasible/permissible range.

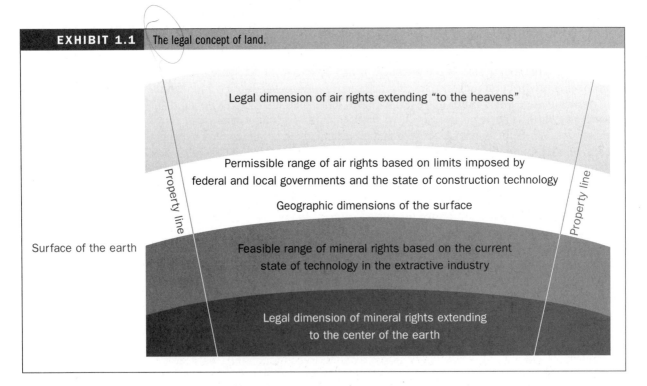

EXHIBIT 1.1 The legal concept of land.

Legal dimension of air rights extending "to the heavens"

Permissible range of air rights based on limits imposed by federal and local governments and the state of construction technology

Geographic dimensions of the surface

Property line

Surface of the earth

Feasible range of mineral rights based on the current state of technology in the extractive industry

Legal dimension of mineral rights extending to the center of the earth

Improvements and Fixtures

The second obvious component of real estate is any building or structure on the land. The term **improvements** is used to denote these buildings and structures as well as other manmade additions, such as fences, driveways, and retaining walls. The general term used to represent all types of permanently erected man-made structures is *improvements-on-the-land* (see Exhibit 1.2).

Another kind of improvement called *improvements-to-the-land* denotes such changes to the land as improving drainage, grading, and filling; providing utilities in the form of water and sewage laterals to the water and sewer mains, natural gas lines, and electricity and telephone lines; and construction of access roads to main arterial streets and highways. These changes make the land suitable for some form of economic or public use, such as homes, stores, industries, schools, and parks.

Improvements-on-the-land and improvements-to-the-land, taken together, are referred to as *on-site improvements*. Thus, the second major physical component of the commodity known as real estate is the entire complex of man-made additions known as on-site improvements.

A **fixture** is personal property that is legally considered real estate because it is attached to the land or to an improvement, which is itself permanently attached to the land. Attachment is only one criterion used to identify a fixture. Other factors that must be considered are the method of attachment, the intention of the party making the attachment, and the purpose for which the personal property is to be used. In terms of the method of attachment, if the item of personal property is firmly attached so that its removal would injure the property, the item is considered to be a fixture.

The intention of the person making the attachment is another criterion for identifying a fixture. When an owner builds an appliance into the counter, the courts view the appliance as a fixture because, by building it in, the owner has expressed an intent

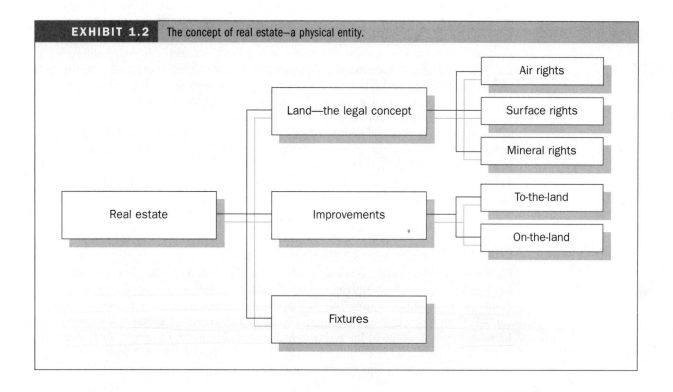

EXHIBIT 1.2   The concept of real estate—a physical entity.

- Real estate
  - Land—the legal concept
    - Air rights
    - Surface rights
    - Mineral rights
  - Improvements
    - To-the-land
    - On-the-land
  - Fixtures

to make the appliance a fixture. In another situation, the owner of a parcel of residential real estate may offer to sell the house with a fully equipped kitchen.

Finally, the purpose for which the property is used also is important. If the item is used to promote the purpose for which the real estate is owned, the presumption is that the owner intended the item to be a fixture regardless of the manner of the attachment. An example of this situation is the sale of a retail store as a clothes store to a buyer who expresses an intention to use the property in the same way.

The question of whether an item of personal property is a fixture arises only if (1) the property to which the item is attached changes owners, (2) the property has been rented to a tenant and is subsequently returned to the owner, or (3) the property is used as security for a loan. If the object does not change hands or if it is not used as collateral for a loan, the character of the item as personal property or a fixture is immaterial because it belongs to the owner in any event.

THE LEGAL DIMENSIONS OF REAL ESTATE

The legal dimensions of the commodity known as real estate are cumulatively called **rights of ownership.** These rights include the right to use the commodity, the right to possess the commodity, the right to exclude others from using the commodity, and the right to dispose of the commodity by selling it or by giving it away as a gift. These rights are intangible factors that exist in law and pertain to the physical or tangible aspects of real estate—land and on-site improvements.

When the ownership dimension is added to the two physical components, a change occurs in the term designating the commodity. Real estate becomes **real property** when the rights of ownership are considered. However, in the generally accepted use of the term *real estate,* most people imply these intangible rights of ownership. In popular usage, the term *real estate,* which denotes only the physical aspect of the commodity, and the term *real property,* which denotes the physical entity and the ownership rights in the commodity, are used as synonyms. The term *realty* is also used by many people. **Realty** typically refers to the physical components of the property and is thereby a synonym for real estate.

Any classification of ownership must be based on the degree to which the rights of use, possession, exclusion, and disposition are held by the owner of the real estate. In other words, the owner of real estate can (1) use the property but only within limits established by the government, (2) have the property in her possession, (3) exclude others from the property, and, finally, (4) choose the means of disposing of the property—for example, by sale or by gift. The material in this section will be presented by analyzing these four rights. However, these same rights can be presented as a classification system of more than four items. For example, the right to dispose of the property could be subdivided into the right to sell, the right to give away, and the right to lease. Of the four rights noted above, the most significant in real estate law are the right of disposition and the right of possession. These two rights are closely intertwined in the body of real estate law (see Exhibit 1.3).

Freehold and Less-than-Freehold Estates

Ownership can be broken down into freehold and less-than-freehold estates. The **freehold estate** is a package of the rights of ownership possessed by the owner for the duration of a lifetime, a time period that must be recognized as indefinite because it can last from a day to many decades. The **less-than-freehold estate** (also known as a **leasehold**) is a package of the rights of ownership obtained by a tenant from an owner; it can last for either a definite period or an indefinite period, depending on the expressed wishes of the landlord and the tenant.

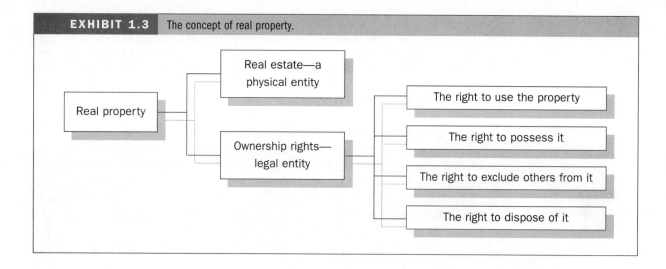

EXHIBIT 1.3 The concept of real property.

Real property

Real estate—a physical entity

Ownership rights—legal entity

The right to use the property

The right to possess it

The right to exclude others from it

The right to dispose of it

FREEHOLD ESTATE.   The owner of a freehold estate may or may not have the right of disposition along with the right of possession. A *freehold estate of inheritance* is a situation in which the owner has all four rights of ownership—to use the land, to possess the land, to exclude others from the land, and to dispose of the land according to the owner's wishes. This is the highest form of ownership and is often called a **fee simple estate.**

A *freehold estate not-of-inheritance* is an estate in which the owner has the rights of use, possession, and exclusion but does not have the right of disposition. The most common form of this type of estate is the **life estate.** The rights of ownership are limited to a lifetime, in this case the lifetime of the owner. As an example of this form of estate, consider the following:

> Your parents retire to Hawaii and give you the family home for as long as you live, an estate based on the duration of your lifetime. Upon your death, the home goes to your younger sister. Your parents owned the home as a freehold estate of inheritance; they have the right to dispose of it. The fact that they gave it to you as a life estate allows you to use, possess, and exclude others from the property for as long as you are alive. However, they did not give you the right of disposition. Regardless of your wishes, your younger sister will receive that property upon your death.

An interesting sidelight of this example is that the creation of the life estate by your parents created two ownership packages. You received an **estate in possession.** Your younger sister received an **estate in expectancy.** You have the right of possession; your sister has an ownership interest that is expected to materialize in the indefinite future. Each of you has a clearly defined package of rights. You can live in the house or rent it out; your sister can sell the property with a delivery date to the new owner that occurs upon or slightly after your death. In this example, you are known as the owner and your sister's estate is legally referred to as a **remainder** while you are alive.

Alternatively, your parents may have arranged to give you the family home for as long as you live and to have it returned to them upon your death. Such an arrangement might be used if your life expectancy, due to illness, is shorter than theirs. In this case, your parents' interest in the property is known legally as a **reversion.**

A second form of freehold estate not-of-inheritance is an **estate *pur autre vie.*** A loose translation of this phrase is "an estate for another's life." An example of this type of estate is a case in which your parents give you the family home for as long as your younger sister's husband is alive. Upon his death, the home goes to your sister. You have an estate in possession; your sister has a remainder. Both estates are based on your brother-in-law's lifetime.

The person in possession of a freehold estate not-of-inheritance has certain obligations to the owner of a remainder or a reversion. The owner of a life estate cannot commit **waste.** The legal term *waste* refers to an act that does permanent injury to the real estate that is owned as a life estate. Examples of waste are the destruction of a building without agreement by the owner of the remainder, failure to make ordinary repairs and to provide necessary maintenance, and failure to pay all of the property taxes and other charges imposed by the local government upon the property.

In addition to the life estate and the estate *pur autre vie,* some states maintain legal life estates known as dower and curtesy. **Dower,** in common law, is the wife's life estate in the real property of her deceased husband. The common-law provision generally held that the wife was given a life estate equal to one-third of all of the real estate that the husband owned at the time of his death. **Curtesy** is the reciprocal of dower; it is the legal life estate created, in common law, for the husband out of the wife's property at her death.

LESS-THAN-FREEHOLD ESTATE.   The less-than-freehold estate is a specified package of the rights of ownership that last for less than a lifetime and do not include the right of disposition. In other words, the owner of a less-than-freehold estate possesses the estate for a prescribed period of time and has no right to sell or give away the property. This form of estate is more commonly known as a **leasehold.**

Stated in positive terms, the rights of the holder of a leasehold are the rights to possess and use the property; the right to exclude others from the property, except that the owner has the right of entry in certain situations; and the right to transfer the use and possession of the property to others through the process of subletting with the consent of the owner.

The body of real estate law defines four categories of leasehold estates. An **estate for years** is a leasehold that continues for a definite period of time. The duration of the leasehold can be for one year (as in a residential lease), for more than a year (as in the case of a commercial or industrial lease), or for a definite period of time that is less than a year.

The second type of leasehold is an **estate from year to year;** it is often referred to as an *estate from period to period.* This estate comes into effect when a tenant maintains possession of the property after an estate for years expires and the owner agrees to the tenant's continued possession of the property by accepting a payment of rent. In this case, the terms of the original, but expired, lease are reestablished for a maximum period of one year if the original lease was for one year or longer. If the original lease was for less than one year, the same shorter period of time is reestablished.

The third type of leasehold is the **tenancy at will.** Under the provisions of this leasehold, the duration is not definitely specified. The agreement between the owner and the tenant exists for as long as both are in agreement. If either party chooses to negate the agreement, the lease arrangement is terminated. The only limitation imposed on the owner and the tenant is that they must give legal notice of their intent. As a general rule, the notice is for 30 or 60 days. Finally, the death of either party terminates the lease under the tenancy at will agreement.

The last type of leasehold is the **tenancy by sufferance.** This form of leasehold comes into existence when a tenant's right under one of the other leaseholds expires and the tenant retains possession against the owner's wishes. In common usage, the tenant at sufferance is called a **holdover tenant.** This situation generally culminates in an eviction of the tenant by the owner of the property. The property owner's right of eviction varies from state to state. At times, the holdover tenant pays the rent, which is accepted by the landlord. In this instance, the tenancy at sufferance usually becomes a tenancy from period to period (see Exhibit 1.4).

EXHIBIT 1.4   The rights of ownership.

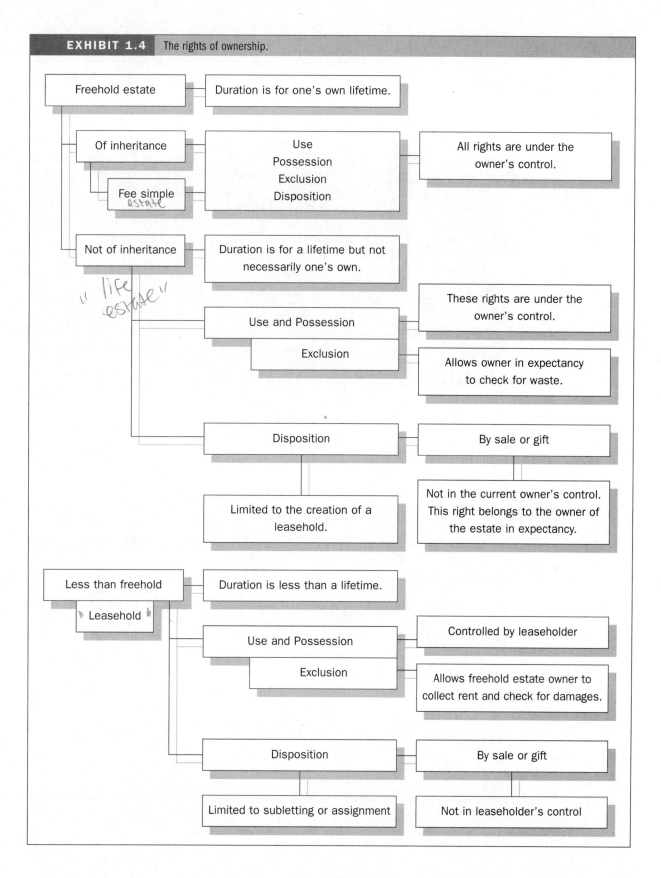

Co-Ownership

The rights of ownership to a parcel of real estate can be held by one person or organization or can be owned by more than one entity. When the rights are held by more than one entity, the persons or organizations are known as co-owners of the property. The principal forms of co-ownership are joint tenancy, tenancy in common, tenancy by the entirety, and community property. They differ in terms of the right of disposition.

The first form of co-ownership, **joint tenancy,** requires the existence of four unities in some states—the unities of title, time, possession, and interest. The **unity of title** implies that individual owners in the joint tenancy arrangement do not have the right of disposition of the entire property. It can only be sold when the co-owners all agree to the sale. Furthermore, upon the death of one of the co-owners, the total number of owners is reduced by one and the deceased person's ownership rights revert to the surviving owners. When all of the other co-owners have died, the last surviving member of the joint tenancy owns the property completely.

Related to the unity of title discussed in the preceding paragraph is the **unity of time:** the joint tenants must receive title to the property at the same time. Moreover, the joint tenants take possession of the property as though they were a single individual, which is called the **unity of possession.** Finally, the joint tenants have a **unity of interest.** They hold an undivided interest in the property; no separate components are identified as the portions of the property owned and possessed by any one of the co-owners. They own equal shares in the entire property, their individual shares cannot be divided, and they all have the same right of possession.

In terms of each individual's right of disposition, the joint tenancy can be viewed as a freehold estate not-of-inheritance that is owned by two or more people. The individual cannot sell the property, give it away, or leave it as an inheritance for his heirs and have this new owner incorporated into the joint tenancy. However, each individual joint tenant can sell her undivided interest. The new owner does not become a member of the joint tenancy but becomes a tenant in common. (The concept of tenancy in common is the next form of co-ownership to be discussed.)

A joint tenancy can be dissolved by specific actions of the tenants (which will not be discussed here). Each joint tenant has the right to destroy the agreement.

In the second form of co-ownership, **tenancy in common,** the individual owners do have the right of disposition within the form of co-ownership and do have separate, identifiable interests, which need not be equal. Each tenant in common owns an explicit percentage of the undivided total interest. The tenants in common can pass their respective interests on to their heirs or can sell their own interest. In other words, tenancy in common is a freehold estate of inheritance among several persons or organizations.

The tenancy in common also differs from the joint tenancy in the way the property passes from a deceased tenant in common. Under a joint tenancy arrangement, the surviving tenant (or tenants) receives the deceased member's interest. Under a tenancy in common, the surviving tenant (or tenants) in common does not automatically receive the interest of the deceased member. In a tenancy in common, each member can dispose of his undivided share by will—that is, by leaving the property interest to an heir.

The other two forms of co-ownership are ways in which property is owned under the institution of marriage. The form known as **tenancy by the entirety** is a joint estate between married people. It is therefore a freehold estate not-of-inheritance; it is an estate in which the marriage partners do not have individual rights of disposition. They can only dispose of the property jointly. Neither the husband nor the wife is able to dispose of the property or any part of it without the consent of the other person.

The other marriage-oriented form of co-ownership is **community property,** property that is jointly acquired and owned by a husband and wife. Each individual may own property separately, but this property is typically property acquired before the marriage.

Nonpossessionary Rights

The freehold estates and the leaseholds discussed in the preceding sections are all estates of possession. The only exceptions are the remainder and the reversion interests, which are estates in expectancy, and even these estates in expectancy are estates of future possession. In contrast to such estates of ownership, which include the rights of use, possession, exclusion, and disposition, certain nonpossessionary rights of use and exclusion can be held by one person in real estate owned by another person. The two types of nonpossessionary rights in real estate are easements and liens, which are discussed in a later chapter.

THE BUNDLE-OF-RIGHTS THEORY

In the discussion of the components of real estate, several rights are identified. Some rights are related to the physical commodity (for example, surface rights, mineral rights, and air rights). Other rights are the intangible rights of ownership, such as the several estates based on the right of disposition (for example, freehold estates of inheritance, freehold estates not-of-inheritance, and leasehold estates). These various rights can be held as either estates in possession or estates in expectancy. If the right of disposition is defined, the separate estates in possession can be disposed of by several methods—sale, gift, or lease.

The commonly accepted analogy is the **bundle-of-rights** theory, which identifies these various rights in real estate as a bundle of sticks, with each stick representing an identifiable right. Each stick can be disposed of as a separate entity. If an individual holds a freehold estate of inheritance, that individual owns the whole bundle of rights. The owner can dispose of these rights in a variety of ways. The use of the surface and mineral rights can be leased to one person, and the air rights can be leased to someone else. At the same time, an easement or several easements can be created and sold to third parties. Then, even while these leaseholds and easements are in force, the entire estate can be sold in expectancy with a delivery date ten, fifteen, or twenty years in the future.

What Are the Characteristics of Real Estate?

The characteristics of the real estate commodity are of two types: physical and economic. The physical characteristics are related to the land itself and to the on-site improvements. The economic characteristics are different in certain respects from those of other commodities.

THE PHYSICAL CHARACTERISTICS

The physical characteristics of land are its immobility, indestructibility, and nonhomogeneity. Once the size and shape of a parcel of land are established, the legal nature of the land is also established with respect to mineral and air rights. Knowledge of the legal concept of land is important for making an analysis of its physical characteristics. Land in its legal sense is *immobile* because it cannot be moved from one place to another. The property owner can spend years moving the earth on the surface, as in the case of a strip mine, but such activity does not move the rights to the minerals in the deeper strata or move the rights to the air above the newly created surface. This point can be reemphasized by saying that the location of the mineral rights and the air rights cannot be moved even if the surface is moved.

Land is *indestructible* in the sense that movement of the surface does not destroy the full package of rights. Moreover, other deliberate human acts, as well as acts of nature, are not capable of destroying land in its legal sense. Fire can char the land. Wind and rain can erode the surface. Earthquakes can rearrange the subsurface strata and cause the surface to rise or fall. Nuclear bombs can dissipate part of the surface. However, in none of these instances is the land destroyed in the legal sense. The land cannot be destroyed because its location cannot be destroyed.

Land is *nonhomogeneous.* Each parcel of land can be distinguished from all other parcels of land on the basis of several physical characteristics. The size and shape can differ. The geological features of elevation, slope, drainage capacity, mineral composition, soil fertility, and bedrock characteristics can be different. However, even if all of these characteristics are perfectly identical, each parcel of land is unique because of its location. No two parcels of land occupy the same space on the earth's surface. The physical feature of location is a very important issue because it is a dominant physical attribute of any property.

THE ECONOMIC CHARACTERISTICS

The economic characteristics of the real estate commodity are somewhat different from those of other commodities. Real estate is the only commodity that the typical consumer buys that is measured in multiples of that individual's or household's income. The home is usually valued at two or three times the household's yearly income, whereas all other commodities—even the automobile—are measured in fractions of the household's yearly income. Because of this first economic characteristic of real estate, its *high price,* the purchase of real estate is generally undertaken with *borrowed funds.* This second characteristic of real estate is shared with many other commodities that the consumer buys.

The third economic characteristic of real estate arises from its physical characteristics of immobility, nonhomogeneity, and location. The *search costs* or *information-gathering costs,* associated with comparison shopping are greater for real estate than for any other product. Each parcel is unique in its location and cannot be moved. Consequently, unless the properties are adjacent, side-by-side comparison is not possible. The purchaser must expend money and time to examine the many different units that are being considered for possible purchase or rental.

The fourth economic characteristic of real estate is *scarcity.* Real estate in both its components of land and improvements is not available in sufficient quantities to meet the desires that all individuals have for it. At any point in time, the total amount of land available is limited. For example, if a local geographic area is defined, within that area there is only a limited amount of available land—as well as a limited number of structures.

A fifth economic characteristic is the concept of **situs,** the economic location of a parcel of real estate. Each parcel is immobile—a physical characteristic. Therefore, each parcel is affected by changes in economic and demographic factors in the surrounding area.

A sixth economic characteristic is the influence that the quantity and the quality of *surrounding structures* and other off-site improvements-to-the-land have on the proper-

ty in question. As the quantity of desirable improvements increases, or as their physical quality improves, the value of the subject property increases. The reverse situation can and does happen if the physical surroundings deteriorate. Many refer to this sixth economic characteristic as "modification" on value caused by adjacent parcels of property.

Finally, the concept of *fixity* is often introduced as an economic characteristic. As land is improved by the addition of on-site improvements (buildings, driveways, water lines, and so forth), the investment is fixed. It cannot be moved or easily altered, and it has a long physical and economic life.

What Is the Real Estate Business?

The purpose of this section is to explore the nature of the real estate business by identifying the participants, explaining their relationships to one another, and describing the services that each offers to a potential buyer or seller and the public in general. This information is important to the potential consumer (buyer or seller) for the following reasons:

- It can eliminate any misconceptions about the real estate business.
- It can assist either the buyer or the seller in deciding whether to handle certain steps of a transaction by using personal knowledge or training or by seeking assistance from a real estate specialist.
- It identifies the specialists from whom the consumer can solicit assistance.
- It helps to illustrate that a real estate transaction can be a very detailed process that could require the services of several individuals within the real estate business to ensure that the needs of all parties are satisfied and protected.

The **real estate business** encompasses all individuals and organizations who receive compensation for providing a service. It includes the carpenter who frames a new structure as well as a life insurance company that loans several million dollars for the construction of a new shopping center. It includes the real estate agent, the real estate lender, the appraiser, the title company, the attorney, the property manager, the insurance company, the developer, the escrow agent, and the contractor. Each plays a special role by providing a service to, and satisfying a need of, the buyer, the seller, or the public in a real estate transaction.

THE REAL ESTATE AGENT

A **real estate agent** is licensed by the state to enter into a contractual relationship with a client in the expectation of a commission. Typically, the agent must satisfy a series of prerequisites prior to receiving a license. Although these prerequisites differ among states, they typically include requirements for education, experience, or both, recommendations from property owners, references covering high morals and good character, and a passing score on an examination.

The agency relationship created in a real estate transaction may be regarded as a **special agency.** The real estate agent may represent the client only according to the special instructions that have been given. For example, the instructions may be to locate a buyer who is ready, willing, and able to purchase the property at a specified price, in a predetermined time period, and under certain other conditions that the client may legally impose. Typically, real estate agents do not function as **general agents,** who have a broader range of authority to represent the client's interests.

Real Estate Commission

In every state a **real estate commission** or, in some cases, a **real estate commissioner** is charged with the responsibility of enforcing the state license law. The commission issues licenses to real estate agents, holds hearings on complaints, issues penalties such as suspensions and revocations against the license, and passes rules and regulations governing the operation of the real estate business.

All license laws contain a description of the activities that distinguish a broker and a salesperson. Typically, there are two essential distinctions of a *broker*. A broker may (1) name the firm after herself and advertise the firm in her name, and (2) employ salespeople as independent contractors or employees. The *salesperson* may not.

National, State, and Local Boards

The **National Association of REALTORS® (NAR)** acts as a parent trade organization for the state association of REALTORS® and local boards. The purpose of these organizations is to promote the real estate business, offer education, express the members' views politically, and support a code of ethics. Any agent has the option of joining all three groups.

Several institutes affiliated with the NAR award several designations to members to indicate completion of a prescribed course of education and the presentation of satisfactory experience in specialized areas. For example, a member may become a Certified Residential Broker (CRB) to indicate a specialty in the brokerage of residential properties. A member may pursue a CCIM (Certified Commercial and Investment Member of the Commercial Investment Real Estate Institute) designation to indicate a specialty in commercial and industrial property brokerage and management. Other specialties are available through affiliate programs in such areas as appraising (Member of the Appraisal Institute) and property management (Certified Property Manager), known respectively as MAI and CPM.

Typically, a client would have good reason to expect a high level of professionalism and performance from an agent who is a **REALTOR®** and holds a designation in the appropriate specialty. For example, a person buying or selling a home would expect a high level of competence from an agent who is a REALTOR® and a CRB.

The NAR website contains information on many of the individual specialties in real estate, including residential, commercial, and management designations. Their web address is found on the website for this text at **http://epley.swcollege.com.**

The registered trademark REALTOR® refers to a full member in good standing of the National Association of REALTORS®, a national trade group. A **REALTOR®-ASSOCIATE** refers to a different category of membership in the NAR. Members of NAR may use the symbol "®" in their advertising, which signifies the membership and adherence to the NAR rules and code of conduct. The public should realize that membership is voluntary. This means that a real estate agent may not be a REALTOR®, but all REALTORS® and REALTOR®-ASSOCIATES must be real estate agents.

THE REAL ESTATE COUNSELOR

A **real estate counselor** typically has the designation CRE (Counselor of Real Estate) following his or her name. It signifies membership in the national organization, which supports required education, experience, and standards of conduct. Counselors serve as problem solvers who rely on their experience and education to determine the best solutions.

REAL ESTATE LENDERS

Real estate lenders provide equity and debt funds to investors and borrowers who do not have sufficient cash to pay the full purchase price of property. These lenders serve a valuable function in the economy by competing with other markets for the investment dollar in order that it can be loaned into real estate. Thus, they serve as a valuable conduit of money into the real estate market and provide loans to potential buyers who otherwise would be unable to purchase real estate.

Typically, a lender loans either equity funds or debt funds for the purchase of real estate. **Equity funds** come from the assets of the potential buyer. If the buyer provides this money from his own resources, it is expressed on that person's balance sheet as an asset. **Debt funds** are supplied from the assets of other people and are added to the equity funds to equal the purchase price of the property. This additional amount is usually in the form of a mortgage, which enters the buyer's balance sheet as a liability because it is a debt that he owes with interest. A buyer usually cannot borrow 100 percent of a property's purchase price. If the buyer does not have enough cash for the down payment (the difference between the purchase price and the mortgage amount), he can sometimes borrow the needed funds.

The Mortgage Bankers Association website contains additional information on real estate lending. Their web address is found on the website for this text at **http://epley.swcollege.com.**

THE APPRAISER

The job of the **appraiser** is to provide an independent estimate of the value of property. The appraiser inspects the premises, gathers data on the local market and trends, and applies a professional approach to determining the property value.

The appraiser must be licensed by the state for the protection of the public. In addition, the appraiser may be designated by one of the professional appraisal organizations. For example, the appraiser may be a Residential Member (RM) or a Member of the Appraisal Institute (MAI), which means that she has successfully completed a course of instruction and satisfied an experience requirement prescribed by the Appraisal Institute.

For additional current information on this specialty, visit the website for the Appraisal Institute (AI). The AI is one of the oldest and largest appraisal trade groups in the United States. Its address is found on the website for this text at **http://epley.swcollege.com.**

THE TITLE COMPANY

The **title company** prepares an abstract (chain of title) containing the complete history of a parcel of real estate. This history includes all title transfers and all encumbrances against the property, including mortgage releases and outstanding liens. The title company compiles this history by searching the public records to locate all recorded documents that pertain to the subject property.

The abstract is very valuable to the buyer in that it gives the buyer and his attorney the facts from which to determine whether the seller actually owns all of the property rights. Also, it informs the buyer of any outstanding encumbrances and shows whether any other parties have interests in the property. Therefore, the title company, by preparing the abstract, is giving the buyer the opportunity to determine whether good title can be acquired from the seller. The abstract is usually sent to the buyer's attorney for an opinion on the seller's ownership rights. It thus protects the buyer.

THE REAL ESTATE ATTORNEY

The **real estate attorney** can provide a number of services to the client. The attorney can write a contract of sale, give opinions about the validity of the present owner's rights of ownership and any outstanding encumbrances, and prepare the deed and any other necessary legal documents. Further, an attorney can perform numerous other services, including providing legal advice or service related to problems with the subject property.

THE PROPERTY MANAGER

The **property manager** is a specialist in the management of real estate. Typically, property that involves a property manager produces income, and the manager is needed to collect rents, negotiate leases, pay mortgage payments for the investors, supervise maintenance, reduce expenses, and advise the investors. A property manager provides the client an income and expense statement periodically. The obvious advantage to an owner is that the property is managed by a professional. Also, the owner is not bothered by the problems of the tenants.

Property managers generally are not required to be licensed by the state, although resident managers living on the premises may be required to hold a real estate agent's license. A property manager may be designated or nondesignated. She may be an Accredited Residential Manager (ARM) or a Certified Property Manager (CPM). To obtain either of these designations, the candidate must complete a course of study and satisfy an experience requirement administered by the Institute of Real Estate Management.

For additional information on real estate management, visit the Building Owners and Managers Association website. The address can be found on the website for this text at **http://epley.swcollege.com.**

THE REAL ESTATE INSURANCE COMPANY

Any improvements on property that have a value should be covered by insurance against loss from common hazards. If the improvements have been mortgaged, the lender will require an insurance policy protecting the lender's interests. The insurance is purchased from a property and casualty insurance company through an agent who has been licensed by the state insurance department.

An insurance company gives protection to the lender and the buyer in the event of a financial loss to the property from a hazard. A typical homeowner's policy covers a home, home fixtures, and any garages on the premises as well as furniture, clothing, appliances, and most other family personal property. The policy specifically identifies the hazards against which the property is insured—for example, fire, lightning, explosion, smoke, vandalism, riot damage, hail, windstorm, vehicle damage, and glass breakage. The policy also lists certain hazards to which the insurance does not apply— for example, acts of war, rebellion, and revolution. No payment is made for damage caused by unlisted hazards.

Additional coverage can include protection against claims by other people for accidental injury or damage to their property on or off the insured's premises, protection against theft hazards not otherwise specified in the policy, and protection (in most states) for second homes, such as seasonal dwellings located in or out of the insured's home state. Earthquake coverage can be provided as additional coverage, and flood insurance may be available through the National Flood Insurance Association.

Through insurance, the risk of any financial loss is transferred from the lender and the homeowner to the insurance company. The lender and the owner can be assured that they will not face the possibility of bankruptcy if damage occurs to a property that is covered by insurance.

THE REAL ESTATE DEVELOPER

The **real estate developer** is any person or firm that transforms property from one stage of use to another. Developers typically start with raw acreage. They have the property subdivided and plotted by an engineer, and they solicit and receive the necessary permits from the city, county, state, and federal agencies to erect a structure on the site. The developer may be a real estate agent who is involved in marketing the properties. Thus, the property is transformed from raw acreage to a site ready for construction, then to a potentially inhabitable structure, and finally to an inhabited structure.

Anyone who can bear the financial burden and has the knowledge can develop property. There are no licensing requirements unless the developer acts as a broker by employing other people to sell the property for a commission and thus becomes subject to the real estate license law.

THE ESCROW AGENT

The **escrow agent** is a neutral, independent third party who agrees to execute the escrow agreement. The escrow agreement typically allows the deed to be given to the buyer and the funds to be paid to the seller once certain predetermined conditions of the sale are satisfied. The essential purpose in using the escrow agent is to assure that the terms negotiated within the contract of sale are satisfied.

The escrow agent provides as a convenient method of assuring that the terms of the escrow agreement are fulfilled. This can include providing an abstract and opinion of title, title insurance, warranty deed, paid utility receipts, evidence of liens that have been paid, completion of construction, predetermined repairs, recording of the deed, and so on. The agent serves as a depository who has the authority to transfer, dispose, and execute according to the predetermined escrow agreement.

OTHER BUSINESSES THAT SERVICE REAL ESTATE

Numerous other individuals and firms service the real estate business, especially in the construction sector. For example, when a structure is built, one contractor is hired to excavate, another contractor lays the sewer pipe, a lumber company supplies the lumber, a carpenter performs the labor, an appliance store provides the appliances and fixtures, a cabinet shop makes the cabinets, a paint store supplies the paint, a painter contracts for the painting, and so on through a wide range of specialists from the architect who designs the structure to the new custodian who is hired to maintain it. A new structure involves a large number of people who sell their supplies or services.

All of these suppliers of products and labor are brought together by the **general contractor** to build one structure. This individual enters into a contract with a prospective occupant to build a structure by supervising all of the individual suppliers of products and services. The general contractor negotiates a fee that is typically a percentage of the cost of construction. This individual can be the future owner, a developer, or someone in business as a general contractor.

UNIQUE FEATURES OF THE REAL ESTATE TRANSACTION

A typical real estate transaction involves several parties working together to ensure that the purchase (or sale) progresses smoothly and everyone's interests are protected. Thus, the transaction is not similar to that carried out by a consumer in purchasing a suit of clothes or a new automobile. In the latter cases, the consumer enters a retail outlet that carries the product, examines the item, and, if it meets his needs, pays for it and takes it home. In a real estate transaction, the buyer must find a seller who possesses the product that she desires or vice versa. A tremendous search cost may be incurred before the two parties find each other. A real estate agent's services can be used to lower this search cost and to enable one or both parties to save time.

Once the buyer finds a seller with acceptable property, a considerable amount of negotiation may transpire before an acceptable selling price is reached. An agent can be asked to help with the negotiations or an attorney can be employed to review the contracts, write them, or both. Next, appropriate financing needs to be arranged. At this point, the local lending institutions become involved. The lender may insist that an appraiser be hired to estimate the market value of the property and in addition may require an abstract with an attorney's opinion or title insurance. A survey may be needed, and an attorney may be called upon to solve any legal problems. The agent can handle the closing, or it can be conducted by the title company or the financial institution.

Thus, a typical real estate transaction involves several specialists who are asked by the buyer or seller to give their services or who are involved because one of the participants requires their services. It differs from a routine retail transaction because it requires a prolonged search, complex negotiations, the services of numerous specialists, and hence more time to complete successfully.

THE MULTIPLIER EFFECT

Since so many individuals supply products and labor to the real estate business, the effect of one person's decision to buy or build a structure is multiplied by the number of people involved directly and indirectly in the project. Moreover, the effect is multiplied by the number of individuals who are making the decision to buy or build at any given time. This is known as the **multiplier effect.** Thus, a change in demand for real estate can have a tremendous impact on both employment and incomes in a city, a region, or the nation. A change in economic conditions, such as a rapid increase in the interest rate, that dampens the demand for ownership or new construction can have a severe and widespread effect. Many products would remain unsold, contractors and laborers would be unable to find work, and the demand for many services would decline. Conversely, a change in economic conditions that increases the demand for real estate can produce a similarly broad effect, stimulating the sale of goods and services and expanding job opportunities.

What Are Current Trends of the Real Estate Business?

Several trends appear to be developing that should influence the structure of the real estate business in the future.

1. *The real estate transaction for a purchase or a sale is becoming more complex.* Numerous lawsuits have shown that any real estate specialists involved in a transac-

tion need a high level of knowledge and competence and must perform their services honestly. Common types of lawsuits are those against agents for misrepresenting the property characteristics, against the buyer for breach of contract, against the seller for breach of contract, against an attorney for an error in rendering an opinion on an abstract, against lenders for discrimination in their lending practices, against an appraiser for overestimating the value of property, against agents for discriminating in the showing of properties to minorities, and against local real estate boards for fixing commissions.

2. *The level of knowledge required by members of the public to evaluate their own interests is increasing.* In the area of real estate finance, for example, several new types of mortgages are appearing on the market. The public will need a certain minimum level of education about these mortgages as a basis for selecting the most suitable alternative.

3. *Entrance requirements to the profession are becoming much more stringent because of rising educational requirements.* In addition, *continuing education requirements for maintaining the license are increasing.*

4. *The small local firm is encountering more competition from the growing number of franchises and larger national or regional firms.*

5. *Lenders are moving toward lending a lower percentage of the purchase price; hence, the new buyer will need more cash.*

6. *Federal and state intervention in real estate transactions is increasing.*

7. *The Internet is starting to significantly influence the real estate transaction.*

Chapter Summary

Real estate is a physical entity consisting of land in its legal definition and the man-made improvements permanently affixed to that land. The legal concept of land includes the surface area of the earth plus the mineral and air rights that extend below and above the surface. Improvements are the structures put on the land as well as changes or additions that are made to the land itself, such as grading, clearing, and landscaping. Fixtures are items of personal property that are either attached to or intended to be part of the land or the improvement. They are viewed as part of real property.

The legal dimension of real estate involves several rights—the rights to use, to possess, to exclude other people from, and to dispose of real estate. When the legal dimension is considered in conjunction with land, improvements, and fixtures, the term *real property* is used.

In addition to these components, real estate has the physical characteristics of immobility, indestructibility (or durability), and nonhomogeneity, as well as several economic characteristics. Its purchase price is typically a multiple of the consumer's yearly income, its purchase is almost always facilitated by the use of borrowed money, and the decision to buy necessitates large expenditures of time, effort, and money in gathering relevant information about the product.

Various individuals, firms, and organizations provide services to the buyer, the seller, and the agent. Examples include the appraiser, title company, real estate attorney, surveyor, lender, real estate agency, and the National Association of REALTORS®.

An agent has the option of joining the local board, the State Association of REALTORS®, and the National Association of REALTORS®. Membership means that the agent subscribes to a code of ethics. In addition, an agent may hold a designation, such as a CRB or CCIM, that shows he has completed a prescribed course of study and acquired satisfactory experience. A buyer or seller could expect a high level of professionalism from an agent who is a REALTOR® and who holds a designation in the appropriate specialty.

Internet Applications

A website has been established for this chapter at http://epley.swcollege.com.

Review Questions

1. What is real estate? As part of your definition, be certain to explain the legal concept of land, as well as the nature of improvements-to-the-land and improvements-on-the-land.

2. What are fixtures and how are they determined?

3. Distinguish between freehold and leasehold estates.

4. Distinguish between freehold estates of inheritance (fee simple estates) and freehold estates not-of-inheritance.

5. Identify and describe the four types of leaseholds.

6. Define and distinguish between joint tenancy and tenancy in common.

7. What are the economic characteristics of real estate?

8. What does the phrase "real estate business" mean?

9. Contrast the roles of the National Association of REALTORS® and the state real estate commission.

10. Are all agents REALTORS®? Why or why not?

11. What is the difference between a general agent and a special agent?

12. Explain the services offered by each of the following that a potential buyer or seller might use:

real estate agent	escrow agent
real estate lender	general contractor
appraiser	real estate attorney
title company	property manager
real estate counselor	real estate insurance company
real estate developer	

13. Describe the multiplier effect of the real estate business.

14. Discuss the trends that could influence the real estate business in the future.

15. Discuss the information found from the Internet applications you explored above.

1. The bundle of rights held by the owner of a freehold estate of inheritance can be manipulated in a variety of ways. Devise at least three different alternatives by which a landowner can sell and rent out the several rights that she possesses.

2. What are the merits of using a real estate agent?

3. Should a prospective buyer or seller always use an agent who is a REALTOR®? Why or why not?

4. Should all of the services described in this chapter be used in a typical real estate transaction? Why or why not?

5. Should all prospective candidates for a real estate license be required to pass a *national* exam? Should they be given a *national* license?

6. Since the real estate business is tied into the economy through many related businesses, should the federal government increase financial support and regulation to minimize the impact of adverse fluctuations in the business cycle?

7. Discuss the information found on the various Internet assignments located on the website for this text.

## CHAPTER 2

Public and Private Controls on the Use of Real Property

1. What public controls and private restrictions may be placed on the ownership rights of property?

2. What is the legal description of property and what are the types that may be used?

OBJECTIVES

When finished with this chapter, the student should be able to:

1. Identify and explain the public controls and private restrictions on real property.

2. Explain the purpose of a legal description.

3. Explain the differences among the plat system, metes and bounds system, government rectangular system, and combination.

acre

air and water controls

antitrust litigation

area regulations

baseline

building code

building permit

certificate of occupancy

closure

commercial easement-in-gross

condemnation

construction code

declaration of restrictions

deed restriction

dominant estate

easement

easement appurtenant

easement-in-gross

economic limits

eminent domain

escheat

express agreement

general lien

general plan restriction

government rectangular system

guide meridians

height regulations

housing code

intestate

just compensation

land use regulations

legal description

legal limits

lien

lot and block system

mechanic's lien

metes and bounds system

nonconforming use

occupancy code

permanent reference marker

plat map

point of beginning

police power

principal meridian

private controls

property tax lien

public controls

range

restrictive covenant

rezoning application

section

servient estate

special assessment

specific lien

standard parallels

subdivision plot

subdivision regulations

tax lien

tier

township

unfair trade practices

variance

zoning ordinance

INTRODUCTION

Chapter 1 discussed the nature and characteristics of the real estate commodity. In addition, it contained an explanation of the real estate business and its various individuals and firms that offer services to assist in solving the real problems and satisfying the needs of a buyer, seller, or agent. The consumer has not yet been introduced to the public controls and private restrictions on real estate ownership. This chapter will explain these controls and typical restrictions.

What Are Public Controls
and Limits on Real Estate?

The rights of ownership described in Chapter 1 are not absolute rights because there are constraints on the owner's ability to use the property. The controls and limits are of two major kinds: public and private. An easy method for remembering the **public controls** is the acronym PETE, as shown in Exhibit 2.1:

P: Police power
E: Eminent domain
T: Taxation
E: Escheat

POLICE POWER

The **police power** of the state is provided for in the federal and state constitutions to enable governments to protect the public by regulating factors that can adversely affect the public health, morals, safety, and general welfare.

Four types of police power can be instituted by a local government under the approval of the state legislative body: (1) the zoning ordinance, (2) the subdivision regulations, (3) the building code, and (4) the housing code. In the following sections, each of these controls is described and the impact of each on an owner's use of property is examined.

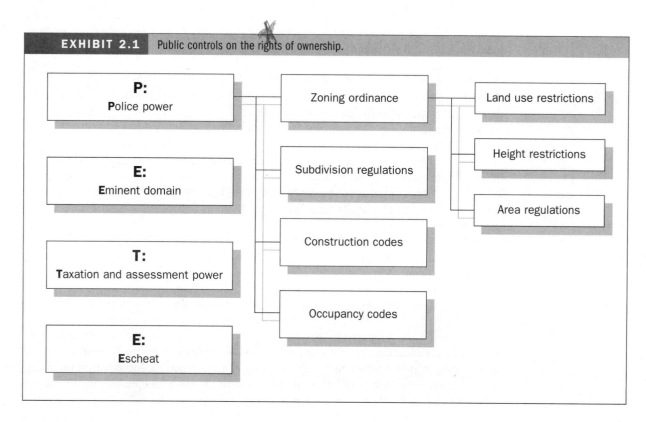

EXHIBIT 2.1 Public controls on the rights of ownership.

The Zoning Ordinance

Initiated by a local community, the **zoning ordinance** usually contains three distinct elements: (1) land use regulations, (2) height regulations, and (3) area, or bulk, regulations.

In the **land use regulations** section of the zoning ordinance, all parcels of property in a community are classified or zoned into four general categories: industrial, commercial, residential, and agricultural. This section of the ordinance establishes a geographic distribution of the land uses in the local community. Once this pattern of land use is stipulated, the land use regulations may legally allow only the use specified and exclude all other land uses (known as *exclusive zoning*), or the land use regulation may legally allow the stated use and all other compatible or suitable land uses, such as residential activity in a commercial zone (known as *inclusive zoning*). The land use categories may contain more specific subcategories, such as single-family detached residences on large lots, single-family detached residences on small lots, duplexes, or multifamily units. Commercial and industrial land use categories may also be broken down into more detailed subclasses.

The **height regulations** in the zoning ordinance specify the legal height of structures by land-use category and by geographic area. They could state a maximum height for apartment buildings in the multifamily residential land use category and a different maximum height for the structures in the single-family detached residential category. The height restrictions could also differ by geographic area. Tall structures could be prohibited near municipal airports but allowed in the central business district.

The **area regulations** (also known as *bulk regulations*) of the zoning ordinance specify the relationship between the structure and the land components on individual parcels of property. In the case of residential property, the area regulations could contain setback rules that establish the minimum distance between the street and the location of the structure. The size of side yards and the minimum size of the building lot could also be established. For commercial property, area regulations could dictate whether the structure is situated at the front or at the rear of the property. They could also regulate the location of parking areas by dictating that parking be provided in front of or behind the building.

Once the zoning regulations are established, the property owner can try to change their impact in either of two ways. One way is to obtain a **variance.** In this case, the owner asks permission to deviate from the current area or height regulation. A request might be made to establish a different setback or a slightly different allowable height. Usually, the argument made by the owner must be based on the fact that a hardship will be incurred if the variance is not granted. The second procedure is the **rezoning application.** In this case, the owner asks for a change in the ordinance to allow a different land use on a specific piece of property. For example, a request can be made to change the zoning from single-family detached to townhouse, to multifamily, or even to commercial use.

When a zoning ordinance is imposed, or when circumstances require a restructuring of the land use restrictions, certain property may not conform with surrounding property under the new zoning ordinance. For example, there may be a single-family detached housing unit in an expanded commercial section, or there may be an apartment building or convenience store in a newly created single-family residential zone. Such a property is known as a **nonconforming use.** As a general rule, the owner can continue using the property as before and can maintain it in good repair. However, unless given express permission, the owner cannot enlarge the structure or undertake an alteration that will lengthen the physical life of that structure. Moreover, if the property is damaged or destroyed, it cannot be repaired or reconstructed unless the zoning ordinance expressly allows such action.

Subdivision Regulations

Subdivision regulations are another type of police power imposed by the local government to promote and protect the health, safety, and general welfare of the community. These goals are accomplished by having a local agency, such as a planning body, review and approve builders' plans for new residential or commercial developments within the local jurisdiction. The regulations are generally designed to prevent construction in floodplains, on land with poor or inadequate drainage capabilities, and on land parcels that have unacceptably steep slopes coupled with soil conditions that could cause land and mud slides.

In addition to requiring an analysis of the geological features of the development site, subdivision regulations require the developer to meet locally acceptable standards for street systems, building lot specifications, and block size. The street system standards include the street layout, the design and frequency of intersections, street widths, maximum slopes and grades, and minimum construction standards for the roadway.

Subdivision regulations are imposed by requiring the prospective developer to file a plat map for approval. The **plat map** is a graphic representation of the subdivision's relative size and shape and includes all of the building lots, the street system, and blocks, all represented in scale. If the plat map is approved, it is recorded and becomes part of the public domain. Prospective buyers of a lot can examine the plat map to verify the shape and the dimensions of the land parcel. One **subdivision plot** is one building lot that is contained in the plat map.

The Building, or Construction, Code

The third police power is the **building, or construction, code** imposed by local government. This code is designed to establish the minimum acceptable standards for construction within the local jurisdiction. It specifies the type and positioning of structural members in the floors, walls, ceiling, and roof of a building (for example, 2 x 4's every 16 inches on center in the walls, 2 x 8 x 12's as floor joists, and so forth). Another section of the building code specifies the minimally acceptable standards for plumbing systems with respect to water supply lines and waste disposal lines. Still another section of the code specifies the minimum gauge of electric wires and the positioning of outlets and switches.

Compliance with the specifications of the building code can be checked by requiring that the contractor apply for a **building permit** with the local government's department of building or construction. In order to complete the application for a building permit, the contractor must submit copies of the construction specifications for examination by local authorities. If the application is approved, the authorities issue a building permit. While the work is under way, inspectors from the building department check the work to see that the contractor is complying with the construction specifications. When the job is completed, a final inspection is performed. If the work is done according to the specifications of the building code, a **certificate of occupancy** is issued and the structure can then be occupied and used.

The Housing, or Occupancy, Code

The fourth police power is the **housing, or occupancy, code.** This code is designed to establish socially acceptable minimum standards for safe and healthy occupancy of existing and newly constructed buildings. One aspect of the housing code is related to the structural quality and physical condition of existing units. Any building that needs major repairs is generally considered in violation of the local housing code. Moreover, any structure that is lacking certain plumbing facilities, such as hot running water and private toilet facilities for individual dwelling units, is considered in violation of the housing code.

Police Power Limits on the Use of Property

Knowing the specific features of the four police powers, a person can easily see that they are indeed limits on the use of individual property. The zoning ordinance limits the use of the site and the height of the structure. The building code specifies the minimal acceptable construction standards for the structure. The housing code specifies the necessary levels of structural quality as well as health and safety features. Property owners must conform to these ordinances and in so doing lose the total control or absolute freedom to use the property as desired.

The various state and federal courts in the United States have supported the legal foundations of the police-power techniques. However, there have been, are, and always will be challenges to the manner in which these powers are used by the local community.

EMINENT DOMAIN

Another public limitation on the rights of property owners is the legal concept of eminent domain. **Eminent domain** is a *right* vested in the state government and given to a local government—and, at times even to private agencies—to acquire possession of (to take) private property. The *act* of converting private property to public property by using eminent domain is called **condemnation.** The property must be acquired for public uses or public purposes, and fair or **just compensation** (compensation equal to the value of the property) must be paid to the owner. The property owner also must be allowed due process of law. Thus, three important factors limit the local government's ability to acquire private property under eminent domain: (1) public use or public purpose, (2) fair or just compensation, and (3) due process of law.

The determination of public use or purpose can be made either by legislation that declares a use to be public or by the courts. In the case of judicial action, the courts can pass judgment on an existing law with its specific statement on public use and purpose, or the courts might be asked to decide on the legality of some specific public purpose.

TAXATION AND ASSESSMENT POWERS

The local county, city, and school districts have the authority to tax real property to provide public services, such as schools and roads. If the property tax is not paid, the local government places a specific lien, the **property tax lien,** against the delinquent property. The local government can sell the property to obtain the delinquent taxes. This forced tax sale overrides the property owner's rights of possession and disposition.

Special assessments are charges that a local government levies against property owners for public services, such as streets, storm-drain systems, and water and sewage disposal systems. These charges directly affect the value of the individual parcels. The major difference between assessment charges and the general property tax is that the services provided and paid for under the assessments are viewed as value enhancers for specific properties, whereas the services provided and paid for under the property tax enhance the value of all property in the community. If the assessments are not paid, a specific lien is established against the property, allowing the property to be sold to obtain the delinquent assessment payments. This forced sale to obtain delinquent assessment payments overrides the property owner's rights of possession and disposition.

ESCHEAT

The last public limit on private ownership is the legal concept of **escheat.** When a property owner dies without leaving a will and legal heirs cannot be found for the property, the real estate tentatively belongs to no one. In this event, the state government can use the power of escheat to claim the land for the state. In this sense, the power of escheat is not really a limit but is a control on ownership rights. When the possession and disposition of property are uncertain because of the lack of heirs, the state assumes possession and all other rights of ownership of the property.

What Public Agencies Influence the Real Estate Business?

The types of controls used by a local government to restrict the use of property are explained in the preceding section. All decisions involving purchases, sales, or use are subject to those controls. This section will describe briefly the influence each level of government can have on the real estate business.

THE ROLE OF FEDERAL GOVERNMENT IN REAL ESTATE

The U.S. Justice Department has a long history of **antitrust litigation** against groups of real estate agents for setting a fixed rate for sales commissions. These cases have resulted in decrees that agents may not establish set or fixed commission rates, may not discuss the setting of rates in groups, may not discriminate against any agent because he will not charge the desired amount, and may not use any educational devices to train members on commission schedules. The listing contract must include a statement, printed on the front in bold letters, that the commission is negotiable between the agent and the owner.

The federal government has attempted to regulate the mortgage application procedure to inform the consumer about the details of the transaction and to ensure that the lender does not discriminate. The Real Estate Settlement Procedures Act (RESPA), the Equal Credit Opportunity Act (ECOA), the Truth-in-Lending Act, and the Mortgage Disclosure Act pertain to interest-rate charges, settlement costs, discrimination, and the region into which loans are originated. All are designed to inform consumers and protect their rights. These acts are implemented through such agencies as the Federal Reserve Board and the Department of Housing and Urban Development.

The federal government also has the right of eminent domain, which was discussed earlier in this chapter in relation to state and local governments. Congress also gives this right to federal agencies to convert private property into public property for the public good. The right is generally used to acquire land for national parks, military installations, and federal office buildings.

The federal government has attempted to establish **air and water controls** on property through such agencies as the Environmental Protection Agency (EPA). For example, the EPA can establish standards regulating the amount of air and water pollutants discharged into the atmosphere and streams.

The Federal Trade Commission has recently focused investigations on several cities in the United States to determine whether **unfair trade practices** are in use. The investigations have been related mainly to the ability of minority group members to earn a living as real estate professionals and the ability of the consumer to buy and sell property without using a real estate agent.

The federal government has a long history of intervention in the real estate business through the financing sector. The government has provided special loan funds to promote housing for low and moderate income families. It has created such agencies as the Federal Housing Administration, the Department of Veteran Affairs, and the Farmers Home Administration to promote standards of quality for the construction of residences and to administer programs to fulfill the housing needs of certain special groups of consumers. The government has created other institutions—such as the Federal National Mortgage Association (Fannie Mae), the Government National Mortgage Association (Ginnie Mae), and the Mortgage Corporation (Freddie Mac)— to establish an orderly secondary mortgage market for the lenders who deal directly with the public. These local lenders who make loans to the public may, under certain conditions, sell the mortgages to institutions in the secondary mortgage market and thus recover their funds to loan again. Congress also has created the Department of Housing and Urban Development to sponsor solutions to the housing needs of the nation. The federal government's long-standing influence on the real estate business undoubtedly will continue into the future.

THE ROLE OF STATE GOVERNMENT IN REAL ESTATE

State legislature and the state courts influence a wide range of real estate uses and decisions. For example, the state legislature recognizes various types of estates that contain bundles of rights that are transferred from the owner to the buyer. The system of recording title documents is determined by the state legislature. The legislature approves the legal descriptions used to identify the unique location of each property, and the property owner's protection from creditors and the creditor's right to place a claim on the value of property for unpaid debts are created by the state legislature. Also, the state retains the right through escheat to claim the property of an owner who dies **intestate** (without a will) and has no heirs.

THE ROLE OF LOCAL GOVERNMENT IN REAL ESTATE

A local government unit, such as a city, county, or school district, typically is given authority by the state to levy a property tax. (The state may also tax real estate for the state general fund.) The state legislature may also give local governments the right to impose other types of controls on property uses. For example, the county can levy a property tax and also may be able to regulate health standards on property and to control land use through a county planning department. The city can levy taxes, can (and usually does) impose zoning requirements to restrict certain land uses to specific locations, and can enforce building codes to maintain a minimum quality of construction, safety, and health standards. As stated earlier, these controls over real estate transactions, uses, and decisions are called police powers. Other local governments, such as school districts, special improvement districts, and townships, typically have only the authority to levy taxes.

What Are Private Controls and Limits on Real Estate?

In addition to the public limits on the rights of ownership, two classes of private limits can affect the use of private property: legal limits and economic limits. **Private controls** restrict real estate ownership rights when non-governmental units, such as private parties, impose the limitation. **Legal limits** are absolute because they deny the right to dispose of, or to use, the property. **Economic limits** are not absolute because they do not deny a right: they just identify a particular use as inefficient or uneconomic.

LEGAL LIMITS

The legal limits in the private sector are the easement, the lien, and the restrictive covenant. The easement and the lien are nonpossessory rights of use and exclusion held by a person who is not the owner of the property. The easement limits an owner's ability to use a predetermined and identified portion of the property. The lien limits the owner's right of possession and disposition because nonpayment of a debt secured by the property will give rise to a forced sale initiated by the creditor.

Easements

An **easement** is the right of one person to use the property of another for a specified purpose and under certain conditions that specify the extent of the allowable usage. The person holding the easement does not possess the property, nor does that person have the right to dispose of that property. However, under certain circumstances, the holder of the easement can dispose of the nonpossessory right by selling it or giving it away.

Two types of easements must be explained to clarify this last point. One type of easement "runs with the land"—that is, possession of the easement passes from one owner to the next. The best example of this form of easement is the **easement appurtenant.** It exists when there are at least two adjacent parcels of land and one of those parcels (the **dominant estate**) receives benefits that derive from the use of the other parcel of land (the **servient estate**). An example of an easement appurtenant is the right of the owner of parcel A to use an access that was created across parcel B. In this case (shown in Exhibit 2.2), the owner of parcel A holds the easement, and parcel A is the estate that receives the benefits from the access road. Parcel B is the servient estate, the estate that provides the benefit or service.

The right of special usage, which the owner of parcel A has in the land described as parcel B, cannot be revoked by the owner of parcel B once the easement is established and is used and maintained. Thus, the easement "runs with the land." This type of easement can be passed from one owner of parcel A to successive owners of parcel A. When parcel B is sold, the successive owners of that parcel take possession of the real estate with the full realization that there is an easement against the property.

The second type of easement does not "run with the land"—instead, it involves only one parcel of real estate. This type of easement is called an **easement-in-gross,** and it conveys only a personal right that cannot be sold or passed on to another person. For example, parcel B is adjacent to a highway, as shown in Exhibit 2.2. An advertising agency asks the farmer for permission to construct a billboard on the property near the highway. The agency will construct and maintain the billboard and will provide a modest yearly payment to the farmer for the use of the space. In exchange, the agency

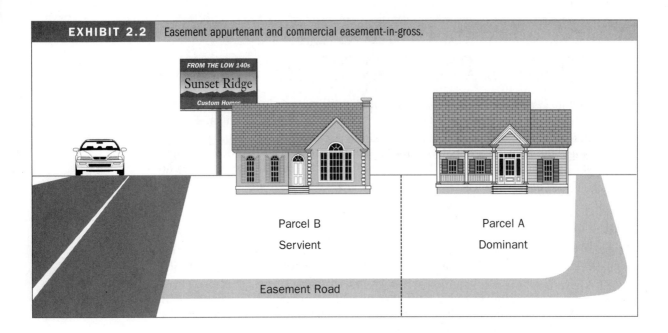

EXHIBIT 2.2 Easement appurtenant and commercial easement-in-gross.

FROM THE LOW 140s

Sunset Ridge

Custom Homes

Parcel B
Servient

Parcel A
Dominant

Easement Road

wishes the right to change the signs periodically. The agency does not wish to rent the land. This agreement provides the agency with an easement to get to the sign (known as an *easement by implication*). The important point is that the advertising agency does not have the right to sell its easement to another agency because the easement is personal in nature. It applies only to the advertising agency.

Some easements-in-gross, however, are not personal in nature, do "run with the land," and involve only one parcel of property. This type is a **commercial easement-in-gross,** which can be sold or transferred to another individual. An example of this type of easement is the right-of-way that a railroad company, pipeline company, or public utility has across an individual parcel of land.

Easements can be created in a variety of ways. The most common way is by **express agreement** between the persons involved. In this situation, the persons involved strike an acceptable agreement about the nature of the use and, in some cases, even the duration of the right to use the property. A second way in which an easement is created is by *necessity* or *implication*. In this case, the easement is created if the circumstances of a real estate transaction indicate that the prudent buyer would require a special use that was not expressly stated because of some error, such as an oversight. For example, Mr. Jones sells Mr. Smith the back 40 acres of his farm. The land that Smith buys is bounded on all sides by land holdings of other people, without access to a road. In this case, most courts would recognize that Smith had an easement across Jones's land by implication or necessity. The courts would recognize that prudent individuals would have decided on the need for such an easement and would have created it.

Liens

The second type of nonpossessionary right in real estate is the **lien.** In general, the lien is the right of a creditor to petition the courts to force the sale of a debtor's property in order to obtain payment. This right is invoked only when the debtor does not fulfill contractual arrangements for the debt's repayment. When the creditor's right to petition to force a sale affects a certain identified parcel of real estate, the lien is referred to as a

specific lien. When the right affects the asset holdings of an individual without specific reference to a certain piece of property, the lien is known as a **general lien.**

In real estate, specific liens are the most important type of lien. The tax lien, the mortgage lien, and the mechanic's lien are the specific liens that are most often incurred. Under a **tax lien,** if a landowner fails to pay the property tax bill against a property, the local government has the right to force the sale of that specific piece of property to obtain the unpaid taxes. A **mechanic's lien** may be filed against the property for an unpaid bill owed to a contractor who has performed work on the property. The mortgage lien is discussed in detail in Chapter 8.

Restrictive Covenants

The **restrictive covenant,** sometimes called a **deed restriction,** is a statement placed in a deed by the current owner when the property is being sold or given to a prospective owner. Since the owner of the property has control of that property subject to public limits, the owner can sell the property on whatever terms he chooses. One of these terms could be the restriction of the future use of the land. However, the owner must be reasonable about such restrictions because they can affect the marketability of the property.

Two major categories of restrictive covenants are used: (1) Restrictions can be imposed on the use of the land by an owner who will sell one parcel but will retain possession of adjacent parcels. In this situation, the owner may not want an industrial site next to her property, so the owner places a restrictive covenant into the deed that expressly forbids the use of the land for industrial purposes. (2) Restrictions can be imposed by a land developer to make a residential subdivision more attractive. In this case, the restrictions could limit the type of dwelling units constructed and the type of nondwelling structures, such as storage buildings and fences, that are allowed on each parcel of land.

This second class of restriction is often referred to as a **general plan restriction.** Under the subdivision regulations determined by the local government, the developer must file a plat, or map, of the subdivision's street layout and building lots. At this point, the developer can also file and record a **declaration of restrictions** that is referenced to the subdivision map. As the building lots are sold, the respective deed for each lot contains clauses stating that the parcel of land is purchased subject to the restrictions that are recorded for the subdivision.

One other type of legal limitation on the use of land is imposed in the various contracts used in real estate transactions. Both the mortgage and the lease, the two most common real estate contracts, contain clauses that restrict the owner's or tenant's right to alter, remove, or demolish portions of the real estate as well as requirements to keep the property in good repair. These clauses thus limit the owner's or tenant's freedom to destroy or ignore the condition of the physical real estate.

What Is the Legal Description of the Site?

Every parcel of property must have a unique description of the amount of surface land that is owned. A unique description that describes only one location is a **legal description.** These descriptions include the lot and block system (also known as the plat map system), the metes and bounds system, the government rectangular system, and a combination legal description, which uses the last two. Each of these systems draws a picture of the land surface that is owned. *A post office address is never used as a unique description of the property.*

EXHIBIT 2.3   Subdivision plat.

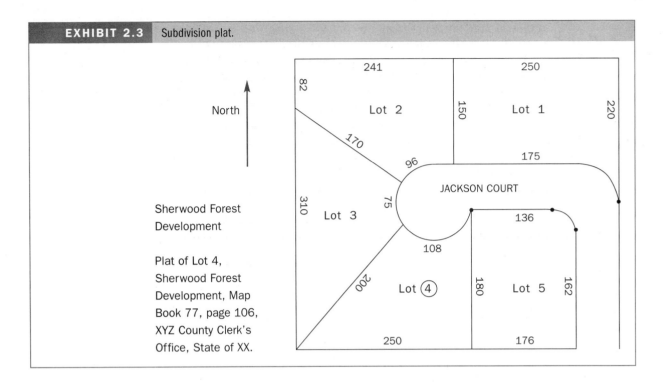

EXHIBIT 2.4   Metes and bounds system.

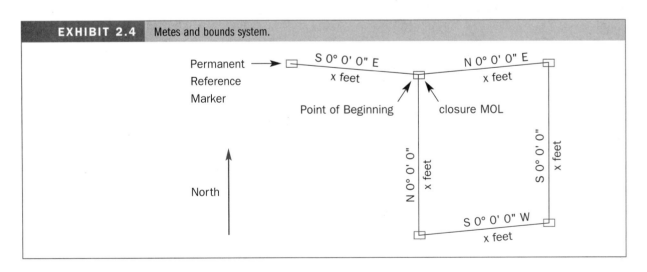

The **lot and block system,** or *plat map system,* for describing land is based on the use of publicly recorded maps, as shown in Exhibit 2.3. Most urban communities require developers to have their tracts surveyed and platted into building lots and blocks. This information is displayed on a plat map, on which each building lot is identified by its size, shape, and location in the tract. The map is placed on file with the local government's records office. The requirements that establish this system are related to the community's subdivision regulations. Under this system, the legal description of a parcel of land would contain the following kind of information: the property is Lot 4 in the Sherwood Forest Development as shown in Map Book 77, page 106, XYZ County.

The **metes and bounds system** describes the exterior perimeter of the property, as shown in Exhibit 2.4. It starts with a **permanent reference marker,** which may be a metal stake in the ground in a safe location such as a roadbed. The description will proceed in one direction to the **point of beginning,** which is one point on the perimeter location. From this point, the property is described usually in a clockwise direction by compass readings and feet such that the entire property is contained. The description ends when the last compass reading and distance arrives back at the point of beginning so that **closure** of the description is obtained. Sometimes the notation "mol" (for "more or less") is used to indicate that the precise location of the beginning point may not be achieved.

Earlier descriptions relied on monuments and other types of natural markers for the metes part of the description. These should not be used today because they could easily change, which means that ownership of the land surface would change with them.

The third legal description technique is the **government rectangular system,** a survey method in which baselines and principal meridians are used to identify tracts of land. **Baselines** are latitude lines running east and west across the face of the earth. **Principal meridians** are longitude lines running north and south. At intervals of 24 miles north and south of the predetermined and recorded baseline are **standard parallels.** At intervals of 24 miles east and west of the principal meridians are **guide meridians.** This system of baselines, standard parallels, principal meridians, and guide meridians is used to mark out plots of land that are 24 miles long and 24 miles wide.

Within each of these 24-mile-square plots of land are 16 subdivisions called townships. (The term *township* in this sense should not be confused with any type of political designation.) A **township** is a plot of land that is 6 miles long and 6 miles wide. It is identified by reference to the baseline and the principal meridian. Townships are arrayed in **tiers** (rows) and **ranges** (columns) and are referred to by their location. Thus, a township that is in the second tier north of the baseline and the second range west of the principal meridian is easy to identify and to distinguish from the township that is in the third tier south of the baseline and the second range east of the principal meridian. This distinction is shown in Exhibit 2.5.

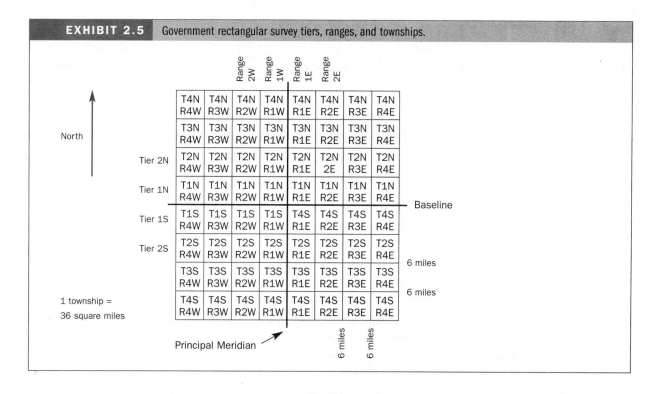

EXHIBIT 2.5 Government rectangular survey tiers, ranges, and townships.

EXHIBIT 2.6 **EXHIBIT 2.6** One township = 36 sections.

6	5	4	3	2	1
7	8	9	10	11	12
18	17	16	15	14	13
19	20	21	22	23	24
30	29	28	27	26	25
31	32	33	34	35	36

1 township = 36 square miles
1 township = 36 sections
1 section = 1 square mile
1 section = 640 acres
1 acre = 43,560 square feet

Each of the townships is in turn subdivided into 36 plots of land that are each one mile long and one mile wide. Each of these one-square-mile parcels is called a **section,** as shown in Exhibit 2.6. Within the township, the sections are numbered from 1 through 36. The convention established for numbering these sections starts with the first section in the northeasternmost corner of the township. The numbers of the sections then run in the order depicted in Exhibit 2.6. The final section, section 36, is in the southeasternmost corner of the township.

Each section may be further subdivided into acres. Each section equals 640 acres, and each **acre** equals 43,560 square feet. The conventional usage is to further subdivide using fractions such as 1/2 and 1/4. For example, a section may be divided into the W 1/2 or E 1/2, or the N 1/2 or S 1/2. In contrast, quarters may be used, for example, the NE 1/4, SE 1/4, SW 1/4, or NW 1/4. Exhibit 2.7 shows various divisions and the acres contained in several of them.

EXHIBIT 2.7 Further division of a section.

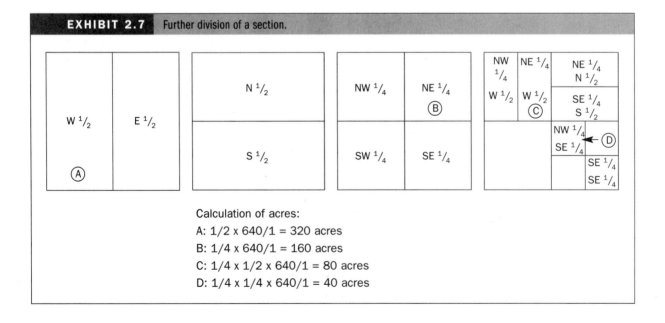

Calculation of acres:
A: 1/2 x 640/1 = 320 acres
B: 1/4 x 640/1 = 160 acres
C: 1/4 x 1/2 x 640/1 = 80 acres
D: 1/4 x 1/4 x 640/1 = 40 acres

The fourth legal system is the *combination legal description,* a combination of the metes and bounds system and the government rectangular system. The government rectangular system is used as the point of beginning for the metes and bounds system.

Chapter Summary

The rights of ownership are not absolute rights because there are constraints on the owner's ability to use the property. The limits and controls are classified into two categories: public and private.

Public controls are police power, eminent domain, taxation, and escheat (represented by the acronym PETE). All place limits on ownership with the purpose of promoting the well-being and interest of society. The most limiting is the police power, which includes various restrictions (such as building codes and zoning requirements) on the construction and use of property. Also, every property pays real estate taxes to some level of government.

Private limits are contractual restrictions between private parties that typically restrict use of the property. An example could be an easement that allows one party to use another's property. Another could be a deed restriction that allows construction on a vacant lot only if it has a minimum value and satisfies a predetermined architectural design.

Every parcel of property must have a unique legal description of the land surface. The four types of descriptions used are the plat map system, the metes and bounds system, the government rectangular system, and the combination legal description. The plat map system is an engineering map that is filed in the local courthouse. It includes the precise location and dimensions of each parcel. The metes and bounds system is a perimeter listing of all sides of the property, normally in a clockwise direction. The government rectangular system relates the location of the parcel to a government-drawn system of coordinates called ranges, tiers, and townships. The combination legal description uses the government rectangular system as a point of beginning for the metes and bounds system.

Internet Applications

A website has been established for this chapter at http://epley.swcollege.com.

Review Questions

1. What are the four types of public controls? What are the two types of private controls?

2. What is the difference between an easement appurtenant and an easement-in-gross?

3. Which is the dominant estate and which is the servient estate in a permanent easement?

4. Define and explain the concept of police power.

5. Define and explain the concept of eminent domain.

6. Explain the differences among the following legal descriptions:

   Metes and bounds system
   Plat map system
   Government rectangular system
   Combination legal description

7. Discuss the meaning of each of the following terms:

Range	Acre
Tier	Principal meridian
Township	Permanent reference marker
Section	Point of beginning

Discussion Questions

1. Are public controls beneficial to society? Why or why not?

2. Are private restrictions beneficial to society? Why or why not?

3. Are the public controls applied equally to all private property? If you answer no, give examples.

4. Should the right of eminent domain be limited? Why or why not?

5. Can a legal description ever be incorrect? If yes, what are the implications?

6. Is one legal description better than another? Who makes the decision?

7. Discuss the material found in the Internet assignments. What are the current land use issues?

## CHAPTER 3

Urban Economics and the Real Estate Market

1. What is a metropolitan area?

2. What is a local economic area?

3. What makes a metropolitan area grow?

4. What is the measure of economic growth?

5. Why are businesses and people attracted to a local economic area?

6. How does economic growth affect the land use pattern of an urban area?

OBJECTIVES

When finished with this chapter, the student should be able to:

1. Identify and describe a metropolitan area.

2. Describe the economic base of a local economy.

3. Identify a local economic area's growth and export industries.

4. Describe the role of basic and nonbasic industries in a local economy.

5. Specify the factors that attract business firms to a metropolitan area.

6. Describe such conceptual land use patterns as the concentric zone, sector, and multiple nuclei models.

7. Discuss the concept of rent bid analysis as a tool for land use analysis.

adaptive reuse

axial model

basic industries

bedroom communities

business climate

circular flow of income model

city

cohort survival method

concentric zone model

county

economic base

edge city

export base theory

functional integration principle

homogeneity principle

housing inventory method

input–output analysis

labor force participation ratio

land use succession theory

local economic area

location quotient (LQ)

meter-set method

metropolitan statistical area

multiple nuclei model

natural increase and migration
    method (MSA)

nonbasic industries

quality of life

ratio technique

rent bid analysis

rent bid function

rent bid gradient

satellite city

sector model

standard industrial classification
    (SIC) system

INTRODUCTION

This chapter focuses on the general topic of metropolitan growth analysis. Several specific questions will be answered by the information provided in this chapter. What makes a metropolitan area grow? What is the measure of economic growth? How does economic growth affect the land use pattern of an urban area? The answers to these questions require an understanding of five major concepts and their accompanying analytical techniques that relate to urban growth analysis. These five concepts are (1) local economic area analysis, (2) industrial location theory, (3) labor force location and migration theory, (4) land use theory, and (5) rent bid theory. The chapter is divided into sections that discuss these concepts.

   An understanding of the relationship among these five analytical techniques is an important first step. Each of the five analytical techniques has both an economic and a geographic, or spatial, component. However, in each study, one of the two components dominates. Local economic area analysis and industrial location theory are primarily economic analytical forms, while land use theory and rent bid theory are primarily spatial forms of analysis.

How Is a Local Economic Area Analyzed?

A metropolitan area, also referred to as an *urban area,* is in fact a **local economic area.** In this sense, it can be viewed as a geographic area that contains consumers of the goods and services provided by local businesses. It is the geographic area that provides the labor services for the production of the goods and the provision of the various services.

An analysis of a local economic area consists of four steps. First, the geographic extent of the local economic area is established. Second, the nature of the economy and its economic components are identified. Third, the magnitude of that economic activity is identified. Fourth, the magnitude and the composition of that economic activity are forecast into the future.

DEFINING THE GEOGRAPHIC ASPECT OF THE LOCAL ECONOMIC AREA

The local economy is defined geographically by political areas, such as the **city** and the **county.** Both a city and a county are political entities because the populations in both have formed local governments that have the ability to govern for the citizens. The city and the county are geographic areas enclosed within the political boundaries established by the residents who have chosen to establish the local jurisdiction. The primary differentiating characteristic between the city and the county is the extent of the geographic area. Counties typically contain more geographic space than cities. Stated in a different way, cities are usually found in counties, sometimes cities cross county lines, but for the most part, cities are political jurisdictions located within the boundaries of a county. The relationship among these concepts is shown in Exhibit 3.1. The exhibit also shows the relationship of census tracts to counties, and counties to the metropolitan statistical area (MSA).

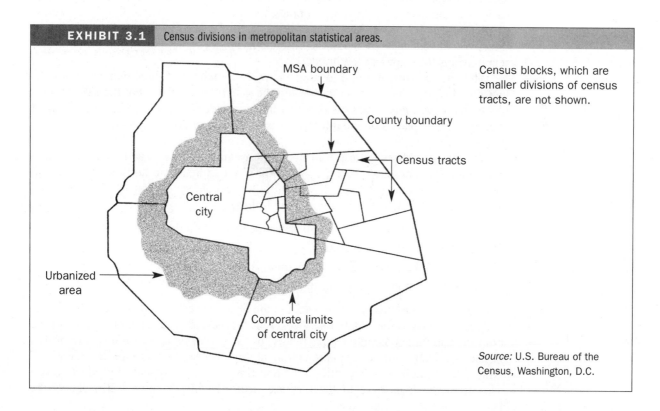

EXHIBIT 3.1   Census divisions in metropolitan statistical areas.

MSA boundary

Census blocks, which are smaller divisions of census tracts, are not shown.

County boundary

Census tracts

Central city

Urbanized area

Corporate limits of central city

Source: U.S. Bureau of the Census, Washington, D.C.

The local economy can be a city, it can be a county, and it often is a combination of counties referred to as a **metropolitan statistical area (MSA).** An MSA is formed by the U.S. Bureau of the Census by combining contiguous counties into a single geographic entity. The basis for making the combination is the functional integration principle and the homogeneity principle. Simply stated, the **functional integration principle** refers to the important economic links and land use similarities that exist between the political-geographic areas known as counties. One such link is the commuting pattern of the population of the counties. For example, two counties are functionally integrated if a high proportion of the labor force in County A commutes to jobs in County B. Two counties also are functionally integrated if their communication and information systems—newspapers, telephone, and TV and radio broadcasting—are linked. The information is broadcast from County A to County B. The **homogeneity principle** focuses on the similarities in economic and physical characteristics between the counties. In this context, two counties with the same approximate population density or land use patterns can be combined into the same MSA.

Depending on where the study is being performed, the local economic area can be described as any one of these three geographic areas: the MSA, the county, or the city. A *local economic area analysis* can be performed, for example, for the Atlanta Metropolitan Statistical Area; Champaign County, Illinois; or the City of Pullman, Washington. In addition, a local economic area analysis can be performed for a large geographic area that crosses county boundaries. For example, a local economic area analysis of "North Atlanta" would involve an analysis of a portion of at least four counties.

DESCRIBING THE NATURE OF ECONOMIC ACTIVITY IN THE LOCAL ECONOMY

Describing the nature of the economic activity that exists in the local economy can be easily accomplished by means of a simple economic model known as the **circular flow of income model.** When the relationships in this model are understood, they lead directly to the concepts of economic base theory, export base theory, and interindustry relationships (the input–output model).

The internal structure of a local economy is composed of three major sectors: the household sector, the business sector, and the government sector. For the sake of simplicity, the government sector is dropped from consideration here so that the focus of attention can be placed on the interrelationships between the household sector and the business sector.

The household sector in the local economy undertakes two activities simultaneously. First, the household sector consists of all individuals and households who own the factors of production. In other words, the household sector consists of those individuals who reside locally and who do the following:

1. Provide labor services to the industries located within the local economy
2. Own land in the local economy
3. Own all of the capital goods and capital funds
4. Provide entrepreneurial talent to local firms

These factors of production are sold to the business sector, and in return the household receives wages for its labor services, rent for the use of its land, dividends for the use of its capital goods, interest payments for the use of its capital funds, and profits for the application of its entrepreneurial ability. These relationships are shown in Exhibit 3.2. Exhibit 3.2(a) identifies the real flows—the movement of productive services from the household to the business sector—while Exhibit 3.2(b) shows the

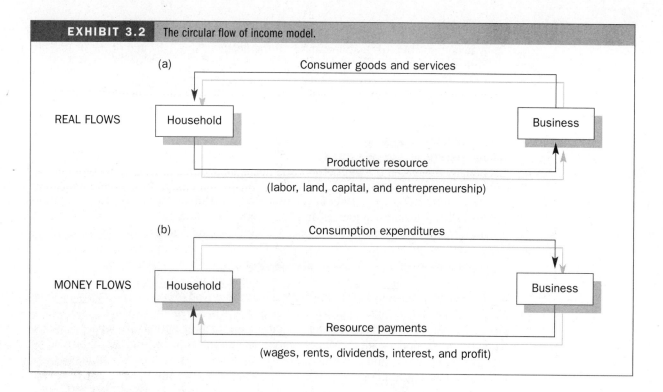

EXHIBIT 3.2 The circular flow of income model.

(a) Consumer goods and services

REAL FLOWS   Household   Business

Productive resource

(labor, land, capital, and entrepreneurship)

(b) Consumption expenditures

MONEY FLOWS   Household   Business

Resource payments

(wages, rents, dividends, interest, and profit)

money flows—the movement of factor payments in the form of wages, rents, interest, dividends, and profits from the business sector to the household sector.

At the same time that the household sector is providing factors of production to the business sector, it is also purchasing consumer goods and services that the business sector produces. This relationship is shown in real terms in Exhibit 3.2(a) as the movement of goods and services from the business sector to the household; it is also shown in money terms in Exhibit 3.2(b) as the flow of money in the form of consumption expenditures from the household to business sector.

The business sector, like the household sector, simultaneously performs two functions in the local economy. First, it uses the productive resources. Second, it produces the consumer goods and services that are purchased by the individuals in the household sector.

The circular flow of income model presented in this form reveals that the local economy is made up of two major sectors and is interrelated by two real flows and two money flows that reflect those real flows. Understanding the composition of the sectors and the composition of the flows is the first major conceptual step in understanding the nature of the economic activity in the local economy.

THE ECONOMIC BASE OF THE LOCAL ECONOMY

The **economic base** of the local economy is the set of characteristics that describe the sectors and the relationships among those sectors in the local economy. It is simply the description of the household and business sectors and the flows shown in the circular flow of income model presented in the previous section. *Economic base theory* simplifies the economy into a few major sectors such as the household and business sectors and postulates their relationships in a local economy. The household sector can be described by identifying variables such as the following:

1. Size of the population, number of families, and number of households
2. Age composition of the population, of the heads of families, and of the heads of households
3. Income composition of the population, families, and households
4. Size of families and households
5. Occupational composition of the population
6. Gender composition of the population
7. Marital status of the population
8. Educational attainment level of the population

This information can be obtained from the U.S. Bureau of the Census and publications of local planning agencies and chambers of commerce.

The structure of the business sector can be described by identifying the industrial classifications that exist in the local economy. This can be accomplished by means of the **standard industrial classification (SIC) system** developed and used by the U.S. Bureau of the Census. The SIC classification system identifies industrial activity according to a numerical code of one to four digits that expresses the type of industrial activity that can occur in an economy. An example of SIC categories is presented in Exhibit 3.3. For example, one local economy may be dominated by the manufacturing SIC codes, while a second local economy with the same approximate population size may be dominated by the finance, insurance and real estate (FIRE) and services SIC codes. Even though these local economies have the same population size and probably the same level of employment, the structure of the business sector is radically different. Focusing attention on the occupational composition of the labor force, one economy is white-collar while the other is blue-collar. These two economies will more than likely face different growth prospects.

EXHIBIT 3.3	Standard Industrial Classification (SIC) Codes.

Division A 0 Agriculture, forestry, fisheries
Division B 1 Mining
Division C 1 Construction
Division D 2 Manufacturing (nondurable)
      20 Food products
          201 Meat products
               2011 Meat-packing plants
               2012
               2013 Sausages and other prepared meat products
               2016 Poultry dressing plants
               2017 Poultry and egg processing
          202 Dairy products [Remainder of 20 series and 21 to 34 series omitted here]
               2021 Creamery butter
               2022 Cheese
               2023 Condensed and evaporated milk
               2024 Ice cream and frozen desserts
               2025 Fluid milk [4-digit breakdown omitted here]
    21 Tobacco manufacturers
    22 Textile mill products
    23 Apparel products
    24 Lumber and wood products
    25 Furniture and fixtures

(continued)

EXHIBIT 3.3 Standard Industrial Classification (SIC) Codes, continued.

26 Paper products
27 Printing, publishing industries
28 Chemicals
29 Petroleum refining

Division D 3 Manufacturing (durable)
30 Rubber and plastics
31 Leather
32 Stone, clay, glass, concrete
33 Primary metals
34 Fabricated metals
35 Machinery, except electrical
    351 Engines and turbines
    352 Farm and garden machinery
    353 Construction and related machinery
    354 Metalworking machinery
    355 Special industry machinery
    356 General industrial machinery
    357 Office and computing machines
    358 Refrigeration and service machinery
    359 Miscellaneous machinery
36 Electrical and electronic machinery
    361 Electric distribution equipment [4-digit breakdown omitted here]
    362 Electical industrial apparatus
    363 Household appliances
    364 Electric lighting and wiring equipment
    365 Radio and TV receiving equipment
    366 Communication and equipment
    367 Electronic components and accessories
    368 Miscellaneous electrical equipment and supplies
37 Transportation equipment
    371 Motor vehicles
        3711 Motor vehicles and passenger car bodies
        3712
        3713 Truck and bus bodies
        3714 Motor vehicle parts and accessories
        3715 Truck trailers [4-digit breakdown omitted here]
    372 Aircraft and parts
    373 Ship and boat building
    374 Railroad equipment
    375 Motorcyles, bicycles, and parts
    376 Guided missiles and space vehicles and parts
    379 Miscellaneous transportation equipment [Remainder of 38 and 39 series omitted here]
38 Instruments, photographic goods, optical goods, watches, and clocks
39 Miscellaneous
Division E 4 Transportation, communication, utilities (electric, gas, sanitary services)
Division F 5 Wholesale trade
Division G 5 Retail trade
Division H 6 Finance, insurance, and real estate
Division I 7 Services (personal, business)
Division I 8 Services (professional, educational)
Division J 9 Public administration (federal, state, and local government agencies)
Division K Nonclassifiable establishments

The real flows and the money flows for consumer goods are closely related. However, it is easier to obtain information on the money flow known as "consumption expenditures" than it is to obtain a list of the consumer goods and services themselves. Therefore, information from several sources is used to describe the composition of this flow. The *Census of Retail Trade* is one such publication in which the composition of retail trade for the MSA is broken down by two- and three-digit SIC codes.

The nature and composition of the productive resource flow and the resource payments flow can also be obtained from government publications. First, the workers can be identified by the type of industry in which they work. This method would yield information about the number of workers in the construction industry, in the manufacturing industries (heavy and light), in the retail and wholesale industries, and in the food processing industry. This information is provided by the *Census of Population,* which identifies the number of employees in one-digit SIC codes for MSAs and counties. Similar information can also be obtained from state offices on a county basis. Second, the labor force can be identified by its skill level and job orientation. This method would yield information about the number of workers who are classified as managerial and professional, technical, clerical, sales, service workers, and production craft and repair workers.

The local economy's real estate can be described by its components. The following kind of information can be provided:

1. The number of land units (acres, lots, and so forth) and specific uses of this land (residential, retail, office, and industrial) can be identified.
2. The area inside existing structures can be stated in square footage available for retail, office, and industrial users.
3. Current vacant real estate can be enumerated in terms of the number of vacant acres zoned for residential, commercial, or industrial use and the square footage of vacant commercial and industrial buildings.

EXPORT BASE THEORY—THE LINK TO THE NONLOCAL AREA

The **export base theory** was formulated in the 1950s and 1960s to analyze the growth of a local economy. This economic model starts with the idea that the business sector of the local economy contains both firms that sell to nonlocal consumers and firms that sell to local consumers. The community's commercial and industrial firms can be classified on the basis of the sales of their goods and services to local versus nonlocal consumers. Those industrial and commercial firms that sell their products to nonlocal consumers are known as the **basic industries** in the local economy. The firms that sell their goods and services to local consumers are known as the **nonbasic industries** in the local economy. In its original formulation, the export base theory held that an expansion in the basic industries of the economy generated the growth of the local economy. As the exportation of goods and services grew to accommodate increased demand by external consumers, the local economy grew for two reasons. First, the basic industries needed more employees to meet increased external demand. Second, the firms producing goods for local consumption also had to expand or new firms had to be started (or both) to meet the demands of the expanded local labor force in the basic industries.

As the basic industries expand their output and employment, they foster the expansion of employment in local producers. The effect of this expansion in the local economy is an increased demand in the various housing submarkets and the markets for commercial services. This increase in demand is brought about by an increase in the number of households and a possible increase in their purchasing power.

The significance of the export base theory lies in its signal to the analyst that external factors play a substantial role in the future of the local economy. As discussed in the previous section, economic base analysis describes the internal structure of the local economy. Export base theory alerts the analyst to the following needs:

1. To find the major growth industries in the local economy.
2. To find the most significant basic industries and firms in the local economy.
3. To identify the important external economic variables affecting the basic industries.
4. To trace the impact of changes in the basic sector the local economy.

IDENTIFYING THE MAJOR GROWTH INDUSTRIES IN THE LOCAL ECONOMY

To identify the major growth industries in the local economy, the analyst needs to compare employment levels. At least two points in time in the recent past should be used. For example, the analysis could be done for 1995 and 2000. The analyst can generate a growth rate for each industrial classification and for the level of total employment. This simple growth table will identify declining, stable, and growth industries. It will also identify growth industries that are growing at levels above the average growth for the local economy. Exhibit 3.4 is an example of such a table.

An examination of Exhibit 3.4 reveals the employment levels by one- and two-digit SIC codes for 1995 and 2000 for the local economy. Columns A and C show the levels of employment at these two points in time. Column E shows the five-year percentage growth for these industries. Notice that four industries are declining: rubber and plastics products; stone, clay, and glass products; fabricated metal products; and membership organizations. Several of the industries are "stable" in that they exhibit relatively low growth over the five-year period—for example, see leather and leather products, which is at 6.67 percent over five years.

The average growth rate for all employment was 50.33 percent for five years. An examination of column E reveals the high-growth industries to be those whose growth rates exceed 50 percent for five years. See transportation equipment, which shows the entry of a new firm. Also see business services, at 188.36 percent, health services, at 132.42 percent, and industrial machines including computers, at 154.09 percent.

Determining the continued growth of these high-growth industries is an important key in judging the future growth of the local economy. The analyst can look into the future prospects of these industries by checking on market trends in the specific industries. For example, if the local economy has a substantial number of firms in the electronics industry that have been growing, a check of the electronics industry through financial reports may reveal that growth in this industry is expected to continue into the future.

Exhibit 3.4 also allows the analyst to see the changing nature of the industrial structure in the local economy. Compare columns B and D for the one-digit SIC codes for both manufacturing and services. Manufacturing fell from 18.37 percent of total employment in 1995 to 15.23 percent in 2000. It is now less significant as a major industrial classification. On the other hand, services rose from 16.92 percent in 1995 to 23.56 percent in 2000. It is now more significant as a major industrial classification. Based simply on these two observations, the nature of the economy is changing from blue-collar to white-collar industry.

Exhibit 3.5 replicates the same SIC codes for the state. An examination of this table in a manner similar to the examination of Exhibit 3.4 reveals the declining, stable, and growth industries for the state. Several interesting observations arise when the local economy is contrasted to that of the state.

EXHIBIT 3.4 County employment.

	A	B	C	D	E
	1995		2000		Empl. Growth
	# EMPL.	% DISTR.	# EMPL.	% DISTR.	Percent
Agriculture, Forestry & Fisheries	1,376	1.00%	2,497	1.20%	81.47%
Mining	60	0.04%	162	0.08%	170.00%
Construction	8,749	6.34%	13,451	6.49%	53.74%
Manufacturing	25,339	18.37%	31,591	15.23%	24.67%
Food and kindred products	234	0.17%	378	0.18%	61.54%
Textile mill products	188	0.14%	254	0.12%	35.11%
Apparel and other textiles	1,053	0.76%	1,265	0.61%	20.13%
Lumber and wood products	617	0.45%	913	0.44%	47.97%
Furniture and fixtures	195	0.14%	305	0.15%	56.41%
Paper and allied products	722	0.52%	1,431	0.69%	98.20%
Printing and publishing	2,043	1.48%	2,772	1.34%	35.68%
Chemicals and allied products	734	0.53%	989	0.48%	34.74%
Petroleum and coal products	0				
Rubber and plastics products	919	0.67%	810	0.39%	-11.86%
Leather and leather products	30	0.02%	32	0.02%	6.67%
Stone, clay and glass products	1,392	1.01%	1,268	0.61%	-8.91%
Primary metal industries	0		0		
Fabricated metal products	1,687	1.22%	1,559	0.75%	-7.59%
Ind. machines including computers	1,405	1.02%	3,570	1.72%	154.09%
Electronics & electrical equipment	5,254	3.81%	6,866	3.31%	30.68%
Transportation equipment	1	0.00%	1,054	0.51%	105300.0%
Instruments and related products	2,522	1.83%	3,963	1.91%	57.14%
Misc. manufacturing industries	1,000	0.72%	1,287	0.62%	28.70%
Transportation and Public Utilities	3,828	2.77%	6,282	3.03%	64.11%
Wholesale Trade	21,723	15.74%	29,841	14.39%	37.37%
Durable goods	16,385	11.88%	22,752	10.97%	38.86%
Nondurable goods	5,338	3.87%	7,088	3.42%	32.78%
Retail Trade	29,573	21.43%	44,256	21.34%	49.65%
Finance, Insurance & Real Estate	7,847	5.69%	10,625	5.12%	35.40%
Services	23,346	16.92%	48,870	23.56%	109.33%
Hotels, other lodging places	1,439	1.04%	1,568	0.76%	8.96%
Personal services	1,201	0.87%	1,973	0.95%	64.28%
Business services	7,494	5.43%	21,610	10.42%	188.36%
Auto repair services, garages	1,301	0.94%	2,049	0.99%	57.49%
Misc. repair services	454	0.33%	680	0.33%	49.78%
Motion pictures	658	0.48%	765	0.37%	16.26%
Amusement and recreatrion	1,103	0.80%	1,900	0.92%	72.26%
Health services	3,621	2.62%	8,416	4.06%	132.42%
Legal services	344	0.25%	583	0.28%	69.48%
Educational	656	0.48%	720	0.35%	9.76%
Social services	1,314	0.95%	2,636	1.27%	100.61%
Membership organizations	668	0.48%	588	0.28%	-11.98%
Engineering and management	2,891	2.10%	5,022	2.42%	73.71%
Private households	96	0.07%	187	0.09%	94.79%
Federal Government	1,744	1.26%	3,423	1.65%	96.27%
Local Government	13,194	9.56%	14,622	7.05%	10.82%
State Government	1,102	0.80%	1,790	0.86%	62.43%
Nonclassifiable Establishments	31	0.02%	6	0.00%	-80.65%
TOTAL for ALL INDUSTRIES	137,971	100.00%	207,414	100.00%	50.33%

EXHIBIT 3.5   State employment.

	A	B	C	D	E
	1995		2000		Empl/ Growth
	# EMPL.	% DISTR.	# EMPL.	% DISTR.	Percent
Agriculture, Forestry & Fisheries	27,260	0.93%	36,040	1.07%	32.21%
Mining	8,702	0.30%	7,688	0.23%	-11.65%
Construction	146,084	4.96%	151,040	4.50%	3.39%
Manufacturing	559,458	19.00%	587,604	17.50%	5.03%
Food and kindred products	60,965	2.07%	67,156	2.00%	10.16%
Textile mill products	109,879	3.73%	111,745	3.33%	1.70%
Apparel and other textiles	60,932	2.07%	50,460	1.50%	-17.19%
Lumber and wood products	31,800	1.08%	37,681	1.12%	18.49%
Furniture and fixtures	9,933	0.34%	10,546	0.31%	6.17%
Paper and allied products	33,732	1.15%	34,534	1.03%	2.38%
Printing and publishing	38,142	1.30%	42,562	1.27%	11.59%
Chemicals and allied products	19,821	0.67%	21,023	0.63%	6.06%
Petroleum and coal products	932	0.03%	826	0.02%	-11.37%
Rubber and plastics products	17,442	0.59%	22,799	0.68%	30.71%
Leather and leather products	1,529	0.05%	1,388	0.04%	-9.22%
Stone, clay, and glass products	18,280	0.62%	19,116	0.57%	4.57%
Primary metal industries	14,961	0.51%	14,159	0.42%	-5.36%
Fabricated metal products	20,649	0.70%	22,943	0.68%	11.11%
Ind. machines including computers	28,645	0.97%	34,204	1.02%	19.41%
Electronics & electrical equipment	32,325	1.10%	33,483	0.997%	3.58%
Transportation equipment	40,916	1.39%	42,675	1.27%	4.30%
Instruments and related products	9,590	0.33%	10,975	0.33%	14.44%
Misc. manufacturing industries	6,154	0.21%	6,689	0.20%	8.69%
Transportation and Public Utilities	188,519	6.40%	209,168	6.23%	10.95%
Wholesale Trade	214,168	7.27%	227,766	6.78%	6.35%
Durable goods	134,979	4.58%	142,890	4.26%	5.86%
Nondurable goods	79,190	2.69%	84,876	2.53%	7.18%
Retail Trade	527,660	17.92%	628,865	18.73%	19.18%
Finance, Insurance & Real Estate	161,433	5.48%	172,172	5.13%	6.65%
Services	588,042	19.97%	772,386	23.00%	31.35%
Hotels, other lodging places	42,144	1.43%	41,165	1.23%	-2.32%
Personal services	28,841	0.98%	31,405	0.94%	8.89%
Business services	147,972	5.03%	222,094	6.61%	50.09%
Auto repair services, garages	24,865	0.84%	28,685	0.85%	15.36%
Misc. repair services	9,066	0.31%	9,659	0.29%	6.54%
Motion pictures	8,954	0.30%	10,609	0.32%	18.48%
Amusement and recreatrion	21,145	0.72%	29,418	0.88%	39.13%
Health services	154,357	5.24%	210,288	6.26%	36.23%
Legal services	19,279	0.65%	21,163	0.63%	9.77%
Educational	26,186	0.89%	32,630	0.97%	24.61%
Social services	27,955	0.95%	40,021	1.19%	43.16%
Membership organizations	14,309	0.49%	15,221	0.45%	6.37%
Engineering and management	53,675	1.82%	67,943	2.02%	26.58%
Private households	7,452	0.25%	9,304	0.28%	24.85%
Federal Government	103,715	3.52%	99,425	2.96%	-4.14%
Local Government	298,730	10.15%	326,387	9.72%	9.26%
State Government	115,947	3.94%	136,325	4.06%	17.58%
Nonclassifiable establishments	4,695	0.16%	3,187	0.09%	-32.12%
TOTAL for ALL INDUSTRIES	2,944,426	100.00%	3,358,052	100.00%	14.05%

1. The local economy's employment level grew by 50 percent while the state's grew by 14 percent.
2. Apparel is a growth industry in the local economy but a declining industry in the state economy.
3. Transportation equipment is a stable industry in the state economy but a growth industry in the local economy.
4. Both rubber and plastic products and fabricated metal products are declining industries in the local economy but are growth industries in the state economy.

IDENTIFYING THE BASIC INDUSTRIES IN THE LOCAL ECONOMY

The basic industries in a small local economy can be identified by means of a direct survey of the major firms, or even all of the firms, in the economy. By a direct survey of the plant manager or the head of shipping, the analyst can determine that all of the output of Firm A is sent out of the local economy. Firm A is a basic firm serving the nonlocal market and is thereby bringing funds into the local economy by exporting its goods or services.

If the local economy contains hundreds or even thousands of firms, the direct survey technique can be very costly and time-consuming. The alternate method used in such a situation is a proxy measure known as the **location quotient (LQ).** It measures the percentage of a local industrial classification to total local employment and compares it to a similar measure for a larger economic entity. For example, if the manufacturing sector of a local economy has 25,000 workers in a total workforce of 220,000, the local percentage is 11.36 percent. For the same period of time, the manufacturing sector of the state has 46,000 workers out of a total workforce of 500,000. The state percentage is 9.2 percent. The LQ is 11.36/9.2 = 1.23. This industry is a basic industry in this local economy. The indicator is that the LQ is greater than one.

The common sense of the LQ technique is that an industry with an LQ greater than one is producing more of a product than the local economy consumes. The additional product is shipped to other areas of the state as an export that generates income for the local economy.

Exhibit 3.6 shows the LQs for each of the one- and two-digit SIC codes in the sample local economy. In 2000, the electronics and electrical equipment industry has an LQ of 3.32. This is calculated by the method discussed above. In Exhibit 3.4, column D, this SIC has a distribution percentage of 3.31 percent in the local economy, and in Exhibit 3.5, it has a distribution percentage of 0.997 percent. Dividing 3.31% by 0.997% yields an LQ of 3.32.

An examination of the LQs of 2000 reveals that the most significant basic industries are construction, industrial machinery including computers, electronics and electrical equipment, instruments and related products, wholesale trade, businesses services, and engineering and management. All of these industries have an LQ greater than or equal to 1.2.

IDENTIFYING THE IMPORTANT EXTERNAL ECONOMIC VARIABLES AFFECTING THE BASIC INDUSTRIES

After the analyst has identified the high-growth industries and the basic industries, the focus of the analysis shifts to the external, or nonlocal, factors that affect these industries. Here the analyst will seek forecasts about these specific industries from various sources of financial information. What are the reports of Wall Street firms projecting

EXHIBIT 3.6   Location quotients.

	1995	2000
Agriculture, Forestry & Fisheries	1.08	1.12
Mining	0.15	0.34
CONSTRUCTION	1.28	1.44
Manufacturing	0.97	0.87
Food and kindred products	0.08	0.09
Textile mill products	0.04	0.04
Apparel and other textiles	0.37	0.41
Lumber and wood products	0.41	0.39
Furniture and fixtures	0.42	0.47
Paper and allied products	0.46	0.67
Printing and publishing	1.14	1.05
Chemicals and allied products	0.79	0.76
Petroleum and coal products		
Rubber and plastics products	1.12	0.58
Leather and leather products	0.42	0.37
Stone, clay and glass products	1.63	1.07
Primary metal industries		
Fabricated metal products	1.74	1.10
Ind. machines including computers	1.05	1.69
Electronics and electrical equipment	3.47	3.32
Transportation equipment	0.00	0.40
Instruments and related products	5.61	5.85
Misc. manufacturing industries	3.47	3.12
Transportation and Public Utilities	0.43	0.49
Wholesale Trade	2.16	2.12
Durable goods	2.59	2.58
Nondurable goods	1.44	1.35
Retail Trade	1.20	1.14
Finance, Insurance & Real Estate	1.04	1.00
Services	0.85	1.02
Hotels, other lodging places	0.73	0.62
Personal services	0.89	1.02
Business services	1.08	1.58
Auto repair services, garages	1.12	1.16
Misc. repair services	1.07	1.14
Motion pictures	1.57	1.17
Amusement and recreatrion	1.11	1.05
Health services	0.50	0.65
Legal services	0.38	0.45
Educational	0.53	0.36
Social services	1.00	1.07
Membership organizations	1.00	0.63
Engineering and management	1.15	1.20
Private households	0.27	0.33
Federal Government	0.36	0.56
Local Government	0.94	0.73
State Government	0.20	0.21
Nonclassifiable Establishments	0.14	0.03

for these industries? How have these industries reacted to changes in national or regional employment levels, personal disposable income, interest rates, and inflation rates? What do macroeconomic forecasts predict for future levels of employment, income, interest rates, and inflation rates? The answers to these questions give the analyst a foundation for making judgments concerning the future of the local economy.

TRACING THE IMPACT OF CHANGES IN THE BASIC SECTOR ON THE LOCAL ECONOMY

After the analyst has gathered information about the external factors affecting the high-growth and basic industries, the forecast change in these industries needs to be related to the change in the local economy. Several approaches are available to accomplish this task. The most straightforward is to check the prospects for growth in only the high-growth and the export industries. The analyst may not have the time or financial resources to examine each SIC code. If the analysis reveals that future prospects are just as good in the next five years as they were in the past five years, then the analyst can assume that the other industries will perform as they have, and can reach the conclusion that the employment growth rate for the local economy will be 50 percent for the five-year period, or 10 percent annually. If the prospects for the high-growth industries are less favorable by a factor of 40 percent, then the employment growth can be scaled back to 6 percent per year. Another approach requires the calculation of an economic impact multiplier for the basic industries and the use of this figure to predict the future level of employment. Two such multipliers can be calculated, but the procedure will not be discussed here.

INPUT–OUTPUT ANALYSIS

Input–output analysis is an alternative technique that allows the analyst to combine the circular flow of income theory and the export base theory. In its simplest use, the input–output model is a description device for the internal relationships in the business sector and an alternative to the circular flow of income theory as a descriptive technique for the economy. The analysis is based upon an input–output table that lists the relationships among all of the industries internal to the economy. A quick look at the table with a focus on a specific SIC code would show the following facts:

1. Inputs into the firms in that SIC code from all other local firms
2. Amount of imports and exports for that SIC code
3. Input of labor services from the household sector and output of the local firms to the household sector

However, as important as input–output analysis is as a descriptive measure for a local economy, a full discussion of this technique is beyond the scope of this chapter.

UPDATING AND FORECASTING POPULATION AND EMPLOYMENT

Economic base theory and export base theory are both descriptive tools. Description is important, but prediction of the future economic status or vitality of the local economy is even more important.

After the real estate analyst describes the nature of the existing economy using the most recent data, the analyst typically faces two additional tasks. First, if the census data are not current—for example, the analysis is being done in 1995, but the census information reflects the economic relationships of 1990—the analyst must update the key variables, such as population, employment, income, and retail sales. Once the information is updated, the analyst can then use this current information as well as past information to forecast the level of population, employment, income, and retail sales for future periods.

As a point of clarification, there is a difference between a projection and a forecast. A *projection* is simply the extrapolation of past values for some variable, such as population, through the present period into the future. A *forecast,* on the other hand, begins as a projection by using historic information but then the analyst uses the most current information that may not appear in the database to make adjustments to the historic projection. Published information is almost never current—some information might be a month old, other data can be a year old. Things change since the last data entry and the present day, and these current period changes are considered in the forecast to the best possible extent. When this analysis is imposed, the trend of the variable into the future may be higher or lower than the value that would arise given a simple projection. The need to make this distinction between a forecast and a projection exists because the real estate market analyst is responsible for forecasting future changes that can affect a parcel of real property or its income stream.

The real estate analyst often makes forecasts based upon projections of the population and employment made by governmental agencies. At times, the real estate analyst must make forecasts concerning the property based upon a projection or a forecast for the national, regional, or local economy. The following sections present information on the traditionally accepted techniques used by the analyst to update and forecast information.

Updating Techniques

Several accepted methods exist for updating population values from a past census to the current period. Five of these methods will be briefly discussed in the following subsections: (1) the housing inventory method, (2) the natural increase and migration method, (3) the cohort survival method, (4) the ratio technique, and (5) graphical/mathematical techniques.

HOUSING INVENTORY METHOD. The **housing inventory method** relies on the use of population and household size figures from the previous census. In addition to the census data, local area data on building permits and demolitions are also used. The method of calculating the current population value starts with the 1990 population for the geographic area in question and the appropriate household size for that geographic area. (The geographic area can be the MSA, the county, or a census tract.) Information from the 2000 census is obtained for household size. Once these data from the past are obtained, the trends in household size are forecast to the current period. The number of current households is estimated by using building permit and demolition data from the local community to get the change in the number of housing units. The analyst produces a population estimate for the current period by multiplying housing units by household size.

A method very similar to the housing inventory method is the **meter-set method.** The phrase "meter set" is a shortened and modified expression that refers to the installation of electric meters. In this method, instead of relying on building permits to estimate new residential construction, the analyst uses information from the local electric power company to estimate the number of new households moving into the geographical area under analysis.

NATURAL INCREASE AND MIGRATION METHOD. The **natural increase and migration method** starts with information from the most recent census of population for age categories and gender composition as they existed in 2000. The net change in population is calculated. First, using demographic information about the fertility rate of women in the prime childbearing age category, the number of births per thousand can be established for each year. Then, the survival rate—or its counterpart, the death rate—is obtained by age category from mortality tables on a year-to-year basis.

The next piece of information required to complete the estimate of current population is an estimate of the net migration of individuals into the geographic area. The best available local source of such information is the net new electrical hookups for the area in question. This information is available from a utility company by broad geographic areas, such as by census tract, zip code, or county. Net new hookups represent the number of households that have established new service at another site in the local area. In other words, it measures the number of households who had electrical service less those households who resided in the area, canceled their service, and never established a new account because they had left the area.

If net new electrical hookups data are not available, the most recent migration (2000 to the current period) must be extrapolated from the previous period (1990–2000). Given the data, this extrapolation can be performed on a year-by-year basis.

The analyst produces the population estimate for the current period by recording the 2000 population, adding the estimated births for the 2000–current period, subtracting out the deaths for the 2000–current period, and then entering the result of migration, which could be positive or negative. If the analyst obtains local statistics on actual births and deaths for the 2000–current period, the updated population figure becomes more accurate.

COHORT SURVIVAL METHOD. This population updating technique also utilizes an age breakdown of the population from the most recent census of population. In the **cohort survival method,** the breakdown in the age category has to be in five-year intervals because the data are presented in the census in five-year groupings. In other words, the age-group that was ages 21 to 25 in 1990 were ages 26 to 30 in 1995 and 31 to 35 in 2000.

This technique uses the survival rate for these five-year cohorts to obtain the surviving members of each age cohort. A calculation is performed for each of the age-groups, and the surviving members of each age cohort are placed forward in time. In other words, the age group that was ages 21 to 25 in 1990 were ages 26 to 30 in 1995, but only about 99.6 percent survived. This age group was ages 31 to 35 in 2000 but only 99.2 percent survived the additional 5 years.

The next major component of the cohort survival method is the calculation of net migration. In the simplest form, the estimate for net migration can be obtained using the net new hookups figure. Once it is obtained, this figure is entered by age-group or simply by its total change (plus or minus) to get the 2000 population estimate.

Finally, births during the update period are estimated from data on women in their prime childbearing years and the fertility rate. Births become the estimate for children in the ages 0 to 5 cohort.

RATIO TECHNIQUE. The **ratio technique** allows the analyst to estimate the value of an unknown value from a known value. The analyst may have past and current data for a larger geographic unit, a county, but only have past data for a specific census tract. The task at hand is to obtain an estimate for the population level in the census tract for the current period. This is accomplished by using the ratio for the known values in the past to estimate the unknown value for the present period in the census tract. For example, the county had a population of 100,000 in 1995 and the census tract had a population of 9,000 in 1995. The planning agency has an estimate of the 2002 population in the county of 140,000 but needs to obtain an estimate for the census tract in 2002. The ratio technique states that 9,000 divided by 100,000 is a 9 percent census tract-to-county ratio in 1995. This 9 percent ratio is then applied to the 140,000 to yield a population estimate for the census tract of 12,600 in 2002.

GRAPHICAL AND MATHEMATICAL TECHNIQUES. The graphical and mathematical techniques for updating population use data from previous periods and project it to the present using either a graph or a mathematical equation that approximates the value of the historical curve. In their simplest form, these techniques use direct observation to project a curve. The analyst looks at a graph of past data and extends the curve. Currently, the most popular technique for approximating the historical values and projecting them is regression analysis. However, a detailed discussion of regression analysis in its mathematical and statistical forms is beyond the scope of this chapter.

Forecasting Techniques

Each of the updating techniques discussed in the previous section can be used to forecast or project into the future. The procedure involves an additional conceptual step. The updating task brings the data series to the present; the forecasting task extrapolates the present into the future by analyzing key variables in each method. The forecast can be made under two initial conditions: the existence of a population projection or the lack of such a projection.

FORECASTING POPULATION FROM AN EXISTING PROJECTION. The ratio technique is the simplest method to use if a legitimate population forecast or projection exists. Usually, such data are provided by an agency of a state government. They also may be available from a regional planning agency.

First, the analyst displays the actual 1990 and 2000 population data for the county and the census tract. From these data, the historical census tract to county population ratio and the current period values are calculated. Then, the analyst displays the county population projection from the state agency for 2000 and 2005.

The forecast for census tract population involves the following steps:

1. The value of the census tract to county population ratio is forecast into the future by checking the current growth potential in the county and the census tract.
2. The future appropriate value of the ratio is applied to the projected county population.

For example, the ratio of population in the census tract to the population in the county in the past was 5 percent in 2000, 4 percent in 1995, and 3 percent in 1990. The analyst has a forecast of county population for the next year of 200,000. How would the ratio technique yield a forecast of population for the census tract for the next year? Based solely on historic values, the population ratio has been increasing by 1 full percentage point every five years. If the analyst is forecasting for 2005, the baseline projection would simply be the application of the historic data into the future. In 2005, the ratio would be 6 percent if no basis change occurred in either the county or the census tract. The projection for the census tract population would be 12,000.

The projection would be a forecast if the analyst checked to see that the economic and demographic situation in the future would be the same as it was in the past. If the circumstances were the same, 12,000 would be the forecast. If the analyst discovered that the supply of vacant residential property was used up in the most recent year, then the forecast would be that the ratio could only increase to 5.25 percent instead of 6 percent for the year 2005.

To obtain the appropriate future value of the census tract to county population ratio, the analyst could check the following supply factors that enable growth in both the county and the census tract:

1. Construction projects under way
2. Available land zoned for residential construction
3. Prospects for rezoning from low-density residential to high-density residential, and from nonresidential to residential, uses
4. County plans for road, water, and sewage system extensions into undeveloped areas
5. State and county plans for the provision of public services that might require eminent domain takings of existing residential units

In addition to these supply variables, the analysis also can check the demand for residential space in the respective areas.

After the level of population in the census tract has been forecast, the number of households also can be forecast. This is accomplished by determining the historic trend in household size for the study area, judging its future value, and dividing this estimate into the population forecast.

FORECASTING POPULATION WITHOUT AN EXISTING PROJECTION. If an independent population projection is not available from a reputable government or private agency, the ratio method is not applicable. In this case, one of the other methods must be used. For discussion purposes, the natural increase and migration method will be used here.

Because relatively short time periods are of major concern for small area forecasting, this forecast will be made for 2005. The first piece of information needed to make the forecast is the number of females in their primary childbearing years, 21 to 35. The exact number of women will depend on the relative number of women in the ages 10 to 20 cohort in 2000 who will move into the ages 21 to 35 cohort by 2010, and the number of women in the ages 25 to 35 cohort in 2000 who will move out of the ages 21 to 35 cohort by 2010. A first approximation would set the inflow equal to the outflow so that the size of the ages 21 to 35 cohort is assumed to be stable at 12,000 women. If this assumption is made, the number of births between 2000 and 2010 can be estimated. Then, the number of deaths between 2000 and 2010 can be estimated. In this way, the net effect of the birth and death components can be established.

The first appropriation for net migration could be the simple reinsertion of the 1990 to 2000 net migration value. However, the more conceptually appropriate approach would be an analysis of the historic migration figures compared to the past growth potential of the study area. If the factors enabling future growth in the area are still favorable, the historic trend can be extended into the future. But, if the ability to grow is retarded because the supply of land for commercial, industrial, and residential use is limited, future growth will be much less than the historic trend. In other words, future levels of net migration will be lower and could even be negative.

In summary, the population can be forecast by combining the natural increase and migration method with the graphical technique to analyze the historic migration trend and compare it to future trends.

What Factors Attract Firms to an Urban Area?

The typical measures of urban economic growth are the rates of change in employment, population, and personal income. Urban areas grow when firms are attracted to the urban area, bringing jobs and income with them. In order to understand the factors that affect the growth of an urban area, the analyst needs to understand the factors that affect the location of firms.

Industrial and commercial firms bring jobs to a locality both when they move into the local economy and when they expand their operations in the locality. They also affect the number of jobs (negatively) when they move out of the local economy or go out of business. Understanding the factors that attract a firm to a geographic area and the factors that repel a firm from the same area is important. The following subsections focus on this issue. In the location decision-making process, each of the following location determinants enters the analysis. Keep in mind that the factors must be evaluated as an interrelated whole, even though the following discussion handles each factor by itself.

GEOGRAPHIC DIFFERENCES IN LABOR COSTS

Labor costs, a major cost in producing a good or providing a service, is an important location determinant. The labor costs to produce a good are a combination of a wage rate and labor productivity. Consider this example: A firm incurs $400 in labor costs to produce 80 units of a product in one hour. Given the current technology of the production facility, this output level is accomplished by using 20 workers at $20 per hour. Working as part of an assembly line, the average output per worker is 4 units per hour. If the firm chose to change the production process, it could hire 40 workers at $10 per hour to produce 80 units per hour. Here, the average output per worker would be 2 units per hour. In both situations, the labor cost would be $400, but the wage rate and the labor productivity would be different. Thus, any discussion of wage rate differences needs to also consider productivity differences.

In order to achieve the lowest production costs, a firm will choose a geographic area in which productivity is high and wages are low rather than an area in which the reverse is the case. If productivity levels are comparable between two possible sites for the firm, the firm will choose the area with the lower wage rate structure. If wage rates are comparable, the firm will choose the site in the higher productivity area.

Wage rates are a function of the demand for labor relative to the supply of labor. The productivity of labor underlies the demand for labor. In turn, the productivity of labor is a function of the amount of education, experience, and on-the-job training that the laborers possess.

When the firm evaluates possible locations, it checks to see what is happening in the local labor market for laborers with the skills that it requires. Important factors are the current wage rate, the projected wage rate in the near future, the availability of labor with the required skill level, and the rate at which new entrants to the labor force with the required skill level are generated by the local secondary school system, technical schools, junior colleges, senior colleges, and universities.

GEOGRAPHIC DIFFERENCES IN SPACE COSTS

The cost of the space in which the product is produced or the service is provided is another important location determinant. The focus rests on the price of land, the rent rate on space, or both.

If a production firm is evaluating the geographic differences in land costs, it checks the asking price for currently available land and the actual transaction price for similar land parcels that have recently sold. Here, the evaluation considers all of the important dimensions of the alternative sites. Land use restrictions in the zoning are checked. Site size and shape are checked. Topography and soil and bedrock characteristics are checked. But, this is only the starting point. In addition to the cost of the raw land, local zoning and subdivision regulations can make a difference in the cost of developed land, even when the cost of raw land is the same. Local differences in construction codes can also make a substantial difference. Local differences in the cost of construction can make a difference. It is quite possible, for example, that the site in Community A, which has the lowest cost for the raw land, can turn out to have the highest cost for the completed space once these other considerations are evaluated.

If the firm is looking for office space, the analysis focuses on the effective rent rate for the office space in the local economy and specifically in the market area. The quoted rent rate is the rent rate the broker advertises for the space. The effective rent rate is the rent the tenant actually pays. The difference between these two rent levels is a function of free rent periods, rent abatements, tenant improvement allowances, free parking space, and other lease negotiation items.

If the advertised rent rate is $20 per square foot of rentable space per year for 12,000 square feet, the total space cost is $240,000 per year, or $20,000 per month. If the owner offers to provide free rent, the effective rent is less than the advertised rent rate. If the owner offers the first two months of rent free on a five-year lease, the total space cost drops from $1,200,000 over the five years to $1,160,000, which is $19,333.33 per month. The effective rent of $19.33 per square foot is less than the advertised rent of $20. The lease will contain the advertised rent of $20 per square foot per year for 12,000 square feet of space and the free rent arrangement for the first two months of the five-year lease. The effective rent of $19.33 per square foot is not stated in the lease but is a figure that the tenant calculates in order to be able to compare this lease offer to other lease offers.

A rent abatement occurs when the owner allows the tenant to pay a reduced rate over a period of time. In the previous case, the owner charges $20 per square foot but will allow the tenant to pay only 50 percent of the rate for the first 9 months. The total space cost drops from $1,200,000 over the five years to $1,110,000, which is $18,500 per month. The effective rent of $18.50 per square foot is less than the advertised rent of $20, which is stated in the lease.

Two geographic areas may be quoting the same rent rate, but the effective rent rate can be substantially different due to actual rent provisions such as free rent and rent abatements. The firm looks for the geographic area that offers the lowest effective rent rate. Typically, the effective rent in a local area is lower when the vacancy rate in the office market is higher.

GEOGRAPHIC DIFFERENCES IN TRANSPORT COSTS

In a manufacturing context, a firm must obtain raw materials or finished inputs in its production process. The firm incurs procurement costs to transport the inputs to the production facility. The firm also must distribute the output of the plant to the user of the product. The ultimate user can be the consumer or another firm that uses this firm's output as an input in its production process. As part of the location decision, the firm needs to try to minimize the total of these transportation costs. For one firm, the transport cost minimization may require a location close to the consumer markets where the product is sold. For another firm, the transport cost minimization may require a location near the location of the raw materials.

For a service provider that requires office space, minimizing transport cost is also a key consideration. Here, the main transport cost is probably the cost of getting personnel to and from an airport that provides easy access to other geographic areas.

GEOGRAPHIC DIFFERENCES IN UTILITIES

The cost and availability of electrical energy, natural gas, water, wastewater treatment, and solid waste removal can vary across different locations. These utility costs affect the level of production costs in the same way as labor costs and space costs and thereby also enter into the location decision of the firm.

GEOGRAPHIC DIFFERENCES IN BUSINESS CLIMATE

The principal location determinants for a firm tend to be the economic considerations that arise regarding geographic differences in labor cost, space cost, transportation cost, and utility cost. Yet, the issue of the local community's business climate is also an important consideration. A community's **business climate** is the attitude of the local population, the business leaders, and the local officials, appointed or elected, toward the firm and its key personnel. Studies of business climate generally focus on issues that can be controlled by the population or its government, such as laws, regulations, public service expenditures, and labor force relationships (unions and strikes). Business climate can be perceived in a general way by focusing on the community's attitude toward all types of commerce and industry. However, the business climate toward a specific firm is much more useful in that firm's location choice. Business climate can be positive, indifferent, or negative. The firm is most concerned about the effects of locating a production plant or distribution facility in a negative business climate.

To a specific firm, the community's attitude is important, because on the surface the community will not be able to discriminate against a specific firm. However, there are many ways that an unwelcome firm can be treated. The assessed value of an unwelcome firm can be disproportionately higher. The public services provided to it can be disproportionately lower than they are for other firms. Slower maintenance and repair of access roads that serve the plant site may occur. The firm may have to spend substantial time and money to obtain fair treatment.

Public attitude can affect legal rulings in local judicial proceedings involving the firm. The unwelcome firm may be found liable when it is not; it may have to pay higher awards than normal or typical if it is in fact liable. Public attitude can slow the process of taking the raw land and developing it. Here, zoning issues, subdivision regulations, and construction codes can be used adversely by local inspectors and other local officials. Future expansion of the firm either on-site or off-site can also meet with government resistance.

The community's attitude toward the firm and its management personnel can affect the costs of operation for the plant by affecting the cost of maintaining upper management at the facility. Salaries of management and key personnel may have to be raised in order to keep them at the plant. This can occur if plant management is excluded from social and community activities because of their affiliation with the unwelcome firm. If an increased salary base is not provided as compensation for community exclusion, the key management personnel will have a high turnover, generating extra expenses for the firm.

Unlike the geographic differentials in labor, space, transport, and utility costs that can be quantified, the various aspects of business climate are not as easily quantifiable. However, in a thorough location study, both the negative and positive effects of business climate need to be made an integral part.

Finally, the rankings of best places to do business are poor substitutes for a business climate study because they focus on general issues of interest to all types of firms, not on the specific interests of a specific firm.

QUALITY OF LIFE FOR KEY PERSONNEL

Quality of life considerations have bearing on both the location decision of the firm and on the location decision of labor and population. In this section, the focus is on those aspects of quality of life that bear directly on the members of management and other key personnel in the firm. The affect of quality of life on individuals in general also has bearing here but will be discussed later in this chapter.

For the firm, quality of life enters the firm's location decision through its key personnel. The firm's location decision may require several upper and middle managers to relocate, and it may require several other key professional staff to relocate. The firm wants to make these people happy or, if not happy, at least content about the move. The firm's location evaluation team needs to know some of the important preferences of these key personnel. For example, these people currently are living in large, modern housing units in well-designed subdivisions that provide recreational facilities. Community A has this housing option, while Community B does not. These people are water-oriented people who enjoy boating, fishing, and other water sports. Community A can provide these amenities. Community B can provide a variety of golf courses, but the key personnel do not like to golf. Based on the preferences of the key personnel, Community A provides a higher quality of life than B.

As part of this quality of life decision, the firm may have to provide some form of financial assistance with the sale of the peoples' current homes and the acquisition of a suitable and comparable home in the new location. The firm might have to provide a loan for a down payment or a reimbursement for a loss on the sale of the existing home. The firm may have to provide assistance with travel and moving expenses.

What Factors Attract Labor and Population to an Urban Area?

The creation of job opportunities attracts labor. As laborers move into the area, some of them bring other members of their families or households with them, causing an increase in population.

Currently, each laborer on average is associated with approximately one additional member of the population. For example, a single or unmarried individual moving into an urban area brings one person, himself or herself, to the population base. A married couple with no children can add either one or two people to the local labor force but does add two people to the local population. A married couple with children typically adds two people to the workforce and four people to the population. These individual situations are reflected in the aggregate for a geographic area by the **labor force participation ratio,** which is the number of workers in the labor force divided by the population. This ratio differs from one area to another, and it changes over time for any given area.

Individuals who move from one location to another do so for economic and psychological reasons, and they generally perform a benefits versus costs analysis to make the decision to relocate.

$$\frac{\text{\# of workers in LF}}{\text{pop}}$$

GEOGRAPHIC DIFFERENCE IN THE SALARY, WAGE RATE, AND WORKING CONDITIONS

An individual examines the difference between the current earnings at her location and the current earnings at the other location. This difference must be positive, and it must be substantial enough to overcome inertia. For example, if everything else were the same between the two locations, but the potential migrant was making $20 per hour where she is and could make $20 per hour at the new location, she has no incentive to move. However, if the wage rate difference were an increase of $2 per hour, the incentive to undergo the challenge of moving could exist.

In addition to the difference in the current wage rate or salary, the potential migrant desires at least the same potential for earnings growth and advancement prospects between the two locations. If the new location provides the same current wage or salary but better prospects for earnings growth, the potential migrant would have an incentive to move.

GEOGRAPHIC DIFFERENCE IN THE COST OF LIVING

In addition to the current wage or salary, the cost of living between the two locations is an important consideration. The potential migrant has a new 2,000-square-foot house that has a current market value of $180,000. The same house in the new location will cost $170,000. The current monthly food bill for the family is $700. The same grocery basket of items in the new location can be purchased for $650. The potential migrant has an incentive to move because the nominal earnings can purchase the same amount of food and shelter for less. This is an increase in the real earnings of the worker.

The cost of living consideration can extend to other major factors such as the property tax on the house and the public services that those dollars fund; the sales tax rate and its treatment of items to be taxed; the costs of commuting as exhibited by gasoline prices; and any other items the potential migrant deems important (for example, entertainment and recreation costs).

QUALITY OF LIFE FOR THE LABOR FORCE

Even though it can be argued that the issue of earnings and cost of living affect the migrant's quality of life, it is better for illustration purposes here to separate them out of the quality of life consideration. With the economic factors considered separately, quality of life can focus on noneconomic factors. People may relocate to experience an improvement in climate and scenery. People may relocate to enhance their access to desired recreation activities. People may relocate to obtain access to better quality education for their children or themselves.

The major point to remember is that the relevant quality of life differential is the one that relates specifically to the potential migrant, not to some nebulously defined migrant. Quality of life rankings of different metropolitan areas always focus on what exists at each location, not on what a specific migrant wants at any location. The number of golf courses in the community gives it a higher ranking, but this means nothing to an avid fisherman looking for a trout stream or a lake. A lower incidence of crime gives one metropolitan area a better ranking than another but makes no mention of the spatial distribution of that crime. The lower incidence of crime could be spread out evenly throughout the metropolitan area, urban, and suburban areas, while the higher incidence of crime could be concentrated in selected areas of the metropolitan area.

The number of sunny days per year or the ratio of sunny to rainy days often is found in these studies as a measure of the climate. The higher the ratio, the better the ranking. But a specific migrant may be susceptible to skin cancer and need to avoid direct sunshine. Moreover, the ratio of sunny to rainy days is not an adequate reflection of climate. Using this ratio as the only measure, Death Valley, California, probably has one of the best sunny day to rainy day ratios, although it is not a hospitable climate.

What Models of Urban Structure Exist?

T hree classic spatial models of urban structure describe the land use pattern in the traditional North American metropolitan area: (1) the concentric zone model, (2) the sector model, and (3) the multiple nuclei model. Every student of urban studies encounters these conceptualizations because they are so widely accepted by the social science disciplines. Exhibit 3.7 presents the traditional views of these land use patterns.

CONCENTRIC ZONE MODEL

The **concentric zone model** emerged from a study of Chicago by sociologists at the University of Chicago in the early 1900s and is attributed to the work of E. W. Burgess.[1] That model positioned a central business district (CBD) at the center (zone 1) of the urban areas around which all other uses formed. Surrounding the CBD, a factory, a slum, and an ethnic community zone existed (zone 2). This area became known as a *transition zone* (or *gray zone*) between the commercial core and the residential communities farther from the center. The transition zone concept refers to the tendency of older residential areas to be converted to commercial uses as the CBD grew. Such an area often attracted immigrants and was generally run-down and a center of crime and vice. Frequently, the land in the transition zone was held by speculators, and the housing function is only an interim use. Zone 3 consisted of lower-income working people's homes. Other successive zones consisted of higher-income residences, with a commuter zone lying on the periphery.

The concentric zone model inadequately accounted for the development of specialized clusters of industrial uses. It also failed to explain the impact of transportation routes on land use. Some later students of the concentric zone model did adjust it to meet these deficiencies by superimposing a radial highway system on it. The highway system had the effect of stretching the zones outward to where they intersected transportation corridors, creating a star-shaped rather than a circular urban form.

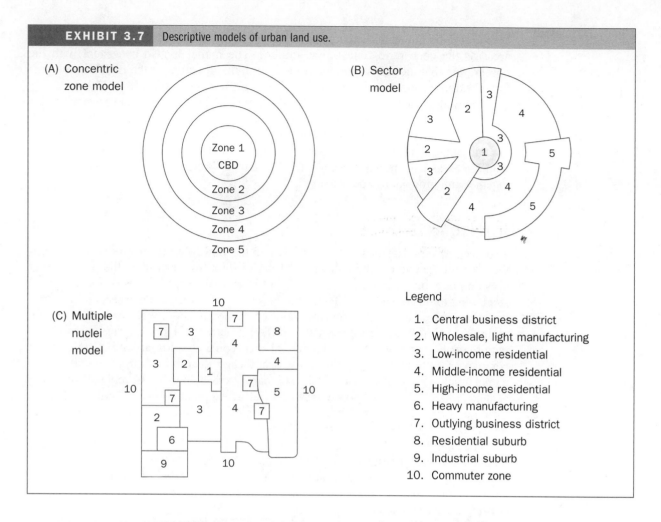

EXHIBIT 3.7 Descriptive models of urban land use.

(A) Concentric zone model

Zone 1
CBD
Zone 2
Zone 3
Zone 4
Zone 5

(B) Sector model

(C) Multiple nuclei model

Legend

1. Central business district
2. Wholesale, light manufacturing
3. Low-income residential
4. Middle-income residential
5. High-income residential
6. Heavy manufacturing
7. Outlying business district
8. Residential suburb
9. Industrial suburb
10. Commuter zone

If the CBD grew, it did so by encroaching on the land in the transition zone adjacent to the CBD. The land users who were displaced moved to the outer edge of the transition zone or to the inner edge of zone 3, where the improvements were older and in depreciated condition. In turn, the displaced land users from zone 3's inner edge moved to the outer edge of zone 3 and the inner edge of zone 4. Growth took place in a ripple effect from the center of the urban area, spreading out to the edge of the urban area.

SECTOR MODEL

In 1939, after an exhaustive study of land use patterns in more than 100 cities, a land economist named Homer Hoyt published a landmark article setting forth the notion of a **sector model** of urban land uses.[2] He suggested that when similar uses had emerged around the CBD (at the center of the city), activities would remain in that particular area and extend outward over time in the same direction that the city grew. The intuitive appeal of this argument is strong because similar uses do in fact grow in specific directions, often following rail or highway arteries or high or low ground, or simply clustering on the same side of the city.

High-income residential areas are notorious for being in high, rolling, or wooded areas, and low-income areas for being in less desirable, low-lying valleys and industrial basins. Hoyt's model also easily accommodates growth because it allows new activities to be added to the periphery rather than requiring redevelopment of existing areas as the concentric zone model implies. The model is also consistent with the observation that the cities grow more rapidly in the direction of the high-income sector as entrepreneurs seek business sites near the affluent market.

The wedges that form the basis of the sector model have particular relevance to the residential function. The distribution of families by income in a metropolitan area is highly differentiated by neighborhood, conforming to a zonal pattern. Even with the random mobility afforded by the automobile, and the locational flexibility it promotes, land use areas have remained relatively distinctive. Particular uses continue to cluster together and grow along specific axes.

MULTIPLE NUCLEI MODEL

Two geographers, Harris and Ullman, created the **multiple nuclei model,** which provides an alternative conceptualization of urban form, one based on the premise that uses do not evolve around a single core but instead at several nodes or focal points.[3] According to this model, the CBD is not necessarily the only place of economic activity in an urban area. Rather, several nodes of economic activity typically evolve. The multiple nuclei model recognizes that different activities have varying accessibility requirements. For example, a commercial area could develop around a government complex, a cultural center, a university, or a theater district. An airport could induce commercial and industrial uses. Today, in many metropolitan areas, regional shopping centers, which grew in response to residential development, have in turn served as a focal point for the development of office complexes. Each of these areas could develop its own satellite residential communities.

The multiple nuclei model acknowledges not only that specific functions have unique locational and functional needs, but also that some activities are detrimental to one another and need widely separated locations. Historical inertia that maintains relatively unique districts can also be an important factor as cities grow and envelop existing industrial and commercial nodes.

Harris and Ullman philosophized that none of the three land use models, including their own, was universally applicable, and that all cities exhibited patterns identifying aspects of one or more of the models.

The multiple nuclei model, which implies that these nuclei appear at the intersection of two streets, is related to the *axial model.* The **axial model** for the land use pattern of an urban area focuses on the transportation corridors, especially the street and road system serving that urban area. In its simplest form, an urban area that is served by, and is centered on, the intersection of two major roads will have a development pattern that shows growth along the two street systems. Then, after the density of population along and close to the major roads increases, the adjacent areas in the quadrants between the roads will fill in as new secondary streets are constructed.

SUBURBIA AND "BEDROOM COMMUNITIES"

Urban areas and suburban areas are differentiated on the basis of both population density and employment opportunities relative to the resident population. Urban areas have a denser population distribution and contain a high proportion of jobs to residents for a specifically defined geographic area. On the other hand, suburbs were developed with larger residential lots and a very high percentage of single-family units relative to multifamily units. Residents of suburbia commuted to the inner, urban area for employment and shopping. In this context, suburbia is a generalized area that is adjacent to the urban area.

As part of suburbia and at the outer edge of most metropolitan areas, communities developed that were primarily residential areas. These communities were local jurisdictions in which the resident population had self-government; they could pass their own zoning and development legislation. At most, these communities contained retail activity that mostly provided convenience goods and services. These areas became known as **bedroom communities.** They typically followed a sector orientation in which communities with higher-priced housing units developed at the edge of the high-income residential sector, and communities with modestly priced housing units developed at the edge of the middle-income residential sector. In these bedroom communities, the ratio of local jobs to resident labor was very low. Residents commuted to the inner, urban area for employment and shopping.

SATELLITE CITIES AND EDGE CITIES

As time passed, some of these bedroom communities in suburbia evolved by developing places of employment and centers of commerce. The ratio of jobs to resident population increased, and thus the ratio of local employees (noncommuters) to commuters increased. When these employment opportunities existed in the local community, the area became known as a **satellite city.** Notice that the concept of the satellite city is related to the multiple nuclei model: The satellite city is a center of economic activity in which employment opportunities exist.

The edge city concept relates to the satellite city concept and the multiple nuclei model. An **edge city** is any area that meets the following criteria:

1. 5,000,000 square feet or more of leasable office space that serves as the workplace of the information age
2. 600,000 square feet or more of leasable retail space
3. More jobs than bedrooms, indicating that people head toward this place when the workday starts
4. Perceived by the population as one place that contains jobs, shopping, entertainment, and so forth
5. Thirty years ago, was simply a bedroom community or even undeveloped agricultural land

The edge city is an advanced satellite city that grew from a bedroom community. As such, it is a major node of economic activity in a metropolitan area as expressed by the multiple nuclei model.

INFERENCES THAT CAN BE DRAWN FROM THESE DESCRIPTIVE MODELS

The descriptive land use models discussed above point out the importance and the effect of several factors in the urban growth process. The factors that will be singled out for discussion are (1) transportation networks, (2) land use succession, (3) clusters of compatible land users, and (4) multiple centers of economic activity.

Transportation Network

Transportation plays a part in each of these descriptive models. The axial pattern of transport routes was superimposed on the concentric zone model, and the growth occurred initially at the intersections of the transport routes and the fringe of the city. Each sector in the sector model was served by at least one main artery, which was extended out to the fringe to enable growth in that direction. Each of the centers of economic activity in the multiple nuclei model was connected to the others and to its surrounding areas by transport routes. Consequently, the land use controls imposed by the local government must rely upon additional transport facilities and their maintenance at high-quality levels as an important development factor.

Land Use Succession

Each model, especially the concentric zone and sector models, recognized the occurrence of land use changes. In the concentric zone model, the land use succession occurred at the border of each zone. In the sector model, the changes in land use took place in the inner segment of each sector, where the sector met the central business district. Consequently, the local land use controls must recognize that economic factors exist that cause land use changes. Land use planners must recognize these factors and then encourage the changes necessary to keep the local economy functioning and to generate favorable effects—while trying to stop, or at least reduce, the adverse effects.

Both land use for a specific property and land use in a broader area of a community can change overtime. **Land use succession theory** is based on the idea that land use patterns are not static (fixed over time) but rather are dynamic in nature. For example, a new residential area being considered starts out at a certain average value per residence. As the area's population and households increase in number, the area begins to grow—and as a result, so does the average value of the housing units. Typically, the value increases over time as the demand for land in general increases and the demand for housing also increases (shown as the movement from point A to point B in Exhibit 3.8). At some point in time, growth will continue but will slow (shown as the movement from point B to point C in Exhibit 3.8).

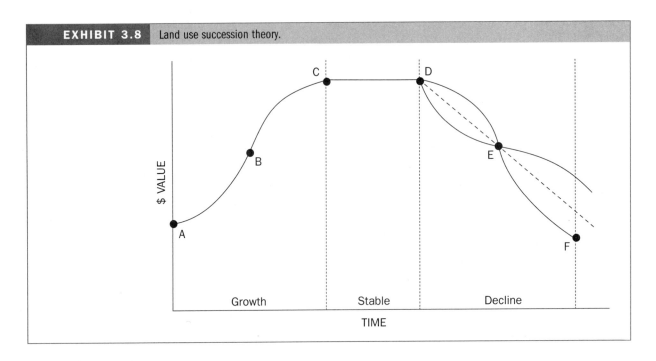

| EXHIBIT 3.8 | Land use succession theory. |

At some point in time, the growth process will reach its peak and stabilize for some time (shown as the movement from point C to point D in Exhibit 3.8). During this phase, there is little if any development because there is very little available land. The population is stable in the sense that families are moving through the family life cycle from small children in elementary school through adolescence into young adulthood.

Eventually, economic, demographic, and physical circumstance come into play to cause a decline in value (shown as the movement from point D to point E in Exhibit 3.8). The families move into the "empty nest" phase as children leave for college or go out on their own. The dwelling units are now older and may be less attractive to current buyers in the market, who in turn offer less for the property. The community infrastructure and uses of adjacent land are also older. This decline in value can occur at many rates; values could decline at an increasing, a decreasing, or a constant rate.

Beyond point E in the declining phase of value, the property value can continue to decline until the ultimate value of the property becomes less than the property's original value and has a very low market value. But, at a time such as that represented by point F, economic circumstances in the market could arise that make it financially feasible to renovate, rehabilitate, and modernize the existing land uses in their current use. Substandard apartments or offices can be renovated. Or, the process of **adaptive reuse** can take place, in which a physically deteriorated current use is replaced by a different use that is supported by the current market. An example of adaptive reuse is the conversion of older industrial buildings near a central business district into loft apartments.

Clusters of Compatible Land Users

Because land users tend to form clusters of similar uses in both the residential and the commercial sectors of the local economy, an area's zoning ordinance should not stand in the way of these economic realities. The zoning ordinance should aid in the process as long as the action does not harm any individual (according to the discriminatory housing provision).

Multiple Centers of Economic Activity

Finally, multiple centers of economic activity will arise in an urban area as a result of the economic climate. Land use controls should not be used as an impediment to these changes, which reflect the necessities of the market. Whether a cluster is one of retail shops, office buildings, industrial plants, or residences, land use planners should first try to understand why the cluster is occurring. Then, they should evaluate their private and social benefits and costs before imposing restrictions or permitting the occurrence of the cluster.

What Is Rent Bid Analysis?

Rent bid analysis focuses on the revenues and costs of a representative firm or economic unit in a particular land use category and measures that firm's ability to pay for the use of land. Thus, the analysis would reveal how much a retail establishment could pay in rent at various sites. The tool used in the analysis is the rent bid function, which is both an algebraic and a graphical representation of a simple economic model that includes a spatial dimension.

THE RENT BID FUNCTION

The **rent bid function** is based on a firm's ability to pay for the use of land—the rent [R]—which in turn depends on the difference between the firm's total revenues [TR] and its total costs for all factors of production and transportation [TC] excluding the cost of the land. Stated as an equation

$$(1) \qquad R = TR - TC$$

TR is the result of the price of the product [P] times the amount of the product that is sold [Q]. TC is composed of (1) the average, nonland costs of producing the product [A]; (2) the cost per unit to receive the inputs that go into the production of the product [T_i]; (3) the distance over which the inputs must be transported [Di]; (4) the cost per unit to ship the output to the customer [T_o]; and (5) the distance over which the output must be shipped [D_o]. Stated as an equation

$$(2) \qquad TR = PQ$$
$$(3) \qquad TC = Q[A + T_iD_i + T_oD_o]$$

When equations 2 and 3 are substituted into equation 1 and the equation is then simplified, the result is shown as equation 4 and then recombined into equations 5 and 6:

$$(4) \qquad R = PQ - Q[A + T_iD_i + T_oD_o]$$
$$(5) \qquad R = PQ - AQ - (T_i)(D_i)Q - (T_o)(D_o)Q$$
$$(6) \qquad R = Q[P - A] - Q[T_iD_i + T_oD_o]$$

Now for the purpose of simplification, let the term [$T_iD_i + T_oD_o$] which contains the transport costs for the inputs and the outputs collapse into a single term given as [TD]. The rent gradient equation becomes

$$(7) \qquad R = Q[P - A] - QTD$$

This equation for a straight line is graphed in Exhibit 3.9 in a coordinate system with R on the vertical axis and D on the horizontal axis. The vertical intercept where D is zero is Q[P−A]: the horizontal intercept is [P−A]/T_0. This graph can be used to show the impact on this representative firm's ability to pay rent when certain economic factors exist, as follows:

1. In Exhibit 3.10(a), the price of the product (P) increases due to an increase in demand. The effect of this change on the rent bid curve is shown as a nonparallel shift up at all distances, creating an increase in the value of each intercept. The firm

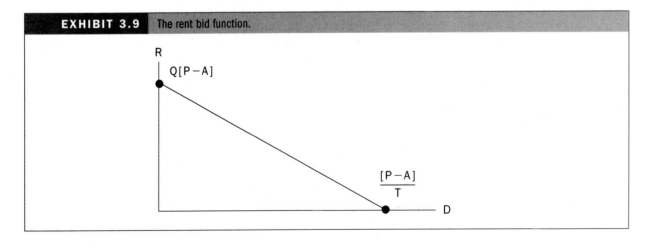

EXHIBIT 3.9   The rent bid function.

is able to pay more for rent at each distance, and rent-paying ability does not fall to zero until D_2 is reached.

2. In Exhibit 3.10(b), the quantity demanded at the current product price increases because the product is in greater demand due to an increase in the number of consumers, a favorable shift in taste and preference toward the product, or an increase in consumer income (or a combination of these factors). The effect of this change on the rent bid curve is shown as a pivot up around the horizontal intercept at all distances less than D_1. The firm is able to pay more for rent at each distance except D_1.

3. In Exhibit 3.10(c), either the cost of production goes up as the firm must pay more for labor, interest on business loans, or input prices. The effect of this change on the rent bid curve is shown as a nonparallel shift down at all distances, creating a decrease in the value of each intercept. The firm can only pay less for rent at each distance, and rent-paying ability falls to zero at D_0.

4. In Exhibit 3.10(d), the transport rate on either the input or the finished product increases. The effect of this change on the rent bid curve is shown as a pivot down around the vertical intercept at all distances. The firm is able to pay rent only if the distance to the market is less than D_0.

If the opposite changes in the economic variables of the product's market occur, or if the costs of production or the transportation costs for either the inputs or outputs change in the other direction, the effect on the rent bid curve or function will be in the opposite direction of the one shown in Exhibit 3.10.

Rent Bid Functions for Property Types

A representative entity in each major property type—residential, retail, office, and industrial—can be represented by the rent bid curve discussed above. However, the interpretation of the variables in the rent bid function changes.

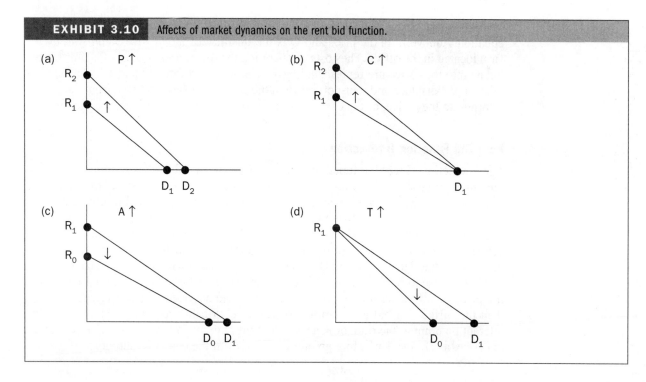

EXHIBIT 3.10 Affects of market dynamics on the rent bid function.

RESIDENTIAL RENT BID FUNCTION. The representative household's ability to pay for the use of land is based on the household's income and its allocation of that income among such major categories as housing, insurance, taxes, retail purchases, and transportation costs. The rent bid function reflects this relationship in a simple, intuitive manner in the form of the following equation:

$$(8) \qquad R = [Y - AY]B - TD$$

Here Y represents the household income level. A represents expenditures made by the household for products and services they require that are not related to housing or transportation. These would include retail products of all kinds, insurance payments, medical costs, education expenses, and various tax payments. The term [Y − AY] represents the amount of income spent for housing and transportation. B represents the benefits the household perceives that it would receive from the house at this location. Consider B equal to 1 as the acceptable situation. If the benefits are not perceived as acceptable, B is less than 1 and the household will not allocate as much of its income to rent. T and D represent the transport rate for commuter costs, school trip costs, and shopping trip costs. The further the household is located from these other land users, the less it is willing to pay for rent.

This equation can be used for households with two different sets of locational preferences. For the representative urban-oriented household, B [urban] is greater than B [suburban], so the vertical intercept for an urban-oriented household is greater than the vertical intercept for a suburban-oriented household, and the slope is also greater for the urban-oriented household.

RETAIL RENT BID FUNCTION. The retail rent bid function takes the form of equation 7 shown earlier. P is the price and Q is the quantity of the product or service being sold by the retail establishment. The costs of operating the store and the cost of acquiring any inputs into the store are represented by A. The transport rate [T] and the distance [D] relate to the distance and transport rate that the consumers have from their point of origin to the store.

OFFICE RENT BID FUNCTION. The office rent bid function also takes the form of equation 7 above. P is the price and Q is the quantity of the service being sold by the firm located in the office. The costs of operating the office and the cost of acquiring any inputs into the office are represented by A. The transport rate [T] and the distance [D] relate to the distance and transport rate that the consumers have to travel from their point of origin to the office, or the cost of travel for office employees to provide the service.

Rent Bid Function Interaction

The interaction of rent bid functions shows the potential effect of economic changes on the entities that bid for the use of the land on the land use patterns of that land. For example, consider a central business district or one of the principal multinuclei areas found in the urban area. Office use currently dominates the center of the area, with retail and suburban-oriented residential uses arrayed at a point in space away from the center. Exhibit 3.11 depicts this situation. Point K is the interaction point between office and retail land users, and D_1 is the point in space at which land use changes from office land use to retail land use. If this status quo is disturbed by an increase in either the price of office services or the amount of those services that consumers demand, then the office rent bid curve shifts up. The effect of this economic change is a new interaction point to the right of K as well as a pressure on land use to switch from retail to office, as D_1 also shifts to a greater distance from the center of activity.

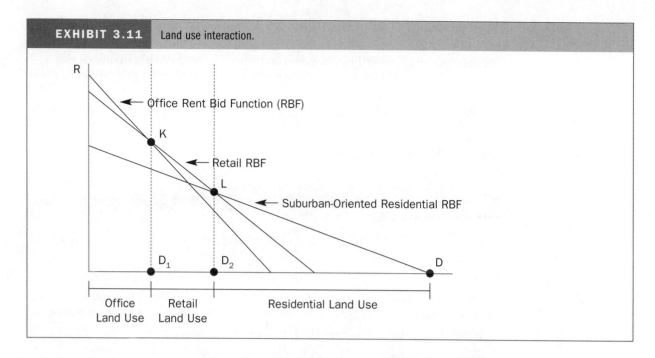

EXHIBIT 3.11 Land use interaction.

Office Rent Bid Function (RBF)

K

Retail RBF

L

Suburban-Oriented Residential RBF

D_1

D_2

D

Office Land Use

Retail Land Use

Residential Land Use

The Rent Bid Gradient

The conceptual **rent bid gradient** is the locus of points representing the highest rent bid across the various land users shown in Exhibit 3.11. The actual rent gradient is a spatial plot of the actual contract rents being paid for space by different land and space users. The conceptual and the actual rent gradients have an inverse relationship with a central node of economic activity. As distance from the center of the node increases, the rent that can be paid conceptually and the rent that is actually paid decline.

Chapter Summary

This chapter has focused on the general topic of metropolitan growth analysis by discussing five major concepts and their accompanying analytical techniques that relate to urban growth analysis. These five concepts are local economic area analysis, industrial location theory, labor force location and migration theory, land use theory, and rent bid theory.

Local economic area analysis provides a way to describe the economic relationships in a metropolitan area. This chapter discussed the significance of local growth industries and local export industries and showed the process of using location quotients to identify the major export industries that foster growth in the metropolitan area.

Industrial location theory provides information on the economic and spatial factors that attract business firms to a metropolitan area. The text discussed the importance of geographic labor, transport, and space cost differences. The concept of business climate also was shown to be an element in the firm's decision process.

Labor force location and migration theory provides information on the economic and spatial factors that attract people to a metropolitan area. The text discussed the importance of geographic earnings, cost of living, and quality of life differences.

Land use theory presented descriptive models for the land use development patterns in metropolitan areas. The concentric zone, sector, and multiple nuclei models were presented. Such concepts as satellite cities and edge cities also were discussed. Finally, rent bid theory was discussed as a theoretical tool to analyze changes in land use patterns as a metropolitan area grows from business and labor migration to a local economy.

Internet Applications

A website has been established for this chapter at http://epley.swcollege.com.

Review Questions

1. What economic and demographic variables describe the economic base of a local economic area?
2. What is the export base theory? How does it relate to the local economy?
3. What techniques are available to update the census data from the most recent census year to the present period? Briefly describe how each technique works.
4. What factors attract business firms to a local economy?
5. What factors attract individuals to a local economy?
6. Describe the models used to explain the land use development patterns in a local economy.
7. Describe the rent bid function.

Discussion Questions

1. You are given an assignment by your employer to describe the local economy in which you live and work. How would you do it and what concepts would you use?
2. After you have described the local economy, your boss now asks you to describe the growth industries in the local economy. How would you do it?
3. Your boss gives you four-year-old population data for the county or counties in which your firm does business. She asks you to get an estimate of the current population. How would you do it?
4. You are asked to make a speech about the quality of life in your local economy. What ideas would you present?

Endnotes

1. R.E. Park, E.W. Burgess, and R.D. McKenzie, *The City* (Chicago: University of Chicago Press, 1925), 47–62.
2. H. Hoyt, *The Structure and Growth of Residential Neighborhoods in American Cities* (Washington, D.C.: U.S. Government Printing Office, 1939).
3. C.D. Harris and E.G. Ullman, "The Nature of Cities," *Annals of the American Academy of Political Science,* vol. LLXLII (1945): 7–17.

The Decision to Estimate Market Value

## CHAPTER 4

Valuation

QUESTIONS TO BE ANSWERED

1. What are the determinants of value for real property?

2. What are the factors that affect the market value of real estate?

3. What is an appraisal and what is the appraisal process?

OBJECTIVES

When finished with this chapter, the student should be able to:

1. Identify the factors that affect the value of real property.

2. Describe the impact of economic, physical, social, and governmental factors in the urban area, the region, and the nation on the value of a parcel of property.

3. Describe the impact of neighborhood and site-specific factors on the value of a parcel of real property.

4. Discuss the valuation process used by professionally designated appraisers.

appraisal	market
appraisal commission	market value
Appraisal Foundation	neighborhood
assessed value	neighborhood analysis
commuter costs	plottage value
cost approach	principle of anticipation
cul-de-sac	principle of substitution
demand	private zone
depth	public zone
environmental determinants of value	purchasing power
frontage	reconciliation
functional efficiency	redlining
gross rent multiplier technique	sales comparison approach
highest and best use	site-specific determinants of value
improvement analysis	supply
income approach	utility
insurable value	valuation process
investment value	value
landscaping	value-in-exchange
linkage	value-in-use

INTRODUCTION

This chapter focuses on the factors that affect the value of a property. The next two chapters consider the methods and techniques to determine the value of the property. This chapter first identifies and discusses the concept of market value; it then discusses the determinants of value. This discussion considers general factors of the community or economy that can affect the value of a property and general factors in the neighborhood that affect the value of a property. When this broad focus is completed, the focus narrows to discuss attributes or characteristics of the property itself that can affect its market value. The chapter ends with a discussion of the appraisal process and its components. This is a logical arrangement of the general and specific factors discussed in the chapter as they relate to the valuation techniques.

What Is Value?

Chapter 1's discussion of real estate as a commodity, including its components and its characteristics, should leave the consumer or potential owner with an understanding of the nature of the real property commodity. The consumer should realize what public and private factors influence his capability to use the product and what circumstances can arise to affect his possession of the product. In addition, the public and private limits on the rights of ownership should show the scope of the consumer's authority or control over the commodity. These concepts from Chapter 1 set the background and are a logical starting point for the following discussion of the aspects of real estate that give it value, and of the market in which it is exchanged.

VALUE DETERMINATION AND ESTIMATION

The value of real estate is established or determined by the participants in the market in which that real estate trades. These participants include the potential buyers and the sellers who offer their property for sale. The buyers determine what they are willing to pay for the property, and the sellers determine the minimum price for which they will sell the property. The discussion in this chapter rests on this simple premise.

Any participant in a market—buyer or seller—can and does have an opinion of market value for properties in the market. The brokers and the sales associates who operate in the market also have opinions of value. These opinions of market value may or may not be accurate, and they may or may not be documented. The opinions can be made by people trained in valuation theory and techniques or by people who are not. The market value of property is determined by the market participants, who consider the attributes of the property in their deliberation. These market participants periodically need an expert opinion of market value. The real estate appraiser provides the unbiased, knowledgeable, and documented opinion of value. The discussions in this chapter and the next two chapters focus on the estimate of market value for a property that is made by an appraiser.

THE NATURE OF VALUE

Value typically is defined as the worth of a commodity, which arises from its utility to an individual or its ability to command other commodities in exchange. This definition means that a commodity can have a value-in-use and a value-in-exchange. **Value-in-use** arises from an individual's ability to obtain satisfaction or utility from the consumption of the product. In this sense, the commodity is valuable even if no other person desires it or recognizes its worth.

Value-in-exchange arises when at least two people recognize the value-in-use or utility of the commodity. The owner of the commodity can then ask for something in exchange for the commodity if she chooses to trade with the other individual. However, for a commodity to have value-in-exchange, two conditions must be met: (1) The commodity must be transferable; it must be capable of being passed to another person. Without this quality, the exchange is impossible. (2) The commodity must not be a free good. It must be relatively scarce so that it is not in everyone's possession, in contrast to air and sunlight.

THE DETERMINANTS OF VALUE

The value of real property is determined by the interaction of supply and demand in the market for the particular real property that is being considered. However, each parcel of real property has its own set of attributes that affect the market participants' opinions of value-in-use and value-in-exchange. These attributes consist of the features of *the real property commodity itself* and the features of *the environment in which it exists.* These two sets of attributes are discussed in subsequent sections of this chapter.

These demand and supply factors operate at three interrelated levels. The local economic area affects the value of the subject property by affecting broad factors such as employment opportunities in the MSA. The neighborhood affects the subject property

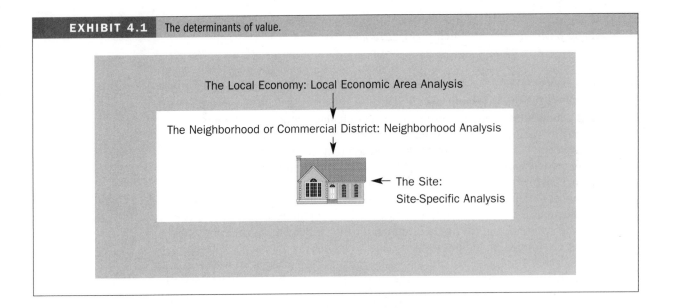

EXHIBIT 4.1	The determinants of value.

The Local Economy: Local Economic Area Analysis

The Neighborhood or Commercial District: Neighborhood Analysis

The Site:
Site-Specific Analysis

with more proximate factors such as the quality of the local schools. The site and the improvements on the site affect the value of the subject proeprty by providing amenities and features that create satisfaction for the owner. Exhibit 4.1 shows these three interrelationships. From the broad perspective to the narrow perspective they point to the subject property.

HOW IS THE MARKET RELATED TO VALUE?

The term *market* represents the willingness and ability of two distinct entities to interact and to exchange one item for another. One entity expresses a need for real estate. The other entity is willing to exchange real estate for something of value. The terms *demand* and *supply* identify the two entities. The **demand** side of the market is composed of the potential buyers. The **supply** side of the market is composed of the current owners or producers of the commodity—that is, the potential sellers. In this context, a **market** can be defined as an economic environment in which a commodity is exchanged.

The demand side of the market is governed by the value-in-use that arises from the property's physical and economic attributes that each potential buyer envisions in the commodity. In other words, the demand side is influenced by the concept of **utility,** which is the inherent quality of the product to provide some form of satisfaction to the buyer. Value-in-exchange is based on the existence of value-in-use for a group of potential buyers. The desire for the commodity must be accompanied by the ability to provide some valuable item in exchange for the product. This ability is known as **purchasing power.** Finally, the demand for the commodity depends on the number of individuals who want the product and who can purchase it.

The supply side of the market is also governed by the property's value-in-use and the resultant value-in-exchange of a parcel of real estate. Value-in-exchange is influenced by the utility of the commodity—the value-in-use as perceived by the buyers. In addition, value-in-exchange is influenced by the availability of the commodity. Real estate in general is not infinitely available; it is economically scarce. No matter what aspect of real estate is examined, only a finite number of units of the commodity exist. For example, consider the following quantities: the number of acres of land in the

United States, the number of building sites in a state, and the amount of land zoned for residential purposes in an urban area. Each of these land parcel types is limited in quantity. An analysis of the structures on land would yield the same result. For example, consider the number of existing housing units in an urban area and the number of new housing units that can be built in a given period of time. A finite number represents each of these categories of housing units.

Thus, the value-in-use and the resultant value-in-exchange that determine the willingness and ability of individuals to buy and sell property affect the value of real estate. In this way, value-in-use and value-in-exchange as perceived by groups of individuals underlie demand and supply in the market. In turn, demand and supply determine the selling price or market value of a parcel of real property. However, a more thorough understanding of the concepts of market value and selling price is required, especially when the consumer is dealing with a real estate appraiser.

WHAT IS MARKET VALUE?

The **Appraisal Foundation** is a private foundation recognized by the U.S. Congress to provide standards for the property appraisal profession. It is discussed in more detail later in this chapter. **Market value** is officially defined by the Appraisal Foundation in its *Uniform Standards of Professional Appraisal Practice* as follows:

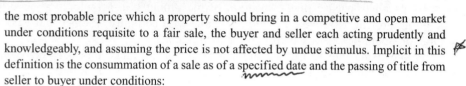

> the most probable price which a property should bring in a competitive and open market under conditions requisite to a fair sale, the buyer and seller each acting prudently and knowledgeably, and assuming the price is not affected by undue stimulus. Implicit in this definition is the consummation of a sale as of a specified date and the passing of title from seller to buyer under conditions:
>
> 1. Buyer and seller are typically motivated.
> 2. Both parties are well informed or well advised, and acting in what they consider their best interest.
> 3. A reasonable time is allowed for exposure in the open market.
> 4. Payment is made in terms of cash in United States dollars or in terms of financial arrangements thereto; and
> 5. The price represents a normal consideration for the property sold unaffected by special or creative financing or sales concessions granted by anyone associated with the sale.

When the appraiser analyzes real estate markets or when a property is analyzed by an investment analyst, the value-in-exchange concept that is typically obtained is the most probable selling price—not necessarily its market value. This occurs because participants in the real estate market are not fully knowledgeable due to inexperience and the high costs of obtaining information about alternative properties as well as alternative uses of a piece of property. In addition, market participants differ in their relative abilities to obtain financing in order to purchase the property. For at least these two reasons, the concept of value generated in the market for any piece of real property is the most probable selling price of the property, which also happens to be a reasonably good estimate of the property's true market value.

COMMON FALLACIES ABOUT VALUE

Two common fallacies about the value of real estate exist. One is that all real estate is valuable. As extreme examples, consider parcels of land in the Sahara Desert and Antarctica. If a building were erected on these parcels, it could have value-in-use to the owner but may have no value-in-exchange because no one else would be willing to buy it. The fallacy that all real estate is valuable was probably an underlying factor in the land frauds that took place in the 1960s in Florida and Arizona. People bought such land "site" unseen with the belief that the land was, and would continue to be, valuable.

The second fallacy is that all urban real estate increases in value. Each parcel of urban real estate does have a market value, but that value can be high or low, and it can increase, decrease, or stay constant over time. The potential buyer should realize that market value is established by demand and supply factors in the market. The fallacy arises when the consumer assumes that urban real estate will always have an increasing market value, and that when it is time to sell, an able and willing buyer will be in the market and will pay the original price plus a significant number of additional dollars as profit to the owner. The visual proof of this mistaken assumption can be seen in every urban area in the form of vacant land and vacant buildings. The owners of some of these parcels of urban real estate chose to give up their rights of ownership through tax foreclosure when they decided not to pay taxes on a structure they could not use or sell. Other owners pay the tax with the hope that, sometime in the future, an individual will appear who has a value-in-use for that parcel and will make a reasonable offer. Still other owners of other vacant land parcels are holding land off the market voluntarily with the expectation of a gain in the future. They expect to obtain an increase in the market value because of the location of the property in a sector that should be undergoing growth. However, they do not know with certainty whether that gain will be large or small, or whether there will be a gain at all.

The knowledgeable real estate purchaser should not make unwarranted assumptions about the market value of real estate in general or urban real estate in particular. These properties have value-in-exchange only when there are potential buyers.

What Are the Environmental Determinants of Value?

The **environmental determinants of value** consist of the economic, locational, social, demographic, physical, and government-political environments that affect the property. These factors are not site or property specific. The effects of these environmental factors start at the level of the local economy and narrow to the neighborhood surrounding the property. The appraiser must keep in mind that the effects of these non-site-specific factors ultimately focus on the value of the subject property. Exhibit 4.2 represents the relationship among the environmental determinants of value and the property. Local economic area analysis (previously discussed in Chapter 3) has a broad focus; neighborhood analysis has a narrower focus that encompasses the immediate area surrounding the property; and site-specific analysis focuses directly on the property.

LOCAL ECONOMIC AREA ANALYSIS

The general focus of local economic area analysis is the impact brought about by the various environmental factors on the urban area as a whole or on a major sector of the urban area (for example, the northern suburbs).

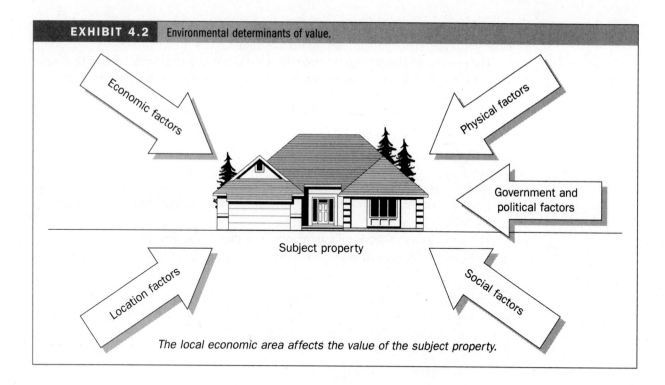

EXHIBIT 4.2 Environmental determinants of value.

Subject property

The local economic area affects the value of the subject property.

Economic Factors

The economic factors include all of the factors identified as part of the economic base of the community (as discussed in Chapter 3). Changes in the community's economic base indicate either the growth or the decline of the local economy. More importantly, changes in the economic base are translated into changes in the level of demand and supply in the market to which the subject property belongs. To analyze a housing market, the appraiser must analyze past trends in the housing market that are reflected in the economic base of the community. With the aid of these past trends, the appraiser can estimate future levels of households by size and age, future levels of disposable income, future credit conditions, the supply of existing housing, and future levels of construction. The appraiser should not merely assume that the past trends will continue unchanged into the future. From the estimates of future levels of the factors affecting demand and supply, the appraiser can estimate the future trend of market value in the housing market for the subject property.

The forecast of market factors is clearly important when the appraiser is estimating market value for some point in the future. For example, assume that a new industrial plant will open in 18 months. This plant opening will create new jobs and should attract new households, thus increasing the demand for existing housing units in the future. Over the next 18 months, some or all of this demand for existing units can be shifted to newly constructed units as the supply side of the market adjusts. However, the influx of people could eliminate vacancies, giving future owners of existing units a stronger bargaining position and thereby increasing future selling prices. Who obtains this increase in market value? Is it the current owner who is selling today or the future owner, or could the total increase be split between the current and future owners? If the current market contains well-informed buyers, they will pay prices that are higher than those offered before the plant opening was announced because these buyers fully expect appreciation of the property's value in the future. Thus, information about the future should affect current market values.

The process of forecasting the probable changes in the economic base of the community is a complex topic that cannot be explored in detail in this text. However, any forecasting technique must start with an analysis of the changes in external market factors. Some of the variables that need to be examined include the following:

1. The impact of increased real income and different preference patterns of nonlocal consumers on the demand for locally produced goods and services
2. The desirability of the local community as a location for new firms that are looking for industrial or commercial sites
3. The ability of the local community to retain present industrial and commercial enterprises
4. The desirability of the local community as a place of residence
5. The impact of nonlocal competitors on the demand for locally produced goods and services

As these factors work in favor of the local economy, economic growth will occur and will enhance the market value—or at least will inhibit a decline in the market value—of the local community's housing units.

Locational Factors

In a geographic sense, every parcel of real estate is located in a unique place on the face of the earth. Moreover, in an environmental sense, every parcel of real estate is also located in a unique place with respect to every other parcel of real estate. Each one of these relationships between two land users is a **linkage.** The relationships between the land users on one parcel and the land users on all the other parcels are known as the *linkage pattern* of that property. For example, a residential user of land is linked economically with employment centers where the husband and wife might work, and with commercial areas where all types of products and services are bought and sold. The residential land user is also linked with the school system, the local church, various social organizations, and area recreational centers.

Maintenance of these linkages requires the household to move through space. The adults in the household must travel to do their jobs, and in so doing they incur travel or transportation costs. Traditionally, these job-oriented transportation costs are known as **commuter costs.** Other transportation costs are incurred to maintain each of the linkages. Because they depend on the household's linkage pattern, such costs are part of a rational household's decision about its dwelling site. Consequently, the composition of these transportation costs in general and the commuter costs in particular should be understood.

Each household has money and nonmoney costs of transportation. The money costs of moving through space are generally obvious—the price of gasoline, oil, tires, tune-ups, repairs, replacement of parts, depreciation, insurance, parking, and licenses for automobiles, and the price of fares for public transportation. The nonmoney costs of moving through space are less obvious. The time involved in travel is a nonmoney cost; however, the anxiety and aggravation associated with travel on congested highways must also be considered a nonmoney or psychic cost. Because the nonmoney costs cannot be quantified directly in dollar terms, they cannot be easily measured. Researchers in the area of commuting costs have typically used the commuter's income level as a proxy for the time cost of travel. The higher the income level of the commuter, the higher the value of leisure time and the higher the commuting cost. The dollar value of freedom from aggravation is also difficult to establish, and few resources have been used to measure it.

Another nonmoney aspect of transportation costs is the environment of the transportation route between the linkages. The route environment must be examined by analyzing the structural characteristics of the transportation system, the aesthetics of the route, and the health and safety features of the route. The structural features include the width of the streets and the number of lanes, the quality of the road surface, the frequency of intersections, the system of lighting, and the level of demarcation. The aesthetics of the route can heighten or ameliorate the aggravation factor of commuting. Driving on a tree-lined highway with greenery and attractive structures can be less aggravating than driving through a congested industrial district flanked by a railroad line on one side and dilapidated industrial structures on the other side. The health of the commuter can also be affected if the industrial district poses an air pollution threat. Finally, the safety factor is included because an irritable driver is a careless, inconsiderate driver who is more prone to irrational and negligent acts behind the wheel. The level of driver irritation may also be a function of the aesthetics, but it is most assuredly a function of the traffic congestion and time delays.

Trip frequency is the multiplier that greatly affects the costs of transportation. Commuter costs are the most frequent travel costs, and they are usually high in both money and nonmoney elements. The linkage pattern and the cost of transportation to maintain the linkages affect the value of a real estate parcel. If all other things are equal, the site that is most conveniently located to minimize the costs of transportation, especially the commuter costs, is the site that will be considered most valuable.

THE DYNAMIC NATURE OF THE LOCATION. With the exception of the attributes of the site itself (such as the geological features), the attributes of the location, the off-site improvements, and to a lesser extent the on-site improvements are susceptible to change over time. Linkage patterns can change as employment opportunities shift and commercial enterprises change sites. The cost of transportation can change as gasoline prices change and as new highways and alternate modes of transportation are initiated. The quality of public services and the neighborhood structures can change. Standards of attractiveness change. Consequently, the value of a parcel of real estate can change over time as its attributes change. For these reasons, real estate analysts must understand the changing locational patterns and physical characteristics of the urban area.

Physical Factors

The physical factors to be considered are those that make the local urban area attractive to households. Two such factors are climate and scenery. A favorable climate and picturesque scenery can attract industry and households and thus increase demand in the housing market. In addition, certain factors affect the ability of the area to support residential units as well as places of employment. For example, the availability of water, the topography, the soil and subsoil conditions (such as drainage), and the bedrock characteristics of the geographic area can affect industrial relocation into the area. An increase in job opportunities can increase the number of households through migration and thereby increase the demand in the housing market. On the supply side of the market, the availability of water affects the size of the stock of housing that can exist in the area. Drainage characteristics can limit the number of buildable sites if much of the land in the area is classified as floodplain.

Governmental and Political Factors

The local government's use of its police powers and eminent domain legislation (for example, condemnation), its provision of public services, and its taxation powers (as described in Chapter 2) also affect the value of a residential unit in the market. The zoning ordinance affects the supply of land that can be used for new residential construction as well as the ability of a contractor to make conversions of existing structures from one form of residential use to another. The construction code affects the supply of new construction because it places a minimum supply price on the new unit.

Eminent domain (previously discussed in Chapter 2) can be used to reduce the stock of one type of housing unit, such as old low-quality apartments in the central city. This action could increase the market value of the remaining units if the level of demand stays constant. In addition, the process of eminent domain can increase the supply of new construction in a geographic area after the older structures are demolished, the land is cleared, and the new units are built.

The provision of public services in the form of utilities such as water, sewerage, and street systems affects the supply of land that can be used for residential units. If such utilities are not extended into new areas, the supply of land for new housing construction will become restricted; the price of both new and existing housing will rise dramatically if demand increases, because additional housing units cannot be built. On the demand side of the market, the provision of such public services as high-quality schools, fire and police protection, trash collection, and street cleaning can make housing more desirable than similar housing in an area that does not provide high-quality public services. This last statement is especially relevant if households in both areas are paying the same level of property tax.

Where the quality of public services is high, households generally pay high property tax bills. However, if the tax level increases in an area without a commensurate improvement in the quality of services, the demand for housing in that area may decline. This decline in demand will occur only if another area exists in which the quantity and quality of public services per property tax dollar are higher.

Social Factors

Certain social and demographic factors are considered in economic base analysis—for example, the differences in employment levels and occupational composition of the labor force, household and population size, age structure, and income structure. However, the social factors examined in area analysis are the preferences of people for material goods, population density, crowding or congestion in dwelling units, crowding of the dwelling units, and the social attitudes of the population toward such matters as marriage, divorce, birth control, integration, and the use of leisure time.

Changes in these social and demographic variables can affect the market value of the subject property. First, an increase in the absolute number of households can increase demand in several submarkets. Second, a change in the households' attitudes toward the desirability of single-family detached housing units can change the level of demand in several different submarkets. For example, demand could decrease in the single-family detached submarket and increase in the townhouse and apartment submarkets if consumer preferences were to shift away from single-family detached housing units. Changes in household attitudes toward city versus suburban lifestyles can cause a change in intra-urban locational preferences. In-town living could become a more popular lifestyle; such a change is occurring in many cities today. Finally, the postponement of marriage and the decision to have fewer children can affect the demand in different residential submarkets—demand for apartments and smaller houses could increase, and the demand for large houses with four or more bedrooms could decrease.

NEIGHBORHOOD ANALYSIS

Neighborhood analysis examines the environmental factors that affect the area surrounding the subject property. Exhibit 4.3 shows the perspective of neighborhood analysis; it is narrower in its focus than local economic area analysis and is not site specific. As a prelude to neighborhood analysis, the analyst or the appraiser must first reach an understanding of the concept of the neighborhood. Then, the features of the neighborhood can be identified and their impact on the subject property evaluated.

The appraisal profession defines a **neighborhood** as a group of complementary land uses or a congruous grouping of inhabitants, buildings, or business enterprises. Any attempt to define the exact boundary of a neighborhood is subject to great difficulty. The two parts of the definition indicate that several factors are used to define a neighborhood. One factor is the land uses on each site. The others are social and economic factors, such as income level, age of the household, and size of the household.

Each of these social and economic factors has a small range of variation within a defined neighborhood. It is not likely that homogeneity of land use and homogeneity of household income or household age would be present at the same points in space. Consequently, many areas could be considered to belong in either of two adjoining neighborhoods. For example, an area may have the income level of one neighborhood and the architectural style and land use of the other. In such situations, the appraiser's judgment and knowledge of the local community are important factors in determining what constitutes the neighborhood of the subject property. One such judgmental definition is the statement that a neighborhood is the area around a lot to a point where changes in land use have no direct effect on the value of the lot.

However, for practical purposes, neighborhood boundaries are frequently defined in terms of political boundaries, zoning districts, planning areas, school districts, subdivi-

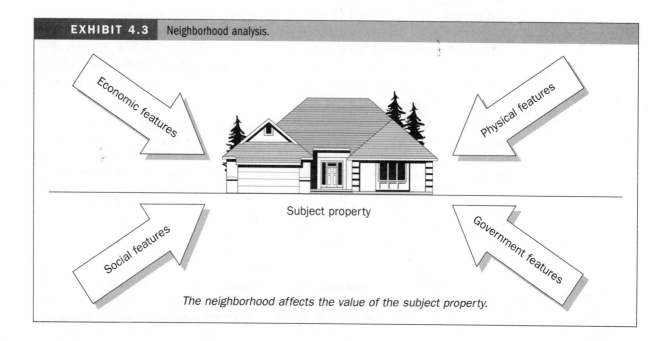

EXHIBIT 4.3 Neighborhood analysis.

Economic features

Physical features

Subject property

Social features

Government features

The neighborhood affects the value of the subject property.

sion boundaries, or some other similar concept. At this point, the appraiser's experience in the community and knowledge of the population's perceptions about neighborhoods become the major determining factors in the definition of a neighborhood.

Neighborhood Analysis Versus Area Analysis

Once the boundaries of the subject property's neighborhood are identified, the appraiser must analyze the impacts of the neighborhood's features on the value of the property being appraised. These neighborhood features are typically categorized as physical, social, economic, and governmental. They are the same factors used in area analysis but in this case are examined in reference to the neighborhood rather than to a larger region.

Physical Features

Neighborhood features that can have an impact on the value of the subject property are the physical features of the immediate environment. Typical physical features include the following:

1. Age, condition, and appearance of residences and other improvements in proximity to the subject property
2. Conformity of structural style
3. Availability and quality of public services and utilities
4. Pattern of the surrounding land uses and the size and shape of the lots (This factor includes the physical density of the structures—-that is, the number of lots per acre.)
5. Street patterns, width, and quality of construction
6. Quality of supporting facilities, such as public transportation, schools, commercial establishments, and social, cultural, and recreational activities
7. Proximity to supporting facilities
8. Proximity to employment opportunities
9. Visual factors, such as topographic features, proximity to lakes and rivers, and the climate
10. Geological factors, such as drainage capacity of the soil and other soil conditions
11. Presence of such nuisances and hazards, as smog, smoke, odors, and pollution (air, water, noise, and visual)

The value of the subject property is affected by each of these physical factors. The best way to visualize their impact is to imagine a parcel of real estate, the subject property, as being situated in two different neighborhoods having different physical features. For example, view Neighborhood A as consisting of 10- to 15-year-old houses in excellent condition both internally and externally, and Neighborhood B as consisting of 10- to 15-year-old houses of the same size and style but that are in poor physical condition. If all other neighborhood factors are the same, the subject property located in Neighborhood A would be valued more highly than the identical property located in Neighborhood B.

The appraiser must evaluate each of the physical features in the same manner. In addition, she must be cognizant of the general public's reactions or tastes and preferences about these physical features. The preceding example is straightforward because it is generally correct to assume that the vast majority of people prefer to live in neighborhoods where the surrounding structures are well maintained. Similarly, it is reasonable to assume that people wish to live in neighborhoods that have a high quality of public services and utilities; a high quality of supporting facilities, such as public transportation and schools; pleasant visual features; and few nuisances and hazards.

No such general assumptions can be made about other physical features. Their presence could enhance the value of the subject property or have no effect on value at all because they might not be universally preferred. For example, some people might prefer conformity of structural style. They would like a neighborhood that consists of all brick split-level houses. Other people, however, might prefer diversity of architectural styles in the neighborhood. The appraiser's task is to analyze such physical features and determine how the typical purchaser would react to them. In other words, the appraiser must understand the public's preference patterns toward housing. These patterns change over time, so the appraiser must also stay in tune with these changes.

Social Features

A second set of neighborhood features consists of social factors that identify the neighborhood's residents. These social factors are listed below.

1. Demographic traits of the neighborhood's population—for example, age, household size, marital status
2. Social attitudes of the population toward child rearing, cleanliness of property, respect for the private property of others, and general interpersonal social conduct
3. Existence and level of involvement of neighborhood organizations, community associations, and religious groups
4. Occupancy level (the number of people per room) of the structure
5. Extent of crime or level of safety in the neighborhood

As in the case of the physical features, certain social features generally are viewed as desirable in a neighborhood. A clean, crime-free neighborhood in which all landowners have respect for the property of others and where interpersonal contact is pleasant should enhance the value of a house.

However, the value-enhancing effect of population density and communal attitudes depends on the potential home buyer's preferences about population homogeneity and interaction. If the potential buyers in the submarket for such housing view these traits as important, the house in the neighborhood that has these social features will be valued more highly.

Economic Features

The third set of neighborhood features consists of the economic factors that identify the residents and the surrounding improvements. A list of these economic factors follows.

1. Economic profile of the neighborhood's residents, including such factors as income level, occupational status, and employment status
2. Proportion of resident owners to renters in the neighborhood
3. Turnover and vacancy levels of the properties
4. Degree of land utilization—that is, the amount of vacant land and the amount of new construction

5. Relationship of the neighborhood to the growth path and development pattern of the urban area

6. Attitude of financial institutions toward the issuance of mortgages in the neighborhood

The economic features of the neighborhood's residents and the surrounding improvements affect the value of the subject property. To analyze the impact of some of these factors, the appraiser must be a market analyst; to analyze the impact of the other factors, the appraiser must keep abreast of public attitudes. In examining the economic profile of the neighborhood's residents, the appraiser must consider the economic homogeneity of the neighborhood. Many people view such homogeneity as an important factor. In addition, the appraiser must consider the economic circumstances of the inhabitants in relation to the value of the structures and the level of maintenance and operating costs, which can determine the eventual physical condition of the improvements. The income level or employment pattern of the residents may be such that they are unable to expend a sufficient portion of their income to either maintain or renovate their homes.

The proportion of owners to tenants residing in a neighborhood also can be related to the current appearance and future condition of the improvements. For a neighborhood that contains single-family detached housing, the common belief is that residences occupied by their owners receive better care than residences owned by absentee owners and occupied by tenants. This generalization is usually but not always true. Therefore, a high proportion of owners to tenants in a neighborhood can have an enhancing effect on the subject property.

However, if the neighborhood in question is a mixed residential-use neighborhood with single-family detached housing units and low-rise apartments, the proportion of owners to tenants is meaningless. A low ratio of owners to tenants in this type of neighborhood does not signal declining values. Tenants as a group are not unclean, destructive, or a public nuisance. Owners as a group do not always expend funds to keep their property in good repair. In this type of neighborhood, the appraiser must analyze the past trend and estimate the future trend with regard to expenditures for upkeep by both the owners of the single-family detached units and the owners of the apartment units.

Generalizations about the turnover rate and the vacancy level must be made with care. A neighborhood can have many houses for sale, but the houses may be on the market for only a short period of time. Very mobile people could inhabit such a neighborhood, and it could be in great demand as a residential site. In this case, high turnover does not have a value-depressing effect. In contrast, a neighborhood with many houses for sale that stay on the market for long periods of time could be a neighborhood with problems. If the high levels of vacancies are due primarily to a relatively low level of demand for the properties, the values in this neighborhood will most likely decline in the future.

The degree of land utilization in the neighborhood is also a difficult factor to analyze. Often, this information is presented as the amount of vacant land in the neighborhood. Potential buyers may fear that this vacant land will be used in such a way that property values in the neighborhood will be reduced. If inharmonious or incompatible uses actually do enter the neighborhood, property values will decline. However, for several reasons, the amount of vacant land should not be considered a proxy for the possibility of invasion by value-depressing land uses. First, some of the vacant land may not be suitable for development (for example, land with excessively steep slopes or land that is in a floodplain). Such land will not be improved and will have no value-depressing or value-enhancing effect on the subject property. Second, for the sake of increased privacy, some private owners voluntarily hold some of the vacant land off the market. This vacant land could be developed ultimately by its owner in a way that could either depress or enhance the value of the subject property. Finally, the local zoning ordinance controls the types of development for which vacant land can be used. The specifications of the land use restrictions may prohibit value-depressing land uses. Moreover, the community may have a history of being value-conscious when allowing variances and rezoning. To analyze the impact of vacant land on neighborhood values, the appraiser should know the zoning ordinance and the probability of rezoning to an inharmonious or nonconforming use.

The growth path of the urban area can also have a major impact on property values in the neighborhood. As decentralization of employment opportunities occurs in an urban area, some neighborhoods become more convenient and others become less convenient in relation to jobs. As decentralization of population continues, newer neighborhoods at the fringe become increasingly popular at the expense of most central city neighborhoods. (In some cities, revitalization of downtown as an employment center has led to rehabilitation of neighborhoods in the central city.) As the transport system is changed to accommodate decentralization, some neighborhoods become more accessible and others become less accessible. A neighborhood that is receiving the benefits of decentralization has a value-enhancing effect on a subject property.

Finally, the willingness of financial institutions to issue mortgages for the purchase of property in a neighborhood can affect property values. The term **redlining** is used to refer to a practice whereby financial institutions delineate certain areas or neighborhoods in which they do not issue mortgage loans. If the redlining practice exists in a community, it is justified on the basis that the financial institution has a responsibility to its depositors to invest in safe assets that retain their value. So, the financial institutions attempt to make loans on properties whose collateral value will exceed the mortgage balance at all times until the loan period is repaid. Therefore, they try to identify and avoid properties and neighborhoods that might not maintain their collateral value at sufficiently high levels in the future. Legally, racial, ethnic, religious, and gender characteristics of the neighbors cannot be used by the financial institutions to determine the future value of such properties. If the redlining does exist and the financial institutions do not issue mortgages in a neighborhood, this unavailability of mortgage funds has a depressing impact on the demand for properties there. Consequently, the value of the subject property falls because of the inability of potential buyers to obtain mortgages.

Governmental Features

The fourth set of neighborhood features is related to local governmental activity. This category consists of the following factors:

1. Quantity and quality of public improvements and services
2. Property taxation and special assessments
3. Public restrictions and regulations

The most significant governmental features affecting the value of the subject property are the off-site public improvements and public services available in the neighborhood. These features have both a quantitative and a qualitative component. Public improvements-to-the-land that are not on, but are adjacent to, the site include the street and sidewalk network, the utility lines, and the storm-drain system that serves the property. This category typically includes improvements provided through special assessments by the local government. These public improvements-to-the-land unquestionably affect the value of the individual parcels they serve.

The second set of off-site improvements that affects a particular site's value is the neighboring improvements-on-the-land. This category includes the neighboring structures and the types of land use nearby. If the quality of the neighborhood is deteriorating because little, if any, repair and maintenance work is done on the surrounding structures, the value of the subject property will be lower than it would be in a neighborhood that is not deteriorating. The proximity of dissimilar or incompatible land uses also has an adverse effect on the subject property. If an industrial district is adjacent to a residential area, the proximity of the dissimilar use could have a value-depressing effect on the residential units. However, a prestigious commercial area could have a value-enhancing effect on an adjacent residential area and the individual parcels of real estate.

The third off-site improvement category consists of the public services that are typically provided through the general revenue or property tax base of the community. The availability and quality of instruction in community schools, the level of fire and police protection, the availability of community parks and recreational areas, and the existence of community-sponsored cultural and recreational activities affect the value of a particular site. The availability of these public services will enhance the value of a parcel of real estate if the potential homeowners view these features as desirable.

In neighborhoods that offer high-quality and high-quantity levels of public improvements and services, the demand for houses is higher and hence their value is greater than in neighborhoods lacking such facilities.

The second governmental feature is property taxation and special assessments. All public services and improvements must be bought and paid for by the consumer through the property tax and the special assessment (previously discussed in Chapter 2). The special assessment should reflect the dollar value of the adjoining public improvement, and the value of the newly constructed adjoining improvement should have a corresponding positive impact on the value of the subject property. The property tax, in contrast, does not have an impact that is directly identifiable. Generally, the property tax is a cost of home ownership. As the total level of this cost increases, the demand for housing should decline unless the higher tax was offset by improved or expanded public services. For example, if two neighborhoods have the same quantity and quality of public services but the tax bill in Neighborhood A is greater than the tax bill in Neighborhood B, the value of the subject property would be lower in Neighborhood A.

The third governmental feature is the full complement of public restrictions and regulations embodied in the zoning ordinance, the subdivision regulations, the construction code, and the occupancy code. Each of these regulations (discussed in detail in Chapter 2) affects the neighborhood and hence the value of the subject property.

For example, assume that the subdivision regulations imposed on the development of Neighborhood A provide this neighborhood with features consumers desire. It could have wide curvilinear streets that heighten the aesthetic quality of the neighborhood and cul-de-sacs that reduce traffic and thereby reduce the noise level and increase the safety of children. It could provide a lot arrangement to maximize privacy without the need for fencing. Assume that Neighborhood B does not have such features. If all other neighborhood features were the same, the value of the subject property would be higher in Neighborhood A than in Neighborhood B because of consumer preferences.

In terms of zoning, assume that Neighborhood A has land use restrictions that are incompatible with low-density, single-family detached housing—for example, high-density apartment complexes, commercial activity that generates a high volume of vehicular traffic (sports arenas, race tracks, large discount stores), and noisy, dirty industrial plants. Moreover, the planning department operates to maintain this feature of the neighborhood by carefully scrutinizing all requests for variances and rezoning. Assume that Neighborhood B does not have a land use plan that is as well prepared and well maintained as that of Neighborhood A. If all other features of the two neighborhoods are the same, Neighborhood A will be more desirable given consumer preferences, and thus the subject property would be worth more if it were located in Neighborhood A instead of Neighborhood B.

The impact of construction codes and occupancy codes on the value of property is transmitted through the quality of the adjoining structures. If improvements in a neighborhood are well maintained because of the occupancy code, and if maintenance is relatively easy because of high-quality construction standards imposed in the past by the construction code, any specific property in that neighborhood is more valuable than it would be in a neighborhood of poorly maintained improvements.

What Are the Site-Specific Determinants of Value?

The **site-specific determinants of value** that the appraiser must analyze consist of the on-site features of specific parcels of real property. In the context of the full scope of the analysis depicted earlier in Exhibit 4.1, the site-specific determinants of value are the ones most focused on the property. The purpose of site-specific analysis is to identify the impact of on-site features on the value of the subject property. Specific data relevant to both the site and the improvements are gathered. Then, the use of the property is analyzed to determine whether a change in the use could generate a higher value than that generated by the parcel in its present usage. Thus, the specific data gathered for parcels of real property are used for site analysis, improvement analysis, and highest-and-best-use analysis.

SITE DATA AND ANALYSIS

The specific data needed for site analysis include legal, physical, and economic and locational features of the site. Each of these three types of data is described below.

Legal Features

The category of legal data consists of the rights of ownership that are held in the property and the public and private limits on those rights. A prospective buyer obviously would pay more for an estate in possession than for an estate in expectancy (both discussed in Chapter 1) if all other aspects of the property were the same. Similarly, the buyer would pay more for a property that does not have an easement than for a property on which an easement eliminates the owner's ability to use all of the site.

Restrictive covenants (discussed in Chapter 2) in the deed also affect the value of the parcel of real estate. The typical prospective buyer will offer less for a property having this type of private land use restriction than a property that is not restricted as to use. For this reason, the person initially establishing the restrictive covenant must understand the impact of the covenant on prospective buyers.

Public limits on the rights of ownership in the form of the zoning ordinance also affect the value of the parcel of property. The most obvious examples are the land use regulations, which disallow a particular land use; the height regulations, which limit the number of floors or stories that can be constructed on a given site; and the area regulations, which limit the amount of land surface that can be used for the improvement. All else being similar, the typical buyer will pay less for property that has the more severe restrictions.

Construction and occupancy codes also place limits on the rights of ownership. These codes affect the property owner because they directly affect the level of construction costs and maintenance and repair costs, respectively. The prudent buyer will pay more for a property that is subject to less demanding occupancy codes because the maintenance and repair costs will probably be lower. However, the prudent buyer will pay less for a property that was subject to less demanding construction codes because the maintenance and repair costs will probably be higher.

LEGAL DESCRIPTION OF THE SITE. Being able to describe the amount of land surface that is owned is a necessity. Typically, the larger the surface, the more valuable the property. Three techniques of legal description currently are used to describe the extent of the land surface: the lot and block (or plat map) system, the metes and bounds system, and the government rectangular survey system. In a sense, each of these techniques draws a picture of the land surface that is owned. (See Chapter 2 for a discussion of these three systems.)

Physical Features

This category of site-specific data is related to the geological and geographical features of the site. The geographical features include the following:

1. Width and frontage
2. Depth
3. Shape
4. Size
5. Corner and cul-de-sac influences

The geological features of the site include the following:

1. Topography
2. Surface-soil quality and landscaping
3. Subsoil and bedrock characteristics
4. Drainage and runoff characteristics
5. Availability of potable water

One purpose of the site analysis is to examine the impact of each one of these physical features on the value of a residential property.

WIDTH AND FRONTAGE. The width and frontage of a site measure the same physical dimension but at different points on the site. **Frontage** is the width of the site where it is adjacent to an access road. Along the road, frontage and width are always the same. If the site is a rectangle or square, then the width of the lot is equal to the frontage of all points. However, for a non-rectangular-shaped lot, the width will differ from the frontage at all points except along the frontage road. The impact of frontage on value is readily identified. All else being equal, the more front footage, the more valuable the site, especially in commercial areas. Similarly, the impact of width on value is readily apparent. Given the same frontage, the wider the site, the more valuable it is, because more square feet of space exist. In other words, two irregularly shaped lots with the same front footage will have different values if the lots have different widths. The wider lot is typically more valuable.

DEPTH. The **depth** of a site is the measurement from the frontage to the back property line. If other aspects of the site are the same, the deeper the site, the more valuable it is. However, appraisers realize that a few extra feet of depth are not as valuable as the first few feet of depth. The addition of a foot of depth increases the total value but by smaller and smaller increments, because the major improvement on most sites is constructed as near to the front of the site as permitted by the area regulations of the zoning ordinance. In this instance, the first 100 feet of depth should be worth more than the next 100 feet of depth, which in turn should be worth more than the next 100 feet of depth. In other words, the first feet of depth are worth more than the last feet of depth.

SHAPE. The impact of the shape of a lot is not as easily determined. If the lot is irregular in shape but large enough to accommodate the planned improvement, the shape does not affect the value in relation to that of a regular rectangular lot if the two lots are approximately the same otherwise. However, a very irregular lot in a neighborhood of regularly shaped lots may be valued less than the other lots.

SIZE. The size of a site has a direct impact on the value of that site. Width and depth of the lot determine size. For a rectangular lot, the product of these measures of distance is the square footage of the site. As a general rule, the larger the lot in square feet, the greater the value. Size, however, is only one of the major physical determinants of value. Frontage is generally more significant as a value determinant than sheer size of the lot. For example, consider two sites. Site A has a 100-foot frontage and a 200-foot depth; therefore, it contains 20,000 square feet. Site B has an 80-foot frontage and a 250-foot depth, and also contains 20,000 square feet. All else being equal, the lot with the greater frontage is more valuable as commercial property. However, it is difficult to generalize about the impact on residential value because the lots are the same size. If the lot is wide enough at 80 feet to provide privacy from the adjacent neighbors, the additional 50 feet of depth can provide an added degree of privacy from the street.

A problem arises for the appraiser when the frontage and the square footage both differ. For example, consider Site A with its 100-foot frontage and 200-foot depth, containing 20,000 square feet, and Site C, with its 90-foot frontage and 222-foot depth, containing 19,980 square feet. Site A has 10 percent more frontage. Site C is 11 percent deeper. Which site is worth more if all other things are equal? The answer depends on the type of land use and the standards for lot width and depth in the surrounding neighborhood. More specifically, the answer depends on the appraiser's knowledge of the neighborhood's land use pattern and experience with consumer preferences about the issue.

A special aspect of size is **plottage value,** the increase in value to each individual site when smaller plots are combined to form a larger one. For plottage value to be realized, the potential use of the combined sites must be an activity that generates a higher return to the land than would result if the small, individual sites were developed separately. For example, five building lots would provide for the construction of five single-family, detached housing units. If a rezoning request were granted, these five small sites could be assembled into one site and developed into 15 town houses. Otherwise, the whole could not be worth more than the sum of its parts. In other words, when several small adjacent lots are purchased and assembled into one large lot, the value of the large lot exceeds the sum of the values of the small lots. However, plottage value occurs only when the large lot can be used to generate a residual income from a highest and best use that exceeds the residual income obtained from the highest and best use of each individual lot summed together. A **highest and best use** is defined as the legally permissible and physically possible use that generates the highest residual income to the property over a reasonable period of time.

CORNER AND CUL-DE-SAC INFLUENCES. The influence of a corner location on the value of a site depends on the type of land use for that site and the manner in which the improvement is related to the space provided on the site. In urban residential neighborhoods of the past, corner lots were considered more valuable because they were viewed as providing more light and air than lots in the interior of the block. The additional exposure provided a positive value increment to residences on corners. However, growth of cities has brought about increased vehicular and pedestrian traffic along the street network and hence, more noise, air pollution, and litter. In addition, corner lots generally are subject to higher public improvement assessments because they front on two streets and may be larger than the typical internal lot, and they may also be subject to higher property tax bills.

Finally, corner lots tend to have less privacy because the backyard is exposed to one of the streets. These adverse impacts counterbalance the positive impacts of sunlight and breezes. The appraiser must consider both the positive and the negative aspects in determining the influence of a corner location on a residential site. The impact of corner locations for commercial property is typically positive because the property faces pedestrian and vehicular traffic on two streets. Consequently, the volume of potential customers passing a corner location is greater than the volume passing an interior location. Moreover, interior lots can benefit from proximity to a corner. The magnitude of the value premium declines quickly as the lot's distance from the corner increases.

A **cul-de-sac** is a street that has one entry point and a dead end that is a circular turnaround area bordered by houses. The increased prominence of cul-de-sac development patterns in new residential neighborhoods reflects the desire to reduce the negative impacts of vehicular traffic as well as to provide safety for children at play and greater backyard privacy.

TOPOGRAPHY. The impact of a site's topography on value is not readily identifiable. This physical feature needs to be closely scrutinized for the benefits provided and the costs that must be incurred. According to current consumer preferences, a desirable residential lot is one that gently rises from the street level so that the house can be situated at a slight elevation above the street. At the back of the lot, consumers like a contour that allows for a patio at the back of the house and flat ground for a play area and possibly a swimming pool. A site having these features should be valued more highly than a flat site.

However, a building lot that is situated above or below the grade of the abutting street level usually encounters additional costs to correct poor drainage, erosion, or accessibility problems. If the site requires such costly corrections, it will have a lower value. Therefore, the appraiser must balance the extra costs for on-site improvements against the additional benefits derived from desirable topographic characteristics of the site.

SURFACE-SOIL QUALITY AND LANDSCAPING. One geological feature that affects a site's value is the quality of the topsoil. The soil supports the life of indigenous trees on the site as well as the man-made improvement called **landscaping,** which includes the lawn, shrubbery, and gardens. In general, this vegetation improves the appearance and the desirability of residential properties. Soil quality is a relative factor, however. If the soil quality of the site is inferior to that of the neighboring sites, it will have a value-depressing effect. If all the sites in the neighborhood or area have uniformly poor soil quality, there should not be a value-depressing effect on any one specific site due to poor soil quality.

SUBSOIL AND BEDROCK CHARACTERISTICS. The nature of the subsoil can affect the costs of building an improvement. It can also affect the height of the major improvement. If the soil is unstable, structural supports must be sunk to the bedrock. The depth of the unstable soil greatly affects construction costs. If the subsurface is solid rock, digging foundations is very expensive. Consequently, a site with geological features that increase construction costs above their level on neighboring properties will command a lower price.

DRAINAGE AND RUNOFF CHARACTERISTICS. The ability of the site's surface contour and subsurface soil to remove stormwater greatly affects the value of that site. If the site is flat or slightly sloped and if it is composed of porous, stable subsurface soil, there is no problem of standing water after a rainstorm or after snow melts. However, if the site is below the level of abutting property and the soil is nonporous (such as clay), the site will experience standing water and flooding. In this case, the developer must incur additional site preparation costs to correct the problem. For example, porous tile pipe might have to be installed from the area of flooding on the site to a point where the water can run off. This project might necessitate digging a trench 1 foot wide and 12 to 18 inches deep for a distance of 100 or more feet, which would clearly add to the site's improvement costs.

Therefore, all else being equal, a site that has good natural drainage and runoff characteristics should be more valuable—that is, have a higher selling price—than a site that does not have these physical characteristics. The difference between the selling prices of the two plots of land represents the cost of the improvements needed to rectify the problem.

If the site with poor natural drainage also is not served with public sewers, the cost of residential construction increases further. Any site not served by public sewers must have a septic tank and leach lines to disperse waste material. On a site with poor drainage, a layer of crushed rock must be placed below the tile pipe and leach lines to increase the drainage capability. The length of the leach line or the size of the leach field also may have to be increased if drainage is poor. These requirements increase the cost of improvements and thus reduce the value of the site. At the extreme, local health ordinances may prohibit the construction of septic tanks and leach lines on sites that have extremely poor drainage capabilities. Such a prohibition would have an obvious detrimental impact on the value of the site.

AVAILABILITY OF POTABLE WATER. The term *potable water* simply means "drinkable water." If a site is not served by a municipal water system, a well must be drilled to obtain water. In most counties, a site cannot be developed until potable water is discovered on that site. The site must have a natural water supply that meets minimum standards of purity imposed by the county health department. A site that is not served by a water system and that does not have a potable water supply is less valuable than a site that is similar in all respects but does have a supply of drinkable natural water. This value difference exists because the latter site can be improved but the former cannot.

Economic and Locational Features

The third category of site data represents the site's relative economic and spatial position in comparison with other sites nearby. One economic factor that must be considered is the price of nearby lots that are similar to the subject property. The principle of substitution (discussed later in this chapter) implies that the selling price of the similar lots sets an upper limit on the most probable selling price of the subject property. A second economic factor is the tax burden imposed on the subject property. If it is higher than that imposed on similar lots in proximity to the subject property, and if all of the lots are receiving the same level of services, the lot with the excessive tax burden is depressed in value by the additional tax payment required. In other words, the subject property may be overassessed in comparison with comparable properties or, if the assessments are the same, the subject property is overtaxed. Overassessment causes a reduction in market value. Conversely, if the subject property is underassessed or undertaxed, its market value will be greater than that of similar properties receiving the same quantity and quality of public services. However, this effect on value lasts only until the assessment and tax burden aspects are corrected.

The locational factors of site analysis are the attributes of location. The location of the site in relation to employment centers and other establishments has a significant impact on the market value of the site. The more accessible the site is to economic activities—that is, the shorter the linkages and the lower the cost of transportation—the more valuable the site.

Another locational factor is the site's position in space relative to scenic views and other preferred natural features. A lakeside lot is more valuable than an identical interior lot. A hillside lot that overlooks a valley is more valuable than a similar lot on a flat plain or in an area without a view.

In addition, hazards and nuisances can affect the value of a site. Hazards may be large volumes of high-speed vehicular traffic, floods, landslides, avalanches, steep cliffs, and fire danger. Typically, these hazards depress the value of a site. Nuisances include noisy highways, industry, and playgrounds full of noisy children. These nuisances in proximity to a site can have a value-depressing effect.

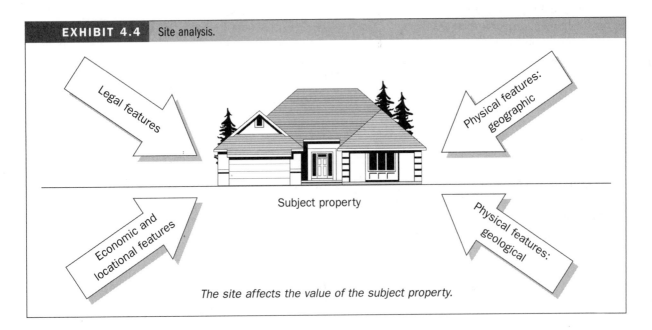

EXHIBIT 4.4 Site analysis.

Legal features

Physical features: geographic

Subject property

Economic and locational features

Physical features: geological

The site affects the value of the subject property.

Aesthetic Features

The final site-specific determinant of value for on-site improvements is the attractiveness of the building. The external measures of attractiveness are typically factors of structural design, positioning of the structure on the lot, landscaping, and the covering of exterior surfaces. The internal measures of attractiveness are room size and shape, placement of windows and doors, orientation of sunlight and natural ventilation, floor plan, wall coverings, fixtures, and the degree of privacy and quiet provided. Because the standards of attractiveness differ among people and also change over time, the influence of this factor is difficult to measure. However, it does affect an individual's decision about the value of a structure.

IMPROVEMENT ANALYSIS

The second phase of analyzing site-specific determinants of value is **improvement analysis,** which focuses on the man-made construction on the physical site. Both improvements-on-the-land and some of the improvements-to-the-land (described in Chapter 1) must be analyzed for their quantitative and qualitative features (see Exhibit 4.5). Improvements-to-the-land, such as landscaping, access roads or driveways, utility connections, water wells, and septic tanks, can have a major effect on the value of a specific property.

Quantity of the Improvements

The size of the structure and the number of structures are the first considerations. The bigger the major improvements and the more of them present on the site affect the value of the real property. Remember from the discussion in Chapter 1 that these on-

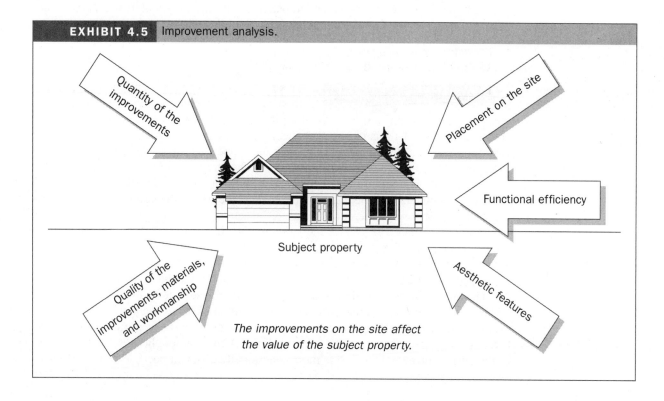

EXHIBIT 4.5 Improvement analysis.

Quantity of the improvements

Placement on the site

Functional efficiency

Subject property

Quality of the improvements, materials, and workmanship

Aesthetic features

The improvements on the site affect the value of the subject property.

site improvements consist of the principal structure and all man-made additions to the land. In a residential context, this includes driveways, sidewalks, fences, patios, decorative landscaping, and so forth.

Quality of the Improvements

Another factor in the category of site-specific determinants of value is the quality of the improvements. Each structure or other improvement is durable. However, durability (or long physical life) does not impart value-in-use or value-in-exchange. What is important is the quality of the material and the workmanship that were used both in construction and in the maintenance and repair routines. If two similar improvements or structures are productive—that is, they render similar services—the structure with the higher quality of construction will be more valuable because the repair and maintenance expenses on a year-to-year basis will be less. In other words, given the same level of maintenance and repair, the higher quality structure should have a longer physical life.

Placement of the Structure on the Site

Two aspects of a structure's placement on the site are conceptually important in an analysis of the subject property's value. One aspect is the arrangement of public and private zones on the property. The **public zone** is the portion of the property that is visible from the street. By good site planning, this zone can be minimized within the area regulations or setback regulations of the local zoning ordinance. The **private zone** is the area of the property used for household activity. It includes playgrounds, patios, and gardens. This area on the site should be made as large as possible. All else being equal, people will view a house with a larger private zone as more desirable.

The second aspect of the structure's placement on the site is the positioning of the structure in relation to the sun and wind patterns. The structure and its windows should be positioned to catch the maximum amount of sunlight.

Functional Description of the Improvements

Functional efficiency is the ability of a structure to meet its current intended use and to be adapted to changing needs. In this sense, a house is functionally efficient if it meets the current and future needs of typical residents. Every improvement is or was constructed to meet a specific need. If the improvement fulfills that need, it has met the first requirement of functional efficiency in this current use. Every improvement is also expected to meet new needs that arise due to changing circumstances in its environment. The ability of the improvement to adapt to changing needs is the second aspect of functional efficiency. The change can occur in the use of the structure or in the attitudes of people toward the correct use. As a general rule, the greater the degree of functional efficiency, the greater the value of the structure. If two structures are currently meeting the same need in an adequate manner, if one structure can be easily adapted to a new use and the other is adaptable only with difficulty and great expense, the structure that can be easily adapted should be more valuable to its owner.

The degree of functional efficiency depends on the services provided by the house and the desires of typical buyers in that housing submarket today and in the future. For example, assume that two houses are identical in every detail except that House A has 8-foot ceilings and House B has 12-foot ceilings. Although both houses meet the needs of the current owners, House A is more functionally efficient because it is less expensive to heat and cool. As a second example, assume that a tall couple built a customized house to meet their needs. They installed a kitchen counter, with a built-in range and a sink, that is six or eight inches higher than normal. This kitchen feature is functionally efficient in its current use for the tall couple. It probably will not be functionally efficient in the future, however, because the typical buyer is shorter and requires a house with a countertop of normal height. In both cases, the functionally efficient house is the more desirable.

Two commercial property examples illustrate the adaptability of structures to changing needs. First, many modern production techniques require single-story industrial plants. Technological change has made multistory industrial plants, which are typically located in the central cities, functionally inefficient as production facilities. Some of these buildings have been adapted for storage and warehousing functions or as industrial space for small manufacturing plants, whose volume of production does not require large amounts of space. However, many of these old industrial buildings are vacant—a sign either of their functional inefficiency or of lack of demand for their services. Second, changing tastes and preferences in housing once made the multistory house with several dwelling units, situated on a small lot in the central city, less desirable than a single-family house on a large lot in a suburban area. However, increases in the costs of transportation, heating, and cooling (coupled with a trend toward much smaller lots in suburban areas) have caused a growing trend in several cities to renovate these multistory houses on small lots. These older structures in the central cities, which did not fill the needs of housing consumers in the 1950s through the 1970s, have begun to fill the needs of today's families.

The physical design and layout of the house and its rooms are another important aspect of functional efficiency. Like the lot, the house is divided into public and private zones. The working (or service) zone is composed of the kitchen, pantry, utility room, and other areas set aside for household-related work. The living (or social) zone is composed of the living room, dining room, family room, den, recreation room, and porch. The private (or sleeping) zone is composed of the bedrooms, bathrooms, and other rooms where quiet and privacy are desired. According to current preferences, these three zones should be separate, distinct parts of the residential unit. Such an arrangement is most desirable to current home buyers and should be a value-enhancing factor.

What Is a Real Estate Appraisal?

A real estate **appraisal** is defined by the Appraisal Foundation as "the act or process of estimating value; an estimate of value." In this definition, the term *real estate* denotes real property—the legal as well as the physical aspects of real estate. Thus, an appraisal of real estate is an estimate of the value of the physical property and the rights of ownership associated with that property.

An expanded definition of a real estate appraisal is that it is an unbiased, knowledgeable, and documented opinion of value. The term *unbiased* here denotes that the appraiser has no personal interest in the value estimate; the market value estimate is not affected by any personal motives or benefits. The appraisal fee is based on the work effort to reach the opinion; it is a fixed amount adequate to do the job and is not based on a percentage of the value estimate. Moreover, the appraiser does not include his personal preferences in the valuation process.

The term *knowledgeable* here means that the appraiser receives both classroom instruction on the principles and procedures involved in real estate appraisal and on-the-job experience under the guidance of a practicing appraiser. All states have an **appraisal**

commission that establishes rules and regulations governing the content and the extent of classroom contact hours, examinations, and experience credit. Beyond this mandated certification by the states, professional organizations offer appraisal designations that expand on the educational aspects and experience requirements imposed by the state.

The term *documented* here means that the appraiser must provide some form of tangible evidence to support the opinion of value. Depending on the nature of the appraisal assignment, the tangible evidence can take the form of a narrative report that provides the data and logic that lead to the value opinion. This is the typical documentation that underlies the value estimate for commercial properties. The documentation for a single-family dwelling unit is typically a report in the format of a prescribed two-page form.

AGENCIES THAT OVERSEE THE REAL PROPERTY APPRAISAL PROFESSION

First, each state has a state agency—the appraisal commission—that oversees the licensing and certification of individuals who are approved to undertake real property appraisals. The process of obtaining a license or a certification involves a formal classroom experience, a competency examination of the educational contact hours, and on-the-job experience. Second, the U.S. Congress recognized the private Appraisal Foundation in 1987 as a nonprofit educational organization that fosters professionalism in appraising. Third, the Congress created the Appraisal Subcommittee to regulate the state agencies.

The Appraisal Foundation (located in Washington, D.C.; 202-347-7722) accomplishes this objective by establishing and promoting professional standards and appraiser qualifications. The Appraisal Foundation believes that public input and public education are essential to achieving its objectives. To this end, the Appraisal Foundation maintains a fax-on-demand service and a website (www.appraisalfoundation.org). These two forms of communication provide access to publications, on-line services, and the ability for the public to communicate with the staff of the organization.

The Appraisal Foundation is sponsored by other nonprofit organizations dedicated to the appraisers and the users of appraisal services. The sponsors include the following appraiser organizations: the Appraisal Institute, the American Society of Appraisers, the American Society of Farm Managers and Rural Appraisers, the International Association of Assessing Officers, the International Right of Way Association, the National Association of Independent Fee Appraisers, the National Association of Master Appraisers, and the Appraisal Institute of Canada. The sponsors also include the following users of appraisal services: the American Bankers Association, the National Association of Realtors, the Farm Credit Council, and the Mortgage Insurance Companies of America.

The major publication of the Appraisal Foundation is the *Uniform Standards of Professional Appraisal Practice (USPAP)*. The Financial Institutions Reform, Recovery and Enforcement Act (FIRREA) requires that appraisals prepared by state-certified and state-licensed appraisers must be prepared according to the standards and rules set out in USPAP. State and federal agencies enforce USPAP through laws, regulations, and ordinances. If an appraiser fails to conform to the rules and standards in USPAP in an appraisal, that appraiser's certificate or license can be invalidated. USPAP is a lengthy document that is revised annually. It is too long to present here, but a short sampling of its ethics statement and the standards of practice appear in Exhibits 4.6 and 4.7. For each of the standards presented in Exhibit 4.7, the USPAP provides further explanations and comments.

ETHICS

Conduct

An appraiser must perform ethically and competently in accordance with these standards and not engage in conduct that is unlawful, unethical, or improper. An appraiser who could reasonably be perceived to act as a disinterested third party in rendering an unbiased appraisal, review, or consulting service must perform assignments with impartiality, objectivity, and independence and without accommodation of personal interests.

Management

The acceptance of compensation that is contingent upon the reporting of a predetermined value or a direction in value that favors the cause of the client, the amount of the value estimate, the attainment of a stipulated result, or the occurrence of a subsequent event is unethical.

The payment of undisclosed fees, commissions, or things of value in connection with the procurement of appraisal, review, or consulting assignments is unethical.

Advertising for or soliciting appraisal assignments in a manner which is false, misleading, or exaggerated is unethical.

The restriction on contingent compensation in the first paragraph of this section does not apply to consulting assignments where the appraiser is not acting in a disinterested manner and would not reasonably be perceived as performing a service that requires impartiality. This permitted contingent compensation must be properly disclosed in the report.

Confidentiality

An appraiser must protect the confidential nature of the appraiser-client relationship.

Record Keeping

An appraiser must prepare written records of appraisal, review, and consulting assignments—including oral testimony and reports—and retain such records for a period of at least five (5) years after preparation or at least two (2) years after final disposition of any judicial proceeding in which testimony was given, whichever expires last.

Competency

Prior to accepting an assignment or entering into an agreement to perform any assignment, an appraiser must properly identify the problem to be addressed and have the knowledge and experience to complete the assignment competently; or alternatively:

1. disclose the lack of knowledge and/or experience to the client accepting the assignment; and

2. take all steps necessary or appropriate to complete the assignment competently; and

3. describe the lack of knowledge and/or experience and the steps taken to complete the assignment competently in the report.

Source: Appraisal Foundation, *Uniform Standards of Professional Appraisal Practice,* Washington, D.C., 1999.

EXHIBIT 4.7 Standards of Professional Appraisal Practice.

1	**Real Property Appraisal**	In developing a real property appraisal, an appraiser must be aware of, understand, and correctly employ those recognized methods and techniques that are necessary to produce a credible appraisal.
2	**Real Property Appraisal, Reporting**	In reporting the results of a real property appraisal, an appraiser must communicate each analysis, opinion, and conclusion in a manner that is not misleading.
3	**Review Appraisal and Reporting**	In reviewing an appraisal and reporting the results of that review, an appraiser must form an opinion as to the adequacy and appropriateness of the report being reviewed and must clearly disclose the nature of the review process undertaken.
4	**Real Estate/Real Property Consulting**	In performing real estate or real property consulting services, an appraiser must be aware of, understand, and correctly employ those recognized methods and techniques that are necessary to produce a credible result.
5	**Real Estate/Real Property Consulting Reporting**	In reporting the results of a real estate or real property consulting service, an appraiser must communicate each analysis, opinion, and conclusion in a manner that is not misleading.
6	**Mass Appraisal and Reporting**	In developing a mass appraisal, an appraiser must be aware of, understand, and correctly employ those generally accepted methods and techniques necessary to produce and communicate credible appraisals.
7	**Personal Property Appraisal**	In developing a personal property appraisal, an appraiser must be aware of, understand, and correctly employ those recognized methods and techniques that are necessary to produce a credible appraisal.
8	**Personal Property Appraisal Reporting**	In reporting the results of a personal property appraisal, an appraiser must communicate each analysis, opinion, and conclusion in a manner that is not misleading.
9	**Business Appraisal**	In developing a business or intangible asset appraisal, an appraiser must be aware of, understand, and correctly employ those recognized methods and techniques that are necessary to produce a credible appraisal.
10	**Business Appraisal Reporting**	In reporting the results of a business or intangible asset appraisal, an appraiser must communicate each analysis, opinion, and conclusion in a manner that is not misleading.

Source: Appraisal Foundation, *Uniform Standards of Professional Appraisal Practice,* Washington, D.C., 2000.

TYPES OF VALUE ESTIMATES

The value estimates obtained from an appraisal can be of several different types. Market value is perhaps the most familiar concept and the value most often desired. Other types of value that can be estimated by appraisal are

- *Assessed value:* a dollar amount assigned to taxable property, both real and personal, by the assessor of the local community for the purpose of taxation

- *Insurable value:* the dollar amount of insurance that may be, or should be, carried on destructible portions of a property to indemnify the owner in case of loss

- *Investment value:* the dollar value to a particular investor based on individual investment requirements, such as financing and taxation, as distinguished from market value, which is impersonal and detached

This chapter explores the appraisal process used to estimate the market value of single-family residential property. The need for such an estimate arises for many reasons. A partial list of the uses of this type of estimate follows.

1. Transfer of ownership: (a) to help prospective buyers decide on offering prices, (b) to help prospective sellers determine acceptable selling prices, (c) to establish a basis for exchange of real property, (d) to establish a basis for reorganization or for merging the ownership of multiple properties, and (e) to distribute the assets of an estate

2. Financing and credit: (a) to arrive at the essential security offered for a proposed mortgage loan, (b) to provide an investor with a sound basis for deciding whether to purchase real estate mortgages, and (c) to establish a basis for a decision about the insuring or underwriting of a loan on real property

3. Just compensation in condemnation proceedings: (a) to estimate market value of property as a whole, that is, before the taking, (b) to estimate value after the taking, and (c) to allocate market values between the part taken and damage to the remainder

4. A basis for taxation: (a) to separate assets into depreciable items, such as buildings, and nondepreciable items, such as land, and to estimate applicable depreciation rates, and (b) to determine gift or inheritance taxes

5. A basis for rental schedules and lease provisions

Thus, the need for a real estate appraisal arises for many reasons pertaining to a decision to purchase or sell real estate, a decision to offer funding for such a purpose, and a decision to insure a structure against casualty losses.

What Is the Real Estate Valuation Process?

The **valuation process** (also known as the appraisal process) for estimating the market value of a parcel of real property is a logical and concise step-by-step process. It is an orderly program by which the problem is defined, the work necessary to solve the problem is planned, and the data involved is acquired, classified, analyzed, interpreted, and translated into an estimate of value. Exhibit 4.8 shows the steps of the appraisal process found in USPAP.

EXHIBIT 4.8   The real property valuation process.

Define the Appraisal Problem
(1) Identify the Intended Use and Users of the Appraisal
(2) Define Value(s) to be Developed
(3) Establish Date(s) of the Value Opinion(s)
(4) Identify and Locate the Real Estate
(5) Identify the Property Rights to be Valued
(6) Identify Limiting Conditions or Limitations

Preliminary Analysis and Plan: Select and Collect Data

General (market):	Subject Property:	Competitive Properties:
Market Analysis	**Property Analysis**	**Comparison Analysis**
Demand Components	Site/Improvements	Sales
Supply Components	Size	Rentals
Trends	Age and Condition	Costs
Forecasts	Location	Elements of Comparison
	Legal (Title, Use)	Units of Comparison

Develop Highest and Best Use Opinion
Land as if Vacant and Available
Property as Improved (Existing or Proposed)

Develop Indicator(s) of Land/Site/Value (As Defined)

Sales Comparison	Income Capitalization	Subdivision/Development

Develop Indicator(s) of Improved Property Value (As Defined)

Cost	Sales Comparison	Income Capitalization

Reconcile Value Indicators; Reach Defined Value Opinion

Report Opinion(s) of Value(s) (As Defined)

Source: Appraisal Foundation, *Uniform Standards of Professional Appraisal Practice*, Washington, D.C., 2000, p. 89.

THE APPRAISAL PROBLEM

The first step in the appraisal process is definitional. Before the appraiser can start any task, the client's needs must be ascertained. The physical entity to be appraised must be identified first in terms of the land parcel and the structures. Then, the bundle of rights (discussed in Chapter 1) must be analyzed, and the mineral and air rights identified. Then, the legal rights of ownership pertaining to the physical property must be specified: Does the owner have the right of disposition and possession (freehold estate of inheritance) or does the owner only possess the property without the right of disposition (life estate)? Is it an estate in possession or an estate in expectancy? Are there easements and restrictive covenants that affect the owner's ability to develop portions of the property? The client must answer these types of questions.

The concept of value also must be specified. Typically, the client wants to know the market value of the property, but she may also be interested in some other type of value, such as insurance value or investment value.

The next important step in defining the assignment is specification of the date of the value estimate. In most cases, the appraiser is expected to estimate the current market value on the date the property is inspected. However, in some situations the appraiser might be requested to estimate the market value in some past period. For example, assume that an individual is given a piece of property as an inheritance but does not receive it until after a prolonged probate process. This property was given to the heir upon the relative's death the previous year, but it is legally received today and the inheritance tax must be paid. The heir would like to know the market value of the property as of the date the gift was made because property values have been rising. As a second example, consider the case of a condemnation trial in which the local government is taking property under eminent domain. The trial date is set four months in the future. The value estimate required is the market value of the property at that future date, specifically on the day of the trial.

PRELIMINARY ANALYSIS AND DATA SELECTION AND COLLECTION

Once the appraiser has clearly defined the assignment, the next step is the establishment of an execution plan for the assignment. In this step, the appraiser identifies the data required to complete the assignment, the public and private sources of the data, the type of personnel required to research and analyze the data and produce the report, and the time requirements for each of the individuals involved in the project. The final task in this step is to make a fee proposal to the client. This fee is quoted as a lump sum charge that reflects the dollar per hour or dollar per day charges for the personnel, overhead, and expenses.

If the client accepts the stated fee for the specified estimate of value, the next step in the appraisal process is the actual gathering of data pertinent to the assignment. Two main categories of data must be gathered—the environmental and site-specific data discussed earlier in this chapter.

HIGHEST AND BEST USE ANALYSIS

As defined earlier in this chapter, a highest and best use is the legally permissible and physically possible use that generates the highest residual income to the property over a reasonable period of time. To determine the highest and best use, the appraiser must examine four factors related to the site. The land use regulations established in the zoning ordinance are one factor of concern. Another concern is the physical capability of the site to support the improvement. In other words, in a legal and geological sense, what restrictions are placed on the construction of the improvement? A third factor is the market for each legally permitted and physically possible land use. Market analysis establishes the level of total revenue to be generated by the permitted project over each of the next several years. Finally, the appraiser estimates the highest and best use by subtracting the expenses from the revenue estimate to obtain the use with the highest residual income figure.

Highest-and-best-use analysis is applied in two steps. First, the site is analyzed as though it were vacant. In this phase of analysis, the investigator can examine all legally permitted and physically feasible land uses that the site can accommodate. By searching through these probable uses, the appraiser can find a highest and best use for the site "as if vacant." Then, the site is analyzed as if it is improved. In this phase of the analysis, the investigator can examine all of the legal uses of the improved site to determine a highest and best use for the site "as improved." This highest and best use "as improved" is the dominant consideration because it prevails even if the highest and best use "as if vacant" yields a higher residual income level. This is because the highest and best use "as if vacant" cannot be realized until the existing improvement is demolished and the site is cleared for construction of the highest and best use identified for the vacant lot. Therefore, the highest and best use "as improved" dominates until the difference between the two residual income streams is great enough to pay for the demolition and clearing of the old improvement. The residual income generated by the highest and best use "as if vacant" must be larger than the residual income generated by the highest and best use of the improved site plus the costs of demolition, clearing, and construction.

LAND VALUE ESTIMATION

After the highest and best use of the site is evaluated, the appraiser must establish the value of the land as vacant. This is a crucial and separate step in the appraisal process. The details of land valuation are discussed in Chapter 5 as part of the sales comparison and cost approaches to value estimation.

THE THREE APPRAISAL TECHNIQUES

The next step in the appraisal process is the application of the appropriate appraisal technique to the assignment. Three techniques are available to the appraiser. These are traditionally known as (1) the sales comparison approach, (2) the cost approach, and (3) the income approach. The purpose of this section is to identify each of these appraisal approaches by describing the format and the underlying principles involved. An appraiser should attempt all three approaches when undertaking an appraisal. However, if data are not available to support an approach, the appraiser can emphasize the other two.

The Sales Comparison Approach

In the **sales comparison approach,** the appraiser verifies the existence of a market for the type of property being analyzed. This means that the appraiser verifies the existence of buyers and sellers who are reasonably well informed about the properties in the market, and verifies that the property would be exposed in the market for a reasonable period of time. To apply the sales comparison approach, an appraiser follows a systematic procedure. A general outline of the basic procedure follows.

1. Research the market for information on sales transactions, listings, and offers to purchase or sell involving properties that are similar to the subject property in terms of such characteristics as property type, date of sale, physical condition, location, and zoning.

2. Verify the information by confirming that the data obtained are factually accurate and that the transactions reflect arm's-length market considerations. Verification may elicit additional information about the market.

3. Select relevant units of comparison (for example, price per acre, price per square foot, and price per front foot) and develop a comparative analysis for each unit.

4. Compare comparable sale properties with the subject property using the elements of comparison, and adjust the price of each comparable property to the subject property or eliminate the sale property as a comparable.

5. Reconcile the various value indications produced from the analysis of comparables into a single value indication or a range of values. In an imprecise market subject to varying occupancies and economies, a range of values may be a better conclusion than a single value estimate.

The underlying principle for this appraisal technique is the **principle of substitution:** an informed buyer will pay no more for a property than the cost of acquiring an equally desirable substitute on the open market. The principle of substitution presumes that the buyer considers all available alternatives and acts rationally on the basis of his information about these alternatives.

The sales comparison method will be discussed in greater detail in Chapter 5.

The Cost Approach

In the **cost approach,** the appraiser separates the physical entity of real estate into its two components of land and improvements. Then, the appraiser estimates the current market value of the land and approximates the value of the improvement. The two components are added to obtain the estimate of value for the entire property.

After inspecting the neighborhood, the site, and the improvements and gathering all relevant market data, an appraiser follows the series of steps below to derive a value by the cost approach.

1. Estimate the value of the site as though vacant and available to be developed to its highest and best use.

2. Estimate the direct (hard) and indirect (soft) costs of the improvements as of the effective appraisal date.

3. Estimate an appropriate entrepreneurial incentive (profit) from analysis of the market.

4. Add estimated direct cost, indirect costs, and the entrepreneurial incentive (profit) to arrive at the total cost of the improvements.

5. Estimate the amount of accrued depreciation in the structure and, if necessary, allocate it among the three major categories: physical deterioration, functional obsolescence, and external obsolescence.

6. Deduct the estimated depreciation from the total cost of the improvements to derive an estimate of their depreciated cost.

7. Estimate the contributory value of any site improvements that have not already been considered. (Site improvements are often appraised at their contributory value—that is, directly on a depreciated-cost basis.)

8. Add the site value to the total depreciated cost of all the improvements to arrive at the indicated value of the property.

9. Adjust the indicated value of the property for any personal property (for example, fixtures, furniture, and equipment) that may be included in the cost estimate and, if necessary, adjust this value, which reflects the value of the fee simple interest, for the property interest being appraised to arrive at the indicated value of the specified interest in the property.

The fundamental underlying principle for the cost approach is also the principle of substitution, but it is restated as follows: a rational person will not pay more for a property than the amount at which an equally desirable and useful property can be obtained without an undue delay.

The cost approach will be discussed in greater detail in Chapter 5.

The Income Approach

To use the **income approach,** the appraiser starts with the realization that the parcel of real estate generates a stream of future benefits to its owner. These benefits are in the form of money received for allowing others to use and possess part or all of the physical property. The appraiser estimates the value of the current and future revenues that can accrue to the owner and then estimates the costs incurred to operate the property. From these figures, the appraiser calculates the value for net operating income that the property could generate for a typical owner. By means of a discounting or capitalizing technique, which is essentially dividing the net operating income value by an interest rate, the appraiser obtains an estimate of the market value.

In more precise terms, the appraiser follows the series of steps below to obtain market value for an income-earning property.

1. Calculate the revenues that the property can generate from rents on space and from other services that the owner of the building can provide.
2. Estimate the probable vacancies that will occur in the structure.
3. Gather information about expenses incurred to operate the property.
4. Calculate a value for net operating income, and estimate the probable duration of time over which this net operating income stream will be positive. (In other words, the appraiser estimates the period of time over which the building will generate revenues that exceed costs.)
5. Select an appropriate capitalization rate and use it to obtain the market value.

The underlying principle for the income approach is the **principle of anticipation:** the recognition that value is created by the benefits to be derived in the future. The principle of substitution also is applicable to the income approach.

The income approach will be discussed in greater detail in Chapter 6.

THE GROSS RENT MULTIPLIER TECHNIQUE. An alternative form of the income approach is the **gross rent multiplier technique.** The underlying assumption of this technique is that the revenue from comparable income-earning properties and their recent sales prices can indicate the current market value of the subject property. To use this approach, the appraiser identifies several comparable properties and divides their sales prices by monthly or yearly rent revenues to get a "multiplier" that is representative of the comparable properties. Then, the appraiser multiplies the revenue to be derived from the subject property by this number to obtain an estimate of the current market value of the subject property. This income technique is often used to estimate value for residential properties that produce income. (A more thorough discussion of the gross rent multiplier technique appears in Chapter 6.)

RECONCILIATION

In summary, the appraisal process is a logical sequencing of activities, which starts with a definition of the task. Once the task is defined, the types of general and specific data required to make the value estimate can be identified. These data are then used as inputs into the three appraisal techniques. If possible, the appraiser obtains an estimate of market value by each technique, or by at least two of the techniques, and uses these value estimates to present the final single or "point" estimate of value to the client.

The process of reaching the final estimate from the multiple value estimates derived from multiple appraisal techniques is the process of **reconciliation.** This process involves the following tasks:

1. A check for the accuracy of the calculations made to obtain the value estimate in each alternative technique

2. An evaluation of the quality of the data and information included in each alternative technique

3. An evaluation of the appropriateness of each alternative technique for the appraisal assignment at hand

After this evaluation process, the appraiser uses her judgment to select the most appropriate technique and thereby the most appropriate value estimate.

Chapter Summary

An appraisal is an unbiased, knowledgeable, and documented opinion or estimate of value. The value that is most often sought is current market value, and a real estate appraisal is typically defined as an estimate of the current market value of a parcel of real property. To provide this estimate, the appraiser utilizes an orderly, logical, step-by-step process known as the appraisal process. As part of this process, the appraiser obtains a definition of the task, estimates data and personnel requirements to accomplish the task, gathers data relevant to the subject property, and utilizes the three appraisal techniques—the sales comparison approach, the cost approach, and the income approach.

As part of the appraisal process, the appraiser must gather and analyze two broad categories of data: general data and site-specific data. The appraiser obtains these data by means of area analysis, neighborhood analysis, site analysis, improvement analysis, and highest-and-best-use analysis. Once this information has been acquired, the appraiser can apply the three appraisal techniques mentioned above.

Internet Applications

A website has been established for this chapter http://epley.swcollege.com.

Review Questions

1. What issues does the appraiser consider in the definitional stage of the appraisal process?

2. What are the two broad classes of data that the appraiser collects and how do they differ?

3. Briefly describe the three appraisal techniques that the appraiser can use.

4. Distinguish between local economic area analysis and neighborhood analysis.

5. Describe the concepts of value-in-use and value-in-exchange.

6. Define the concept of highest and best use, and then describe the thought process used by the appraiser in determining the highest and best use for an improved parcel of real estate.

Discussion Questions

1. How could changes in the national economy affect the value of your home? Consider the following situations:

   (a) A recession in which income levels decline and unemployment increases

   (b) Abnormally high levels of inflation for food, transportation, and shelter

   (c) High interest rates that will continue to rise in the future

2. How could changes in the city's economy affect the value of your home? Consider the following situations:

   (a) A new major industrial firm moves into the area

   (b) The town's major employer suffers a significant reduction in the volume of output sold

   (c) A decline in the population of the area occurs because of out-migration of young and middle-aged individuals

3. How could changes in the neighborhood affect the value of your home? Consider the following situations:

   (a) A deterioration in the physical appearance of surrounding housing units

   (b) An increase of the crime rate caused by increased levels of vandalism, robbery, and muggings

   (c) An upgrade in the quality and quantity of such public services as schools, streets, and police and fire protection

4. Is the highest and best use for a property the use that places the most expensive improvement on the property? Explain your answer.

## CHAPTER 5

Residential Property Appraisal

How does the appraiser estimate the current market value of a single-family residence?

OBJECTIVES

When finished with this chapter, the student should be able to:

1. Explain the nature and structure of the sales comparison approach as it is used by the appraiser to estimate the current market value of residential property.

2. Explain the nature and structure of the cost approach as it is used by the appraiser to estimate the current market value of residential property.

IMPORTANT TERMS

accrued depreciation	market comparison procedure
allocation procedure	physical deterioration
arm's length sale	quantity survey method
comparable property	replacement cost
comparative method	reproduction cost
external obsolescence	subject property
functional obsolescence	unit-in-place method

INTRODUCTION

Chapter 4 described the process used by an appraiser to estimate market value for a specific parcel of real property and identified the kinds of information the appraiser requires. The information consists of general data on the environmental conditions that surround the subject property as well as specific data on the particular site and its improvements.

A large appraisal company may do appraisal work in an entire urban region, whereas an individual appraiser may work only with a certain portion of that region. Some appraisers do both residential and commercial work, and others focus exclusively on the appraisal of single-family residences. Regardless of the scope of the appraiser's work, it requires a current database with relevant information about the economic, social, physical, and governmental factors in area analysis and neighborhood analysis. It also requires site-specific factors, such as the geographical and geological features of the land and the physical and functional features of the improvement.

The purpose of this chapter is to explore the principal methods used to estimate the current market value of a single-family residence. The underlying assumption of the methods is that the owner-occupied single-family residence is not used as an income-earning asset. In other words, the dwelling unit is inhabited by its owner, who does not intend to rent the premises. The two techniques used to appraise such property are the sales comparison (market data) approach and the cost approach.

What Is the Sales Comparison Approach?

Once the general and specific data have been gathered, the appraiser can start the analysis of market value for a single-family residence, also referred to as the **subject property** (the property under consideration). The most commonly used technique is the sales comparison approach. The fundamental concept of this approach is that current market data provide the best indication of market value for a property. The appraiser's task is to discover the recently sold *comparable properties* in the local market and, through an appropriate *adjustment process,* to develop indications of what these properties would have sold for if they possessed the same physical and economic characteristics as the subject property. The key terms *comparable properties* and *adjustment process* will be explained in the following sections.

SELECTION OF COMPARABLE PROPERTIES AND THE ELEMENTS OF COMPARISON

The selection of **comparable properties** (or competitive properties) to use in the sales comparison approach is based on an analysis of various aspects of the subject property and of the whole profile of properties that have sold in the recent past in the local market area. From this very heterogeneous group of previously traded properties, the appraiser finds the ones that are as similar as possible to the subject property in terms of the *elements of comparison.* The following elements of comparison are considered:

1. Real property rights conveyed
2. Financing terms
3. Conditions of the sale
4. Expenditures made immediately after the purchase
5. Market conditions
6. Location

7. Physical characteristics (such as size, construction quality, and condition)
8. Economic characteristics
9. Use (zoning)
10. Nonrealty components of value

These elements of comparison will be discussed in the following subsections of this chapter.

Real Property Rights Conveyed

In residential real property appraisal, the most prevalent set of property rights encountered by the appraiser is the fee simple estate (introduced in Chapter 1). So, the appraiser must make certain that all of the comparable properties are fee simple ownership if the subject property is fee simple ownership. On rare occasions, the residential appraiser may encounter the task of valuing something other than a fee simple estate, such as an estate in possession or an estate in expectancy created by a life estate.

As part of the examination of the real property rights conveyed, the appraiser needs to determine the existence of easements and to evaluate the effect of any easements on the value of the respective property. Ideally, if the subject property is not affected by an easement, the comparable properties should not be affected by an easement. If one of the comparable properties commands an easement on an adjacent property, the appraiser needs to estimate the effect of this easement on the dominant estate (the land receiving the benefits of the easement). If one of the comparable properties provides an easement to an adjacent property, the appraiser needs to estimate the effect of this easement on the servient estate (the land providing the benefits of the easement to the adjacent property).

Financial Terms of the Sale

This aspect of the search for comparable properties does not involve changes in the mortgage interest rate over time. The financial terms to be considered are the characteristics of the financing arrangement. When the comparable property sales are compared with the property being appraised, some of the properties might have been purchased with a conventional mortgage, while others could have been purchased with FHA financing. (The various forms of financial arrangements are discussed in Chapters 9 and 10.) The type of financial arrangement the buyer can obtain can affect the sales price of the property. Therefore, to avoid inconsistencies, the subject and the comparable properties should be financed under the same arrangements—for example, a conventional mortgage, an FHA/VA mortgage, or a purchase money mortgage. If the financial arrangements are generally the same, minor variations in the mortgage interest rate, in the length of the loan, or in the amount of the down payment required can be reconciled by the adjustment process. The essential question asked by the appraiser is, "Has the price of a sold comparable property been increased as compensation for below-market financing terms?"

Conditions of the Sale

Five necessary conditions define a competitive market.

1. The buyer and seller are typically motivated and free of any undue pressure.
2. Both parties to the transaction must be informed about the market in which they are dealing.
3. Given this market information, both parties must act rationally, and their actions should be in their own self-interests.

4. The property must have been on the market for a reasonable amount of time.
5. Financing is on terms generally available and typical for the property type.

If these market conditions did not apply in the sale of a certain property, that property must be rejected for use as a comparable property, even if it is similar in all other respects to the property being appraised. For example, an appraiser would reject from a list of comparable properties the ones that sold with unusually low down payments and below-market interest rates.

Expenditures Made Immediately After Purchase

A knowledgeable buyer of property will make a thorough inspection of the property prior to its purchase. A property inspector may be hired to undertake this inspection. Armed with this information, the buyer will attempt to have the seller handle any problems as part of the contract negotiations. If the seller does not take care of the problems, the buyer will offer a lower price for the property. In a residential context, the problems will be predominantly issues of structural repair or interior finishing, such as painting, replacing carpeting, and removing wallpaper. In a commercial context, these issues can expand to cover the costs of a rezoning application, demolition and removal of obsolete structures, construction of necessary site improvements, and remediation of environmental contamination.

Market Conditions (Time of Sale)

The date of the comparable property's sale is an indication of the market circumstances under which the comparable property sold. Ideally, the comparable properties should have sold within the current market period, which is the typical need for an estimate of value for the subject property. Realistically, the dates of sale can be weeks, even months, apart for residential properties. Unlike financial securities such as common stocks, real property does not have daily quotes for its sale price.

If the comparable properties did sell in the last few days, there may be little need for an adjustment in their sales prices. However, if comparable properties must be chosen that were sold several months in the past, an adjustment could be made for changes in the economic and demographic conditions that affect both the demand and the supply sides of the market.

Typically, a time adjustment is applied to the comparable sale price to reflect any change in the market between two dates. If the prices of such construction inputs as labor, construction loans, and building materials increase, market analysis reveals that the supply of new construction decreases and causes the price of new housing to rise. This price change for new housing units is reflected in a price rise for existing units because these two markets are interrelated. As the price of the new units increases, the demand for existing units increases.

Inflation is not the only economic change that must be recognized. A change in local economic conditions can also affect the price of housing. Assume, for example, that two months ago a major employer announced a plant closing. When the plant closes in the very near future, 400 household members will be out of work. Assume that all 400 people own similar houses in the community and that only 300 of these people will be able to find alternative employment in the general area. The other 100 households must migrate to other localities. The supply of existing houses for sale will increase. If demand is constant or (more realistically) declining, increased supply will cause the price of the existing units in the market to fall.

Because the vast majority of properties are purchased with borrowed funds, and because the interest rate and degree of credit availability affect the level of demand, changes in financial terms over time are important if the changes influence demand for the property. To analyze this factor, the appraiser must know the financial conditions both in the present market and in the market when the comparable properties were sold. The adjustment process involves an understanding of the impact of mortgage interest charges on the demand for housing in the submarket. As interest rates drop, demand increases and, all else being equal, the price of housing increases.

In the process of performing the appraisal, the appraiser has to deal with *several different dates* that must be clearly identified. These dates include:

1. The *closed sales date* for the comparable properties
2. The date the appraiser finishes the analysis, draws the value conclusion, and signs the report: the *date of the report*
3. The date on which the appraiser does a physical inspection of the property: the *effective date* of the value estimate

Location

Ideally, the comparable properties should be adjacent to the subject property. Realistically, the comparable properties should be drawn from the same neighborhood or, if this is not possible, from another neighborhood that is very similar to that of the subject property in all of the pertinent components of neighborhood analysis.

Physical Features of the Site and the Improvements

The comparable properties should be as similar as possible to the subject property in site-specific factors. There should be little, if any, difference in the physical character- istics of the sites as typified by geological and geographical features. The improvements should match closely in physical features, physical condition, and struc- tural description. Moreover, there should be virtually no difference in the quality of construction between the subject property and the comparable properties. Any minor differences in physical features between the subject property and the comparable prop- erties are recognized by an adjustment to the sales price of the comparable property.

Economic Characteristics

The economic characteristics of the comparable properties are those characteristics that affect the income-earning potential of an income property. For a residential property, these characteristics would include the resale potential of the property as stated by the appreciation rate, the property tax level, and the operating costs for the property as measured by utility costs and maintenance and repair. These same characteristics would relate to commercial properties. Additional characteristics for a commercial property include rent agreements such as free rent, concessions, and abatements; lease expira- tion and renewal provisions; the operating expenses of the property; the tenant mix in retail space; and the quality of the property management. In the sales comparison approach, the subject property and the comparable properties need to be as similar as possible on the basis of these economic characteristics.

Use and Zoning

In the ideal situation, the subject property and the comparable properties need to have the same zoning classification and the same potential for any rezoning of the proper- ties. For single-family residential property already improved with a house, the current zoning must be checked so that all the properties are zoned for "large" lots and do not have a mixture of "large" and "small" lot sizes. All of these properties should reflect the highest and best use of the land (a concept discussed in Chapter 4). If one of the "comparable" properties has a house on a lot that is zoned for commercial use, it is not a comparable property for the subject property being analyzed. If retail properties are being evaluated as comparable properties, it is not enough that all of them are zoned "C" for "commercial"; they should all be zoned "C1," which represents "commercial land for retail use as a shopping center."

Nonrealty Components of Value

If a comparable real property sold but the sale included other items beyond the real property itself, the appraiser must estimate the contribution to the sale price made by these items. For example, a house might sell with furniture and fixtures of higher than normal quality. The appraiser must subtract the value of these items from the sales price to determine the value of the real property. In a retail context, a freestanding store might sell with the retail trade fixtures in place (display counters, shelves, and racks; floor covering; wall decorations; and ceiling tiles), while the subject property does not offer any of these items. Again, the appraiser must subtract the value of these items from the sales price to reach the value of the real property.

THE ADJUSTMENT PROCESS

In the ideal situation, the subject property and all the comparable properties are identical in every detail. However, this ideal situation is very unlikely. Generally, the comparable properties differ in some way from the subject property, and adjustments must be made to their sales prices to compensate for the differences. The process for making these adjustments is straightforward. First, the appraiser asks the following question: What effect does the presence or absence of a property feature or characteristic have on the probable sales price of the property? If the subject property contains an item or a characteristic that the comparable property does not have, the sales price of the comparable property is adjusted upward. This process can be easily remembered by applying the acronym CPA: if the Comparable property is Poorer, Add to the comparable property's sale price. In this case, the appraiser asks the following question: What would have been the comparable property's sales price if it had possessed this additional factor? If the comparable property contains a feature that the subject property does not have, the sales price of the comparable property is scaled down by the dollar value of that feature. This process can be easily remembered by applying the acronym CBS: if the Comparable property is Better, Subtract from the comparable property's sale price.

Because one of the physical characteristics of real estate is heterogeneity, it is not surprising that perfect substitutes are difficult to find. There are always some differences in the physical features of the on-site improvements. If the physical features are similar, there are differences in locational and neighborhood features. Finally, if the locational and neighborhood features are similar, there are differences in the time of sale.

The appraiser should understand which features are most amenable to the adjustment process and thereby yield accurate results, and which features are difficult to measure and thus are difficult to specify as a dollar adjustment. One of the factors most difficult to measure in dollar terms is the impact on value of neighborhood and locational features. Consequently, the appraiser should be diligent in choosing comparable properties that are in the same neighborhood as the subject property. Use of such properties eliminates the need for adjustments to overcome differences in the quality of the physical environment around the subject property, the safety of the area, and other variables discussed in the section on neighborhood analysis in Chapter 4.

Another factor difficult to measure in dollar terms is the difference in the economic and demographic variables of the markets in which the subject and comparable properties sell. To eliminate the need for adjustment, the appraiser attempts to find comparable properties that sold in the immediate past. A close temporal relationship validates the assumption that the subject property will sell in the same market as the comparable properties.

If the appraiser can control the neighborhood factors and date-of-sale considerations and thereby minimize, or totally eliminate, differences in these categories, the adjustment process can be limited to features that are much easier to measure in dollar terms. Consequently, the accuracy of the adjustments is increased, and the adjustment process is subject to fewer criticisms. The adjustments that the appraiser can document and justify most easily are those representing differences in the physical features of the lot and the improvement. The documentation and justification are accomplished by referring to cost data or market evidence in the form of sales-price differences for houses with different features.

Exhibit 5.1 is a numerical example of the adjustment process. The items listed along the left side of the table are the elements of comparison. The appraiser is commissioned to estimate current market value for the subject property, a single-family residence. The appraisal problem is defined, and the property and the market data are identified, and the subsequent analysis and the adjustment grid for the subject property are shown.

Information for the Case

The subject property is owned as a fee simple estate, and there are no easements against the property. When the property sells, it will probably be financed under a conventional mortgage at an interest rate of 8 percent per year, a loan maturity of 30 years, and a down payment of 20 percent. The sale is verified by the appraiser as an **arm's length sale,** meaning that each participant operated of his own free will, there was no coercion, and there were no extenuating circumstances such as a sale between two family members. This is a transaction between well-informed and willing participants. None of the buyers saw a need to spend money after the purchase on the property.

Comparable property #1 sold five months ago. Comparable property #2 sold one month ago. Comparable property #3 sold two weeks ago.

The location/neighborhood features of the subject property are stated in general terms—"good," "average," and "fair"—in descending order. The neighborhood is served by a school system that is considered to be of good quality. Other public services provided by the local government are also considered to be good. The neighborhood contains off-site improvements that are in good physical condition. Finally, the neighborhood's location in the urban area provides an average level of accessibility to employment opportunities.

The most significant physical features of the subject property's lot are the size of the lot, the shape of the lot, its landscaping, and its cul-de-sac location. The most significant physical features of the subject property's structure are the square feet of livable space in the structure, the structural condition, the age of the structure, and the age and condition of the mechanical systems. In addition, the subject property has three special features—a fireplace, a deck, and a patio.

The economic characteristics do not apply because the subject property is not an income-earning asset. All of the properties have the same current zoning. The subject property is offered for sale without any nonrealty items. Comparable property #1 sold with a lawn tractor included in the transaction.

EXHIBIT 5.1   Comparative sales data for the sales comparison approach.

Characteristic	Subject Property	Comparable #1		Comparable #2		Comparable #3	
Sales Price	?		$ 93,900		$ 98,500		$ 96,300
Property Rights Conveyed							
Fee Simple	yes	yes	0	yes	0	yes	0
Easements against the Property	no	no	0	no	0	no	0
Financial Terms of the Sale							
Type of Loan	Conventional	Conventional	0	Conventional	0	Conventional	0
Term of the Loan	30 years	30 years	0	30 years	0	30 years	0
Interest Rate on the Loan	8%	8%	0	7.6%	-1200	8%	0
Down Payment Requirement	20%	20%	0	20%	0	20%	0
Condition of Sale	arm's length	arm's length	0	arm's length	0	arm's length	0
Expenditures after Purchase	none	none	0	none	0	none	0
Market Conditions (time of sale)	Current	5 months ago	850	1 month ago	0	2 weeks ago	0
Location/Neighborhood Features							
Quality of Public Schools	Good	Inferior	6000	Inferior	6500	same	0
Provision of Other Public Services	Good	same	0	Inferior	3000	same	0
Proximity to Employments Centers	Average	same	0	Superior	-4000	same	0
Proximity of Shopping	Good	same	0	same	0	same	0
Physical Condition of Neighborhood	Good	Superior	-5000	same	0	same	0
Physical Features of the Site							
Size	100' by 250'	100' by 250'	0	100' by 300'	-2000	100' by 250'	0
Shape	Regular	same	0	same	0	same	0
Landscaping	Average	same	0	Superior	-500	Inferior	500
Cul de Sac	Yes	No	2000	Yes	0	Yes	0
Physical Features of the Improvement							
Size in Square Feet	2000	2000	0	2200	-8000	2000	0
Condition	Good	Inferior	1000	same	0	same	0
Age	5 yrs	Inferior	2500	Inferior	1500	Inferior	500
Mechanical Systems	5 yrs old	new	-1000	Inferior	300	6 yrs old	100
Fireplace	yes, brick	yes, brick	0	no	3000	yes, brick	0
Deck	yes	yes	0	yes	0	yes	0
Patio	yes	no	1000	yes	0	yes	0
Economic Characteristics	none	none	0	none	0	none	0
Use/Zoning	R 75	R 75	0	R 75	0	R 75	0
Personal Property in the Transactio	none	lawn tractor	-500	none	0	none	0
Net Adjustment			$ 6,850		$ (1,400)		$ 1,100
Adjusted Sales Price			$ 100,750		$ 97,100		$ 97,400

The Search for the Comparable Properties

The first step in the process is gathering the information about the subject property. This information is the basis on which the appraiser can then search for comparable properties. From a large pool of properties that have been sold, the appraiser first checks the records for sales that match the characteristics of the subject property. Three such sales are found. One sale took place a week ago, a second took place a month ago, and a third took place five months ago. In addition, the three properties all sold under conventional financing with roughly the same interest rate and exactly the same loan maturity and down payment requirements. They are all freehold estates of inheritance with no easements against the property. The condition and the age of the improvements are roughly the same as those of the subject property. The appraiser has found the comparable properties required for the sales comparison approach.

In the past, the appraiser would check the records in her personal files and ask colleagues to share their data. This sharing was routinely done. Today, the search is done in a computerized database. The appraiser specifies the appropriate elements of comparison as inputs into the database, and the database provides the comparable properties that match on those characteristics.

The Adjustment Grid

The appraiser can now begin the analysis phase of the sale comparison approach. The first step in the adjustment process is the construction of an adjustment grid that is similar to the grid in Exhibit 5.1. The adjustments follow along the elements of comparison in the left-hand column of the exhibit. For the sake of the subsequent discussion, comparable property #1 is compared to the subject property.

PROPERTY RIGHTS CONVEYED. In real property respects, comparable property #1 is identical to the subject property. Both are fee simple estates, and so no adjustment is necessary. Comparable property #1, like the subject property, is not affected by easements.

FINANCING TERMS. Comparable property #1 sold under conventional mortgage financing at the interest rate and other terms that still prevail in the current market. No adjustment is necessary.

CONDITION OF SALE. The subject property is expected to sell as an arm's length transaction, and comparable property #1 did sell as an arm's length transaction. No adjustment is necessary.

EXPENDITURES AFTER THE PURCHASE. No such expenditure is expected for the subject property, and no such expenditure was made for the comparable property.

MARKET CONDITIONS (TIME OF SALE). The next difference between the subject property and comparable property #1 is the date of sale. The comparable property sold five months ago; the subject property is expected to sell today. The appraiser knows from recent experience on the job that house prices in the market and in the neighborhood have been rising by 2 percent per year. This translates into an approximate $2,000 increase for the year, or approximately $850 for the five-month period.

LOCATION/NEIGHBORHOOD FEATURES. Next, the appraiser analyzes the neighborhood features and finds that the neighborhood surrounding comparable property #1 is inferior to the neighborhood surrounding the subject property with regard to the quality of the public schools but is superior with regard to the physical condition of structures in the neighborhood. The quality of the school system is only average for comparable property #1, but it is good for the subject property. Based on market information, the appraiser adds a $6,000 adjustment to the sales price of comparable property #1. Comparable property #1 would have sold for $6,000 more if it were located in the same public school district as the subject property.

Regarding the physical condition of the neighborhood, the neighborhood surrounding the subject property is rated good, but the neighborhood surrounding comparable property #1 is rated superior. This can occur because the local government is doing a better job repairing the roads, caring for the public parks and playgrounds, and keeping the streets clean. This situation also can occur if property owners are taking better care of their lots and improvements. Based on market information, the appraiser subtracts a $5,000 adjustment to the sales price of comparable property #1. Comparable property #1 would have sold for $5,000 less if it were located in the same neighborhood as the subject property.

PHYSICAL FEATURES OF THE SITE. First, the physical comparability of comparable property #1 with the subject property is checked. The two properties are the same in terms lot size, shape of the lot, and landscaping. But they are different on the site characteristic of cul-de-sac. The subject property has a cul-de-sac location, which is considered a positive aspect of the property in subdivisions containing families with young children. The cul-de-sac serves as a highly visible playground that is relatively free of auto traffic—a positive characteristic that adds value to the property. The appraiser asks, what would comparable property #1 have sold for if it were located on a cul-de-sac? From market information, the appraiser knows that the cul-de-sac premium is $2,000 in this neighborhood. So, if comparable property #1 were located on a cul-de-sac it would have sold for $2,000 more than its actual $93,900 sale price based on this single characteristic. The adjustment is a positive $2,000.

PHYSICAL FEATURES OF THE STRUCTURE. The appraiser now considers the physical features of the improvements on the property. The subject property and comparable property #1 are the same with regard to the square feet of livable space—2,000 square feet. The first difference is the condition of the structures. The subject property is in better condition than comparable property #1. Applying the "CPA" guideline explained earlier, the appraiser adds an adjustment to the sales price of comparable property #1. From market experience, the appraiser judges the adjustment at $1,000.

The next physical characteristic is the age of the structures. The subject property is 5 years old, while comparable property #1 is 10 years old. This difference in age establishes a need for an adjustment. The appraiser asks, what would comparable property #1 have sold for if it were 5 years old and not 10 years old? Comparable property #1 has 5 additional years of wear and tear on its structural members, its fixtures, and its mechanical systems. This additional wear and tear is evaluated at $2,500, and the appraiser adds $2,500 as the adjustment to the sales price of comparable property #1. The underlying assumption is that comparable property #1 would have sold for $2,500 more if it had been 5 years old instead of 10.

Next, the appraiser notices that comparable property #1 contains the same mechanical system as the subject property, but that a new furnace was recently installed. The new furnace has an expected life of 10 years, and its cost was $2,000. The dollar adjustment, to be deducted in this case, is $1,000, half the value of the furnace, because the subject property's five-year-old furnace still has five years of expected life. Then, the appraiser notices that comparable property #1 does not have a concrete block patio and the subject property does. If comparable property #1 did have a concrete block patio and its installation cost had been $1,000, the sales price of the comparable property would have been $1,000 more if the patio were in "brand-new" condition.

In making these adjustments, the appraiser is applying a rather straightforward rule of operation and comparison: "Make the comparable property like the subject property." If the comparable property is inferior to the subject property on one of the characteristics, improve the comparable to the level of the subject and ask what would the comparable sell for under this improved condition.

ECONOMIC CHARACTERISTICS. These do not apply to single-family, owner-occupied properties.

USE/ZONING. The subject property and comparable property #1 are similarly zoned as R-75, which typically means a residential lot with 75 feet of frontage. No adjustment is necessary.

NONREALTY COMPONENTS IN THE TRANSACTION. The final difference between the subject property and comparable property #1 is the personal property that was exchanged in the sale. The buyer of comparable property #1 purchased an old riding lawn tractor that the seller no longer needed. The appraiser estimates that the lawn tractor is in the final third portion of its useful life and would cost approximately $1,500 to replace. The resale value of the old tractor is set at $500. The adjustment is a negative $500 to remove the effect of this personal property on the real property's sales price.

The Adjusted Sales Price Estimate

The net value of the adjustments to comparable property #1 yields a positive adjustment of $6,850. By adding this figure to the actual price of $93,900, the appraiser obtains an adjusted sales price for comparable property #1 of $100,750. This adjusted sales price is interpreted as the current sales price of comparable property #1 under the condition that it is as similar to the subject property as possible given the selection of the comparable and then the adjustments.

The appraiser then goes through a similar analysis for comparable property #2 and the subject property. The necessary dollar adjustments are made in a similar manner. Comparable property #2 sold under conventional mortgage financing, but the mortgage interest rate was 7.6 percent instead of the current market rate of 8 percent. Under the condition of below-market interest rate, the buyer could have bid more for that property. This adjustment results in a negative $1,200 adjustment. Comparable property #2 is in a neighborhood where the quality of schools is inferior to the quality of schools in the neighborhood surrounding the subject property, and the provision of public services is inferior. Therefore, a positive dollar adjustment is made to the sales price of comparable property #2 to reflect these two neighborhood features. Comparable property #2 sold one month ago, and the appraisers best estimate is that the current and past markets are the same, so no adjustment is required. Comparable property #2 has a bigger lot with better landscaping than the subject property, so a negative dollar adjustment is needed for the physical features of the lot. The structure on comparable property #2 is larger, so a negative dollar adjustment is made for that physical feature of the improvement. Comparable property #2 is older by three years and does not have a fireplace, so these features generate positive adjustments to its sales price. The net value of the adjustments to comparable property #2 yields a negative adjustment of $1,400. Subtracting the net adjustment from the actual sales price of comparable property #2 gives an adjusted sales price of $97,100.

The appraiser then turns to an analysis of comparable property #3. The property rights involved in the sale of comparable property #3 are the same as those for the subject property. Comparable property #3 sold two weeks previously under exactly the same financial terms as would apply to the subject property. Comparable property #3 is in the same neighborhood as the subject property, and no adjustment is required for neighborhood features. This property has the same size and shape as the subject property, but the quality and the quantity of its landscaping are inferior. The structure is the same size as that of the subject property, and it is in approximately the same physical condition, but it is one year older. Due to the one-year age difference, the mechanical systems in comparable property #3 are a year older, and a small positive dollar adjustment is required. Combining all of these dollar adjustments yields a positive adjustment of $1,100, which is added to the actual sales price of comparable property #3 for an adjusted sales price of $97,400.

The Estimation of the Market Value of the Subject Property

After making these adjustments, the appraiser has three adjusted sales prices for the three comparable properties. The sales price of the subject property is now estimated from the adjusted sales prices of the comparable properties. Several methods can be used to obtain an estimate of value for the client. One method is to select the adjusted comparable price that used the *smallest number* of adjustments. The rationale is that it *must be* the most comparable since the adjustments were the fewest in number.

A second important numerical measure for the appraiser to calculate is the absolute dollar adjustment; the total dollar adjustment without regard for the direction of the adjustment. For comparable property #1, the absolute adjustment is $19,850. For comparable property #2, the absolute adjustment is $30,000. For comparable property #3, the absolute adjustment is $1,100. Comparable property #3 is the most similar to the subject property because the absolute adjustment is the smallest. Furthermore, on the basis of the absolute adjustments, comparable property #2 could be considered an inappropriate selection for the analysis of this subject property because the size of the absolute adjustment is too big relative to the sales price or the adjusted sales price.

The accepted procedure is to review each sale and judge its comparability to the subject property. The comparable property with the fewest adjustments and the smaller total dollar adjustment is considered to be the best evidence for the market value of the subject property. In the example, comparable property #3 requires the smallest net adjustment, at $1,100, and is also the most similar to the subject property in terms of the time of sale, the financial terms of the sale, and neighborhood features.

Given these facts, the appraiser would establish the market value as a single estimate of $97,400 based on the evidence from comparable property #3.

THE APPLICABILITY OF THE SALES COMPARISON APPROACH

The sales comparison approach for estimating the current market value of a piece of residential real estate is subject to certain limiting conditions that affect its applicability. The cornerstone of this valuation approach is the existence of comparable properties. If comparable properties can be found that are very similar to the subject property, the sales comparison approach is applicable. However, if comparable properties cannot be found, the sales comparison approach is inapplicable. An example of a property for which the sales comparison approach is not applicable is a property that is unique and does not sell frequently in the market. In this case, the comparable properties may have to be found among a limited number of nonlocal properties that may have sold several years in the past. Rather large adjustments would need to reflect differences in the economic and demographic features of the temporal and spatial markets.

The sales comparison approach also is not applicable if the subject property and the potential comparable properties have some features that are very similar and some features that are very different. For example, the physical features of the lots and the improvements may be the same, but the neighborhood features, the bundle of rights exchanged, or the financial terms of the sale may be dissimilar. In this situation, the adjustments would be so severe that the properties may be very dissimilar and the accuracy of the value estimate would be suspect.

The sales comparison approach also is not applicable when the sale is not based on competitive market conditions (for example, well-informed participants, no undue pressures on the participants, a reasonable exposure time for the property in the market). Finally, the sales comparison approach is not applicable when the financial arrangements surrounding the sale are highly dissimilar because different types of mortgages are used to facilitate the purchases.

What Is the Cost Approach?

The cost approach for estimating current market value is based on the recognition that a parcel of real estate is composed of two parts: the land and the improvements. The appraiser separates these two components of the real estate commodity and attempts to place a dollar value on each. To obtain a dollar estimate of market value for a specific residential site, the appraiser must analyze the market for residential land sales. To the value of the land, the appraiser adds the cost of constructing a building and all improvements for the subject property. Finally, if the subject property is not new, the cost of constructing the building must be reduced by an estimate of the depreciation that the subject property has undergone. Each of these steps is described in the following sections.

ESTIMATION OF SITE VALUE

The appraiser knows six techniques to value the site. However, only two of these procedures for estimating the market value of the residential site will be discussed here, both of which rely on market data. One technique is the **market comparison procedure,** in which comparable sites are compared with the land component of the subject property. The second technique is the **allocation procedure,** which requires an initial estimation of the market value of the full residential property and then the division of the overall market value between land value and the value of the improvements on the site.

The Sales Comparison Procedure

The sales comparison procedure to value land is similar to the sales comparison appraisal approach previously discussed. The only difference is that there is no analysis of the physical features of an improvement. The elements of this procedure are the analysis of the physical features of the lot, analysis of the locational attributes of the site, and neighborhood analysis. The geological features of the site, the location of the site, the availability of public services, and the quality of adjacent improvements can affect the market value of the site.

Once the appraiser finds comparable sites that are very similar to the subject property with respect to physical, locational, and neighborhood features, an adjustment process can be undertaken to compensate for any differences. Then, the appraiser can examine the other aspects of comparability—the market conditions under which the comparable properties were purchased, the financing used in the purchase, and the bundle of rights that was transferred in each of the sales.

The Extraction Procedure

The extraction procedure is based on an analysis of parcels of real estate that have sold in the recent past. The land component of the comparable property must be very similar to the land component of the parcel that is being appraised. The sales price of the comparable parcel of real estate is then separated into the value of the land and the value of the improvement in the following way. The appraiser estimates the depreciated construction cost of the improvement and subtracts this figure from the actual sales price of the whole property. The difference between these two figures is the value of the land. If the subject property is viewed as a vacant parcel of land and is similar to the land component of this recently sold property, the appraiser has an estimate of the value of the subject land. To use this procedure effectively, the appraiser must analyze several comparable properties.

In actual practice, the sales comparison procedure is used more often than the extraction procedure.

ESTIMATION OF IMPROVEMENT VALUE

In the cost approach, the estimation process used to obtain a value for the structure is based on the cost to construct an exact replica of the subject property or a close substitute for it with the same utility. A distinction must be made between *an exact replica* and *a close substitute* for the subject property. The key to this distinction is an understanding of the difference between reproduction cost and replacement cost.

Reproduction or Replacement Cost of New Improvements

The **reproduction cost** is the current cost to construct a building that is an exact replica of the subject property at current prices. In the physical sense, reproduction denotes the fact that the replica is built with the same materials, workmanship, and technology as were used in the original construction of the subject property. Reproduction cost is typically requested by a client as it represents what currently rests on the site. The quality of building materials, the type of materials used, the workmanship involved in the construction process, and the techniques used in construction do not change drastically in short periods of time.

If the subject property is not fairly new, replacement cost is used. The **replacement cost** is the current cost to construct a new improvement that serves the same purpose as the subject property at current prices. The new building is constructed with currently available building materials, workmanship, and technology.

The appraiser can estimate the cost to construct the subject property to its actual physical specifications but with current materials, workmanship, and construction techniques. For example, if the house has 10-foot ceilings instead of 8-foot ceilings, the alternative reproduction cost would include the dollar expenditure of making the ceilings in all rooms 10 feet high. Moreover, if the subject property has solid concrete foundation walls instead of cement block foundation walls, the alternative reproduction cost would estimate the dollar expenditure to reproduce the poured concrete foundation walls using current materials, workmanship, and standards of construction.

Direct Cost Versus Indirect Cost

In addition to the knowledge and use of the reproduction cost and replacement cost concepts, the appraiser also must recognize the existence of *direct construction costs* (also known as "hard" costs) and *indirect construction costs* (also known as "soft" costs). These two categories sum to total construction costs.

Direct construction costs are the expenditures for materials, equipment, and labor of all types used to actually construct the improvement. Indirect construction costs are other expenditures related to the construction process and an important component of taking the construction process from start to finish; they include expenditures such as fees (attorney, architectural, engineering, inspection, legal, etc.), permits, marketing expenses, contractor's overhead expenses, and contractor profit.

When using the cost approach, the appraiser needs to realize that total construction costs are the appropriate reproduction or replacement costs. If indirect costs are not fully considered, the market value estimate using the cost approach will be an underestimate.

Methods of Estimating Reproduction Cost

Three methods can be used by the appraiser to estimate the cost of a new structure—(1) the quantity survey method, (2) the unit-in-place method, and (3) the comparative method.

THE QUANTITY SURVEY METHOD. The **quantity survey method** is the most comprehensive of the three methods used to estimate construction cost. It is based on the premise that an appraiser can identify the quantities of all materials and labor used in the construction process. The appraiser must identify the units and the quantities of all materials used—for example, the number of cubic yards of concrete or the number of cement blocks (or both) used to construct the foundation. The number of 2 x 4 x 8 boards used in the construction of the structural frame must be specified. The number of plywood panels used to construct the exterior walls and the flooring must be identified. In essence, the appraiser identifies all the major and minor material items that go into the construction of the residential unit. In addition, the appraiser enumerates the labor required to assemble these materials. The appraiser ascertains the number of hours that concrete masons, brick masons, carpenters, plumbers, and electricians will work to construct the finished product. When all of the material and labor inputs have been enumerated, they are multiplied by the current input price (for example, each 2 x 4 x 8 costs $1.35 and each hour of a carpenter's time costs $11.25) to give the appraiser an estimate of the major direct costs incurred in the construction of the residential unit.

In addition to the direct costs of construction, the appraiser must estimate a dollar value for the indirect costs of construction. The components of indirect costs are fees for professional services of architects, engineers, surveyors, and lawyers; overhead expenditures of the developer; the cost of building permits and licenses; insurance premiums and property tax outlays during the construction process; interest payments on the construction loan; and selling expenditures if the developer undertakes the marketing process. When these indirect costs of construction are added to the direct costs of construction on a per unit basis, the appraiser has a detailed estimate of the reproduction cost of a structure that is a replica of the subject property.

Because of the enormous degree of specificity required and the need to know construction techniques, the quantity survey technique is rarely used in actual practice. However, an understanding of its structure does set the basis for an understanding of what the appraiser is attempting to accomplish in the estimation process to obtain the value of the improvement.

THE UNIT-IN-PLACE METHOD. The **unit-in-place method** (also called the *subcontractors' method*) of estimating the reproduction cost of a new improvement is based on the realization that a structure consists of major components. The reproduction cost for the new improvement is estimated by calculating the cost of constructing each of the major components of the structure (the foundation, the frame and exterior walls, the flooring, the plumbing system, the electrical system, the roof, and so forth). Each of these major components is installed by a construction firm that specializes in the installation of one or two of these structural members. When requested to perform such a service, each specialized construction firm or subcontractor calculates the full cost to construct or install the structural component. Each subcontractor estimates the cost of materials, the cost of labor, and the cost of equipment, as well as all the indirect costs. Upon completion of the direct and indirect cost estimates, the subcontractor specifies a price to install the component.

From the prices quoted by each of the subcontractors, the appraiser can obtain an estimate of the reproduction cost for a new improvement by simple addition. The unit-in-place method measures or estimates the same quantities as are estimated in the quantity survey method. The difference between these techniques is in their underlying assumptions. The quantity survey method is based on the premise that a single entity constructs the house from beginning to end, whereas the unit-in-place method is based on the premise that the house is constructed by a group of specialists whose individual inputs are integrated in the completed structure.

THE COMPARATIVE METHOD. The **comparative method** for deriving the cost of a new structure is based on the availability of published data on construction costs for standard residential units and on the appraiser's knowledge of local costs of construction. For example, assume that a four-bedroom brick ranch house with 2,000 square feet of livable space and a two-car attached garage can be constructed for $80 per square foot. If the subject property is a similar type of residence with the same quality of materials but contains only 1,900 square feet of livable space, a rough approximation of its construction cost can be obtained by multiplying 1,900 square feet by $80 per square foot. This multiplication yields a reproduction cost for the new structure of $152,000. If $80 per square foot accurately represents current prices, and if the construction techniques and materials used to build a 1,900-square-foot house are approximately the same as those used to construct a 2,000-square-foot house, then $152,000 is a fairly accurate estimate.

The appraiser can draw upon various data sources that provide construction costs per square foot for various sizes and types of residential structures. In addition, data services provide figures on changes in the prices of building material and in the wage rates of construction labor. By using these data sources and local information, the appraiser can quickly estimate the reproduction cost of a residential structure in the local market. Conceptually, the comparative method is the least accurate of the three cost estimating techniques because the appraiser must adjust the cost-per-square-foot figure to compensate for quality and quantity differences between the standard house and the subject property. However, in practice, the comparative method may be the most accurate because the appraiser's expertise is not in the area of construction techniques that are required for the quantity survey and unit-in-place methods. The appraiser is probably more adept at making the adjustments required by the comparative method.

ESTIMATION OF ACCRUED DEPRECIATION

When the cost has been estimated for a new structure, the appraiser recognizes that there are differences between the new structure and the subject property (which is not a newly constructed unit). These differences require an adjustment to account for all of the possible value-reducing phenomena that have affected the subject property. The dollar adjustment made to account for the value reduction is known as the **accrued depreciation.** As a background for the estimation of accrued depreciation, the appraiser examines three categories of value-reducing factors: physical deterioration, functional obsolescence, and external obsolescence.

Physical Deterioration

Physical deterioration is defined as the reduction in value caused by wear and tear or by disintegration of the structural components and fixtures of the building (or by both). Examples of physical deterioration are doors and windows that are difficult to open and close, cracks in plaster or wallboard caused by unusual amounts of settling, deterioration of roof shingles causing leaks and discoloration of ceilings, cracks in concrete foundations due to uneven settling, and a general wearing out of mechanical systems in the house caused by continued use over time.

Physical deterioration is either *curable* or *incurable,* depending on the costs of repairing or replacing the deteriorating items in the structure. If the repair cost is less than or equal to the increase in the structure's value after the repairs are made, the physical deterioration is considered curable. However, if repair cost exceeds the increase in value consequent upon that repair, the physical deterioration is incurable.

The dollar estimate of physical deterioration is simply the cost to repair or replace the deteriorated component of the structure. Regardless of whether physical deterioration is curable or incurable, the appraiser must take note of it and estimate its value-reducing impact on the market value of the structure.

Functional Obsolescence

Functional obsolescence is the reduction in value generated by inherent defects in the design of the structure or by changes in consumer attitudes toward the design of the structure and its fixtures. Regardless of the cause, functional obsolescence reduces the utility or satisfaction that the typical consumer derives from the property. Examples of functional obsolescence are 10-foot ceiling heights instead of the 8-foot ceiling heights now used to reduce heating and cooling costs, small room sizes and irregular room layouts that make it difficult to use currently desirable sizes and styles of furniture, and antiquated fixtures (such as bathroom lighting) that are not considered desirable by current standards.

Functional obsolescence is also subdivided into curable and incurable aspects. As in the case of physical deterioration, the distinction between the curable and incurable categories depends on the relation between the cost to replace and the value-enhancing effect that the replacement may have on the market value of the structure. If the replacement or addition of a factor in the house adds more to the market value than the cost of the change, the functionally obsolescent factor is considered curable. If the cost to replace, remove, or add exceeds the value-enhancing impact on market value, the functionally obsolescent factor is considered incurable.

The following definitions provide an excellent list of factors that are classified as curable functional obsolescence versus those that are classified as incurable functional obsolescence:

- *Curable functional obsolescence:* an inadequate heating, electrical, plumbing, and/or air conditioning system, an insufficient number of electrical outlets, insufficient cabinet space, too few doors or windows, inadequate water heating capacity, undesired plumbing and kitchen fixtures, and undesired floor and wall coverings.
- *Incurable functional obsolescence:* may include a structure's basic design and layout including ceilings that are too high or too low, rooms that are too small, inefficient traffic patterns among the rooms, and an insufficient number of bathrooms.

Placing a dollar value on curable and incurable functional obsolescence is not as straightforward as it is in the case of curable and incurable physical deterioration. To establish a dollar value for functional obsolescence, the appraiser must ascertain three facts:

1. The cost to replace, remove, or add the feature to the structure as it is today
2. The cost to remove or add the feature when the structure was originally built
3. The increase in property value that results from the removal, addition, or replacement of the functionally obsolescent feature

Once these pieces of information are known, an estimate of functional obsolescence can be made. The dollar estimate of curable functional obsolescence is the difference between points 1 and 2 in the preceding list. It is the difference between (1) the construction cost of adding a missing factor, or removing a factor, in the house as it is today, and (2) the construction cost of adding or removing this factor when the house was originally constructed. The underlying premise is that additions or removals after the initial construction are more expensive than inclusion or exclusion during the original construction phase.

To estimate the dollar value of incurable functional obsolescence, the appraiser must determine the difference between points 2 and 3. The dollar estimate of incurable functional obsolescence is the difference between the value-enhancing aspect of the feature and the cost to include that feature in the original construction of the house. For example, suppose the appraiser knows from experience that four-bedroom houses of a certain size, style, and quality located in a certain neighborhood typically sell for $2,500 more than three-bedroom houses of the same style and in the same neighborhood. This information reveals that the value enhancement created by the fourth bedroom is $2,500. Suppose that the appraiser also knows that the reproduction cost of that fourth bedroom is $3,500; in other words, there is a $3,500 difference in the construction costs of the four-bedroom and the three-bedroom residences. Given these two facts, the appraiser knows that the dollar value of incurable functional obsolescence in this case is $1,000, the difference between the $3,500 reproduction cost and the $2,500 market premium that is attached to a fourth bedroom.

External Obsolescence

External obsolescence is the value-reducing effect of changes in economic, demographic, or locational influences outside the property itself. It can be caused by changes in the economic, social, physical, and governmental factors of neighborhood analysis; by changes in the locational attributes of the site; and by changes in the economic and social factors of area analysis. External obsolescence is not considered curable, because the source of the problem is not part of the property. The dollar value of incurable external obsolescence is determined by an analysis of the market. The appraiser should identify comparable properties that are *not* affected by the value-reducing external obsolescence features and obtain the market value of such properties. Then, comparable properties must be found that *are* affected by value-reducing external features, and the market value of these properties must be ascertained. The dollar estimate of external obsolescence is the difference between the market values of these two sets of comparable properties. For example, assume that the factor causing external obsolescence is deterioration in the quality of adjacent structures. If comparable properties in the neighborhood are selling for $35,000, whereas comparable properties in a neighborhood that does not contain deteriorating structures are selling for $42,000, the dollar estimate of external obsolescence is $7,000. This figure is subtracted from the cost of the new improvement to represent incurable external obsolescence.

In the case of an income-earning property, the value reduction can be established by examining the difference between rents of properties in a good neighborhood and those in a poor neighborhood. The difference in rent revenues between comparable properties serves as an indication of the value-depressing factors operating in the poor neighborhood. To calculate the value reduction, the appraiser determines the current worth of the difference in rent revenues.

The cost approach for estimating market value requires three pieces of information: the market value of the site, the cost of a new improvement, and a dollar value for accrued depreciation. Once these three figures are known, the cost of the new unit is reduced by the dollar estimate for accrued depreciation and then the estimated market value of the site is added. The resultant figure is the estimate of the subject property's market value based on the cost approach.

The applicability and the accuracy of the cost approach depend on the following factors:

- The availability of market data for estimating site value
- The accuracy of the cost estimate
- The availability of data on repair costs to estimate physical deterioration
- The availability of market data and the accuracy of cost data for the calculation of dollar values for functional and economic obsolescence

The applicability and the accuracy of the cost approach also are influenced by the age of the subject property. The estimate for accrued depreciation is less accurate for an older structure because it is more difficult to calculate functional and economic obsolescence for an older structure that was built using different standards of construction and different construction materials.

An example of the cost approach to estimate market value by the comparative cost method is presented in Exhibit 5.2.

Chapter Summary

To estimate the current market value of a single-family residential unit occupied by its owner, the appraiser generally relies on the sales comparison approach and the cost approach. To use the sales comparison approach, the appraiser identifies at least three recently sold comparable properties and examines them in relation to the subject property. Adjustments are made to the sales prices of the comparable properties to compensate for any differences from the subject property. The appraiser thus estimates current market value on the basis of information about the recent sales prices of very similar properties.

EXHIBIT 5.2   Example of cost approach.

INPUT DATA				COST
House Characteristics	**sq.ft.**	**Reproduction Cost New**	**$/sq.ft**	**Calculation**
Size	1800	Basic Construction Cost	$ 76.50	$ 137,700.00
Exterior Material Brick	1800	Brick Veneer Exterior	$ 4.45	$ 8,010.00
Exterior Material Vinyl	0	Vinyl Siding Exterior	$ 4.20	$ –
Finished Basement	600	Finished Basement	$ 22.00	$ 13,200.00
Two-Car Garage	400	Garage	$ 25.00	$ 10,000.00
				$ 168,910.00
Add-on Costs		Add-on Costs		
Carpeting	1350	Carpeting	$ 2.35	$ 3,172.50
Hardwood Floors	400	Hardwood Floors	$ 3.00	$ 1,200.00
Ceramic Tile	50	Ceramic Tile	$ 3.25	$ 162.50
Brick Walkway	60	Brick Walkway	$ 4.75	$ 285.00
Patio	100	Concrete Patio	$ 1.50	$ 150.00
Deck	140	Deck	$ 7.25	$ 1,015.00
				$ 5,985.00

EXTRA FEATURES	# ITEMS	$/ITEM	
Brick Fireplace	1	$ 3,600	$ 3,600.00
Storm Windows	14	$ 150	$ 2,100.00
Extra Windows	2	$ 180	$ 360.00
Cabinet Upgrade	1	$ 700	$ 700.00
Countertop Upgrade	1	$ 500	$ 500.00
Vanity Upgrade	2	$ 125	$ 250.00
Toilet Upgrade	2	$ 80	$ 160.00
Bathtub/Shower Upgrade	2	$ 100	$ 200.00
			$ 7,870.00

Total Reproduction Cost			$ 182,765.00
Accrued Depreciation Data			$ (52,208.30)
Physical Det.		$ 12,000.00	
Functional Obso.	12%	$ 21,931.80	
External Obso.	10%	$ 18,276.50	
Land Value			$ 32,000.00
MARKET VALUE ESTIMATE			$ 162,556.70

In the cost approach, the appraiser first estimates the land value by using a sales comparison approach. The cost of the structure then is obtained by either the quantity survey method, the unit-in-place method, or the comparative method. Typically, the comparative method is used. Once the cost of a new structure similar to the subject property is obtained, the appraiser adjusts it to reflect the value-reducing impact of the factors causing accrued depreciation of the subject property. These factors are physical deterioration, functional obsolescence, and external obsolescence, and they may be curable or incurable. The dollar value of these factors is estimated and subtracted from the cost. Finally, the appraiser adds the value of the land to this figure to estimate the current market value of the property.

A website has been established for this chapter at http://epley.swcollege.com.

Review Questions

1. List the elements of comparison that the appraiser uses to find properties comparable to the subject property.

2. After the comparable properties are selected, the appraiser uses an adjustment process in the sales comparison approach. Explain the purpose of the adjustment process and the manner in which the adjustments are made.

3. How does the appraiser obtain a value for the land when using the cost approach?

4. Differentiate between reproduction cost and replacement cost. Which does the appraiser typically use in the cost approach?

5. What is the relationship between the quantity survey method and the unit-in-place method for estimating reproduction costs?

6. What is accrued depreciation? What three elements does the appraiser consider in determining the value-reducing impact of accrued appreciation?

Discussion Questions

1. How does the appraiser estimate the market value of a unique residential unit? (The term *unique* implies that there are no comparable properties.)

2. What adjustments might the appraiser make when using the comparative method for estimating reproduction costs?

3. What are the most difficult types of adjustments needed in the sale comparison approach?

4. If the appraiser is using the cost approach, can the original sales price of a building lot be used as an estimate for the value of the land?

Problems

1. How would the adjustment grid shown in Exhibit 5.1 change, and what would the value estimate become if the following changes reflected comparable property #3? It sold for $84,000 and was inferior to the subject property in the following manner:

Characteristic	Adjustment to Comp. #3
Quality of Public Schools	+ $6,000
Other Public Services	+ $3,000

Proximity to Employment Centers	+ $5,000
Proximity to Shopping	+ $2,000
Physical Condition of Neighborhood	+ $5,000

2. How would the adjustment grid shown in Exhibit 5.1 change, and what would the value estimate become if the following changes reflected comparable property #1? It sold for $102,000 and was similar to the subject property in the following manner:

Characteristic	Adjustment to Comp. #1
Market Conditions	0
Quality of Public Schools	0
Physical Condition of Neighborhood	0
Cul-de-sac	0
Age	0
Mechanical Systems	0
Patio	0
Condition	0

3. What would the market value estimate by the cost approach as shown in Exhibit 5.2 become if the following changes were made to the characteristics of the structure and the data for reproduction costs?

Reproduction Costs – Basic	$68.75 per sq. ft.
Finished basement = 800 sq. ft.	$20 per sq. ft.
Carpeting = 1,350 sq. ft.	$3 per sq. ft.
Garage = 460 sq. ft.	$24 per sq. ft.
Functional Obsolescence	8%
External Obsolescence	5%
Land Value	$36,000

4. What would the market value estimate by the cost approach as shown in Exhibit 5.2 become if the following changes were made to the characteristics of the structure and the data for reproduction costs?

Size of Basic Structure	2,000 sq. ft.
Reproduction Costs – Basic	$80.75 per sq. ft.
Finished Basement = 900 sq. ft.	$23 per sq. ft.
Carpeting = 1,550 sq. ft.	$2.75 per sq. ft.
Garage = 420 sq. ft.	$21 per sq. ft.
Functional Obsolescence	12%
External Obsolescence	6%
Land Value	$38,000

## CHAPTER 6

Income Property Appraisal

1. How is the direct capitalization technique used to estimate the current market value of a property that is an income-earning investment?

2. How is the gross rent multiplier technique used to estimate the current market value of a property that is an income-earning investment?

3. How are the property's operating expenses evaluated in the valuation process?

When finished with this chapter, the student should be able to:

1. Identify the revenue sources of an income-earning property.

2. Identify the operating expenses of an income-earning property.

3. Explain the concepts of potential and effective gross income as well as net operating income.

4. Explain the nature and derivation of the capitalization rate.

5. Explain how the capitalization rate is used in the income approach to generate an estimate of market value.

6. Discuss the gross rent multiplier technique for estimating market value.

INTRODUCTION

The value of income property is the overall focus of this chapter. Although the current market value is the typical focus of an income property appraiser, real property investors also want to know the investment value of a property. An owner would like to know both of these values. When you are reading and studying this chapter, keep these points in mind. The material is relevant for appraisers, investors, lenders, and owners.

What Is Income Property Appraisal?

An **income property appraisal** estimates value for a property that generates an income payment to its owner. The typical income-earning properties are residential real estate in the form of apartment buildings, and commercial real estate in the form of offices and retail space in office buildings, shopping centers, and commercial districts. The owner of such a property negotiates a lease with another person for a portion, or in some cases all, of the parcel of real estate. The owner retains the right of disposition of the property, and the leaseholder obtains the rights of possession and use and, to a limited extent, the right to exclude others (as discussed in Chapter 1). In return for giving away the rights of possession and use, the owner receives a payment known as **rent.**

The appraiser has three appraisal techniques that can be applied to income-earning properties. These three techniques are:

1. The gross rent multiplier technique—a sales comparison approach
2. The direct capitalization technique—a single-period cash flow analysis
3. The yield capitalization technique—a multiperiod cash flow analysis

Each of these techniques is discussed in the following sections of this chapter.

What Is the Gross Rent Multiplier Technique?

The **gross rent multiplier (GRM)** technique can be used to estimate current market value of an income-earning property by converting annual gross rental income into an estimate of market value. To apply the GRM, the appraiser assumes that investors in income-earning properties are rational and well-informed market participants, and that the sales price of recently sold comparable properties adequately reflects the investor's judgments about the future income to be derived from those properties. Inherent in this assumption is the idea that the sales price paid for these comparable properties also adequately reflects future trends in operating expenses, vacancy rates, and the market value of the space being provided by those structures.

To use the GRM technique, the appraiser takes her knowledge of the elements of comparison to obtain comparable properties and applies it to income-earning properties in a manner similar to the application in the case of the single-family residence. In this case, the appraiser first finds comparable properties that were rental properties at the time they were sold and obtains their sales price and their rent revenue at the time of sale. These properties are the **sales of comparable properties.** The appraiser divides the sales price of each of the comparable properties by the rent level for its space. If the division is done on the basis of annual rent, then the appraiser calculates the *annual* GRM. If the division is done on the basis of monthly rent, then the appraiser calculates the *monthly* GRM.

To determine the **market value** (MV) for the subject property, the following formula is used:

MV = GRM from sales of comparables x Market Rent for the subject property

CALCULATING THE GRM FROM SALES OF COMPARABLE PROPERTIES

Exhibit 6.1 shows a worksheet that an appraiser could construct to make an explicit statement of the GRM calculation.

EXHIBIT 6.1   Determination of the Gross Rent Multiplier (GRM).

Comparables have same number of units					
Sales Comparable Property	Sales Price	Monthly Rent Revenue	# units	Monthly GRM	Annual GRM
#1	$ 960,000	$ 10,400	24	92.3	7.69
#2	$ 985,000	$ 10,700	24	92.1	7.67
#3	$1,000,000	$ 11,100	24	90.1	7.51
#4	$ 990,000	$ 10,900	24	90.8	7.57
#5	$ 975,000	$ 10,600	24	92.0	7.67

In Exhibit 6.1, the comparable properties have the same number of similar units (24 two-bedroom units). This situation is the ideal situation because the degree of comparability is heightened. The GRM can be used when the number of units differs. But the degree of difference needs to be as small as possible. A 20-unit complex can be compared to a 28-unit complex, but a comparison of a 20-unit complex to a 40-unit complex is less desirable because it will be less accurate.

Just as the number of units varies, the rent revenue and the sales price vary due solely to the difference in units. In the case where the number of units is the same, the rents and sales prices also vary but for reasons associated with the physical, neighborhood, financial, and date of sale characteristics. In other words, difference in the GRMs for the comparable properties can reflect physical differences in age, condition, special features, and room size; differences in such locational features as proximity to jobs, shopping, and entertainment; differences in date of the property's sale; and financial arrangements that facilitated the purchase of the property. For this reason, the appraiser typically does not adjust GRMs.

By establishing GRMs for several comparable properties that have recently sold in the market, the appraiser obtains an order of magnitude for the current GRM as shown in Exhibit 6.1. If the comparable properties were chosen correctly, the several GRMs established for them may deviate from one another by a relatively small amount. This small level of deviation more than likely reflects differences that the market has detected in the properties. In Exhibit 6.1, the monthly GRM varies from 90.1 to 92.3. The appraiser can identify the comparable property that is most like the subject property and use its GRM to estimate the market value of the subject. The GRMs of the other comparable properties serve as a check on the accuracy of the market, in other words, on the consistency of the different investors' judgments about the market value of the properties that are very similar. Using the latter approach, the appraiser identifies comparable property #2 as the most similar to the subject and so uses the monthly GRM of 92.1 in the analysis.

CALCULATING MARKET RENT FOR THE SUBJECT PROPERTY

The second component of the GRM technique is an estimate of the subject property's market rent. The first step in this phase of the procedure is to find all properties that are comparable to the subject property. This includes the sales comparables used to calculate the GRM as well as all other comparable properties that are renting but did not sell. This latter group is the **rent comparables.**

Exhibit 6.2 presents a simple rent adjustment worksheet for the rent comparables. Unlike the GRM, which is not adjusted, the search for the market rent for the subject property allows for an adjustment process. As in the adjustment process for the single-family residence, the rent comparables are adjusted to the subject property. In Exhibit 6.2, comparable property #1 has the least amount of absolute adjustment, so it is identified as the best of the rent comparables and its adjusted rent of $535 is determined to be the best estimate of market rent for the subject property.

CALCULATING MARKET VALUE BY THE GRM TECHNIQUE

Market value of the subject property is obtained in the GRM technique by the following formula: MV = GRM × Market Rent. The monthly GRM estimate is 92.1 and the monthly market rent estimate is $535 per unit for each of the 24 two-bedroom apartments, which yields a market value estimate for the subject property of $1,182,564. The appraiser would most likely round this figure to $1,200,000.

EXHIBIT 6.2 — Adjustment worksheet to obtain market rent for the subject property.

Property Characteristics	Subject Property	Comparable Properties #1		#2		#3		#4	
Monthly Rent	?	$520		$500		$440		$410	
Sq. Feet	800	800	$ -	800	$ -	750	$ 40	750	$ 40
Condition	Good	Good	$ -	Good	$ -	Superior	$ (25)	Fair	$ 25
Aesthetics	Good	Good	$ -	average	$ 15	Good	$ -	Fair	$ 20
Security	Good	Good	$ -	Good	$ -	Good	$ -	Poor	$ 30
Pool	Yes	Yes	$ -	Yes	$ -	No	$ 30	Yes	$ -
Tennis Courts	Yes	Yes	$ -	No	$ 15	Yes	$ -	Yes	$ -
Health Club	Yes	No	$ 15	No	$ 15	No	$ 15	Yes	$ -
Neighborhood	Good	Good	$ -	Good	$ -	Fair	$ 45	Good	$ -
Adjusted Monthly Rent		$535		$ 545		$ 545		$525	

THE GROSS INCOME MULTIPLIER TECHNIQUE

There are several other forms of the multiplier technique. If the appraiser uses the income to the subject property from sources other than the rental of space in addition to the rental income, the gross income of the property is being used. In this event, the **gross income multiplier (GIM) technique** is being used. For an example of this technique, look ahead to the first year in the revenue section of Exhibit 6.6, p. 158. If these numbers represented a comparable property, the GRM would be based on the rent revenue from the 24 apartment units. The GIM would be based on this rent revenue plus the revenue from parking and laundry room collections.

Two other multipliers are based on the effective—rather than the potential—income from the property. These additional multipliers are discussed later in the chapter after the concepts of potential and effective income are presented.

ISSUES AND CONCERNS REGARDING THE GRM

Gross Income Orientation Versus Net Income Orientation

The appraiser must recognize limitations when using the GRM technique. Since the GRM technique relates the appraiser's estimate of market value to a gross income concept (that is, to potential gross income or to effective gross income rather than to net operating income), its use is valid only under certain conditions. The properties used for comparison must exhibit a high degree of uniformity among their operating expenses and financial characteristics, and this uniformity must be present among the whole set of comparable properties and the subject property itself. Without uniformity in operating expenses, the gross income estimate cannot reflect comparability in net operating income among the properties and the subject property. If uniformity among operating expense ratios exists, the assumption of comparability among the net operating incomes of the comparable properties and the subject property is warranted.

Remaining Economic Life

The GRM ignores the **remaining economic life** of the property, which is a judgment made by the appraiser about the length of time into the future over which the property will generate a cash flow. Use of the GRM technique is based on the assumption that the comparable properties and the subject property have the same remaining economic life span. In reality, comparable properties of the same actual age in the same physical condition may have different levels, different patterns, and different durations of income into the future. If the appraiser is to use the GRM concept appropriately, this difference in remaining economic life must be incorporated in some way into the selection of comparable properties.

Applicability of the GRM

Despite these limitations, the GRM technique is very appealing because of its simplicity. By obtaining estimates of GRM from the comparable properties, checking to be sure that the divergence among these estimates is not excessively large, and identifying the comparable property most like the subject property, the appraiser can determine a GRM to use in placing a value on the subject property. However, the accuracy and the applicability of the GRM technique rests on the availability of good comparable properties that are similar to the subject property for each of the elements of comparison.

What Is Direct Capitalization?

The rent payment is the basis for estimating market value by all of the income property appraisal approaches. As a very brief overview of the **direct capitalization** appraisal process, consider the following steps that the appraiser follows. First, the appraiser obtains an estimate of the rent revenues that the owner receives from the subject property. Then, the operating expenses of the property are subtracted from this income. The resultant dollar figure is the **net operating income (NOI).** It is the number of dollars that the income property generates after meeting its expenses of operation.

The appraiser now needs a technique to convert NOI into an estimate of value. The traditional technique is borrowed from the valuation of fixed-income securities in the bond market. The value of a bond that has a very long maturity (usually considered to be many decades but conceptually considered as perpetuity) is estimated by using the following formula:

$$V = I/i$$

where
V = the value estimate,
I = a periodic constant income received by the owner of the asset less any expenses of ownership or operation, and
i = a constant interest rate appropriate for prevailing conditions in the financial markets in that period of time.

Using this formula, a corporate or government bond that pays the owner $1,000 per year for the next 40 years is worth $10,000 if the current market rate of interest on alternative and comparable investments is 10 percent ($V = \$1,000/10\% = \$10,000$).

When this equation is adopted as the formula for estimating the value of real property by the direct capitalization method, the terms of the equation become:

$$V = NOI/R_0$$

where   V   =   the value estimate
          NOI   =   constant net operating income for the subject property
          R_0 =   constant capitalization rate derived from the sale of
                      comparable properties.

This equation simply states the following relationship. The value of the income-generating parcel of real property is equal to the NOI generated by the property divided by the capitalization rate appropriate for prevailing conditions in the property and financial markets in that period of time. By this formula, if a parcel of real estate generates an NOI of $10,000 per year and the appraiser uses a capitalization rate of 10 percent per year, the value of the real property is $100,000.

Although the concept of income property appraising as it appears in the formula for direct capitalization is relatively simple, the actual process is very complex. One of the purposes of this chapter is to consider the many factors that must be analyzed in the process of identifying the property's sources of income, its operating expenses, and the selection of the appropriate capitalization rate.

INCOME ANALYSIS

An appraisal of income property starts with **income analysis,** which is the process of identifying the sources of revenue and level of income that will be earned by the property. Income analysis includes an understanding of two relationships—contract rent and market rent—as well as the two income concepts of potential gross income and effective gross income.

Potential gross income is the total number of dollars that the income-producing property could generate in the form of rent revenue. **Effective gross income** is an estimate of the number of dollars that might be received by the property owner after reducing potential gross income by an estimate of vacancy and rent collection losses.

Contract Rent and Market Rent

Contract rent is the rental income to the property as a result of contractual commitments, which bind owners and tenants for a specified future period of time. Contract rent is the rent payment actually being paid by the tenant and received by the property owner. In contrast, **market rent** is the rental income that a property would obtain in the open market as indicated by current rents being paid for comparable space. Market rent is the payment the property owner would receive if a tenant were found for the property in the current market.

At any time, market rent and contract rent need not be the same. The current market rent can be greater than, equal to, or less than the contract rent, which may have been established 1, 2, or even 10 years ago. The level of contract rent based on market circumstances 2 years ago most likely is different from the current market rent level.

The Concept of Potential Gross Income

The potential gross income (PGI) is obtained by adding the rent revenues per unit of space for all units of space that are available for occupancy. If the property is an apartment building of 12 two-bedroom apartments, and the rent is $600 per unit per month, the PGI is $7,200 per month, or $86,400 per year. If the property is a retail building containing 8,000 square feet of leasable space at $14 per square foot per year, the PGI is $112,000 per year.

Fee Simple or Leased Fee Valuation

If the appraiser uses market rent as the basis for establishing PGI, the resulting value estimate is a *value of the fee simple estate* in the real property. If, on the other hand, the appraiser uses contract rent as the basis for establishing PGI, the resulting value estimate is the *value of the leased fee estate* in the real property.

The decision to use contract rent or market rent in the valuation process is based on the specific circumstances of the property and the information needed by the client. If the property will always have short-term leases in effect, then market rents should form the basis for PGI in a valuation of a fee simple estate. If the property has a long-term lease in effect, and the tenant has a good credit rating signaling a small chance of defaulting on the lease, then contract rents should form the basis for PGI in a valuation of a leased fee. However, in this latter case, the client might like to have an idea of the value of the fee simple estate and the leased fee estate. If contract and market rents are not the same, then the value of the fee simple estate and the leased fee estate are not the same.

Revenue Sources

To determine the level of PGI that a property can generate, the appraiser must identify all rentable space in that structure. This space, whether it is the number of apartment units or the floor area in square feet, must be priced at the prevailing market rate for similar space in competitive properties. In addition to the rentable space in the structure, the appraiser must identify other sources of PGI, such as parking facilities for the tenants of the building. If the structure is an apartment building, the tenants may receive one parking space as part of the package of services they buy with their rental payment. However, a second parking space for the household's second car or a covered parking space may cost an additional $15 per month.

Another source of revenue that can add to potential gross income is the provision of other services, such as washing machines and dryers in apartment buildings, and vending machines in office buildings and commercial retail facilities. The owner of the property can receive such revenue in either of two ways. The fixtures can be purchased and operated by the owner, or the owner can sell the right to provide these services to some other person. In either case, the owner receives additional income. However, additional expenses are also incurred when the owner decides to purchase the equipment and provide the services. These additional expenses must be considered and in some way charged against the revenues that they generate.

When market rent is multiplied by the rentable space in the building and when other sources of revenue are added to this figure, a quantitative measure of potential gross income is obtained. In addition to this quantitative aspect of the income stream, the appraiser must consider a qualitative aspect. The major factor that affects the quality of the PGI generated by the property is the uncertainty surrounding the actual receipt of rent payments. The owner and the appraiser are always uncertain about the exact level of future PGI that the property will generate. Market rents can change unexpectedly. They may actually decline when expectations are that they will increase, or rents may increase but not as much as anticipated. In addition, tenants might default on their agreement and not pay the stipulated contract rent. The degree of uncertainty determines the quality of the income stream. The higher the level of uncertainty, the lower the quality of the PGI generated by the property.

These quantitative and qualitative aspects of PGI are examined in greater detail in the next two sections.

Revenue Characteristics and Patterns that Affect the Quantity of Potential Gross Income

Several characteristics of an income stream affect the absolute number of dollars that the income-producing property generates. An income-producing property generates PGI for the current year and for many years into the future. To estimate the market value of an income-producing property, the appraiser must take both current and future PGI into account. For the most part, the revenue characteristics described in this section are related to this time element.

Duration of the Income Stream

The duration of the potential gross income stream of a property is related directly to the remaining economic life of the structure or improvement on the parcel of real property. The concept of remaining economic life is premised on the understanding of the economic life of the structure.

The **economic life** of a structure can be defined in two ways. First, it is the number of years that the structure is expected to provide useful service (sometimes called **useful life**). In terms of income or revenue, economic life is the number of years over which a positive net operating income will be realized. Another definition of economic life involves the generation of a competitive level of net operating income. Here, the economic life would be the number of years during which the property generates financial returns to its owner that are competitive or comparable to the returns generated by similar types of income-earning property. Whichever definition is chosen in order to predict the economic life of the improvement, the appraiser must consider the physical and functional features of the building, as well as the economic and demographic factors that affect the market in which the building's services are sold. If the building provides space for several uses, such as apartments and office space, then the economic factors in each market must be analyzed.

The physical characteristics of the improvement determine the **physical life** of the improvement, the period over which an improved property may be expected to remain in existence and to be capable of generating any income. The physical life of the improvement establishes an upper limit to the economic life of the structure. The economic life of the improvement cannot exceed the physical life of the improvement. Therefore, a discussion of the duration of the potential gross income stream is in fact a discussion of the economic life of the improvement of the property. The appraiser is concerned with the length of time over which the property will generate an income that is sufficiently large to cover the costs associated with the building if the first definition of economic life is used or, alternatively, with the time required to provide a competitive return on the investment if the second definition of economic life is used.

The factors that affect economic life are the economic and demographic variables that affect the market in which the services of the building are sold. The economic life of the improvement can also come to an end if the building is sold. The economic life of the improvement can come to an end if the demand for its services declines while the number of buildings providing space for those services remains constant. In this situation, the market rent must decline, causing a decline in PGI. When the income level falls to the point where it just barely covers the costs of operating the building, or even falls below the level of those costs, the economic life of that improvement has ended. The same result can occur if the demand for the improvement's services is constant, but the number of buildings providing the services increases. In this situation, market rent may fall or vacancy rates may rise to the point where PGI does not exceed the costs of operating the structure. Clearly, a prediction of economic life must be based on an analysis of the dynamic aspects of the market.

An improvement can have several economic lives within the span of its physical life. As one economic life ends, another economic life may start. The ability of the structure to adapt to changes in demand for its use is a functional characteristic of that structure. The greater the building's adaptability to change (known as functional efficiency), the greater the possibilities of lengthening the total economic life of the structure by establishing a second or a third economic use. The structure's ability to adapt to changing demands for its services depends on its design and space layout.

The longer the total economic life of the improvement, the greater the PGI that can be generated. A building that generates positive or competitive returns for 30 years should generate more total PGI than a building that receives the same market rent but has an economic life of only 25 years.

For a newly constructed building, the judgment about its economic life is the same as the judgment about its remaining economic life. However, for an existing 10-year-old building, the simplicity of the relationship fails. Consider the following situations.

First, 10 years ago, the building could have been judged to have an economic life of 40 years. Today, the remaining economic life judgment could be 30 years if the original judgment were absolutely correct. Second, 10 years ago, the building was judged to have an economic life of 40 years, but today the appraiser sees that the building has been repaired and maintained to the highest standards; it does not show any significant physical deterioration. Even though its actual age is 10 years, the appraiser judges the building to have an **effective age** of 2 years based on its current physical condition. Based on this judgment of effective age, the appraiser attributes a remaining economic life of 38 years to the building.

The third situation is the reverse of the second situation. Today, the 10-year-old building shows substantial deterioration because of a lack of maintenance and repair. Its actual age is 10 years, but its effective age is judged to be 15 years. Based on this physical evidence, the appraiser could judge the remaining economic life to be 25 years.

Timing and Pattern of the Rental Payments

If a building has a given economic life, and if a dollar received today is worth a little more than a dollar received next year, the pattern by which the rental payments are received becomes an important consideration in estimating PGI. For example, assume that the economic life of the building is one year and the owner can use one of two rent payment patterns:

1. An annual payment made by the tenant at the beginning of the year, or
2. An annual payment made by the tenant at the end of the year.

These two rent payment schemes generate two different levels of PGI. To calculate the levels of PGI, assume that the annual rental payment is $1,200, which can be paid in monthly installments of $100, and that the current interest rate is 10 percent (chosen here for simplicity of arithmetic). Under payment pattern #1, when the owner receives the $1,200 on January 1, she places that $1,200 in the bank for the full year. On December 31, the PGI generated is $1,200 plus 10 percent of $1,200, a total PGI of $1,320. Under payment pattern #2, the tenant delivers $1,200 to the landlord on December 31. In this case, the PGI is $1,200 because no interest is earned. The timing of the payment between the start of the period and the end of the period affects the level of PGI by a rate that is equal to the market rate of interest. Thus, an owner can maximize total PGI over the economic life of the structure by receiving payment in advance, at the beginning of whatever payment interval is used.

Variability of the Payment Pattern Over Time

In the previous example, the rent payment is assumed to be constant over time. However, changes in the magnitude of the payment over time can affect the total amount of income to be received. If the economic life of the improvement is five years, and over the five-year period the property generates $6,000 in rental payments, the manner in which the full $6,000 is paid to the owner affects total income. For example, assume that the tenant can make payments to the landlord in any of the three patterns shown in Exhibit 6.3.

EXHIBIT 6.3 Three hypothetical payment patterns.

A

Year	1	2	3
1	$ 1,200	$ 2,000	$ 400
2	$ 1,200	$ 1,600	$ 800
3	$ 1,200	$ 1,200	$ 1,200
4	$ 1,200	$ 800	$ 1,600
5	$ 1,200	$ 400	$ 2,000
Total Receipts	$ 6,000	$ 6,000	$ 6,000

B Present Value Calculation

Year	1			2			3		
1	$ 1,200	0.9434	$ 1,132	$ 2,000	0.9434	$ 1,887	$ 400	0.9434	$ 377
2	$ 1,200	0.8900	$ 1,068	$ 1,600	0.8900	$ 1,424	$ 800	0.8900	$ 712
3	$ 1,200	0.8396	$ 1,008	$ 1,200	0.8396	$ 1,008	$ 1,200	0.8396	$ 1,008
4	$ 1,200	0.7921	$ 951	$ 800	0.7921	$ 634	$ 1,600	0.7921	$ 1,267
5	$ 1,200	0.7473	$ 897	$ 400	0.7473	$ 299	$ 2,000	0.7473	$ 1,495
Total Receipts	$ 6,000		$ 5,055	$ 6,000		$ 5,251	$ 6,000		$ 4,859

Discount Rate	6.0%								

C Future Value Calculation: End of Period Payments

Year	1			2			3		
1	$ 1,200		$ 1,515	$ 2,000		$ 2,525	$ 400		$ 505
2	$ 1,200		$ 1,429	$ 1,600		$ 1,906	$ 800		$ 953
3	$ 1,200		$ 1,348	$ 1,200		$ 1,348	$ 1,200		$ 1,348
4	$ 1,200		$ 1,272	$ 800		$ 848	$ 1,600		$ 1,696
5	$ 1,200		$ 1,200	$ 400		$ 400	$ 2,000		$ 2,000
Total Receipts	$ 6,000		$ 6,765	$ 6,000		$ 7,027	$ 6,000		$ 6,502

Discount Rate	6.0%								

In Exhibit 6.3, part A, the three rent payment options differ over time, but the total rent over the five year period is the same for each option at $6,000. There is no basis for choice if total rent over time is the only decision criterion. However, tenants know that it is better to pay more at the end of the lease period while landlords desire more of the rent at the front of the lease period. Thus, the tenant prefers rent payment option 3 while the landlord prefers option 2.

For those students who are familiar with compound interest theory, parts B and C of Exhibit 6.3 reveal this fact. The example is constructed at an interest rate of 6 percent. The determination made at the present time is shown in part B. The present value of option 3 is $4,859; this is the tenant's desired rent payment scheme. The present value of option 2 is $5,251; this is the landlord's desired rent payment scheme. The determination made at the end of the five-year period (the future value) is shown in part B. The future value of option 3 is $6,502; this is the tenant's desired rent payment scheme. The future value of option 2 is $7,027; this is the landlord's desired rent payment scheme.

Factors That Influence the Quality of PGI

The factors that influence the qualitative aspect of PGI are related to the degree of uncertainty about the actual receipt of the rental payments by the owner. One qualitative factor that the appraiser considers is the financial responsibility of the tenant. The owner of the property anticipates very little uncertainty in collecting the rental payment if the tenant is considered to be financially responsible or has a good credit rating. In other words, the owner of the property faces very little risk that the tenant's financial position will interfere with ability to pay the rent.

A second qualitative factor related to the tenant is the degree of that person's nonfinancial responsibility. Lease agreements contain clauses that require the tenant to perform such stipulated actions as keeping the property in good repair by avoiding undue wear and tear. A tenant who does not act in the prescribed manner may have to be removed by the landlord. If such an action does take place, the rent payment is interrupted until a new tenant is found.

The nature of the rental agreement itself also can affect the level of certainty about the future rent payments. The lease may contain provisions that could nullify the rental agreement. One such provision is known as the **transfer clause** in a residential lease. If the tenant is transferred to a new job that is at least 50 miles away from the apartment building, the tenant can void the lease. Such statements in the lease increase the risk that the owner will not be receiving the market rent over the full term of the lease.

Another qualitative factor that affects PGI is the degree of accuracy associated with the projections of future market rent levels. In the process of determining PGI, the appraiser must make forecasts about future market rent levels. Therefore, the appraiser must forecast the economic and demographic factors that affect both demand and supply in the market for the space provided by the subject property. All such forecasts are based on uncertainty. Thus, the risk factor associated with forecasting future market rent rates—the risk of forecast error—affects the quality of the PGI figure.

Quality of management also can affect PGI. The basic assumption made by the appraiser is that the subject property and comparable properties in the market are under "good management." Efficient systems for rent collection can maintain a stable flow of income. In addition, an effective tenant selection process can reduce problems associated with rent collection, vacant apartments, and the turnover rate of tenants. The risk associated with the management function is that the assumption of high-quality management is erroneous or will be incorrect in the future. In either case, the actual level of PGI may not be as high as it should be if an inefficient manager does not know the market rent and leases the space at less than market rates.

Income Projections and Their Effects on the Quantity of PGI

The preceding discussion on quantitative factors affecting PGI (the duration, timing, pattern, and variability of the rental payment) is based on the assumption that the exact magnitude of rent payments is known. However, future market rents and thereby future levels of PGI are known with only limited certainty. The appraiser must forecast these future market rent levels by analyzing the market in which the property's services are sold. All the pertinent economic and demographic features affecting both demand and supply must be analyzed. The dynamic changes in these variables must be anticipated.

In essence, the appraiser must consider the economic factors used in both area analysis and neighborhood analysis as well as the full scope of factors used in locational analysis. At a minimum, the appraiser must be able to forecast future levels of real disposable income; the number and composition of the households in the community; the number of properties in competition with the subject property; changes in locational attributes based on shifts in residential, employment, and commercial locations; and changes in neighborhood factors that would make the subject property more or less desirable to the consumer. If the appraiser can forecast an increasing level of demand for the services provided by the subject property, a constant supply of competitive space, a stable neighborhood that maintains its present quality, and little, if any, change in other significant variables, the appraiser can forecast an increase in market rents. However, the exact level of those future market rents is subject to error whether the appraiser uses an educated guess or undertakes some sophisticated mathematical or statistical projection of the future rent level.

VACANCY AND INCOME LOSS CONSIDERATIONS

Potential gross income is an estimate of the subject property's maximum income-earning potential given current and future market conditions. However, the appraiser is not interested in what the property could generate in the form of income as an end product. The appraiser is interested in the income level that the property actually should generate from its full potential. In other words, the appraiser calculates PGI as the starting point but makes an adjustment to PGI to obtain an income figure that represents the revenues of the property that are actually received. This adjusted income level is known as effective gross income, the income from operation of the real estate after allowance for vacancy and collection loss.

To estimate vacancy and collection loss, the appraiser considers the following information:

1. The vacancy rate by type of residential unit or type of commercial space
2. Rent payment problems, such as nonpayment or partial payment of rent
3. Special concessions made to the tenant that have a monetary value
4. Losses due to vandalism or theft

When the earning potential of an income property is considered, the appraiser must realize that some space in that structure may be vacant for some period of time during its economic life. This situation could occur even if the property is fully occupied in the current period. A tenant may have to be evicted because the rent is not paid or for some other violation of the lease arrangement. Also, demand for such space may decline. In this case, there will be an abundance of available rental space and a shortage of tenants at the current market rent. The owner of the property may have to make such concessions as a rent exemption (a free first month), free parking for the household's second car, or even a contract rent below the current market rent to attract enough tenants to keep the property fully rented. If the owner is not successful with these concessions, space will be vacant in the building. Finally, even if damage by vandals and theft of fixtures have never occurred, such losses can be incurred in the future. Therefore, to establish the effective gross income projections for the property, the appraiser must make a negative adjustment to PGI to reflect the events that can cause vacancy and income loss for the property.

Three general sources of information about the magnitude of these vacancy and income losses are available. One source of data is the historical record of the subject property itself. The appraiser can analyze the property's records over the last four or five years to establish a figure for annual losses in the four categories. Then, the appraiser can assume that the magnitude of such losses will be the same in the future if the financial quality of the tenants, the quality of the neighborhood, and the relative market activity of the buyers and sellers remain constant in the future.

The historical records of comparable properties represent the second source of information on these income losses. The appraiser obtains figures for such losses from comparable properties and uses them as a check against the estimates for the subject property.

The third data set consists of surveys that are occasionally made by trade associations, brokerage firms, or universities. Such surveys are usually made on a national or regional basis for different types of residential and commercial property. Such surveys sometimes can be found for the local economic area. They provide an understanding of the vacancy and income losses for similar kinds of property in the nation, or at least in the region in which the subject property is located. If the data are for nonlocal comparable properties, this information is a less important and less definite check against the data gathered about the subject property and local comparable properties.

PGI is the first element of analysis in income property appraisal. From this income figure, the appraiser subtracts vacancy and income losses to obtain a revenue estimate known as effective gross income. Having obtained this figure, the appraiser can examine the next important component of income property appraisal—the current and future operating expenses of the property.

OPERATING EXPENSE ANALYSIS

The **operating expenses** incurred by the owner of an income-producing property are the annual cash payments that are a necessary cost of generating effective gross income. The important phrase in this definition is "necessary cost of generating effective gross income." To identify the operating expenses of the property, the appraiser must consider only expenditures that are necessary for the operation of the property and that are associated with the property. If an expenditure is associated with the owner's personal needs or the operation of another property, the appraiser must ignore it in the appraisal of the subject property.

Classification of Operating Expenses

Operating expenses traditionally have been grouped into variable expenses, fixed expenses, and reserves for replacement. **Variable expenses** include cash outlays that change with the level of occupancy in the structure. As more residential units or more commercial space is leased to tenants, certain cash outlays increase in magnitude. There are several major expenditure items in this category:

1. *Payroll and personnel expenses* include salaries, social security contributions, payments to unemployment insurance, and all other fringe benefits provided by the property owner to the employees working in the subject property. In some instances, the fringe benefits include a rent concession on the maintenance superintendent's apartment in the subject property.

2. *Management fees* are the expenditures incurred by the owner for rent collection, tenant selection, marketing the property, and other such administrative work. The payments for these management services can be made to an independent property manager, or they may be made to the owner for the time and effort expended in this activity.

3. *Utilities expenses* include all payments made by the owner for electricity, natural gas, heating oil, water, sewer service, and trash collection.

4. *Supplies and materials expenses* include only those items that are used in the normal operation of the property. These supplies and materials are not fixtures of the property; they are the owner's personal property used to make the property habitable and clean. This expense category includes the payments made by the owner for light bulbs, rug cleaning solutions, floor wax, paint, and other general cleaning and repair supplies.

5. *Grounds care expenses* are the maintenance expenditures for improvements made on the property other than to the main building. Maintenance expenditures for parking lots, access roads, and sidewalks would be included in this category, as would expenditures incurred in connection with the lawn, landscaping, swimming pools, tennis courts, and patios.

The second type of operating expenses is known as **fixed expenses.** These cash outlays do not vary with the level of occupancy in the structure. Their magnitude is relatively constant whether the property is fully occupied or whether the property is entirely vacant. Traditionally, the most important fixed expenditures are as follows:

1. *Property taxes* are the actual tax dollars paid by the owner of the property. Property taxes are considered a fixed operating expense because they are levied by local governments as payments for public services provided to the inhabitants of that property. A well-maintained street network, reliable police protection, and an up-to-date school system, for example, affect both the desirability and satisfaction of the structure to the tenants.

2. *Property insurance* requires a cash outlay by the owner to insure the property against such hazards as fire, theft, and vandalism. In addition, the owner must carry liability insurance on those portions of the property for which the courts hold the owner responsible. The property owner should carry *liability insurance* to cover the common areas against personal injury incurred by tenants and their guests. However, the owner need not carry liability insurance for the space leased by the tenants. The courts hold the tenant responsible for personal injury incurred within the leased space.

3. *Long-term ground lease.* The underlying site may have been leased for a lengthy time rather than purchased. This annual payment must be deducted.

The third category of operating expenses is **reserves for replacement.** These expenditures are the payments made by the owner for short-lived items that need to be replaced periodically. These short-lived items include the following:

- Appliances that are provided with the apartment unit
- Heating and cooling equipment in the structure
- Roof covering
- Elevators and escalators
- Light fixtures
- Revolving doors
- Carpeting and other floor coverings
- Plumbing fixtures

The economic lives of these fixtures are much shorter than the economic life of the major improvement or structure. Every 5 years or so, some of them must be replaced. Those that are not replaced on a 5-year cycle are typically replaced about every 10 years. Therefore, the owner must have a reserve of funds from which money can be drawn to replace these items as they wear out.

Expense Items Excluded from the Appraiser's Operating Expense Statement

The operating expense statement used by the appraiser does not include many items that are viewed as expenses by the owner of the property. Conventional profit and loss statements do include all expenses incurred by the owner with respect to the property. Some of these expenses are inappropriate for the appraiser's purposes because they are not cash outlays that are a necessary cost of generating the effective gross income from the property. Consequently, the appraiser excludes the following expenses in preparing an operating expense statement for the purpose of income property appraisal.

INCOME TAXES. Personal and corporate income taxes are excluded from the appraiser's operating expense statement because they are expenses of the owner, not of the income-producing property. The exact level of the income tax payment varies with the taxable earnings of the individual or the corporation. Even though these expenditures are important to the owner, and even though they can influence the decision to buy the property, the value estimate must not include them in the total of operating expenditures.

DEBT SERVICE. Debt service is the annual payment made by the owner of the property to repay the loan. It is the sum of the annual interest charge on the mortgage and the principal repayment made during the year. Even though this payment is an expense incurred by the owner of the property, the expenditure is not necessary to generate effective gross income. The property has the same income-generating potential whether it was purchased with borrowed money or purchased by the owner with cash. If borrowed funds were used, the property has the same income-generating potential whether it was purchased on a 30-year mortgage or a 5-year mortgage. Moreover, the property has the same income-earning potential whether the interest rate on the borrowed funds is 9.5 percent per year or 3 percent per year. Consequently, the operating expense statement should not include the mortgage repayment or debt service payment.

The exclusion of debt service from operating expenses can be justified for another reason. The more sophisticated techniques used to generate the rate of capitalization incorporate the debt service consideration into the process of calculating the capitalization rate. In this way, mortgage features are reflected in the appraisal process even though the exact mortgage payment is not considered an expense.

TAX DEPRECIATION EXPENSES. Capital recovery or depreciation expenses are an important item and must be considered by the appraiser at some point in the income property appraisal process. The generally accepted manner of treating this expense item is to consider it as a deduction when computing federal income taxes and not as a separate expense item in the appraiser's operating expense statement.

CAPITAL IMPROVEMENTS OR CAPITAL OUTLAYS. Capital improvement expenditures are made by the owner to improve the property. They typically include payments for remodeling, replacing functionally obsolescent equipment that still operates but does not suit consumer preferences, and upgrading the level of services by including patios, covered parking, and other amenities. Capital improvement expenditures are made only when the owner is certain that the property's income-producing potential will increase sufficiently to cover the cost of the improvement. This increase in the income-producing potential can occur if market rent, and thus the contract rent, can be increased, or if the economic life of the improvement is extended. The appraiser does not treat these expenditures as operating expenses for purposes of income property appraisal. Capital improvement expenditures do not generate current effective gross income as do the products or services provided by operating expenses. Capital improvements increase the level of future effective gross income by raising rent revenues or lengthening the economic life of the property. Thus, the impact of capital improvement expenditures is seen as an increase in the income-generating potential of the property, which is how they are reflected in the appraisal process.

OTHER EXPENSES OF THE OWNER. A distinction must be made between certain other expenses that the owner charges against the property and the operating expenses used by the appraiser in the income property appraisal process. True operating expenses are instrumental in generating effective gross income. For this reason, such expenditures as charitable contributions, traffic or other fines, entertainment expenses, cost of lawsuits, damage awards, and personal expenditures must be excluded from the list of operating expenses used by the appraiser. In addition, any payments made by the owner for supervisory or management activities that are neither performed for nor essential to the operation of the property must also be excluded.

RECONSTRUCTION OF THE INCOME AND OPERATING EXPENSE STATEMENT

Exhibit 6.4 is a numerical representation of the property owner's income and operating expense statement based on acceptable accounting procedures. Exhibit 6.5 is a reconstruction of this statement into an income property operating statement that is appropriate for calculating NOI. Comparison of these two exhibits reveals that the accountant's level of net income is significantly different from the estimation of net operating income. First, market rents are used, not contract rents. In situations where the lease agreements are short term as they are for apartments, market rents give a more accurate estimate of value. If a property contained tenants that had long-term leases of 20 years or more, then the contract rent stated in the lease would be more realistic as a value determinant.[1]

Second, as discussed in the previous section, expense items that are not directly related to the generation of effective gross income are excluded. Third, a vacancy and collection loss factor that does not appear in the accountant's statement is included.

The end result of these adjustments to the property's income and operating expense records is a change from a net income of $656 to a net operating income of $82,203.

EXHIBIT 6.4 Property owner's income and expense statement.

Revenues: 24 apartment units							Annual receipts
Rent receipts:							
	14 two bedroom units @ monthly rent			$ 400			$ 67,200
	10 one bedroom units @ monthly rent			$ 320			$ 38,400
Parking fees:							
	$15 per month for second car						$ 2,520
	$25 per month for covered parking						$ 2,400
Laundry room collections							$ 1,500
				Total Revenues			$ 112,020
Expenses:							
Management fees		6.50% of rent receipts					$ 6,864
Property taxes							$ 6,400
Insurance premiums							$ 2,500
Maintenance and repairs							$ 9,400
Supplies and materials							$ 2,400
Mortage payments							$ 34,000
Building custodial costs							$ 15,000
Depreciation							$ 9,800
Utilities							$ 3,000
Income tax payments							$ 11,000
Replacement of appliances, carpeting, etc.							$ 5,200
Lawn and grounds maintenance							$ 3,300
Misc. administrative costs							$ 2,500
				Total Expenses			$ 111,364
Net Income							$ 656
INPUTS							
# two bedroom units		14					
# one bedroom units		10					
Two bedroom rent	$ 400						
One bedroom rent	$ 320						
Management fee	6.50%						

EXHIBIT 6.5   Property owner's reconstructed income and expense statement.

Revenues: 24 apartment units								
							Annual receipts	
Rent receipts:								
	14 two bedroom units @ monthly rent			$	525		$	88,200
	10 one bedroom units @ monthly rent			$	425		$	51,000
Parking fees:								
	$15 per month for second car						$	2,520
	$25 per month for covered parking						$	2,400
Laundry room collections							$	1,500
				Total Revenues			$	145,620
				less vacancies @		3.50%	$	(5,097)
				Effective Gross Income			$	140,523
Expenses:								
Management fees		7.25%	of rent receipts				$	10,092
Property taxes							$	6,400
Insurance premiums							$	2,500
Maintenance and repairs							$	9,400
Supplies and materials							$	2,400
Mortage payments							$	-
Building custodial costs							$	15,000
Depreciation							$	-
Utilities							$	3,000
Income tax payments								-
Replacement of appliances, carpeting, etc.							$	4,500
Lawn and grounds maintenance							$	3,300
Misc. administrative costs							$	1,000
				Total Expenses			$	57,592
Net Operating Income NOI							$	82,931
INPUTS								
# two bedroom units		14						
# one bedroom units		10						
Two bedroom rent	$	525						
One bedroom rent	$	425						
Management fee		7.25%						
Market vacancy rate		3.50%						

OPERATING EXPENSE RATIO

Knowledge of the subject property's operating expense ratio is useful to the appraiser for two reasons. First, it can provide a check or a benchmark against which the appraiser can judge the reasonableness of the estimation of the subject property's operating expenses. This task is accomplished by examining operating expense and effective gross income data for comparable properties in the local community and in the nation as a whole. Several publications provide this information to the appraiser. Second, the operating expense ratio is useful in judging the property's operating performance.

The typical **operating expense ratio** used by investors and appraisers is found by dividing total operating expenses by effective gross income. In Exhibit 6.5 it is 41 percent ($57,592 ÷ $140,523). An acceptable value for the ratio depends on the nature of the improvement. Apartment buildings that differ in numbers of units, size of the rooms, and elevator systems will have different acceptable operating expense ratios. The ratio for apartments is different from the operating expense ratio for commercial buildings. As a general operational procedure, the appraiser assumes that competent property management acts to keep the level of effective gross income high and the level of total operating expenses low. Therefore, a low operating expense ratio is the ideal.

The appraiser should realize that the level of operating expenses can be lowered by minimizing or reducing operating expenses. For example, the operating expense ratio can be reduced by lowering the level of repairs and maintenance. This action makes the financial ratio look better in the short term. However, such deferred maintenance is not beneficial to the structure. If necessary repairs are not made, both the level of operating expenses and the operating expense ratio fall; this should make the property appear more desirable. But, if the repairs are not made, the physical deterioration can cause increased vacancy levels or reduced contract rents in the future. At some point in the future, the deferred maintenance must be corrected. If it is not corrected, the remaining economic life of the building is shortened. The net effect may well be a reduction in future levels of effective gross income.

The appraiser and the investor should know the variables used to construct the operating expense ratio. The numerical value of the ratio could be lower if potential gross income, instead of effective gross income, is used as the denominator of the ratio, because vacancy losses are not considered in PGI. The operating expense ratio can also be low if some category of operating expenses, such as reserves for replacement, is not included in the numerator of the ratio. Therefore, the appraiser and the investor should ask for a definition of the terms and values used in generating the operating expense ratio.

THE CONCEPT OF NET OPERATING INCOME

After the appraiser has calculated effective gross income and total operating expenses, net operating income can be calculated. NOI is simply effective gross income minus total operating expenses. The importance of NOI to the appraiser is simple to understand. It is the numerator in the valuation formula discussed at the beginning of this chapter, in which NOI is divided by a capitalization rate to obtain an estimate of the property's market value.

DERIVATION OF THE CAPITALIZATION RATE

The **capitalization rate** is always composed of two rates of return that serve different purposes. One of these rates is the **basic rate of interest.** It reflects current phenomena in the financial markets where the investor will borrow funds while simultaneously representing a rate of return on the investment. The second rate is the **capital recovery rate** for the investment, which represents the accrued depreciation of the improvement over its economic life. It is a return of the investment.

A typical investor who purchases income-producing property fully expects to receive a rate of return on the equity that is put into the investment. The reasoning process is similar to that of an investor who puts $40,000 into a savings account with the expectation of receiving a rate of return on that money.

In addition, the typical investor wants a return of the investment. Unlike a savings account, the income-producing property can undergo a loss in the value of the equity over time. As the property ages, it becomes less valuable. The investor therefore needs some way to recover the equity put into the investment. For example, assume the investor holds the property for 10 years, and that after 10 years the property is worth 75 percent of its current value. Consequently, the investor needs to have that 25-percent reduction in value returned over the period of ownership. In this case, the investor would want 2.5 percent of $10,000 returned each year. This 2.5 percent is a capital recovery rate that is calculated using a straight-line depreciation technique.

Regardless of whether the basic rate of interest and the capital recovery rate of the investment are stated explicitly as two separate entities, they are both conceptually included in the rate of capitalization.

The Overall Rate of Capitalization Derived from the Property Market

The overall rate of capitalization is derived from the market. The appraiser identifies several comparable properties that have sold in the recent past and obtains both their sales prices and levels of net operating income. For example, assume that a duplicate property to the subject property recently sold for $1,100,000 and that its NOI in year 1 is $88,000. In this case, the overall rate of capitalization is obtained by using the following simple equation:

$$\text{NOI/Sales Price} = \$88,000/\$1,100,000 = 0.08 \text{ or } 8\%$$

If reliable market data are available for comparable investment properties, the overall rate of capitalization from such market comparisons can be used. However, the necessary data on such comparable properties are frequently not available. Moreover, if the properties are not similar, a significant number of adjustments to the sales price would have to be made, and this technique for obtaining the rate of capitalization would lose its validity and its applicability. The subject property and the comparable properties must have the following elements of similarity if the overall rate of capitalization is to be used:

1. Similar types of property with essentially the same remaining economic lives, physical condition, and relationship of the site to the improvement
2. Similar neighborhood and locational characteristics
3. Similar terms of financing involved in the purchase
4. Similar terms of sale and market conditions prevailing at the time of the sale
5. Similar income streams that represent the same timing, stability, and risk
6. Similar types of buying motivations underlying their purchase
7. Arm's-length transactions surrounding the sale (The term arm's length transaction denotes a transaction that takes place in a free and open market. The transaction is not affected by undue influence and duress on either party to the

transaction, and the transaction exhibits a normal competitive negotiation that does not include a transaction between family members and friends.)

If the use of an overall capitalization rate cannot be obtained from the market because of the lack of comparable properties, the appraiser must turn to alternative methods of deriving the rate of capitalization. These alternative approaches are beyond the scope of this text, but are taught in real estate appraisal courses.

ESTIMATING MARKET VALUE USING DIRECT CAPITALIZATION

Given the income and expense figures presented earlier in Exhibit 6.5, the appraiser can estimate current market value. First, the appraiser makes an estimate of an income figure called the *stabilized NOI*. This is a single value of the NOI that represents the NOI figures that should arise in the current as well as future years. The rationale used to develop the stabilized NOI is based on the establishment of a single number that typifies the stream of future NOI figures. It is neither the highest NOI nor the lowest, and it is not the average NOI value. Conceptually, the stabilized NOI is a single figure whose present value, if it were received in each year, would equal the present value of the actual NOI figures. In the numerical example being used in this chapter, an initial period NOI of $82,200 has been established.

Second, the appraiser divides the initial period NOI by a capitalization rate to obtain an estimate of market value. Remember that the capitalization rate consists of a return on the initial investment, a return of the investment, and should include an estimate of the change in sales price over the ownership period. If the future sales price is expected to increase, then the capitalization rate decreases, causing a rise in the estimated present market value.

Even though this final step in the direct capitalization process seems simple, also remember that the capitalization rate is established only after a large number of important factors are analyzed. A list of these factors should serve as a reminder of the complexity of the underlying thought process. The following factors are either directly or indirectly considered in the calculation of a capitalization rate.

1. The typical mortgage interest rate
2. The length of the typical mortgage
3. The typical size of the mortgage as a percentage of sales price
4. The typical investor's expected rate of return, which in itself considers the rate of return on a safe, riskless investment plus premiums for risk, illiquidity, and management
5. The typical investor's equity as a percentage of sales price
6. The return on the equity increase as the mortgage balance is paid down
7. A price appreciation factor for an investment that gains value over the ownership period

The complexity in the direct capitalization technique is in the generation of the capitalization rate and the appropriate NOI. Once these two magnitudes are known, the simple $V = NOI/R$ equation provides the market value estimate. The formula for estimating market value of the subject property by the direct capitalization technique is $MV = (NOI)/R$. If the NOI is taken from Exhibit 6.5 to be $82,000 and the R is 8 percent, then the estimate of the market value is $82,200/0.08 = $1,027,500, rounded to $1,000,000.

What Is Yield Capitalization?

Yield capitalization is the logical expansion of direct capitalization. It takes the initial period estimate of rent revenue and operating expenses and adds future values of these items in the analysis. From market evidence, the appraiser discovers information about changes into the future and directly uses this information in the analysis. Exhibit 6.6 shows the revenue and expense information that goes into the generation of future values of NOI. A discussion of the several changes that take place in the transition from direct to yield capitalization appears below.

Yield capitalization can be performed by using two different methods. The first method uses the stream of NOI figures, a capitalization rate, and a discount rate. This is the method that will be discussed here. The second method uses concepts that are introduced in Chapter 11. Consequently, the discussion of this second technique will be delayed until Chapter 11, which contains a section on yield capitalization.

CURRENT PERIOD NOI AND THE NEED TO FORECAST FUTURE LEVELS OF NOI

In the preceding discussion of effective gross income and operating expenses, the appraiser calculated these income and expense figures for the current period. However, an estimate of current period NOI is not the conceptually appropriate income figure to use in the income property appraisal process. The income approach for estimating the current market value of a property is based on the principle of anticipation which states that the market value of a property is created by the expectation of benefits to be obtained in the future. The significance of past experience arises from its use as a reference point for estimating future conditions. The current operating statement prepared by the appraiser is the assembled data from the past that can be used as an aid in forecasting future levels of NOI.

Because the income property appraisal process is based on the principle of anticipation, the appraiser must analyze future levels of NOI. However, the only readily available information is historical data about the operation of the subject property and historical data about the operation of comparable properties. From these data, the appraiser can evaluate short-term and intermediate-term trends in the historical operating expense items. In addition, the appraiser must evaluate the probable impact of dynamic changes in economic and demographic variables on future levels of potential gross income, effective gross income, and net operating income.

FORECASTING FUTURE LEVELS OF POTENTIAL AND EFFECTIVE GROSS INCOME

To forecast future levels of potential gross income for the subject property, the appraiser must forecast future trends in the economic and demographic factors that affect that property market of which the subject property is a part. In other words, the appraiser must analyze the future level of market rent and vacancies for the comparable properties. Once these trends are forecast, the appraiser can determine their impact on market rents. For example, assume that the subject property is a small apartment complex in a desirable section of the city. The appraiser can forecast an increase in market rents if the following market trends occur: an increase in the number of households in the age-groups that desire apartment living; a continuation of the neighborhood's desirability and accessibility to employment opportunities; and stability in the local zoning pattern that deters construction of competing properties.

EXHIBIT 6.6 Property owner's reconstructed income and expense statement.

Revenues: 24 apartment units					Year 1	2	3	4	5	6
Rent reciepts:										
	14 two bedroom units @ monthly rent		$ 525		$ 88,200	$ 91,287	$ 94,482	$ 97,789	$ 101,212	$ 104,754
	10 one bedroom units @ monthly rent		$ 425		$ 51,000	$ 52,275	$ 53,582	$ 54,921	$ 56,294	$ 57,702
Parking fees:										
	$15 per month for second car				$ 2,520	$ 2,520	$ 2,520	$ 2,520	$ 2,520	$ 2,520
	$25 per month for covered parking				$ 2,400	$ 2,400	$ 2,400	$ 2,400	$ 2,400	$ 2,400
Laundry Room Collections:					$ 1,500	$ 1,500	$ 1,500	$ 1,500	$ 1,500	$ 1,500
Total Revenues					$ 145,620	$ 149,982	$ 154,484	$ 159,130	$ 163,926	$ 168,876
less vacancies @	3.50%				$ (5,097)	$ (5,249)	$ (5,407)	$ (5,570)	$ (5,737)	$ (5,911)
Effective Gross Income					$ 140,523	$ 144,733	$ 149,077	$ 153,561	$ 158,189	$ 162,965
Expenses:										
Management fees	7.25% of rent receipts				$ 10,092	$ 10,408	$ 10,735	$ 11,071	$ 11,419	$ 11,778
Property taxes					$ 6,400	$ 6,624	$ 6,856	$ 7,096	$ 7,344	$ 7,601
Insurance premiums					$ 2,500	$ 2,550	$ 2,601	$ 2,653	$ 2,706	$ 2,760
Maintenance and repairs					$ 9,400	$ 9,682	$ 9,972	$ 10,272	$ 10,580	$ 10,897
Supplies and materials					$ 2,400	$ 2,448	$ 2,497	$ 2,547	$ 2,598	$ 2,650
Building custodial costs					$ 15,000	$ 15,300	$ 15,606	$ 15,918	$ 16,236	$ 16,561
Utilities					$ 3,000	$ 3,060	$ 3,121	$ 3,184	$ 3,247	$ 3,312
Replacement of appliances, carpeting, etc.					$ 4,500	$ 4,590	$ 4,682	$ 4,775	$ 4,871	$ 4,968
Lawn and grounds maintenance					$ 3,300	$ 3,366	$ 3,433	$ 3,502	$ 3,572	$ 3,643
Misc. administrative costs					$ 1,000	$ 1,020	$ 1,040	$ 1,061	$ 1,082	$ 1,104
			Total Expenses		$ 57,592	$ 59,048	$ 60,544	$ 62,079	$ 63,656	$ 65,276
Net Operating Income					$ 82,931	$ 85,684	$ 88,533	$ 91,482	$ 94,532	$ 97,689

INPUTS		
# two bedroom units	14	
# one bedroom units	10	
two bedroom rent	$ 525	
one bedroom rent	$ 425	
management fee	7.25%	
market vacancy rate	3.50%	
two bedroom unit rent growth		3.50%
one bedroom unit rent growth		2.50%
property tax growth rate		4.00%
maintenance & repair growth rate		3.00%
all other operating expenses		2.00%

If, however, the appraiser forecasts a reduction in the absolute size of the 18- to 25-year-old and the over-55 age-groups in the population, if changing neighborhood factors will make the property less desirable, and if comparable properties are being constructed in other more desirable neighborhoods, the appraiser can forecast declining market rent. Many other combinations of market and neighborhood factors could indicate changes in market rent levels. The examples are used to illustrate how market and neighborhood analyses are used in forecasting future market rent.

Having established a probable direction of change in the level of market rents, the appraiser can estimate the change in the level of market gross income. However, the exact magnitude of the change is still an educated guess.

The appraiser can develop proxy relationships to represent future economic and demographic changes. For example, the appraiser may determine the future increases in the number of households over the next 5 to 10 years. In addition, the appraiser may determine that construction of new apartments over the next 10 years will be approximately equal to construction of new apartments over the past 10 years. These two pieces of proxy information provide a basis for forecasting future market rent levels. Similarly, the appraiser can assume that the market rent increase in 1- or 2-year increments in the future will be equal to the percentage increases by similar increments over the past 5 years. The appraiser may assume that after the five-year period market rent will remain constant for a decade and then gradually decline as the building reaches the end of its projected economic life of about 40 years.

Alternatively, the appraiser may forecast that future levels of the economic and demographic variables will stay approximately as they are today and have been in the recent past. In addition, historical data for the subject property and comparable properties may reflect that the rent level has been constant over the last five years. In this case, the appraiser can assume that the rent level will stay constant for at least the next five years. After that point, the market rent may decline as the building ages and nears the end of its projected economic life.

The assumption that at some point in time market rents will decline is logical, even if the initial forecast shows an increase in market rent. The structure will age, and all economic and demographic factors affecting the property will not remain stable for the remaining economic life of the property. As the building ages, less will be offered for its space because its floor plan and design are less popular (an example of functional obsolescence). Furthermore, as the subject property ages, the adjacent structures in the neighborhood also age. This economic obsolescence of neighborhood features and services reinforces the inevitability of declining market rent in the later years of the property's economic life in its current use. The phrase "in its current use" is important because it indicates that the property is not improved, rehabilitated, or renovated. If capital improvements are made, the building is in a different market after the rehabilitation and enters another period of economic life in the new use.

FORECASTING FUTURE LEVELS OF OPERATING EXPENSES

The appraiser must also forecast future levels of operating expenses. In the majority of cases, the appraiser can rely on published data to obtain a reasonable estimate of what happens to various operating expense items as the building ages. The appraiser can apply this information as a first step in forecasting future levels of expense items, starting with the current year's figures as the base. For example, as the building ages, the expenditures for maintenance and repair on a per-unit basis increase if the owner is attempting to keep the structure in good condition.

However, the data available from published sources may not be adequate unless past trends can be determined. For example, payments for utilities, property tax, and insurance will have increased steadily for several years. Therefore, the appraiser can reasonably assume that utility costs will continue to rise in the near future at a rate that is comparable to their increase in the last three or four years. Insurance rates will have been steadily rising as the cost to reconstruct the improvement continues to rise. Thus, a good proxy for changes in the insurance payment would be an extrapolation into the future of changes in building material and construction labor costs over the previous three or four years.

A projection of property tax payments is more difficult to make because of the apparent trend to shift the revenue-generating structure of local government away from real property taxes to taxes such as an income tax or a sales tax. In addition, future levels of property taxes are difficult to predict because of the movements to put a ceiling on local governmental budgets. If such actions are likely or have already been taken in the local community of the subject property, the appraiser can assume that the current property tax bill will not be exceeded in the future, and that the future property tax bill for the subject property may decline. If the local community has established a ceiling for the property tax bill as some percentage of the property's market value, the appraiser can assume that the property tax payment will in some way reflect the path of potential gross income.

Exhibit 6.6 (introduced earlier) shows the potential gross income, effective gross income, and net operating income pattern generated for a hypothetical subject property over a six-year ownership period. It serves as a basis for the following discussion of the yield capitalization process. The underlying assumptions used to generate the figures in Exhibit 6.6 are as follows:

1. Market conditions are such that market rent will rise over the initial six years of the economic life of the property and then level off in the later years. The rent on two-bedroom units will increase by 3.5 percent, while the rent for one-bedroom units will increase by 2.5 percent per year.

2. Vacancy losses for the subject property will always reflect the rate comparable to that of similar properties in the market. The vacancy rate is 3.5 percent for each year into the future.

3. All operating expense items will increase over time at a rate of 2 percent, except that property taxes will grow by 3.5 percent and maintenance and repair expenditures will grow by 3 percent per year.

ESTIMATING MARKET VALUE

The estimation of market value by the yield capitalization technique starts with the generation of the rent revenue. Exhibit 6.6 will be used as the example here. For the 14 two-bedroom units, the current market rent is $525 per month per unit, which generates $88,200 per year. This rent level is expected to increase by 3.5 percent per year, so the rent revenue in the second year is $88,200 times 1.035, which equals $91,287. Successive years are handled in the same way. For the 10 one-bedroom units, the current market rent is $425 per month per unit, which generates $51,000 per year. This rent level is expected to increase by 2.5 percent per year, so the rent revenue in the second year is $51,000 times 1.025, which equals $52,275. Successive years are handled in the same way.

For simplicity sake, the revenues from parking fees and laundry room collections are held constant over time. The vacancy rate is also being held constant over time at 3.5 percent.

Given the changes in rent revenue, the level of effective gross income increases from $140,523 in the first year to $144,733 in the second year and $162,965 in the sixth year.

Operating expenses change by the specific rates shown above. Property taxes increase by 3.5 percent, from $6,400 in the first year to $6,624 in the second year and $7,601 in the sixth year. Maintenance and repair expenditures increase by 3 percent, from \$9,400 in the first year to \$9,682 in the second year and \$10,897 in the sixth year. All of the other operating expenses change by 2 percent per year.

Based on these changes in operating expenses and the changes in effective gross income, NOI increases from \$82,931 in the first year to \$85,684 in the second year and \$97,689 in the sixth year. Using the capitalization rate of 8 percent calculated previously, the value from yield capitalization can now be determined. However, several major factors are handled in yield capitalization that were not a part of direct capitalization.

TERMINAL CAPITALIZATION RATE

The initial capitalization rate for the direct capitalization technique is a rate that is used at the time the analysis is undertaken. It is a rate that is applicable to the initial year. However, in yield capitalization, the capitalization rate is applied several years in the future. In the case shown in Exhibit 6.6, it is in the sixth year, which is the last explicit year in the cash flow statement. The capitalization rate is referred to as the **terminal capitalization rate** when it is applied in this last year.

The terminal capitalization rate differs from the initial period capitalization rate in magnitude because of risk arising from uncertainty about the future circumstances that can affect the property. The appraiser is quite certain about current rents and operating expenses. However, as time passes, the judgments made about the change in rents and operating expenses displayed in Exhibit 6.6 become more uncertain. This uncertainty increases risk, and this increased risk is reflected in the terminal capitalization rate as an increase in the rate. If the appraiser knew with absolute certainty that the market and financial circumstances in the sixth year would be the same as they are in the current year, then the initial and the terminal capitalization rates would be the same at 8 percent.

CAPITALIZED VALUE OF THE LAST EXPLICIT NOI

In yield capitalization, the next step after the generation of the explicit cash flows is to use the last of these cash flows to estimate the value of all future NOI beyond the last explicit NOI; in this example, the last explicit cash flow is the sixth year. At this point, the appraiser applies direct capitalization to that last NOI. The implicit assumption is that the remaining economic life is a relatively long period of time, such as 25 or more years.

CALCULATING THE PRESENT VALUE OF CASH FLOWS
AND THE CAPITALIZED VALUE OF THE LAST EXPLICIT NOI

Exhibit 6.7 shows the calculation procedure used to determine the market value estimate for the property. The inputs into the analysis are the initial capitalization rate at 8 percent, the adjustment of 0.75 percent for uncertainty, and the terminal capitalization rate of 8.75 percent, which is the sum of these two figures. The cash flow of \$97,689 in the sixth year is divided by the terminal capitalization rate, which gives \$1,116,449.

The other input is the **discounting interest rate,** or simply the *discount rate,* which the appraiser views as the rate of return the typical investor would like to obtain from a real property investment. The conceptual components of the discount rate are as follows:

EXHIBIT 6.7 Market value by yield capitalization.

		Desired	Portion			
Initial Period Cap. Rate			8.00%			
Risk Adjustment			0.75%			
Terminal Cap. Rate			8.75%			
		Desired	Portion			
		Rate of Return				
Debt Position		9.00%	80%			
Equity Position		14.00%	20%			
Discount Rate		10.00%				
	Year	NOI	Capitalized Value	Cash Flow	Present Value	Present Value Cash Flows
	1	$ 82,931		$ 82,931	0.9091	$ 75,392
	2	$ 85,684		$ 85,684	0.8264	$ 70,814
	3	$ 88,533		$ 88,533	0.7513	$ 66,516
	4	$ 91,482		$ 91,482	0.6830	$ 62,483
	5	$ 94,532	1,116,449	$ 1,210,982	0.6209	$ 751,924
	6	$ 97,689				
Market Value Estimate						$ 1,027,130

1. A "pure" rate of return that reflects the delay of consumption (It is usually considered to be the rate of return on a safe, risk-free investment, such as a U.S. government bond or a federally insured passbook account.)

2. A risk premium to compensate the typical investor for the uncertainty associated with real estate investment (This topic will be discussed in Chapter 11.)

3. A premium for factors associated with real estate investment that are not associated with a safe, riskless investment—for example, illiquidity of the investment, financial management of investment, and asset acquisition costs, including transactions costs and search and information gathering costs

4. A premium for expected inflation rates[2]

For example, if the safe rate on U.S. government bonds is 5 percent, the expected rate of inflation into the future is 2 percent, the investors' perception of risk is 2 percent, and the additional premium for the nonrisk factors is 1 percent, the discount rate is the sum of these items, 10 percent.

The numerical value of the discount rate changes with changes in the property market, the financial markets, and the participant's perception of risk. Several such changes are discussed below:

1. As the economic conditions in a specific property market area under analysis change, the subject property in that market is subjected to variation in market rents over time. For example, the current market rent in the apartment market is $525 for two-bedroom apartments. In the future, new comparable units will be built to

accommodate a growing population. The uncertainty, and thereby the risk, is higher in this market than it is for an apartment market that will have a stable supply of units and a stable population that desires these units. The instability and the uncertainty would carry a higher risk. In the financial market, this risk would be reflected in a higher mortgage interest rate on the loan to buy the apartment complex and a higher expected rate of return for the investors (known as the *intraproperty market effect*).

2. If the subject property were an office building in the same market area as the apartment project, but office buildings had higher vacancy levels and less predictable space absorption of new space, the risk for the office property type would be higher than it is for apartment projects. Here the discount rate would also be greater for the office market, reflecting the added risk (known as the *interproperty market effect*).

3. In most instances, a property is bought when a buyer and a lender participate in the acquisition of the property. The lender wants the loan repaid and expects a return on the loan in the form of the mortgage interest payment. The property is security for the repayment of the loan even if the borrower defaults on the loan. The buyer wants to have his down payment returned as well as a rate of return on the money invested in the property that is greater than the mortgage interest rate. However, there is no guarantee or safety net for the buyer. If the future value of the property declines, the buyer loses the return on the investment. If the future value of the property declines far enough, the buyer loses not only the return on the investment but also may lose some or all of the down payment. The risk is greater for the equity investor than it is for the lender.

If the appraiser does not use this intuitive summation process to establish directly a numerical value for the expected rate of return, how is a numerical value determined? The answer depends on the appraiser's understanding of the property market in which this type of property is sold and of the financial market, which provides debt and equity funds to acquire the property. From discussions with clients and colleagues, the appraiser can obtain information about the anticipated rates of return and the actual rates of return that typical investors have received from similar investments. From the financial community, the appraiser can get information on mortgage interest rates and the loan-to-value ratio that the lenders are using. Such information might show that most investors in this class of property are receiving between 14 and 16 percent on their investments, and most lenders are receiving between 8 and 9 percent on their loans. Therefore, the appraiser can deduce that the appropriate discount rate is 12 percent.[3]

The first column of Exhibit 6.7 shows the years. The second column shows the NOIs taken from Exhibit 6.6. The third column shows the result from the direct capitalization of the sixth year's NOI by the terminal capitalization rate. The fourth column is the sum of columns two and three. The fifth column displays the **present value factors** at the discount rate of 10 percent. These present value factors are calculated by simple division. For the first year $(1/1.10) = 0.90909$. The common sense of this calculation is that a dollar to be received a year from now is worth only 91 cents today at an interest rate of 10 percent. For year two, the present value factor is $(0.90909/1.10) = 0.82645$. The present value factors for the remaining years are calculated by continuing the process. For year three, the present value factor is $(0.82645/1.10) = 0.75131$.

The right-hand column shows the present value of the cash flows. It is the product of the annual cash flow in each of the years 1 through 4 and the annual cash flow in year

5 plus the capitalized value derived from the NOI in the sixth year. The sum of this column, $1,027,130, is the market value estimate by this first form of yield capitalization.

Additional Considerations in Estimating the Discount Rate

In the simple procedure, the loan/sales price ratio, the equity/sales price ratio, the interest rate on the loan, and the investor's expected rate of return on the investment are used in calculating the discount rate. However, the typical investor also considers other factors. First, the investor would be concerned about the maturity date of the mortgage loan. If $50,000 were borrowed at a rate of 10 percent for 40 years, the monthly repayment of this loan would be less than the monthly payment required to pay back a loan of $50,000 at 10 percent for 10 years. Consequently, the length of the mortgage loan is an important consideration for the investor because it affects the size of the monthly mortgage payment.

Second, the investor would be concerned with the fact that over time the equity/sales price ratio increases as the mortgage loan is paid off. Assume, for example, that the buyer invests 10 percent of the value of the property on the day of purchase; over time, as the mortgage loan is paid off, the owner's funds account for more than 10 percent of the original sales price. The investor's equity increases because the principal of the loan is being paid off. In a sense, the investor is investing additional equity funds in the property. The simple discount rate estimation technique ignores this phenomena of increasing equity caused by mortgage loan payment. Hence, the discount interest rate is understated, and the value of the property is overstated.

A related matter of concern to the investor is that this equity increase caused by the mortgage repayment is taking place at the mortgage rate of interest and not the investor's expected rate of return. In other words, instead of receiving 16 percent as a return on the increase in equity, the investor receives only a 10-percent return.

Another factor that the typical investor considers is the length of time that property will be held. The simple technique does not consider this point. However, it is an important consideration to the investor because the length of ownership of the investment determines the amount of equity increase caused by mortgage repayment. If the investor holds the property for 10 years instead of 5 years, the investor's equity increase is greater.

Multiplier Concepts Revisited

The GRM and the GIM were discussed in the first major section of this chapter. In addition to these multipliers, the appraiser can employ the potential gross income multiplier (PGIM), the effective gross income multiplier (EGIM), and the net income multiplier (NIM). Consider Exhibit 6.6 as the income and expense statement for a sales comparable property that sold recently for $980,000. The PGIM would be the sales price of $980,000 divided by the total revenue. It would be $980,000/$145,620 = 6.73. The EGIM would be the sales price of $980,000 divided by the effective gross income. The EGIM would be $980,000/$139,795 = 7.01. The NIM is simply the sales price divided by the net operating income. It is $980,000/ $82,203 = 11.92.

These multipliers can be used by the appraiser in the same manner as the GRM and GIM. Sales comparable properties are used to calculate the multiplier, which is multiplied by an estimate of market rent to obtain an estimate of the value of the subject property.

This chapter explains the three procedures used by the appraiser to estimate a current market value for income-earning real estate. The GRM technique relies on the use of sales comparable properties to obtain the GRM estimate and rent comparable properties to obtain the estimate of market rent. These two terms are multiplied to get the value estimate.

Direct capitalization and yield capitalization rely on the market rent capabilities of the property both in the current period and in the future. The level of current and future vacancy losses must be estimated. The appraiser must identify the operating expenses of the property and estimate changes in these expenses over time. Then, the appraiser obtains an estimate of net operating income for each year in that property's remaining economic life.

After generating these net operating income figures, the appraiser establishes the capitalization rate and the discounting interest rate that will be used to determine the present value of the future stream of NOI. The capitalization rate is a composite of many factors that reflect typical property market situations and typical financial market situations. Once the capitalization rate is obtained, it is used in direct capitalization to establish the market value of the property as well as in yield capitalization to capitalize the NOI in the last year of the cash flow statement. Once the discount rate is obtained, it is used to established the present value of the future stream of NOI and the capitalized last period NOI. Based on the principle of anticipation, the current market value of the property is equal to the present value of the stream of future benefits.

Internet Applications

A website has been established for this chapter at http://epley.swcollege.com.

Review Questions

1. Distinguish between market rent and contract rent. How is potential gross income determined?

2. Explain the nature and purpose of the appraiser's view of operating expenses. Identify and discuss the several categories of operating expenses.

3. Identify the expense items that are not included on the appraiser's operating expense statement.

4. Identify the components of the capitalization rate, and discuss the technique by which each of these components can be calculated.

5. Explain how the appraiser uses revenues, operating expenses, and the capitalization rate to make an estimate of the current market value for an income-earning property.

6. Identify the shortcomings of the simple band-of-investment technique by explaining the factors that more sophisticated techniques consider in the process of deriving the capitalization rate.

Discussion Questions

1. Differentiate between capital improvement expenditures and reserves for replacement.

2. Discuss the impact of rising energy costs on the market value of income-earning property. First assume that revenues do not increase while energy costs rise; then assume that rent revenues increase at a rate that is greater than the increase in the energy costs.

3. Analyze and comment on the following statement: It does not matter whether the appraiser is accurate in making projections of income and operating expenses for the last years of the property's economic life; what matters is that the projections made for the first decade are accurate.

Problems

1. Consider the analysis of the GRM in Exhibit 6.1. Calculate the monthly GRM and the annual GRM for the following comparable properties containing 200 units each.

Comparable Property	Sales Price	NOI
#1	$14,000,000	$1,440,000
#2	$14,500,000	$1,520,000
#3	$14,900,000	$1,600,000
#4	$15,000,000	$1,650,000

2. Using Exhibit 6.6, focus on the initial year of the analysis. Use the direct capitalization technique to estimate current market value under the changes shown for the following scenarios:

Cash Flow Items	Scenario #1	Scenario #2	Scenario #3
Rent for two-bedroom units	$550	$600	$625
Vacancy rate	3%	5%	5.25%
Management fee	8%	9%	10%
Property tax	$8,000	$10,000	$16,000
Maintenance and repair	$11,000	$14,000	$20,000
Utilities	$4,000	$5,000	$7,000
Capitalization rate	8.25%	8.4%	9%

3. Consider Exhibit 6.7. What happens to the market value estimate under the changes shown for the following scenarios?

Item	Scenario #1	Scenario #2	Scenario #3
Initial Period Cap. Rate	8%	8%	9%
Risk Adjustment	0.5%	0.5%	0.6%
Discount Rate	11%	9%	9.75%

1. The use of market rent or contract rent in the valuation process is a more complex consideration than is stated in this paragraph. If you are interested in this topic, check an appraisal methodology text for the discussion of valuing a fee simple versus a leased fee.

2. An expanded discussion of the discount rate is contained in the following material. Every investor realizes that there are certain types of investment for which there is very little risk of losing all or even part of the invested funds. Two such investments are government bonds and savings accounts in insured savings and loan associations and commercial banks. The federal government provides the ultimate backing for both of these safe, virtually riskless savings opportunities. Government bonds are considered safe because the federal government's power to tax and thereby raise revenues insures that it will not become bankrupt. Deposits in insured savings accounts are backed by two agencies of the federal government, the Federal Deposit Insurance Corporation (FDIC) and the Federal Savings and Loan Insurance Corporation (FSLIC). Each of these safe investments pays a return to the saver in the form of an interest payment. The interest payment on these riskless or safe investments forms the lower limit of the typical investor's expected rate of return. As an example, assume that government bonds are paying a higher rate than savings accounts, and that the rate is 6 percent per year.

The Safe Rate and the Risk Premium

A typical investor who places accumulated savings into a real estate investment would expect to receive a rate of return that is at least equal to the interest rate on a safe or riskless investment. However, real estate is not a safe or riskless investment. Therefore, some additional return must be generated to compensate for the risk of loss faced by the investor and future owner of the property. There are no guarantees that in two, three, or five years the property can be sold for an amount of money equal to its current sales price. There are no guarantees that the gross effective income generated by the property will continue at its current level. How much does the typical investor require to compensate for such risk? Evaluation of this risk is highly subjective and may vary greatly from one investor to another. The appraiser, however, must recognize the importance of such risk and must obtain some intuitive understanding of its magnitude for the type of property being appraised.

The Illiquidity Premium

The investor who fully considers the real estate market must also evaluate the economic characteristics of the real estate commodity. First, the typical well-informed investor realizes that, unlike the government or the savings account, real estate cannot be converted into cash quickly. In other words, it is not a liquid asset. Real estate is a very illiquid asset. A long period of time usually is required to convert real estate investments into cash without taking a loss in the value of the investment. A government bond can be converted into cash in several business days. A "day-to-day" savings account in a savings and loan association can be converted into cash within a matter of hours. In the case of a long-term savings certificate, the investor may lose an interest payment in order to convert the certificate into cash but does not suffer any loss in the value of the investment.

At most, it may take 30 days to turn such a long-term savings account into cash. However, in the case of real estate, it may take several months to convert the property into cash. The typical investor in real estate therefore requires an additional return over the safe rate to compensate for the loss of liquidity.

The Administrative/Management Return

The next factor that the investor recognizes is that a real estate investment requires a certain degree of management that a government bond or savings account does not. Someone must make the disbursements associated with the various categories of operating expenses. Utility bills, tax bills, repair bills, and salaries must be paid. In many cases, an account must be established to hold funds for replacing fixtures and major components of the structure. Someone must maintain the financial records associated with the property. All these activities are time-consuming tasks. They can be performed by the owner or by a property manager. In either case, the owner incurs an additional expense. Time must be devoted to this activity, or money must be paid to hire the services of a property manager. The appraiser can estimate the compensation required by the typical investor for the burden of management associated with real estate. Property management companies charge a percentage of the property's gross income. The appraiser can use these management fees as a proxy for the premium that the typical investor would expect as compensation for the extra burden associated with investment in real estate. The management fee depends on the type of property and the volume of services that the property owner requests.

The preceding numerical example indicates how the investor could decide upon an expected rate of return, which is the sum of the interest payment on the safe riskless investment plus the risk premium, plus the illiquidity premium, plus the percentage of gross income established as the management fee. However, the subjectivity associated with determining the risk of loss and the illiquidity premium makes this summation process an unacceptable technique for an appraiser to use to calculate the investor's expected rate of return.

3. The appraiser could use a weighted average of the expected rates of return for the lender and the investor. If the lender loans 80 percent of the sales price and desires a 9-percent rate of return, and if the investor puts up 20 percent as the down payment and desires a 14-percent rate of return, the discount rate is obtained from the following weighted average calculation:

$$(80\%)(9\%) + (20\%)(14\%) = 0.072 + 0.028 + 0.10 = 10\%$$

Real Estate Market Analysis

1. How is a market analysis conducted?

2. What are the major elements of a market analysis?

3. What is a marketability study?

4. What are the major elements of a marketability study?

When finished with this chapter, the student should be able to:

1. Identify the nature and major elements of a market study.

2. Describe the nature of the market analysis process.

3. Discuss the concept of linkages.

4. Describe the survey of competition.

5. Describe the nature and components of a marketability study.

construction cost study	market analysis
convenience goods	market disaggregation
cumulative attraction	market segmentation
design study	market value impact study
economic impact study	marketability analysis
financial feasibility study	operating cost study
fiscal impact study	product differentiation
infrastructure impact study	psychographic factors
location inducement and incentive study	rehabilitation cost study
location study	survey of the competition

INTRODUCTION

Chapter 3 introduced local economic analysis as a way to analyze and identify the economic vitality of a metropolitan area. The analysis of historic employment trends and a forecast of the future changes in employment were the prime economic issues of concern. The local economic study leads to a conclusion as to whether the metropolitan area has grown in the past and whether it will grow in the future. Growth is based on an increase in the number of jobs offered by the businesses in the area.

This chapter focuses on two other studies that relate to local economic analysis but are substantively different because they focus on more narrowly defined concepts. These studies are the market analysis and the marketability analysis.

What Are Market and Marketability Studies?

A **market analysis** examines the demand and supply factors that affect the market for a specific type of real estate, such as single-family housing units or retail space in a specific geographic area. A market analysis can be performed at various levels of product and spatial aggregation. For example, a highly aggregated residential market analysis is a market study for housing units in a metropolitan area. There is no distinction among the various types of housing units, such as single-family detached, single-family attached, or multifamily. Nor is there any distinction among the various areas or neighborhoods in the metropolitan area. At the other end of the spectrum, a market analysis can be highly disaggregated for the product type and the geographic area. An example of a highly disaggregated study is a market analysis of two-story, brick veneer, traditionally styled single-family detached housing in the Fairhaven neighborhood in the northeast sector of the metropolitan area.

A market analysis is a research project that obtains facts about the demand and the supply for that product type in the specified geographic market area. A very important supply-side component of the market study is an estimate of the activity of the competition. How many similar projects are in existence or under construction? Are any competitors ready to initiate a similar project? How does the subject property compare with one that is being placed on the market by the competition? A market analysis can be used to answer these types of questions focusing on the supply side of the market.

The supply side of the market analysis is the **survey of the competition,** which identifies the major financial, site, structural, and locational characteristics of the existing competitive properties and the competitive properties that are currently under construction or in the planning stage. If the subject of the market analysis is new multifamily housing projects of 250 or more units, then the survey of the competition includes all existing new and relatively new multifamily housing projects of substantial size. If the subject of the competition is a new neighborhood shopping center anchored by a supermarket, then the survey of competition focuses on all of the other existing and to-be-built neighborhood shopping centers containing a supermarket.

The demand side of the analysis consists of an identification of the consumers and their ability to acquire the real estate commodity. It is a measure of the effective demand for the real estate commodity. The effective demand is different for each major type of real estate commodity. Residential housing demand is a function of households and household income. Retail space demand is a function of population and per capita disposable income. Office space demand is a function of the number of office workers requiring work space.

The demand side of a market study is a research effort to determine whether there are enough customers of the product or service provided on the property to generate an income stream that meets the investor's financial goals. This study is used to measure the demand for the product or service and to delineate a geographic market area. It is used to project market prices or market rent and to determine the quantity, quality, and duration of the income stream for the property, its tenants, or both. Quantity is the magnitude of the potential income stream. Quality is related to the nature of the flow—that is, to the financial position of the tenants renting the space and to the capabilities of the management to obtain leases and to keep down operating expenses. The duration of the income flow is the length of time that the necessary level of income is expected to be generated. More specifically, it is a measure of the economic life of the investment.

A **marketability analysis** is a market analysis directed to a specific site. For example, a market analysis for additional retail space in the northeast sector of the metropolitan area can reveal that the population will support additional retail space. However, the marketability analysis asks the next question. What is the best site in that geographic market area to put the additional space? Is the best site at the intersection of Main Street and Broad Avenue, or is it two miles east at the intersection of Sycamore Street and Broad Avenue?

THE ORIENTATION OF THE STUDIES

The first step in structuring a market analysis and a financial study is to define the orientation of the study. The analyst must identify the starting assumptions and the limiting conditions involved in the study. The analyst must ascertain whether the analytical task at hand is:

1. A site or a building in search of a user
2. A user in search of a site and certain improvements
3. An investor looking for an involvement in either of the first two situations

By making this distinction, the analyst can establish the logical starting point for the study and thereby eliminate many unnecessary considerations. For example, a site in search of a use may involve an analysis of the residential market and the retail market that the site could serve. Here, two product types in the same geographic market are analyzed. A retail user in search of a site focuses on product type but may require an analysis of multiple sites in multiple market areas. This analysis could be limited to a single metropolitan area, or it could have regional, national, and even global considerations. An investor looking for an opportunity focuses on all of the above.

A market analysis and marketability analysis can provide the answers to the following five basic questions.

1. What price will the market support for the space being provided? In other words, what is the market rent for the space in the property?

2. What is the optimum size and type of structure for the use involved in the property? The analyst examines the issue of building a new structure, remodeling an existing structure, or renting space in an existing structure.

3. What level of amenities and services should be provided in the structure? The analyst evaluates the size and quality of construction, fixtures placed within the structure, parking space requirements, transportation and access requirements, utility requirements, and any other special features that may be appropriate.

4. When should the structure be built, rented, or remodeled? The analyst could recommend that new space is needed immediately, that space should be rented for a period of time to build cash flow, or that remodeling is the best alternative.

5. Where should the building be located? The answer to this question depends on the transportation needs, the location of competitors, the growth of the market area in geographic and economic terms, and any special financial circumstances, either current or anticipated.

A financial study can provide the answers to the following basic questions.

1. What is the anticipated range of return that the investment will generate? Estimates can be derived showing the return on the investment at various levels of income and expenses; various economic circumstances in the local, regional, and national economy; and various individual tax considerations.

2. How does the return generated by the property compare to the investor's required rate of return? Should the investor make this investment?

What Other Types of Studies are Performed?

There are many other studies that a real estate market analyst can perform. These studies are typically performed as separate studies. However, they can be linked to a market analysis or a marketability analysis. Some of these studies are presented below.

THE FINANCIAL FEASIBILITY STUDY

A **financial study** is an analysis of all pertinent facts and variables to show whether a project, either proposed or existing, will allow all parties involved to accomplish their investment objectives. A financial study requires gathering all relevant economic and financial information and putting these data together in a logical form to reach a conclusion about risk. If the project is deemed *feasible,* this means that the risk can be reasonably assumed and that the investor's objectives can be reasonably fulfilled.

The financial study is a combination of a marketability analysis and an investment analysis represented in a cash flow statement, such as the one shown previously in Exhibit 6.1. The market analysis and marketability analysis generate information to form potential gross income and vacancy and thereby the effective gross income. The market analysis and marketability analysis can also generate information about some of the operating expenses, such as property taxes and labor costs for repairs and maintenance. The investment analysis takes the analysis further by calculating the various performance and profitability ratios and the measures of investment yields (which will be discussed in Chapter 11).

The next step in the financial study is a comparison of the investor's financial requirements to the financial returns generated by the property given the current and future conditions in the product market. The analysis views the property from the standpoint of a client to determine whether the client's objectives can be satisfied, and it includes a recommendation to the client that covers the potential success or failure of the project. In other words, the investor wants a 12-percent annual return on the investment, while the investment property may generate a financial yield of 10 percent. In this situation, the investment is not financially feasible for this investor. However, if a second investor only needs a 10-percent return because she is more of a risk taker, this investment would be financially feasible for that investor.

LOCATION STUDY

A **location study** is an attempt to locate all possible sites that will satisfy the needs of the project. The analyst must ascertain the minimum physical on- and off-site requirements of the project—for example, topography, drainage, transport access, open space for parking, transportation facilities for the shipment of materials, and perhaps open space for visibility to enhance market appeal. All possible sites within the geographic area that have these characteristics are identified. Then, a market analysis is done for each of the potential sites. Finally, the financial features of each site are compared with the funds allocated to purchase the land. The investors are attempting to decide the best location in relation to the funds available for land acquisition.

DESIGN STUDY

A **design study** examines the impact of site and structural features on revenues and operating cost of the property. The study examines the impact on revenues and costs of different structural designs, floor plans, building heights, exterior surface materials, interior finishes, and density of construction on the site. The end result of the study is a determination of the structural design and building lot layout that will best meet the client's financial objectives.

CONSTRUCTION COST STUDY

A **construction cost study** (or **rehabilitation cost study**) can be used to obtain an estimate of the construction (or rehabilitation) costs for a structure designed to satisfy the needs of the user. The analyst examines all of the possibilities allowed by the zoning ordinance and subdivision regulations for minimum building requirements as well as the types of building materials and specifications that will satisfy those requirements.

The cost estimates of each are evaluated against the income and operating expense projections to determine whether investment objectives can be met.

OPERATING COST STUDY

In an **operating cost study,** the analyst examines the operating costs of a proposed or existing structure to determine whether operating expenses can be reduced. A questionable proposed project may be made feasible through such cost reduction even if revenue is stable. Topics of analysis could be the extent to which utilities are provided by the landlord, the use of maintenance and supervisory personnel, the level of maintenance and repair, and special business practices, such as inventory policies and distribution arrangements to customers. In addition, different financing techniques and practices can affect the debt service payment by reducing the interest expenses.

MARKET VALUE IMPACT STUDY

The **market value impact study** determines the potential impact of a commercial or industrial facility on the market value of real property in a specifically defined geographic area or a local community. The study answers the following question. What will it do to market values of real property in this neighborhood or the geographic area in close proximity to the facility or firm? The study is designed to accomplish the following tasks:

- Identify the characteristics and attributes of the facility that is the subject property
- Identify comparable properties and analyze their location attributes in the community in which they exist
- Analyze the impact of the comparable facilities on the property values in their respective communities

The results of this study are an estimate of the net economic costs or benefits that can accrue to the property owners from the operation of the corporate facility, and information that can be used in a public relations campaign in the local community to overcome negative impressions about the facility.

LOCATION INDUCEMENT AND INCENTIVE STUDY

The **location inducement and incentive study** determines types and conditions of community programs available to defray costs or provide other assistance in developing corporate facilities. The study is designed to identify and evaluate the following:

- Types of financial assistance programs provided by the community
- Any tax incentive or tax abatement programs
- Land and space acquisition or provision programs
- Labor force training programs
- Programs that provide incentives or assistance in achieving or complying with pollution or environmental controls

This study produces information about potential benefits of economic development programs designed to attract industry and employment to a community. This information can be used as a differential input to the financial feasibility study for each community under consideration.

ECONOMIC IMPACT STUDY

The **economic impact study** initially determines the increase in total jobs and total income generated by the operation of the facility in the community. Then, it can allocate the increase in total income to the local retail activity and estimate the effect of the increased employment on the demand for housing. The study is designed to do the following:

- Analyze the direct employment at the facility during construction and operation
- Estimate the magnitude of the local economy's multiplier
- Calculate the total change in local employment and income
- Determine the percentage of the household budget spent on various categories of retail goods and services
- Determine the impact on the demand for additional housing units and the impact on existing vacancies in the housing market

The results of the study include an estimate of the economic benefits that can accrue to the local economy from the operation of the corporate facility, and generation of information that can be used in a public relations campaign in the local community to overcome negative impressions about the facility.

FISCAL IMPACT STUDY

The **fiscal impact study** determines both the increase in property tax revenues generated by the facility for the local jurisdiction(s) in which it is located and the increase in public service costs generated by the facility for the local jurisdiction. The study is designed to do the following:

- Analyze the historic and current tax assessment practices and the assessments on comparable properties
- Determine the current millage rate that would apply to the facility, and estimate its future levels
- Determine the use of public services and facilities by the corporation
- Calculate the direct net cost and benefit to the local jurisdiction's operating budget from the operation of the facility
- Calculate the indirect and induced net cost and benefit to the local jurisdiction's operating budget from the facility's effect on the housing stock and retail establishments

The study estimates the economic benefits that can accrue to the local economy from the operation of the corporate facility and generates information that can be used in a public relations campaign in the local community to overcome negative impressions about the facility.

INFRASTRUCTURE IMPACT STUDY

The **infrastructure impact study** determines the effects of a new production or office facility on the physical capacities and service levels of public services and facilities provided by the local government. The study is designed to accomplish the following tasks:

- Identify and describe types of public services and facilities available in the community and quantify the capacity of each

- Analyze operating conditions, standards, requirements, and excess capacity for each public service and facility
- Identify existing service level and expansion needs and costs for each public service or facility affected by the corporate facility

This study estimates the impact on service levels of existing public services and facilities and the amount of improvements and costs needed to meet the needs of the new corporate facility. It also generates information on impacts and potential benefits the new corporate facility will have on public services and facilities in the community to use as a public relations tool to overcome public concerns about negative impacts of the facility.

What Are the Components of the Market and Marketability Analyses?

The market analysis and marketability analysis process requires the completion of the major tasks listed below. Each of these topics can become a component of the market and marketability studies. However, the typical report also contains, and typically starts with, a discussion of the local economy that incorporates the concepts and ideas that were presented in Chapter 3.

1. Analysis of the legal and physical characteristics of the subject property
2. Market disaggregation
3. Market segmentation
4. Delineation of the area of competition
5. Survey of the competition
6. Location analysis—linkage pattern analysis
7. Consumer research
8. Demand analysis

Each of these major tasks will be discussed in general in the following subsections. Later in this chapter, the tasks will be related to specific property types.

ANALYSIS OF THE LEGAL AND PHYSICAL CHARACTERISTICS OF THE SUBJECT PROPERTY

The legal characteristics of the subject property that must be identified and analyzed have been discussed in greater detail in earlier chapters. At this point, these characteristics will simply be identified and briefly examined. The first concern of the market analyst is a determination of what activity is legally permissible on the subject property. To obtain information pertinent to this aspect of inquiry, the analyst must examine the following:

- Zoning ordinance—land use regulations, height regulations, and area regulations
- Zoning ordinance changes—rezoning applications and variances
- Construction code requirements
- Occupancy code requirements
- Environmental and pollution restrictions
- Availability of public services

When the analyst examines the various restrictions and requirements imposed by these ordinances and governmental activities, the legally permissible uses that can be placed on the subject site are identified. In addition to these restrictions and requirements, the local government can also impose other conditions that affect the land cost component of the project. The local government can require the developer of the property to contribute funds to pay for the construction of streets, water lines, sewer lines, new water treatment facilities, and new schools. These charges are known as *impact fees*. The local government can also require the developer of a large residential complex to set aside a portion of the acreage for the development of a park, a fire station, or a school. This process of contributing a portion of the property to the government to provide a public service is known as a *set aside*.

Once the legal restrictions are known, the analyst checks the physical restrictions imposed by the subject site. The factors that are analyzed in this section of the study are the following geographic and geological features of the site:

- Geographic features of the land, which include size, shape, frontage, width, depth, and corner influences
- Geological features of the site, which include topography, surface soil quality and landscaping, subsoil and bedrock characteristics, and drainage and runoff characteristics
- Physical characteristics of the improvement, which include the placement of the structure on the site, quantitative and qualitative construction details, an analysis of the mechanical systems in the improvement, and an analysis of the physical design and layout of the space within the improvement

These physical features associated with the site and the improvements on the site establish the second set of limiting requirements. Not only must the economic activity be legally permissible, but it also must be physically possible given the physical characteristics of the site and the improvement.

After the legal and physical characteristics of the subject property are analyzed, many potential uses are eliminated. The legally permissible and physically possible uses for the subject property can now be analyzed in greater detail to determine their financial feasibility. The following tasks are instrumental in making this determination.

MARKET DISAGGREGATION

In order to analyze a market for a specific type of real estate, that product must be defined. Real estate is not a standardized commodity; in other words, all real estate is not the same. The general term *real estate* incorporates residential, retail, office, industrial, and hotel and motel property. The first step to facilitate market analysis involves the selection of one of these broad types of real estate. Then, within this broad category, additional distinctions must be made. If the inspection of the subject property reveals that it is zoned as, and is physically suitable for, single-family residential real estate but not multifamily residential, the first logical distinction is made. When the specific site has been identified, the second distinction for location or neighborhood has been made. To make finer distinctions, the analyst can make distinctions based on physical characteristics of the site or structure. For example, distinctions can be made on the basis of new versus existing units, one-story versus two-story, large versus small, and brick versus frame. The end result of this refinement process is the identification of a relatively standardized commodity that is a distinct submarket under the general heading of residential real estate.

One submarket could be new, large, brick, two-story, single-family detached units in the Fairhaven subdivision in the northeast sector of the urban area. A second sub-market could be 5- to 10-year-old, small, frame, single-family detached units in the Fairhaven subdivision in the northeast sector of the urban area. A third submarket could be new, large, brick, two-story, single-family detached units in the Bellwood subdivision in the eastern sector of the urban area. The process of identifying a standardized submarket from a general, less standardized market is called **market disaggregation.**

Market analysis can occur at all levels of disaggregation. A developer might ask a real property market analyst to evaluate several metropolitan areas to determine the best local economy to enter with his type of residential unit. Another developer may already have selected a metropolitan area to enter but hires the analyst to evaluate the several different geographic submarkets to determine which one has the greatest demand for his type of product. A third developer might hire an analyst to determine what type of housing unit to build in a predetermined geographic submarket. These are all examples of highly aggregated studies. At the disaggregated end of the spectrum, a developer hires the analyst to determine the best geographic submarket to build new, 2,000-square-foot, two-story, traditionally styled, brick front, single-family units with a two-car attached garage on a small lot. This is a more disaggregated study.

MARKET SEGMENTATION

Market segmentation is the process of forming more standardized groups of con-sumers from a larger population. Demographic, economic, and psychographic characteristics of the population are used to form the various market segments. If age is selected as a segmentation variable, the population can be segmented into the under 21 group, the 21 to 29 group, the 30 to 45 group, and so forth. Size of the household can be selected as a segmentation variable, creating the segments of one person per house-hold, two people per household, and so forth. If income is selected as a segmentation variable, the population can be segmented into the less than $10,000 per capita income group, the $10,000 to $20,000 group, and so forth. These demographic and economic segmentation variables can be combined to form segments—for example, a 2-person household in the 30 to 45 age bracket with a household income exceeding $50,000. This market segment can be further segmented by psychographic factors. Consider lifestyle. This type of household can be found in certain areas of the inner city, such as the resi-dential areas of the central business district, and it can also be found in the suburbs. This is a lifestyle choice not reflected in the demographic or economic characteristics. Market segmentation can also occur for the customers of retail facilities, office space consumers, industrial and distribution space users, and hotel and motel patrons.

The significance of market segmentation is that it allows the analyst to match real estate product attributes to consumer attributes. Product disaggregates can be matched to market segments. Consider the large, expensive single-family house. Who buys such a house? Is it the young married couple with a low household income or the older, married couple with children and a relatively high household income? The latter market segment buys this type of housing unit. The market disaggregate is matched to a market segment.

DELINEATION OF THE AREA OF COMPETITION

The procedure needed to define the competitive trade area for any property type, such as housing or retail activity, has some common characteristics. First, the most appro-priate geographic area to analyze is the area that lies immediately adjacent to, or in close proximity to, the subject site. This geographic area has physical, locational, economic, and psychographic dimensions. From a physical perspective, this area may be readily identified by the analyst because of such natural barriers as rivers, ridgelines, mountains, and hills, and such man-made barriers as railroad tracks, expressways, and open space in the form of golf courses and parks.

From a locational perspective, the distance or the travel time might be too great for the consumer to travel. At its most basic level, consumer behavior is affected by the desire to minimize the inconvenience of travel. If the consumer can find the same thing at two different places, the consumer will go to the place that is closer in either distance or travel time, whichever is most important to the consumer. For the purchase of frequently used, routine items such as groceries and personal care products (known as **convenience goods**), the consumer typically chooses the closest of the alternative sites. For the purchase of goods or services that require a wide selection from which to choose (known as *shopping goods*), the consumer will travel farther than for convenience goods.

From a psychographic perspective, consumers will develop attitudes, habits, preferences, and tastes that affect their behavior. Consumers may prefer scenic routes to work or shopping rather than routes through less aesthetic industrial areas. Consumers like to accomplish several things with a single stop. For example, they want to drop off their dry cleaning and get a haircut in the same shopping center at which they buy their groceries. If they cannot accomplish this multipurpose, single-stop shopping, they organize their route to minimize the aggravation of the trip. For example, they may plan the route so that all turns are right-hand turns in and out of the various parking lots to avoid turning left across heavy traffic. Consumers also have preferences for certain trade names; a certain supermarket or department store is perceived to be better than others.

The spatial pattern of the subject property's competitors is also an important component in the delineation of the area of competition. If two identical neighborhood shopping centers containing supermarkets that are perceived by the consumer to be fully equivalent are located four miles apart along Main Street, where will the consumers located along Main Street shop? With the competitors being identical, the trade area will split the difference between the retail establishments. If Shopping Center A is perceived to be better than Shopping Center B, then consumers at the two-mile mark from Shopping Center B will no longer be indifferent and will more than likely decide to go to Shopping Center A. This might also occur for those consumers who live a mile and a half from Shopping Center B. The greater the difference between Shopping Centers A and B, the greater the incentive for consumers living close to B to travel to A. In the event that Shopping Center B is grossly inferior to Shopping Center A, consumers may drive by B to get to A.

The information to make the comparison between the subject property and each of its most proximate competitors is gathered during the survey of the competition.

SURVEY OF THE COMPETITION

When the survey of the competition is performed, as much information as possible is gathered about the competitors of the activity on the subject property. If the subject property is going to provide housing units, the market researcher must define the competitive geographic trade area and identify all of the comparable properties as well as all of the strong substitutes for the type of housing units on the subject property. If, on the other hand, the subject property is providing retail activities, the market researcher must identify the retail trade area and all of the direct competitors for the retail establishment located on the subject property.

In general, the structure of the information to be gathered in either the residential case or the retail case is quite similar. In either case, the information that should be gathered concerning the competitive and substitute establishments is shown in the classification system below:

1. Physical and functional characteristics of the structure, which include:

   - age and condition of the structure
   - special features, such as covered walkways, enclosed entryways, and location of the units within the structure
   - traffic patterns inside the structure
   - special characteristics that are viewed as attractive (this could include design features, floor layouts, positioning of window openings, lighting, carpeting, size of the individual units in terms of square footage as well as the type of space being provided for bedrooms, bathrooms, living room, and dining room)
   - special structural features, such as balconies, patios, and screen porches in residential units, and atriums, walkways, and rest areas in retail and office units

2. Amenities, which include:

   - parking features, such as the number of spaces, location of the parking facilities relative to the entrance of the structure, covered areas, and quality of the parking surface
   - security and safety factors

3. Accessibility features, which include:

   - proximity to employment centers, shopping facilities, and entertainment, recreational, and cultural activities
   - proximity to major streets and public transportation
   - proximity to fire and police stations, hospitals, and medical facilities
   - proximity to schools, especially if the subject property contains residential units

4. Financial characteristics, which include:

   - sales prices or rent levels for the space
   - special financial arrangements associated with the sale or rental of the space (could include price discounts, rent escalations, below-market rent rates, and the provision of special or supplementary fixtures and appliances)
   - special charges that may take place in the future (could include special assessments for public improvements, cost of living increases in rent levels, and so forth)
   - occupancy and vacancy levels
   - common area charges in regional malls

The market analyst must obtain as much of this information about the subject property and its competitors as possible given the time and money constraints that may be imposed. The end result of the analysis should be the construction of a table that allows the analyst to compare each establishment with regard to each characteristic identified in the previous discussion. This table is the starting point for the establishment of a market standard and the identification of a competitive differential for the subject property as well as a key element in the delineation of the area of the competition.

LOCATION ANALYSIS—LINKAGE PATTERN ANALYSIS

Location decisions by individual entities such as households are based on an interrelationship among different land users. Every household and business firm is a land user, and in their normal activity they relate to other households and businesses on other parcels of land or real property. This spatial relationship among land users is called a linkage. Location theory is an understanding of these linkages and their economic context.

The Concept of Linkages

Linkages (previously introduced in Chapter 4) are the spatial relationships that exist between different land users. The household (the user of residential land) maintains a link or a spatial relationship with an employer (an industrial or commercial land user). The household also has other links to schools, shopping, and so forth. In the case of a retail establishment, there are links between the commercial land user and the residential land users as customers. Households, as providers of labor services, represent another link. Office users often depend on both nearby households and nearby businesses to patronize the services provided in offices, thereby generating the demand for office space at a particular location.

These examples point out the economic nature of a linkage as well as its spatial relationship. A linkage also denotes the movement over space that is necessary to maintain the spatial relationship. The household must commute to work. The shopper must travel to the store.

Considerations in Evaluating Linkages

Three principal considerations are involved in analyzing the quality of a linkage on the development potential of a site: costs of friction, amenity, and convenience. Information gained from the analysis is used to make a locational decision and to select a site.

Costs of friction, or transfer costs, are travel costs that users of a site must incur to maintain the linkages identified. The first of these costs is the direct money or pecuniary costs of travel. These include the dollar costs of the following:

- The price of a vehicle allocated over its economic life
- Fuel
- Insurance
- Maintenance and repair
- License and inspection fees and taxes
- Parking
- Tolls and other user fees
- Public transportation fares
- Ad valorem or personal property tax on the vehicle
- Other direct costs of travel

Another consideration is the nonmoney costs of friction, which can be measured by identifying the value of time spent in traveling to complete the links. The value of time varies with the individual type of traveler and may be very expensive if considerable productive time is consumed in traveling. In other cases, such as transportation of school children, cost of travel time is relatively unimportant. Besides the relinquishing of leisure time spent traveling, however valued, the other basic nonpecuniary cost is the anxiety, aggravation, and frustration of encountering congestion and delays—often called distress costs. Although difficult to measure, these costs are very real concerns that must be taken into account. Proxies such as traffic volumes and operational characteristics are used to estimate the impact of these types of factors.

Site users attempt to minimize costs of friction in two ways. First, each user must identify the relative importance of each type of trip and establish a priority to determine when a trip for a singular purpose is necessary. Then, controlling the frequency of trips and combining trips can be accomplished to minimize costs. The relative importance of trips (or links) and the frequency with which each type of trip must be taken provide a major consideration in selecting a desirable location.

Each site user establishes a preference pattern for certain sets of amenities. These preferences are used by the land use decision maker to analyze the trade-offs and costs associated with the operation of a specific site. Some amenities, such as a panoramic view, are locationally specific, while others, such as architectural features, can be provided at almost any site.

Convenience is usually associated with the proximity, access, and visibility a site has relative to its surrounding features. It deals with the relative freedom of movement from off-site areas to on-site areas. Convenience is more important for such uses as retail facilities than for a house, for example, because of the number of site users who are affected and the capability of site users to go elsewhere if site visitation becomes inconvenient or problematic. Thus, the importance of convenience ranges from critical to minor depending on the use and the preferences and needs of the site user.

Residential Linkage and Location Theory

Residential location is a trade-off between the amenities and benefits to be derived from locating at a specific site and the costs of maintaining the linkage pattern the household desires at that site. Each household, be it a single-person household or a family, needs to have a job and a linkage to the site on which that job exists. The job provides an income. To earn that income, one or two members of that household must travel to the job site. Each household also desires a linkage to shopping opportunities, schools, recreation, entertainment, and other relationships deemed important to the household and its individual members. Each of these relationships exerts an influence on the location decision. Very often, they pull in different directions. The desire to minimize the cost of two adults commuting to two jobs every day may be counterbalanced by the desire to provide the children with high-quality education in close proximity to the home. In this situation, the household not only recognizes the linkages, but the members of the household have placed differential weights on the important of maintaining the linkages. The positive impact of proximity to the school has been given priority over the negative impact of the two commuting patterns.

Retail Linkage and Location Theory

Retail location is analyzed by considering the economic and spatial relationships of a retail establishment. For any site, a retail store must maintain a linkage with its customers who travel the linkage route(s) to get to the store. Like the commuter cost, the monetary and the nonmonetary shopping trip cost needs to be considered. For consumers living near the store, the costs of travel are minimal. At some distance or travel time from the store, the travel costs become high enough to deter the consumer from making the shopping trip. For this reason, retail establishments seek to locate close to their potential customers so that the costs of travel do not unnecessarily eliminate part of the population of potential customers. The linkage to the customers is a critical consideration in the retail location decision.

Retail establishments also require products to sell. So, the retail store must maintain a linkage to a set of distribution facilities that will ship the product to the store. In most instances, this linkage is not used extensively. A supermarket will receive daily (sometimes multiple) shipments of such perishable products as dairy products, seafood, meats, and produce. In most instances, the supermarket receives less frequent shipments of nonperishable products. Canned goods may come in once a day or a couple of times a week. A store selling pianos may get one shipment a month. With regard to the piano store's location decision, the cost to maintain this link between two different sites is not substantial, so it plays a very small role in the retail location decision.

A retail establishment also requires employees. In the past, labor services that could be readily used in retail stores were considered available everywhere. There was no shortage of qualified workers regardless of the location of the store. Today, in many metropolitan areas, labor services are not so readily available. As suburban growth continues in areas that do not have public transportation, retailers are faced with a shortage of labor. Residents in close proximity to the retail store are either employed elsewhere or have no interest in retail employment. Available labor generally lives in the central portion of the metropolitan area and has a very high commuter cost to get to the jobs in the suburbs. So, in some areas labor is not a significant variable in the retail location while in others labor plays a very important role.

Retail location is dominated by the need to service customers by being in close proximity and providing acceptable levels of service. Thus, the discovery of the site that minimizes the travel costs of the population of customers is critical. The retail establishment will seek the center of its market or trade area, with the hope of maintaining an adequate number of qualified employees.

An important element of retail location is the search for the benefits to be derived from **cumulative attraction.** Many retail establishments seek locations that are in close proximity to other retailers that sell similar products. Automobile dealerships are the classic example of this concept. Each dealer believes that its share of the potential customers coming to the "auto dealers row" will be greater as part of the group than it would be if the dealership is located away from all other auto dealers. Furniture stores also show a tendency to form such geographic clusters, but to a lesser extent. Cumulative attraction is a result of these clusters of products that a typical consumer wishes to inspect and compare. A product for which the consumer desires a variety from which to make a selection forms the clusters, which generate the benefits of increased customer traffic from cumulative attraction.

Food courts in shopping centers are another example of cumulative attraction. If shoppers are hungry and do not know exactly what they want, the aggregation of food dealers in a food court generates an attraction for the customer.

The principle of cumulative attraction is based on the economic concept of **product differentiation.** Products that are similar in many of their attributes are still viewed as different in the mind of the typical consumer. These differences can be imagined or perceived, or real, or they can involve conditions that surround the sale. In the example of the auto dealerships, consumers view many different cars as being generally the same. Fords, Chevrolets, and Plymouths are not much different, the consumer would say. But even while they believe this to be true, they still see differences among the three brand names. For one such consumer, the differences may be based on real facts about the production of the automobile. For another consumer, real differences may not exist but he believes that the differences do in fact exist. A third consumer may view the cars as interchangeable but consider the service department or sales personnel at one dealership as better than those at another dealership.

Office Linkage and Location Theory

Office location theory is an evaluation of the linkages to land users that facilitate and complement the proper and successful functioning of the office space user. Offices need to be linked to the residential choices for the upper management and the other employees in the firm. Upper management personnel desire good access to higher-valued housing options. Employees and middle managers need appropriately priced housing in locations suitable for them. Offices need to be linked to an employee pool that contains the skill set that the firm requires. The labor pool must have a good "general education" and be sufficiently large to serve the needs of the office market. In the past, a good general education was a high school diploma and an ability for the 3 Rs—reading, writing, and arithmetic—tied to the use of the typewriter. Today, "general education" means at least the same plus a fourth R for reasoning and the ability to use a word processor and a spreadsheet software package. For many firms, the ability to use a database management software program and a desktop publishing software program is also important.

Office space is also linked to customers if the firm serves the local market. This is true for local insurance sales offices, doctors' offices, lawyers' offices, real estate offices, and so forth. In this situation, minimizing the customers' travel time to the office is an important consideration. If the local firm serves a nonlocal market area—such as the state or the nation—then the linkage to modes of travel is important. A local firm serving the nation would require a very convenient linkage to an airport. A local firm serving a statewide market would require a linkage to a good highway system.

Office space also needs complementary land uses to serve the needs of office space users. Out-of-town visitors to the office space need hotels for overnight stays. Restaurants are needed as a place of doing business as well as a place for entertaining both local and out-of-town visitors.

Industrial Linkage and Location Theory

Industrial space users rely on linkages to material or input sources, output users, and employees. The linkage with employees is a linkage to a labor market area that has a sufficient supply of adequately skilled workers in demand by the firm. An industrial plant most likely requires personnel skilled in using tools and various types of machinery. Thus, a good technical education system in the area is important as a continued source of such skilled employees. The presence of other firms that have trained and use this type of worker is also an important consideration.

If the facility is an assembly plant, then the link to the source of inputs into the assembly line is important. The input provider should be linked to the assembly plant by a very dependable mode of transport so that the parts arrive as planned. The dependability is probably more important than the distance or travel time from the input provider. If the facility is a processing plant turning a raw material into a finished product, then the plant needs a dependable link to the source of the raw material. If the raw material input weighs more than the output, the plant might need to be located near the source of the raw material. On the other hand, if the raw material weighs less than the output or is less fragile or valuable than the output, then the firm could choose a site near its market area.

If the facility is a distribution facility, the firm will choose a location that allows it to receive bulk loads by truck or railroad and enough space to break down those bulk loads for shipping. If the shipment is within a local market area, then the site is centrally located, meaning it has good access to all parts of the market area. The central location could literally be the center of the market area, or it could be a location that is at a crossroads of major highways that allows good access to all parts of the market area. If the shipment goes to a specific region, the distribution facility is typically located at the intersection of major highways leading to the various regional markets.

CONSUMER RESEARCH

A market analysis may require specific information about the nature of the consumers in the area of competition. The demographic and economic characteristics of the group of consumers can be obtained from census data and from vendors of census-based data. However, if the attitudes, behaviors, habits, lifestyles, preferences, or tastes of the consumer (known as **psychographic factors**) are important determinants of the financial success of the real estate project, then primary data about the consumer needs to be obtained. This is accomplished by surveying the consumer. These psychographic factors may be inferred from economic and demographic data, but for enhanced accuracy, the consumers should be asked about these matters directly.

The data gathered in the survey of the competition identify the various characteristics of competitive and substitute properties. However, in an indirect fashion, the data gathered from the survey of the competition also identify consumer tastes and preferences. This information is obtained by checking the absorption rate of the units against the financial, structural, site, and neighborhood and location characteristics. Presumably, the dwelling units in the comparable properties that best satisfy consumer tastes and preferences will have the higher absorption rates, given the relative price of the property. So, the market analyst can start the process of creating a competitive differential by advising the client to design the subject property to include features that are at least as good as those in the properties with the highest historical absorption rates. In this way, the analyst can make the judgment that if consumer tastes and preferences are constant, or are at least highly similar, they will currently select those properties that have the same amenities as the properties with the high absorption rates.

However, information about consumer tastes, preferences, and attitudes taken from the survey of competition is indirect knowledge. The analyst infers present and future taste and preference patterns from past taste and preference patterns. Situations will occur in which the analyst will require direct knowledge about consumer attitudes, tastes, and preferences. As stated above, the only way this information can be obtained is through the process of *consumer research*, in which the analyst uses some form of surveying to go directly to the potential consumer and ask questions that will reveal the pertinent information about desirable characteristics and, in general, about the subject property.

DEMAND ANALYSIS

Once the analyst delineates the geographic area for the analysis, the demand for the space being offered to the market needs to be determined. The exact nature of the demand analysis depends on the type of space under analysis. The demand for residential space is estimated differently from the demand for retail and office space.

However, the first step in demand analysis is the determination of the space consumer. The second step is the determination of the need for the space, and the third step is the determination of the ability to obtain the space. A discussion of the nature of demand analysis for different property types appears in the following sections.

How Is Market Demand Analysis for Real Property Done?

In order to analyze a market for a specific type of real estate, that type of real estate must be defined. Real estate is not a standardized commodity; in other words, all real estate is not the same. The general term *real estate* incorporates residential, retail, office, industrial, and hotel and motel property. The process that is generally applicable for all market and marketability analyses includes the following steps.

1. The first step in all forms of market analysis is an understanding of the degree of *market disaggregation* that the client desires. If the market analysis is coupled with a marketability analysis, the degree of disaggregation is defined by the physical, legal, regulatory, locational, and economic attributes of the subject property. If the subject property exists, it needs to be inspected.

2. Once the nature of the property is identified, then the *survey of the competition* needs to take place. It must evaluate and record the direct competitors for the property being analyzed. The survey can also consider less direct competitors because changes in their market may affect the market for the subject property. For example, the market for new single-family housing can be affected by the market for existing single-family housing; high vacancies in existing units will affect sales of new units.

3. The *linkage pattern* that the subject property can provide for its space user needs to be identified and compared to the linkage pattern that the competition can provide. The analyst may determine that the subject property is closer to a high-quality school and closer to employment opportunities than the competition is.

4. Given the information about disaggregation, the subject property's linkage pattern, and the survey of the competition, the analyst makes a judgment about the subject property's *area of competition*.

5. *Consumer research* and *market segmentation* enter the analysis to reach a deeper understanding of the consumers in the subject property's area of competition.

6. *Demand analysis* is performed to estimate the amount of space that the consumers in the market will absorb.

The nature of demand analysis for several selected real property types will be discussed in the following subsections.

RESIDENTIAL DEMAND ANALYSIS

Residential demand analysis (which has a high level of aggregation) is principally based on the number of households. Households, not population, are the key demand side variable. Under normal circumstances, the number of households should equal the number of residential units. Effective demand in this highly aggregated market comes into the analysis by establishing that the household has an income (that it is employed) and that the income level is at least what needs to be achieved in order to enter the market. This income is needed to make the minimum mortgage payment on the lowest-priced owner-occupied house or to pay the lowest rent level in the market. If the lowest monthly rents are $500 and rents are assumed to be one-third of the household's monthly expenditure, then the lowest income level that the household needs to enter the rental market is $500 × 3 × 12 months = $18,000 per year.

Using a simple rule of thumb that a household can buy a house that is approximately three times its annual income, with a loan payment of $500, the household could buy a $54,000 house. If minimum house prices are more than $54,000, the household cannot be a home buyer. If the $500 per month were the mortgage loan payment, then at an interest rate of 8 percent per year for 30 years, the household could borrow $68,141.75. Adding a 10-percent down payment into the analysis establishes the minimum house price in the market area of approximately $74,955.92, rounded to $75,000.

In its most aggregated form, the principal factor affecting demand in the residential market is the number of employed households with an income of at least $18,000 per year. Residential demand in the future is a forecast of the number of employed households at that point in time. Households will increase because new households are formed from the existing population by children leaving home to live on their own, and by net migration of households.

Single-Family Residential Demand Analysis

At a higher level of disaggregation, the demand analysis becomes more complex. As an example, consider the demand for additional single-family detached housing units in the $120,000 to $150,000 price range in the northern suburbs of the metropolitan area five years into the future. The following estimates need to be made:

1. Estimate the number of employed households in the metropolitan area with income levels of at least $40,000 and in the range of $40,000 to $60,000 for the present period and forecast this number five years into the future.

2. Estimate the number of such households currently in the northern suburbs, and estimate the number of households five years in the future.

3. Determine the distribution of such households in alternative housing, such as equivalently priced condominium units and luxury apartments (rent at $1,000 or more per month) presently and five years in the future.

4. Subtract the number of existing housing units from the future level of households. The result is the number of additional single-family detached housing units in the $120,000 to $150,000 price range in the northern suburbs of the metropolitan area five years into the future.

5. Consider the effect of a change in the mortgage interest rate over the next five years. What will happen to the demand for additional units if the interest rate increases from 8 percent to 10 percent over the five-year period?

In this disaggregated demand analysis, the analyst needs to consider the number of households, the household income level, the distribution of the households among the alternative housing options, changes in the household income level, and changes in the mortgage interest rate.

An example of this single-family residential demand analysis appears as Exhibit 7.1. This example is presented to highlight the nature of the analysis, but it is not an in-depth analysis. Such an analysis is beyond the scope of this text.

EXHIBIT 7.1   Single-family residential demand analysis illustration.

Current Period Data:

1. There are 300,000 households in the metropolitan area with 40 percent in the $40,000 to $60,000 income bracket; 35 percent of these live in the northern suburbs.

2. Households are forecast to increase by a total of 10 percent over the next five years with 50 percent of this increase in the $40,000 to $60,000 income bracket and 40 percent in the northern suburbs.

3. There are 41,500 housing units in the $120,000 to $150,000 price range in the northern suburbs distributed as follows: 38,000 occupied single-family detached housing units, 2,000 occupied condominiums, and 450 occupied luxury apartments. Vacancies are 800 vacant single-family detached housing units, 200 vacant condominium units, and 50 vacant luxury apartments.

4. There are 2,000 single-family units and 400 condominium units in this price range under construction.

Current households in the metropolitan area in the $40,000 to $60,000 income bracket:

$$300,000 \times 40\% = 120,000$$

Current households in the metropolitan area in the $40,000 to $60,000 income bracket living in the northern suburbs:

$$120,000 \times 35\% = 40,200$$

Additional households in the $40,000 to $60,000 income bracket living in the northern suburbs:

$$300,000 \times 10\% \times 50\% \times 40\% = 6,000$$

Distribution of the 6,000 additional units:

	OCCUPIED		VACANT	TOTAL	
Single Family Detached	37,800	94%	1,000	38,800	93.5%
Condominiums	2,000		200	2,200	
Apartments	400		100	500	
	40,200		1,300	41,500	

Additional single-family detached housing units needed in the $120,000 to $150,000 price range for those in the $40,000 to $60,000 income bracket living in the northern suburbs:

$$6,000 \times 94\% = 5,640$$

Additional single-family detached housing units needed to be constructed:

$$5,640 - 1,000 = 4,640$$

The increase in the mortgage interest rate from 8 percent to 10 percent over the five-year period will reduce the demand for single-family housing units in the $120,000 to $150,000 price range. The exact magnitude of the reduction is not known, but it should be recognized as a very strong possibility. The groups that would be most affected are the households who would seek larger or newer housing units. Some of these households would choose to delay their change. A reasonable estimate would be a decline in demand of approximately 10 percent. So, the final estimate for new, additional single-family housing units would be approximately 5,000 less the 1,000 vacant units.

Multifamily Residential Demand Analysis

Multifamily residential demand analysis is principally based on the number of households in the market area. In suburban areas, where single-family housing units dominate the market as in the previous example, multifamily residential demand analysis is a form of repeating the success of the immediate past. For example, if household growth in the market area were 10,000 last year, and if last year the industry built 1,000 new apartment units and 800 were occupied, then this year—if household growth in the market area is forecast to be 10,000—800 units would seem to be appropriate. Multifamily housing demand in the future is a function of the absorption of multifamily units by households in the recent past.

In market areas where multifamily housing is a reasonably high percentage of the housing alternatives, then multifamily housing demand takes on more of an analytical form. However, the structure of the analysis is still based on projecting the recent past into the future. The following tasks need to be undertaken.

1. Check the most recent census year for the distribution of housing units in the market among single-family detached condominiums and apartments.
2. Check the construction and absorption figures for these housing alternatives in the past several years. Include the rent level for the newly constructed and occupied apartments.
3. Estimate the growth of households in the market area over the next five years.
4. Distribute the increase in households among the three alternatives.
5. Factor out the effect of excess vacancies in the market.

An example of this multifamily residential demand analysis appears as Exhibit 7.2. This example is presented to highlight the nature of the analysis, but it is not an in-depth analysis. Such an analysis is beyond the scope of this text.

RETAIL DEMAND ANALYSIS

The demand variables that are most important in an analysis of retail goods and services are the number of consumers in the form of population and their per capita income level. Using these data, the level of purchasing power can be calculated as the product of population times per capita income in the market or trade area. As purchasing power increases, the demand for retail goods and services increases, and, as a consequence of the demand for the retail goods and services, the demand for retail space also increases. This cause-and-effect relationship from the demand for the retail goods to the demand for retail space is known as the *concept of derived demand*.

In addition to purchasing power, two other important demand-side variables are the consumer's taste and preference pattern for the products that can be purchased and the spatial distribution pattern of purchasing power. Considering changes in taste and preferences, the consumer rearranges the combination of retail goods purchased from time to time. For example, as new products are offered for sale (cell phones, video-cassette recorders, personal computers, DVD players, new styled clothes, and so forth), they are added into the consumer's market basket, and the quantity of other products purchased either decreases or is discontinued. In addition, as the consumer moves through his life cycle, different products are bought. For example, the young consumer may spend proportionally more for recreation and entertainment activities, while the older consumer may spend proportionally more for home furnishings, education expenses, and insurance.

EXHIBIT 7.2   Multifamily residential demand analysis illustration.

Past and Current Period Data:

1. There were 70,000 housing units in the market area in 1990 (the most recent available census year). The distribution of these units in single-family detached units, condominiums, and apartments was 50,000, 3,000, and 17,000, respectively. The percentages were 71.4 percent, 4.3 percent, and 24.3 percent, respectively.

2. The estimates for the current year are 66,000, 3,500, and 24,000 for single-family detached units, condominiums, and apartments, respectively. The percentages are 70.6 percent, 3.7 percent, and 25.7 percent, respectively.

3. Data for construction, absorption, and vacancies in the market area for the last three years are given in the table.

	LAST YEAR (T-1)		(T-2)		(T-3)	
	Construction	Absorption	Construction	Absorption	Construction	Absorption
Single-family	1,800	1,750	1,600	1,590	1,500	1,500
Condominiums	0		100	60	150	130
Apartments						
$600–$800	900	900	700	700	600	600
$800–$1,000	200	200	150	150	100	100

4. Household growth in the market area for the next five years is forecast to be 10,000.

5. The distribution of new construction in the last year is 61.4 percent to single-family detached units and 38.6 percent to apartments. These distribution percentages are reasonable given the experience of the last three years. Condominium units are a minor element and have a relatively low level of absorption. The 38.6-percent share to apartments is in turn distributed as 81.8 percent to the $600 to $800 range and 18.2 percent to the $800 to $1,000 range.

6. The distribution percentage obtained from recent construction and absorption activity is deemed more appropriate than the historic distribution percentages.

7. Vacancies in the apartment market are currently at 6 percent of the current stock of 24,000 apartments. The rate has been declining over the past few years. New units have been fully absorbed in the recent past.

Additional apartments needed in the market area:

$$10,000 \times 38.6\% = 3,860$$

Additional apartments by rent level needed in the market area:

$$3,860 \times 81.8\% = 3,157$$
$$3,860 \times 18.2\% = 703$$

The market analyst can obtain information about consumer purchase patterns from two government publications: *Consumer Expenditure Survey* and *Relative Importance of Components in the Consumer Price Index*. Here, several distinct retail categories and the percentage of before-tax income spent on each retail category are identified. In addition, within each of the broad retail categories (for example, men's clothing), different income groups purchase different quality of product lines. For example, the low-income household may buy men's clothing exclusively in discount stores, while the upper-income household may buy men's clothing exclusively in specialty men's shops. The *Census of Retail Trade* can also provide these percentages.

An example of retail demand analysis appears as Exhibit 7.3. This example is presented to highlight the nature of the analysis, but it is not an in-depth analysis. Such an analysis is beyond the scope of this text.

EXHIBIT 7.3   Retail demand analysis illustration.

Current Period Data:

1. After performing a survey of the competition, the analyst defines the retail trade area for a site on which a proposed neighborhood shopping center is being considered. The analyst evaluates the financial feasibility of opening a new supermarket on this site. The retail trade area is matched to two census tracts, and the population and per capita income for these census tracts are a total population of 14,000 with a per capita income of $18,000.

2. The portion of total purchasing power spent on grocery items in this market area is 12 percent. However, only 90 percent of these funds is spent for groceries in stores in the retail trade area.

3. The subject supermarket will require sales of $250,000 per week to be financially feasible.

4. One other competing supermarket shares the retail trade area. This competitor is a quarter of a mile north of the site, at the next major intersection. Consumers view the supermarket in the competing neighborhood shopping center to be similar to the supermarket chain considering the subject site. The analyst decides that the two supermarkets would share the market equally.

Total purchasing power in the trade area:

   14,000 × $18,000 = $252,000,000

Purchasing power allocated to grocery items in this retail trade area:

   $252,000,000 × 90% × 12% = $27,216,000

Share of the grocery expenditures estimated for the subject site:

   $27,216,000 × 50% = $13,608,000

Required sale for the supermarket on the subject site:

   $250,000 × 52 = $13,000,000

The estimated share of the total purchasing power directed toward groceries from the retail trade area toward the subject property is $13.6 million. This figure exceeds the required sales volume of $13 million, so the project is financially feasible.

OFFICE MARKET DEMAND ANALYSIS FOR LOCAL MARKET SERVICES

Office space is developed and designed for use in activities that serve the local market. This category of activities contains the following services: legal, insurance, medical, dental, tax, accounting, general accounting, real estate brokerage, and other such professional services that are provided for local residents. In this situation, disaggregation can occur by analyzing these activities for a particular location within the local economy.

Market analysis for the services and activities provided in this category of commercial property is very similar to the analysis for retail activities. These office services also consist of a certain percentage of the consumer's income. Consequently, as the market analyst obtains data for purchasing power, she can apply those percentages to calculate the local residents' demand for medical, legal, dental, and other services.

A numerical example of this type of analysis could follow the same pattern of logic as the retail example shown earlier. The major change would be the application of the relevant allocation percentage for the specific category of service for the 12-percent grocery allocation. For example, based on national averages, people spend approximately 0.45 percent for legal services, 1 percent for dental services, and 1.75 percent for physician services. Would a general purpose legal services office serving the local population be financially feasible in this trade area if one such office already existed? This analysis is shown in Exhibit 7.4.

EXHIBIT 7.4	Office demand analysis illustration for local services.

Current Period Data:

1. After performing a survey of the competition, the analyst defines the retail trade area for a site on which a law office is being considered. The analyst evaluates the financial feasibility of opening a law office on this site. The retail trade area is matched to three census tracts, and the population and per capita income for these three census tracts are a total population of 14,000 with a per capita income of $18,000.

2. The portion of total purchasing power spent on legal services in this market area is 0.45 percent. However, only 70 percent of these funds is spent for locally provided legal services. One other competing law office shares the trade area. This competitor is a quarter of a mile north of the site, at the next major intersection. Consumers would more than likely view the law offices to be similar, so they would share the market equally.

3. Two lawyers would require annual salaries of $100,000 each and one legal assistant at $35,000, with an overhead allocation for the space, insurance, telephone services, and so forth of 60 percent of salaries.

Total purchasing power in the trade area:

14,000 × $18,000 = $252,000,000

Purchasing power allocated to legal services in this trade area:

$252,000,000 × 70% × 0.45% = $793,800

Share of the legal service expenditures estimated for the subject site:

$793,000 × 50% = $396,900

Required revenue for the law office on the subject site:

$235,000 × 1.6 = $376,000

The estimated share of the total purchasing power directed toward legal services from the trade area toward the subject property is $396,900. This figure exceeds the required revenue volume of $376,000, so the project is financially feasible.

OFFICE MARKET DEMAND ANALYSIS FOR GENERAL USE OFFICE SPACE

The demand for general use office space requires knowledge about the types of industries located in the local economy, the relative cost of comparable space between the local economy and the nonlocal economy, the relative wage rate between the local economy and the nonlocal economy, and the locational amenities that may attract firms to the local economy. The starting point is knowledge about the reasons that firms choose the local economy (these reasons were discussed in Chapter 3). The major reasons include geographic differences in wages, salaries, space costs, utility costs, transportation costs, business climate, and quality of life.

The analysis to determine the need for additional office space starts with an employment growth forecast because the consumer of office space is the office worker. The analysis also requires judgments about the amount of space each office worker requires and the relationship between office employees and total employees in the market area.

An example of office demand analysis appears in Exhibit 7.5. This example is presented to highlight the nature of the analysis, but it is not an in-depth analysis. Such an analysis is beyond the scope of this text.

EXHIBIT 7.5   Office demand analysis illustration.

Current Period Data:

1. Total employment growth is forecast at 9,000 new jobs over the next five years. These new jobs will mostly arise in the financial, legal, and business services sectors of the economy. The analyst estimates that 80 percent of the jobs will be in these areas, and the other 20 percent will be in other employment areas that are not as intensive in the use of office space.

2. The analyst estimates that 90 percent of employees in the financial, legal, and business services sectors of the economy are office workers, while only 30 percent of the other employees work in offices.

3. Because of changes in office technology (computers, electronic storage, and so forth) and office space utilization patterns (modular space, "hotelling," telecommuting, and so forth) to reduce occupancy costs, the office space per employee will decline by five square feet per employee.

4. There are currently 100,000 office employees in 18 million square feet of office space. Employees in the existing office space are utilizing approximately 180 square feet per employee.

Total employment allocated to industrial classification sectors:

$9,000 \times 80\% = 7,200$ in financial, legal, and business services

$9,000 \times 20\% = 1,800$ in other employment

Total employment allocated to office employment:

$7,200 \times 90\% = 6,480$ office employees

$1,800 \times 30\% = \underline{\quad 540}$ office employees

                  7,020 additional office employees

Office space utilization per employee:

$7,020 \times (180 - 5) = 1,228,500$ square feet of new demand for office space

$100,000 \times (-5) = \underline{\quad -500,000}$ square feet of previously used space that will become vacant

                 728,500 net additional new space required

Additional office space in demand:

728,500 square feet for the next 5 years; approximately 145,700 per year

---

How Is the Market Analysis Process Related to Investment Analysis?

The data obtained from the process of market and marketability analysis lead the analyst to a determination of the current market rent and vacancy level as well as a forecast of future levels of market rent and vacancy. This information is used as the "top line" of the discounted cash flow analysis presented for both income property valuation and equity investment analysis.

In general terms, the data for current market rent come from an analysis of the existing competition by means of their current price quotes and the negotiated price for space. Care must be taken to ensure that the information is not historic contract rent, because market analysis points to the future, not to the past. Vacancy data are also obtained from the market analysis process in the same manner as the rent data.

In addition to this current data for rents obtained from the survey of the competition, the analyst can get an idea of what consumers are willing to pay for the space in the subject property by using appropriately designed questions in the consumer survey. These data can even provide information on the differentials that consumers will be willing to pay for certain types of structural amenities, such as extra rooms, extra square footage, balconies, and fireplaces.

The survey of the competition and the survey of the consumer also can provide information about the type of product—its qualitative aspects—that is most desired. The survey of the existing competition can show the analyst what product the market provided in the past by identifying its structural features and its location. Moreover, the survey of the competition can show the analyst the absorption rate, or how responsive the market was to that product.

The survey of the consumers can tell the analyst what current consumers want in the way of location, neighborhood, and structural amenities, and what they are willing to pay for the space they desire. Special features can be evaluated for inclusion in the units. The importance of on-site recreational amenities also can be determined.

Armed with these data, investors can determine whether the investment meets their financial objectives, mortgage lenders can determine whether the property passes their standards for acceptable loans, and developers can determine what to build and where to build it.

Chapter Summary

The market analysis and the marketability analysis are major components of a feasibility study. Other components are the financial feasibility study, the location, design, construction cost, operating cost, market value impact, location inducement and incentive, economic impact, fiscal impact, and infrastructure impact studies. Using these specialized studies, the feasibility study evaluates the property's ability to meet the investor's financial objectives.

The market analysis addresses several important topics. It identifies the local economy and describes its nature and structure. It analyzes the market(s) in which the subject property will compete. This is accomplished by first studying population and income levels in the past, present, and future. Then, the marketability of the space or service of the subject property is evaluated by a study of the characteristics of the property, a delineation of the competitive market area, a survey of the competition, and a survey of the tastes, preferences, purchase habits, and so on of the consumers.

This information allows the analyst to forecast the levels of revenues and vacancies for the subject property. These forecasts are utilized in the financial study that underlies the investment decision.

Internet Applications

A website has been established for this chapter at http://epley.swcollege.com.

Review Questions

1. Discuss the nature and content of a feasibility study. Be certain to describe the various component studies that can be included in a feasibility study.
2. Define market analysis and describe the market analysis process.
3. Identify the tasks to be accomplished to analyze a specific subject property.
4. What are the legal and physical characteristics that can affect the marketability of the subject property?
5. Describe the nature and content of the survey of the competition.
6. What is consumer research?

Discussion Questions

1. How does the condition of the local economy affect the marketability of a single-family home and the marketability of retail space?
2. How does the condition of the "outside world" (the nonlocal economy) affect the marketability of retail space and local housing?
3. Why might the analyst need consumer research to do a complete marketability study for a new apartment project?

The Decision to Finance the Transaction

Mortgages and Borrowed Capital

acceleration clause

amortization

- assignment

- assumption

balloon payment

blanket mortgage

consideration

covenants

debt capital

debiting factor

deed in lieu of foreclosure

deed of trust

deed to secure debt

default

defeasible title

deficiency judgment

discount points

down payment

due-on-sale clause

equitable right of redemption

equity capital

escrow

estoppel certificate

fees

fixed-rate mortgage loan

foreclosure

homestead

installment note

interest

intermediate theory

judicial foreclosure + NON...

leasehold mortgage

lien theory

loan-to-value (LTV) ratio

mortgage

mortgagee

mortgagor

nonrecourse clause

note

open-end mortgage

package mortgage

points

power-of-sale clause

prepayment

prepayment penalty

promissory note

purchase money mortgage (PMM)

recasting

reconveyance deed

refinancing

release

second mortgage

secured loan

seller financing

statutory right of redemption

subject to

subordination clause

sweat equity

title theory

trustee

trustor

unsecured loan

usury

INTRODUCTION

For most individuals and companies, acquiring a home, office, warehouse, or factory is an expensive transaction. Due to this relatively high cost, most residential real estate transactions would not be possible without a mortgage loan. The same is true for most commercial property acquisitions, although there are some institutions, especially pension funds and real estate investment trusts, that purchase income properties on an all-cash basis. In most instances, though, buyers and sellers need to be familiar with the mortgage application process and the characteristics of mortgages. Real estate agents also must be knowledgeable about these matters because they often counsel buyers about local mortgage terms and availability as well as possible sources of cash for a down payment.

This chapter introduces mortgage loans, covering many loan aspects that are applicable to both single-family home loans and income-producing property loans. Chapter 9 then concentrates on the topics that are specific to home loans, while Chapter 10 adds material on commercial or income-producing properties.

What Funds Are Needed to Purchase Property?

Without the availability of real estate financing instruments and procedures, it would be very difficult for purchasers to buy property. They would have to save enough money to be able to afford to pay all cash for their acquisitions. The relatively high prices of houses and most income-producing properties generally require that real estate purchasers use borrowed money for at least a portion of the acquisition price. Moreover, construction costs have increased dramatically over the past several years, driving up the amount necessary to have a new improvement built. Prospects for the future do not indicate any permanent decreases in costs.

EQUITY CAPITAL VERSUS DEBT CAPITAL

Money belonging to someone else that is borrowed from that person and then used to buy property is called **debt capital.** The prospective borrower approaches a lender and borrows a sum of money that is added to his own funds (which are often called **equity capital**); the sum of the two amounts equals the total purchase price. Sometimes, the purchaser is able to borrow the total purchase price so that all of the capital is debt capital provided by the lender, but generally the purchaser must provide some equity capital.

The debt capital is often called a *mortgage loan.* The lender generally requires some collateral from the borrower in return for making the loan, and the borrower offers the real estate as the security for the loan. The security (or collateral) instrument, which gives the lender the right to sell the real estate if the borrower defaults on the loan, is called a **mortgage.** The borrower is called the **mortgagor** because he creates the debt, promises to repay it, and *gives* the security instrument to the lender. The lender is called the **mortgagee** because it *receives* the security instrument and accepts the borrower's offer to create and repay a financial obligation.

The equity capital at the time of the purchase is known as the **down payment.** The equity funds are personal or company assets used for the purchase of the property. These are funds that have not been borrowed from the mortgage lender. In most cases, the equity capital used has been saved from past earnings. For example, a potential homeowner may have to live in an apartment for a time until she has saved enough income to afford the down payment on a house. These debt and equity capital relationships are illustrated in Exhibit 8.1. The top set of labels indicates that the total capital is the sum of the debt capital and the equity capital. The bottom set shows that, at the time of purchase, the purchase price equals the sum of the mortgage loan (debt capital) plus the down payment (equity capital).

EXHIBIT 8.1   Debt and equity capital relationships.

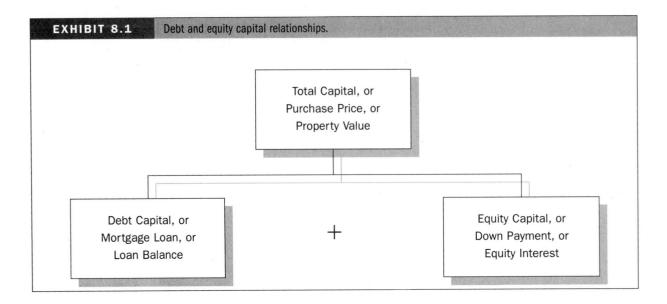

Of course, the relationship among purchase price, loan amount, and down payment is applicable only at the time of purchase. After the purchase, the loan amount is gradually repaid, and the property value generally increases. Because the equity investor's interest plus the loan balance equals the property value, the equity interest must increase to offset the declining loan balance and sum to the property value. The equity **interest** can be calculated by subtracting the amount of any debt owed on the property from its estimated selling price or, equivalently, its market value. We might call this the *final-value* approach. The third set of labels in Exhibit 8.1 illustrates this relationship.

There is a second method for determining the amount of equity capital the owner has invested in the property. It is called the *value-added* approach and gives the same answer as the final-value approach. This approach consists of adding the down payment, the periodic (usually monthly) repayments of the mortgage loan that have been made since the property was purchased, and the increase (appreciation) or decrease (depreciation) in property value since the purchase.

For example, James and Judy Smith have owned their home for two years. They paid $80,000 for it, borrowed $72,000 on a mortgage, and currently owe $69,000. They estimate that the home has increased 10 percent in value since they purchased it. Their equity interest can be computed either of the following ways:

Final Value

Estimated selling price [$80,000 + .10(80,000)]	$ 88,000
Minus the current mortgage balance	69,000
Equals equity interest	$ 19,000

Value Added

Down Payment	$ 8,000
Plus principal repayments to the mortgage lender ($72,000 − $69,000)	3,000
Plus price appreciation ($80,000 × 0.10)	8,000
Equals equity interest	$ 19,000

EQUITY CAPITAL

The equity capital required to acquire real estate either comes from the purchaser's past savings or is borrowed. Moreover, the borrowed equity capital may come from an unsecured or a secured loan.

Savings

The ultimate source of the purchaser's equity funds is the money saved from past income. The purchaser may be an individual looking to buy a home. Perhaps the savings come from successful investments in which the purchaser keeps all or a portion of her capital gains income so that she can buy a home. If the purchaser is a business, it will have earned income in the past that it did not pay to its owners in terms of salary, dividends, or other distributions. The company keeps a portion of its income so that it can have a large enough down payment to afford to acquire the business property needed to house its operations.

Unsecured Loan

A potential homeowner may have a good credit history, good employment stability, and good prospects for income, but not enough cash to make the down payment on the property desired. Assume that in the foregoing example, James and Judy Smith had only $4,000 in cash available for the down payment when they first looked at their present home instead of the $8,000 required down payment. They would have faced an immediate need to raise additional equity funds.

If the purchaser has not saved enough equity capital to purchase the property, one alternative for any purchaser, whether a business, a real estate investor, or a potential homeowner, is to obtain a short-term, unsecured loan from a commercial bank. An **unsecured loan** does not have any collateral pledged to cover the loan in case of default, is typically for a small amount, and has a short term until maturity.

Secured Loan

Another alternative is to obtain a secured loan from a commercial bank. A **secured loan** is one in which the borrower pledges collateral (other than the property being acquired) to cover the risk of default. Examples of collateral that a bank might find acceptable include other parcels of real property, stock owned as an investment, stock in the borrower's company, and the borrower's car, boat, or other personal property in his ownership. Proof of ownership of the collateral is left in the possession of the bank until the loan is paid in full. Typically, the loan is larger in amount than an unsecured loan, and the term to maturity is longer.

Sweat Equity

Finally, a purchaser may be able to provide some of the work on the transaction or the property rather than employing others to do it. This is known as **sweat equity.**

DEBT CAPITAL

Despite the purchaser's efforts to save money so that there is enough cash available to purchase the property, the relatively high prices of individual parcels often dictates that the purchaser will have to use debt capital to supplement his equity capital. In fact, purchasers often want to use as little equity capital as possible for a single transaction, perhaps to save their limited equity for other purposes. The prospective homeowner may need his money for other living expenses, or the business purchaser may need to invest as much in her business as possible. Perhaps a company needs to purchase additional real estate that it will use in its business, but it wishes to conserve its cash so it must borrow part of the down payment as described in the previous section.

Purchasers frequently want to use as much debt capital as possible by obtaining large mortgage loans. Individuals and families who buy homes often want to purchase as large a house as they can afford. To do so, they invest all of their equity capital in the down payment, then borrow as much debt capital as the lender will give them. Sometimes a single investor, a group of investors, or a real estate investment company is interested in diversifying their real estate investments by purchasing several income-producing properties. They want to stretch their investment dollars further by using a large amount of debt financing to accompany their equity capital.

What Are the Key Characteristics of a Fixed-Rate Mortgage Loan?

A mortgage loan carrying an interest rate that does not change during the loan's life is called a **fixed-rate mortgage loan.** This is the most common type of mortgage loan available and has been in widespread use in the United States since the 1930s. The fixed-rate mortgage loan has the following four key characteristics:

1. The mortgage interest rate remains constant throughout the term of the mortgage, provided that the mortgage debt is not taken over (assumed) by a new mortgagor prior to maturity.

2. The loan's maturity date is set at origination and then does not change during the life of the loan, unless a prepayment clause exists that gives the mortgagor the right to repay the loan early.

3. The periodic payments of debt service, that is, mortgage interest and principal amortization, remain the same each period throughout the life of the loan.

4. **Amortization** is complete during the term of the loan. In other words, the loan is fully repaid by maturity through the periodic debt service payments of interest and principal.

The newer contemporary residential mortgage loans, such as the adjustable rate mortgage and the graduated payment mortgage, involve changes to one or more of these characteristics and will be discussed in the next chapter. Commercial mortgages today are often partially amortized loans requiring that the loan balance be paid on a specific date prior to maturity. The balance owed is called the **balloon payment.**

DEBT SERVICE PAYMENT

The first two characteristics of fixed-rate mortgage loans are largely self-explanatory. A fixed-rate mortgage, which you might see abbreviated as FRM, is designed to have an unchanging interest rate and an unchanging maturity. For example, it might carry an 8-percent interest rate and have a 30-year maturity. During those 30 years, the borrower must make periodic (usually monthly) payments, which, in turn, remain the same for each period. In the common case, that would be 360 monthly payments of the same amount each month. The amount of the monthly debt service payment can be calculated with your financial calculator.

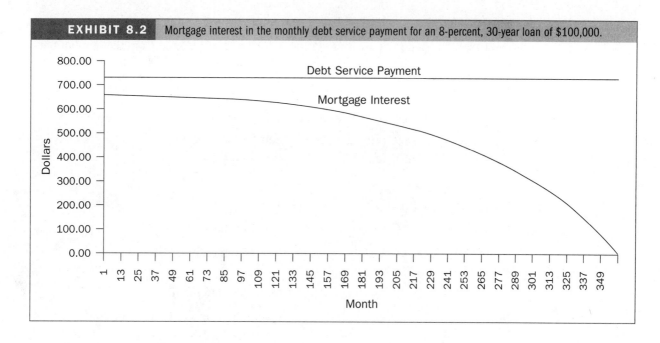

Consider a borrower who wants a new first loan with the following terms:

New first loan amount	$100,000
Annual interest rate negotiated	8%
Term to maturity	30 years
Frequency of payments	monthly

Each student should use a calculator to calculate the exact amount of the monthly payment. The answer is $733.76. That figure remains constant throughout the 360 payments, as shown in Exhibit 8.2 by the horizontal line labeled "Debt Service Payment."

MORTGAGE INTEREST VERSUS PRINCIPAL AMORTIZATION

To find out how much of the payment goes to mortgage interest and how much to principal amortization, one calculates a **debiting factor** for the loan. This is found by dividing the annual interest rate by the number of payments per year. In this example, the debiting factor equals 0.006666667 (0.08 ÷ 12). The allocation of the $733.76 monthly payment between principal amortization and mortgage interest now can be calculated as follows for the first months.

$$\begin{array}{ll} & \$\ 100,000.00 \quad \text{loan balance for the first month} \\ \times & \underline{\quad 0.0066667 \quad} \text{debiting factor} \\ = & \$\quad\quad 666.67 \quad \text{mortgage interest for the first month} \end{array}$$

Because the debt service equals the principal amortization plus the mortgage interest, one can solve for the first month's principal amortization as long as one knows the amount of mortgage interest.

$$\begin{array}{ll} & \$\quad\quad 733.76 \quad \text{monthly debt service} \\ - & \underline{\$\quad\quad 666.67 \quad} \text{mortgage interest for the first month} \\ = & \$\quad\quad\ 67.09 \quad \text{principal amortization for the first month} \end{array}$$

LOAN BALANCE

The first month's principal amortization will now be subtracted from the amount borrowed during the first month in order to calculate the amount of the loan that remains outstanding for the second month. It is the outstanding balance upon which interest must be paid.

$ 100,000.00 loan balance for the first month
− $ 67.09 principal amortization for the first month
= $ 99,932.91 loan balance for the second month

PERIOD BY PERIOD

The entire calculation process is now repeated for the second month.

$ 99,932.91 loan balance for the second month
−   0.0066667 debiting factor
= $ 666.22 mortgage interest for the second month

Notice how the mortgage interest declined slightly from the first month to the second month, from $666.67 to $666.22. Still, the bulk of the debt service payment is devoted to mortgage interest.

$ 733.76 monthly debt service
− $ 666.22 mortgage interest for the second month
= $ 67.54 principal amortization for the second month

Just as the interest component of the debt service declined by 45 cents during the second month, the principal amortization part increased by 45 cents.

$ 99,932.91 loan balance for the second month
− $ 67.54 principal amortization for the second month
= $ 99,865.37 loan balance for the third month

Subsequent months can be calculated similarly, or the "AMORT" key on the calculator may be used by following the instructions that accompanied the calculator.

The four key characteristics of a fixed interest rate, fixed maturity date, fixed monthly payment, and full amortization imply several other characteristics. First, the debiting factor remains constant over the term of the loan. Second, as illustrated above, the interest component of the monthly payment is large at first and gradually declines. The principal component is small at first and gradually increases. Third, as the example shows, the debiting factor is applied to the declining mortgage balance. The loan will be completely repaid (with the possible exception of a few pennies due to rounding since the borrower makes his payments to the nearest penny) through the 360 monthly debt service payments.

GRAPHICAL REPRESENTATIONS

These relationships are also shown in Exhibits 8.2, 8.3, and 8.4. In Exhibit 8.2, the downward-sloping line labeled "Mortgage Interest" represents the amount of the level monthly debt service payment of $733.76 that is mortgage interest. It shows that $666.67 of the first monthly payment goes toward mortgage interest, but the amount allocated for

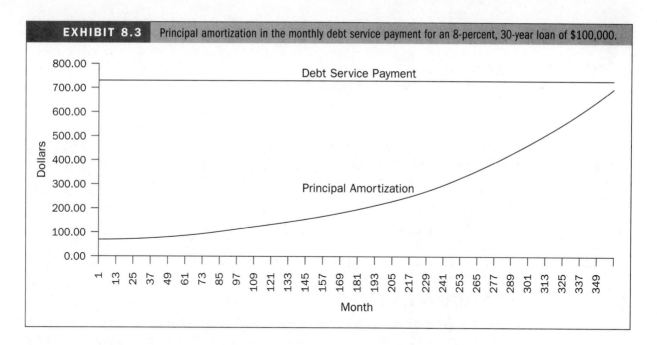

EXHIBIT 8.3 Principal amortization in the monthly debt service payment for an 8-percent, 30-year loan of $100,000.

interest declines at an increasing rate as the mortgage ages. The distance between the declining mortgage interest line and the level debt service payment line is the amount of the monthly payment that goes to reduce the loan balance. This amount is shown separately in Exhibit 8.3 as the upward-sloping line labeled "Principal Amortization." In the first mortgage payment of $733.76, only a small sum of $67.09 is paid toward reducing the debt, but Exhibit 8.3 shows this amount increasing steadily. The declining loan balance is shown separately in Exhibit 8.4, which indicates that the remaining mortgage debt declines at an increasing rate as the mortgage approaches maturity.

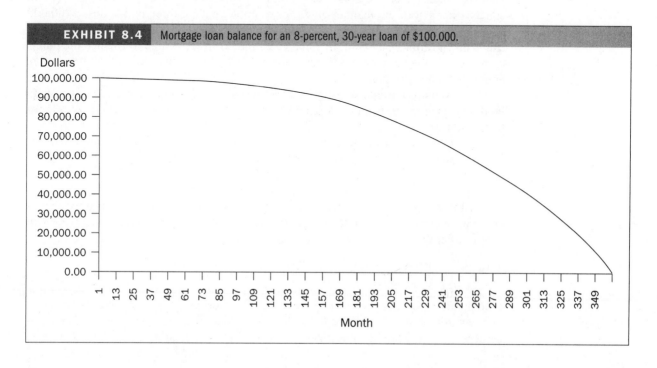

EXHIBIT 8.4 Mortgage loan balance for an 8-percent, 30-year loan of $100.000.

EXHIBIT 8.5 Amortization table: $100,000 loan, 8-percent interest, 30 years, monthly payments.

Fixed Payment Plan

MONTH	BEGINNING BALANCE	PAYMENT	INTEREST	PRINCIPAL	ENDING BALANCE
1	100,000.00	-733.76	666.67	67.10	99,932.90
2	99,932.90	-733.76	666.22	67.55	99,865.36
3	99,865.36	-733.76	665.77	68.00	99,797.36
4	99,797.36	-733.76	665.32	68.45	99,728.91
357	2,886.79	-733.76	19.25	714.52	2,172.27
358	2,172.27	-733.76	14.48	719.28	1,452.98
359	1,452.98	-733.76	9.69	724.08	728.91
360	728.91	-733.76	4.86	728.91	0.00

AMORTIZATION TABLE

An amortization table contains the beginning balance of the loan, the monthly payment, the interest component of the payment, the debt component of the payment, and the ending balance for each month. Exhibit 8.5 shows these numbers for the first four months and the last four months of the $100,000 loan. Each student should generate these numbers using a calculator of choice.

POINTS AND FEES

The prepaid interest the borrower pays when he obtains the loan is known as **points** (or **discount points**). The more points the borrower pays, the lower the interest rate on the loan. This helps keep the borrower's monthly payment as low as possible. Each point equals 1 percent of the loan amount. For example, paying three points on a $100,000 loan results in a $3,000 payment to the lender at the time the loan is granted, often called an "up-front" payment. In some cases the borrower is able to finance the points by borrowing the money used to pay them from the lender, but most situations involve an up-front cash payment.

Borrowers pay points seeking a lower interest rate. Lenders make use of points to hold mortgage interest rates reasonably constant by adjusting the points daily relative to capital market rates.

A number of up-front **fees** are paid as part of the closing costs, including fees for loan origination, credit report, survey, appraisal, title insurance premium, property damage insurance premium, recording, property inspection, legal services, allocation of prepaid expenses, and any mortgage insurance premium and owner's association dues. Most of these fees are paid for services rendered by professionals prior to the purchase of the property, such as the survey and appraisal, or for benefits the owner will receive after the purchase, such as the various insurance policies.

TRUE COST OF FINANCING

If no points or fees are involved, the true cost of a mortgage loan is its interest (or **note**) rate, regardless of when it is repaid. This can be demonstrated using the $100,000, 8-percent, 30-year, monthly amortized mortgage loan in the earlier example. When there is a level payment (also called a level annuity), the five financial function keys of the calculator can be used to calculate the loan's interest rate.

Each student should use a calculator of choice to reestimate the monthly payment of $733.76. The second step is to solve for the interest rate on the loan, which equals 8 percent. It is quicker and easier to use a calculator's financial function keys, as opposed to its cash flow keys, when the problem involves a level payment.

Prepayment

Most borrowers do not keep their mortgage loans until the monthly debt service payments have completely amortized the loan amount (30 years in the preceding example). Instead, they pay them off early. For example, the borrower might consider **refinancing** the loan, that is, to repay it early with the money from a new loan (presumably) carrying a lower interest rate.

Any money paid in addition to the monthly payment that reduces the loan balance is called a **prepayment.** The terms of the loan may include a **prepayment penalty,** which gives the lender the right to assess an additional fee when extra money is paid. Prepayment penalties exist because the lender is projecting a loss in total interest on this loan, and the penalty is a method of reducing the expected loss. Typically, the prepayment amount equals either a percent of the unpaid loan balance, or a percent of the last month's interest.

If points, fees, or both were paid when the loan was first obtained, then the loan's true cost will vary depending upon how long it has been outstanding when it is prepaid. The shorter the holding period prior to prepayment and the larger the points and fees, the greater is its cost. Fortunately, the true cost of such a loan can also be easily calculated. The borrower generally knows what the points and fees will be but is uncertain about how long the loan will be held.

True Cost with Points and Fees and a Prepayment

If the points and fees total $5,000 and the borrower's best guess is that the loan will be prepaid after five years, the following calculations show how the true cost of the 8-percent loan will increase. Recall that the monthly debt service payment is $733.76. If the borrower must pay $5,000 in points and fees, only $95,000 will be received from the $100,000 loan. Moreover, the loan balance of $95,069.26 must be paid at the end of five years. Thus, the net cash inflow when the loan is obtained is a little over $95,000, the monthly cash outflow for debt service is –$733.76, and the cash outflow at the end of the sixtieth month to pay off the loan balance is –$95,069.26. The time-value-of-money keys on a financial calculator can be used to calculate the loan's true cost of 9.28 percent. (Hint: Solve for i with –$95,000 PV, $95,069.26 FV, 60 n, and $733.76 payment.)

What Legal Issues Are Involved with a Mortgage Loan?

After the buyer has enough financial resources for the down payment, he then must obtain a mortgage loan. Recall that the term *mortgage* is used to define a type of long-term real estate loan wherein the property that is purchased is used as collateral for the loan. It can be thought of as a conditional ownership of property that is contingent upon the buyer satisfying the terms of the mortgage, which include a promise to make the payments when due. If this condition is not satisfied, the mortgagee (lender) can follow predetermined steps of **foreclosure** to have the property sold in order to raise the funds necessary to repay the loan.

TITLE THEORY VERSUS LIEN THEORY

A state legislature generally enacts a set of laws interpreting the mortgage according to either of two concepts. One is called **title theory** and refers to the older common-law notion that the mortgagee (lender) is given a deed to the property as collateral for the loan and thus actually owns the property. The mortgagor (buyer) is given possession and all other rights of ownership, including the right to collect income from the property, as long as the monthly payments are made when due. Once the final payment is rendered, title is transferred to the mortgagor via a reconveyance deed. In this case, the mortgage is an instrument to identify the terms of the arrangement when a debt is made.

According to the other concept, which is known as **lien theory,** title to the property is kept by the buyer with the mortgagee receiving only a lien right. The lien can be exercised upon mortgagor default by foreclosing upon the mortgagor and selling the property in order to obtain the funds necessary to repay the loan. To the borrower, the differences between the two concepts may appear to be technical and have no effect. But the differences are important because they involve claims to the rights of possession and the collection of rents in the case of default.

A third concept is followed in a few states where the state statute interprets the mortgage under title theory and the courts interpret it under lien theory. These states are called **intermediate theory** states.

ESTOPPEL CERTIFICATE

An **estoppel certificate** is provided either by the mortgagor or, more commonly, by the mortgagee. It states the precise amount of debt owed as of a certain date and any other outstanding claims on the property of which the maker is aware. By requiring this certificate, the buyer and future lender are aware of the exact dollar amounts owed by the mortgagor on the current financing.

DUE-ON-SALE CLAUSE

Most residential mortgage loans, but not income property loans, include a **due-on-sale clause.** Whenever any interest in the property is transferred to another party without the lender's approval, the due-on-sale clause gives the lender the right to accelerate the mortgage note so that the remaining principal balance immediately becomes due and payable. As the name suggests, the transfer of an "interest" in the property occurs when the property is sold. However, this transfer also occurs in other situations. For example, the land contract (contract for deed), discussed in Chapter 1, and the lease, discussed in Chapter 15, both involve a transfer of an interest in the property. Because such transactions could jeopardize the lender's security interest in the property, the lender reserves the right to call its loan due whenever such a transaction occurs.

ASSUMPTION

A buyer does not have to obtain a new mortgage loan when she purchases a property, although the widespread use of due-on-sale clauses in residential mortgages certainly encourages it. Instead, especially with government-insured and govern-ment-guaranteed loans (discussed in Chapter 9) and most commercial property loans (discussed in Chapter 10), it is possible to *assume* an existing loan. This means the buyer can purchase property by *buying* the equity and *assuming* the remaining debt. This type of transaction is called an **assumption** because the lender typically requires that the buyer accept responsibility for making the future payments on the existing indebtedness. During a time of rising interest rates, the due-on-sale clause also gives the lender the leverage to increase the interest rate on the assumed mort-gage. The buyer pays in cash a sum equal to the difference between the selling price and the current mortgage balance.

BUYING SUBJECT TO THE MORTGAGE

Sometimes the lender is not notified about the sale of the property. In that case, a pur-chaser may buy the property by agreeing with the seller to take over the existing payment and paying the owner her equity in the property. However, the purchaser does *not* sign the promissory note. In the event of foreclosure, the seller will be liable to the lender for the amount of a possible deficiency judgment. Thus, the buyer has purchased the property **subject to** the existing loan as opposed to assuming any liability for it. If the loan includes a due-on-sale clause and the lender subsequently learns about the sale, the lender could call the loan due at any time.

ASSIGNMENT

An **assignment** is a document that transfers certain rights from one party to another party. For example, when a mortgage loan is sold, an assignment can be written and recorded to show that the promissory note and security instrument have been trans-ferred to another owner. Also, an assignment can be written and recorded to provide proof that the right to collect rents on a parcel has been transferred. This document is used to provide proof of legitimate transfer without fraud.

DEFAULT AND FORECLOSURE

When the borrower receives the mortgage loan, he promises to repay it, typically by monthly payments over an extended period. With residential loans, the period is usu-ally 30 years; with commercial loans, it is frequently much shorter, often 7 or 10 years with a large balloon payment because the monthly payments are only large enough to fully amortize the mortgage over 20 or 25 years. Although the borrower makes other promises (also called **covenants**), which will be discussed later in this chapter, the most important covenant is the payment one. If a borrower fails to make a payment by its due date, then he has broken his promise and is said to be in **default** on the loan.

The mortgagee almost always gives the borrower an opportunity to make up the missed payment (plus pay a late fee). The **equitable right of redemption** gives the bor-rower the right to pay all defaulted payments and costs, and stop the move to foreclosure. When the lender finally concludes that the borrower will not bring his account current, the lender's remedy is to foreclose on the borrower's interest in the property by having the property sold and applying the sales proceeds toward repayment of the defaulted debt. In some states, the foreclosure sale is conducted only upon order of a court; in others, the lender may bypass the court and conduct the sale itself.

Judicial Foreclosure Versus Power of Sale

In some states, the mortgagee must file a foreclosure suit alleging the mortgagor's default on the mortgage note. It must then prove to the court that such a default occurred before the court will order the property sold at a public auction by an officer of the court. Known as **judicial foreclosure,** this is a time-consuming and costly process. An alternative procedure allowed in some states gives the lender the power of sale. With a **power-of-sale clause** in the mortgage document, the lender may conduct the foreclosure sale without resorting to the court for approval. Because this clause greatly reduces foreclosure time and expense, lenders rely solely on it wherever it is available.

After the Sale

If the property does not sell for enough at the foreclosure sale to repay the lender what is owed, in some states the lender also has the right to petition the court for a **deficiency judgment** for the amount not repaid from the sale. If granted, this judgment attaches to the borrower's other assets. In some states, deficiency judgments are available only if a judicial foreclosure was used. In those states, the fact that a power-of-sale clause exists does not necessarily mean it will be exercised upon default. Instead, the lender may still use the judicial foreclosure procedure and file a foreclosure suit. Then, if the selling price is less than the unpaid balance of the debt, the beneficiary may go back to the court and sue to obtain a deficiency decree against the borrower.

Some states also offer another safeguard to borrowers, although borrowers are not often able to take advantage of it. This safeguard is the **statutory right of redemption,** which gives the mortgagor the option of repaying whatever the purchaser at the foreclosure sale paid for the property, plus interest and court costs, within a specific time period *after* a foreclosure sale, thereby reclaiming ownership of the property. Purchasers in states that offer a statutory right of redemption receive only a certificate of title indicating they will receive a deed transferring ownership to them upon expiration of the statutory period of redemption. They rarely make any improvements to the property until after this period expires.

SUBORDINATION

Subordination is the act of reducing one's priority. For example, a lender who is making a large loan on a parcel may demand to have a more senior position in case of default than a lender who has lent only a small amount. If the latter lender were to record his claim first, he would have the first mortgage unless there was a **subordination clause** in his security instrument reducing his interest to one that is inferior to the major lender's interest. Of course, an additional document could be created that does the same thing. Filing these documents in the county courthouse gives constructive notice of the subordination and changes the ranking of the claims involved.

What Alternatives to Foreclosure Are Available to the Borrower?

If the mortgagor finds that default is imminent, there are other alternatives he will likely pursue that have fewer adverse consequences to his credit rating than does a mortgage foreclosure. The foreclosure action remains on his credit record for seven years, during which time it may be difficult to borrow additional money. Instead, the mortgagor is likely to pursue what are known as "workouts." Successful implementation of one or more of these strategies will not only assist the mortgagor in recovering from the default but also enable the lender to resolve the bad loan on its books.

RECASTING THE LOAN

Recasting a loan involves changing one or more of its terms. After negotiation, the lender may agree to stop the monthly debt service payment for a time, giving the borrower an opportunity to recover from the adverse situation causing the default. Another alternative might be to extend the amortization period, thus lowering the monthly payment to make it more affordable. The interest rate might be lowered, either temporarily or permanently, to reduce the mortgagor's payments. The loan might be converted from a fixed interest rate to a floating interest rate if that would result in a lower current rate and hence a lower monthly payment. The lender might even agree to forgive a portion of the debt. In fact, any change in any of the terms is possible, depending upon what the mortgagor and mortgagee agree upon.

PROPERTY SALE WITH A LOAN ASSUMPTION

If the mortgagor is unable to negotiate a recasting of the loan with the mortgagee, then he might try to sell the property. If the property's value is greater than the loan balance, the mortgagor could sell it, repay the loan, and thus recover his equity interest in the property. Of course, transaction costs might make this an untenable solution even with a higher property value if the costs more than offset all the profits from the sale.

If a financially strong purchaser viewed the current depressed price as temporary, he still might be willing to purchase the property and assume the existing mortgage. He would make the payments the defaulting mortgagor was unable to make in the hopes that the property value would recover enough to rise back above the loan balance. Given the purchaser's financial strength, the lender would be likely to approve his assumption of the loan without exercising the due-on-sale clause. Of course, the borrower would like to obtain a **release** of his obligation under the loan from the lender so that his credit record would improve.

EXTENSION AGREEMENT

The lender may agree to an extension agreement, which may be one of two different types. The first occurs when the lender forgoes the payments, for example, for two months, and adds them to the maturity date. In this example, a 360-payment loan becomes a 362-payment commitment. The second type of extension agreement occurs when the lender offers a second loan that is secured by the property. The missed payments are paid to the lender by the amount in the second loan.

DEED IN LIEU OF FORECLOSURE

If the lender and borrower are unable to reach agreement on recasting the loan and the borrower cannot sell the property, the lender may have only one remaining option before foreclosing on the borrower. One route left open to the lender is to accept a deed to the property transferring ownership to the lender without the time and expense of a foreclosure sale. This **deed in lieu of foreclosure** also will avoid a foreclosure blemish on the borrower's credit report and thus may be acceptable to him, too. If the value of the property has dropped below the loan balance, then the lender will have to write off the difference. Still, this may be a less expensive alternative for the lender than undertaking a foreclosure.

What Is a Promissory Note?

When the purchaser borrows money from a lender, the lender demands that the borrower sign a **promissory note.** This note serves as evidence of the debt and is the borrower's personal IOU to repay. The borrower agrees to a schedule for repayment of the borrowed money. Most often, this means monthly payments over several years. One promissory note signed by the borrower always accompanies the mortgage.

One of the key accomplishments of the two major purchasers of residential mortgage loans—the Federal National Mortgage Association (FNMA or Fannie Mae) and the Federal Home Loan Mortgage Corporation (FHLMC or Freddie Mac)—is their requirement that purchased loans use standardized documents. One of these mortgage loan documents is the promissory note. A typical Fannie Mae/Freddie Mac multistate fixed-rate note to accompany a residential mortgage is shown in Exhibit 8.6. Although promissory notes for loans on commercial real estate are not standardized and thus differ from lender to lender, many of their features are similar to those described below. Some of the recurring distinctions are identified in the paragraphs immediately following the discussion of Exhibit 8.6.

1. *Date and property address.* The date of the note and the location of the property are identified near the top of the form.

2. *Borrower's promise to pay.* The amount of the loan and a promise to repay the loan, with interest, to the lender are stated in the first paragraph of the note. Because notes are frequently sold, the promise to pay is explicitly extended to anyone holding the note. The borrower is identified by name and signature near the bottom of the note.

3. *Interest.* The interest rate is specified, as well as the borrower's promise to pay interest on the outstanding loan balance amount at that rate, in the second paragraph.

4. *Payments.* The note's third paragraph identifies the amount of the borrower's monthly payment, the day of the month upon which the payment must be made, the loan's maturity date when any remaining amounts owed must be paid, and the place where the payments must be made.

5. *Borrower's right to prepay.* The fourth paragraph is known as the prepayment clause. It specifies that the borrower has the right to make additional payments (prepayments) that reduce the loan balance more quickly than agreed upon in the third paragraph. Although the note in Exhibit 8.6 allows prepayments, some notes do not allow them, others do allow them but require they be made in a certain way, and still others may accept them only if the borrower pays a penalty.

6. *Loan charges.* **Usury** is the charging of an unlawfully high rate of interest. Because the penalties for usury are severe, the fifth paragraph protects the lender by reducing the rate to a nonusurious level and refunding any amounts previously paid that are subsequently determined to be too high.

7. *Borrower's failure to pay as required.* The sixth paragraph gives the borrower a grace period after the payment due date during which late payments will be accept-

NOTE

_____, _____   _____, _____
　　　　　　[Date]   [City]   [State]

_____
[Property Address]

1. BORROWER'S PROMISE TO PAY

In return for a loan that I have received, I promise to pay U.S. $_____ (this amount is called "Principal"), plus interest, to the order of the Lender. The Lender is _____
_____. I will make all payments under this Note in the form of cash, check or money order.

I understand that the Lender may transfer this Note. The Lender or anyone who takes this Note by transfer and who is entitled to receive payments under this Note is called the "Note Holder."

2. INTEREST

Interest will be charged on unpaid principal until the full amount of Principal has been paid. I will pay interest at a yearly rate of _____%.

The interest rate required by this Section 2 is the rate I will pay both before and after any default described in Section 6(B) of this Note.

3. PAYMENTS

(A) Time and Place of Payments

I will pay principal and interest by making a payment every month.

I will make my monthly payment on the _____ day of each month beginning on _____, _____. I will make these payments every month until I have paid all of the principal and interest and any other charges described below that I may owe under this Note. Each monthly payment will be applied as of its scheduled due date and will be applied to interest before Principal. If, on _____, 20____, I still owe amounts under this Note, I will pay those amounts in full on that date, which is called the "Maturity Date."

I will make my monthly payments at _____
_____ or at a different place if required by the Note Holder.

(B) Amount of Monthly Payments

My monthly payment will be in the amount of U.S. $_____.

4. BORROWER'S RIGHT TO PREPAY

I have the right to make payments of Principal at any time before they are due. A payment of Principal only is known as a "Prepayment." When I make a Prepayment, I will tell the Note Holder in writing that I am doing so. I may not designate a payment as a Prepayment if I have not made all the monthly payments due under the Note.

I may make a full Prepayment or partial Prepayments without paying a Prepayment charge. The Note Holder will use my Prepayments to reduce the amount of Principal that I owe under this Note. However, the Note Holder may apply my Prepayment to the accrued and unpaid interest on the Prepayment amount, before applying my Prepayment to reduce the Principal amount of the Note. If I make a partial Prepayment, there will be no changes in the due date or in the amount of my monthly payment unless the Note Holder agrees in writing to those changes.

5. LOAN CHARGES

If a law, which applies to this loan and which sets maximum loan charges, is finally interpreted so that the interest or other loan charges collected or to be collected in connection with this loan exceed the permitted limits, then: (a) any such loan charge shall be reduced by the amount necessary to reduce the charge to the permitted limit; and (b) any sums already collected from me which exceeded permitted limits will be refunded to me. The Note Holder may choose to make this refund by reducing the Principal I owe under this Note or by making a direct payment to me. If a refund reduces Principal, the reduction will be treated as a partial Prepayment.

6. BORROWER'S FAILURE TO PAY AS REQUIRED

(A) Late Charge for Overdue Payments

If the Note Holder has not received the full amount of any monthly payment by the end of _____ calendar days after the date it is due, I will pay a late charge to the Note Holder. The amount of the charge will be _____% of my overdue payment of principal and interest. I will pay this late charge promptly but only once on each late payment.

(B) Default

If I do not pay the full amount of each monthly payment on the date it is due, I will be in default.

(C) Notice of Default

If I am in default, the Note Holder may send me a written notice telling me that if I do not pay the overdue amount by a certain date, the Note Holder may require me to pay immediately the full amount of Principal which has not been paid and all the interest that I owe on that amount. That date must be at least 30 days after the date on which the notice is mailed to me or delivered by other means.

MULTISTATE FIXED RATE NOTE—Single Family—Fannie Mae/Freddie Mac UNIFORM INSTRUMENT　　　　Form 3200　1/01　*(page 1 of 2 pages)*

(D)   No Waiver By Note Holder

Even if, at a time when I am in default, the Note Holder does not require me to pay immediately in full as described above, the Note Holder will still have the right to do so if I am in default at a later time.

(E)   Payment of Note Holder's Costs and Expenses

If the Note Holder has required me to pay immediately in full as described above, the Note Holder will have the right to be paid back by me for all of its costs and expenses in enforcing this Note to the extent not prohibited by applicable law. Those expenses include, for example, reasonable attorneys' fees.

7.   GIVING OF NOTICES

Unless applicable law requires a different method, any notice that must be given to me under this Note will be given by delivering it or by mailing it by first class mail to me at the Property Address above or at a different address if I give the Note Holder a notice of my different address.

Any notice that must be given to the Note Holder under this Note will be given by delivering it or by mailing it by first class mail to the Note Holder at the address stated in Section 3(A) above or at a different address if I am given a notice of that different address.

8.   OBLIGATIONS OF PERSONS UNDER THIS NOTE

If more than one person signs this Note, each person is fully and personally obligated to keep all of the promises made in this Note, including the promise to pay the full amount owed. Any person who is a guarantor, surety or endorser of this Note is also obligated to do these things. Any person who takes over these obligations, including the obligations of a guarantor, surety or endorser of this Note, is also obligated to keep all of the promises made in this Note. The Note Holder may enforce its rights under this Note against each person individually or against all of us together. This means that any one of us may be required to pay all of the amounts owed under this Note.

9.   WAIVERS

I and any other person who has obligations under this Note waive the rights of Presentment and Notice of Dishonor. "Presentment" means the right to require the Note Holder to demand payment of amounts due. "Notice of Dishonor" means the right to require the Note Holder to give notice to other persons that amounts due have not been paid.

10.   UNIFORM SECURED NOTE

This Note is a uniform instrument with limited variations in some jurisdictions. In addition to the protections given to the Note Holder under this Note, a Mortgage, Deed of Trust, or Security Deed (the "Security Instrument"), dated the same date as this Note, protects the Note Holder from possible losses which might result if I do not keep the promises which I make in this Note. That Security Instrument describes how and under what conditions I may be required to make immediate payment in full of all amounts I owe under this Note. Some of those conditions are described as follows:

If all or any part of the Property or any Interest in the Property is sold or transferred (or if Borrower is not a natural person and a beneficial interest in Borrower is sold or transferred) without Lender's prior written consent, Lender may require immediate payment in full of all sums secured by this Security Instrument. However, this option shall not be exercised by Lender if such exercise is prohibited by Applicable Law.

If Lender exercises this option, Lender shall give Borrower notice of acceleration. The notice shall provide a period of not less than 30 days from the date the notice is given in accordance with Section 15 within which Borrower must pay all sums secured by this Security Instrument. If Borrower fails to pay these sums prior to the expiration of this period, Lender may invoke any remedies permitted by this Security Instrument without further notice or demand on Borrower.

WITNESS THE HAND(S) AND SEAL(S) OF THE UNDERSIGNED

_____ (Seal)
                                                  - Borrower

_____ (Seal)
                                                  - Borrower

_____ (Seal)
                                                  - Borrower

[Sign Original Only]

MULTISTATE FIXED RATE NOTE—Single Family—Fannie Mae/Freddie Mac UNIFORM INSTRUMENT   Form 3200   1/01 *(page 2 of 2 pages)*

ed with no penalty. If payments are received after the specified number of days, then the borrower also owes a late payment fee. However, this paragraph also states that any missed or partial payments constitute a default on the borrower's part. The note then includes an acceleration clause, which the lender has the option of exercising upon the borrower's default. The **acceleration clause** gives the lender the right to move the loan's maturity date to the current date as a first step in the foreclosure process.

8. *Giving of notices.* The seventh paragraph sets out the mechanisms both the mortgagor and mortgagee must follow if either wishes to provide legal notice to the other party. For example, any notice to the borrower must be mailed to the property address by first-class mail.

9. *Obligations of persons under this note.* Paragraph eight states that each of the parties that signs the note is personally obligated to repay it, even if the other signers do not do their part.

10. *Waivers.* The borrower foregoes some of his rights by not forcing the lender to demand payment of each payment when due and by not requiring the lender to give notice to other parties that certain amounts due have not been paid.

11. *Uniform secured note.* The last paragraph in the note identifies it as an instrument that is used nationwide with only limited variations. It also references the mortgage, or other security instrument, that provides collateral protection for the lender. Finally, it includes a due-on-sale clause, which gives the lender the option to force the borrower to repay the loan immediately if the property, or any interest in it, is sold.

Promissory notes for loans secured by commercial properties may differ in some of the key components described above. The most common difference is that the mortgagor is frequently organized as a corporation or limited liability company so that the borrower has limited personal liability. The lender accepts this because the income-producing capability of the property, not the borrower's personal income (as in a residential loan), is the source of the debt service payments. The loan may include a specific **nonrecourse clause,** which limits the mortgagee from seeking recourse against the borrower's other assets in case of default.

Under the basic mortgage terms, the commercial property loan may not be a fully amortizing one, in which case the required periodic payment will be insufficient to completely repay the loan. Hence, the promissory note will call for an additional payment due upon loan maturity. Late payment penalties frequently are more severe with income-producing property mortgages than with residential loans. Finally, most commercial real estate loans either do not allow prepayments for the first several years of the loan's life or have prepayment penalties that are so large that they effectively close the loans to prepayment.

How Does the Borrower Give the Lender Collateral?

When a lender gives a borrower a mortgage loan, it not only requires that the borrower sign a promissory note acknowledging the debt and promising to repay it, but it also requires the mortgagor to provide the lender with collateral for its loan. Typically, the collateral is a security interest in the property being acquired. The security interest gives the lender the right to sell the property and use the sales proceeds to repay the loan if the borrower should default on the promissory note. The security interest is passed to the mortgagee with another of the Fannie Mae/Freddie Mac standardized documents, typically either a mortgage or a deed of trust. About two-thirds of the states use the mortgage as their security instrument, while the remaining one-third use a deed of trust. The sole remaining state, Georgia, uses the deed to secure the debt (security deed).

MORTGAGE

Fannie Mae/Freddie Mac have developed a standardized, conventional single-family residential mortgage instrument that is used in many states as a representative document. The first pages define several terms used in the security instrument, identify the borrower and lender, tie the mortgage back to the promissory note, and identify the property serving as collateral for the loan. This section also identifies any riders attached to the mortgage instrument, including those applicable to adjustable rate mortgages, condominium properties, second homes, and so forth. Using general warranty language, the mortgagor also offers the property as security for the loan.

This document contains the four essential characteristics of a legal contract: (1) the parties are competent in that they are sane, of legal age, and not under the influence of drugs; (2) **consideration** (something of value) is given; (3) the object of the contract is legal; and (4) there is mutual assent in which there has been a meeting of the minds with an offer and an acceptance. Moreover, the document is in writing, and the makers have affixed their signatures so that the statute of frauds is not violated.

Uniform Covenants

The remaining pages of the mortgage instrument include 21 *uniform covenants,* which apply to mortgages in every state but frequently have slight wording changes from state to state. Additional nonuniform covenants may be added for each state. Each has its own security instrument and often its own variation of both the uniform and nonuniform covenants. Another term for **covenant** is *promise.* Among other items, the lender asks the borrower to make certain promises to protect the collateral value of the asset and to eliminate the possibility that a tax lien will be imposed on the property. A general description of each of these promises follows.

1. *Borrower's promise to pay.* The borrower agrees to pay the debt service (principal amortization and mortgage interest) when due, as well as any prepayment and late charges due under the promissory note.

2. *Application of borrower's payments and insurance proceeds.* Payments made by the borrower are credited first to the interest due on the mortgage loan, second to the principal amortization due, third to the taxes and insurance escrow account and then to any late charges, fourth to any other past due charges, fifth to any prepayment charges due under the promissory note, and finally to reduce the principal balance of the promissory note.

3. *Monthly payments for taxes and insurance.* Unless the lender approves otherwise, the borrower must pay monthly 1/12 of the annual property tax payment, 1/12 of any annual hazard, flood, and mortgage insurance premiums, 1/12 of any annual ground rent, and 1/12 of any annual community association dues or fees. This **escrow** payment is deposited into an account from which the lender subsequently makes the annual payments when they come due.

4. *Borrower's obligation to pay charges, assessments, and claims.* The borrower must give notice to the lender of all claims to the property that may become senior to the lender's mortgage as well as agree to pay those claims.

5. *Borrower's obligation to maintain hazard insurance or property insurance.* The borrower must maintain one or more insurance policies to protect the collateral against the risk of loss. If the property does suffer a loss, insurance proceeds will be used either to restore or repair the property or to repay the loan.

6. *Borrower's obligations to occupy the property.* The borrower must occupy the property as her principal residence for at least the first year.

7. *Borrower's obligations to maintain and protect the property and to fulfill any lease obligations.* The borrower agrees to keep the property in good repair and gives the lender to right to inspect it to make sure it is being kept in good repair.

8. *Borrower's loan application.* The borrower agrees to provide a truthful loan application. If the lender subsequently discovers any false, misleading, or inaccurate statements, their occurrence will be considered a loan default.

9. *Lender's right to protect its rights in the property.* If the borrower breaks any of the covenants, the lender may take whatever action is necessary to protect its interests. If this involves investing money in the property, the lender may add the amount to the loan balance.

10. *Mortgage insurance.* If the lender required mortgage insurance as a condition to make the loan, then the borrower must pay the premium required to keep the mortgage insurance policy in effect.

11. *Agreements about miscellaneous proceeds; forfeiture.* Any monies paid to the lender (for example, insurance or condemnation proceeds) will be used to restore the property or reduce the amount owed; any excess goes to the borrower.

12. *Continuation of borrower's obligations and of lender's rights.* Even though the lender agrees to recast one or more terms of the loan, the borrower is not released from the liability to repay the loan unless the lender expressly does so. Furthermore, if the lender chooses not to immediately pursue one or more of its legal remedies upon a borrower default, then the lender retains the right to pursue such remedies later.

13. *Obligations of borrower and of persons taking over borrower's rights or obligations.* If the lender should sell the loan or the borrower should sell the property with the purchaser assuming the borrower's obligations under the loan, then these covenants bind the future parties. In addition, the borrower and each co-signer is bound by each and all of the covenants, except a co-signer may sign the security instrument without co-signing the note.

14. *Loan charges.* This parallels the "Loan Charges" section in the promissory note. It gives the lender the right to reduce the loan charges if they would be construed as being usurious.

15. *Notices required under this security instrument.* This parallels the "Giving of Notices" section in the promissory note, setting out the required procedure for each party to give notice to the other.

16. *Law that governs this security instrument; word usage.* This mortgage is governed both by federal law and by New York state law. Should any part of this instrument conflict with applicable laws or judicial opinions, the remainder of the mortgage remains valid.

17. *Borrower's copy.* The borrower will be given a copy of this mortgage and the promissory note.

18. *Agreements about lender's rights if the property is sold or transferred.* This covenant introduces the due-on-sale clause into the mortgage, just as it was introduced into the promissory note earlier. Whenever any interest in the property is transferred to another party without the lender's approval, the lender has the right to accelerate the mortgage note so that the remaining principal balance immediately becomes due and payable.

19. *Borrower's right to have lender's enforcement of the security instrument discontinued.* The borrower can stop any of the foreclosure proceedings prior to the judgment by rectifying the default (often called "curing the default") and paying the lender any monies owed as if no acceleration had occurred. This is sometimes called the borrower's *equitable right of redemption* because the borrower is redeeming his equity interest in the property prior to the foreclosure sale.

20. *Note holder's right to sell the note or an interest in the note; borrower's right to notice of change of loan servicer; lender's and borrower's right to notice of grievance.* This covenant allows the note holder to sell the loan to some other party without notice being given to the borrower. In addition, the party to whom the borrower makes the monthly payment may also change, but the borrower will be notified so that he may make the monthly payment to the correct party in a timely fashion.

21. *Continuation of borrower's obligations to maintain and protect the property.* Sometimes known as the hazardous substance covenant, the borrower is prohibited from having hazardous or toxic substances on or in the property.

Nonuniform Covenants

Recall that the uniform covenants are applied in each of the states and the District of Columbia, although there are technical wording variations to account for different state laws. Other state law differences that are more substantive than technical are covered in a section of *nonuniform covenants.* Examples of these covenants are shown below.

22. *Lender's rights if borrower fails to keep promises and agreements.* As described earlier, this covenant includes an acceleration clause, called an "immediate payment in full" clause, giving the lender the right to move the maturity date to the current date if the borrower breaches any of the covenants. In addition, this covenant is very important because it sets out the process the lender must follow to foreclose upon the borrower's property interest.

23. *Lender's obligation to discharge this security instrument.* The lender promises that it will release its security interest in this property when the loan is repaid.

24. *Agreement about (state) lien law.* The borrower agrees that the loan proceeds will be used to acquire or improve the property serving as collateral. If the property has existing improvements, the borrower owes a special duty to those improvements under the law.

25. *Borrower's statement regarding the property.* The borrower specifies the number of dwelling units in the improvement that is either currently on the property or to be constructed on the property.

A number of other nonuniform covenants exist that might be included in a mortgage, but these apply in only a limited number of states. For example, one might find an *assignment of rents,* in which the borrower assigns any rents generated from the property to the lender to serve as additional security for the loan. The mortgage might include a *future advances covenant,* which retains the property as security for any additional advances the lender may make to the borrower as long as the advances are made before the expiration of the mortgage. There might also be a *subrogation covenant,* in which the borrower is refinancing existing indebtedness. The lender advancing the money receives all the rights that the lender being repaid had.

Despite the many covenants in the mortgage instrument, the nonpayment of the monthly obligation in covenant #1 is the most common cause of default on a mortgage loan. Moreover, the borrower should remember that covenant #9 gives the lender the right to take whatever action is necessary to protect its security interest in the property if the borrower violates *any* of the covenants.

DEED OF TRUST

In about one-third of the states, a **deed of trust** (trust deed) is used as the security instrument in lieu of a mortgage. The property purchaser (**trustor**) transfers **defeasible title** (the property interest held by the trustee) to a neutral third party (**trustee**), who holds the property as security for the periodic payments made to the lender *(trust beneficiary)*. In contrast, in a mortgage, a nonpossessory security interest is given to the lender, who holds it until the debt is repaid. With a deed of trust, defeasible title is released from the trust upon payment of the debt.

Because no mortgage exists that gives the lender a security interest and because the trustee is legally obligated to make sure that a default by the borrower has indeed occurred, a time-consuming foreclosure process designed to verify the default can be avoided. In addition, the holder of the promissory note can easily sell (and then transfer) the instrument without an assignment, as required under a mortgage. On the other hand, with a deed of trust the borrower may not enjoy a statutory right of redemption in some states. Moreover, the trustee generally is an independent third party selected with the consent of all parties. The trustee has a fiduciary relationship with both the trustor and the trust beneficiary and must accept liability for the terms of the trust.

Power-of-Sale Clause

A deed of trust usually contains a provision that gives the trustee the power to sell the property without any court proceedings in the event of a borrower default on the promissory note. For example, in Colorado, a deed of trust state, the trustee is known as a public trustee, and that party must exercise the power-of-sale clause. In Texas, also a deed of trust state, someone on the lender's staff typically serves as the trustee. By contrast, in New York, a judicial foreclosure state, the sale is made by the sheriff or a deputy upon order of the court. In Georgia, the **deed to secure debt** (also known as a security deed) is used in lieu of both a mortgage and a deed of trust; upon default, it is foreclosed by the lender through exercise of its power of sale.

Foreclosure by exercise of the power-of-sale clause is illegal in a number of states. In other states, laws do not forbid the use of this method, but it is not the customary method of foreclosure. In states where the method is employed, the mortgage or trust deed outlines the events of default that will give the trustee or mortgagee power to sell the premises. Also, it specifies the notice of sale that must be given and the other formalities that must be followed in making the sale.

When the promissory note is repaid in full, the lender sends the trustee a request for reconveyance. The trustee then issues a **reconveyance deed** to the trustor, who records it to give constructive notice that he now owns the property free of the mortgage indebtedness.

Typical Deed of Trust

Most of the uniform covenants of a deed of trust cover the same categories as those in the mortgage document, but a few are different and are identified below.

1. *Deed of trust document.* The security instrument is indeed a deed of trust, as opposed to a mortgage, and warranty deed language is used at the bottom of page two and the top of page three.

2. *Three parties to the contract.* The borrower, public trustee, and lender (beneficiary of the trust) are identified on the first page.

3. *Power-of-sale clause.* The power-of-sale clause is included in the deed transfer clause at the top of page three.

4. *Foreclosure procedures.* The first nonuniform covenant, #22 in the previous list, outlines the foreclosure process the lender and trustee must follow if there is a default by the borrower.

5. *Release.* Upon payment of all sums under this mortgage, the lender will cancel the note and then give it to the trustee so that he can release the property as security for the loan.

6. *Waiver of homestead.* In some jurisdictions, the lender is unable to foreclose on property serving as the borrower's **homestead** (official residence). This clause waives the borrower's right to exempt the property from the collateral.

What Other Types of Loans Are Available?

So far, this chapter has concentrated on what those in the real estate industry would call "plain vanilla" mortgages, or promissory notes and security instruments that vary little from the standardized model. However, there are other types of mortgage loans, specialized mortgage clauses, and nonmortgage instruments designed to serve specific purposes. The following sections introduce some of the more common ones.

BLANKET MORTGAGE

A **blanket mortgage** loan is secured by several parcels of real property. It is most often used by land developers as they first plat a large tract into several smaller lots, then receive a development loan that is secured by all of the lots. Because the blanket development loan contains a release clause, the developer is able to repay a portion of the loan when he sells a lot and then have that lot released from the security backing the development loan. The lot purchaser requires the lot to be unencumbered by any loan so that she may obtain a construction loan to fund the construction of improvements on the lot and give the construction lender a first lien position.

PACKAGE MORTGAGE

A **package mortgage** loan may be used when the borrower acquires both the real estate and certain long-lived pieces of personal property used with it and wants to finance both with one mortgage loan. This type of mortgage is attractive to the borrower because he does not have to negotiate a separate loan to finance his acquisition of the property and another one (or more) to cover his purchase items, such as a refrigerator, a clothes washer and dryer, and carpets. This mortgage is commonly used in the financing of homes by the builder or in the acquisition of hotel, motel, and apartment projects.

OPEN-END MORTGAGE

An **open-end mortgage** loan is one mortgage document providing for future advances of additional funds. An advance can be automatic or optional with lender evaluation before more funds are extended. This type of mortgage might be used when the total amount to be borrowed is unknown at the time the loan documentation is prepared, perhaps because a project is being developed using "fast-track" project management, in which construction begins before total project design is completed.

LEASEHOLD MORTGAGE

Not all mortgage loans are secured by the owner of a parcel. For example, someone may obtain a long-term lease on a parcel and then spend a substantial amount of money either building or renovating the improvements. Frequently, the lessee (tenant) wants to finance the cost of the improvements and so obtains a loan secured by those improvements. This type of loan, used primarily with commercial ventures, is called a **leasehold mortgage.** It will be repaid from the sale of the improved space or from the rental income generated from the space.

SELLER FINANCING

Another method of raising cash to supplement the purchaser's existing equity funds is to ask the seller to extend credit for the difference (or for part of the difference) between the selling price of the property and the amount lent by the financial institution. This method is known as **seller financing.** The seller can do this by using such instruments as a second mortgage or an installment note. A **second mortgage** is a loan that is in second position behind the first loan in case of default.

A **purchase money mortgage** (PMM) is a mortgage offered to the seller as consideration for a portion of the purchase price. The seller is asked to extend financing for part of the equity. The existing mortgage may be assumed as a part of the consideration. The motivation for this type of financing occurs when the buyer is short of cash, or the terms of the first loan are attractive relative to those found in the current market.

INSTALLMENT NOTE

An **installment note,** while less commonly used than the second mortgage, also helps the buyer bridge the gap between the purchase price and the available down payment. The buyer gives the seller "paper" instead of cash. The note is a promise to pay the amount due with periodic payments (usually monthly) during an agreed-upon time period. The payments generally include interest and may include principal amortization. Just as with the second mortgage, the installment note often must be completely repaid within a relatively short time. The major difference between a second mortgage and an installment note is that the second mortgage has the property as security and the installment note does not.

How Can a Borrower Get the Benefit of Lower Interest Rates?

ecause long-term interest rates fell from more than 16 percent in the early 1980s to around 6 percent in the late 1990s, borrowers have sought ways to take advantage of mortgage rates that are lower than the rates on their loans. The term *refinancing* means taking out a replacement mortgage at prevailing market interest rates and using at least part of the money from the new loan to repay the current mortgage indebtedness. This method has been widely used by residential borrowers during the past 20 years, but income property loans largely restrict prepayments of loan balances ahead of their due dates.

BENEFITS OF REFINANCING

One of the major benefits to refinancing is the ability to obtain a new loan with a lower interest rate, thus reducing the borrower's mortgage payment. This is why purchasers generally have not wanted to assume existing mortgages during the past 10 years. They could obtain a new loan with a lower interest rate than the current one carried. Further, they could often obtain a larger **loan-to-value ratio (LTV)** (the amount of debt divided by the value of the property) with a new loan than the current loan's balance afforded them, thus decreasing the amount of equity capital needed.

Both of these benefits are also available to current owners, not just to purchasers. An owner can obtain a new loan with a lower interest rate and repay the current one that carries a higher rate. This enables the borrower either to reduce his monthly payment or to shorten the amortization period necessary to fully repay the loan and keep the debt service payment nearly the same. Many owners traded in their current 30-year loans for 15-year mortgages when they took advantage of the lower rates. In addition, an owner may want to refinance the current mortgage to raise cash. He could take out a mortgage with a larger loan amount than the current mortgage's loan balance. With the lower interest rate, his payment may stay the same or increase only marginally. After repaying the current loan, he will be left with additional cash to use as he sees fit.

COSTS OF REFINANCING

Although there are clear benefits to the borrower from refinancing, it is usually not a costless transaction. A number of closing costs are involved, including a loan origination fee, points, credit report, survey, appraisal, title insurance premium, recording fee, property inspection fee, legal fees, and any mortgage insurance premium. Either the borrower can pay these fees in cash, or the lender might be willing to include them in the loan amount. Although the latter approach may appear to be costless, the cost is the smaller amount of cash available to the borrower when the closing costs are financed.

ARE THE BENEFITS WORTH THE COSTS?

The answer to this question can be fairly complex because it depends upon the interaction of a number of factors:

1. the savings in monthly payments with the new loan

2. any increase in up-front cash available if the new loan is greater than the existing loan
3. the closing costs that must be paid upfront to achieve the future savings
4. the borrower's income due to the associated income tax consequences
5. whatever investment opportunities are available to the borrower
6. how long the borrower expects to keep the new loan
7. any prepayment penalties on existing loan

Although several considerations are involved, the answer may be found through use of the time-value-of-money functions on a financial calculator.

Let us simplify the problem in order to more readily show how to solve it. Assume we are dealing with a single-family house valued at $100,000 with a current mortgage loan carrying a 10-percent interest rate and having a balance of $61,807.57 after five years of payments. The owner could probably refinance the existing mortgage by taking out an $80,000 loan at 8-percent interest for 25 years, provided the neighborhood continues to show prospects for future growth and the owner's income remains satisfactory. It would cost the owner $3,000 in closing costs to refinance the loan. This new loan is expected to be kept for its full life of 25 years.

Ignoring the income tax ramifications (that is, the monthly payments are tax-deductible expenses), so that we do not need to know the owner's tax bracket, we see that the owner has reduced the interest rate on the loan from 10 to 8 percent. The old debt service payment based on the existing mortgage (which was a $64,000, 10%, 30-year loan when originated) was $561.65. The existing mortgage now has a balance of $61,807.57. Each student should verify on a calculator of choice that the loan balance equals this amount.

The new payment is $55.80 more per month, at $617.45 per month ($80,000, 8%, 25-year). Each student should verify this amount.

Of course, the borrower keeps the additional up-front cash of $15,192.43 from the refinancing ($80,000 from the new loan less $61,807.57 to repay the existing loan less $3,000 in closing costs) to offset the greater monthly debt service payment costs. The owner has "taken out part of the equity" in this refinancing example.

Is it a good deal or not? Using the period of the new loan as N (25 years), the up-front cash as PV ($15,192.43), and the additional mortgage payment as PMT ($55.80), we can calculate the interest rate from this transaction that is equal to 0.79 percent. Each student should verify this amount on a calculator of choice.

This calculation shows that 0.79 percent per year has been received from this refinancing, so this is not a good choice.

Chapter Summary

This chapter presents the key characteristics of mortgage loans for real property. Typically, the mortgage loan consists of two parts: equity and debt. Equity represents the down payment from the borrower, and debt is the mortgage from a lender. The debt portion, or the mortgage, is repaid in periodic payments that remain fixed or may be adjusted relative to changes in the market rate of interest. Either type of loan requires an amortization payment that is composed of a payment to the debt and another that pays the interest to the lender.

Amortization is the periodic debt service paid to the lender. This chapter has shown how to construct an amortization table and discussed the underlying characteristics. The fixed-rate mortgage is the most common type of mortgage, and it contains a constant interest rate and a constant payment to the end of the loan.

The typical uniform clauses found in a loan were discussed. Simultaneously, the clauses located in the accompanying note were identified. The note represents the borrower's personal bond to repay the debt. Further, the mortgage was contrasted to the deed of trust that is used in some locations.

Other types of loans were also discussed. For example, the borrower may need a blanket loan on a number of parcels of real property as opposed to a package loan that can include personal property.

Internet Applications

A website has been established for this chapter at http://epley.swcollege.com.

Review Questions

1. Explain the difference between equity and debt funds.

2. What are the sources of equity funds? Of debt funds?

3. Define and explain the function of each of the following:
   mortgage interest
   principal payment
   monthly payment
   loan amortization

4. Explain the direction of change over time in the monthly interest paid, monthly debt paid, and remaining balance owed.

5. Explain the economic characteristics of a fixed-rate mortgage loan.

6. Given the following, calculate an amortization table for the first three payments:

First loan:	$60,000
Interest rate:	10.25%
Term:	30 years
Payments:	monthly

7. Using problem #6 above, answer each of the following:
   Total interest paid in months 73 to 84
   Total paid to debt in months 73 to 84
   Ending balance of loan after month 84
   Payment to debt in month 84
   Payment to interest in month 84

8. In problem #6 above, the owner wants to refinance the remaining loan balance after the 84th payment is made. The new interest rate will be 8 percent for the remaining months. What is the new monthly payment?

9. In problem #6 above, what should the remaining loan balance equal after the 360th payment is made? Prove it by calculating the balance.

10. In problem #6 above, change the interest rate to 8.25 percent. What is the new monthly payment?

11. In problem #6 above, change the term to 20 years. What is the new monthly payment?

12. Compare the monthly payments in problem #6 to those found in questions #10 and #11. Do they change? Why or why not?

13. Outline the major components of a Fannie Mae/Freddie Mac note. Discuss the covenants that a borrower makes to the lender. What is the purpose of each?

14. Outline the uniform covenants found in a typical mortgage. What is the meaning of each?

15. What is the difference between a deed of trust and a mortgage?

Discussion Questions

1. Define and discuss each of the following:
   acceleration
   assumption
   balloon payment
   blanket mortgage
   discount points (give an example)
   due-on-sale clause
   loan-to-value (LTV) ratio (give an example)
   package mortgage
   prepayment
   refinancing (give an example)
   statutory right of redemption
2. Discuss the information found in each of the Internet assignments.

Financing Single-Family Homes

1. What types of residential loans are available?

2. What are the features of the amortization schedules of the fixed-rate and the adjustable rate loans?

3. What is contained in the typical residential application?

4. What federal laws apply to the loan application process?

When finished with this chapter, the student should be able to:

1. Describe the types of residential loans available.

2. Discuss the sources of a residential loan and compare the differences.

3. Calculate the amortization schedules for a fixed-rate and an adjustable rate mortgage.

4. Discuss the features of the Uniform Residential Loan Application.

5. Describe the features of the federal RESPA, ECOA, Truth-in-Lending, HMDA, CRA, and Fair Credit Reporting acts.

adjustable rate mortgage (ARM)

annual percentage rate (APR)

balloon loan

buydown mortgage

certificate of eligibility

closing

closing costs

Community Reinvestment Act (CRA)

conventional mortgage loans

Equal Credit Opportunity Act (ECOA)

Fair Credit Reporting Act

Federal Home Loan Mortgage Corporation
(FHLMC or Freddie Mac)

Federal National Mortgage Association
(FNMA or Fannie Mae)

finance charge

Government National Mortgage Association
(GNMA or Ginnie Mae)

government-sponsored enterprises (GSEs)

graduated payment mortgage (GPM)

growing equity mortgage (GEM)

home equity loans

Home Mortgage Disclosure Act (HMDA)

interest rate cap

margin

mortgage banker

mortgage broker

mortgage-backed security (MBS)

negative amortization

nonconventional loans

pass-throughs

primary mortgage market

private mortgage insurance (PMI)

Real Estate Settlement Procedures Act
(RESPA)

reverse annuity mortgage (RAM)

savings and loan associations (S&Ls)

secondary mortgage market

total obligations ratio

Truth-in-Lending Act

underwriting

Uniform Residential Loan Application

INTRODUCTION

Obtaining a single-family home loan, whether it is used to purchase a property or to replace a loan on a home the borrower already owns, is usually done infrequently by the borrower. Consequently, most borrowers are not knowledgeable consumers when it comes to home loans. To overcome this lack of knowledge, prospective borrowers should allocate sufficient time to shop among financial lenders and compare terms to find the lender that offers a mortgage loan containing terms that fit the individual's needs. An excellent summary of the home purchasing process, including the mortgage financing decision, is available from Fannie Mae's HomePath website. The address for this and for others related to this chapter can be found on this book's website for this chapter.

What Should a Purchaser Consider When Shopping for a Home Loan?

A real estate loan is likely to be the single largest debt that a person will incur in a lifetime, and the terms of that debt should suit the borrower. The following typical loan terms can vary among lenders.

1. *Size of the down payment.* The size of the required cash down payment typically equals 3, 5, 10, or 20 percent of the smaller amount: the house's selling price or its appraised value. In some cases, the down payment may even be zero.

2. *Mortgage interest rate.* The exact mortgage interest rate may vary by up to 1 percentage point as the amount of the loan and the size of the down payment change. The larger the loan and the smaller the amount of the down payment, the higher the interest rate on the loan.

3. *Rate lock period.* The lender will guarantee the availability of a loan with a quoted interest rate for a period of time. The longer the rate lock period, the higher the fees the borrower must pay.

4. *Length of the grace period.* A *grace period* is the number of days after the payment's due date in which the borrower can make the mortgage payment and the lender will still count it as paid on time. Grace periods typically range from 7 to 30 days.

5. *Late charge for overdue payments.* This clause within the promissory note identifies the penalty that the borrower is assessed if the mortgage payments are not made within the grace period. This penalty is usually calculated as a certain percentage of the overdue debt service payment.

6. *Prepayment clause.* When the borrower signs the promissory note, he agrees to make monthly payments of a certain amount for several years. If he should subsequently decide to make a greater payment that would prepay part or all of the loan balance, he would be in violation of his note agreement. Fortunately, most single-family home loans now include a prepayment clause in which the lender gives the borrower permission to prepay the loan—without charging him a penalty if he does so.

7. *Amount of mortgage deficiency insurance, if any.* If the borrower defaults on the loan and the property is eventually sold at a foreclosure sale, it is possible that it will not be sold for enough to fully repay what the borrower owes the lender. This would create a deficiency after the foreclosure. To cover the possibility of a deficiency, the lender may require that the borrower purchase mortgage deficiency insurance. The amount of deficiency insurance required by the lender depends on the size of the down payment. The larger the down payment, the smaller the amount of insurance (and hence the less expensive the coverage).

8. *Due-on-sale clause.* The due-on-sale clause requires that the borrower must obtain the lender's prior written consent to transfer any interest in the property. If the borrower fails to do so, the lender may accelerate the loan balance so that it becomes immediately due and payable.

As the prospective borrower begins shopping for a loan, the first step is for the borrower to determine how much cash can be made available for a down payment and the roughly 3 percent of the purchase price necessary to pay **closing costs,** such as the loan origination fee, credit report, survey, appraisal, title insurance premium, homeowner's insurance premium, recording fee, property inspection fee, legal fees, allocation of prepaid expenses, any mortgage insurance premium, points, and so forth.

An extremely important second step is to shop among lenders, either in the borrower's local community or on the Internet using a service such as Microsoft's Home Advisor or Quicken's Mortgage Center (among others) to locate those lenders who will grant the amount of loan needed by the buyer to purchase the desired property. The third step is to select from this group of lenders the one who offers the best combination of terms and service. This may be done after the purchase contract is signed by the buyer, or the buyer may prefer to be "prequalified" by a lender so that he knows what financing is available prior to shopping for a house. Most borrowers want the lowest interest rate, the longest maturity, the longest grace period, no prepayment penalty, the smallest late charge, and no due-on-sale clause, all coupled with superb service available whenever the borrower wants it.

What Types of Home Loans Are Available?

As the borrower begins to shop for a home loan, the type of loan selected will depend primarily upon the amount of down payment she has saved and can apply toward the purchase price. If the borrower is fortunate enough to have saved at least 20 percent of the purchase price for a down payment or has a large down payment from the sale of another home, then the lender most likely will view this as a relatively low-risk loan and will *not* require any additional protection from a foreclosure loss than the 20-percent down payment will provide. On the other hand, loans on homes with down payments of less than 20 percent of the home's value are generally considered high-risk loans, and the lender will demand foreclosure loss protection either from a company that specializes in mortgage deficiency insurance or from the federal government.

The second decision the borrower must make is whether he wants a loan that requires fixed monthly payments or one that has payments that change during the life of the loan. Some of the varying payment mortgage loans change in a predetermined way (that is, the borrower knows when he obtains the loan what the future payments will be), and others change as market interest rates vary. While the former may help the borrower by tailoring the future payments to his expected income stream, the latter introduce a significant increase in uncertainty into the borrower's budgeting process. We will assume the borrower wants a fixed-rate mortgage during the first part of this chapter, then explore other alternative loans later in the chapter.

CONVENTIONAL MORTGAGE LOANS

Most mortgage loans have neither government default insurance nor a government guarantee against default losses. These are called **conventional mortgage loans.** Although conventional loans may offer the mortgage lender deficiency protection from a private mortgage insurance company, most do not. They are low-risk loans in which the borrower has invested equity capital of at least 20 percent of the purchase price in terms of a down payment.

Application Procedure

Anyone can apply for a conventional, single-family home loan. The application procedure for a conventional mortgage loan typically includes the following five steps.

1. The applicant submits a residential loan application form, frequently the widely accepted **Uniform Residential Loan Application** shown in Exhibit 9.1 and found on-line at www.fanniemae.com/singlefamily/doingbusiness/forms/formlist.

EXHIBIT 9.1   Uniform Residential Loan Application.

Uniform Residential Loan Application

This application is designed to be completed by the applicant(s) with the lender's assistance. Applicants should complete this form as "Borrower" or "Co-Borrower", as applicable. Co-Borrower information must also be provided (and the appropriate box checked) when ☐ the income or assets of a person other than the "Borrower" (including the Borrower's spouse) will be used as a basis for loan qualification or ☐ the income or assets of the Borrower's spouse will not be used as a basis for loan qualification, but his or her liabilities must be considered because the Borrower resides in a community property state, the security property is located in a community property state, or the Borrower is relying on other property located in a community property state as a basis for repayment of the loan.

I. TYPE OF MORTGAGE AND TERMS OF LOAN

Mortgage Applied for:	☐ VA ☐ FHA	☐ Conventional ☐ FmHA	☐ Other:	Agency Case Number	Lender Case No.

Amount $	Interest Rate %	No. of Months	Amortization Type:	☐ Fixed Rate ☐ GPM	☐ Other (explain): ☐ ARM (type):

II. PROPERTY INFORMATION AND PURPOSE OF LOAN

Subject Property Address (street, city, state, & zip code)	No. of Units

Legal Description of Subject Property (attach description if necessary)	Year Built

Purpose of Loan	☐ Purchase ☐ Refinance	☐ Construction ☐ Construction-Permanent	☐ Other (explain):	Property will be: ☐ Primary Residence ☐ Secondary Residence ☐ Investment

Complete this line if construction or construction-permanent loan.

Year Lot Acquired	Original Cost $	Amount Existing Liens $	(a) Present Value of Lot $	(b) Cost of Improvements $	Total (a + b) $

Complete this line if this is a refinance loan.

Year Acquired	Original Cost $	Amount Existing Liens $	Purpose of Refinance	Describe Improvements ☐ made ☐ to be made Cost: $

Title will be held in what Name(s)	Manner in which Title will be held	Estate will be held in: ☐ Fee Simple ☐ Leasehold (show expiration date)

Source of Down Payment, Settlement Charges and/or Subordinate Financing (explain)

III. BORROWER INFORMATION

Borrower	Co-Borrower
Borrower's Name (include Jr. or Sr. if applicable)	Co-Borrower's Name (include Jr. or Sr. if applicable)

Social Security Number	Home Phone (incl. area code)	Age	Yrs. School	Social Security Number	Home Phone (incl. area code)	Age	Yrs. School

☐ Married ☐ Separated ☐ Unmarried (include single, divorced, widowed)	Dependents (not listed by Co-Borrower) no.	ages	☐ Married ☐ Separated ☐ Unmarried (include single, divorced, widowed)	Dependents (not listed by Borrower) no.	ages

Present Address (street, city, state, zip code) ☐ Own ☐ Rent ___ No. Yrs.	Present Address (street, city, state, zip code) ☐ Own ☐ Rent ___ No. Yrs.

If residing at present address for less than two years, complete the following:

Former Address (street, city, state, zip code) ☐ Own ☐ Rent ___ No. Yrs.	Former Address (street, city, state, zip code) ☐ Own ☐ Rent ___ No. Yrs.

Former Address (street, city, state, zip code) ☐ Own ☐ Rent ___ No. Yrs.	Former Address (street, city, state, zip code) ☐ Own ☐ Rent ___ No. Yrs.

IV. EMPLOYMENT INFORMATION

Borrower	Co-Borrower
Name & Address of Employer ☐ Self Employed	Yrs. on this job	Name & Address of Employer ☐ Self Employed	Yrs. on this job
	Yrs. employed in this line of work/profession		Yrs. employed in this line of work/profession
Position/Title/Type of Business	Business Phone (incl. area code)	Position/Title/Type of Business	Business Phone (incl. area code)

If employed in current position for less than two years or if currently employed in more than one position, complete the following:

Name & Address of Employer ☐ Self Employed	Dates (from - to)	Name & Address of Employer ☐ Self Employed	Dates (from - to)
	Monthly Income $		Monthly Income $
Position/Title/Type of Business	Business Phone (incl. area code)	Position/Title/Type of Business	Business Phone (incl. area code)

Name & Address of Employer ☐ Self Employed	Dates (from - to)	Name & Address of Employer ☐ Self Employed	Dates (from - to)
	Monthly Income $		Monthly Income $
Position/Title/Type of Business	Business Phone (incl. area code)	Position/Title/Type of Business	Business Phone (incl. area code)

Freddie Mac Form 10/92	ITEM 7300L1 (9210)	Page 1 of 4 pages	"I/We acknowledge that the information provided on this page is true and correct ____ ."	Fannie Mae Form 1003 10/92

(continued)

EXHIBIT 9.1 Uniform Residential Loan Application, continued.

V. MONTHLY INCOME AND COMBINED HOUSING EXPENSE INFORMATION

Gross Monthly Income	Borrower	Co-Borrower	Total	Combined Monthly Housing Expense	Present	Proposed
Base Empl. Income*	$	$	$	Rent	$	
Overtime				First Mortgage (P&I)		$
Bonuses				Other Financing (P&I)		
Commissions				Hazard Insurance		
Dividends/Interest				Real Estate Taxes		
Net Rental Income				Mortgage Insurance		
OTHER (before completing, see the notice in "describe other income," below)				Homeowner Assn. Dues		
				Other:		
Total	$	$	$	Total	$	$

*Self Employed Borrower(s) may be required to provide additional documentation such as tax returns and financial statements.

Describe Other Income   Notice: Alimony, child support, or separate maintenance income need not be revealed if the Borrower (B) or Co-Borrower (C) does not choose to have it considered for repaying this loan.

B/C		Monthly Amount
		$

VI. ASSETS AND LIABILITIES

This Statement and any applicable supporting schedules may be completed jointly by both married and unmarried Co-Borrowers if their assets and liabilities are sufficiently joined so that the Statement can be meaningfully and fairly presented on a combined basis; otherwise separate Statements and Schedules are required. If the Co-Borrower section was completed about a spouse, this Statement and supporting schedules must be completed about that spouse also.

Completed ☐ Jointly   ☐ Not Jointly

ASSETS Description	Cash or Market Value	Liabilities and Pledged Assets. List the creditor's name, address and account number for all outstanding debts, including automobile loans, revolving charge accounts, real estate loans, alimony, child support, stock pledges, etc. Use continuation sheet, if necessary. Indicate by (*) those liabilities which will be satisfied upon sale of real estate owned or upon refinancing of the subject property.	Monthly Payt. & Mos. Left to Pay	Unpaid Balance
Cash deposit toward purchase held by	$	**LIABILITIES**		
		Name and address of Company	$ Payt./Mos.	$
List checking and savings accounts below				
Name and address of Bank, S&L, or Credit Union				
		Acct. no.		
		Name and address of Company	$ Payt./Mos.	$
Acct. no.	$			
Name and address of Bank, S&L, or Credit Union				
		Acct. no.		
		Name and address of Company	$ Payt./Mos.	$
Acct. no.	$			
Name and address of Bank, S&L, or Credit Union				
		Acct. no.		
		Name and address of Company	$ Payt./Mos.	$
Acct. no.	$			
Name and address of Bank, S&L, or Credit Union				
		Acct. no.		
		Name and address of Company	$ Payt./Mos.	$
Acct. no.	$			
Stocks & Bonds (Company name/number & description)	$			
		Acct. no.		
		Name and address of Company	$ Payt./Mos.	$
Life insurance net cash value	$			
Face amount: $				
Subtotal Liquid Assets	$			
Real estate owned (enter market value from schedule of real estate owned)	$	Acct. no.		
		Name and address of Company	$ Payt./Mos.	$
Vested interest in retirement fund	$			
Net worth of business(es) owned (attach financial statement)	$			
Automobiles owned (make and year)	$			
		Acct. no.		
		Alimony/Child Support/Separate Maintenance Payments Owed to:	$	
Other Assets (itemize)	$	Job Related Expense (child care, union dues, etc.)	$	
		Total Monthly Payments	$	
Total Assets a.	$	Net Worth (a minus b) → $	Total Liabilities b.	$

Freddie Mac Form 65 10/92   Page 2 of 4 pages   "I/We acknowledge that the information provided on this page is true and correct _____."   Fannie Mae Form 1003 10/92

(continued)

EXHIBIT 9.1 Uniform Residential Loan Application, continued.

VI. ASSETS AND LIABILITIES (cont.)

Schedule of Real Estate Owned (If additional properties are owned, use continuation sheet.)

Property Address (enter S if sold, PS if pending sale or R if rental being held for income)	Type of Property	Present Market Value	Amount of Mortgages & Liens	Gross Rental Income	Mortgage Payments	Insurance, Maintenance, Taxes & Misc.	Net Rental Income
		$	$	$	$	$	$
Totals		$	$	$	$	$	$

List any additional names under which credit has previously been received and indicate appropriate creditor name(s) and account number(s):

Alternate Name	Creditor Name	Account Number

VII. DETAILS OF TRANSACTION

a. Purchase price	$
b. Alterations, improvements, repairs	
c. Land (if acquired separately)	
d. Refinance (incl. debts to be paid off)	
e. Estimated prepaid items	
f. Estimated closing costs	
g. PMI, MIP, Funding Fee	
h. Discount (if Borrower will pay)	
i. Total costs (add items a through h)	
j. Subordinate financing	
k. Borrower's closing costs paid by Seller	
l. Other Credits (explain)	
m. Loan amount (exclude PMI, MIP, Funding Fee financed)	
n. PMI, MIP, Funding Fee financed	
o. Loan amount (add m & n)	
p. Cash from/to Borrower (subtract j, k, l & o from i)	

VIII. DECLARATIONS

If you answer "yes" to any questions a through i, please use continuation sheet for explanation.

	Borrower Yes No	Co-Borrower Yes No
a. Are there any outstanding judgments against you?		
b. Have you been declared bankrupt within the past 7 years?		
c. Have you had property foreclosed upon or given title or deed in lieu thereof in the last 7 years?		
d. Are you a party to a lawsuit?		
e. Have you directly or indirectly been obligated on any loan which resulted in foreclosure, transfer of title in lieu of foreclosure, or judgment? (This would include such loans as home mortgage loans, SBA loans, home improvement loans, educational loans, manufactured (mobile) home loans, any mortgage, financial obligation, bond, or loan guarantee. If "Yes," provide details, including date, name and address of Lender, FHA or VA case number, if any, and reasons for the action.)		
f. Are you presently delinquent or in default on any Federal debt or any other loan, mortgage, financial obligation, bond, or loan guarantee? If "Yes," give details as described in the preceding question.		
g. Are you obligated to pay alimony, child support, or separate maintenance?		
h. Is any part of the down payment borrowed?		
i. Are you a co-maker or endorser on a note?		
j. Are you a U.S. citizen?		
k. Are you a permanent resident alien?		
l. Do you intend to occupy the property as your primary residence? If "Yes," complete question m below.		
m. Have you had an ownership interest in a property in the last three years?		
(1) What type of property did you own - principal residence (PR), second home (SH), or investment property (IP)?		
(2) How did you hold title to the home - solely by yourself (S), jointly with your spouse (SP), or jointly with another person (O)?		

IX. ACKNOWLEDGMENT AND AGREEMENT

The undersigned specifically acknowledge(s) and agree(s) that: (1) the loan requested by this application will be secured by a first mortgage or deed of trust on the property described herein; (2) the property will not be used for any illegal or prohibited purpose or use; (3) all statements made in this application are made for the purpose of obtaining the loan indicated herein; (4) occupation of the property will be as indicated above; (5) verification or reverification of any information contained in the application may be made at any time by the Lender, its agents, successors and assigns, either directly or through a credit reporting agency, from any source named in this application, and the original copy of this application will be retained by the Lender, even if the loan is not approved; (6) the Lender, its agents, successors and assigns will rely on the information contained in the application and I/we have a continuing obligation to amend and/or supplement the information provided in this application if any of the material facts which I/we have represented herein should change prior to closing; (7) in the event my/our payments on the loan indicated in this application become delinquent, the Lender, its agents, successors and assigns, may, in addition to all their other rights and remedies, report my/our name(s) and account information to a credit reporting agency; (8) ownership of the loan may be transferred to successor or assign of the Lender without notice to me and/or the administration of the loan account may be transferred to an agent, successor or assign of the Lender with prior notice to me; (9) the Lender, its agents, successors and assigns make no representations or warranties, express or implied, to the Borrower(s) regarding the property, the condition of the property, or the value of the property.

Certification: I/We certify that the information provided in this application is true and correct as of the date set forth opposite my/our signature(s) on this application and acknowledge my/our understanding that any intentional or negligent misrepresentation(s) of the information contained in this application may result in civil liability and/or criminal penalties including, but not limited to, fine or imprisonment or both under the provisions of Title 18, United States Code, Section 1001, et. seq. and liability for monetary damages to the Lender, its agents, successors and assigns, insurers and any other person who may suffer any loss due to reliance upon any misrepresentation which I/we have made on this application.

Borrower's Signature	Date	Co-Borrower's Signature	Date
X		X	

X. INFORMATION FOR GOVERNMENT MONITORING PURPOSES

The following information is requested by the Federal Government for certain types of loans related to a dwelling, in order to monitor the Lender's compliance with equal credit opportunity, fair housing and home mortgage disclosure laws. You are not required to furnish this information, but are encouraged to do so. The law provides that a Lender may neither discriminate on the basis of this information, nor on whether you choose to furnish it. However, if you choose not to furnish it, under Federal regulations this Lender is required to note race and sex on the basis of visual observation or surname. If you do not wish to furnish the above information, please check the box below. (Lender must review the above material to assure that the disclosures satisfy all requirements to which the Lender is subject under applicable state law for the particular type of loan applied for.)

BORROWER

I do not wish to furnish this information

Race/National Origin:
- American Indian or Alaskan Native
- Asian or Pacific Islander
- White, not of Hispanic origin
- Black, not of Hispanic origin
- Hispanic
- Other (specify)

Sex: Female / Male

CO-BORROWER

I do not wish to furnish this information

Race/National Origin:
- American Indian or Alaskan Native
- Asian or Pacific Islander
- White, not of Hispanic origin
- Black, not of Hispanic origin
- Hispanic
- Other (specify)

Sex: Female / Male

To be Completed by Interviewer	Interviewer's Name (print or type)		Name and Address of Interviewer's Employer
This application was taken by:			
face-to-face interview	Interviewer's Signature	Date	
by mail			
by telephone	Interviewer's Phone Number (incl. area code)		

Freddie Mac Form 65 10/92   Page 3 of 4 pages   Fannie Mae Form 1003 10/92

(continued)

EXHIBIT 9.1 Uniform Residential Loan Application, continued.

Continuation Sheet/Residential Loan Application

Use this continuation sheet if you need more space to complete the Residential Loan Application. Mark **B** for Borrower or **C** for Co-Borrower.	Borrower:	Agency Case Number:
	Co-Borrower:	Lender Case Number:

I/We fully understand that it is a Federal crime punishable by fine or imprisonment, or both, to knowingly make any false statements concerning any of the above facts as applicable under the provisions of Title 18, United States Code, Section 1001, et. seq.

Borrower's Signature	Date	Co-Borrower's Signature	Date
X		X	

Freddie Mac Form 65 10/92   Page 4 of 4 pages   Fannie Mae Form 1003 10/92

2. Within three business days, the lender gives the loan applicant the following:

- Good Faith Estimate of Settlement Costs (Exhibit 9.2), which has estimated amounts for all the items the borrower must pay in cash at the **closing,** when title is transferred from the seller to the purchaser, including numerous fees, points, insurance premiums, and reimbursements for any property taxes, association dues, and insurance prepaid by the seller (form is on-line at www.hud.gov:80/fha/sfh/res/1.pdf)

- Truth-in-Lending disclosure statement showing the annual cost of the mortgage financing considering all of the borrower's financing costs and assuming the loan will not be repaid ahead of schedule

- booklet prepared by the U.S. Department of Housing and Urban Development explaining the borrower protections under the Real Estate Settlement and Procedures Act (discussed later in this chapter)

3. The lender requests a unified report on the applicant's credit history from the three national credit bureaus, along with a fee from the borrower to cover the cost of the credit reports. A *credit bureau,* sometimes called a credit repository, is a company that maintains historical information about how well borrowers handle credit, including amounts they have borrowed and how regularly they make payments on their debts. The borrower can contact Equifax, Experian, and TransUnion to obtain a copy of his credit report.

The applicant then must provide information to the lender so that the loan may be underwritten. Loan **underwriting** is the process of evaluating the loan application, including both the applicant and the property being offered as collateral, to determine how risky a loan to this applicant would be. Both the applicant and the lender would prefer that the *alternative documentation system* be used. It allows the potential borrower to provide less information than the complete documentation system (to be covered later) would require, making it easier for the applicant and enabling the lender to make a more timely lending decision.

4. The applicant is asked to provide his employer-supplied W-2 tax information statements for the past two years, which show how much income he has earned, plus the two most recent pay stubs to show he is still employed and his current wages. In addition, the lender need only obtain the employer's verbal, rather than written, verification of current employment.

5. The applicant must provide the most recent months' bank statements to show how much he has in savings.

The lender then underwrites the loan application, a process described later in the chapter, conveys its decision to the applicant, and funds the loan if the risk is deemed acceptable.

If the applicant does not have the income information listed in step 4 or the bank statements requested in step 5, then the lender will be forced to use the more detailed and time-consuming *standard documentation system.* It requires the following steps instead of steps 4 and 5 listed above.

- The applicant and lender complete a Request for Verification of Employment form, which is sent to the applicant's employer. The employer is asked to provide employment and income information for the applicant in order for the applicant to demonstrate that he has had steady and permanent employment over the past two years.

- The applicant and lender complete a Request for Verification of Deposit form, which is sent to the various financial institutions with which the appli-

EXHIBIT 9.2 Good Faith Estimate of Settlement Costs.

A. Settlement Statement

U.S. Department of Housing
and Urban Development

OMB Approval No. 2502-0265

B. Type of Loan

1. ☐ FHA 2. ☐ FmHA 3. ☐ Conv. Unins. 4. ☐ VA 5. ☐ Conv. Ins.	6. File Number:	7. Loan Number:	8. Mortgage Insurance Case Number:

C. Note: This form is furnished to give you a statement of actual settlement costs. Amounts paid to and by the settlement agent are shown. Items marked "(p.o.c.)" were paid outside the closing; they are shown here for informational purposes and are not included in the totals.

D. Name & Address of Borrower:	E. Name & Address of Seller:	F. Name & Address of Lender:

G. Property Location:	H. Settlement Agent:	
	Place of Settlement:	I. Settlement Date:

J. Summary of Borrower's Transaction		K. Summary of Seller's Transaction	
100. Gross Amount Due From Borrower		**400. Gross Amount Due To Seller**	
101. Contract sales price		401. Contract sales price	
102. Personal property		402. Personal property	
103. Settlement charges to borrower (line 1400)		403.	
104.		404.	
105.		405.	
Adjustments for items paid by seller in advance		**Adjustments for items paid by seller in advance**	
106. City/town taxes to		406. City/town taxes to	
107. County taxes to		407. County taxes to	
108. Assessments to		408. Assessments to	
109.		409.	
110.		410.	
111.		411.	
112.		412.	
120. Gross Amount Due From Borrower		**420. Gross Amount Due To Seller**	
200. Amounts Paid By Or In Behalf Of Borrower		**500. Reductions In Amount Due To Seller**	
201. Deposit or earnest money		501. Excess deposit (see instructions)	
202. Principal amount of new loan(s) 502.		Settlement charges to seller (line 1400)	
203. Existing loan(s) taken subject to 503.		Existing loan(s) taken subject to	
204.		504. Payoff of first mortgage loan	
205.		505. Payoff of second mortgage loan	
206.		506.	
207.		507.	
208.		508.	
209.		509.	
Adjustments for items unpaid by seller		**Adjustments for items unpaid by seller**	
210. City/town taxes to		510. City/town taxes to	
211. County taxes to		511. County taxes to	
212. Assessments to		512. Assessments to	
213.		513.	
214.		514.	
215.		515.	
216.		516.	
217.		517.	
218.		518.	
219.		519.	
220. Total Paid By/For Borrower		**520. Total Reduction Amount Due Seller**	
300. Cash At Settlement From/To Borrower		**600. Cash At Settlement To/From Seller**	
301. Gross Amount due from borrower (line 120)		601. Gross amount due to seller (line 420)	
302. Less amounts paid by/for borrower (line 220)	( )	602. Less reductions in amt. due seller (line 520)	( )
303. Cash ☐ From ☐ To Borrower		**603. Cash** ☐ To ☐ From Seller	

Section 5 of the Real Estate Settlement Procedures Act (RESPA) requires the following: • HUD must develop a Special Information Booklet to help persons borrowing money to finance the purchase of residential real estate to better understand the nature and costs of real estate settlement services; • Each lender must provide the booklet to all applicants from whom it receives or for whom it prepares a written application to borrow money to finance the purchase of residential real estate; • Lenders must prepare and distribute with the Booklet a Good Faith Estimate of the settlement costs that the borrower is likely to incur in connection with the settlement. These disclosures are manadatory.

Section 4(a) of RESPA mandates that HUD develop and prescribe this standard form to be used at the time of loan settlement to provide full disclosure of all

charges imposed upon the borrower and seller. These are third party disclosures that are designed to provide the borrower with pertinent information during the settlement process in order to be a better shopper.

The Public Reporting Burden for this collection of information is estimated to average one hour per response, including the time for reviewing instructions, searching existing data sources, gathering and maintaining the data needed, and completing and reviewing the collection of information.

This agency may not collect this information, and you are not required to complete this form, unless it displays a currently valid OMB control number. The information requested does not lend itself to confidentiality.

Previous editions are obsolete

Page 1 of 2

form **HUD-1** (3/86)
ref Handbook 4305.2

cant has accounts. The institution is asked to provide depository and loan account information for the applicant so that the applicant can demonstrate that he has enough money on hand to cover the down payment and closing costs and these funds can be readily transferred to the seller and lender, respectively.

After the lender receives the information from the employer(s) and the financial institution(s), it then underwrites the loan application, a process described later in the chapter, conveys its decision to the applicant, and funds the loan is the risk is deemed acceptable.

Conventional Mortgage Loans with Private Mortgage Insurance

As long as a sizable down payment of 20 percent or more is involved, mortgage lenders accept the risk of default. Because most single-family mortgage loans are sold to investors in what is called the **secondary mortgage market,** the lender's decision to require deficiency protection is often driven by the secondary market investors' requirements. The two dominant investors are the Federal National Mortgage Association (FNMA or Fannie Mae) and the Federal Home Loan Mortgage Corporation (FHLMC or Freddie Mac). Each of these investors requires deficiency protection if the borrower fails to make a down payment of at least 20 percent of the house's value.

If the borrower wanted to obtain a conventional loan having a low down payment and a loan-to-value (LTV) ratio greater than 80 percent (and thus a down payment of less than 20 percent), then the lender would require that the borrower obtain **private mortgage insurance (PMI)** when the loan is granted. PMI is available from eight nationwide specialized insurance companies, which insure lenders against deficiency losses on mortgages that are considered risky because they are loans with low down payments.

How Does Private Mortgage Insurance Work?

PMI typically insures the top 20 to 25 percent of a loan, not the whole loan. When the lender makes a 90-, 95-, or 97-percent LTV loan, he is protected against losses totaling 20 to 25 percent of the loan amount. Using a 90-percent LTV loan as an example because it is the most common high-ratio loan, the borrower places 10-percent cash down and thus assumes the top 10 percent of risk exposure to falling real estate prices. If the lender is protected by 20-percent PMI coverage, the PMI company covers the next 20 percent of the loan or, equivalently, 18 percent ($90\% \times 20\% = 18\%$) of the original purchase price. The sum of the borrower's first 10-percent risk coverage plus the PMI company's 18-percent coverage means the lender's risk exposure is limited to 72 percent ($100\% - 10\% - 18\% = 72\%$) of the original value of the property. This would be the same risk exposure as making a 72-percent LTV conventional loan without any deficiency protection. More information about PMI can be found on the website for this text.

In summary, any request by the borrower for a conventional mortgage with an LTV ratio in excess of 80 percent (typically, 90 or 95 percent and, occasionally, 97 percent) will almost always necessitate the purchase of PMI. The amount of the coverage depends on the amount loaned, the lender's need for deficiency protection, and what the lender's competitors are requiring. A request for a mortgage with an LTV ratio of 80 percent or less rarely involves PMI.

LOANS INSURED BY THE FEDERAL HOUSING ADMINISTRATION

So far, we have been exploring the borrower's preference for conventional mortgage loans. These loans have neither government deficiency insurance nor a government guarantee against deficiency losses, although we have seen that they may offer deficiency protection from a private mortgage insurance company. If the borrower has only a very small down payment to invest, then he may find the equity capital requirements of the conventional loan to be too great. Instead, he may find that a nonconventional loan better meets his needs. **Nonconventional loans** have deficiency protection provided by the federal government, typically by either the Federal Housing Administration or the Department of Veterans Affairs.

The Federal Housing Administration (FHA), created in 1934 during the Great Depression, is a government agency housed today within the U.S. Department of Housing and Urban Development (HUD). Among other things, the FHA provides deficiency insurance on mortgage loans that are amortized over several years. The FHA does *not* lend money; it merely insures loans made by supervised lending institutions, including mortgage companies, commercial banks, savings and loan associations, and savings banks. If the borrower defaults on the promissory note and the loan is proceeding to foreclosure, the lender has the same options as it does with a conventional loan protected by PMI. The lender may apply to the FHA to purchase the loan for the amount the lender has invested in it, or the lender may undertake the foreclosure sale itself and then seek reimbursement from the FHA for any deficiency loss.

Maximum Loan Amounts

Although a borrower can obtain FHA insurance on many types of mortgage loans, the most common insurance covers loans for construction or the purchase of single-family dwellings. These loans are known in the real estate business as FHA 203(b) loans after the section of the National Housing Act authorizing their use. Unless the property is located in a high-cost area, Section 203(b)–insured loans are limited to $121,296 for single-family homes as of the year 2000; the loan limit for high-cost areas is $219,849. If the sales price is over $50,000, the FHA requires a down payment of only 2.25 percent of the sales price or appraised value, whichever is lower. The buyer must invest a minimum of 3 percent, but closing costs may count in that total, making an FHA-insured loan one that requires a very small investment by the home purchaser.

Insurance Premium

Just as with PMI, the borrower must pay an insurance premium for FHA coverage. However, the borrower's required premium is larger with FHA insurance. The borrower must pay an up-front premium equal to 2.25 percent of the loan amount on 30-year loans. However, this premium may be financed, that is, added to the loan balance and paid over the 30-year life of the loan. In addition to the up-front premium, the borrower also must pay an annual premium of 0.5 percent of the loan amount. This premium is paid monthly along with the *P*rincipal amortization, mortgage *I*nterest, 1/12 of the annual property *T*axes, and 1/12 of the annual homeowners *I*nsurance premium (often abbreviated PITI). The borrower's monthly property tax, homeowners insurance, and FHA insurance payments are deposited into an escrow account and then paid on the borrower's behalf to the appropriate parties by the lender when the payments are due. (To review, *escrow* is an item of value, money, or documents deposited with a third party to be delivered upon the fulfillment of a condition. Another example would be the deposit of funds or documents with an attorney or escrow agent to be disbursed upon the closing of a sale of real estate.)

LOANS GUARANTEED BY THE DEPARTMENT OF VETERANS AFFAIRS

Another attractive program is available to a borrower who is a veteran. Instead of deficiency protection being provided by mortgage insurance, the U.S. Department of Veterans Affairs (VA) offers veterans a guaranty that achieves much the same effect. To show its appreciation to servicemen and servicewomen returning from World War II, Congress in 1944 passed far-reaching legislation to aid veterans in education, hospitalization, employment training, and housing. In the area of housing, the G.I. Bill of Rights empowered the federal government to guarantee the repayment of a portion of any first-mortgage home loan made to a veteran. For this guaranty, no fee would be charged the veteran, and the government would suffer any losses. The objective of the original law was to enable a veteran to buy a home with *no cash down payment* by making the loan less risky for the lender, and the "zero-down" mortgage remains the distinctive feature of VA-guaranteed loans today.

Eligibility

To be eligible for a VA guaranty, the borrower must have served at least 90 days on active duty, and not have been dishonorably discharged, during World War II, the Korean conflict, or the Vietnam era. Veterans with service only during peacetime periods and military personnel who currently are on active duty must have had more than 180 days' active service prior to September 7, 1980, or 24 months of active duty service after that date. Some exceptions to these requirements are made for veterans who served during the Persian Gulf conflict and for reservists and National Guard members. The veteran looking for more detailed information, including these exceptions, should check the VA's Home Loan Program website and visit with a loan officer at a VA-approved mortgage lender. Not only can these lenders provide the veteran with the current status and details of the VA's programs, but they also will be knowledgeable about the availability of state veterans benefits. Several states offer special advantages, including mortgage loan assistance, to their residents who have served in the armed forces. Information on this topic can be found on the website for this text.

Application Procedure

Just as with FHA-insured loans, borrowers obtain VA-guaranteed loans from local lenders, including mortgage companies, commercial banks, and savings and loan associations, *not* from the VA. The veteran's application procedure is the same as the standard documentation system described earlier, although there is one noteworthy difference. The applicant must obtain a **certificate of eligibility** from the VA, preferably prior to searching for a house to purchase. In this certificate, the VA certifies that the individual is indeed a veteran and notes the amount of the guaranty (called the veteran's *entitlement*) for which the veteran is eligible. The lender then underwrites the loan application, a process described later in the chapter, conveys its decision to the applicant, and funds the loan if the risk is deemed acceptable.

VA Guaranty Amount

The veteran is able to obtain a loan carrying a VA guaranty ranging from 50 percent of the loan amount for loans up to $45,000 down to 25 percent for loans in excess of $144,000. Because the maximum guaranty amount in 1999 was $50,750 and because secondary market investors who purchase VA-guaranteed mortgages want the guaranty to cover at least 25 percent of the loan amount, the maximum guaranty limits the borrower's "zero-down" VA loan to $203,000 (50,750 ÷ 0.25). The figures assume the veteran is eligible for the maximum guarantee, but his "entitlement" may be less than that.

VETERAN'S ENTITLEMENT. When the G.I. Bill was enacted into law, the veteran's maximum entitlement was $2,000, but legislation enacted since 1944 has increased the veteran's entitlement up to the present maximum of $36,000 (or up to $50,750 for loans over $144,000). Once all or part of the $36,000 has been used to obtain a VA-guaranteed loan, the veteran's entitlement is reduced. The amount of remaining entitlement, if any, can be determined by subtracting the amount of entitlement used from the *current* maximum available entitlement of $36,000. Moreover, it is possible for the veteran to have his entitlement restored by

1. selling the house and repaying the loan in full,
2. selling the house to a qualified, credit-worthy veteran who "assumes" the outstanding balance on the loan and agrees to "substitute" his entitlement for the same amount of entitlement originally used to obtain the loan, or
3. repaying the loan in full, even though the veteran still owns the property. This restoration option may be used only once.

Unless used, the veteran's entitlement never expires.

Since these terms and amounts can change, students should examine the VA website for current information (www.homeloans.va.gov/mission/htm).

How Does the Lender Decide Whether to Make the Loan?

Once the borrower decides what type of loan is needed, a decision based largely on the amount of down payment he has available and the size of the loan he wants, an application is submitted for a conventional loan (with or without PMI), an FHA-insured loan, or a VA-guaranteed loan.

The lender is concerned about whether the borrower will have enough income to make the monthly debt service payments necessary to repay the mortgage loan according to the payment schedule. Even if the borrower has enough income, the lender is concerned the borrower will not use the income to repay the loan. Finally, regardless of the cause, the lender is worried about loan default. If the borrower should default and never bring the payments current again, the lender will have to foreclose and thus is concerned about the value of the property that serves as collateral for the loan.

BORROWER CAPACITY

Does the applicant have the financial wherewithal to make the monthly debt service payments on the loan? The prospective borrower's income should be sufficient to meet not only the mortgage debt service and escrow payment but also the monthly payments on the applicant's other debts. The lender typically uses two ratios to address the income adequacy question: the housing expense ratio and the total obligations ratio. The *housing expense ratio* is the total monthly housing expenses, including principal amortization, mortgage interest, and one-twelfth of the annual property taxes, hazard insurance, mortgage insurance (if any), flood insurance (if any), association dues (if any), special assessments (if any), and so forth, divided by the borrower's monthly gross income. If the housing expense ratio exceeds 28 percent, there should be a demonstrable reason why the borrower can afford to devote more than 28 percent of her monthly income to housing expenses.

The second ratio, the **total obligations ratio,** is the sum of the housing expenses and the monthly payments on other debt that will take more than 10 months to repay divided by the borrower's monthly gross income. If the total obligations ratio exceeds 36 percent, again there should be a good reason for the lender to assume the borrower is not overextended.

AUTOMATED UNDERWRITING

Just a few years ago, the analysis of the borrower and the property was done by loan officers. This process changed dramatically during the last half of the 1990s as computerized loan underwriting became commonplace, but the essential underwriting process—whether performed manually or by a computer program—remains the same. After the borrower follows the five-step alternative documentation system discussed earlier in the chapter, the lender uses a computer to submit the information to an automated loan underwriting system. The automated system evaluates this information, much as was done manually in the past, and reaches a loan decision within a matter of minutes rather than within weeks.

If the lender does a large enough volume of loan originations to have developed its own automated underwriting system, as several large nationwide lenders have done, the analysis will be done using that system. More likely, the information will be submitted electronically to either Fannie Mae's or Freddie Mac's automated underwriting system, known as Desktop Underwriter and Loan Prospector, respectively.

UNDERWRITING VA-GUARANTEED LOANS

Although the VA does not have an automated underwriting system similar to Fannie Mae's or Freddie Mac's, it does authorize many of its approved lenders to do what it calls automatic processing. This means that the lender, after receiving the deposit and employment verifications, the credit report, and the appraiser's estimate of value (or certificate of reasonable value), is able to approve the loan without waiting for the VA's review of the credit application. Approximately 90 percent of VA applications are handled this way, accelerating the loan approval process as a way for VA-guaranteed loans to compete with conventional loans.

What Other Types of Residential Loans Are Available?

Other types of residential loans exist. A selected sample are discussed below.

THE 15-YEAR LOAN

Although mortgage loans may have any amortization schedule and maturity that the borrower and lender agree upon, most single-family home loans are sold to investors in the secondary mortgage market. Because these investors prefer a limited number of standardized mortgages, most FRM loans have the same amortization period as their maturity—typically 30 years or 15 years. The only difference, then, between a 30-year and a 15-year mortgage loan is that the latter has a shorter amortization period and corresponding maturity.

The shorter period makes a significant difference for the borrower. Although 30-year interest rates are usually higher than 15-year rates, the shorter period during which the 15-year loan must be repaid results in a larger monthly payment. On the other hand, if the borrower calculates the total interest that would be paid during the loan, he will see that he will be paying much less interest with the 15-year loan.

Assume again that the borrower can obtain a $100,000 mortgage that requires monthly debt service payments, but the loan now will be fully amortized over a 15-year period. Because the loan has a shorter term, it will have a lower interest rate; 7.625 percent rather than 8 percent would be a reasonable rate. Due to the shorter amortization period, the borrower will have to pay a higher monthly payment of $934.13 instead of $733.76 with the 30-year loan. However, the total interest the borrower will pay over the 15-year life of the loan is only $68,143.38, a significant savings when compared to the $164,155.25 in interest payable with the 30-year loan.

THE 7-YEAR BALLOON LOAN

So far, the mortgages we have covered have had equal amortization terms and maturities, either a 30-year amortization schedule and 30-year maturity (sometimes called a 30-year "term") or a 15-year amortization term and 15-year maturity. Sometimes, however, the term (or maturity or life) of the loan is less than the scheduled amortization period. For example, the borrower might want to obtain a loan with a 30-year amortization period and a 7-year maturity, known as a 7-year balloon loan. The loan balance remaining when the loan matures is known as the *balloon*. This type of mortgage is called a **balloon loan** because the final payment must include the balloon in addition to the regular debt service payment. Balloon loans of 5, 7, 10, and 15 years are widely available options for the borrower.

Why would a borrower be interested in a balloon loan? Typically, the shorter the maturity of a loan, the lower the interest rate. Borrowers want a lower interest rate because it results in a lower monthly debt service payment, as long as they can keep the lengthy amortization schedule. For example, if the borrower obtains a $100,000, 7-year balloon loan with a 30-year amortization schedule, the interest rate could be approximately 7.25 percent instead of 8 percent for the 30-year loan or 7.625 percent for the 15-year loan. The 30-year amortization would result in a monthly payment of only $682.18 instead of $733.76 for the 30-year loan with a 30-year amortization period.

In return for the $51.58 of monthly savings, the borrower has a balloon payment to make at the loan's maturity at the end of 7 years of $91,496.22 because the loan balance will not have been paid down very far. How will the borrower make the balloon payment? He generally expects either to sell the property before the balloon payment comes due and repay the loan with the sales proceeds, or to refinance the loan at maturity and repay the balloon with the proceeds from a new loan. In the meantime, he has the benefit of a lower monthly payment.

THE ADJUSTABLE RATE MORTGAGE LOAN

Mortgage loans do not have to have fixed interest rates. In fact, loans that have interest rates that vary over time may be attractive to both borrowers and lenders. For borrowers, an **adjustable rate mortgage (ARM)** frequently is available at a lower interest rate than is a fixed-rate mortgage, partly because lenders no longer have to bear the risk of being locked into a low-rate mortgage while market interest rates (and the cost of their funds) increases. The trade-off, of course, is that the borrower now may have to pay escalating interest rates instead of savoring the low, fixed interest rate she once could have obtained. Nevertheless, a borrower might find an ARM attractive if she plans to move in a few years and can enjoy the lower interest rates (and payments) during the interim. Or, perhaps the borrower's income is such that she needs the lower rate to qualify for a mortgage loan.

ARM Features

ARMs are very flexible instruments, limited only by the standardization requirements imposed by mortgage investors in the secondary mortgage market or lenders' own policies. The ARM's key features include the following.

1. *Adjustable interest rate.* The heart of an ARM is an interest rate that may change several times during the life of the mortgage. Although the borrower and lender must agree upon the frequency with which the rate changes, it usually changes once or twice a year. With some plans, it changes every three or five years, or even just once during the life of the loan. Often, an **interest rate cap,** or maximum rate, exists to protect the borrower from the possibility of rapid and continual increases in the mortgage rate. Caps may relate to the periodic interest rate, to the total of all rate changes over the life of the loan, or both. For example, a loan may have an annual rate cap of 1 or 2 percentage points and a lifetime rate cap of +4, +5, or +6 percentage points. Caps enable the borrower to better budget for a worst-case scenario.

2. *Mortgage interest rate index.* Changes in the loan's interest rate are tied to changes in an index that is public information available to the borrower. Both the borrower and lender must agree to use a particular index prior to the loan being made. For the borrower's protection, the lender must not be able to affect the values of the index. Common indexes used include the following:

- Yields on U. S. Treasury securities adjusted to a constant maturity of six months, one year, three years, or five years
- The cost of funds index (COFI) based on costs for lenders in the Eleventh Federal Home Loan Bank District, which covers member institutions in the Far West
- The six-month London Interbank Offered Rate (LIBOR)

Because it frequently results in lower mortgage rates than do the other indexes and because incomes often change on an annual basis, historically consumers have preferred the one-year Treasury index.

3. *Margin.* When calculating the borrower's interest rate, an amount called the **margin** is added to the selected index rate. The borrower and lender must agree on the margin when the loan is obtained, and it then remains constant throughout the life of the loan. The index may change, but the constant margin is added to the revised index to derive the borrower's new mortgage interest rate.

4. *Monthly payment changes.* Regardless of how frequently the mortgage interest rate changes, most ARMs keep the borrower's monthly payment the same for at least six months. If the interest rate changes less often than annually (say, once every three years), then debt service payments remain the same for the longer period before their first adjustment (for example, changing only after three years) but typically change

annually thereafter. Some plans even require only one or two payment changes by the borrower during the life of the loan. In addition, ARMs may include an annual payment cap, similar to the interest rate caps, limiting the payment increase to 7.5 percent. Knowing what the maximum increase in monthly payments might be makes it easier for the borrower to budget for those future mortgage payments.

5. *Initial year's interest rate.* Sometimes lenders offer a so-called *teaser rate* for the first year of the ARM loan. Instead of using the sum of the index plus the margin for the first year's interest rate, the lender may base the initial year's payments on a lower interest rate to encourage borrowers to choose an ARM over a fixed-rate loan. This may lead to "payment shock" for the borrower because the next year's payments are based on the sum of the index plus the margin. Even if the index remains the same or decreases somewhat, the payment may still increase because the loan no longer has the benefit of the teaser rate.

6. *Negative amortization.* **Negative amortization** occurs when the borrower's monthly payment does not cover the total amount of interest owed to the lender. The amount of interest owed, but not paid, is added to the loan balance. This might occur on an ARM loan if the interest rate increases enough to cause the payment to go up by more than the allowable payment cap.

These features make the ARM loan attractive to borrowers because their debt service payments can be noticeably lower or, alternatively, they can afford to purchase a more expensive home. However, the trade-off for the lower rate is that the borrower faces several risks with an ARM. First, misunderstandings may occur between the lender and the borrower over the loan's terms because of the greater complexity of the ARM. Second, the payment changes can be large, especially if no cap exists, making it difficult for the borrower to meet his obligations. Third, negative amortization can cause the borrower to owe more on the loan at the end of the year than he does at the beginning.

ARM Payments

Exhibit 9.3 shows the borrower's monthly payments for a $100,000 ARM, using the 1-year Treasury index with a ±1 percentage point annual interest rate cap and a +5 percentage point lifetime interest rate cap, but without a payment cap. Recall that the interest rate used in the FRM example was 8 percent; a comparable ARM rate in this situation might be 6.4 percent. The calculations assume a worst-case scenario in which the borrower's ARM interest rate increases to 7.4 percent at the end of the first year, 8.4 percent at the end of the second year, 9.4 percent at the end of the third year, 10.4 percent at the end of the fourth year, and 11.4 percent at the end of the fifth year, and then remains at that level for the remaining 24 years of the loan's life. Based on past history, the likelihood of such a worst-case scenario occurring is remote, but the borrower should recognize that this is indeed a possibility.

SPECIALIZED MORTGAGE LOANS

Although 30- and 15-year FRMs, balloon loans, jumbo mortgages, and ARMs are widely available and widely used, they do not solve the needs of every borrower. Because mortgage lending is such a competitive business, lenders are frequently designing new mortgages with specific features targeted to particular market segments. Most of these specialized mortgages lower the monthly payments during the early years of the mortgage so that more borrowers are able to afford a mortgage loan.

EXHIBIT 9.3 Adjustable rate mortgage loan calculations.

$100,000 loan, 30-year term, monthly payment.

	FIXED PAYMENT MORTGAGE			ADJUSTABLE RATE MORTGAGE		
Year	Interest Rate (%)	Monthly Payment ($)	Loan Balance at End of Year ($)	Interest Rate (%)	Monthly Payment ($)	Loan Balance at End of Year ($)
1	8.00	733.76	99,165	6.40	625.51	98,861
2	8.00	733.76	98,260	7.40	690.99	97,851
3	8.00	733.76	97,280	8.40	757.66	96,944
4	8.00	733.76	96,219	9.40	825.26	96,119
5	8.00	733.76	95,070	10.40	893.54	95,357
6	8.00	733.76	93,826	11.40	962.31	94,643
Remaining years	8.00	733.76	N.A.	11.40	962.31	N.A.

N.A. indicates "not applicable."

The Graduated Payment Mortgage

The **graduated payment mortgage (GPM)** allows younger borrowers to enter the home-buying market sooner than they would otherwise be able to do. It accomplishes this by deferring part of the mortgage payments during the early years of the mortgage until later years, when the borrower presumably can better afford to make the payments. The lender adds any deferred interest onto the loan balance so that the balance grows over time. The lender eventually increases the borrower's monthly payment as well, gradually raising it until it is large enough to fully amortize the higher loan balance over the remaining life of the mortgage.

The most common GPM plans increase the borrower's monthly payments by 2, 5, or 7.5 percent annually for 5 years, or by 2 or 3 percent annually for 10 years. Assume the loan applicant is a recent college graduate with currently limited income but excellent prospects for income growth. Given today's relatively low inflation and depending upon her risk preferences, the recent graduate might consider a GPM with either a very aggressive 7.5-percent annual payment increase over 5 years or a conservative 2-percent annual increase over 10 years. Exhibit 9.4 shows two examples of the different monthly payments and associated loan balances for a $100,000, 30-year, monthly amortized, 7-percent GPM loan, presuming the borrower plans to keep that loan for 10 years.

Exhibit 9.4 also includes the standard FRM's level monthly debt service payment of $665.30 and shows the loan's balance steadily declining until it reaches $85,813 at the end of 10 years. The two graduated payment mortgages both require substantially *lower* debt service payments from the borrower during the initial year: either $496.62 with the mortgage that has payments increasing by 7.5 percent annually or $583.16 with the mortgage that has payments increasing by 2 percent annually. Given the borrower's limited income, this would help her to meet more comfortably the monthly payment requirement early in the loan's life. However, the payment increases each year,

$100,000 loan, 7-percent interest, 30-year term, monthly payment.

Year	FIXED PAYMENT MORTGAGE		GRADUATED PAYMENT MORTGAGES			
			7.5% Increase/Year for 5 Years		2% Increase/Year for 10 Years	
	Monthly Payment ($)	Loan Balance at End of Year 1 ($)	Monthly Payment ($)	Loan Balance at End of Year 1 ($)	Monthly Payment ($)	Loan Balance at End of Year 1 ($)
1	665.30	98,984	496.62	100,075	583.16	100,002
2	665.30	–	533.86	–	594.83	–
6	665.30	–	712.96	–	643.86	–
10	665.30	–	712.96	–	696.93	–

surpassing the fixed payment loan's $665.30 in year 6 for the first GPM and in year 8 for the second one, as shown in Exhibit 9.4.

The first month's required *interest,* regardless of the type of loan, is $583.33 (100,000 × 7% ÷ 12). The FRM's monthly debt service payment of $665.30 is in excess of the required interest, thus reducing the loan balance by $81.97 (665.30 − 583.33) at the end of the first month. The 7.5 percent GPM has a monthly payment of only $496.62 during the first year, so with it the borrower fails to pay $168.68 (665.30 − 496.62). This amount is *added* to the loan balance at the end of the first month, making this a negative amortization loan.

Any GPM will lower the monthly payments during the early years of a mortgage. However, the borrower should be aware of two characteristics of any GPM plan:

1. The payments will take an increasing proportion of the family income unless the income rises at a faster rate than do the payments. To accommodate this increase, the borrower should be able to project an increasing family income, which should allow the percentage going to the mortgage payment to remain constant or decrease.

2. Over the life of the loan, the borrower will pay more interest than would be paid on a conventional loan that had same loan amount and interest rate.

The Buydown Mortgage

A **buydown mortgage** is similar to the GPM in that its debt service payment starts low and increases the first few years. However, the borrower's payments do not increase above the payment that a fixed-payment mortgage would have. The payments increase in a stair-step fashion until they reach the same level as the standard mortgage's payments. In a typical buydown loan, a party to the transaction, usually the seller, pays part of the borrower's interest in advance to give the borrower a lower interest rate—and thus a lower monthly payment—during the early years of the loan. Using this technique, the borrower may be able to qualify for a loan if the family income is insufficient to qualify for a standard FRM loan.

$100,000 loan, 7-percent interest, 30-year term, monthly payment.

	FIXED PAYMENT MORTGAGE (USING A 7% INTEREST RATE)		BUYDOWN MORTGAGE (USING A 3-2-1 RATIO OF LOWER INTEREST RATES)		
Year	Monthly Payment ($)	Loan Balance at End of Year ($)	Interest Rate (%)	Monthly Payment ($)	Amount Below FPM ($)
1	665.30	98,984	5.5	567.79	97.51
2	665.30	97,895	6.0	598.83	66.47
3	665.30	96,727	6.5	629.88	35.42
4 and later	665.30	N.A.	7.0	660.87	4.43

N.A. indicates "not applicable."

A typical buydown uses a 3-2-1 ratio of lower pay rates (see Exhibit 9.5). Using a 7-percent market rate, the borrower's first year rate might be 1.5 percentage points less than the 7-percent interest rate (or 5.5 percent), the second year's rate would be 1 percentage point less (6 percent), and the third year's rate would be 0.5 percentage point less (6.5 percent). After the third year, the borrower's payments would be based on a 7-percent interest rate for the remaining life of the loan. The difference between the borrower's payments based on the lower interest rates and the payment due based on the 7-percent rate would be paid to the lender in a lump sum at closing, after discounting the differences at the 7-percent mortgage rate to reflect the fact that the lender is receiving the payments sooner.

Notice how the borrower's debt service savings last for only 3 years, as compared to the 5 or 10 years of savings with the GPM. The lower monthly payment is between the aggressive savings available under the 7-percent GPM and the savings available with the more conservative 2-percent GPM. In both GPM cases, however, the payments rise above the FRM debt service of $665.30, while the buydown payments never do.

The Growing Equity Mortgage

A **growing equity mortgage (GEM)** is a loan arrangement in which the borrower makes larger payments each year, just as is done with a GPM or buydown loan, but *all of the increase* in payments is applied to the loan balance. The more rapid reduction in the loan balance from the increasing payments means that even less of each debt service payment goes to mortgage interest and more to principal amortization. This serves to further shorten the loan life. For example, if the borrower obtains a $100,000, 7-percent, 30-year, monthly paid GEM that calls for payments to increase by 3 percent annually for 10 years, this will decrease the loan's life from 30 years to a much shorter maturity. Not only does this repay the loan sooner, but it also results in less total interest being paid to the lender.

In most cases, it is not necessary to use the GEM's formal arrangement specifying the increases in monthly payments. If the borrower wants to make additional payments,

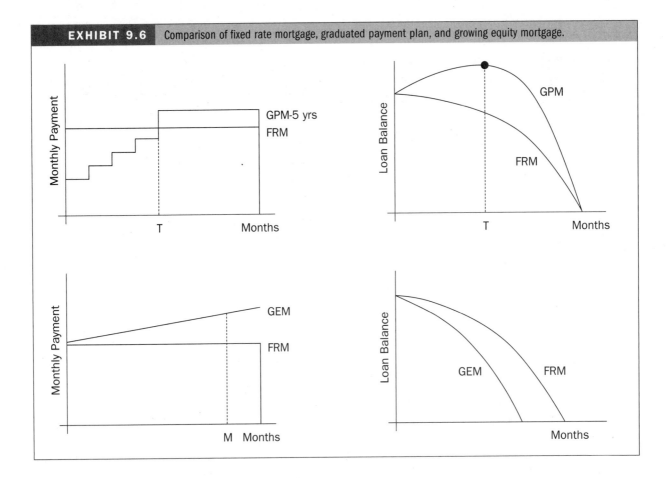

the promissory note discussed in the preceding chapter allows the extra payments to be made. Moreover, the lender automatically will apply them to reduce the loan balance, presuming the borrower is current on his obligations to the lender.

Exhibit 9.6 is a summary comparison of the characteristics among the FRM, GPM, and GEM. The 5-year GPM contains a stair-step system of predetermined payments that begin the sixth year at a payment that is higher than the FRM. This causes the loan balance to continue to increase in the first five years, and begin to decline at time T.

The GEM payments begin at the same level as the FRM and steadily increase. The loan payout month, M, in which the balance is completely paid will be much shorter than the maturity date for the FRM. This system of payments causes the loan balance to decline more rapidly than the traditional FRM pattern.

The Reverse Annuity Mortgage

Each of the preceding loans was designed to help the borrower buy or build a home. The borrower received the loan amount at closing, had to pay closing costs (including the down payment), and used the rest of the cash to pay for the single-family home. Each of the loans could also be used to refinance an existing mortgage, either lowering the monthly debt service payment by taking advantage of falling interest rates or pulling some equity out of the property by taking out a larger loan than the current loan's balance. Suppose, however, that the house is owned free and clear, (that is, any loan used to acquire the home has been completely repaid). Could a borrower then get a new loan based on the 100-percent equity she owns in the home, perhaps receiving 80 percent or more of the value of the house?

This, in part, is the motivation behind the **reverse annuity mortgage (RAM).** Many older consumers have repaid their home loans and now own their homes debt-free. In their retirement years, they may need additional cash to supplement their retirement incomes, to pay for unexpected medical expenses, to complete home repairs, or for whatever purpose they choose. Because they often have a substantial amount of equity tied up in a rather illiquid asset—their home—a reverse mortgage loan would enable them to tap that equity by borrowing against it. An even better option for the consumer would be to borrow just the amount of cash they needed, rather than receive the cash in a lump sum at closing, as in a traditional loan. The RAM solves these problems for the older consumer. The loan can be funded in a lump sum, but more frequently it is advanced either as a line of credit (where a borrower writes a check and the money to cover the check comes from increasing the loan balance) or as scheduled monthly payments made directly to a borrower in the form of an annuity.

Second Mortgage

A second mortgage (previously introduced in Chapter 8) is a second loan using the same property as collateral. The key difference between a first and a second mortgage is who gets repaid first in case the borrower ever defaults on the loan. If the borrower should default and the property is subsequently sold in order to raise the funds to repay the loan, the second mortgage lender does not receive *any* money until the first mortgage lender has been fully repaid. Thus, the second mortgage lender must accept *more risk* than does the first mortgage lender.

A second mortgage often differs from a first mortgage in several key ways. First, due to its higher risk, a second mortgage should carry an interest rate that is higher than the rate charged on the first mortgage. Second mortgages, however, are used for many different purposes. Not only may a buyer use a second mortgage to raise additional cash to help pay the down payment, but an owner may later take out a second mortgage from a lender to borrow against the equity in the property without disturbing the first mortgage. In the first case, the second mortgage may be obtained from an institutional lender or it may be a loan offered by the seller in order to entice the buyer to purchase the property. If it is provided by the seller, he frequently offers a *lower* interest rate in spite of the higher risk involved because his primary goal is to sell the property. In other situations, the second mortgage lender charges a higher rate because she wants compensation for the additional risk of being second in line in case of borrower default.

Another way a second mortgage differs from a first mortgage is that its maturity frequently is shorter than that of the first mortgage because the seller wants to encourage the buyer to repay the loan as soon as possible. A third difference is that the second mortgage may contain a *subordination clause,* which states that the second loan will always remain secondary to the first mortgage and to any new first mortgage that may be placed on the property in the future. Fourth, a second mortgage often includes a *default in prior payment clause.* If the buyer should ever default on the first mortgage, this clause allows the seller to make the payments for the buyer, add the missed first mortgage payments to the indebtedness of the second loan, and foreclose on the second loan. In this manner, the seller (or any second mortgage lender) can judge the appropriate time to foreclose to avoid losses.

What Federal Legislation Affects Mortgage Loans?

Regardless of what type of mortgage loan or which mortgage lender the borrower selects, there are several pieces of federal legislation designed to protect naive consumers from questionable activities by more knowledgeable lenders. Enacted over a period of years, this legislation provides additional information to consumers that allows them to find the best possible loan for their situations. It also prohibits certain lender activities that Congress has deemed to be discriminatory.

TRUTH-IN-LENDING ACT

The intent of the **Truth-in-Lending Act** is to inform borrowers about the true cost of credit, which is knowledge they can use to compare costs of different loans. Customers are encouraged under the act to shop at different lenders for credit terms most appropriate to their needs. Because the act is administered by the Federal Reserve Board as Regulation Z, it is sometime referred to as "Reg Z." The finance charge and the resulting annual percentage rate (APR) must be disclosed to the borrower. The **finance charge** for real estate loans includes interest and the following charges, if present: finder's fee, loan origination fee, discount fee, time price differential, points, carrying charge, and credit life insurance premium. It does not include acquisition charges that are paid regardless of whether credit is extended, such as legal fees, a survey, recording fees, and a title insurance premium.

The **annual percentage rate (APR),** which only approximates the true cost of financing computed in the previous chapter since it assumes loans are never repaid ahead of schedule, can be calculated by using the time-value-of-money keys on a financial calculator. Using the same set of assumptions introduced earlier in this chapter (a $100,000 mortgage carrying an 8-percent interest rate and requiring monthly debt service payments of $733.76 over a 30-year period), now add the information that the total of all finance charges equals $3,000. The APR is based on the loan amount less the finance charges, or $97,000. Each student should use a calculator of choice to verify that the APR is 8.3 percent. A much more comprehensive APR calculation program that accommodates a number of situations is available for the Windows operating system from the U.S. Comptroller of the Currency. Information can be found at the website for this text.

FAIR CREDIT REPORTING ACT

As shown in the loan underwriting section earlier in this chapter, one of the ways in which a lender judges whether the borrower is likely to repay the loan is to look at how the borrower has handled credit in the past. This is done by examining a report provided by a credit bureau. Because the borrower's credit history is a crucial part of the underwriting process, Congress enacted the **Fair Credit Reporting Act** to ensure that erroneous and irrelevant information was not included in a borrower's credit report. Further, because negative information can damage a borrower's financial reputation, Congress insisted upon the confidential treatment of this information. Finally, if a borrower is refused credit based on the information in a report provided by one of the credit bureaus, then the borrower must receive a copy of the report containing the information. If the report is in error, then the borrower can instruct the credit bureau to research the erroneous information. If the credit bureau verifies the information as being accurate and the borrower still believes it is wrong, then the borrower has the right to provide a 100-word statement telling why he thinks the report is in error, and that statement must be transmitted to any lender who requests credit information about the borrower.

REAL ESTATE SETTLEMENT PROCEDURES ACT

The **Real Estate Settlement Procedures Act (RESPA)** has two main purposes. First, it requires the lender to give the loan applicant a good faith estimate of the charges she is likely to face at closing. She must be given this estimate within three days of making the loan application, and then again one day before the closing. Knowing the loan's costs early in the process enables the borrower to compare credit terms and costs among lenders so that an informed decision may be made. Second, the consumer is given the right to select the individuals or firms providing services required by the lender, such as an attorney, an appraiser, and a title insurance company, rather than being forced to use providers selected by the lender. Moreover, those providers are not allowed to share any of their fees (a practice commonly called "kickbacks") with the lender. Third, lenders must use a uniform settlement statement prepared by the U.S. Department of Housing and Urban Development. Using a uniform statement increases the likelihood that all costs are included as well as makes it easier for the lender to describe the costs facing the borrower. Fourth, RESPA limits the amount that lenders can require the borrower to place in escrow for property taxes, hazard insurance premiums, and so forth to a two-month cushion in excess of prorated costs. Of course, lenders may require a smaller cushion, no cushion at all, or not even require an escrow account because such accounts are one of the negotiable items that borrowers look at when comparing one lender's mortgage loan offerings to another lender's. RESPA requirements are included in a prepared form that can be reviewed at the address www.hud.gov:80/fha/sfh/res/1.pdf.

EQUAL CREDIT OPPORTUNITY ACT

The intent of the **Equal Credit Opportunity Act (ECOA),** implemented under the Federal Reserve Board's Regulation B, is to prevent lenders from discriminating against borrowers. It makes it illegal for lenders to use certain borrower characteristics in the loan underwriting process. For example, lenders cannot take the borrower's gender into account (for example, by making it harder for women to qualify for a loan), nor the borrower's marital status (for example, by making it harder for single people to qualify), nor the borrower's age, national origin, race, color, or religion. Furthermore, the borrower's income from sources such as alimony or a public assistance program must be examined and counted as qualifying income for the loan if there is a sufficiently reliable pattern of receipt. In fact, the thrust of the law is to require the lender to look solely to the level and stability of a borrower's future income, as well as to claims against that income, as the measure of the borrower's ability to repay the mortgage. To emphasize the importance of these requirements, lenders must provide written justification to the borrower for each denial of credit.

COMMUNITY REINVESTMENT ACT

The **Community Reinvestment Act (CRA)** prohibits lenders from discriminating against borrowers whose homes are located in lower-income neighborhoods as long as the lenders accept deposits from individuals residing in those same neighborhoods. Provided that the borrower is creditworthy and the collateral's value is satisfactory, the lender cannot refuse to make the loan. Consequently, this act is intended to encourage depository institutions to help meet the credit needs of the communities in which they operate, including low- and moderate-income neighborhoods. To enforce the act, the lender's regulators periodically conduct examinations that are then taken into account when the lender wants to establish additional deposit facilities.

HOME MORTGAGE DISCLOSURE ACT

The **Home Mortgage Disclosure Act (HMDA)** is related to the CRA in that its goal is also to ensure that adequate financing is available for creditworthy borrowers, regardless of the location of the property. It does this by requiring lenders to file government reports detailing loan application information, including the collateral property's location. Reports summarizing a lender's loan rejections by race and location are then available for the public to use not only in assessing whether the financial institutions are serving the housing needs of their communities, but whether they are engaging in possible discriminatory lending patterns.

Whom Does the Borrower Compete Against for Mortgage Money?

O bviously, one single-family home loan borrower competes against other home loan borrowers for mortgage funds from local lenders. What may not be quite so obvious is that the mortgage markets are an integral part of the overall capital markets. This means that home mortgage borrowers must not only compete among themselves but also compete with other users of capital market funds who need money for a variety of reasons.

GOVERNMENT

The home loan borrower's biggest and most formidable competitor is the government at the federal, state, and local levels. Until recently, the federal government was operating at a substantial deficit because it spent more than it was receiving from taxes and fees. Most state and local governments operate near breakeven, sometimes with a surplus of revenues over expenses, and sometimes at a deficit. Because it has the power to levy taxes, the government can pay however high an interest rate it must pay in order to borrow its needed funds. That means home loan borrowers can be priced out of the market as, during the loan underwriting process, lenders consider the required debt service payments too large for the prospective borrowers' incomes.

BUSINESS

Business is also a major competitor because firms borrow to meet their need for debt capital to expand and satisfy their customers' demands. Whether the firms are adding new manufacturing facilities, equipment to go in the new facilities or to replace outmoded existing equipment, warehouse space to temporarily store their expanding range of products, vehicles to deliver their products to warehouses or retail sites, or any other major expenditures, businesses borrow a substantial amount of their capital needs. Included in the business category is the need for income-property mortgage loans to build office buildings, retail centers, multifamily housing, and hotels and motels. When businesses borrow funds to meet these needs, or even when they tap the equity markets by issuing new stock, they are competing with home loan borrowers for funds.

HOUSEHOLDS

Finally, other households are competing against the home loan borrower for funds. Not only are some of these households trying to borrow mortgage money, but they are also borrowing money to pay education expenses, take vacations, pay medical bills, make improvements to their existing homes, buy second homes, invest in the stock market, and purchase automobiles, trucks, and boats. Credit card loans also are a major component of household debt. Lenders must decide whether to use their scarce resources to make single-family home loans or some other form of household loan.

WHO GETS THE LOAN?

A lender who has to choose between loan applicants selects the applicant who offers the highest return considering the risk associated with the loan. That means the single-family home loan borrower must provide a high enough return to the lender to not only justify the lender's risk from making that loan but also provide the lender with a better return than another loan carrying an equivalent level of risk. If the borrower cannot make this return, the funds-constrained lender will make the other loan rather than the home loan.

SAVINGS ARE THE KEY

Ideally, lenders have access to all the money they need and can satisfy all borrowers. Realistically, they are constrained by labor availability, management capability, capital deficiency, and aggressive competitors. The amount of capital available in the U.S. financial system as a whole depends upon the savings of governments (surpluses or deficits), businesses (retained earnings), households (disposable income less consumption expenditures), and the foreign sector (net foreign investment in the United States). Because it is a part of the financial system, the fundamental source of mortgage money is the savings of the four sectors of the economy. As savings increase, more money flows into the money and the capital markets. This money is then available for lenders to allocate to their various borrowers.

In a macro sense, government, business, and household consumer attitudes toward saving are the fundamental source of funds. In economies where cultural norms favor saving, interest rates are generally low because there is a large amount of capital available for lenders to loan. Moreover, consumer attitudes toward saving and the allocation of savings is another factor that frequently is overlooked. The U.S. political system offered many incentives to encourage single-family home lending after World War II because home ownership was an important goal. Since many families now have achieved that goal, the political system does not favor home loans to the extent it once did.

What Lenders Offer Mortgage Loans?

After deciding what kind of mortgage loan he wants, the borrower must find a lender that offers a satisfactory combination of service and mortgage loan terms. Service might include the lender's willingness to help the borrower prepare a loan application at a time convenient to the borrower, the speed with which the lender is able to underwrite the loan and reach a decision on the borrower's application, and the lender's attitude during the application process. Important mortgage loan terms to the borrower might include the loan amount; interest rate; loan-to-value ratio and, conversely, required down payment; points, fees, and other charges; interest rate lock period, closing costs, which can vary substantially from lender to lender; and escrow requirements.

In real estate circles, one name for a lender that makes loans directly to the public is *mortgage originator.* A mortgage originator may be a common mortgage lending institution, an individual mortgage banker or mortgage broker, or a mortgage loan site on the Internet. Although there are other originators, they have insignificant shares of the market. When the mortgage loan originator makes a single-family home loan to a borrower, the transaction is said to occur in the **primary mortgage market.** Sometimes, these loans are sold to an investor by the originating mortgage lender in what is called the **secondary mortgage market.** In other words, home loans are made in the *primary* mortgage market, and investors may purchase the same loans in the *secondary* mortgage market.

MORTGAGE COMPANY

The group of mortgage originators with the largest single-family home loan market share is the *mortgage companies.* This group began the 1990s with slightly more than 35 percent of the market and finished the decade with almost 58 percent of the single-family home loan origination market. A mortgage company often does not have a recognizable name (unless it is owned by a financial institution such as a commercial bank and uses the bank's name as its own), but the mortgage company often includes the word *mortgage* in its name. Although they are not yet being tracked in the government's statistics as a separate category because their loan volumes are still too small, the Internet mortgage lenders most often fall in this category.

Mortgage companies range in size from websites having no physical presence for borrowers to visit to one-person businesses operating with minimal overhead expenses on a contract basis out of the originator's home to large nationwide companies with offices in many states and several thousand employees. Most mortgage companies specialize in single-family home loans and are quite good at what they do. After all, what the borrower wants most is competitive terms with outstanding service, and the size of the firm that can deliver that combination is immaterial.

The category of mortgage companies includes both mortgage bankers and mortgage brokers. Both operate under the laws of the states in which they do business (as opposed to being chartered or regulated, or both, by the federal government), except for the federal consumer protections described earlier. Both traditionally have operated with relatively small amounts of equity capital. They have no deposits, no premiums, no contractually guaranteed cash inflows such as retirement contributions, and no other sources of readily available funds other than what they are able to borrow. Yet they originate almost $6 out of every $10 of single-family home loans each year. The key is that they originate mortgage loans for others.

Mortgage Banker

A retail **mortgage banker** acts as a loan originator for various other institutions, including wholesale mortgage bankers, savings and loan associations, commercial banks, savings banks, Fannie Mae, and Freddie Mac. A retail mortgage banker typically makes several single-family home loans, accumulates them until there are enough loans to attract a larger institution (commonly called an investor), and then sells the package of loans to the investor. The process begins by finding borrowers, qualifying them by doing a preliminary loan underwriting, preparing the necessary loan papers, and making the loans. Because the mortgage banker does not have its own funds, it usually borrows them from a commercial bank until it can sell the package of mortgages to an investor. These temporary funds are called *warehouse loans,* and the commercial bank is the typical *warehouse lender,* although large mortgage companies may tap the money markets themselves and issue corporate paper to obtain their short-term debt. Once the single-family mortgage banker has accumulated a large number of loans, the loans are packaged together and sold. The sales proceeds are then used to repay the warehouse loan. The mortgage banker is often retained by the mortgage purchaser to service the loans by collecting the monthly payments from the borrower, forwarding the debt service payments (less a servicing fee that the mortgage banker keeps) to the investor, and handling the insurance and property tax escrow, any delinquencies, early loan payoffs, and mortgage releases once the loans have been fully repaid.

Each type of loan investor is discussed later in this chapter, with the following exception. Wholesale mortgage bankers are the same as the retail mortgage bankers described in the preceding paragraph, except they do not originate loans. Instead, they purchase loans from other loan originators, including the retail mortgage bankers. A large mortgage banking firm may have both retail and wholesale divisions, but most single-family mortgage banking firms specialize in one or the other function.

Combining all mortgage company purchases and originations and then comparing the total to the dollar amount of loans they sell, mortgage companies sell virtually all of the loans they originate and purchase. Given that they have relatively small amounts of capital, this is a logical conclusion.

Mortgage Broker

A **mortgage broker** is an individual or firm who takes a mortgage application from the prospective borrower and attempts to find an investor who will fund the loan. The investor might be a wholesale mortgage banker, savings and loan association, commercial bank, savings banks, or even a wealthy individual. The broker does not make the loan with its own funds or with funds it has borrowed. Thus, it has no need for warehouse loans. The broker originates the loan in the name of the investor who provides the money for the borrower and is paid a commission by the investor for locating an acceptable borrower. Moreover, the broker does not service the loan for the investor.

COMMERCIAL BANK

The second largest single-family mortgage loan originator is the *commercial bank.* Most banks include the word *bank* as part of their name, and those chartered by the federal government often have the word *national* as part of their company name. Commercial banks' market share dropped from around one-third in 1990 to slightly less than one-quarter of the originations during most of the 1990s.

Commercial banks offer all kinds of lending services, including commercial and industrial loans to businesses (18 percent of assets), real estate loans (25.4 percent), and consumer loans for cars, boats, and other personal expenses (9.6 percent), as well as investing some of their funds in government securities (22.5 percent). Real estate loans, the largest single category, includes single-family home loans, income-property loans, construction loans, and land acquisition and development loans. Single-family home loans are often a more important proportion of the business for smaller, community banks than they are for regional or national money center banks.

Another way in which commercial banks can match changes in their short-term liability costs with revenues that vary with these costs is to make adjustable rate mortgages. They are careful to offer ARMs with rates tied to indexes that reflect changes in their deposit costs and to force frequent enough adjustments in the ARM rate so that their mortgages produce revenues that vary at approximately the same time as do their costs. Further, about 13 percent of the commercial banks' real estate loans are **home equity loans,** second mortgages that carry noticeably higher interest rates than do first mortgages so that they are compensated for the increased risk of longer-term loans. Finally, in smaller towns and rural areas where longer term savings deposits make up a larger portion of a bank's funds, the town bank is a major source of long-term real estate loans. The loans they do sell are often the 25- and 30-year fixed interest rate loans they have originated but do not want to keep in their portfolio of loans and investments, most likely because they do not wish to accept the interest rate risks associated with such loans. When they do this, they are acting much like the mortgage banker discussed earlier.

THRIFT INSTITUTIONS

The third largest group of mortgage originators is the *thrift institutions*. This category commonly encompasses savings and loan associations, savings banks, mutual savings banks, and credit unions. Although they too may use the word *bank* in their names, federally chartered savings and loan associations and credit unions often include the word *federal* in their names while federally chartered savings banks include the abbreviation F.S.B. in small capital letters after their names. Thrift institutions began the 1990s with around a 30-percent market share but quickly dropped below 20 percent and ended the decade at less than an 18-percent share.

Savings and loan associations (and savings banks and mutual savings banks) have been widely known as single-family home loan specialists, usually with the largest market share, for most of this century. But the savings and loan associations in particular suffered losses from making loans outside their specialty during the 1980s and shrunk significantly in size during the late 1980s and early 1990s as they tried to recover from the losses. It would be hard for the mortgage borrower to distinguish between savings and loan associations, savings banks, and mutual savings banks, although there are technical differences among them. Credit unions have made some mortgage loans, but usually only the larger ones offer these while the midsized and small credit unions have tended to stay with personal loans for their members. As before, the borrower is searching for the optimal combination of loan terms and service, and the local thrift institution, regardless of its size or name, may offer the best combination.

In contrast to the commercial banks at 25 percent, the majority of the thrift institutions' assets (59.2 percent) are invested in real estate mortgage loans. Thrifts invest about the same proportion of their assets (24.8 percent) in government securities as do the banks but only half as much in consumer loans (4.8 percent) and one tenth as much in business loans (1.9 percent). The following sections briefly examine each lender in the thrift institution category.

Savings and Loan Associations

Long known as *the* housing market lender, **savings and loan associations (S&Ls)** have specialized in accepting individual borrowers' savings deposits and then lending those monies to borrowers who want to build or buy a single-family home. Stung by profitability problems as deposit costs soared while revenues stagnated due to fixed interest rates on long-term mortgage loans already on the books, S&Ls looked to riskier types of loans, including commercial real estate mortgages, to try to boost profitability. Unfortunately, the United States entered a severe recession during the last half of the 1980s and the early 1990s. It soon became evident that the S&Ls had made too many poor quality loans during the 1980s, and many became insolvent, ultimately going out of business as the government disposed of their remaining loans and foreclosed real estate. Their influence as real estate lenders waned at that time, and they continue to play a supporting role to the mortgage companies and commercial banks today.

To avoid the profitability problems of the past, S&Ls have moved to shorten their loan maturities and secure higher returns. Just as the commercial banks are doing, they offer ARM loans with suitable indices and higher yielding home equity loans. Moreover, S&Ls make over 25 percent of single-family construction loans. They now sell about 54 percent of their loan acquisitions (originations plus purchases), many of which are the 30-year fixed-rate mortgage loans that carry the higher interest rate risks. With the exception of a few large lenders, most S&Ls are locally oriented, collecting their deposits and making loans within their communities. Specialization in limited geographic areas and in property types with which they are familiar appears to be a major factor in thriving S&Ls' ongoing successes.

Savings Banks

While there are technical differences in the charter (the government's permit to operate) granted to an S&L and the one granted to a *savings bank,* the differences are inconsequential for borrowers. Similarly, savings banks and S&Ls may be chartered by the federal government or by one of the states, but again the differences largely turn on relatively minor changes in the rules and regulations under which they operate. In terms of their activities as real estate lenders, a savings bank is indistinguishable from an S&L.

Mutual Savings Banks

Another seemingly minor difference is the addition of the word *mutual* prior to the words *savings bank,* but a *mutual savings bank* is significantly different than a savings bank, at least to its depositors if not to its borrowers. The word *mutual* connotes the ownership of the savings bank by its depositors rather than by stockholders. The importance of this difference for the stockholder-owned savings bank appears to be related both to the attraction of superior management that can be motivated by stock options and to the greater fiscal discipline imposed by stockholders. For both reasons, many mutual savings banks and mutually owned S&Ls have converted to stockholder ownership during the past 20 years.

Another difference is historical accident. Mutual savings banks grew to prominence in the northeastern part of the United States, and almost 75 percent of the existing mutual savings banks still are located in Massachusetts, New York, and Connecticut. In locales where mutual savings banks are strong institutions in the marketplace, S&Ls are usually weak. Many see the two as substitutes for each other, even though mutual savings banks have slightly more flexible lending and investing strictures placed on them by their state regulators.

Credit Unions

The last of the thrift institutions is the *credit union,* which is a state or federally chartered organization of people with a common bond who pool their savings and make loans to members. Credit unions typically are established at a place of employment with employees as both members and owners of the credit union because credit unions are mutual institutions. They have a local presence in that they concentrate on making loans that satisfy their members' needs, including auto loans (25.3 percent of assets), personal and credit card loans (14.3 percent), and real estate loans (24.5 percent). They also maintain 30.9 percent of their assets in investments.

Due to their relatively short-term shares (deposits), credit unions have concentrated on making shorter term loans. Recently, more than 55 percent of their mortgage loan originations either carried an adjustable rate or matured within three years. Of the remaining 45 percent, which consisted of fixed-rate loans, credit unions sold more than one-third to other institutions. Although they are not known as mortgage loan specialists, credit unions have learned well the lessons of the other thrifts and are keeping their growing role in real estate lending mostly short term.

INDIVIDUALS

Finally, individuals are sometimes a source of loans for residential real estate purchases. Generally, maturities on loans made by individuals are shorter than those obtainable from institutional lenders, and interest rates are competitive. Individuals, including sellers, are particularly helpful in granting short-term loans extending up to five years. In some cities, persons can be found who specialize in making or buying second and third mortgage loans with a maximum of 10-year maturities.

Where Does the Lender Obtain the Money to Lend the Borrower?

Lenders must either have an internal source of funds, such as deposits, that they use to originate mortgage loans, or must sell the loans they originate to others. Many of the loan originators identified in the previous section are indeed depository institutions, but some are not. Even those who do have deposits to fund their loans may prefer to sell them to others.

DEPOSITS

The preceding section briefly compared the different primary mortgage market lenders that the borrower might approach for a single-family home loan. The commercial banks funded the bulk of their loans from deposits and other short-term sources, leading them to prefer ARM loans, construction loans, and home equity loans. They sold some of the loans, however, in the secondary mortgage market, a market in which single-family home mortgages can attract funds from sources other than the lender who originated the loan. The thrift institutions sold over half of their loans in the secondary market and funded the remaining mortgages from deposits just as the commercial banks did. By contrast, the mortgage companies sold virtually all of the loans they originated because they are nondepository institutions with no other funding sources.

SECONDARY MORTGAGE MARKET

The housing sector of the economy is able to compete for funds with other investment outlets—such as the stock and bond markets—through the secondary mortgage market. This is the marketplace where mortgages are sold by the loan originators and bought by various investors. Secondary market investors include Fannie Mae, Freddie Mac, securities dealers (as distributors), life insurance companies, pension and retirement funds, mutual funds, commercial banks, and thrift institutions. Some of the institutions that buy mortgages in the secondary market sell bonds and, in some cases, stock to attract money that they can use to purchase the loans originated by the local lenders. By paying competitive rates of return on the bonds, these institutions compete for money and channel it into housing, thus stimulating the housing market.

The secondary market for single-family home loans is composed of two groups of players—the buyers and the sellers. The buyers purchase mortgages and mortgage-related securities for cash. They are interested in receiving the future cash flows that come from the homeowners who make their monthly payments on the mortgages. As will be discussed in more detail in the following sections, the buyers are primarily government-sponsored enterprises, nontraditional mortgage investors, and primary market lenders who either have more money to invest than there is loan demand in their local markets or want the greater liquidity that comes with purchasing mortgage-related securities.

As covered in the previous section, the sellers are the primary mortgage market lenders who originated the single-family home loans because these originators seek to acquire new funds to loan to new customers. For example, consider an aggressive thrift institution that conducts a campaign to attract new retail depositors and receives $1 million in new funds. Within the following month, the institution receives 20 new loan applications in the amounts of $100,000 each. The lender can accept the first 10 loan applications received and turn down the others, or it can accept the first 10, sell those mortgages in the secondary mortgage market, and recover funds that can be re-loaned to the second 10 applicants. Thus, the secondary mortgage market enables the local lender to service its customers, regain loanable funds, and stimulate the local housing market.

Federal Government Assistance

The Federal National Mortgage Association and the Federal Home Loan Mortgage Corporation are two **government-sponsored enterprises (GSEs)** that are active as residential mortgage purchasers in the secondary markets. The Government National Mortgage Association is a government-owned company. It is not a purchaser of mortgages, but a guarantor of certain secondary mortgage market products.

FEDERAL NATIONAL MORTGAGE ASSOCIATION. One of the two major GSEs active in the secondary mortgage market is the **Federal National Mortgage Association (FNMA or Fannie Mae).** Instead of being chartered by a state government, as most companies are, Fannie Mae operates under a U.S. congressional charter. Its charter specifies that it is to make a secondary market for residential mortgages and to encourage the provision of affordable housing finance for low- and moderate-income borrowers, especially in underserved areas. It is a stockholder-owned company with its stock trading on the New York and other stock exchanges. Fannie Mae is the country's third largest corporation in terms of assets and has more than 12 million mortgages on its books.

Fannie Mae raises the funds necessary to purchase this large volume of mortgages in several ways. First, it issues short- and long-term debt in the credit markets. This debt is priced to give the investor a spread above the comparable-maturity U.S. Treasury instrument. Because Fannie Mae has a $2.25 billion unused line of credit with the U.S. Treasury, market participants allow it to borrow at U.S. government agency rates, which are lower credit market rates than those available to any other private company (other than Freddie Mac, discussed below). Fannie Mae regularly issues warnings to investors in its debt that the instruments carry only Fannie Mae's backing, not that of the U.S. government or any of its agencies or instrumentalities. Still, the market believes the government will come to Fannie Mae's rescue if that should ever become necessary. This lower cost debt enables Fannie Mae to borrow at rates substantially below the interest rates that it is receiving on the mortgages in its portfolio.

Another way Fannie Mae can afford to purchase mortgages is by creating mortgage-backed securities and then swapping them to the lenders in return for several of their loans. Because the **mortgage-backed security (MBS)** is a single piece of paper evidencing an ownership interest in the cash flows coming from a pool of loans, it is a much less cumbersome way to obtain the future cash flows than it would be to own the mortgages themselves. Furthermore, Fannie Mae guarantees the holder of the MBS that it will receive the payments due it on time and that any early payoffs by the borrower will be passed through to the investor as soon as they are received. Because there are a large number of MBSs outstanding, a secondary market for them has developed, making them substantially more liquid (and thus less risky) than the whole mortgage loans the lender swapped to Fannie Mae. Yet a third way Fannie Mae obtains the monies used to purchase the mortgages is by creating MBSs out of its portfolio of purchased mortgages and then issuing these to the marketplace. It then uses the cash it raises to buy mortgage loans outright.

Finally, Fannie Mae has a mortgage portfolio of almost one-half trillion dollars of mortgage loans. The borrowers on these loans are continually making debt service payments, including both mortgage interest and loan amortization. Recently, Fannie Mae received almost $100 billion in loan amortization that could be reinvested in additional mortgages from primary market lenders.

FEDERAL HOME LOAN MORTGAGE CORPORATION. The **Federal Home Loan Mortgage Corporation (FHLMC or Freddie Mac)** is the other GSE active in the secondary mortgage market. Created in the early 1970s, Freddie Mac is very similar to Fannie Mae. Both have similar charters and are stockholder-owned companies. Freddie Mac is more active in support of the multifamily mortgage market than is Fannie Mae, but they differ mainly in their approach to funding their mortgage purchases. Whereas Fannie Mae places heavy reliance on the issuance of debt to fund its mortgage acquisition program, Freddie Mac relies just as heavily on the issuance of mortgage-backed securities. The issuance of MBSs, which Freddie Mac calls Participation Certificates (PCs), almost equaled the total of Freddie Mac's mortgage purchases from 1996 through 1999.

GOVERNMENT NATIONAL MORTGAGE ASSOCIATION. The bulk of the mortgages that Fannie Mae and Freddie Mac purchase are conventional loans, although they are also permitted to purchase FHA-insured and VA-guaranteed loans. Most of the latter loans, however, are packaged into MBSs that are eligible for a guarantee by the **Government National Mortgage Association (GNMA or Ginnie Mae).** Although its name is similar, Ginnie Mae is decidedly different from the GSEs. Ginnie Mae is owned by the government. It does *not* buy mortgages; rather, its major function is to insure the investors in certain MBSs that they will receive the monies due them in a timely fashion. Furthermore, its guarantee carries the "full faith and credit of the U.S. government," which means that investors in Ginnie Mae–guaranteed MBSs face *no* default risk on their investments. These securities are sometimes called Ginnie Mae **pass-throughs** because the issuer serves as a conduit to pass through to the investor its proportionate share of interest payments and principal repayments (including any pre-payments) from the borrowers whose mortgages are in the pool backing the security. If any mortgage borrowers are delinquent in their monthly payments, the delinquencies must be covered by the mortgage banker and collected later from the borrower when the payments are brought up to date.

Securities Dealers

Another extraordinarily important party to the residential secondary mortgage markets is the *securities dealer*. The securities dealer provides the lubrication that allows the markets to operate by aggregating MBSs from Fannie Mae and Freddie Mac and those guaranteed by Ginnie Mae, repackaging the MBSs into mortgage derivative securities with cash flow patterns best suited to various investors' needs, and distributing the repackaged securities to those investors who are willing to pay the highest price for the cash flows. Moreover, the debt issued by Fannie Mae and Freddie Mac is also sold to the securities dealers for placement with investors. Thus, the securities dealers are not investors but distributors who do their jobs with an incredible efficiency that results in lower interest rates in the primary mortgage market for the home buyer.

Investors

The preceding institutions—Fannie Mae, Freddie Mac, Ginnie Mae, and the securities dealers—play a direct role in the secondary mortgage market. There are a host of investors that buy Fannie Mae and Freddie Mac debt, MBSs, and derivative mortgage securities who are not considered to be a part of the secondary mortgage market but rather are a part of the broader money and capital markets. These investors are seeking the highest risk-adjusted yields they can find in the financial markets, and they invest in mortgage products only if they provide such yields.

LIFE INSURANCE COMPANIES. Life insurance companies, which must invest insurance premiums and other contractually guaranteed cash inflows for several years until needed to fulfill their insurance obligations, were making loans for real estate purchases as long ago as the 1800s. Such loans are advantageous to life insurance companies for several reasons: (1) loans from various sections of the country allow a life insurance company to take advantage of different growth rates throughout the nation; (2) rates of return on real estate loans may be attractive in comparison with those of competing investments; and (3) real estate loans provide diversification for the company's portfolio. Today, most of the single-family home loans life insurance companies acquire are purchased from securities dealers as MBSs or derivative mortgage instruments.

PENSION AND RETIREMENT FUNDS. Pension funds accumulate private sector workers' savings for several years so that sufficient funds are available to provide a retirement income to the worker. Retirement funds do the same for public sector workers. A portion of fund assets traditionally has been devoted to mortgage debt, with a larger share being invested by the retirement funds. Just as with life insurance companies, these investments today are being made via MBSs or the derivative mortgage instruments.

MUTUAL FUNDS. Mutual funds serve as intermediaries for investors who want the diversification and professional management that the funds offer without the time and knowledge commitments that individual investing requires. They invest in a variety of instruments from conservative stocks to aggressive stocks, from short-term money market instruments to long-term bonds, and from mortgage-backed securities to real estate investment trusts. Of course, the funds that concentrate on MBSs and derivative mortgage instruments are natural investors in secondary mortgage market products. But mutual funds are marketed on the basis of their historical returns. Consequently, they constantly seek as high a return as possible within their investment charter. One way to achieve this high return is with mortgage derivatives; thus many different types of funds may be in the market seeking high-yielding mortgage-related investments.

TRADITIONAL MORTGAGE LENDERS. Finally, traditional mortgage lenders—the commercial banks and thrift institutions—are also mortgage investors. They may make long-term fixed-rate mortgage loans but need short-term adjustable rate investments to match the short-term nature of their liability structure (primarily short-term deposits). To avoid the maturity mismatch, they may sell their loan originations in the secondary market, then purchase mortgage derivative instruments that provide them with the necessary short-term maturities. Even Fannie Mae and Freddie Mac will buy some mortgage derivatives to help balance their asset–liability structure.

What Determines the Borrower's Mortgage Rate?

The interest rate and other lending terms that borrowers can expect from mortgage lenders are determined by a number of factors. First, the terms any borrower will be offered depend upon that borrower's creditworthiness. Second, for a particular borrower, the offered terms will depend further upon what loan terms are available from the competition. Mortgage lending is a very competitive business, and mortgage originators rarely have markets to themselves. Third, if the loan is an adjustable rate mortgage that the originating lender expects to keep in its portfolio of loans and other investments, then the mortgage rate will have to be competitive with the other lending and investing opportunities available to the lender. Thus, mortgage rates have to compare favorably with rates available on commercial and industrial loans, construction loans, auto and other personal loans, credit card loans, home equity loans, and various investment securities for commercial banks and thrift institutions.

SECONDARY MORTGAGE MARKET REQUIREMENTS

Because so many single-family home loans are sold in the secondary mortgage market, lenders must also take this market into consideration. The fourth determinant of the primary market loan terms the single-family borrower must pay is the yield that secondary market investors demand. These investors often have a number of investment opportunities available in several different money and capital markets. Consequently, the borrower's mortgage must successfully compete with the expected yields available on these other investments, at least after the purchaser takes into account the differences in risk among investment alternatives. This is a very important, although indirect, influence because it operates through a mortgage-related security.

To determine how yield requirements in the secondary mortgage markets affect primary mortgage market rates, recall that mortgages sold in the secondary market are usually fixed interest rate mortgages. With any fixed-rate instrument, lowering the price paid for the future stream of fixed cash flows raises the yield on the investment. This is precisely what investors do when buying MBSs or derivative mortgage instruments. If the price has to be lowered to attract investors, then the securities dealer selling the instruments will want to pay lower prices to Fannie Mae and Freddie Mac for their MBSs or to the mortgage banker issuers for Ginnie Mae–guaranteed MBSs. If Fannie Mae and Freddie Mac cannot sell their securities for their face values, then they will be unwilling to pay the originating lenders face value for the mortgages they are asked to purchase. Similarly, if the GNMA pass-through issuer cannot sell the Ginnie Maes for face value, then it will have to take a loss on the FHA-insured and VA-guaranteed mortgages it has originated.

POINTS

How does the mortgage originator keep from suffering a loss when originating mortgages at face value (meaning the borrower receives $100,000 in cash when he takes out a $100,000 mortgage) and then selling them for less than face value (for example, $98,000)? The lender charges points, which are sometimes called discount points. Recall that each point equals 1 percent of the loan amount. In our example, the lender would charge 2 points, or 2 percent of $100,000, to make up the $2,000 difference between the $100,000 the lender gives the borrower and the $98,000 that the lender receives when it sells the mortgage. Do not forget the competitive factor; competition may not allow the lender to charge the full 2 points. The lender is indifferent as to who pays the points. It may be the borrower, the seller, or anyone else. But if the lender does not receive the full $2,000, then it will lose money when it sells the mortgage in the secondary market.

The final question is, how did the secondary market participants determine that they were going to pay only $98,000 for the mortgage? Part of the answer is that they expected the mortgage investment would pay them a certain amount of cash flows. For example, using the situation from earlier in this chapter in which the borrower can obtain a $100,000 mortgage carrying an 8-percent interest rate and requiring monthly debt service payments that will fully amortize the loan over a 30-year period, the investor would compute the required monthly payment to be $733.76. Each student should use a calculator of choice to verify that the payment is $733.76.

Chapter Summary

The potential borrower should feel a responsibility to acquire as much information on real estate mortgages as possible to apply for the type that best meets her needs. An application could be submitted for a conventional FRM, conventional ARM, FHA FRM, FHA ARM, or VA FRM. Also, the borrower could inquire for information on a GPM or a GEM. A property with a large amount of equity could qualify for an RAM. Each of these loan types has been designed and offered to the public to satisfy the borrower's needs and potential risk of default.

Further, does the borrower want or need PMI? If so, an application could be submitted for a conventional FRM with PMI. This chapter has attempted to provide the necessary information to enable a potential borrower to make an intelligent decision.

Major influences on the logistics of the residential application are the many federal requirements that have been imposed over time on the processing of the information and the manner in which the loan is approved. These include requirements on the types of questions that may be asked by the lender, the criteria for processing that information in the decision, and the correct disclosure of the terms of the financing. Examples of these laws, such as RESPA and the Truth-in-Lending Act, were discussed.

Local real estate lenders historically have been concerned about the ability of the real estate industry to compete for capital funds with other parts of the economy. The result has been the creation and support of the secondary mortgage market and of special securities such as the CMO. The CMO provides a security that can be sold to investors to channel money into real estate. The secondary mortgage market provides an outlet for local lenders to sell the loans originated at the local level. These funds may be re-loaned to new borrowers.

Internet Applications

A website has been established for this chapter at http://epley.swcollege.com.

Review Questions

1. Calculate the amortization schedule from the following terms:

Loan:	$100,000
Rate:	6.85%
Term:	25 years
Payments:	monthly

2. At the end of the 53rd payment, the interest rate rises to 7.5 percent. Calculate the monthly payment for the remaining term. Prove that the balance of the debt equals zero after the last payment is made. Recalculate the figures in the table shown in Exhibit 9.3.

3. In Exhibit 9.4, change the interest rate to 7 percent and redo the table. Compare it to the answers in questions 1 and 2 above.

4. What is a RAM? A GEM? A buydown? A GPM? A 7-year balloon?

5. Under what circumstances would each of the loan types in question 4 have a benefit to the buyer?

6. Describe the terms of an ARM.

7. What is the meaning of the following terms to an ARM?

   margin
   annual cap
   lifetime cap

8. What is the role of the loan underwriter?

9. What is the purpose of points?

10. If the property sells for $200,000, the first loan is $160,000, and the borrower agrees to pay 3 points, how much money is actually loaned from the lender's own funds?

11. What is a prepayment? How does it influence the monthly payment? Interest paid? Interest rate? Maturity date?

Discussion Questions

1. Discuss the information found in the various Internet assignments.

2. You want to apply for a residential loan. Present all of the alternative types of applications. Give a reason why a potential borrower would apply for each. For example, one type would be a conventional FRM with PMI. Why would a borrower want this type of loan?

3. Discuss the federal laws that cover the residential application.

4. Discuss the sources of capital for a potential real estate loan.

5. Is FHA needed? Why? Present an argument to eliminate any government involvement with housing.

Commercial Loans and Lease Analysis

6. Explain the key financial ratios often used to evaluate a commercial loan application.

7. Contrast the types of amortization typically used to repay commercial loans.

8. Explain the purpose of a second mortgage and the subordination and default in prior payment clauses.

9. Explain the assignment contract and the estoppel certificate.

10. Explain the nature of the commercial lease agreement.

11. State the rights and responsibilities of the landlord and the tenant in a lease.

12. Explain the types of rent payment arrangements.

IMPORTANT TERMS

commercial lease	individual ownership
commercial loan	joint ownership
construction draws	leverage
construction loan	limited partnership
corporation	net lease
equity participation	nondisturbance clause
escalated lease	option to purchase clause
financial ratios	percentage lease
gap financing	permanent loan
general partnership	positive leverage
graduated payment lease	real estate investment trust (REIT)
gross lease	retainage
ground lease	sale and leaseback agreement
holdback	subchapter S corporation
income participation	takeout commitment
indexed lease	

INTRODUCTION

Commercial real estate loans are used in the purchase and development of all types of income-producing property. Many individuals use such loans to purchase property for their own business enterprise or as part of the financing for a real estate investment. Therefore, the consumer needs to understand the nature of the commercial loan, the types of commercial investment organizations, the sources of commercial funds, commercial loan requirements, and the financial ratios used to evaluate commercial loan applications. The consumer will use this knowledge to make a sound decision about buying or investing in commercial property, choosing the most suitable type of investment organization, finding a lender, and preparing a loan application.

Commercial leases are discussed here for two purposes. First, the commercial lease is the source of income to the owner in payment for rental of the space. The product sold in the market place by the owner/landlord is space that is designed to satisfy the current market demand, for example, multifamily rental, retail, office, or industrial. Second, the clauses in the lease reflect the type of market risk and its magnitude. For example, typical commercial leases include an annual adjustment of the rent subject to a rate of inflation such as the consumer price index (CPI). If the renter accepts this type of adjustment, he is accepting the market risk that influences the CPI. This chapter will spend time on commercial property leases to provide a background on these critical subjects.

What Are Commercial Investment Organizations?

Any individual or group contemplating a real estate investment must decide which form of investment organization is most suitable. The type of organization selected should be determined after careful consideration has been given to the *marketability of the properties* that the organization or individual will sell, the *liability* of the individual investors, the *tax benefits,* and the *requirements of the lenders* with whom the group or individual must work. These factors can be used to evaluate the following forms of investment organizations.

LIMITED PARTNERSHIP

A **limited partnership** is composed of a general partner(s) and a number of limited partners. The general partner typically is the organizer (syndicator) who has the real estate expertise, and the limited partners are the investors who supply the investment funds.

This investment vehicle has several advantages: (1) It provides income tax benefits in that profits and deductions from the investment can pass through the partnership to the individuals to be used on their personal tax returns. (2) Each limited partner has limited liability against lawsuits in the amount of her investment funds. (3) The limited partners do not participate in the management of the investment; management is left solely to the general partner.

A limited partnership organization must be distinguished from a corporation for taxation purposes. The tests used to differentiate the two are the continuity of the organization, centralization of management, limited liability, and transferability of the ownership interest. *Continuity of the organization* is a corporate characteristic—the organization persists after the resignation, death, or other departure of an officer that would cause a true partnership to be dissolved. If the state law provides for a technical division of the partnership, the organization qualifies as a limited partnership and the partnership agreement can be used to establish its continuity in the event of death, resignation, and so forth. *Centralization of management* means that management is essentially separated from the ownership. A typical criterion for a corporation is that all management decisions are made and administered by the board of directors. In a partnership, this function is carried out by the general partner. *Limited liability* typically exists for a corporation if the directors do not have substantial assets in the corporation or simply work as agents for the shareholders. In a partnership, the general partner must not own substantial assets or simply work as an agent for the limited partners. *Transferability of interests* means that shares of the corporation can be transferred in the open market. In a partnership, the transferability of interest must not be substantially restricted by the partnership agreement.

These four criteria are used by the IRS to determine whether an organization is a corporation or a limited partnership. A ruling that the organization is in essence a corporation means that the limited partnership loses its tax advantages.

GENERAL PARTNERSHIP

A **general partnership** is a group of investors who pool their investment funds to participate in real estate ownership collectively. Each investor is viewed as a co-owner. The profits and losses are distributed on a proportional basis according to each partner's share of the ownership.

The general partnership has three characteristics: (1) A test for continuity of the organization requires that the partnership be dissolved if a partner dies, resigns, or otherwise leaves the partnership. However, if the state law provides for a technical division upon death, resignation, or other departure of a partner, the organization qualifies as a partnership. A contractual agreement can be written to continue the organization. (2) Each partner has unlimited liability for any obligations of the organization. (3) All members of the partnership have equal management rights to contractually commit and bind the whole organization. This principle can hold even though the partnership may centralize its management by an internal agreement.

REAL ESTATE INVESTMENT TRUST

An association or a trust that invests primarily in real estate and mortgages may elect special tax treatment as a **real estate investment trust (REIT).** REITs provide for a pooling of investment funds under the guidance of a real estate specialist. However, because of limitations placed on a trust or an association to qualify as a REIT, this type of organization may not suit the needs of many investors, especially those searching for a tax shelter. A REIT, unlike a limited partnership, does not pass losses through to the individual investor.

Historically, REITs have been identified according to the types of real estate investments they purchase. _Equity REITs_ supply equity funds by specializing in equity purchases in property. _Mortgage REITs_ supply debt funds by granting long-term mortgages on property.

CORPORATION

A **corporation** is an organization that exists separately from the shareholders and can own assets. Individual shareholders cannot use corporate property, have liability limited to the amount of their investment, can transfer ownership of their shares by selling them to any willing buyer, and expect continuity of the organization in the event of death of a shareholder.

A corporation does not offer the same advantages as a partnership with respect to income taxes. The corporation is a separate entity and must pay corporate income taxes on its income. However, the corporation does offer several benefits, such as diversification of real estate owned. Several different types and amounts of property can be readily purchased. The shares give some degree of liquidity to the owner because they can be resold for cash. The corporation can establish its own credit and potentially raise more capital than a partnership. The corporation may be in a position to extend additional fringe benefits to the person or group organizing the syndication.

SUBCHAPTER S CORPORATION

A corporation that qualifies under the tax code as a **subchapter S corporation** offers some of the tax benefits of a partnership. Congress attempted to give the small businessperson the advantages of limited liability and fringe benefits while retaining the pass-through deduction of the partnership. A subchapter S corporation is viewed as a corporation that has special characteristics.

JOINT OWNERSHIP

Joint ownership refers to joint tenancy, tenancy in common, and tenancy by the entirety. Tenancy ownership provides several advantages. One is the right of survivorship in joint tenancy whereby ownership automatically goes to the surviving tenant(s). Second, under tenants in common, each owner can make his own election of accounting methods, depreciation schedules, and so on without regard to the choices made by other owners. Third, an audit of the tax return of one owner does not necessarily cause an audit of the returns of the other owners as it could in a partnership. Perhaps the greatest single advantage of a joint tenancy ownership is the right of survivorship.

INDIVIDUAL OWNERSHIP

Individual ownership (legally referred to as tenancy by severalty) is used when no benefits are to be gained from pooling an individual's funds with those of others.

What Is the Nature of the Commercial Loan?

A commercial loan differs from a residential loan in several respects. A **commercial loan** is given on property that produces an income stream from the sale of a product. The product can be rental space, the sale of portions of the property such as condominium units, or such items as pizzas, clothing, and chemicals. The income stream to the property is used to make the loan payments, pay expenses, and generate a profit. In addition, part of the owner's return may be generated from an expected increase in property value over time.

The application for a commercial loan is evaluated by the lender on the basis of a combination of factors, including the expected future income from the sale of product(s), the past earnings and credit record of the borrower, the location of the site, and the number of potential buyers in the market. These factors are evaluated jointly, and various weights are applied to each to determine potential success or failure. Consequently, a commercial loan application is more difficult to evaluate than a residential loan application. Residential lending is based on a smaller number of factors, such as past credit, nature of employment, and expected wage earnings, which are easier to measure.

Commercial loans are usually much larger in amount than a residential loan and may carry a comparable maturity period. In addition, the lender may impose requirements on the borrower such as a restriction limiting expenses, as a condition for receiving the loan.

THE NEED FOR COMMERCIAL FINANCING

The need for *commercial financing* is similar to the need for residential financing. The economy needs commercial businesses just as it needs residential properties. Commercial businesses produce and sell products to satisfy the demands of the public. The flow of income generated from the sale of these products earns the investor a profit that is a return on the investment.

Commercial financing can be viewed as an outlet for investment funds that is comparable to other competing outlets, such as the stock market. In both cases, the investor looks for the highest return on her money.

Commercial lenders may band together to underwrite a single commercial loan because it may be larger than the amount a local regionalized lender would be able to grant in one loan. A failure and foreclosure of a commercial loan for a larger amount could bankrupt a small lender because the amount could represent a large percentage of the institution's assets.

DEBT VERSUS EQUITY FUNDS

Commercial financing consists of the same equity and debt components discussed in earlier chapters. One is *equity financing,* the amount of a buyer's own assets used to purchase a parcel of property. The other is *debt financing,* the amount of another party's assets used to help purchase the property. Often, a potential buyer raises equity funds from personal assets for the down payment and borrows the mortgage amount from a debt lender (or group of lenders). For example, Tom Kennedy has $100,000 cash, which he plans to use as equity for a down payment on a small business. He needs an additional $400,000 for a mortgage (debt funds) to pay the required purchase price of $500,000. Tom obtains the loan from the First National Bank at the current market rate of 10.5 percent.

Equity funds can be raised from an individual's own assets or provided by several investors pooling their assets. Similarly, debt funds can be raised from a lender or a group of lenders. An investor can be a demander or a supplier of equity and/or debt funds. Which role the investor decides to assume depends on her objectives, motives, and expected return on each individual project.

LEVERAGE

Any commercial investor should be aware of the use of borrowed funds to magnify the amount of return on the equity invested in the project. In general, **leverage** is considered to be *favorable* when the return on the equity is larger than the cost of the money and *unfavorable* when the opposite holds true. In a rising market, the purchase of property with debt funds as opposed to a purchase with all cash will normally result in a larger rate of return on the amount of equity paid by the investor.

For example, consider property that is purchased for $200 million with all cash, held for one year, and sold for $210 million. The return would be

	Purchase	Sale
Market value	$200,000,000	$210,000,000
Debt	0	
Equity	$200,000,000	

The gain is 10,000,000/200,000,000 = .05, or 5 percent on the cash invested, which is **positive leverage** because 5 percent is greater than 0 cost of debt.

Now consider the purchase where the buyer paid $20 million down, financed the balance with a $180 million mortgage at 10.5 percent for 20 years, and sold the property in 1 year. The return would be

	Purchase	Sale
Market value	$200,000,000	$210,000,000
Debt	$180,000,000	
Cash down	$20,000,000	

The gain is $10,000,000/20,000,000 = .5, or 50 percent, which is greater positive leverage from the use of debt.

An investor can achieve a high rate of return on the equity funds invested in real estate by combining where possible a small down payment with a large mortgage. In this manner, the two combined can be used to purchase high-priced property. Real estate is unique in that the investor can acquire higher-priced property with a small down payment to achieve the maximum leverage.

How Do Commercial Loan Payments Differ?

Amortization of a commercial loan can be negotiated with the lender. Typically, the results will fall into one of the following categories:

constant level payment with monthly, quarterly, or semiannual payments

term payment

partial payment with a balloon

constant level payment with income participation, equity participation, or both

Consider the following example:

$50,000,000 first loan

9.5% annual interest

20-year maturity date

With a *constant level payment, monthly payments* equal $466,065.59, which remain constant to reduce the debt to 0 by maturity and pay 9.5 percent on the monthly declining balance. *Quarterly payments* equal $1,401,887.80, and *semiannual payments* are $2,814,837.27.

With a *term payment,* the borrower pays the debt balance at the end of the loan period. Normally, the lender will require the interest to be paid in periodic payments. Using the same loan above:

$50,000,000 × .095 = $4,750,000 interest owed annually, **or**

$4,750,000/12 months = $395,833.33 paid monthly, **or**

$4,750,000/4 months = $1,187,500 paid quarterly, **or**

$4,750,000/2 months = $2,375,000 paid semiannually.

A *partial payment with a balloon* plan allows the borrower to delay a portion of the debt until the end. The purpose of this arrangement is to give the borrower (1) a lower payment that results in a higher level of return during the period of ownership, and (2) additional time to increase the value of the property so that a potential re-sale or refinancing will generate the needed funds to repay the debt balance.

Consider the figures used above. The borrower and lender agree to a debt repayment plan where $10 million is written as a separate loan that matures in 10 years, and interest is paid quarterly. The remaining debt of $40 million is due in 20 years at 9.5 percent with quarterly payments. The quarterly amount owed to the lender is as follows:

$1,121,510.24 quarterly amortization payment at 9.5% for 20 years on $40,000,000

\+ 237,500.00 interest only on $10,000,000 at 9.5% paid quarterly

\= $1,359,010.24

The borrower has saved

$1,401,887.80 quarterly payment on $50,000,000 at 9.5% for 20 years

\- 1,359,010.24

\= $ 42,877.56 per quarter

A *constant level payment with lender participation* may be used when the risk of the project may be higher because the lender wants an additional return above the interest rate charged in a typical loan. This additional payment to the lender can be any of three different types. The first is an **income participation,** in which the lender receives the negotiated amortization payment on a first loan plus a percentage of the property's net operating income. The second is an **equity participation,** in which the lender receives a percentage of the net equity returned to the owner on a predetermined date when the property is to be either sold or refinanced. The third is a *combination* of the previous two types.

Participation financing of any type greatly increases the rate of return to the lender as compensation for risk in the project. The amount and type must be negotiated to assure that the final returns to the borrower and lender are acceptable.

Consider the example in Exhibit 10.1. The borrower has agreed to a debt that requires an amortization payment of $30,000 annually. An additional income participation equal to 1/5 of the net operating income (NOI) must also be paid. Further, when the property is sold at the end of year 5, the borrower must pay 20 percent of the net equity. The lender's rate of return for the risk in this project has increased substantially.

EXHIBIT 10.1	Participation financing.					
	Year 1	Year 2	Year 3	Year 4	Year 5	Year 5 Sale Net Equity
NOI	$50,000	$50,000	$50,000	$50,000	$50,000	$100,000
Debt Pay	30,000	30,000	30,000	30,000	30,000	
Participation Pay	10,000	10,000	10,000	10,000	10,000	20,000
Cash Flow	10,000	10,000	10,000	10,000	10,000	80,000

What Are Key Financial Ratios?

Several key **financial ratios** can be used by the potential borrower or the lender to evaluate the worthiness of the application. Exhibit 10.2 illustrates the magnitude of ratios that one large underwriter has used to evaluate applications for a loan for an office building, apartment building, shopping center, and warehouse. Considered collectively, these ratios provide a "ballpark" estimate of the worthiness of the application. These ratios are defined below.

Debt service coverage ratio: Net operating income divided by the annual debt service.

Loan-to-value (LTV) ratio: Loan amount divided by the value of the property or the sales price.

Default ratio: Loan debt service and operating expenses divided by the gross potential income.

Stabilized vacancy ratio: Income lost from vacancy divided by gross potential income. Some analysts may use effective gross income as it includes an adjustment for vacancy losses.

Land-to-building ratio: Square footage of the building's ground floor divided by the square footage of the site.

Building area ratio: Square footage of the building that can be leased divided by the total square footage of the building.

Overall cap rate: Net operating income divided by the estimate of market value or the sales price.

EXHIBIT 10.2	Key financial ratios for evaluating commercial loans.			
Ratio	**Office Buildings**	**Apartments**	**Shopping Centers**	**Warehouses**
Debt service coverage ratio	1.25%–1.3%	1.2%–1.25% minimum	1.25%–1.3%	1.25%–1.3%
Loan-to-value ratio	75% of economic value but not to exceed 90% of cost of purchase price	80% of economic value but not to exceed 90% of replacement costs or purchase price	75% of economic value but not to exceed 90% of cost or purchase price	75% of economic value but not to exceed 90% of cost or purchase price
Default ratio	70%–80%	80%–85%	70%–80%	70%
Stabilized vacancy ratio	10% of gross income	—	5%–10% of gross income	5%–10% of gross income
Land-to-building ratio	Not to exceed 100%	—	—	—
Building area ratio	85%+	—	—	—
Overall cap rate	1% over interest rate	—	1% over interest rate	1%–2% over interest rate

Source: Survey conducted by authors among commercial lenders.

Consider a mortgage application for an office building that has the following characteristics.

Debt service coverage ratio: 1.3
Loan-to-value ratio: 75% of the income approach is $825,000
Default ratio: 78.4%
Stabilized vacancy ratio: 8%
Land-to-building ratio: 90%
Building area ratio: 88%
Overall cap rate: 11.5%

All of the financial ratios are within acceptable ranges or exceed the minimum. Therefore, the mortgage application for $825,000 would probably be approved if the remainder of the application were satisfactory.

These financial ratios enable the borrower to evaluate the mortgage application before presenting it to the lender. Also, by comparing these figures with figures for similar projects, the borrower can determine whether the proposed project is competitive.

What Is Commercial Loan Underwriting?

The process of underwriting the loan involves the lender's risk assessment of potential loan default by the borrower. The commercial lender will use several of the ratios defined above to help assess this risk and determine the maximum amount of the loan. For example, consider the following situation:

Jack Jones Construction Co. applies for a commercial loan on a proposed apartment development that the appraiser values at $2 million. Jack estimates the first year's NOI to equal $255,000. First National tells Jack that the bank's required debt service coverage ratio for apartments equals 1.25 percent. If the current rates on this type of loan equal 9 percent for 20 years with monthly payments, what is the maximum loan that the bank will offer Jack?

One ratio that is helpful here:

Annual debt service = NOI/DCR
Annual debt service = $255,000/1.25
                     = $204,000/12 months
                     = $17,000 monthly

The maximum amount of the loan equals the present value of the monthly payments at 9-percent interest for 20 years. A financial calculator shows this amount to equal $1,889,464. The difference of $110,536 (2,000,000 − 1,889,464) represents the amount of cash or equity that the company has invested in the property.

Further, the lender may discuss an additional requirement with the construction company that involves the loan-to-value ratio. For example, in the problem above, the bank may tell Jack that it will grant a loan either on the amount determined from the calculations above, or a 75-percent LTV, *whichever is lower.* If the appraiser estimates a value of $2,000,000, the LTV ratio is

$2,000,000 × .75 = $1,500,000 loan, and
LTV = $1,500,000/$2,000,000 = .75

The result is that the bank will grant a maximum loan of only $1,500,000. The annual debt service at 9 percent for 20 years with monthly payments will equal $13,495.89.

UNDERWRITING AND FEASIBILITY

Underwriting and feasibility are decisions that can be made together. Continuing with the previous example, Jack has estimated that the costs of the apartment development are the following:

Size of building:
    389,340 sq. ft.

Cost of construction:
Building	$3.90 per sq. ft.
Utilities	$1.10 per sq. ft.

Sales price:
    Anticipated $5.50 per sq. ft.

Total cost:
    389,340 × $3.90 = $1,518,426 bldg.
    389,340 × $1.10 = $ 428,274 utilities
    Total   = $1,946,700

Anticipated sales price:
    389,340 × $5.50 = $2,141,370

Because the estimate of market value by the appraiser is $2,000,000 and the total cost of the project is $1,946,700, the project creates excess profit, which means that it is feasible. The construction company must contribute any amount over the $1,500,000 loan from its own funds, or equity.

What Is Construction Finance?

CONSTRUCTION LOANS AND GAP FINANCING ✏

A **construction loan** is a short-term loan given for the construction of an improvement on the property. The builder-developer may require **gap financing** (another loan from another lender) if the lender supplying the permanent, first-lien mortgage will not pay the full amount of the mortgage until the newly constructed building attains a predetermined occupancy or usage level. This *retainage* or *holdback,* which is described in the following paragraph, must be covered by the building-developer with gap financing.

PERMANENT LOANS ✏

A **permanent loan** is the first-lien mortgage on the property. Permanent lenders give the construction lender a **takeout commitment,** agreeing to pay off the construction loan once the building is complete. No takeout will occur until the building is free of potential liens. In addition, the permanent lender may insist on a **retainage,** or **holdback,** from the amount of funds paid to the borrower. This amount protects the lender from the risk of failure to complete the job or of bankruptcy of the borrower. Typically, the permanent loan is approved prior to the construction loan to assure the interim lender of the "takeout" once the project is complete. The construction loan is paid out in increments based upon stages of completion.

Evaluating the application for a permanent loan is much more subjective than evaluating a residential application because so many additional factors are involved and their quantification is difficult. To assist the lender in processing the loan application and to ensure a fair evaluation, the borrower should provide supporting documents. The application can be divided into four basic parts.

The Overall Project

The overall project report should contain a description of the physical features and design elements of the entire project. Although the borrower may be asking for funds to cover only an initial phase of the development, the lender needs a total view of the entire project. This report should include the *feasibility study,* which shows that the proposed project will support itself once constructed. It could be a financial, market, site, or cost study depending on the project and the use of funds. This information assists the lender in evaluating the risk involved in the loan. The overall project cost that the borrower thinks is realistic should be stated.

The Borrower and Advisors

A past record of successes in real estate projects is good evidence that the borrower can interpret the local market trends correctly. All previous projects that the borrower has developed or constructed and the names of the loan offices should be provided.

The Completed Project

Additional documents describing physical details of the completed project should be presented—a street map serving the site, a property survey, aerial photos, present zoning, an appraisal, and a description of general and special amenities. A set of building plans and a specifications manual should be provided. The lender also would like to have a detailed breakdown of the projected income and expenses.

Financing

A complete financing plan should be presented to the lender. The amount of equity the borrower is providing, the amount of loan the lender is asked to commit, the payback periods, the amount of amortization, and the suggested interest rate should be stated.

CONSTRUCTION DRAWS

Construction loans are scheduled in a series of **construction draws.** For example, the lender may commit up to 33 percent of the total once the foundation is poured. A second 33 percent may be paid after the roof, windows, and doors are installed. A third 33 percent may be requested when both parties are ready to close.

The total construction cost approved in the loan must include the interest on the construction loan. For example, the total out-of-pocket costs for materials and labor may be equal to $841,500. The amount actually approved by the bank might be closer to $900,000 maximum to account for interest owed on the various draws during the construction.

For example, consider the maximum loan of $900,000 over 210 days, three equal draws, and estimated out-of-pocket expenses projected to be $841,500. What is the expected amount of interest to be owed at a rate of 10 percent annually? Compute the interest owed as simple interest (not compounded).

Amount Drawn	Date Drawn	Interest Owed at the End of Month 6
$280,500	today	$280,500 \times .10/365 \text{ days} \times 210 \text{ days}$ = $16,138
280,500	beginning of month 2	$280,500 \times .10/365 \text{ days} \times 150 \text{ days}$ = $11,527
280,500	beginning of month 6	$280,500 \times .10/365 \text{ days} \times 30 \text{ days}$ = $2,305
		Total simple interest owed = $29,970

The total amount of interest owed depends on the date the draw was actually used. The total amount that the lender would transfer to permanent financing for repayment would equal the $841,500 plus the $29,970, or $871,470 total.

How Is a Second Mortgage Used?

A second mortgage is a second loan using the same property as collateral. In a purchase, the buyer may use a second mortgage to raise additional cash to pay the purchase price or the down payment. In addition, an owner may take out a second mortgage from a lender to borrow against the equity in the property without disturbing the original loan.

The second mortgage lender can be a third party, such as a second financial institution or even the seller, who is subject to possible restrictions within the first mortgage. The mortgage document contains many of the same terms as a first mortgage but with several differences. A second mortgage typically carries an interest rate that is higher than the rates charged on first mortgages. The lender wants compensation for the additional risk of being second in line in case of borrower default. The maturity is shorter than that of the first mortgage. Also, the second mortgage may contain a subordination clause or a default on prior mortgage clause.

Assume, for example, that Janette Worley is attempting to purchase a building on East Huntsville Street in Springdale, Georgia. Jack Hugley, the owner, is asking $100,000 for the building, and Miss Worley has agreed to the price provided that she can obtain the necessary financing. The building has a good income and would easily pay for itself. However, Miss Worley has only $2,000 cash. Miss Worley and the agent handling the transaction apply to the First Mortgage Company in Savannah for a commercial loan in the amount of $80,000 for 20 years at 11 percent. Also, they ask the Second National Bank of Springdale for a second mortgage on the building in the amount of $18,000 for 10 years at 13.5 percent. First Mortgage accepts the venture because of Miss Worley's good financial statement. Her employment and income potential are good, and the Second National Bank approves the second mortgage. The property also is well located, which will cause the value of the collateral to grow with time.

What Are Common Special Clauses Used in Commercial Loans?

A SUBORDINATION CLAUSE

A *subordination clause,* usually found within the second mortgage, states that the second loan will always remain secondary to the first mortgage and to any new first mortgage that may be placed on the property in the future.

A DEFAULT IN PRIOR PAYMENT CLAUSE

A *default in prior payment clause,* usually found within the second mortgage, allows the second lender to correct a default in the first mortgage by making the payments, adding the amount to the indebtedness of the second loan, and foreclosing on the second loan. In this manner, the second lender can judge the appropriate time to foreclose to avoid losses in certain situations, such as an interruption of the income flows from rentals that are in turn paid to the lender for mortgage payments.

ASSIGNMENT AND ESTOPPEL

The buyer can protect rights to the income stream by requiring the seller to produce an abstract (previously introduced in Chapter 1). This document shows whether the seller legally has the right to sell the income stream. Also, the buyer can require the seller to sign and file in the county courthouse an *assignment* (also discussed in Chapter 8), which gives the buyer the legal right to collect the income stream. Third, the buyer can require the seller to produce an *estoppel certificate.* This certificate requires the seller to state the exact balance of the mortgage that the mortgagor is paying and whether the seller has any claims against the income stream that are unknown. This certificate "stops" the seller from changing the balance or making other claims later.

Assume, for example, that the Land Auction Real Estate Company has recently missed three payments on a mortgage for a duplex from which they receive about $5,500 net income per month. The lender is holding a $300,000 outstanding mortgage on the unit. Exercising the right to claim the income stream in the event of default under a *mortgagee in possession clause* in the mortgage, the lender, First State Bank, requests an abstract and asks Land Auction to pay the costs. An estoppel certificate and an assignment are signed by the Land Auction Real Estate Company. The First State Bank knows that it has the legal right to collect the rents by the abstract, gives constructive notice of this right by filing the assignment contract, and stops Land Auction from changing their claim or mortgage balance by the estoppel certificate.

A NONRECOURSE CLAUSE TO THE BORROWER

A *nonrecourse* (or *exculpatory*) *clause* limits the borrower's liability in the permanent loan to the proceeds from the sale of the property. If the borrower should eventually default on the loan, the lender could not pursue any personal assets that the borrower might own. The existence of this clause in the loan document means that the lender has devoted a significant amount of time and resources to an examination of the underlying merit of the overall project.

What Is the Nature of the Commercial Lease?

The **commercial lease** is a legal document that describes the agreement reached between a landlord who owns property that can be rented as commercial space and a tenant who is a private businessperson. Commercial leases are written for such tenants as retail stores, restaurants, movie theaters, and drug stores. In addition, commercial leases are written for office space that is needed by doctors, dentists, optometrists, attorneys, appraisers, real estate brokers, and other professional individuals. The commercial lease is generally similar to the residential lease but differs in certain respects. The following discussion of the commercial lease explains the significant points of difference.

TYPES AND CONDITIONS OF COMMERCIAL LEASES

In a commercial lease, the landlord and the tenant must reach an agreement about the rent to be paid and the space to be provided. Unlike the residential lease, in which the rent payment is usually stated as a flat fee, the commercial lease can stipulate any of a variety of payment schemes. Moreover, the commercial lease includes special provisions about the space.

Rent Payment Schemes

The commercial lease takes a special name that reflects the rent payment scheme agreed to by the landlord and the tenant. Hence, commercial leases are referred to by the following names:

    gross lease
    net lease
    percentage lease
    escalated or indexed lease
    graduated payment lease

Each of these rent payment arrangements is described hereafter.

GROSS LEASE. The **gross lease** is a commercial counterpart of the flat or fixed rent payment lease for residential property. Under a gross lease arrangement, the tenant pays a predetermined fixed amount for the space on a periodic basis. This fixed amount of rent covers all of the financial responsibilities that the tenant incurs for possessing and using the space. For example, the payment can be stated as $5,000 per month or as $12 per square foot of space per year.

NET LEASE. The **net lease** breaks the rent payment into components; one component is fixed, and the other one can change over time. In this arrangement, the tenant promises to pay the landlord a fixed sum on a periodic basis and in addition promises to pay some of the expenses that the landlord incurs against the property. The most typical expenses paid by the tenant under a net lease arrangement are the real property taxes and insurance premiums. A net lease can be written in which the tenant promises to pay a flat fee plus the real property taxes, a flat fee plus the hazard insurance premiums, or a flat fee plus the real estate taxes and the hazard insurance premiums. If the tenant pays two expense items, the leasing arrangement is often called a *net-net lease.* In this instance, the tenant might be paying a flat fee plus property taxes and insurance.

Other charges also may enter into a net lease arrangement. The lease can require the tenant to bear the financial responsibility for maintaining and repairing the structure. If the tenant is required to pay the real estate taxes, the insurance premium, and the maintenance and repair costs, the lease is often referred to as a *net-net-net,* or *triple-net, lease.* Many people in the real estate industry use the *triple-net lease* phrase to imply that the tenant is in essence paying all of the landlord's normal operating expenses.

PERCENTAGE LEASE. In a **percentage lease,** the landlord and the tenant agree that the rent payment will reflect the gross sales or gross revenues of the tenant's commercial establishment. The landlord must specify or define the concept of gross sales revenue. To do this, the landlord must understand the nature of the tenant's business. For example, a retail store may sell merchandise directly over the counter to customers on the premises and in addition sell merchandise by mail.

The landlord's income under a percentage lease is affected by the success of the commercial establishment. Consequently, an astute landlord would like the following two provisions incorporated into a percentage lease:

1. *A fixed minimum rent payment.* The landlord should insist that the lease contain a statement establishing the rent payment as a fixed minimum amount to which the percentage is added; or, the lease should require the tenant to pay whichever is the higher sum—the minimum payment decided by agreement between the two parties or the percentage of the gross sales.

2. *A recapture clause.* This clause enables the landlord to regain the property if the tenant's business is not successful over a predetermined time. For example, the landlord may want the lease to terminate if the tenant has paid only the minimum rent for twelve consecutive months. In this way, the landlord regains possession of the property and is able to search for another tenant whose business may be more successful.

ESCALATED OR INDEXED LEASE. When the **escalated lease** (or **indexed lease**) arrangement is used, the landlord and the tenant agree that the first year's rent will be a flat or fixed amount, but that this amount will change on a periodic basis, usually yearly, when some index changes. This agreement necessitates a second agreement on the index that will be used to adjust the gross rent. The index can be the consumer price index, the wholesale price index, or any other index related to commodity prices.

GRADUATED PAYMENT LEASE. Under a **graduated payment lease,** the landlord and the tenant mutually agree on a rent payment pattern that will continue into the future. The agreement may stipulate, for example, that the tenant will pay $3,500 per month for use of the commercial space in the first year of operation, $4,500 per month in the second and third years of the lease, and $6,000 per month in the remaining years of the lease. This agreement is established at the outset of the leasing period and remains in force for the remainder of the lease. The graduated payment can take any one of a multitude of forms. For example, an alternative could be a rent payment of $3,500 per month for the first year, $4,500 per month in the second and third years, and a minimum of $5,000 per month plus 1 percent of the gross sales per month for the remainder of the lease. In this case, the lease is a hybrid of the graduated payment and the percentage leases.

Agreement on Competitive Space

In addition to the negotiations about the rent payment scheme, the landlord and the tenant may need to reach an agreement about space usage. Such agreements are common in leases for space in shopping centers. If the shopping center is small in total rentable floor space, or if the shopping center does not attract many customers, certain tenants may want a clause in the lease that eliminates the landlord's right to rent space to a competitor.

Term of the Lease

Commercial leases are generally regarded as medium-term leases whose expiration date is set between 3 and 10 years in the future. The term of the lease is negotiated between the landlord and the tenant. Usually, the term of the lease is considered in relation to the rent payment scheme and the future state of the economy. For example, if inflation is expected to continue into the future, the tenant would like a gross lease at the lowest possible rate for the longest term that can be negotiated.

Legal Description

The description of the premises that the tenant leases must be clearly stated. If the tenant leases an entire property, the mailing address may be sufficient description for the tenant's purposes, but only if the tenant has no use for the external surroundings. Because a future need may arise for that space, the tenant may want the lease to define some portion of the surrounding land as being in the tenant's possession.

THE GROUND LEASE

The **ground lease** is an agreement between a landlord and a tenant for the lease of vacant land. An important provision of the lease is the tenant's promise to erect a building on the vacant land. This promise necessitates a thorough discussion between the two parties about the length or term of the lease and the disposition of the improvement when the lease expires. Generally the ground lease is a long-term lease. Few such leases are written for less than 20 years, and in some cases 50 years is stipulated as the minimum term of a ground lease.

When the tenant fulfills the promise to build the structure, the structure legally becomes the property of the landlord. Consequently, the tenant should discuss the financial settlement that will occur when the lease terminates. The tenant may insist on compensation for the value of the structure at the expiration of the lease. The landlord and the tenant may agree that an appraiser will be consulted to estimate the replacement value of the structure at that future date. If the term of the lease is long enough, the replacement cost of the structure may be insignificant. For example, a 50-year-old industrial plant may be so functionally obsolete and physically deteriorated that its replacement cost less depreciation is zero. Whatever the situation at the end of the lease, the landlord and the tenant should reach some agreement at the beginning of the lease about the value of the improvement and whether the landlord will compensate the tenant for the improvement.

In the majority of cases, the ground lease is written as a triple-net lease agreement. The tenant typically incurs the obligation to pay a flat rate to the landlord plus all property taxes and assessments against the property, construction costs of the building, insurance on the improvement, and all expenses for maintenance and repair. In addition, the tenant assumes all responsibility for personal injury to third parties. Consequently, the landlord is relieved of all expenses associated with the property. The landlord receives a fixed periodic payment of rent; more importantly, all value increases to the land accrue to the landlord. The tenant receives the use of the land and the long-term use of the building specifically designed to meet her needs.

Most provisions in a ground lease are very similar to those in a commercial lease. The topics discussed between the landlord and the tenant in a commercial lease form the basis of the agreement between the landlord and the tenant in the ground lease.

The ground lease is beneficial to both parties. The landlord receives a periodic rent payment, is freed of major expenses associated with owning vacant land, and receives any increase in the value of the land. The tenant receives the use and possession of the land; use and possession of the building, which in most cases is specifically designed for her needs; and may receive compensation for the value of the structure at the expiration of the lease. The tenant can also receive income tax benefits derived from deductibility of depreciation allowances, interest payments on the leasehold mortgage, and ground rent as a business expense.

THE SALE AND LEASEBACK AGREEMENT

The **sale and leaseback agreement** is an arrangement whereby a current owner and user of commercial or industrial property decides to offer the property for sale, but only on the condition that the prospective buyer simultaneously enters into a lease in which the current owner retains the rights to use and possess the property. The current owner initially must make an own-or-rent decision. The owner must analyze the company's financial position to see whether the ownership of the real estate asset is or is not more beneficial than leasing the rights to use and possess that same property. Each of these options has advantages and disadvantages. The owner must consider the following items:

1. *The equity in the property.* The owner of commercial or industrial real estate has an equity position in the property. The question to be resolved is whether that equity is needed in the operation of the business. The owner must weigh the relative benefits of keeping the equity in real property or converting it to personal property such as machines and inventory.

2. *Income tax consideration.* Generally, the owner of income-producing property is able to deduct the interest payments on the mortgage, real property taxes, and depreciation allowances from income earned in the current year. If the same property is leased, the entire rental payment becomes an expense of the business and thereby a deduction against the income of the business.

3. *Fixed asset holdings.* The fixed asset can be converted to a cash asset. The liquidity position of the business is improved, and thus the capacity to borrow funds is increased.

4. *Change in role from landlord to tenant.* When the property is sold and leased back, the owner of the business is no longer the owner of the property. The landlord becomes a tenant. Consequently, that businessperson is obligated to the provisions of the lease with its stipulated rent payment and other terms.

The other party to the sale and leaseback arrangement is the prospective buyer or the future owner of the property. This individual's decision is based on the factors that will be discussed in Chapter 11. The investor in a sale and leaseback agreement should analyze the rate of return to be obtained from the investment and compare it to the rates of return available from alternative investments. In this context, the investor is analyzing the periodic cash flow, the equity increase through mortgage reduction, the price appreciation, and all of the other factors and considerations involved in the real estate equity investment decision.

What Are Special-Purpose Clauses in a Commercial Lease?

The commercial lease can be affected by several special situations. In medium- and long-term leases, the tenant and the landlord both have rights of ownership that can be used as collateral for a loan. The landlord owns the freehold estate and the tenant owns a leasehold estate. The two parties must agree to the manner and method by which each will be treated if the other uses the ownership rights he controls as security for a loan. If condemnation proceedings take place against the property, the fact that the tenant owns a leasehold may establish the tenant's right to make a claim against the compensation paid by the local government to the property owner. The extent and nature of the tenant's claim under condemnation must be analyzed and understood by the two parties in the lease. Finally, the tenant may wish to purchase the freehold estate at some point in the future. The tenant could have this right stated in the lease in the form of an option-to-purchase clause.

THE LANDLORD'S RIGHT TO MORTGAGE THE PROPERTY

When a lease is written and signed, it is automatically subordinate to all current mortgages that are recorded or that the tenant knows exist. The lease is superior, however, to a future mortgage that may be created unless the lease contains a provision expressly stating a subordinate relationship. Obviously, a landlord desires this type of subordination clause in the lease, and printed lease forms generally include such a clause. Few landlords would be willing to waive this subordination clause.

The effect of the subordination clause on the tenant is profound. If a new mortgage is made, the subordination clause allows the lender to terminate the lease and evict the tenant if the landlord defaults on the mortgage. If the tenant is evicted because of the landlord's default on a mortgage that was executed after the lease came into force, the tenant may or may not have a right to sue the landlord for damages. The grounds for the suit would be the landlord's breach of contract, specifically, breach of the landlord's promise of "quiet enjoyment." However, the tenant's rights in this situation depend on the language of the lease and the wording of the quiet-enjoyment clause.

The tenant should seek to limit his risk in the event that the landlord defaults on a mortgage that is issued subsequent to the lease. The tenant can attempt to insert a clause limiting the future mortgage to a specific sum. Alternatively, the tenant may agree to subordinate the lease only to a mortgage that is made by a financial institution. Also, the tenant who is in possession of the entire property can seek to limit the mortgage in such a way that the mortgage payment or the debt service does not exceed the rent paid on a monthly or yearly basis when added to the property's operating expenses.

The tenant may be able to insert a **nondisturbance clause** into the original lease. This clause would state that the lease shall be subject to and subordinated to any future mortgage but that the lender must agree not to terminate the lease in the event of a foreclosure proceeding. Such a clause clearly states that the lease is subordinate to the future mortgage. It therefore should be agreeable to the landlord and the future lender, but it also accords the tenant some degree of assurance that possession of the property will not be disturbed in the event of the landlord's default on the mortgage.

The tenant who is unsuccessful in obtaining a nondisturbance clause in the lease, and who consequently must sign a lease that subordinates her interest to future mortgages, can minimize the risk of eviction by inserting a clause that gives the tenant the right to pay the mortgage if the landlord defaults. This clause should also contain an agreement giving the tenant some way of shifting the burden back to the landlord, for example, by subtracting the mortgage payments from the tenant's rent responsibilities.

THE TENANT'S RIGHT TO MORTGAGE THE LEASEHOLD

Just as in the cases of assignment and sublet, the tenant has the right to mortgage the leasehold unless a specific prohibition is stated in the lease. The tenant may find it desirable to maintain the right to mortgage the leasehold. If the property is in a good location, the use and possession of the property are valuable assets. For example, if a tenant holds a long-term lease on a building at the corner of the busiest commercial intersection in town, and if the business is successful because of the ideal location, the space is valuable not only to the current tenant but also to a new tenant who could establish the same retail operation. Consequently, a lender might issue a loan for which the collateral is only the right to use and possess that property.

THE OPTION TO PURCHASE

The purchase option can be viewed as a series of clauses in a commercial lease giving the tenant the possibility of buying the leased property. Probably the most important element of the **option to purchase clause** is the determination of the purchase price. The landlord and the tenant can agree on a definite, future sales price at the time the property is leased and simultaneously can identify the manner in which payment will be made. Alternatively, the landlord and the tenant may agree to stipulate the sales price as being equal to the market value of the property on the day of sale at some time in the future. In this case, the landlord and the tenant should also agree on the manner in which the future market value of the property will be determined. Other issues to be settled are the manner in which the appraiser is chosen and whether either party has the right to withdraw if the estimated market value is too high for the tenant or too low for the landlord.

The purchase option should also specify the manner in which the tenant exercises the option. To avoid any future confusion or unnecessary legal complications, the parties should agree that the option is exercised in writing. The tenant drafts a note to the landlord in which she clearly states the intention of accepting the purchase option as specified in the lease. Many option to purchase clauses require that the tenant give advance notice of intent to exercise the option. The nature of the advance notice should be clearly described within the purchase option, and the tenant's written statement concerning the exercise of the option should be dated and delivered to the landlord within the specified time period.

The potential investor should select in advance of the investment the proper type of organization to achieve his objectives. A group of investors can pool their money with a professional in real estate to purchase property, or they can rely on some form of joint ownership.

In searching for a commercial loan, the potential investor should find a lender that has a history of providing the type of funds (debt or equity) needed. In addition, the investor should examine the type of loans typically granted by the lender as a guide to current approval of the loan application.

No standardized loan application procedure is used by all commercial lenders. However, several components of an ideal application can be identified. The application should thoroughly describe the overall project, the borrower and advisors, the completed project, and the financing.

Several key financial ratios can be used to develop an overall indication of the worthiness of the project: the debt service coverage ratio, loan-to-value ratio, default ratio, stabilized vacancy ratio, land-to-building ratio, building area ratio, and overall cap rate. These ratios should be considered as a group rather than individually to make judgments on specific aspects of the project.

The amortization schedule of a commercial loan can be negotiable. The repayment of a commercial loan and its interest typically is a constant level payment, a partial payment with a balloon note, a term payment, or a participation agreement. The first requires a fixed periodic payment, usually monthly, where the interest owed is computed on the declining balance. By maturity, the remaining debt is equal to zero. Under partial payment, a periodic repayment is required and interest is computed on the declining balance. By maturity, the repayments have not reduced the balance to zero so a single large payment is required with interest. Under term payment, the whole loan plus interest is repaid in one payment when the loan matures. In a participation agreement, the borrower agrees to pay the lender a payment on a loan plus a percentage of either the net operation income or the net equity at the sale or both.

In a commercial lease, each party—the landlord and the tenant—has certain rights and responsibilities related to the delivery of possession, the use of the leased property, the responsibility for maintenance and repair, the liability for personal injury, the right to enter the property, and the right to assign or sublet the lease. Both parties to the lease must be concerned and informed about their legal responsibilities and their rights in these matters.

In addition to these rights and responsibilities, the commercial lease contains numerous clauses pertaining to matters of mutual concern to the landlord and the tenant. In a commercial lease, the parties must agree on provision for commercial fixtures, improvements made by the tenant, the landlord's right to relocate the tenant after the lease is signed, and breakdowns of mechanical equipment.

Commercial leases are typically written for space in a structure. A ground lease is a special lease agreement to establish a leasehold for vacant land. It generally lasts for a longer period of time than the average commercial lease, and it contains clauses pertaining to the tenant's right to any structures or improvements erected on the landlord's property. Another special arrangement is the sale and leaseback agreement, whereby the owner of the property sells the property to a prospective buyer while maintaining a claim on the leasehold.

A website has been established for this chapter at http://epley.swcollege.com.

Review Questions

1. What is positive leverage? Why does it exist?
2. Why would a lender want a participation loan? What types are available?
3. Describe the types of repayment plans that are typical to commercial loans.
4. Explain the meaning of "construction loan draws." How is the interest computed?
5. What are the typical parts of a commercial loan application?
6. What types of organizations are used for commercial loans?
7. What is the purpose of a second mortgage?
8. Explain the meaning of each of the following:

   sale leaseback

   ground lease

   takeout commitment

   percentage lease

   net-net lease

   income participation

   equity participation

   nonrecourse clause

   equity funds

9. Does a commercial lease reflect market risk? How?
10. Identify the difference between a gross lease and a net lease.
11. ABC Development Co. has negotiated a construction loan for $5,500,000 at 9 percent annually for a maximum of 365 days. The lender wants to issue the money for the $4,800,000 out-of-pocket costs in three equal draws. The first will be taken when the loan is signed, the second in 180 days, and the third at the closing on the 365th day. What is the total simple interest owed on the 365th day?
12. Given a loan on income-producing property at $45,000,000, 9.5-percent annual interest, payable over 20 years, illustrate the difference in the payments and the remaining loan balance at the end of year 10 under the following payment plans:

    monthly payments

    quarterly payments

    semiannual payments

    annual payments

    At the end of year 10, what is the difference in the total amount of interest paid under each payment plan?

How does a change in the interest rate influence the payments and remaining balance after year 10? Find the current rate on the Internet and illustrate the differences.

13. Greystone Development Co. estimates that the first-year NOI on its new building will equal $280,000. A private appraiser estimates that the building will be worth $2,550,000 when completed. AB Bank is willing to grant a loan on either the 75-percent LTV, or using a 1.3 debt coverage ratio. The current rates are 9.5 percent for 25 years with monthly payments. What is the loan, and what are the monthly payments?

Discussion Questions

1. Are there any circumstances in which an individual would want to invest in property as an individual? Identify them.

2. Explain the differences between the application process for a residential loan and the process for a commercial loan.

3. Can you identify any additional financial ratios that might be used to evaluate a commercial loan application for a specific use?

4. Should a commercial borrower ask for an amortization schedule that is not at a constant level like the residential mortgage? Is it more efficient management to repay the debt on a regular basis, which reduces the balance to zero by maturity? Explain.

5. Explain the market conditions that would create an incentive for a borrower to request a second mortgage rather than refinancing.

6. When should a tenant ask for a gross lease as opposed to a net lease? Or a net lease as opposed to a gross lease?

7. When should a sale and leaseback agreement be used?

8. What market circumstance would cause the owner of a site to refuse an offer to buy a site and ask for a ground lease?

## PART IV

The Decision to Invest in the Property

CHAPTER 11

Real Estate Equity Investment

QUESTIONS TO BE ANSWERED

1. What factors must an individual investor consider in deciding whether to purchase income-earning real property?

2. What financial relationships should the investor consider when evaluating real property for acquisition?

3. What technique should the individual investor use as part of the decision-making process?

OBJECTIVES

When finished with this chapter, the student should be able to:

1. Explain the nature of an equity investment in real estate.

2. Understand the various objectives that typical investors wish to achieve.

3. Identify and discuss the risks and obstacles associated with real estate equity investment.

4. Explain the generation of before-tax cash flow.

5. Describe the nature and uses of financial and profitability ratios.

6. Describe the nature and uses of present value and internal rate of return calculations.

7. Explain feasibility analysis.

IMPORTANT TERMS

amortization table	internal rate of return (IRR) technique
before-tax cash flow (BTCF)	investment
before-tax equity reversion (BTER)	investment analysis
breakeven ratio	liquidity
business or income risk	net present value (NPV) comparison
cost of capital	net proceeds from the sale
discounted cash flow analysis	payback period
equity	periodic cash flow
equity capitalization rate	present value technique
equity investment	price appreciation
equity yield rate	principal risk
estate building	purchasing power risk
financial risk	pyramiding
gross rate of return	sensitivity analysis
holding period analysis	tax-deferred exchange
interest or money market risk	tax shelter

INTRODUCTION

Investment analysis is a personal consideration. It focuses on the economic and financial characteristics of a specific property and it also considers the specific needs or requirements of a specific individual. Investment analysis is similar to income property valuation because both focus on the specific economic and financial characteristics of a specific property. Investment analysis differs from income property valuation because investment analysis focuses on an individual while income property valuation focuses on the actions of a market—a group of potential investors.

Each individual investor needs to know (1) what level of risk he or she is willing to accept for an investment and (2) the rate of return that, in their opinion, adequately covers this risk. This chapter asks and answers these two related questions by showing the analytical techniques used by real estate investors.

What Are the Major Investment Considerations?

Every potential investor in real estate must have pertinent information about the investment opportunity and the various economic and financial factors that can affect it. In addition, the investor should establish personal goals about the financial returns to be derived from the investment. Neither real estate investments nor any other investment can fulfill everyone's financial objectives. The investor should evaluate the strengths and weaknesses of each available real estate investment.

When private individuals or corporations accumulate savings, they investigate various uses to which this unspent money can be applied. In other words, private individuals and corporations look for investment opportunities. The term *investment* is used in this sense throughout this textbook. **Investment** is the use of accumulated savings to purchase an income-earning asset.

TYPES OF INVESTMENT OPPORTUNITIES

Individuals can choose from a large number of investment alternatives for accumulated savings. A person can enter some investments directly by assuming ownership of a document that is an income-earning asset—for example, saving accounts, corporate bonds, government bonds, and common and preferred stocks. The expected return for the savings accounts and bonds is greater than zero and is fixed in magnitude. The interest payment is stated in advance when the asset is purchased. In contrast, common and preferred stocks are investments for which the rate of return is variable. The dividends paid by the corporation depend on the company's earnings level and profits.

In addition to financial assets, an individual can invest in many types of nonfinancial assets, such as commodities, business ventures, precious metals, gems, art objects, and antiques. The rate of return on each of these investments varies because the yield depends on such factors as the investor's bargaining ability, the establishment and operation of a business concern, and knowledge about future levels of demand and consumer tastes.

Real estate provides opportunities for investment in both financial and nonfinancial assets. An investor who purchases part or all of a parcel of real property makes an **equity investment.** An investor who purchases a financial asset called a mortgage makes a mortgage investment. Both types of real estate investments are examined in detail in the following section.

Real Estate Equity Investment Versus Mortgage Investment

The real estate equity investor owns real property. The investor typically pays part of the sales price from savings and borrows the remainder. The extent to which borrowed funds are used does not affect the level of the investor's ownership rights. Whether the investor pays 10 percent, 50 percent, or 100 percent of the sales price from savings, the rights to use and dispose of the property do not change. At the time of purchase, the buyer's funds or assets that are used to acquire the property are known as **equity.** If a 20-percent down payment is made from the investor's savings, the equity in the property is equal to 20 percent of the sales price.

The income-earning capability of an equity investment in real estate depends on a multitude of factors than can affect potential gross income, effective gross income, and operating expenses, and thereby affect the level of net operating income (NOI). The individual investor's income tax considerations also affect the level of earnings that can be derived from a specific parcel of real estate.

Mortgage investment is very rarely chosen by an individual. Financial institutions such as commercial banks and life insurance companies generally utilize this type of investment. Mortgage investment is not ownership. The financial institution lends money to a person to buy real estate. In return, the financial institution receives an asset or legal document called the mortgage. The rate of return that the financial institution receives is known as the *mortgage interest payment.* In the past, the mortgage has typically yielded a fixed rate of return to the financial institution if the mortgage is held to maturity. The return is determined by the interest payment that is calculated at the time the mortgage instrument is signed by the borrower and the lender. Some forms of mortgage, however, have a rate of return that is not fixed or constant (the adjustable rate mortgage). In this situation, the interest payment made by the borrower changes over time to reflect fluctuations in the level of interest rates in the economy.

The purpose of this chapter is to examine the equity investment in real estate because it is the type of investment chosen by people who wish to invest in real estate. In later chapters, the mortgage investment and the viewpoint of the mortgage investor will be explored because the equity investor needs to understand the considerations and objectives of the financial institutions that loan money for the purchase of real estate.

What Are the Investor's Objectives?

The rational investor analyzes all available opportunities for the use of savings. This analysis takes place in the framework established by the investor's individual financial goals and objectives. Some investors will assume more risk if there is a strong possibility of a high rate of return. Other investors will give up a periodic income flow for the prospect of an increase in the value of the asset over time. These investors are willing to take the risk that the investment will increase in value if the right economic or market circumstances occur.

The rational investor considers not only the income flow, the rate of return, and the growth of the investment's value, but also the possibility of converting the asset into cash without a loss during the transaction—known as the **liquidity** of the asset. As a general rule, an asset that is traded in an organized, active market tends to be more liquid than an asset that must be traded in a disorganized or fragmented market. Consequently, common stocks, preferred stocks, corporate bonds, and government bonds tend to be more liquid than real estate.

Once the investor decides what traits are desirable in a specific investment, a choice can be made from many alternatives. The purpose of this section is to identify the various objectives that typically pertain to the real estate investment. Some of these objectives are appropriate to an investment decision in financial securities, such as stocks and bonds, and other objectives are applicable only to real estate investments.

PERIODIC CASH FLOW

One investor objective is a return of dollars from the investment on some definite periodic basis, known as **periodic cash flow.** In the case of a common stock, this periodic return (or cash flow) is the quarterly or semiannual dividend check that may be issued by the company. For the investor in corporate or government bonds, the periodic cash flow is the interest payment received quarterly or annually. For the equity investor in real estate, the periodic cash flow is that portion of actual gross income that remains after operating expenses and other expenses associated with the property are paid. (A complete discussion of cash flow from a real estate investment is presented later in this chapter).

LIQUIDITY

A second investor objective is the ability to convert the asset into cash without a loss of value in the transaction. Common and preferred stocks that are listed with a major stock exchange can be converted into cash at the prevailing market rate within several business days. The investor receives the market value as of the time the asset was sold. From these funds, the investor pays the selling costs associated with the transaction. Corporate and government bonds can also be sold in organized markets for the current market value established in those markets. No organized national market is available for equity investments in real estate.

Real estate markets are local; they are differentiated on the basis of the physical characteristics of the property. Moreover, at any one time, the number of potential buyers may be small. In some instances, there may not be even one buyer for the property. The process of converting the real estate asset to cash will probably take a relatively long time—60 to 180 days for residential property, several months for commercial property, and perhaps a year or more for industrial property. Consequently, real estate is probably the most illiquid investment alternative.

PRICE APPRECIATION

Some investors may not be concerned about a periodic income flow or even the liquidity of the asset because the primary objective is to hold the property while its market value increases—a situation known as **price appreciation.** The investor expects the sales price of the property to increase over the next 5 or 10 years by an amount that is greater than the earnings that might be received from alternate investments. The underlying assumption made by the investor in this case is that the real estate investment is part of an active market both currently and during the entire time the property is held. An investor whose main objective is price appreciation also might seek a periodic cash flow as a secondary objective.

INCREASE IN EQUITY THROUGH MORTGAGE REDUCTION

This investment objective is related to the need for cash flow from the property. What the investor hopes to achieve is an actual gross income level from the property that is great enough to cover all expenses as well as the mortgage payment. If the investment is paying for itself, the investor need not divert any income from other sources to pay off the mortgage on the property. The investor's equity, or percentage of ownership, increases as the borrowed funds are repaid over time. If the property is held for 10 years, and if at the end of that time the investor must sell the property for its original price, the investor still has a financial gain because the equity is a greater percentage of that price at the end of the 10-year period than it was on the day of purchase.

As an objective, this form of equity increase makes sense only in a market where the price of the commodity is increasing or at least staying constant. If the price of the property declines over the ownership period, the investor is really getting a larger percentage of a smaller number of dollars. If prices are declining, equity increase through mortgage reduction as an objective may be futile because the decline in the property's price may be greater than the increase in equity over the period of time that the property is held by the investor.

TAX SHELTER

The tax laws of the federal and state governments have created another investment objective—obtaining a **tax shelter.** Because an income-producing structure is viewed as a wasting asset, the Internal Revenue Code allows the property owner to subtract a percentage of the value of that structure from the property's income stream. The tax codes allow several different methods for the calculation of this depreciation rate. A tax shelter is achieved when the income subject to taxation that is generated by the property is negative (taxable income is negative). When the taxable income from the property is negative, the investor is able to shelter or protect income that is received from other sources—even salary—from federal and state income taxation. Furthermore, to the extent that the depreciation charges taken as an income tax deduction are not measures of actual accrued depreciation (physical deterioration, functional obsolescence, and economic obsolescence), the investor is able to shelter part of the net operating income generated by the property from taxation.

HIGH RATE OF RETURN ON EQUITY

Many people choose real estate as an investment to obtain high rates of return on equity. Typically, a good, financially sound real estate investment generates a positive periodic cash flow that can create a higher rate of return than an investment in stocks or bonds. However, the investor should realize that this higher rate of return is a compensation for factors that negatively affect real estate investment. Real estate investments are riskier than the typical investment in a financial asset, such as stocks and bonds, because real estate investments involve a greater degree of uncertainty about the income stream. A portion of the higher rate of return is designed to compensate the investor for this risk. In addition, real estate investments are less liquid and require more personal attention on the part of the investor than investments in financial securities.

Two important rates of return are used in a discussion of real estate equity investments. The first is the **equity capitalization rate.** This rate is formed by dividing the periodic cash flow by the investor's equity. A more technically precise definition will be offered later in this chapter. However, conceptually, this definition is applicable. The other rate of return is the **equity yield rate.** In simple terms, this is the rate of return to the investor's equity obtained from periodic cash flow, price appreciation, and reduction in the unpaid balance of the mortgage. A more precise definition of this rate of return will also be offered later in this chapter.

[handwritten margin note: periodic cash flow / investor's equity]

LEVERAGE

The term *leverage* refers to a technique that can allow the investor to achieve objectives of high periodic cash flow, price appreciation, tax shelter, and so on by using borrowed funds. A frequently used measure of leverage is the relationship between the rate of return generated by the property and the rate the investor must pay on the money borrowed to purchase that property. Another way to explain this concept of leverage is to say that the NOI from the investment property exceeds the mortgage payment by enough to produce a return on the equity greater than the mortgage rate of interest. In this situation, the investor is utilizing funds obtained from a lender to generate an income flow that is large enough to pay all operating expenses plus the cost of borrowed funds and still provide a positive cash payment. This positive cash flow is divided by the equity invested in the property to determine the investment's equity capitalization rate. If this rate exceeds the mortgage rate on borrowed money, the investor is benefiting financially by using other people's funds to purchase investment property. Consequently, the investor wishes to find a property that provides positive leverage—a rate of return on the investment that is greater than the mortgage interest rate. Another form of leverage is the amount of funds the investor can borrow as a percentage of the property's value. The higher the loan-to-value ratio, the greater the leverage.

ESTATE BUILDING AND PYRAMIDING

Estate building is another technique than can be used to achieve certain investment objectives. It is based on the premise that the investor currently owns a property that generates a gross income large enough to cover all operating expenses and the mortgage payment and still return a positive cash flow. The investor can use such property in a trade for another piece of property that is larger or more profitable and thus more valuable. This process of estate building is encouraged by a tax code provision known as the **tax-deferred exchange** that allows the investor to defer capital gains taxation into the future.

Pyramiding is also dependent on prior ownership of a good investment. However, the investor does not exchange one property for another. Instead, the equity increase in the initial investment is used as collateral to acquire an additional property. When equity has increased, the original property can be refinanced to free cash that can be used to buy a second property, or the increased equity in the first property can be used as collateral for a loan to buy the second property.

HEDGE AGAINST INFLATION

The investor also wishes to protect the purchasing power of the equity investment. This objective can be accomplished by a combination of price appreciation and rate-of-return considerations. The investor would like to earn a return from the periodic cash flow and price appreciation that is great enough to offset alternative opportunities, illiquidity, management expenses, and risk. In addition, the investor would like the same return to be large enough to cover increases in the price level, as measured by the consumer price index, as well as provide a reasonable rate of return. So, if the investor desires a 16-percent return when inflation is 2 percent per year, the same investor wants a 24-percent return when inflation is 10 percent per year. This investment objective is typically achieved in an active real estate market when demand is increasing.

PSYCHOLOGICAL FACTORS

Some investors may derive nonmonetary benefits from the prestige associated with ownership of real property. Friends and relatives tend to be more impressed by ownership of an apartment building than with the possession of an account at the local savings and loan association, even if the equity position in the apartment complex is the same as the dollar value deposited in the savings account. Thus, the prestige of ownership can be an incentive for real estate investment for some individuals.

Conversely, certain psychological considerations can deter an investor from owning real property. Some people view the prospect of being somebody's landlord as troublesome. Tenants can be demanding and difficult to deal with; they can also be irrational and unreasonable. Thus, the fear of ownership responsibilities of a physical asset that affects the lives of individuals can deter some potential investors.

What Risks and Obstacles Affect the Equity Investment?

Most types of investments are affected by risks and obstacles. The risks faced by the real estate investor tend to be greater than those faced by investors in financial securities. However, a parcel of real estate in a good location that has very little competition from other properties and is traded in an active market is likely to be a safer investment than many common stocks. Moreover, such a real estate investment is possibly safer than a bond issued by a corporation that has a small portfolio of assets and whose expenses have exceeded income for the past several years.

RISKS

In general, risk is the possibility of financial loss in an investment opportunity arising from uncertainty about the future. The basic sources of risk are unfavorable changes in the economic environment affecting an investment with a fixed location, and a poor information flow coupled with high information search costs. The risks described in this section affect all investment alternatives, but they are examined with specific references to the real estate investment.

Business or Income Risk

Every real estate investment has a **business or income risk.** Future levels of actual gross income may not be as large as forecast. In addition, the pattern or timing of future actual gross income flows may not be as forecast. Such risk arises from both internal and external sources. The external sources are unanticipated changes in economic and demographic market factors that cause the level of market rent to fall below the investor's expectations. The internal source of business risk is the assumption of competent management. If this assumption does not hold true in the future, the vacancy loss will be higher if the inefficient manager is unable to find suitable tenants and accepts tenants with poor credit ratings.

Financial Risk

Financial risk occurs when the level of income remaining after the property pays for all of the operating expenses is not sufficient to cover the debt service on the property. In other words, financial risk occurs when future levels of NOI are not sufficient to allow the owner to pay the mortgage from the revenues generated by the property. This problem can arise as a repercussion of business risk when the level of effective gross income in future periods is less than the amount forecast. Financial risk also can arise because the levels of future operating expenses were underestimated in the forecast. Operating expenses are affected by internal and external factors. Internally, the assumption of competent management may be erroneous, and operating expenses for the property may increase at a greater rate than operating expenses for comparable properties that have competent management. Externally, operating expenses can be underestimated because the investor was unable to project rapid or sharp increases in such expense items as utilities, maintenance, property taxes, insurance, and the price of replacements for appliances and structural components.

Principal Risk

The future sales price of the property may be less than anticipated. **Principal risk** can arise because the property's value is expected to increase when, in fact, the market value of that property declines. Also, principal risk can arise if the investor unrealistically forecasts a rate of price appreciation greater than the rate that actually occurs. In the second case, the actual future sales price may be higher than the current price but still significantly less than the sales price forecast.

Interest or Money Market Risk

Every real estate investment also has an **interest or money market risk.** The future value of the investment may be less because the basic rate component of a capitalization rate may be higher in the future than it was at the time of the initial appraisal and investment decision. In terms of the band-of-investment technique, this risk can arise if mortgage interest rates rise in the future, if the expectations about typical rates of return increase, or if the typical loan in the future is made with a lower equity to value ratio. All of these changes are difficult to calculate for the future. If future capitalization rates are higher than current capitalization rates and this increase is not expected, the actual value of the property in the future may be much less than the future value forecast.

Purchasing Power Risk

The dollars the investor will receive in the future may have less purchasing power than anticipated. The cause of this **purchasing power risk** is inflation. Such risk arises when the investor underestimates the rate of inflation in the future and thereby uses a discount rate that is too low and has an expected rate of return that is too low.

OBSTACLES

Many obstacles can affect the investor's ability to analyze a real estate investment opportunity thoroughly. In general, these obstacles are the problems the investor faces in gathering adequate information to make an accurate forecast of future income and expenses. Certain difficulties inherent in the real estate sales transaction do not occur in the purchase of a financial security. The following list of obstacles is representative of the problems of the real estate investor.

1. Objective information sources about the subject property are difficult to find.
2. The amount of usable data on comparable properties is limited.
3. Reliable price quotations are not available on a frequent basis.
4. There are typically only a few buyers and sellers.
5. Real estate transactions are typically cumbersome, time-consuming, and very often inefficient.
6. Each transaction is usually undertaken after a search of ownership records because of the possibility of title errors.
7. The exchange typically requires much negotiating and bargaining, which can be difficult and time-consuming.
8. Specialized legal factors and tax considerations increase the complexity and costs of the transaction.

Generally, these obstacles do not affect investment alternatives in the stock and bond markets or in savings accounts. The information and data problems associated with real estate investment increase business and financial risks above the levels faced by investors in stocks and bonds. The extra time and dollar costs associated with the real estate transaction either serve as a disincentive to enter into the real estate investment or necessitate a higher rate of return to compensate for the increased time and money expenditure involved.

How Does the Income Approach to Market Value Relate to Investment Analysis?

The income approach to determining current market value is very similar to the approach used to determine investment value. In this section, the similarities and differences between the two approaches are explored. First, the nature and purpose of investment analysis are compared with the nature and purpose of estimating current market value of an income-earning real estate asset. Then, the income and expense items included in each technique are examined.

NATURE AND PURPOSE OF INVESTMENT ANALYSIS

The income approach for estimating the current market value of a specific parcel of real estate focuses on market forces and their effect on the subject property. The appraiser attempts to analyze the typical investor, whose expectations are reflected in the demand side of the market for this class of property. Within this frame of reference, the appraiser primarily examines market phenomena that affect all aspects of this type of property. Market rents are analyzed. The mortgage rate and loan-to-value ratio available to the typical investor are used in the construction of the capitalization rate. The typical investor's expected rate of return is also used in determining the capitalization rate. In this process, the appraiser does not consider the income and expense items of the specific investor. In **investment analysis,** the investor is concerned not only with market phenomena but also with personalized income and expense factors that are specific to the property under analysis. In other words, the income property appraisal technique (discussed in Chapter 6) informs the investor of the price the market will pay for the property whereas investment analysis leads the investor to a conclusion about the specific price that he should offer for the property.

Another way to consider the relationship between market value and investment value is to assume that there are many possible investors for a specific property. Each investor is competent and rational, but each has a different set of objectives. If each investor receives sufficient information, each can make an evaluation of the value of the property to him—the investment value. Now, if these investment values were plotted along a line, a normal (bell-shaped) curve should result. Many investors will calculate approximately the same investment value. A few calculations will yield very high or very low investment values. In this sense, market value (or most probable selling price) can be explained as the mean or median of the distribution of possible investment values.

INCOME ITEMS IN INVESTMENT ANALYSIS

In general, investment analysis involves the same revenue considerations that are used in income property appraisal. However, the distinction between contract rents and market rent is important. To the appraiser, market rents dominate the analysis. Contract rents are merely viewed as an adjustment to make potential gross income a more reasonable representation of the property's income-earning capability. In investment analysis, the contract rents are given more weight. The investor uses them to calculate the level of income for the length of the contract period. After these rental agreements terminate, the investment analyst, like the income property appraiser, searches to identify market rent levels and utilizes these figures to forecast revenues.

Generally, the other sources of revenue that are not affected by contractual agreement and are not related to the provision of space within the structure are treated the same way in investment analysis as they are in income property appraisal. These other income sources are forecast on the basis of the investor's understanding of their future market trends. Thus, as the cost of appliances increases, so does the charge for doing a load of wash in the complex's laundry facility.

Vacancy and collection losses in investment analysis also are viewed in relation to the rental agreements that are in force for the first years of ownership. An investor can identify specific tenants and examine the leases they signed. If the tenants are individuals or corporations with good credit ratings, the investor can assume collection losses over the rental agreement period will be zero. If the leases do not contain escape provisions for the tenant, the investor can assume the vacancy rate for that space will also be zero for the length of time the rental agreement is in force. Upon termination of the rental agreements, the investment analyst, just like the income property appraiser, must turn to the market to forecast future levels of vacancy and collection losses.

EXPENSE ITEMS IN INVESTMENT ANALYSIS

The purpose of investment analysis is to obtain an estimate of the value of the property to the specific investor. An evaluation of the expense items in investment analysis starts with the owner's income statement from the subject property. The investor must use the same expenses that the income property appraiser uses. In addition, the investor must consider those expense items that are excluded from the appraiser's reconstructed income statement for the subject property. In other words, the investor does consider income taxes, depreciation allowances, capital improvement expenditures, and the exact level of the interest payment on the mortgage. All four of these excluded items are considered to obtain the investor's "before-tax" cash flow.

The following section examines the before-tax cash flow concept. First, the process of generating before-tax cash flow is explained, and then it is used to judge the performance of the real estate investment in the initial period as well as in the future. Chapter 12, which covers the income tax aspects of the investment decision, includes an explanation of the income tax considerations that allow the investor to obtain after-tax cash flow from before-tax cash flow.

How Is Before-Tax Cash Flow Determined?

An investor obtains a numerical value for before-tax cash flow by calculating NOI and subtracting the annual mortgage payment or debt service from that figure. The underlying reason for calculating before-tax cash flow is the investor's desire to obtain an estimate of the revenue generated by the property after all operating expenses and mortgage expenses are subtracted from revenue. In other words, **before-tax cash flow (BTCF)** represents the dollars that the investor would receive after the revenue from the property has been used to cover the major outlays the investor incurs.

A numerical example illustrates the aspects of real estate equity investment analysis. The property and market information gathered by the investor is displayed in Exhibit 11.1.

Property Attributes				
Asking price			$ 950,000	
				Rent
		#	Rent	Growth
# two-bedroom units		14	$ 525	3.50%
# one-bedroom units		10	$ 425	2.50%
Management fee			7.25%	
Property tax growth rate			3.50%	
Maintenance & repair growth rate			3.00%	
All other operating expenses			2.00%	
Market Characteristics				
Market vacancy rate			3.50%	
Appreciation rate per year			1.25%	
Financial Market Inputs				
Interest rate			8.00%	
Loan term			30	
Loan to value ratio			80%	
Loan amount			$ 760,000	
Loan payment per month			($5,576.61)	
Initial equity			$ 190,000	
Discount rate		14.0%		

DERIVATION OF NOI FOR INVESTMENT ANALYSIS

The income and expense items analyzed by the investor to obtain NOI are the same as those the appraiser uses in establishing NOI for income property appraisal. The investor must establish a level of potential gross income for the property in the current year and estimate levels of potential gross income for future years. These income figures are established by referring to contract rents while the contracts or leases are in force. Then the investor relies on market analysis to establish market rent levels in those future periods for which no leases are in effect. Vacancy and collection losses also must be determined just as the appraiser determines such losses. Other sources of revenue must be identified and the magnitude of these funds must be estimated for future periods. Then the investor must establish the level of operating expense for the current period and prepare a forecast of the level of operating expenses by category. Once this is done, the investor has an income statement for the current and future levels of NOI.

This process appears in Exhibits 11.1 and 11.2. For simplicity, Exhibit 11.1 lists the relevant information obtained by the investor about the market and the property, including information about market rents, growth rates in rent, appreciation, growth rates for the operating expense categories, and financial information about the loan. The assumption made in Exhibit 11.2 is that the investor will analyze only the data for the first or initial year. In Exhibit 11.3, the analysis is made more realistic as the assumption is that the investor will hold the property for the next six years. (This numerical example is consistent with the example presented in Chapter 6 on income property appraisal).

Revenues: 24 apartment units								
Rent receipts:							Year 1	
		14 two-bedroom units @ monthly rent			$	525	$	88,200
		10 one-bedroom units @ monthly rent			$	425	$	51,000
Parking fees:								
		$15 per month for second car					$	2,520
		$25 per month for covered parking					$	2,400
Laundry room collections							$	1,500
Total Revenues							$	145,620
Less vacancies @		3.50%					$	(5,097)
Effective Gross Income							$	140,523
Expenses:								
Management fees	7.25%	of rent receipts					$	10,092
Property taxes							$	6,400
Insurance premiums							$	2,500
Maintenance and repairs							$	9,400
Supplies and materials							$	2,400
Building custodial costs							$	15,000
Utilities							$	3,000
Replacement of appliances, carpeting, etc.							$	4,500
Lawn and grounds maintenance							$	3,300
Misc. administrative costs							$	1,000
					Total Expenses		$	57,592
Net Operating Income NOI							$	82,931
Debt Service							($66,919)	
Before Tax Cash Flow BTCF							$	16,012

(handwritten note beside Debt Service: "not on 6.5")

The market and property related data obtained for the analysis shown in Exhibit 11.1 is summarized below:

1. All 14 of the two-bedroom apartment units are currently rented for $525/month on a one year lease.

2. All 10 of the one-bedroom apartment units are currently rented for $425/month on a one year lease.

3. Market analysis shows that the level of demand for this type of property in this part of town will grow moderately into the future. This information translates into the fact that in the second year the market rent will increase by 3.5 percent and 2.5 percent on the two-bedroom and one-bedroom apartments, respectively.

4. The vacancy rate for comparable properties in the local market is 3.5 percent.

5. Property taxes will increase by 3.5 percent per year, maintenance and repairs by 3 percent per year, and all other operating expenses by 2 percent per year.

On the basis of these income and expense items, NOI can be generated for the current year and each of the five future years.

Revenues: 24 apartment units					Year 1	2	3	4	5	6
Rent receipts:										
	14 two bedroom units @ monthly rent		$ 525		$ 88,200	$ 91,287	$ 94,482	$ 97,789	$101,212	$104,754
	10 one-bedroom units @ monthly rent		$ 425		$ 51,000	$ 52,275	$ 53,582	$ 54,921	$ 56,294	$ 57,702
Parking fees:										
	$15 per month for second car				$ 2,520	$ 2,520	$ 2,520	$ 2,520	$ 2,520	$ 2,520
	$25 per month for covered parking				$ 2,400	$ 2,400	$ 2,400	$ 2,400	$ 2,400	$ 2,400
Laundry room collections:					$ 1,500	$ 1,500	$ 1,500	$ 1,500	$ 1,500	$ 1,500
Total Revenues					$ 145,620	$149,982	$154,484	$ 159,130	$163,926	$168,876
Less vacancies @	3.5%				$ (5,097)	$ (5,249)	$ (5,407)	$ (5,570)	$ (5,737)	$ (5,911)
Effective Gross Income					$ 140,523	$144,733	$149,077	$ 153,561	$158,189	$162,965
Expenses:										
Management fees	7.25%	of rent receipts			$ 10,092	$ 10,408	$ 10,735	$ 11,071	$ 11,419	$ 11,778
Property taxes					$ 6,400	$ 6,624	$ 6,856	$ 7,096	$ 7,344	$ 7,601
Insurance premiums					$ 2,500	$ 2,550	$ 2,601	$ 2,653	$ 2,706	$ 2,760
Maintenance and repairs					$ 9,400	$ 9,682	$ 9,972	$ 10,272	$ 10,580	$ 10,897
Supplies and materials					$ 2,400	$ 2,448	$ 2,497	$ 2,547	$ 2,598	$ 2,650
Building custodial costs					$ 15,000	$ 15,300	$ 15,606	$ 15,918	$ 16,236	$ 16,561
Utilities					$ 3,000	$ 3,060	$ 3,121	$ 3,184	$ 3,247	$ 3,312
Replacement of appliances, carpeting, etc.					$ 4,500	$ 4,590	$ 4,682	$ 4,775	$ 4,871	$ 4,968
Lawn and grounds maintenance					$ 3,300	$ 3,366	$ 3,433	$ 3,502	$ 3,572	$ 3,643
Misc. administrative costs					$ 1,000	$ 1,020	$ 1,040	$ 1,061	$ 1,082	$ 1,104
			Total Expenses		$ 57,592	$ 59,048	$ 60,544	$ 62,079	$ 63,656	$ 65,276
Net Operating Income					$ 82,931	$ 85,684	$ 88,533	$ 91,482	$ 94,532	$ 97,689
Debt Service					($66,919)	($66,919)	($66,919)	($66,919)	($66,919)	($66,919)
Before Tax Cash Flow					$ 16,012	$ 18,765	$ 21,614	$ 24,562	$ 27,613	$ 30,770

DEBT SERVICE

Once NOI is calculated, the next step in generating BTCF is the deduction of debt service (or the mortgage payment) from NOI. This process is also shown in Exhibit 11.2. Debt service has two components, the interest payment made on the loan and the principal repayment. Assume that the mortgage repayment scheme for the mortgage is the fixed-rate mortgage, whereby the total monthly mortgage payment stays constant over time. However, as the loan matures, part of the principal is paid back, and thus the interest rate applies to a smaller unpaid balance in each of the successive years. Consequently, in each successive year, the interest payment declines. Because the total payment on a monthly basis is constant, the principal repayment increases over time.

The seller of this 24-unit apartment project is willing to sell the property for $950,000. The investor is able to obtain a first mortgage loan under the following conditions: 8-percent interest rate on funds for investment property, 30-year term, 80-percent loan-to-sales price ratio. Under these terms, the loan amount will be $760,000, the monthly payment will be $5,576.61, and the annual debt service will be $66,919.33.

If a financial calculator is used, the monthly payment is solved by entering the following information into the calculator:

Loan amount as the present value = $760,000

Interest on a monthly basis = .08/12 = 0.006667 monthly

Term of the loan = 30 years of 12 months each = 360 periods

Solve for the monthly payment that gives the answer of $5,576.61/month

Multiplying by 12 gives $66,919.33 as the annual debt service

When the total debt service payment is subtracted from NOI, the resultant figure is BTCF. In the first year of the ownership period, BTCF is $15,284.

What Are the Initial Period Rates of Performance?

When BTCF is calculated for the current year, several financial and profitability ratios can be derived. These ratios are determined from the various income and expense items used in the calculation of BTCF. At the most rudimentary level, the investment decision can be based on an analysis of initial period financial and profitability ratios that are calculated from the first year's income and expense items. Although a strict adherence to these initial period ratios is viewed as conceptually inadequate, an understanding of the facts displayed by these ratios is important for the investor.

FINANCIAL RATIOS

The investor needs to understand three financial ratios: the operating expense ratio; the debt service coverage ratio; and the breakeven, or default, ratio. Each provides information about the financial capability of the investment opportunity. The common focus of these financial ratios is the ability of the investment's income stream to support the different expenses that the investor incurs for the property.

Operating Expense Ratio

The *operating expense ratio* was first explained in the discussion of income property appraisal in Chapter 6. It is the level of operating expenses divided by either potential gross income or effective gross income. The numerical value of the operating expense ratio generated by effective gross income is always larger than the value of the ratio generated by potential gross income. This difference is obvious because vacancy and collection losses are usually positive, making effective gross income a smaller number than potential gross income when these losses are subtracted out. In appraisal analysis, the operating expense ratio is important as a check on the efficiency of operation of the subject property. The underlying assumption is that the subject property should have an operating expense ratio similar to that of the comparable properties in the local market.

For the typical investor, the operating expense ratio indicates the property's capability of generating income large enough to cover the full operating expenses. Ideally, the investor should seek a property with the smallest possible operating expense ratio. At the extreme, the investor would want the operating expenses to be as little as possible without jeopardizing the physical maintenance of the building and the desirability of the units within that building. However, the acceptable operating expense ratio depends on the type of property. Obviously, high-rise apartments with elevators have a higher operating expense ratio than low-rise apartments without elevators because elevators run on electric power and they require repair and maintenance. An operating expense ratio for retail space will be different from the operating ratio for an apartment building or an office building.

If the operating expense ratio is very low, this would appear to be a favorable situation. However, the investor should seek information about the reasons for the low rate. The seller could be operating a sound, high-quality building that requires few repairs and is energy efficient. But, the low operating expense ratio could occur if the seller is deferring maintenance, cutting back on utilities, and reducing reserves for replacing such short-lived items as appliances and mechanical systems. In this latter situation, the investor would be buying high future operating expenses. As a safety measure, the investor should obtain information about the operating expense ratio for comparable properties to use as a check on the subject property.

The initial period operating expense ratio for the numerical example in Exhibit 11.2 is 41 percent. This ratio is calculated by dividing the $57,592 in total operating expenses by the $140,523 effective gross income.

Debt Service Coverage Ratio

The *debt service coverage ratio* (introduced in Chapter 10) is the level of NOI divided by the annual mortgage payment. This financial ratio indicates whether the property is able to generate a level of NOI large enough to cover the full mortgage payment. If the numerical value of this ratio is less than 1.0, the mortgage payment is greater than the amount of effective gross income remaining after operating expenses have been paid. If the ratio exceeds 1.0, the property is capable of meeting all of its operating expenses and the mortgage payment and still providing the investor with a positive level of BTCF. Conceptually, the minimum acceptable debt service coverage ratio for the investor should be equal to 1.0 plus enough cash to provide for that investor's expected rate of return before taxes. However, a common rule of thumb is that a debt service coverage ratio of 1.25 or more on residential income property is acceptable, but, as financial and market factors change, lenders may require a higher debt service coverage ratio. Finally, the magnitude of the ratio changes with different types of investment properties.

The initial period debt service coverage ratio is calculated by dividing NOI by the annual mortgage payment. Using this debt service information and the value of NOI calculated in Exhibit 11.2, the ratio is the NOI of $82,931 divided by the debt service of $66,919. The value of the debt service coverage ratio is 1.24 and is considered an acceptable level.

Breakeven Ratio

The numerator of the **breakeven ratio** (or default ratio; introduced in Chapter 10) is the sum of operating expenses and the mortgage payment. In other words, the numerator of the ratio identifies all expense items plus the mortgage payment that must be made from the income generated by the property. The denominator of the ratio is either potential or effective gross income. If the value of this ratio is greater than 1.0, the investor knows that the property is not generating a level of income adequate to pay the expenses incurred in the operation and the purchase of the property. If the ratio is less than 1.0, the property is generating an income stream large enough to cover all operating expenses and the debt service as well as to maintain some level of vacancy within the property.

The initial period breakeven ratio for the numerical example in Exhibit 11.2 is 88.6 percent. It is calculated by dividing the sum of operating expenses ($57,592) and debt service ($66,919) by the effective gross income of $140,523.

Obviously, the investor desires the lowest possible breakeven ratio. The typically acceptable breakeven ratio on a residential income-producing property is a figure below 90 percent of effective gross income. This level of the ratio would allow enough remaining cash to cover an unexpected increase in the vacancy rate and to provide a positive cash flow to the investor before income tax impacts are calculated.

PROFITABILITY RATIOS

The financial ratios described in the preceding section indicate the property's ability to generate an income flow large enough to cover operating expenses and mortgage payments. The profitability ratios discussed in this section show the relationship of income and expense items to the investor's equity in the property. In other words, the profitability ratios can be viewed as measures of the rate of return on the investment.

Equity Capitalization Rate

The equity capitalization rate is the before-tax rate of return on equity in the investment. It is BTCF divided by the dollars of equity invested in the property. The before-tax equity capitalization rate for the first year as shown in Exhibit 11.2 is 8.4 percent ($16,012/$190,000). Once it is calculated, this rate of return can be compared with the investor's expectations about a rate of return that should be obtained from the investment. The actual return should be large enough to provide for the interest payment available from a safe, riskless investment plus premiums for illiquidity, risk, and management of the property. If the initial period equity dividend ratio exceeds the investor's expected rate of return, the investor realizes that some burden, such as risk or illiquidity, is being borne without compensation.

The reciprocal of the equity capitalization ratio is known as the **payback period.** For example, the before-tax equity dividend ratio for the property in Exhibit 11.2 is 8.4 percent. The reciprocal of this figure is 1 divided by 0.084, which yields 11.87 years. The payback period is an estimate of the number of years that the property must be held before the total cash flow equals the equity position of the investor. It is not considered a return of the investment because at the end of 11.87 years the investment still has a positive value.

Gross Rate of Return on Equity

The equity capitalization rate pertains only to BTCF. However, two other payments accrue to the investor each year that the property operates and generates funds to pay the mortgage. Each mortgage payment is composed of an interest payment and principal repayment. Consequently, the equity increases each year as the principal repayment is added to the original equity of the investor. Also, each year the property operates it can either appreciate or depreciate in value. The **gross rate of return** on equity represents the relationship between the total yearly return and the original equity position. The gross return on equity is the ratio of BTCF plus the mortgage principal repayment (the equity increase through mortgage reduction) plus the appreciation amount divided by the investor's initial equity.

In the first year, the investor owes the lender the total interest payment of $760,000 times 8 percent; this is $60,800. The total debt service for the first year is $66,919. The difference between these two figures of $6,119 is the first year's loan repayment, the equity increase through mortgage reduction. Each year, the property is expected to appreciate by 1.25 percent. This is an appreciation amount of $11,875 for the first year ($950,000 × .0125).

The gross rate of return is the sum of the BTCF of $16,012 plus the first-year loan repayment of $6,119 plus the first-year expected appreciation of $11,875, which equals $33,278, divided by the $190,000 down payment, or 17.9 percent.

As long as the principal repayment and the appreciation are greater than zero, the gross rate of return on equity exceeds the equity capitalization rate. The importance of the gross rate of return is simply that it shows all three elements of the property's earning potential. It includes the increase in equity due to mortgage loan repayment and the price appreciation in the initial period ratio analysis.

DISADVANTAGES OF INITIAL PERIOD RATES OF PERFORMANCE

Several shortcomings are associated with the use of initial period ratio analysis to evaluate the attractiveness of a property as an investment opportunity. First, there may be a difference between the level of income and expense items in the initial period and their level in future time periods. Many factors can change between the first and second year. For example, if contract rents in the first year exceed market rents, when the leases terminate at the end of the first year future income will decline. The level of potential gross income in year 2 will be less than it is in year 1. In this case, all other things being equal, the level of BTCF is less in the second year. This decline will cause the equity capitalization rate and the gross rate of return on equity to be lower in the second year. Alternatively, potential gross income in the second and successive years may increase while expense items in those years increase even more. In this situation, BTCF will fall, causing a reduction in the value of the equity capitalization rate and the gross rate of return in the second year.

The second problem with initial period ratio analysis is that the actual value of the property at the time of the sale is not considered directly. The gross rate of return, an initial period ratio, considers only the expected rate of appreciation and applies it to the acquisition price to get a dollar amount for the first year's appreciation. The full analysis of appreciation requires an analysis of the costs involved in selling the property.

The third disadvantage of initial period ratio analysis is that the investor needs to know what the future levels of cash flow and the future sales price of the property are worth in dollar terms at the time the investment is being made. In other words, the investor needs to know the present value of payments that will be made at different times in the future. Only when the present values of these future payments are known can the investor evaluate the financial desirability of the investment.

The underlying concept for establishing the present value of future income flows can be seen in the following example. If you know that the current interest rate is 5 percent on a savings account at a local savings and loan association, you are in a position to make the following decision. A friend of yours offers to give you either $100 today or $104 a year from now. Which option do you take? At the 5-percent rate of interest, you are $1 ahead if you take the $100 today and place it in the savings account at 5 percent. This action would yield $105 at the end of the year instead of the $104 offered. Now turn this example around. Your friend offers you $95.24 payable today or $100 at the end of a one-year period. Which offer do you accept? The answer is simple: it does not matter because the present value of both payments is the same. If you take the $95.24 and place it in the bank at 5-percent interest per year, the value at the end of the year will be $100. Thus, $95.24 is the present value of $100 to be received one year from now if the interest rate is 5 percent.

MAKING A DECISION BASED ON INITIAL PERIOD RATIOS

An analysis of the initial period financial and profitability ratios for the example contained in Exhibit 11.2 reveals the following facts: the operating expense ratio, based on effective gross income, is 41.2 percent; the debt service coverage ratio is 1.23 percent; and the breakeven ratio is 89.07 percent. Each of these financial ratios is within the reasonable range for a good investment.

The two profitability ratios, however, provide what appears to be conflicting information. The equity capitalization rate of 8 percent is less than the investor's required return of 14 percent. This ratio does not indicate that the investment can be considered good on the basis of this initial period analysis. The gross rate of return on equity of 17 percent exceeds the investor's expected rate of return of 14 percent. If the decision is made at this point in the analysis, the investor would buy the property for $950,000 because the gross rate of return reflects the three parts of the total return to the investor.

Because of the three disadvantages of initial period ratio analysis, the investor must seek measures of performance that reflect future circumstances of the investment. The two methods for determining the investment's performance in the future are *present value analysis* and *internal rate of return analysis.*

How Is the Investment's Future Performance Evaluated?

The process of evaluating the investment's future performance involves an analysis of the present and future benefits derived from the property. Two new concepts enter the analysis and must be examined before the numerical analysis takes place. These concepts are the *holding period* and the *discounting interest rate.*

THE HOLDING PERIOD

Every investor must make a decision about the length of time the real estate equity investment will be owned, a process known as **holding period analysis.** Various economic and financial factors affect the decision about the planned holding period for any particular real estate investment. For simplicity's sake and to accommodate the general investor population, many commercial property brokers will prepare a cash flow statement for a 10-year holding period. The investor should realize that this 10-year holding period may be irrelevant to her specific investment need. The 10-year holding period calculations are only a matter of convenience.

Several alternative strategies for establishing the holding period are presented in the following statements. These strategies are not mutually exclusive but can be used in consort. They can be appropriate for investors who view periodic cash flow as the primary investor objective.

1. The investor links the holding period to the length of time until a certain event requires the funds. Examples of this approach include the following: hold the property for 20 years until I retire; hold the property for 12 years until our child starts college; hold the property for 8 years and see whether the equity is enough for us to buy that summer resort.

2. The investor holds the property while the BTCF growth occurs and sells it when the BTCF stabilizes.

3. The investor holds the property as long as BTCF is positive.

4. The investor holds the property as long as tax sheltering occurs.

If the investor's primary objective is price appreciation, the property is usually acquired for one of the following reasons:

1. The investor sees the opportunity to buy a property that is currently being sold for less than its market value and whose NOI should remain stable or experience future growth.

2. The investor sees the opportunity to buy a property that should experience favorable future conditions as the surrounding neighborhood improves.

3. The investor sees the opportunity to buy a property with a strong expectation of a significant change in its economic use in the near future. Such a change in use can occur, for example, because of market factors that create a higher investment use, or because a possible zoning ordinance change can allow a change in the use of the land.

If the investor's objective is price appreciation, the planned holding period is equal to the time required for the anticipated future benefit to occur—at which time the property is sold. If a hedge against inflation is the reason for the purchase, the holding period is the length of time over which either the equity dividend ratio or the equity yield rate of return exceeds the rate of inflation. This time horizon could be one year or two decades. An example of this situation occurs when the investor sees that the rate of return is well above the current rate of inflation and believes it will increase as the rate of inflation increases. This situation can arise when the rental payment for commercial property is tied directly to changes in the consumer price index, or when the market for the residential property is strong and rents and NOI have the potential to increase by more than the consumer price index.

The holding period is established at the time the investor is analyzing the property for purchase. However, the sophisticated investor will recalculate the holding period, quite possibly on a yearly basis, to see what impact the changing economic environment has on the levels of cash flow and future sales price.

In conclusion, each investor needs to determine a holding period for each specific investment property. The underlying reason for the holding period differs from investor to investor and from property to property. Two investors analyzing the same property more than likely would have different holding periods, two properties being analyzed by the same investor more than likely also would have different holding periods.

THE DISCOUNTING INTEREST RATE

One way to establish the discounting interest rate (introduced in Chapter 6) is to use the investor's expected rate of return on the investment. In this way, the analysis would reflect the investor's knowledge about safe rates and expected needs for risk, illiquidity, and management coverage.

Another concept for defining the discounting interest rate is the concept of cost of capital. An entity such as a corporation can borrow in a variety of ways; it can issue bonds, common stock, or preferred stock or it can borrow it directly from a bank. The **cost of capital** is the rate of return that the corporation must pay for such funds. For the real estate equity investor, the minimum cost of capital is the cost of borrowed funds; that is, the mortgage interest rate is 8 percent in the example shown in Exhibit 11.2. However, the real estate investor knows that more risk is associated with the equity position in real property than there is with the loan or debt position in that same property. So, the real estate investor uses the cost of capital and then adds an adjustment for the risk and illiquidity faced in using equity funds in real estate investment instead of some other investment opportunity. This approach could add approximately 6 percent to the 8-percent cost of funds to yield a discounting rate of 14 percent.

The numerical example used in Exhibit 11.2 assumes that the investor in question is a typical investor in the market. Typical investors in this market for this property type require a 14 percent rate of return. Therefore, his expected return from the investment would be 14 percent. If the investor is risk adverse, a high value would be assigned to the risk and illiquidity premiums, causing an expected return greater than 14 percent. If the investor is a risk taker, a low value would be assigned to risk and illiquidity, and the expected equity yield rate might be less than 14 percent. In conclusion, assume that the individual making the investment decision in the example used here is a typical investor and is seeking a 14-percent return.

DISCOUNTED CASH FLOW ANALYSIS

In the numerical example in Exhibits 11.3–11.6, the six-year holding period reflects the investor's expectations about price appreciation and periodic cash flow. Expectations are that the market value of the property will increase over the six-year period and that simultaneously the BTCF will be positive and increasing. The investor establishes a 14-percent discounting interest rate to reflect the generally held belief about the magnitude of a safe rate, risk, illiquidity, and administrative tasks associated with the investment.

Determining the Before-Tax Cash Flows

As noted earlier, Exhibit 11.1 contains the information about the property, the property market, and the financial market that the investor was able to obtain. Rents and rent growth rates are known from a check of comparable properties and the general economic circumstances affecting the property. The rent for two-bedroom apartments is $525 per month, and it is expected to grow by 3.5 percent per year. The rent for one-bedroom apartments is $425 per month, and it is expected to grow by 2.5 percent per

---

EXHIBIT 11.4   Estimation of before-tax equity reversion.

Appreciation Rate per Year		1.25%
Future Sales Price		$1,023,514
Less selling costs	6.00%	(61,411)
Net Proceeds from the Sale		$ 962,103
Less the loan balance at end of sixth year		$713,072
Before Tax Equity Reversion		$ 249,031

EXHIBIT 11.5	Estimation of future sales price.

Appreciation Rate	1.25%
Appreciation Factor	1.0125

Yr.	Acquisition Price	Appreciated Price
0	$ 950,000	
1		$ 961,875
2		$ 973,898
3		$ 986,072
4		$ 998,398
5		$ 1,010,878
6		$ 1,023,514

year. Operating expenses are reconstructed from the financial records of the property to reflect current and future circumstances. Property taxes are set at $6,400 in the initial year, and they are expected to grow by 3.5 percent per year. The annual price appreciation rate of 1.25 percent per year is discovered from evidence in the recent market and anticipation of future economic circumstances.

As shown in Exhibits 11.2 and 11.3, the BTCF in the initial year is $16,012. After each of the revenue sources and each of the operating expenses is adjusted by its appropriate annual rate of change, the BTCF in the second year through the sixth year is shown in Exhibit 11.3. The BTCF in the second year is $18,765. The BTCF for years 3 through 6 are calculated on a year-by-year basis in the same manner as the transition from year 1 to year 2.

Determining the Before-Tax Equity Reversion

The calculation of the **before-tax equity reversion (BTER)** is shown in Exhibit 11.4. The BTER reflects the affect of price appreciation and the increase in equity from mortgage loan reduction in the cash flow analysis. The starting point in the calculation is the determination of the anticipated future sales price. It is the acquisition price or asking price of $950,000 times the annual price appreciation rate for the six-year holding period. The arithmetic calculation of the future sales price is shown in Exhibit 11.5. At the end of the first year, the asking price is increased by 1.25 percent by multiplying $950,000 by 1.0125. This same step is then repeated for each of years 2 through 6. At the end of the holding period, the future sales price is $1,023,514. The problem can be solved using the future value function of a financial calculator.

The next step is the estimation of the selling costs at the end of the six-year holding period. The most typical situation is the use of a commercial real property brokerage firm and the payment of a real estate commission. In this example, the assumption is that the investor will have to pay a 6-percent sales commission that is established after a negotiation between the seller and the broker. A possible alternative is a for sale by owner arrangement in which the investor, who is the owner, undertakes the sales activity. Remember that if this option is taken, it is not without cost. The investor would have to devote a substantial amount of time to the sales activity, time that would have to be taken away from some other income-earning activity or from leisure. Also, the investor would incur expenses associated with the sales activity. The usual approach is to use the sales commission alternative in the calculation process.

When the selling cost is subtracted from the future sales price, the result is the **net proceeds from the sale.** Selling costs at a 6-percent commission against a future sales price of $1,023,514 amount to $61,410.84, rounded to the dollar at $61,411. Net proceeds from the sale are $962,103.

Next, the investor must subtract out the unpaid mortgage loan balance. Each year of ownership brings a reduction in the unpaid balance of the loan as the tenants pay for the operating expenses and the debt service. The arithmetic procedure to obtain the loan balance at the end of the six-year holding period is the **amortization table** for the loan. Because the mortgage loan is a monthly payment loan, the amortization table must reflect the 72 months that make up the six-year holding period. Once the calculation procedure is understood for the first month in the amortization table, all of the calculations for the successive months is pure repetition.

At the outset of the loan, the investor owes $760,000. At the end of the first month, the investor makes a loan payment of $5,576.61 but owes an interest payment of only $5,066.67. The difference between the loan payment and the interest payment owed is the loan repayment of $509.94. So, the unpaid loan balance after the first monthly payment is $759,490.06. At the end of the second month, the investor makes a loan payment of $5,576.61 but owes an interest payment of only $5,063.27. The difference between the loan payment and the interest payment owed is the loan repayment of $513.34. So, the unpaid loan balance after the second monthly payment is $758,976.71. The calculations for the subsequent years follow the same procedure. The loan balance at the end of the 72-month holding period is $713,072.23. The investor can easily obtain this loan balance information and the data on how each payment is split between interest payment and principal repayment by asking the lender for an amortization table or schedule for the loan. Or, the investor can use the calculator procedures shown in Chapters 8 and 9.

The BTER is estimated when the loan balance at the end of the holding period is subtracted from the net proceeds from the sale. As shown in Exhibit 11.4, the BTER is $249,031. As stated earlier, the BTER reflects the sales price appreciation and the equity increase through loan balance reduction. The BTER also reflects the investor's initial equity in the property. If BTER is broken down into these components, price appreciation is $73,514 ($1,023,514 − $950,000), equity increase through loan reduction is $46,928 ($760,000 − $713,072), and initial equity is $190,000, for a total of $310,442. Subtracting out the selling costs of $61,411 yields the BTER of $249,031.

Investment Decision Criterion

The *investment decision criterion* is a comparison of the initial equity that has to be put into the investment to the present value of the financial benefits to be derived from the investment. This comparison can be made in several ways. The first is the direct comparison of the financial benefits to the initial equity. This comparison is made at the investor's required or anticipated rate of return, 14 percent in this illustration. The criterion is shown below.

(PV of all BTCFs) + (PV of BTER) > Initial Equity

A second form of this analysis is the **net present value (NPV) comparison,** in which the difference between the financial benefits and the initial equity is highlighted. This criterion is shown below.

[(PV of all BTCFs) + (PV of BTER)] − Initial Equity > 0

Discounted Cash Flow Analysis

The investment decision is made when the future is analyzed in addition to the present and the past. The answer is determined by utilizing a method known as **discounted cash flow analysis,** which is based on the present value, the BTCFs for the holding period, and the BTER at the end of the holding period. The analysis requires the calculation of these present values. This analysis is performed in Exhibit 11.6.

In Exhibit 11.6, the BTCFs are taken from Exhibit 11.3 and the BTER is taken from Exhibit 11.4 and displayed in the appropriate column in Exhibit 11.6. A major point to notice is that the BTER is used in the analysis at the end of the sixth year because that is when it will be received. The BTER is not the seventh-year cash flow; if it were mistakenly treated as a cash flow in the seventh year, the present value would be incorrectly calculated. The six total cash flows are displayed in a separate column.

The next step in the procedure is the calculation of the present value factor at the investor's expected rate of return, which is 14 percent in this example.

In simple terms the "present worth of one" tells us what a $1 payment in the future is worth in the present at a given interest rate. To reach a simple understanding of the **present value technique,** consider the following example. An investor is given a choice. Take $90 dollars today or receive $100 a year from now, when the market rate of interest is 10 percent. What option should the investor take to maximize the financial return? The first point to recognize is that the decision has to be made at a predetermined point in time. If the investor chooses to make the decision in the future, one year from now, then the $90 has to be moved to that point in time. The future worth of the $90 is the principal plus the interest for one year at 10 percent. The interest is $9. So, a year from now the investor chooses between $100 and $99. If the investor chooses to make the decision now, then the $100 has to be moved to the present. The present worth of $100 is the amount of money that must currently exist in order for it to be worth $100 a year from now at a 10-percent interest rate. This can be expressed in a simple one-period formula in which x is the unknown and i is the interest rate.

$$\$100 = x + ix = (1+i)x$$

$$x = \$100 / (1+i)$$

$$x = \$90.91$$

EXHIBIT 11.6	Calculation of the present value of the investment.

Discount Rate			14.00%		
Year	BTCF	Reversion	Total Cash Flows	Factor	PV Cash Flows
1	$ 16,012		$ 16,012	0.8772	$ 14,046
2	$ 18,765		$ 18,765	0.7695	$ 14,439
3	$ 21,614		$ 21,614	0.6750	$ 14,589
4	$ 24,562		$ 24,562	0.5921	$ 14,543
5	$ 27,613		$ 27,613	0.5194	$ 14,341
6	$ 30,770	$ 249,031	$ 279,801	0.4556	$ 127,474
	Present Value of Cash Flows + Reversion				$ 199,431
	Initial Equity				$ 190,000
	Net Present Value at the Discount Rate				$ 9,431

If $90.91 is placed into a savings account for one year at 10 percent per year, it would accumulate to $100. So, the investor's decision is between $90.00 and $90.91.

When more than one period of time enters into the analysis, the present worth of one formula expressed for the value of a dollar becomes

$$PV = 1 / (1+i)^n$$

where *n* represents the time period. If *n* equals two, then

$$PV = 1 / (1+i)^2 = 1/ (1.1)(1.1) = 1 / 1.21 = 0.8264$$

Exhibit 11.6 shows the calculation of the "present worth of one" factors for the first six years at 14 percent. The numerical value of $1/1.14$ is equal to 0.8772 in year 1, and the BTCF of $16,012 is multiplied by 0.8772, yielding the present value of the BTCF of $14,046. In the second year, the present value factor is $1/ (1.14)(1.14)$ equals $1 / 1.2996$ equals 0.7695, and the present value of $18,765 becomes $14,439.

The present value of all six BTCFs and the BTER is $199,431. The initial equity is $190,000. The net present value is $9,431. The significance of the NPV being greater than zero is that the investor's rate return is greater than the 14 percent that was used in the analysis.

The Investment Decision

The initial period financial and profitability ratios indicate that the investment is not a good opportunity because the profitability rates of return were less than the investor's required rate of return of 14 percent. On the other hand, the present value calculations of BTCFs, equity increase from mortgage balance reduction, and future sales price indicate that the investment is a good opportunity. The investor could purchase property and feel reasonably assured that the total return to be derived warrants the use of the initial $190,000 in equity. The present value calculation of $196,413 at a 14-percent rate shows the investor that the future stream of benefits to be derived from the property over the next six years is adequate to cover the investor's desire for a safe return plus premiums for risk, illiquidity, and management expenses.

"Things to Come"

A real property investment needs to make financial sense for before-tax considerations. This is the same as saying that the decision to invest should be made on property and market characteristics that generate the profitability of the property. One remaining fact that needs to be considered before the investor knows the full scope of possible returns is the impact of the Internal Revenue Code. The actual investment return can only be known after calculation of the after-tax cash flows and the after-tax reversion. The federal income tax aspects of the investment decision are the subject of the following chapter, where the analysis takes the before-tax concerns of this chapter and includes the income tax code considerations.

THE INTERNAL RATE OF RETURN

An alternative approach to the NPV that can be used to make the investment decision is the calculation of the rate of return instead of the net present value of the investment. This process is known as the **internal rate of return (IRR) technique.** The IRR is the rate of return that equates the cash flows and reversion to the initial equity. To apply the IRR technique, the investor must have an estimate of cash flow, equity increase through mortgage balance reduction, and the expected sales price of the investment. However, the investor does not need to state a discounting interest rate (as is the case in the present value technique). The discounting rate is the unknown to be estimated in this procedure. It is the IRR.

The calculation of the IRR is not simple because our numerical example involves the solution of an equation that contains the discounting rate raised to the sixth power. Currently, the sophisticated investor uses spreadsheet software to solve this problem. First, a discount factor is chosen, then is incorporated into the analysis, and finally is utilized to calculate the present value of future return to be received. If the present value of future benefits is less than the initial equity, the discount factor that was chosen is too large. If the present value of the benefits is greater than the initial equity, the discount factor that was chosen is too small. By a process of elimination, a discount factor can be identified that brings about an equality between the future returns and initial costs of the investment. In the example depicted in Exhibits 11.1 through 11.6, the IRR is approximately 14.75 percent. At this discounting interest rate, NPV becomes or approaches a value of zero.

Sensitivity Analysis

Both the NPV and the IRR are affected by the factors used in the generation of BTCFs as well as by the market factors that affect the future sales price of the property. Because of possible changes in these factors, the investor must undertake two related studies. First, the impact of changes in these factors on the investment decision should be understood. The investor must study the sensitivity of the NPV calculation or the IRR calculation to changes in revenue, operating expenses, and the future sales price. The investor should also examine the expected length of time that the property may be owned. This study is known as **sensitivity analysis.**

The investor does not know with certainty the future level of any income or operating expense item; nor does the investor know with certainty the future resale price of the property. However, a most probable range of these income, expense, and resale figures can be determined. The investor must identify the most volatile income and expense items and establish both the most pessimistic and the most optimistic estimates to recalculate the level of present value or the IRR under these opposite conditions. Thus, the investor establishes a range for either the present value or the internal rate of return within which the actual present value or internal rate of return should fall.

From the present value calculation, the investor can make several kinds of decisions. If, under the most pessimistic conditions, the present value of the investment exceeds the initial equity, the investor can feel very confident that the investment opportunity is good on the basis of both initial period estimates and analysis of future performance. On the contrary, if the present value of the investment calculated under the most optimistic circumstances is less than the initial equity, it is undesirable.

REFINANCING

Over the six-year holding period, a change in the mortgage market might cause the investor to seek refinancing of the original mortgage. In other words, because of economic circumstances in the mortgage market, the mortgage interest rate in the third year or so could be substantially less than the 8-percent rate that the investor initially obtained to purchase the property. Assume that in the third year, the mortgage rate in the market falls to 6 percent. In this case, the investor could go to a lender, obtain a new mortgage on the property, and use the funds received to pay off the original mortgage.

The investor's benefit from this financial change is a reduction in the total debt service requirement. As the level of the mortgage payment declines, the level of BTCF increases if all other expenses and income items stay the same.

OTHER CONSIDERATIONS

The owner controls very few of the income and expense items shown in Exhibit 11.1. The market controls potential rent receipts and vacancy losses. The market also controls parking fees and, to a lesser extent, laundry room revenues. The owner can negotiate the management fee, but only within limits. The property tax bill is beyond the investor's control even with the right to argue for a reduction in the assessment value of the property. The insurance premiums are quoted, and the only choice is to underinsure the property; but even this choice is limited by the demands of the lender to keep the property insured to the value of the unpaid loan.

The items most directly controlled by the investor are dollars paid for maintenance and repairs, expenditures for utilities (in this case, utility expenditures to heat and light the common areas, not the apartments themselves), and replacement of appliances. If the investor minimizes maintenance and repair expenditures, the value of BTCF in each year can increase. Similarly, measures to reduce utility costs—such as eliminating lights in the parking area between the hours of twelve and six in the morning, and lowering the thermostat on the heating unit serving the common areas of the property—can increase the level of BTCF. Finally, as appliances wear out over the holding period, leases can be renegotiated so that the landlord does not provide kitchen appliances. In this way, the investor eliminates the need to accumulate funds to replace worn-out refrigerators, ranges, and dishwashers and hence increases BTCF.

The investor can influence the level of BTCF substantially by manipulating the few items on the income and expense statement that are under her control. However, the investor should realize that minimizing these expense items will have future repercussions on the profitability and marketability of the property. As maintenance and repair expenditures are reduced, the degree of physical deterioration increases and reduces future resale value. As fully equipped kitchens are eliminated from the units, the rent potential in future years may decline or at least not rise at a rate comparable to that of units providing fully equipped kitchens. In a sense, the investor is trading the savings on expense items for future losses in rent receipts or resale value.

THE FEASIBILITY STUDY

The feasibility study was introduced in Chapter 7. At that point, two important components of a feasibility study were identified—the market analysis and the financial study. To review, the market analysis yields information about current revenues and vacancies as well as forecasts of future levels of rents and vacancies. The financial study takes data from the market analysis, combines it with expense data, and calculates performance and profitability ratios. The two studies work hand in hand to help the investor make a rational decision about involvement in an investment project.

FORMS OF OWNERSHIP IN A REAL ESTATE EQUITY INVESTMENT

In the preceding discussion of equity investment, the owner and investor were viewed as a single individual. However, in many situations, a single individual cannot raise enough money to be the only person involved in an equity investment. For example, the purchase of a large apartment complex or a small shopping center would require an investor to raise several million dollars. Some of this money would be used as a down payment, and the remainder would be in the form of a mortgage. In this situation, if the best mortgage term available is an 80-percent loan-to-value ratio and the sales price of the property is $3 million, the initial down payment would be $600,000. A single individual may not be able to raise $600,000 to enter this specific investment opportunity. Consequently, other ownership forms are utilized in real estate equity investments. Three of these forms are the partnership, the corporation, and the real estate investment trust (REIT), all of which were introduced and discussed in Chapter 10.

YIELD CAPITALIZATION

Yield capitalization was introduced in Chapter 6. At that time two methods for yield capitalization were identified, but only one method was discussed. That method was the one that relied on the use of the NOIs, the terminal capitalization rate, and the discount rate. The second method of yield capitalization relies on the use of the BTCFs, the reversion, and the discount rate. Now that these concepts have been discussed, the second yield capitalization method can be presented.

Exhibit 11.6 is the form of the numerical analysis for yield capitalization. It calculates the present value of the BTCFs and the reversion, which are the returns to the equity position. As shown, the present value of these cash flows is $196,413, at a discount rate of 14 percent. This analysis can be used to estimate the current market value as long as two important assumptions hold true. First, the financing terms must represent the terms and the rate that are typically available in the financial market for the type of property being purchased. The mortgage interest rate cannot be affected by any special considerations associated with any specific investor. Second, the 14 percent is the appropriate discount rate as long as it reflects the desire of the typical or representative investor in these types of properties and not any special considerations associated with any specific investor.

Because the focus is on the equity position in the investment, the investor's expected return is the appropriate interest rate to use as the discount rate. In the other yield capitalization approach that relied on the NOIs, a weighted discount rate was used. That discount rate had to reflect the desires of both the lender and the investor, so it turned out to be a weighted average of 10 percent—which reflected the lender's 8-percent desired return and the investor's 14-percent rate of return.

Chapter Summary

An individual can choose from among many kinds of investment opportunities—savings accounts, common stocks, corporate bonds, government bonds, and real estate equity investments. To make a rational choice, each investor must define his investment objectives, which may be price appreciation, periodic cash flow, equity increases through mortgage reduction, tax shelter, leverage, estate building, or a combination of these objectives. In addition, the investor must understand the risks inherent in the various investments.

Having chosen real estate equity as the desired type of investment, an individual must examine the financial aspects of the potential investment property. The first step in this process is the estimation of revenues, total operating expenses, and the debt service to obtain a value for before-tax cash flow. Then, initial period rates of performance are used to calculate the operating expense ratio, the debt service coverage ratio, and the breakeven ratio to determine whether the income generated by the property is great enough to cover various categories and combinations of the property's expenses. Next, the investor can calculate the profitability ratios, such as the equity dividend ratio, as a measure of the return on the investment.

However, the initial period performance ratios do not provide projections of future levels of income and expenses, the time value of money, price appreciation, and such income tax factors as capital gains and depreciation recapture that only come into effect upon sale of the property. Consequently, more sophisticated tools are used in the investment decision—present value or internal rate of return techniques.

Finally, the investor should realize that a feasibility study may be needed. By using a financial study and market analysis, the investor can develop a full understanding of the investment opportunity and its desirability as a method of achieving her financial objectives.

Internet Applications

A website has been established for this chapter at http://epley.swcollege.com.

Review Questions

1. Discuss the difference between financial and nonfinancial assets. How does this distinction relate to real estate investment opportunities?

2. What is a real estate equity investment?

3. Identify and explain the various objectives that a real estate equity investor may have.

4. Identify and explain the various risks that a real estate equity investor may face.

5. Explain the process by which before-tax cash flow (BTCF) is obtained.

6. Identify the initial period rates of performance.

7. Explain the disadvantages or shortcomings of initial period rates of performance.

8. Describe the present value and internal rate of return techniques. How do these techniques overcome some of the disadvantages of initial period ratio analysis?

9. Define feasibility study and describe its component parts.

Discussion Questions

1. Discuss the significance of the initial period ratios. Are they good indicators of an investment's potential? Why or why not?

2. Is multiperiod discounted cash flow analysis a better analytical tool for investment analysis? Why or why not?

3. What is sensitivity analysis and how might an investor use it?

4. What is holding period analysis and how is it related to investor objectives?

5. When might it be reasonable for the investor to refinance the property?

Problems

1. Refer to the numerical example presented in the chapter. Analyze the investment on the assumption that total operating expenses in the second through the sixth year are 10 percent more in each year than those appearing in Exhibit 11.3. So, in the second year, operating expenses are $64,953, and, because of price appreciation, the expected sales price in the sixth year is $1,100,000.

2. Analyze the investment decision portrayed in Exhibits 11.1 through 11.6 given the new assumptions shown in the following scenarios:

Cash Flow Item	Scenario #1	#2	#3	#4
Rent for two-bedroom units	$550	$600	$635	$650
Vacancy rate	5%	6%	7%	10%
Property tax	$9,000	$10,000	$6,000	$9,000
Maintenance and repair	$12,000	$14,000	$15,000	$18,000
Utilities	$5,000	$7,000	$7,000	$8,000
Appreciation rate	0	1%	1.5%	2%
Investor's required rate of return	14.5%	16%	16.5%	17%

Taxation of the Real Estate Investment

QUESTIONS TO BE ANSWERED

1. What are the effects of the Internal Revenue Code on the single-family homeowner?

2. What are the effects of the Internal Revenue Code on the investor who owns income-producing real property?

3. How does the investor incorporate income tax factors into the investment decision?

OBJECTIVES

When finished with this chapter, the student should be able to:

1. Explain the Internal Revenue Code's concepts of useful life, adjusted basis, and original basis and describe their impact on the owner of real estate.

2. Explain the nature and purpose of depreciation techniques permitted in the Internal Revenue Code.

3. Define taxable income and show how it is used in the investment decision.

4. Explain the concept of capital gain upon sale of the property.

5. Describe the capital gain tax deferral techniques permitted in the Internal Revenue Code.

accelerated depreciation method

adjusted basis

after-tax cash flow (ATCF)

after-tax equity reversion (ATER)

alternative depreciation system (ADS)

at-risk rules

basis

capital gain

capital gain exclusion

capital loss

declining balance depreciation methods

deductions

deferred exchange

depreciation recapture

effective tax rate

fair market value

general depreciation system (GDS)

home equity debt

installment sale

like-kind property

marginal tax rate

modified accelerated cost recovery system (MACRS)

net tax savings

nontaxable exchange

ownership test

partially nontaxable exchange

participation

passive activity

passive activity rules

placed in service

qualifying property

recovery property

replacement property

retired from service

return of the investment

secured debt

straight-line depreciation

taxable income

use test

INTRODUCTION

One of the four investment returns discussed in Chapter 11 was tax shelter, referring to tax shelter for income from both the federal and the state income tax codes. In this chapter we discuss only the federal tax code. Because it is more inclusive than most state tax codes, an understanding of the federal code will also enhance understanding of any of the state tax codes.

The federal tax code affects both owners of residential property and owners of investment property. Some of the effects are similar between these two groups while many are not. This chapter first discusses the tax code effects on residential homeowners. The emphasis then shifts to individual investors.

Real estate investors typically are not tax accountants or tax attorneys specializing in tax codes. Real estate investors are often generalists, lacking specific tax knowledge. However, investors do need to know enough about the tax code to judge its effects on the investment analysis, and that is the purpose of this chapter. Real estate investors need to know if the return of the investment *including the tax effect* is "in the ballpark." Then, if it is, investors can obtain the needed specific information about the tax code by hiring the tax accountant or attorney.

What Are the Effects of the Income Tax Code on Owner-Occupied Residential Real Estate?

O wners of a single-family house who occupy that house for their own purposes are significantly affected by income tax provisions of both the federal and state governments. The purpose of this section is to describe the typical tax effects on such individuals during ownership and at the time the property is sold. The information in this section is drawn mainly from four publications issued by the U.S. Department of the Treasury's Internal Revenue Service: *Tax Information for First-Time Homeowners* (Publication #530), *Selling Your Home* (Publication #523), *Home Mortgage Interest Deduction* (Publication #936), and *Basis of Assets* (Publication #551). The homeowner should review these free publications frequently to discover any changes in the federal income tax code that affect owner-occupied units. These publications as well as other IRS publications are available on the IRS website at www.irs.ustreas.gov.

TAX SAVINGS DURING OWNERSHIP

The IRS code affects the federal income tax position of the homeowner during the ownership period, including the handling of itemized deductions and costs associated with the purchase of the property and the typically related activity of using the property as collateral for a new loan, a home equity loan, or a refinancing the existing loan. These items are discussed in the following sections.

Home Acquisition and Home Equity Debt

The IRS recognizes two types of debt that relate to a taxpayer's home. The first loan is the *home acquisition loan* the taxpayer took out to buy, build, or substantially improve a qualified home that is the collateral for the loan. The qualified home can be either a main home or a second home. The home acquisition loan is limited to the price of the home plus the cost of any substantial improvements to that home. If the actual debt is greater than the price of the home plus the cost of any substantial improvements, the additional debt may qualify as home equity debt. The **home equity debt** is a loan that does not qualify as a home acquisition debt but is still secured by the home. The home equity debt is taken out for reasons other than to buy, build, or substantially improve a qualified home. The IRS specifically mentions tuition, medical costs, and debt consolidation as reasons to obtain a home equity debt. The distinction between these two categories of debt comes into play when the IRS imposes limits on the maximum debt allowed for consideration of mortgage interest payment deductions.

Annual Itemized Deductions

The federal income tax code allows a homeowner to take certain annual deductions during the ownership period. **Deductions** are itemized expenditures associated with home ownership that are made by the homeowner; they can be subtracted on the income tax form from the owner's earnings for the year. The IRS allows the following expenditures as annual deductions.

MORGAGE INTEREST PAYMENTS. The taxpayer can deduct the mortgage interest that is paid on the money borrowed to purchase the qualified home, which is a secured debt. A **secured debt** is one in which the taxpayer signs a legal instrument—such as a mortgage, deed of trust, security deed, or land contract—that:

1. Makes ownership in a qualified home the security for repayment of the loan.
2. Provides that the home could satisfy the debt in case of default on the loan.
3. Is recorded or otherwise perfected under any state or local law that applies.

The loan can be a first or a second mortgage loan. However, the mortgage interest deduction may be limited under two conditions:

- *Adjusted gross income limitation.* The current limitation on the deduction is imposed if the homeowner's adjusted gross income (AGI) is more than $124,500 if married and filing jointly, or $62,250 if married and filing separately. The limitation is imposed on the following itemized deduction categories shown on Schedule A: taxes, mortgage interest, gifts to charity, job expenses, and other miscellaneous expenses. The limitation is obtained by making the following two calculations and applying the smaller of the two options. Consider a case in which the homeowner has an AGI of $150,000, total itemized deductions including the mortgage interest are $40,000.

1. Three percent of the difference between the homeowner's AGI and the $124,500 figure (For example, if the homeowner's AGI is $150,000, the difference is $25,500. Three percent of the difference is $765. Subtracting $765 from $40,000 leaves $39,235.)
2. Eighty percent of the itemized deductions subject to the limitation (For example, 80 percent of $40,000 is $32,000.)

Choosing the smaller of the two figures, the homeowner's total itemized deductions (which include the mortgage interest) are limited to $32,000.

- *Total mortgage loan limitation.* If the total of all home acquisition mortgages on the taxpayer's qualified homes (main and second homes) is $1 million or less if married and filing jointly or $500,000 or less if married and filing separately, the full amount of the mortgage interest is deductible but limited by the AGI limitation above. If the total of all home acquisition mortgages exceeds $1 million, the homeowner needs to consult *Home Mortgage Interest Deduction* (Publication #936) regarding how to treat the deductibility of the mortgage interest.

The limit on all home equity mortgages is the smaller of (1) $100,000 if married and filing jointly or $50,000 if married and filing separately, or (2) the total of each home's fair market value reduced by the amount of its home acquisition debt. The interest paid on the smaller of these two values is deductible in the tax year. Interest paid on the loan over the limit is treated as personal interest and as such is not deductible.

HOME IMPROVEMENT LOAN FINANCING ITEMS. The interest payments and points paid on the money borrowed as a home improvement loan or an equity line of credit, which use the real property as collateral, are allowed as annual deductions. The money can be used to fund improvements or additions to the house as well as expenditures for education.

REAL PROPERTY TAX. The real property tax that is paid to the local government or local taxing jurisdiction during the year is deductible.

LATE PAYMENT CHARGES AND PREPAYMENT PENALTIES. Mortgage finance items such as late payment charges and prepayment penalties are allowed as annual deductions.

CASUALTY LOSSES. The portion of fire and other casualty loss to the home that exceeds $100 after any insurance reimbursement is deductible. Casualty or theft loss on personal property in the home is deductible to the extent that the loss exceeds $100 for each casualty or theft and 10 percent of the homeowner's adjusted gross income. When real property has been damaged, the loss is calculated by the following steps: (1) determine the adjusted basis of the property before the loss; (2) determine the difference between the fair market value of the property before the damage and the fair market value of the property after the damage; (3) select the smaller of the two values from #1 and #2. This value is then reduced by the amount of the insurance compensation received. If the remaining figure is positive it is reduced further by a $100 statutory minimum and is also reduced by 10 percent of the taxpayer's AGI. The remaining figure is an itemized deduction.

Casualty losses for furniture and fixtures not entirely destroyed are also deductible. In this case, the deductible amount is computed for each item, as it was above. The amount of the deduction is the decrease in value, less any insurance compensation and less $100 and 10 percent of AGI for each casualty loss.

OTHER ITEMIZED DEDUCTIONS. Other itemized expenditures not related to the cost of home ownership are deductible. These deductions can be taken by tenants as well as landlords. For example, the tax code allows deductions for taxes paid on personal property, medical and dental expenses, educational expenses, union or employee organization dues, charitable contributions, and interest on consumer loans.

Expenditures Not Allowed as Annual Deductions

Certain expenditures made by the homeowner cannot be deducted as an annual expenditure. These expenditures include the following:

1. Certain costs or charges for services associated with the purchase of the house, such as appraisal fees, notary fees, preparation costs for the legal documents, mortgage insurance premiums, and Department of Veteran Affairs (VA) funding fees
2. Expenses for maintenance and repairs to the house
3. Payments for special assessments imposed for construction of streets, sidewalks, and water and sewer systems (However, special assessments for the maintenance and repair of these same public improvements are deductible.)
4. Insurance premiums paid for the homeowners' hazard and liability insurance
5. Transfer taxes
6. Depreciation charges
7. Utility payments
8. Certain costs or charges for services associated with the real property, such as trash collection and removal
9. Certain costs associated with compliance with the zoning ordinance, the subdivision regulations, or any other local ordinance imposed by the local government, such as the cost of yard cleanup to comply with a local ordinance
10. Homeowner association charges, fees, or assessments

The federal tax code makes a distinction between repairs and improvements. It defines a *repair* as an expenditure made to maintain the house in an ordinarily efficient operating condition. A repair expenditure does not add to the value of the property or increase its physical life. Examples of repairs are painting, fixing gutters, repairing the roof, plastering walls, and replacing broken windows. In contrast, an *improvement* expenditure materially increases the value of the property, lengthens its economic life, or adapts it to a new use. Examples of improvement expenditures are the construction of a room addition or new wing, modernizing a bathroom or kitchen, finishing the basement, putting up a fence, installing new plumbing or electrical wiring, replacing an old roof, and paving the driveway. If ordinary repairs are done as part of an improvement project, the tax code allows the entire expenditure to be treated as an improvement. Improvement expenditures are a major consideration when the property is sold, but repair expenditures are not.

Costs Incurred During the Purchase

In addition to the annual itemized deductions, certain expenses incurred by the homeowner when the property is purchased are deductible in the year of the purchase.

REAL PROPERTY TAXES THAT ARE PRORATED. One of these items is any real property tax proration paid by the buyer on the day the property is bought. This payment from the buyer to the seller arises because the seller usually pays the property taxes on an annual basis. If the property is sold six months into the tax period, the seller will require a payment of half of these taxes from the buyer. This expenditure is a tax deduction in the year of purchase because it is a property tax payment made by the buyer.

POINTS—THE IRS GENERAL RULE. A second expenditure associated with the purchase of a house is any additional interest charge, typically known as origination fees and points on the loan. The lender makes such charges when the mortgage interest rate is less than the return the lender could receive on alternative nonmortgage type loans (business loans) and investments. These charges allow the lender to receive an effective interest rate that exceeds the interest rate stated on the mortgage. Therefore, depending on the type of mortgage, the buyer, the seller, or both may have to pay some small percentage of the value of the loan at the time the property is purchased and the loan is made. (Points are examined in greater detail in Chapter 8.)

If points are paid on the value of the loan that was obtained to purchase the taxpayer's principal residence, these funds are not annual expenditures and cannot be deducted in the year of purchase. This is the general rule stated by the IRS. However, the amortized portion of the origination fees or loan discount points associated with the loan to purchase the home are deductible. In other words, if the homeowner took out a loan for $100,000 for 30 years and paid three points on that loan, the $3,000 paid to the lender as points could be deducted at a rate of $100 per year for 30 years.

POINTS—EXCEPTIONS TO THE GENERAL RULE. The IRS does allow an exception to the general rule. The full amount of the points can be deducted in the year of purchase if the following set of nine tests is passed.

1. The loan is secured by the home.
2. The charging of points is an established business practice in the geographic area where the loan was made.
3. The number of points claimed by the taxpayer does not exceed the number generally charged in the area.
4. The cash method of accounting is used by the taxpayer.

5. The points are not paid in place of amounts that are ordinarily stated separately on the closing statement, such as appraisal fees, inspection fees, title fees, attorney fees, and property taxes.

6. The loan is used to buy or build the taxpayer's principal residence.

7. The points are computed as a percentage of the loan amount.

8. The amount of points is clearly shown on the closing documents.

9. The funds provided by the buyer at or before the closing, plus any points paid by the seller, are at least as much as the points charged. They can include a down payment, an escrow deposit, earnest money, and other funds. These funds cannot be borrowed from the lender or mortgage broker.

If the first eight of these tests are passed, but the ninth test is not, then the IRS allows the homeowner to deduct the amount of points in the year of purchase up to the amount of funds that the homeowner provided. For example, the homeowner obtains a 30-year loan for $100,000 with two points charged by the lender. The homeowner provides $1,400 as a down payment. The homeowner can claim $1,400 of the $2,000 in points in the year of purchase and must amortize the remaining $600 over the 30 years at $20 per year.

If all the nine tests are passed with the exception of test #3, the IRS allows the homeowner to claim the points generally charged as a deduction in the year of purchase. The points in excess of those generally charged in the market must be amortized over the remaining term of the loan. For example, the homeowner obtains a 30-year loan for $100,000 with three points charged by the lender. The amount of points generally charged in the market is two points. The homeowner can claim $2,000 of the $3,000 in points in the year of purchase and must amortize the remaining $1,000 over the 30 years of the loan.

POINTS AT THE TERMINATION OF THE EXISTING LOAN. The mortgage loan may not run its full term because the homeowner sells the property and pays off the loan balance or the property is refinanced. In these situations, the points that were being amortized over the 30-year term of the loan and have not yet been claimed as annual deductions can be summed and claimed in the year the original loan is repaid. For example, the homeowner obtains a 30-year loan for $100,000 with three points charged by the lender. The homeowner must follow the general rule of the IRS and amortize all of the points because the nine tests are not passed. The homeowner can claim $100 of the $3,000 in points every year of the term of the loan. The homeowner sells the house in the eleventh year of ownership after claiming $1,000 of the points. In the eleventh year, the homeowner can claim the remaining $2,000.

PREPAID INTEREST. The tax deductibility for prepaid interest is parallel to the tax deductibility of points. It must be amortized over the term of the loan unless it passes the nine-step test presented for points.

CONCLUSION REGARDING COSTS INCURRED DURING THE PURCHASE. For more information on the tax deductibility of points and prepaid interest, see IRS Publications #523 and #936. The tax savings generated by the annual deductions and other deductible expenses can be significant. The homeowner should keep records on both the annual deductions and the year-of-purchase deductions to extract the maximum benefit from the tax code. Depending on the property owner's effective tax rate, these deductions could amount to an annual deduction of $8,000 to $15,000, and a tax savings of $2,000 to $5,000 per year for the homeowner.

Points Under Special Circumstances

Points also come into play in situations other than the acquisition of a new mortgage loan to purchase a main or principal residence. Two of these situations are the points on a home improvement loan and the points on a refinancing.

POINTS PAID ON A HOME IMPROVEMENT LOAN. The points paid on a home improvement loan are fully deductible in the year the loan was obtained if the first five tests listed earlier are passed. Also, if part of the funds received from a refinancing are used for a home improvement, that portion can be deducted as an expenditure in the year of the refinancing.

POINTS PAID ON A REFINANCING OF THE EXISTING LOAN. Generally, points the taxpayer pays to refinance a mortgage are not deductible in full in the year of the refinancing. The points must be amortized over the term of the loan. However, if a portion of the funds obtained from the refinancing are used to improve the main or principal residence, and if the first five tests listed earlier are passed, the points paid on that portion of the loan can be deducted in the year of the refinancing. The remaining points must be amortized.

TAX LIABILITY AT TERMINATION OF OWNERSHIP

The homeowner should know about four important concepts when the property is sold—(1) the basis of the property, (2) the adjusted basis of the property, (3) the capital gains, and (4) techniques for the deferral of capital gains.

Basis of the Property

In the Internal Revenue Code, the basis of the property is the value of that property for tax purposes. The basis is determined as the sum of the following components.

ACQUISITION PRICE OF THE PROPERTY. The first important component of basis is the acquisition price of the property. If the home was purchased on the open market, this first element of basis is the price paid for the property. If the home was constructed new, it consists of the price of the land plus the construction costs of the improvements of the land. These construction costs include labor, materials, contractor payments, architect's fees, building permit fees, utility meter and connection charges, and legal fees connected with the building of the house and other improvements on the property.

If the property was received as a gift, the basis is either the fair market value of the property at the time of the gift or the adjusted basis of the property of the person from whom it was received. See IRS Publication #530 for more details about the basis of property received as a gift or through inheritance.

POINTS PAID BY THE SELLER. If the seller of the property paid any of the points associated with the buyer's loan to acquire the property, the buyer must reduce the basis of the property by the dollar amount of the points the seller paid. For example, if the $100,000 loan had two points and the seller paid one point equal to $1,000, and if the buyer bought the house for $120,000, then the basis of the house would be $119,000. This requirement applies for any house bought after April 3, 1994, even if the buyer did not deduct the points as an annual deduction in the year of the purchase as discussed above. If the house was bought prior to April 3, 1994, the IRS allows the points to be handled differently. See IRS Publication #530 for more detail.

If the seller of a property paid any of the points associated with the buyer's loan to acquire the property, the seller's tax situation is also affected. For the seller, the points paid on the buyer's loan are considered as selling costs and reduce the net proceeds from the sale.

SETTLEMENT FEES OR CLOSING COSTS. The IRS's general rule with regard to settlement fees or closing costs is that these items are included in the basis if they are associated with buying the home, but they are not included if they are associated with getting the mortgage loan. The IRS provides three lists of settlement costs to guide the homebuyer.

Settlement fees and closing costs that can be included in the basis of the property because they are associated with the purchase of the house include the following:

1. Abstract fees
2. Charges for installing utility services
3. Legal fees, including the fees for title search and preparation of the sales contract and the deed
4. Recording fees
5. Surveying fees
6. Transfer taxes
7. Owner's title insurance
8. Amounts the seller owes that the buyer agrees to pay, such as back taxes or interest, recording fees, mortgage fees, charges for improvements or repairs, and sales commissions

Settlement fees and closing costs that cannot be included in the basis of the property because they are associated with obtaining the mortgage include the following:

1. Mortgage insurance premiums
2. Loan assumption fees
3. Cost of a credit report
4. Appraisal fee
5. Fees for refinancing a mortgage

The IRS also identifies other settlement fees and closing costs that cannot be included in the basis of the property. These items include the following:

1. Fire insurance premiums
2. Rent for the buyer's occupancy of the house before the closing
3. Utility charges or other services associated with the buyer's occupancy of the house before the closing
4. Moving expenses

REAL ESTATE TAXES. The real estate taxes in the year that the home is purchased can affect the basis in the following two ways:

1. If the buyer pays the real estate taxes that the seller owed on the house up to the date of the sale, and the seller does not reimburse the buyer for these taxes, then the taxes are added to the basis of the house.

2. If the seller pays real estate taxes for the buyer for some period after the sale to the buyer, and the buyer does not reimburse the seller, then the taxes are subtracted from the basis of the house.

Basis Other Than Cost

If the homeowner received the property as a gift, as an inheritance, or in a trade, then the basis of the property is established by its fair market value at the time the property is received. The IRS explains **fair market value** as the "price at which property would change hands between a willing buyer and a willing seller, neither having to buy or sell, and both having reasonable knowledge of the relevant facts." In this instance, IRS Publication #530 explains some of the special considerations for the situation involving a gift, an inheritance, or a property trade.

Adjusted Basis Calculation

In addition to the sales price or construction costs, seller-paid points, settlement fees associated with the property purchase, and selected real estate tax situations that form the IRS's basis of the property, other items change the basis of the property after the sale has occurred. When these changes are recorded in the homeowner's tax records, the resulting IRS concept is the **adjusted basis** of the property.

The expenditures that increase the IRS's basis to generate higher value for the adjusted basis are as follows:

1. Expenditures made for improvements and additions to the property that have a useful life of more than one year
2. Special assessments for off-site improvements by the local government
3. Amount of money spent after a casualty to restore the damaged property

Improvements are added to the adjusted basis; repairs are not. The IRS specifically identifies the following examples of improvements that increase the basis of the property.

Additions:	Bedroom, bathroom, deck, garage, porch, patio, fireplace, storage shed
Lawn and grounds:	landscaping, driveway, walkway, fence, retaining wall, sprinkler system, swimming pool, exterior lighting
Heating and air:	heating system, central air conditioning, furnace, duct work, central humidifier, filtration system
Plumbing:	septic tank system, water heater, soft water heater, filtration system
Electrical:	lighting fixtures, wiring upgrades
Interior upgrades:	built-in appliances, kitchen modernization, bathroom modernization, flooring, wall-to-wall carpeting
Insulation:	attic, walls, floor, pipes, duct work
Communications:	satellite dish, intercom, security system
Miscellaneous:	storm windows and doors, new roof, central vacuum system

If the improvement was made and counted as an increase in the adjusted basis but now is no longer a part of the home because the item was removed, then the adjusted basis should not include the item and the adjusted basis should be reduced.

The expenditures that decrease the IRS's basis to generate a reduced value for the adjusted basis are as follows:

1. Deductible casualty losses not covered by insurance
2. Insurance payments received for casualty losses
3. Payments received for granting an easement or right-of-way
4. Depreciation allowed if the home is used for business or rental purposes
5. Energy conservation subsidy received from a public utility after 1992 to buy or install any energy conservation measure that reduces the consumption of electricity or natural gas or improves the management of energy demand for a home

Depreciation (cost recovery) is not allowed as a deduction from the adjusted basis for an owner-occupied residential unit, but if the property owner rents the property or uses some portion of the property for business purposes, a depreciation deduction is allowed. In the case of rental property, the full structure can be depreciated. If part of the property is used for business purposes, only that part can be depreciated.

The homeowner should keep accurate records to prove the adjusted basis of the property, including the following:

1. Proof of the purchase price, seller-paid points, and the settlement items associated with the purchase of the property that determine the basis of the property
2. Receipts for all improvements, additions, and other items that affect the adjusted basis
3. Worksheets and records that were used to calculate the adjusted basis of a property that was sold

These records are also important in making calculations of casualty losses or damage to property. In addition, these figures serve as the starting point for calculating capital gains on the property.

Exhibit 12.1 provides a summary of the preceding discussion of interest payments, points, settlement costs, and real property taxes.

Capital Gain or Loss

A taxable **capital gain** is generated when the net proceeds from the sale of the property exceeds the adjusted basis of the property. The reverse relationship between these two concepts generates a **capital loss.** If the property has been owned for more than one year, it is a long-term capital gain or loss as opposed to a short-term capital gain or loss.

The IRS publications discuss the concepts of a realized capital gain and a recognized capital gain. *A realized capital gain* is the total of all cash, property, and financial benefits that the seller receives for the property. For example, as part of the agreement with the buyer, the seller receives $100,000 in cash, personal property worth $10,000, the buyer pays $4,000 in real estate taxes for the seller, and the buyer assumes the $50,000 mortgage loan on the property. The realized capital gain is $164,000. However, the *recognized capital gain* for federal income tax purposes is the sale price of the property (in this case, $164,000) less selling costs and less the adjusted basis of the property. If the adjusted basis is $84,000, and selling costs are $10,000, the recognized capital gain is $70,000. The recognized capital gain is subject to taxation.

The calculation of either a recognized capital gain or a loss requires the homeowner to start with the exact sales price and to subtract the selling costs to get the net proceeds from the sale. For example, a homeowner bought a home 10 years ago for $100,000, spent $3,000 in property acquisition settlement costs, spent $8,000 to mod-

	Annual Deduction	Amortized Deduction	Basis/Adjusted Basis
Interest payment on a secured debt	*yes* as long as the limits on the home acquisition and home equity debt are met	no	no
Points paid by buyer	*yes* on a qualified home if the nine tests are passed	*yes* if the nine tests are not passed	no
	yes on a home improvement loan		no
	no on a refinancing loan	yes	no
Points paid by seller	no	no	*yes;* the buyer's basis is reduced by the points paid
			no effect on seller's basis or adjusted basis (the points are considered selling costs)
Prepaid interest	*yes* on a qualified home if the nine tests are passed	*yes* if the nine tests are not passed	no
Settlement costs to acquire the property	no	no	*yes;* basis is increased
Settlement costs to acquire the loan	no	no	no
Real property tax—current year	yes	no	no
Real property tax at closing	yes	no	If buyer pays back taxes and is not reimbursed by the seller, the sum of these taxes can be added to the basis.
			If the seller pays taxes for the buyer for the time beyond the sale date, the buyer must deduct this sum from the basis.
Special assessment	no	no	*yes;* basis is increased
Casualty loss	no	no	*yes;* the amount of the loss not covered by insurance is a reduction to the basis

ernize the kitchen and $4,000 to build a porch, and sold it yesterday for $145,000. The brokerage commission was 6 percent of the sales price. Is there a capital gain or a capital loss? What is the magnitude of the gain or loss?

Basis = $100,000 + $3,000 = $103,000
Adjusted Basis = $103,000 + $8,000 + $4,000 = $115,000
Brokerage commission = $8,700
Net proceeds from the sale = $145,000 − $8,700 = $136,300
Capital gain or loss = $136,300 − $115,000 = $21,300, a capital gain

What would be the result if the original purchase price were $110,000, and the sales price were only $130,000?

Basis = $110,000 + $3,000 = $113,000
Adjusted basis = $113,000 + $8,000 + $4,000 = $125,000
Brokerage commission = $7,800
Net proceeds from the sale = $130,000 − $7,800 = $122,200
Capital gain or loss = $122,200 − $125,000 = −$2,800, a capital loss

Capital Gain Exclusion

The material in this section generally applies to all homeowners who sell their home in 1998 or in later years. However, IRS Publication #523 also provides for the implementation of the old rules rather than the current rules. A short discussion of these old, special circumstances appears in the subsection following the current rules.

THE CURRENT CASE: HOME IS SOLD IN 1998 OR IN LATER YEARS. The IRS rules governing the exclusion of a capital gain depend on the homeowner passing an **ownership test** and a **use test.** The discussion that follows focuses on the major themes of the IRS code; for more comprehensive coverage of complicating situations, refer to IRS Publication #523.

The ability of the homeowner to exclude the payment of a tax on the capital gain from the sale of the home in 1998 or later depends on the following conditions:

- *Ownership test:* the homeowner owned the home for at least two of the preceding five years
- *Use test:* the homeowner lived in the home as a main residence for at least two of the preceding five years

The ownership and use tests can be met at different times within the preceding five-year period. Consider the following examples:

1. The homeowner sold the house in December 2000 and bought it in September of 1998. The homeowner lived in the property during this time. The ownership and use tests are passed in the two years preceding the sale.

2. The homeowner sold the property in September 1999 and used it as a rental property investment from October 1996 until September 1999 (passing the ownership test). The homeowner lived in the house as the main residence from September 1994 until October 1996 (passing the use test).

In order for the homeowner to claim a capital gain exclusion, the homeowner must pass the ownership and use tests as stated above. The IRS allows for a partial exclusion of capital gains if either one, but not both, of the ownership and/or use tests are passed. A full discussion of this point appears in IRS Publication #523.

The amount of the **capital gain exclusion** is a maximum amount of $250,000 per homeowner. However, if all of the following conditions are met, then the exclusion can go up to a maximum amount of $500,000. The conditions are as follows:

1. The homeowner is married and files a joint return for the year of sale.
2. Either the husband or the wife meets the ownership test.
3. Either the husband or the wife meets the use test.
4. Neither the husband nor the wife excluded a capital gain from the sale of another home after May 6, 1997.

The homeowner can claim this capital gain exclusion each time a principal residence is sold as long as only one such home is sold in a two-year period. According to the IRS, an owner cannot exclude gain on the sale of the home if, during a two-year period ending on the date of sale, the owner sold another home at a gain and excluded all or part of the gain. However, the owner can claim a reduced level of the capital gain exclusion if the property was sold due to health considerations or a change in employment. The IRS offers a special Reduced Exclusion Worksheet in IRS Publication #523.

If the capital gain is not excluded either in whole or in part, then the gain must be added to the homeowner's adjusted income for the year of the sale and taxed at the homeowner's effective tax rate.

THE OLD RULE FOR POSTPONEMENT OF CAPITAL GAIN TAX. If a capital gain was realized from the sale of the property, the seller had a 24-month period in which to utilize that capital gain for the purchase of a replacement residence before reporting it to the IRS as a taxable capital gain.

If the seller chose to purchase a replacement home within 24 months of the sale of the original home, and this replacement was of equal or greater value than the residence that was sold, the capital gains tax was deferred into the future. The capital gain continued to be deferred until the principal residence was sold and an equally valuable substitute was not purchased.

If an individual sold his or her principal residence and bought a residence of lower value, the difference between the adjusted sales price and the adjusted basis was subject to taxation in the current year; part of the capital gain was deferred and part of the capital gain was subject to taxation in the current year. The entire capital gain could be deferred if the homeowner undertook improvements to the replacement residence, such as adding a room or remodeling the basement into a den or extra bedroom.

Fix-up expenditures are incurred to make the house more saleable. They may include such expenses as painting the interior and exterior surfaces of the house, wallpapering, installing new carpets, and installing new appliances or fixtures.

The following established rules regulate which fix-up expenses could be used in the adjustment process when calculating capital gain under the old rules.

1. The work must be performed during the 90 days preceding the day upon which the sales contract is signed by both parties.
2. The expenditures cannot be made later than 30 days after the date of sale as it appears on the contract.
3. The expenditures cannot be considered as improvement expenditures.
4. The expenditures cannot be deducted by the individual as operating expenses when calculating taxable income in the year of sale. They are deducted in the process of establishing the capital gain.

To calculate the capital gain, the seller first subtracts the selling expenses from the sales price of the property to get the net proceeds from the sale. Then, the seller subtracts the adjusted basis from the net proceeds from the sale. The remainder is a capital gain if the amount is positive and is a capital loss if the amount is negative.

To calculate the tax on the capital gain, the seller first subtracts the selling expenses and the fix-up expenses from the sales price of the property to get the adjusted sales price. Then the seller subtracts the adjusted basis from the adjusted sales price. The remainder is the capital gain subject to taxation in the year of sale.

Under the old rule, if the property was sold during the first six months of ownership, any gain was not considered a long-term gain and was treated as ordinary income and was taxed at its full value.

How Does the Federal Income Tax Code Affect Income-Producing Real Properties?

The tax impact on income-earning property is related to three key concepts within the tax law: basis and adjusted basis, depreciation, and the recovery period. Much of the information from the previous section applies in the income-property situation, especially the concepts surrounding basis and adjusted basis as well as the calculation of capital gain. However, this section also has new information that is based on the following IRS publications: *Residential Rental Property* (Publication #527), *How to Depreciate Property* (Publication #946), *Sales and Other Disposition of Assets* (Publication #544), and *Installment Sales* (Publication #537).

The major concepts involved with the federal tax treatment of income-producing property are discussed below as part of the modified accelerated cost recovery system.

RULES GOVERNING PROPERTY DEPRECIATION

The IRS allows the taxpayer to depreciate properties such as buildings, site improvements costs (parking surfaces, fences, landscaping, and so forth), improvements to the structure, furniture, appliances, equipment, machinery, vehicles, patents, and copyrights. To be eligible for depreciation, the property must meet all of the following requirements. The property must:

1. be used in business or held to produce income,
2. have a useful life longer than one year, and
3. wear out, decay, get used up, become obsolete, or lose value from natural causes.

In addition to specifically identifying the characteristics of property that can be depreciated, the IRS also specifically identifies types of property that cannot be depreciated. These types are as follows:

1. Property placed in service and sold in the same year
2. Land, including the cost of clearing, grading, planting, and landscaping[1]
3. Real property leased to a tenant. The tenant cannot claim property depreciation, but the property owner can . The rule involves the consideration of the "incidents of ownership," which include the following items:
   - Legal title
   - Legal obligation to pay for the property

- Responsibility to pay for maintenance and operating expenses
- Duty to pay any taxes
- Risk of loss if the property is destroyed, condemned, or diminishes in value through obsolescence or exhaustion

4. Inventory that is defined as property held for sale to customers in the ordinary course of the business
5. Equipment used to build capital improvements

IRS DEFINITIONS OF "PLACED IN SERVICE" AND "RETIRED FROM SERVICE"

Rental property is considered to be **placed in service** when it is ready and available for use as a rental facility, such as an apartment or an office. Once the property is placed in service, it starts the depreciation period even if the property is vacant for the first few months.

As part of the process of claiming depreciation for a property placed in service, the IRS requires that both residential and nonresidential rental real property must adopt the "mid-month convention" for placement in service and property disposal. This simply means that any residential property placed in service or sold on any day in the month must be treated as if it sold on the 15th day of that month. If, for example, the holding period is six years, the impact is half a month out of 72 months, which is a 0.07-percent effect.

Other income-producing property must adopt a half-year convention. A mid-quarter convention can be used for nonresidential rental property if 40 percent of the property placed in service is placed in service in the last three months of the tax year.

Any property is **retired from service** when the taxpayer permanently withdraws it from use in the production of income or in a trade or business. Depreciation must stop when the property is retired from service. A property can be retired from service by selling it, exchanging it, abandoning it, or destroying it.

COST RECOVERY PERIODS ALLOWED IN THE MODIFIED ACCELERATED COST RECOVERY SYSTEM

The **modified accelerated cost recovery system (MACRS)** contains an identification of the classes of **recovery property,** which means tangible property that depreciates when it is used in a trade or business or as an investment held for the production of income. Exhibit 12.2 shows the classes of recovery property and the type of property in each class of recovery property. The exhibit identifies two cost recovery systems. The **general depreciation system (GDS)** is the system used by most taxpayers to depreciate income-producing rental properties. However, the taxpayer can elect to use the **alternative depreciation system (ADS).** Because the GDS allows shorter recovery periods, the annual depreciation that can be taken is greater under the GDS.

The taxpayer identifies the cost recovery category in which the property belongs and then uses the specified number of years over which the cost of the property can be depreciated. For example, under current rules, a recently acquired apartment building can be depreciated over 27.5 years, while a recently acquired office building can be depreciated over 39 years. The furniture, appliances, and carpet in a fully furnished apartment can be depreciated over 7 years. A rewiring and replumbing job on an apartment building can be depreciated over 27.5 years.

EXHIBIT 12.2 MACRS recovery periods for property used in rental activities.

Type of Property	GDS Recovery Period	ADS Recovery Period	Depreciation Method Allowed
3-year property (not applicable to rental property)			
5-year property			
Computers and peripheral equipment	5 years	5 years	150% declining
Office machinery (copiers, calculators, etc.)	5	6	balance or
Automobiles and light trucks	5	5	straight line
7-year property			
Office furniture	7	12	150% declining
Appliances	7	12	balance or
Carpets	7	12	straight line
Furniture in rental property	7	12	
Any property unclassified by the MACRS	7	12	
10-year property (not applicable to rental property)			
15-year property			
Roads	15	20	150% declining
Shrubbery	15	20	balance or
Fences	15	20	straight line
20-year property (not applicable to rental property)			
Residential rental property (buildings and structures) and structural components such as furnaces, water pipes, venting, etc.	27.5	40	straight line
Nonresidential real property			straight line
1. placed in service before May 13, 1993	31.5		
2. placed in service after May 13, 1993	39		

BASIS AND ADJUSTED BASIS

The **basis** of income-earning property is the acquisition cost of the real estate, either the purchase price or the price for land and construction, plus seller-paid points, allowable settlement fees, and allowable real estate taxes. These aspects of the original basis of real property were discussed earlier in this chapter regarding the tax impact on the homeowner. That discussion also applies to this material.

The adjusted basis of residential rental property is obtained by adding the following items to the original basis:

1. Expenditures made for improvements and additions to the property that have a useful life of more than one year

2. Special assessments for off-site improvements by the local government that increase the value of the property (Utility service lines, streets, sidewalks, curbing, and so forth qualify.)

3. Amount of money spent after a casualty to restore the damaged property (Insurance compensation is handled as a separate deduction.)
4. Legal fees, such as the cost of defending the title to the property and litigation to argue the decrease in an assessment.

The following items must be subtracted from the original basis in order to obtain the adjusted basis:

1. The amount of any money received from insurance as a result of a casualty or theft
2. Any deductible casualty loss not covered by insurance
3. Any amount received from granting an easement
4. The amount of depreciation that could have been deducted on the tax forms under the method of depreciation that could have been selected (If the owner does not claim any depreciation, the IRS requires the adjusted basis to be reduced by the amount that could have been calculated.)

The adjusted basis can be reduced for any casualty loss to the property. However, in the calculation of both the annual depreciation and the casualty loss, the investor must realize that real estate is composed of both a depreciable and a nondepreciable component. Real estate consists of the improvement, which is depreciable, and the land, which is not depreciable. The investor, therefore, must apportion the original basis or acquisition price of the property into two components—the acquisition price of the land and the acquisition price of the improvement(s). The investor is not allowed to depreciate more than the value of the improvement, nor is the investor allowed to claim a casualty loss that exceeds the value of the adjusted basis of the improvement at the time the loss occurs.

One major subtraction from the original basis that needs additional discussion is the depreciation that is allowed during the period of time the property is owned. The investor *must* deduct depreciation from the basis. If a depreciation claim is not made by the owner, the Internal Revenue Code implies that a depreciation charge calculated by means of the straight-line technique (discussed below) will be subtracted from the basis. If the investor deducts more than the straight-line depreciation charge, either intentionally or unintentionally, the basis is reduced by the actual amount of depreciation that is deducted.

The unadjusted or original basis is used to calculate the annual depreciation charge. The adjusted basis is used for the calculation of capital gains. This distinction is very important to keep in mind.

DEPRECIATION METHODS

Two depreciation methods are allowed under the Internal Revenue Code: (1) straight-line depreciation and (2) accelerated depreciation in the form of the 150 percent declining balance method. Exhibit 12.2 identifies the depreciation method allowed for each of the types of property. To a limited extent, investors can choose the type of depreciation method that best meets their investment objectives. Therefore, an understanding of each technique and the manner in which the annual depreciation charge is determined is important for real estate investors.

Straight-Line Depreciation

Assume that the recovery period of a residential rental real estate equity investment is 27.5 years. The investor learns from the appraisal report that the estimated market value of $1 million is divided into its two components in such a way that the value of the land is $200,000 and the value of the improvements is $800,000.

The annual depreciation percentage under the **straight-line depreciation** method is very simple to calculate. Over the 27.5 years, the investor would like to receive a **return of the investment.** In other words, over this 27.5-year period, the owner would like to write off the value of the structure. The straight-line depreciation method is based on the fact that in each of the 27.5 years, an equal percentage of the improvement's value is charged against the income that the property generates. An annual percentage charge of 0.036364 for 27.5 years will recover 100 percent of this value ($1/27.5 = 0.036364$). This establishes a depreciation charge of $29,090.91 per year for each of the 27.5 years ($800,000 \times 0.036364 = $29,090.91$).

The IRS provides a depreciation table for residential (27.5-year) property in Publication #946 that is structured for the mid-month convention and the date the property is placed in service. Once these considerations enter the analysis, the dollar value of the annual depreciation charge changes in the first and the last year. This depreciation table is presented in Exhibit 12.3.

150-Percent Depreciation Method

In contrast to the straight-line method, the 150-percent depreciation method generates an annual depreciation charge in the first years of ownership that exceeds the annual depreciation charge in the straight-line method and generates an annual depreciation charge in the last years of ownership that is less than the straight-line method. For this reason, the 150-percent declining balance method and any other **declining balance depreciation method** (such as the 200-percent declining balance method) is called an **accelerated depreciation method.**

The 150-percent method applies to 5-, 7-, and 15-year property types. Let us use the 15-year property type in our example for an improvement value of $500,000. Under

---

EXHIBIT 12.3 Residential rental property mid-month convention; straight line—27.5 years.

Year	\multicolumn{12}{c}{Month property placed in service}											
	1	2	3	4	5	6	7	8	9	10	11	12
1	3.485%	3.182%	2.879%	2.576%	2.273%	1.970%	1.667%	1.364%	1.061%	75.800%	45.500%	15.200%
2 - 9	3.636%	3.636%	3.636%	3.636%	3.636%	3.636%	3.636%	3.636%	3.636%	3.636%	3.636%	3.636%
10	3.637%	3.637%	3.637%	3.637%	3.637%	3.637%	3.636%	3.636%	3.636%	3.636%	3.636%	3.636%
11	3.636%	3.636%	3.636%	3.636%	3.636%	3.636%	3.637%	3.637%	3.637%	3.637%	3.637%	3.637%
12	3.637%	3.637%	3.637%	3.637%	3.637%	3.637%	3.636%	3.636%	3.636%	3.636%	3.636%	3.636%
13	3.636%	3.636%	3.636%	3.636%	3.636%	3.636%	3.637%	3.637%	3.637%	3.637%	3.637%	3.637%
14	3.637%	3.637%	3.637%	3.637%	3.637%	3.637%	3.636%	3.636%	3.636%	3.636%	3.636%	3.636%
15	3.636%	3.636%	3.636%	3.636%	3.636%	3.636%	3.637%	3.637%	3.637%	3.637%	3.637%	3.637%
16	3.637%	3.637%	3.637%	3.637%	3.637%	3.637%	3.636%	3.636%	3.636%	3.636%	3.636%	3.636%
17	3.636%	3.636%	3.636%	3.636%	3.636%	3.636%	3.637%	3.637%	3.637%	3.637%	3.637%	3.637%
18	3.637%	3.637%	3.637%	3.637%	3.637%	3.637%	3.636%	3.636%	3.636%	3.636%	3.636%	3.636%
19	3.636%	3.636%	3.636%	3.636%	3.636%	3.636%	3.637%	3.637%	3.637%	3.637%	3.637%	3.637%
20	3.637%	3.637%	3.637%	3.637%	3.637%	3.637%	3.636%	3.636%	3.636%	3.636%	3.636%	3.636%
21	3.636%	3.636%	3.636%	3.636%	3.636%	3.636%	3.637%	3.637%	3.637%	3.637%	3.637%	3.637%
22	3.637%	3.637%	3.637%	3.637%	3.637%	3.637%	3.636%	3.636%	3.636%	3.636%	3.636%	3.636%
23	3.636%	3.636%	3.636%	3.636%	3.636%	3.636%	3.637%	3.637%	3.637%	3.637%	3.637%	3.637%
24	3.637%	3.637%	3.637%	3.637%	3.637%	3.637%	3.636%	3.636%	3.636%	3.636%	3.636%	3.636%
25	3.636%	3.636%	3.636%	3.636%	3.636%	3.636%	3.637%	3.637%	3.637%	3.637%	3.637%	3.637%
26	3.637%	3.637%	3.637%	3.637%	3.637%	3.637%	3.636%	3.636%	3.636%	3.636%	3.636%	3.636%
27	3.636%	3.636%	3.636%	3.636%	3.636%	3.636%	3.637%	3.637%	3.637%	3.637%	3.637%	3.637%
28	1.970%	2.273%	2.576%	2.879%	3.182%	3.485%	3.636%	3.636%	3.636%	3.636%	3.636%	3.636%
29							0.152%	0.455%	0.758%	1.061%	1.364%	1.667%

EXHIBIT 12.4 Depreciation methods for 15-year property.

Recovery period		15
Straight-line depreciation rate		6.667%
150% declining balance rate		10.00%
Depreciable value		$500,000

Year	Straight-Line Method		150% Declining Balance Method			150% Declining less Straight-line	
	Rate	$ Depreciation	Rate	$ Balance	$ Depreciation		
1	6.667%	$33,333.33	10.00%	$500,000	$50,000.00	$16,666.67	$16,666.67
2	6.667%	$33,333.33	10.00%	$450,000.00	$45,000.00	$11,666.67	$28,333.33
3	6.667%	$33,333.33	10.00%	$405,000.00	$40,500.00	$7,166.67	$35,500.00
4	6.667%	$33,333.33	10.00%	$364,500.00	$36,450.00	$3,116.67	$38,616.67
5	6.667%	$33,333.33	10.00%	$328,050.00	$32,805.00	($528.33)	$38,088.33
6	6.667%	$33,333.33	10.00%	$295,245.00	$29,524.50	($3,808.83)	$34,279.50
7	6.667%	$33,333.33	10.00%	$265,720.50	$26,572.05	($6,761.28)	$27,518.22
8	6.667%	$33,333.33	10.00%	$239,148.45	$23,914.85	($9,418.49)	$18,099.73
9	6.667%	$33,333.33	10.00%	$215,233.61	$21,523.36	($11,809.97)	$6,289.76
10	6.667%	$33,333.33	10.00%	$193,710.24	$19,371.02	($13,962.31)	($7,672.55)
11	6.667%	$33,333.33	10.00%	$174,339.22	$17,433.92	($15,899.41)	
12	6.667%	$33,333.33	10.00%	$156,905.30	$15,690.53	($17,642.80)	
13	6.667%	$33,333.33	10.00%	$141,214.77	$14,121.48	($19,211.86)	
14	6.667%	$33,333.33	10.00%	$127,093.29	$12,709.33	($20,624.00)	
15	6.667%	$33,333.33	10.00%	$114,383.96	$11,438.40	($21,894.94)	
		$500,000.00			$397,054.43		

the straight-line depreciation method, the annual depreciation rate is (1/15), which is 0.06667 per year over a 15-year recovery period. So, each year the annual depreciation is $33,335 ($500,000 $\times$ 0.06667).

Under the 150-percent declining balance method, the annual depreciation is 150 percent of 0.06667, which is equal to 0.1. But, unlike the straight-line method in which the annual depreciation charge is applied each year to the total improvement value of $500,000, the charge here is applied to the undepreciated value of the improvement in each of those years. A numerical calculation of the straight-line and the 150-percent declining balance methods is shown in Exhibit 12.4.

In the first year of ownership, the undepreciated balance is $500,000. Applying the 0.1 depreciation rate generates a depreciation charge for the first year of $50,000. After the investor writes off this amount in the first year, the undepreciated balance in the second year is $450,000. Applying the annual rate of 0.1 to this amount yields a depreciation charge in the second year of $45,000. This procedure continues for each year to establish the annual deprecation charge from the first through the 15th year of the recovery period.

Comparing columns 1 and 2 in Exhibit 12.4 clarifies the concept of accelerated depreciation. For the first four years of the recovery period, the 150-percent declining balance method allows an annual depreciation charge that exceeds the straight-line depreciation charge. In the fifth year, the annual depreciation charge under the 150-percent declining balance method is less than the annual depreciation charge under the straight-line method. The adjective *accelerated* implies that under the declining balance method, the investor can depreciate the project more rapidly than under the straight-line method. In a sense, the investor accelerates the maximum allowable depreciation charge over the useful life by taking large write-offs in the first year and small write-offs in the last years.

Depreciation Recapture

The concept of **depreciation recapture** does not arise for both residential rental real estate (27.5-year property) and nonresidential rental real estate. This is explicitly stated by the IRS in *How to Depreciate Property* (Publication #946). For residential and nonresidential investment property, the IRS allows all of the depreciation taken in each of the years of the holding period. However, under special circumstances that involve properties with shorter recovery periods, such as the 15-year property, some of the depreciation taken must be added back to the taxpayer's adjusted income for the tax year. Referring to Exhibit 12.4, at the end of a 4-year holding period, the taxpayer would have claimed $38,617 more than the straight-line depreciation would allow. This represents additional or extra depreciation that would need to be recaptured in the year of the sale. The extra depreciation is eliminated in the middle of the 11th year.

CAPITAL GAIN OR LOSS

The capital gain or loss for investment property is calculated in the same manner as the capital gain for the homeowner. Review the capital gain section in the earlier part of this chapter. To review, the capital gain or loss is the future sale price of the property less the selling costs and the adjusted basis of the property. If the property has been owned for more than one year, it is a long-term capital gain or loss as opposed to a short-term capital gain or loss.

CAPITAL GAIN TAX ON INVESTMENT PROPERTY

Unlike the capital gain treatment for the homeowner who can exclude all, or a part of, the capital gain, the investor must pay taxes on the capital gain. As of this writing, the capital gain tax as it applies to a real estate investment is 20 percent if the investor's income tax bracket is 28 percent or higher.

LIMITS ON CAPITAL LOSSES: THE AT-RISK RULES

Real estate investments are subject to the **at-risk rules.** If the future sale price of the property less the selling costs and the adjusted basis of the property yields a loss, the IRS imposes the at-risk rules. Generally, any loss subject to these rules is allowed only to the extent of the total amount the investor has at risk in the investment at the end of the tax year. The amount that is at risk is the sum of the following:

1. Money and adjusted basis of property contributed to the investment, and
2. Amounts borrowed for use in the investment if the taxpayer is personally liable for repayment, or if the taxpayer pledged property other than this investment as security for the loan. A *nonrecourse loan* for which the taxpayer is not held personally liable cannot be considered part of the at-risk amount.

Consider the following example. A taxpayer buys a property for $300,000 with $60,000 initial equity and a 80-percent loan for $240,000. The loan is secured by the property, and the taxpayer is held responsible for the loan's repayment. If a capital loss of $50,000 occurs from the sale of this real estate investment, then the entire loss of $50,000 can be treated as a loss in the tax year. If the loss were $100,000, it could be treated as a loss in the tax year. If the loss amounted to $350,000, only the amount at risk ($300,000) could be treated as a loss. However, the actual amount of the loss that can be claimed in the tax year depends on the passive activity rules discussed in the following section. The at-risk rules identify the magnitude of a loss that can be considered as a capital loss, while the **passive activity rules** identify the amount of that capital loss that can be claimed in the tax year. The full discussion of the at-risk rules appears in the IRS publication entitled *Passive Activity and At-Risk Rules* (Publication #925).

LIMITS ON CAPITAL LOSSES: THE PASSIVE ACTIVITY RULES

The IRS limits the capital loss deductible in the year of the loss if the real property investment is classified as a passive activity. In simple terms, a **passive activity** is any business activity in which the taxpayer does not show material participation (defined below) during the tax year, or is a rental activity. A real estate investment is by definition a passive activity in this simple IRS definition. However, to fully understand the IRS passive activity rules, the taxpayer must understand what the IRS means by the terms *participation, active participation, material participation,* and *rental activity.*

Participation

To the IRS, **participation** means any work performed by the taxpayer in connection with an activity in which the taxpayer has or owns an interest. It must be work customarily done by owners of this type of activity, and it must not be done in order to avoid the disallowance of a loss under the passive activity rules.

PARTICIPATION AS AN INVESTOR. This type of participation requires involvement in the day-to-day management or operations of the activity. Work done as an investor includes the following:

- Studying and reviewing financial statements or reports on the operation of the activity
- Preparing or compiling summaries of analyses of the finances or the operation of the activity
- Monitoring the finances or the operation of the activity in a nonmanagerial capacity

ACTIVE PARTICIPATION. According to the IRS, *active participation* in a real estate investment occurs if the taxpayer makes management decisions in a significant and bona fide sense. Management decisions that count as active participation include approving tenants, deciding on rental terms, approving expenditures, and similar decisions.

MATERIAL PARTICIPATION. According to the IRS, a trade or business activity is not a passive activity if the taxpayer materially participated in the activity. *Material participation* occurs for a specific tax year if the taxpayer satisfies any one of the following tests. The taxpayer's participation was:

1. More than 500 hours in the activity for the year.
2. Substantially all the participation in the activity of all individuals for the tax year.
3. More than 100 hours in the activity for the year and was at least as much as any other individual for the tax year.
4. Performed for 5 of the last 10 years preceding the tax year. The 5 years do not have to be consecutive.

5. Regular, continuous, and substantial. It had to be performed for at least 100 hours during the tax year. No other individual put in more hours than the taxpayer, and no individual other than the taxpayer received compensation for managing the activity.

The Real Estate Professional and Real Property Rental Activity

The IRS considers real property rental activity a passive activity even if the taxpayer materially participated in that activity unless the taxpayer participated as a *real estate professional*. According to the IRS, the taxpayer qualifies as a real estate professional for the tax year if both of the following requirements are met:

1. More than half of the personal services performed by the taxpayer in all trades or businesses were performed in real property trades or businesses in which the taxpayer materially participated.
2. More than 750 hours of services were performed in real property trades or businesses in which the taxpayer materially participated.

The taxpayer cannot count any personal services performed as an employee in real property trades or businesses unless the taxpayer was at least a 5-percent owner.

A real estate trade or business is defined by the IRS as any of the following activities: development, construction, acquisition, conversion, brokerage, operation or management, and renting or leasing.

In conclusion, if the taxpayer qualifies as a real estate professional, rental real estate activities in which the taxpayer materially participates are not passive activities and therefore are not subject to the passive activity loss limitations. This is the orientation assumed for the investment discussion in the remaining portion of this chapter. However, the issues of passive activity loss and at-risk limits on capital losses come into play when the investment orientation changes to such ownership forms as real estate investment trusts (REITs), limited partnerships, joint tenancies, and tenancies in common.

What Are the Tax Aspects of the Investment Decision?

The Internal Revenue Code has a major impact on the real estate equity investment decision. The potential investor must examine the effects of the tax code during the period of ownership and at the time the property is sold. Moreover, these effects must be evaluated in relation to the investor's own effective tax rate.

TAX LIABILITY DURING OWNERSHIP

During the ownership period, the investor is primarily interested in how the tax code treats the operating expense and debt service items that are considered in establishing the level of before-tax cash flow (BTCF), and what benefits may be received in the form of a tax shelter. The investor first calculates the taxable income that will be received from the property, then calculates the value of after-tax cash flow, which is considered to be the "bottom line" of the income and expense statement.

The starting point of the analysis is the BTCF statement established in the previous chapter as Exhibits 11.1 and 11.3. These two exhibits are repeated in this chapter as Exhibits 12.5 and 12.6.

Property Attributes				
Asking price		$ 950,000		
			Rent	
	#	Rent	Growth	
# two bedroom units	14	$ 525	3.50%	
# one bedroom units	10	$ 425	2.50%	
Management fee		7.25%		
Property tax growth rate		4.00%		
Maintenance & repair growth rate		3.00%		
All other operating expenses		2.00%		
Market Characteristics				
Market vacancy rate		3.5%		
Appreciation rate per year		1.25%		
Financial Market Inputs				
Interest rate		8.00%		
Loan term		30		
Loan to value ratio		80%		
Loan amount		$ 760,000		
Loan payment per month		($5,576.61)		
Annual debt service		($66,919.33)		
Initial equity		$ 190,000		
Discount rate		14.00%		

Depreciation Data

For residential property placed in service in January

1st year	3.485%	
Years 2 - 9	3.636%	

Depreciation allocation to land and improvements

Land		15%
Improvements		85%

Settlement Costs

Discount points		1.5%
Discount dollars	$	11,400
Amortized disc. dollars/yr	$	380.00
Unclaimed amortized disc. dollars/yr	$	9,120.00
Settlement costs	$	18,000
Improvements	$	40,000
Special assessment	$	15,000

Investor's tax rate on income	28%
Investor's tax rate on capital gain	20%

EXHIBIT 12.6 Property's reconstructed income and expense statement.

Revenues: 24 apartment units

Rent reciepts:				Year 1	2	3	4	5	6
14 two bedroom units @ monthly rent	$	525		$ 88,200	$ 91,287	$ 94,482	$ 97,789	$ 101,212	$ 104,754
10 one bedroom units @ monthly rent	$	425		$ 51,000	$ 52,275	$ 53,582	$ 54,921	$ 56,294	$ 57,702
Parking fees:									
$15 per month for second car				$ 2,520	$ 2,520	$ 2,520	$ 2,520	$ 2,520	$ 2,520
$25 per month for covered parking				$ 2,400	$ 2,400	$ 2,400	$ 2,400	$ 2,400	$ 2,400
Laundry Room Collections:				$ 1,500	$ 1,500	$ 1,500	$ 1,500	$ 1,500	$ 1,500
Total Revenues				$ 145,620	$ 149,982	$ 154,484	$ 159,130	$ 163,926	$ 168,876
less vacancies @	3.5%			$ (5,097)	$ (5,249)	$ (5,407)	$ (5,570)	$ (5,737)	$ (5,911)
Effective Gross Income				$ 140,523	$ 144,733	$ 149,077	$ 153,561	$ 158,189	$ 162,965
Expenses:									
Management fees	7.25%	of rent receipts		$ 10,092	$ 10,408	$ 10,735	$ 11,071	$ 11,419	$ 11,778
Property taxes				$ 6,400	$ 6,624	$ 6,856	$ 7,096	$ 7,344	$ 7,601
Insurance premiums				$ 2,500	$ 2,550	$ 2,601	$ 2,653	$ 2,706	$ 2,760
Maintenance and repairs				$ 9,400	$ 9,682	$ 9,972	$ 10,272	$ 10,580	$ 10,897
Supplies and materials				$ 2,400	$ 2,448	$ 2,497	$ 2,547	$ 2,598	$ 2,650
Building custodial costs				$ 15,000	$ 15,300	$ 15,606	$ 15,918	$ 16,236	$ 16,561
Utilities				$ 3,000	$ 3,060	$ 3,121	$ 3,184	$ 3,247	$ 3,312
Reserves for replacement of appliances, carpeting, etc.				$ 4,500	$ 4,590	$ 4,682	$ 4,775	$ 4,871	$ 4,968
Lawn and grounds maintenance				$ 3,300	$ 3,366	$ 3,433	$ 3,502	$ 3,572	$ 3,643
Misc. administrative costs				$ 1,000	$ 1,020	$ 1,040	$ 1,061	$ 1,082	$ 1,104
			Total Expenses	$ 57,592	$ 59,048	$ 60,544	$ 62,079	$ 63,656	$ 65,276
Net Operating Income				$ 82,931	$ 85,684	$ 88,533	$ 91,482	$ 94,532	$ 97,689
Debt Service				($66,919)	($66,919)	($66,919)	($66,919)	($66,919)	($66,919)
Before Tax Cash Flow				$ 16,012	$ 18,765	$ 21,614	$ 24,562	$ 27,613	$ 30,770

EXHIBIT 12.7   Taxable income calculation.

						Year 1	2	3	4	5	6
Net operating income						$ 82,931	$ 85,684	$ 88,533	$ 91,482	$ 94,532	$ 97,689
plus Reserves for replacement						$ 4,500	$ 4,590	$ 4,682	$ 4,775	$ 4,871	$ 4,968
less mortgage interest payment						($60,571)	($60,044)	($59,473)	($58,855)	($58,186)	($57,461)
less depreciation						($28,141)	($29,361)	($29,361)	($29,361)	($29,361)	($29,361)
less amortized points on the loan						($380)	($380)	($380)	($380)	($380)	($380)
less unclaimed amortized											$ (9,120)

Calculating Taxable Income

Exhibit 12.7 shows the procedure for calculating **taxable income** for the real estate investment. The procedure starts with the amount of net operating income (NOI), as shown in Exhibit 12.6. Then, the first step for the investor is to add back the amount of money claimed as reserves for replacement of short-lived items in the operating expenses portion of the BTCF schedule. The IRS requires this because the reserves are not actual operating expenses in the tax year. Next, the investor subtracts the mortgage interest payment, the annual depreciation charge, the amortized points on the loan, and in the last year of the holding period, the unclaimed amortized points are subtracted.

The first deduction from NOI is the mortgage interest payment. The full value of the mortgage payment is not deducted. The tax code does not allow the investor to deduct the principal repayment component of debt service because the IRS does not view the principal repayment as an expense incurred by the owner of income-earning property. The IRS considers it a repayment of the individual's obligation to the lender. The mortgage interest payment, in contrast, is considered to be an expense of ownership and, consequently, is a tax-deductible item. In the example shown in Exhibit 12.8, the interest deduction in the first year is $60,571, while the debt service is $66,919. This is a loan balance repayment of $6,349 during the first year. In the second year, the interest deduction decreases because the loan balance declines $6,348. The interest payment in the second year is $60,044, and the loan repayment is an additional $6,876. Exhibit 12.8 is the monthly amortization for the loan and shows the interest payment and loan repayment on a monthly basis for the six-year holding period.

The second deduction from NOI is the annual depreciation charge. Depreciation is not a true expense of ownership because it does not represent funds that the owner pays out each year. It is a tax concept used to recognize the fact that a real estate investment will undergo physical deterioration, functional obsolescence, and external obsolescence over its useful life. The IRS code recognizes that the investor both desires and deserves a return of the investment over the useful life of the property. In Exhibit 12.5, the allocation of the property value is 15 percent to the land and 85 percent to the improvements. The annual depreciation rates for the holding period are taken from the IRS publication entitled *How to Depreciate Property* (Publication #946), which is replicated as Exhibit 12.3. These rates are 3.485 percent for a property put in service in January of the first year, and 3.636 percent for years 2 to 9.

The Internal Revenue Code allows the deduction of the points paid on the loan. This deduction is an amortized deduction of the dollar value of the points paid over the term of the loan. In Exhibit 12.5, the amortized points are deducted in the calculation of taxable income on an annual basis. In addition, the unclaimed unamortized points are deducted in the final year of the holding period.

Once the mortgage interest payment, depreciation, and amortized points deductions have been calculated over the holding period, they can be used to determine

EXHIBIT 12.8   Mortgage amortization table.

Month	PMT	Interest Paid	Principal Repaid	Loan Balance		Interest Paid for the Year	Principal Repaid for the Year
1	$5,576.61	$5,066.67	$509.94	$759,490.06			
2	$5,576.61	$5,063.27	$513.34	$758,976.71			
3	$5,576.61	$5,059.84	$516.77	$758,459.95			
4	$5,576.61	$5,056.40	$520.21	$757,939.74			
5	$5,576.61	$5,052.93	$523.68	$757,416.06			
6	$5,576.61	$5,049.44	$527.17	$756,888.89			
7	$5,576.61	$5,045.93	$530.68	$756,358.20			
8	$5,576.61	$5,042.39	$534.22	$755,823.98			
9	$5,576.61	$5,038.83	$537.78	$755,286.19			
10	$5,576.61	$5,035.24	$541.37	$754,744.82			
11	$5,576.61	$5,031.63	$544.98	$754,199.85			
12	$5,576.61	$5,028.00	$548.61	$753,651.23		$60,570.56	$6,348.77
13	$5,576.61	$5,024.34	$552.27	$753,098.96			
14	$5,576.61	$5,020.66	$555.95	$752,543.01			
15	$5,576.61	$5,016.95	$559.66	$751,983.36			
16	$5,576.61	$5,013.22	$563.39	$751,419.97			
17	$5,576.61	$5,009.47	$567.14	$750,852.82			
18	$5,576.61	$5,005.69	$570.93	$750,281.90			
19	$5,576.61	$5,001.88	$574.73	$749,707.17			
20	$5,576.61	$4,998.05	$578.56	$749,128.60			
21	$5,576.61	$4,994.19	$582.42	$748,546.18			
22	$5,576.61	$4,990.31	$586.30	$747,959.88			
23	$5,576.61	$4,986.40	$590.21	$747,369.67			
24	$5,576.61	$4,982.46	$594.15	$746,775.52		$60,043.62	$6,875.71
25	$5,576.61	$4,978.50	$598.11	$746,177.42			
26	$5,576.61	$4,974.52	$602.09	$745,575.32			
27	$5,576.61	$4,970.50	$606.11	$744,969.21			
28	$5,576.61	$4,966.46	$610.15	$744,359.06			
29	$5,576.61	$4,962.39	$614.22	$743,744.85			
30	$5,576.61	$4,958.30	$618.31	$743,126.53			
31	$5,576.61	$4,954.18	$622.43	$742,504.10			
32	$5,576.61	$4,950.03	$626.58	$741,877.52			
33	$5,576.61	$4,945.85	$630.76	$741,246.76			
34	$5,576.61	$4,941.65	$634.97	$740,611.79			
35	$5,576.61	$4,937.41	$639.20	$739,972.59			
36	$5,576.61	$4,933.15	$643.46	$739,329.13		$59,472.94	$7,446.39
37	$5,576.61	$4,928.86	$647.75	$738,681.38			
38	$5,576.61	$4,924.54	$652.07	$738,029.31			
39	$5,576.61	$4,920.20	$656.42	$737,372.90			
40	$5,576.61	$4,915.82	$660.79	$736,712.11			

(continued)

taxable income over the investor's planned holding period. Exhibit 12.7 shows the calculation of the taxable income level for the six-year holding period. In the first two years, the taxable income is a negative number. This situation provides a tax shelter.

Tax Shelter

The IRS code allows the owner of the property to subtract the negative taxable income figure from his adjusted gross income figure as reported on Form 1040 in each year of ownership. In other words, the negative taxable income generated by the investment reduces the investor's adjusted gross income and thereby the tax liability from other income sources in those years. In the first year, for example, Exhibit 12.7 shows that the investment property is sheltering the individual's other earnings to the extent of $1,661. For individual investors, application of this tax shelter depends on adjusted gross income

EXHIBIT 12.8   Mortgage amortization table, continued.

41	$5,576.61	$4,911.41	$665.20	$736,046.91			
42	$5,576.61	$4,906.98	$669.63	$735,377.28			
43	$5,576.61	$4,902.52	$674.10	$734,703.18			
44	$5,576.61	$4,898.02	$678.59	$734,024.59			
45	$5,576.61	$4,893.50	$683.11	$733,341.48			
46	$5,576.61	$4,888.94	$687.67	$732,653.81			
47	$5,576.61	$4,884.36	$692.25	$731,961.56			
48	$5,576.61	$4,879.74	$696.87	$731,264.69		$58,854.89	$8,064.44
49	$5,576.61	$4,875.10	$701.51	$730,563.18			
50	$5,576.61	$4,870.42	$706.19	$729,856.99			
51	$5,576.61	$4,865.71	$710.90	$729,146.09			
52	$5,576.61	$4,860.97	$715.64	$728,430.46			
53	$5,576.61	$4,856.20	$720.41	$727,710.05			
54	$5,576.61	$4,851.40	$725.21	$726,984.84			
55	$5,576.61	$4,846.57	$730.05	$726,254.79			
56	$5,576.61	$4,841.70	$734.91	$725,519.88			
57	$5,576.61	$4,836.80	$739.81	$724,780.07			
58	$5,576.61	$4,831.87	$744.74	$724,035.33			
59	$5,576.61	$4,826.90	$749.71	$723,285.62			
60	$5,576.61	$4,821.90	$754.71	$722,530.91		$58,185.55	$8,733.78
61	$5,576.61	$4,816.87	$759.74	$721,771.17			
62	$5,576.61	$4,811.81	$764.80	$721,006.37			
63	$5,576.61	$4,806.71	$769.90	$720,236.47			
64	$5,576.61	$4,801.58	$775.03	$719,461.43			
65	$5,576.61	$4,796.41	$780.20	$718,681.23			
66	$5,576.61	$4,791.21	$785.40	$717,895.83			
67	$5,576.61	$4,785.97	$790.64	$717,105.19			
68	$5,576.61	$4,780.70	$795.91	$716,309.28			
69	$5,576.61	$4,775.40	$801.22	$715,508.07			
70	$5,576.61	$4,770.05	$806.56	$714,701.51			
71	$5,576.61	$4,764.68	$811.93	$713,889.58			
72	$5,576.61	$4,759.26	$817.35	$713,072.23		$57,460.65	$9,458.68
							$46,927.77

as reported on IRS 1040 form. If AGI is less than $100,000, the taxpayer receives the full benefit. When AGI is $150,000 or more, the tax sheltering benefit does not exist. Between these two income levels the impact of tax sheltering declines from 100 percent to zero.

After the taxable income is calculated, the next step in the investment decision is to calculate the value of the **net tax savings.** This calculation yields a dollar figure to represent either the tax benefits provided by a negative taxable income or the tax obligation created by a positive taxable income. To make this calculation, the investor must know the effective tax rate that she will pay in each year over the holding period.

The investor's effective tax rate is not the investor's marginal tax rate. The **marginal tax rate** is the portion of each extra dollar of income that is subject to the income tax; the **effective tax rate** is the portion of the investor's AGI that is paid as income taxes. Because the investor probably has deductions that are not associated with the real estate investment, the effective tax rate is less than the marginal tax rate. For example, the investor who is a homeowner can deduct the mortgage interest payments on the home as well as the real property taxes on the home. In addition, the investor can deduct charitable contributions, a portion of medical expenses, and personal property casualty losses on Schedule A of Form 1040. These deductions could be sufficiently high to lower the effective tax rate below the marginal tax rate on the investor's income.

Consider the following example to show the difference between the effective and the marginal tax rates. If a household is earning $50,000 and they earn one more dollar, the marginal tax rate on that dollar would be 28 percent; the tax on that additional dollar would be 28 cents. But, because of itemized deductions for property taxes, mortgage interest payments, and charitable contributions, the household's adjusted income for tax purposes could be $40,000. After all calculations are made, the household pays $8,000 in taxes for the year. The effective tax rate is $8,000/$40,000 equal to 20 percent. Consequently, the investors' effective rate is the critical rate for analyzing the tax considerations for the "small-time" individual investor in real property.

However, in common practice, the marginal tax rate is used much more frequently than the effective tax rate. When the marginal tax rate is used, the investor should realize that all of the cash flow from the property may not be subject to the same marginal tax rate. This rate increases as AGI increases. So, if the cash flow is small, it will all probably be taxed at the same marginal rate. But, if the cash flow is large, part of it could be taxed at a lower rate and the other part of it at a higher rate as the investor moves into a higher income bracket.

In the numerical example given in Exhibit 12.9, the investor's effective tax rate is assumed to be 28 percent. The net tax savings attributable to the investment is calculated by treating 28 percent of the taxable income as an addition to BTCF if taxable income is negative, or as a reduction in cash flow if the taxable income is positive. The net tax savings in each of the six years is calculated at a rate of 28 percent.

After-Tax Investment Decision: The After-Tax Cash Flows

After the net tax savings is calculated, its numerical value can be added to BTCF. The resultant figure is **after-tax cash flow (ATCF).** It represents the numerical value of the cash flow that the investor can expect in each of the years of the holding period after the income tax impact has been determined. The ATCF figures are also presented in Exhibit 12.9. In the first year, the BTCF is $16,012, and the taxable income is a negative $1,661 (as shown in Exhibit 12.7). Because the taxable income figure is negative, it reduces the investor's AGI and generates a reduction in total taxes that need to be paid; this is the tax savings. The amount of the tax savings in this case is $1,661 times 28 percent, which equals $465. ATCF is the sum of BTCF and the tax savings, which equals $16,447. In the third year, the taxable income figure is a positive $4,002, so tax must be paid on this amount at the rate of 28 percent. The amount of the tax is $1,120, which reduces the BTCF in year 3 of $21,614 by $1,120 to yield an ATCF of $20,494.

After-Tax Investment Decision: Profitability Ratios

The investor can use the ATCF figures in Exhibit 12.9 to evaluate the desirability of the investment. Initial-period profitability ratios can be examined just as they were in the case of the BTCFs. For example, the after-tax equity dividend rate is equal to the initial

| EXHIBIT 12.9 | After-tax cash flow calculation. |

				Year 1	2	3	4	5	6
Before Tax Cash Flow				$ 16,012	$ 18,765	$ 21,614	$ 24,562	$ 27,613	$ 30,770
Net Tax Savings				$ 465	$ (137)	$ (1,120)	$ (2,145)	$ (3,214)	$ (1,774)
After Tax Cash Flow				$ 16,477	$ 18,628	$ 20,494	$ 22,417	$ 24,399	$ 28,996
	Equity Capitalization (Dividend) Rate			8.67%					

period ATCF divided by equity. In the calculations, $16,447 divided by $190,000 equals 8.67 percent. A second initial-period profitability ratio is the after-tax gross return on equity, which is a measure of the ATCF plus mortgage principal repayment plus appreciation. In the example, $16,477 plus $6,349 plus $11,875 divided by $190,000 yields a rate of 18.3 percent. These two initial-period profitability ratios suggest that the investment is not a financially sound opportunity because they do not exceed the investor's 14-percent expected rate of return on equity. The initial-period performance ratios—the operating expense ratio, the debt service coverage ratio, and the breakeven ratio—are the same as they were in the calculations in the BTCF situation earlier in this chapter because they are not affected by the tax savings implications.

TAX LIABILITY FROM THE SALE OF THE PROPERTY

The tax liability from the sale of the property involves the calculation of the capital gain and the tax on that capital gain. The process start with the estimation of the future sales price of the property and the net proceeds from the sale of the property. The analysis continues with the calculation of the adjusted basis. The difference between the net proceeds and the adjusted basis establishes either the capital gain or the capital loss.

Future Sales Price and the Net Proceeds from the Sale

The calculation is the same calculation that was made in Chapter 11 as the first step in calculating the before tax equity reversion (BTER). The information that the investor gathered was that price appreciation in the property's market area was expected to be 1.25 percent per year. Over the anticipated six-year holding period, the future sales price would increase from the acquisition price of $950,000 to $1,023,514. Selling costs of 6 percent amount to $61,411. Net proceeds become $1,023,514 less $61,411 equals $962,103. This calculation originally appeared as Exhibit 11.4 and is replicated here as Exhibit 12.10.

Adjusted Basis

The original basis of income-earning property is determined just as in the case of the home discussed in the first part of this chapter. The basis starts with the purchase price of the property, regardless of the type of financial arrangements used in the acquisition. If the purchase price of the property is $950,000, the basis is $950,000 whether the buyer buys the property for cash or only pays 10 percent of the purchase price in cash and uses

EXHIBIT 12.10	Estimation of before-tax equity reversion.

Appreciation Rate per Year		1.25%
Future Sales Price		$1,023,514
Less selling costs	6.00%	($61,410.84)
Net Proceeds from the Sale		$ 962,103
Less the loan balance at end of sixth year		$713,072
Before Tax Equity Reversion		$ 249,031

a mortgage for the remaining 90 percent. If the property was constructed new, this component of basis consists of the price of the land plus the construction costs of the improvements of the land. These construction costs include labor, materials, contractor payments, architect's fees, building permit fees, utility meter and connection charges, and legal fees connected with the building of the house and other improvements on the property. The basis also includes seller-paid points on the loan and settlement items. If the property is inherited or received as a gift, the basis for the property is its market value on the date it is received. Review the material on the original basis of property as well as the material on the adjusted basis of property presented in the homeownership section of this chapter for both the additions and subtractions that change original basis to adjusted basis.

In addition to the acquisition price, the original basis included $18,000 in settlement costs to acquire the property. The $18,000 included legal fees, title insurance, and other settlement fees. The original basis is $968,000.

During the anticipated six-year period of ownership, the investor assumes that the property will require $40,000 in improvements and that the city will charge $15,000 for a special assessment to install a storm drainage system. The original basis is increased by $55,000.

During the six-year holding period, the depreciation claimed is $28,141 in the first year and $29,361 in each of years 2 through 6. The total amount of depreciation claimed is $174,946. The investor has no expectation of a casualty loss or the receipt of money for selling a right-of-way or an easement.

The adjusted basis becomes $950,000 + $18,000 + $40,000 + $15,000 − $174,946 = $848,054.

Capital Gain or Loss

The capital gain or loss is the difference between the net proceeds from the sale and the adjusted basis. The calculation is shown in Exhibit 12.11. In this case, $962,103 less $848,054 equals $114,049, the capital gain. The tax on the capital gain is 20 percent, so the investor has to pay $22,810 in tax on the capital gain in the year of the sale.[2]

After-Tax Investment Decision: The After-Tax Equity Reversion

The **after-tax equity reversion (ATER)** is simply the BTER adjusted for the capital gain or capital loss effect. In this case, the BTER was estimated as $249,031, and the capital gain tax was $22,810. The resulting figure of $249,031 less $22,810 equals $226,221 which can be considered the ATER.

EXHIBIT 12.11	Estimation of the capital gain or loss.

Item	Original basis at time of purchase	Adjustments during the ownership period	Adjusted net basis at time of sale	Net proceeds at sale	Capital gain	Capital gain tax payment at 20%
Acquisition price	$950,000					
Setlement costs	$18,000					
Improvements		$40,000				
Special assessment		$15,000				
Depreciation		($174,946)				
Total	$968,000	($119,946)	$848,054	$962,103	$114,049	$22,810

What Is the Investment Decision?

In Exhibit 11.6 of Chapter 11, which focused on the BTCF considerations, the investor discovered that the present value of the cash flows and the equity reversion discounted at 14 percent, the investor's required rate of return ($199,431), was greater than the initial equity investment ($190,000). The decision based on before-tax consideration is to buy.

It is now time to see what the effect of the tax considerations have on the investment decision. To handle this task, the investor simply substitutes the ATCFs and the ATER into the structure of Exhibit 12.12 (which is a replication of Exhibit 11.6). At the 14-percent discount rate, the present value of the financial benefits is $182,665, while the initial equity is $190,000. The decision after the federal income tax considerations are brought into the picture is to not buy the property at the price of $950,000.

However, if the price declined to $920,000, then the present value of the financial benefits would be $184,748 while the initial equity would be $184,000. At the price of $920,000 with all other things held constant, the investment becomes financially feasible for the investor.

HANDLING A CAPITAL LOSS

If the investment property generates a capital loss when it is sold, the capital loss figures into the tax calculation in the year of the sale. Two issues are part of this discussion—the limit on the capital loss deduction and the capital loss carryover of the loss to subsequent tax years.

LIMIT ON THE DEDUCTION. The capital loss that can be claimed in the year of sale is limited to the smaller of the following values:

1. $3,000 ($1,500 if married and filing separately)
2. the net loss suffered from the sale of all long-term assets (This includes the investment property and other assets such as stocks and bonds.)

CAPITAL LOSS CARRYOVER. The effect of the capital loss carryover can be shown by the following example. First, the taxpayer suffers an $8,000 loss on the sale of the prop-

---

EXHIBIT 12.12   Calculation of the present value of the investment.

Discount Rate		14.00%				
Year	ATCF	Reversion	Capital Gain Tax	Total Cash Flows	Factor	PV Cash Flows
1	$ 16,477			$ 16,477	0.8772	$ 14,453
2	$ 18,628			$ 18,628	0.7695	$ 14,334
3	$ 20,494			$ 20,494	0.6750	$ 13,833
4	$ 22,417			$ 22,417	0.5921	$ 13,273
5	$ 24,399			$ 24,399	0.5194	$ 12,672
6	$ 28,996	$ 249,031	$ -	$ 278,027	0.4556	$ 126,665
						$ 195,230
	Initial Equity					$ 190,000
	Net Present Value at the Discount Rate					$ 5,230

erty but has a $9,000 gain on the sale of stocks in the tax year. Here the "net loss" does not occur because the long-term gain from the stock sale eliminates the long-term loss from the sale of the investment property. If the taxpayer did not have the long-term gain from the sale of the stock, then the long-term capital "net loss" would be $8,000. The limit on the deduction for the loss is the smaller of $3,000 or $8,000. The taxpayer could deduct $3,000 in the year of sale and carry over $5,000 to the next year. If the taxpayer had a long-term capital gain of $5,000 in the second year, the "net loss" would be zero because the $5,000 gain balances out the $5,000 loss carried over to the second tax year.

What Are Capital Gain Deferral Techniques?

The Internal Revenue Code allows the investor to defer realization of long-term capital gain and to defer the payment of capital gains tax until the time the capital gain is actually received. The deferral of these gains is a very important consideration to the investor because of the tax savings in the year of the transaction or sale. The capital gain deferral techniques are the *nontaxable exchange,* the *partially nontaxable exchange,* and the *deferred exchange.* For more information about these deferral techniques, refer to the IRS publication entitled *Sales and Other Dispositions of Assets* (Publication #544).

NONTAXABLE EXCHANGE

The **nontaxable exchange** relies on an understanding of two important concepts—**like-kind property** and **qualifying property.** The first requirement for a nontaxable exchange is that the income-earning properties being traded are of "like kind." The term *like kind* refers to the nature of the income-producing property. The tax code does not require consideration of the quality of the property in terms of its construction or its condition, nor does the tax code require consideration of the size of the properties that are being exchanged. What the tax code does require is that real estate be exchanged for real estate. This ruling would allow a trade of investment property for investment property (commercial space for an apartment building), investment property for business property (an apartment building for a retail store that the investor will now operate), and improved property for land. However, it would not allow an exchange of investment real estate for a residence. Moreover, real estate cannot be exchanged for personal property because these assets are not viewed as like kind.

The second requirement for a nontaxable exchange is that the property that the taxpayer gives up and the property received in exchange must be held for investment or productive activity in a trade or business. This is what is meant by the term *qualifying property.*

The nontaxable exchange occurs in its simplest form when the like-kind, qualifying properties have the same fair market value. Here, the two taxpayers simply retain the adjusted basis of the property they had before the exchange and apply it to the new property received in the exchange. However, in an exchange, one investor may receive a property that is worth more than the property currently owned and the other investor may receive property that is worth less than the property currently owned. In this situation, the financial arrangement must contain a cash payment or an exchange of personal property as well as real property. This cash payment or personal property is offered as part of the trade by the individual who currently owns the lower-valued property. The cash is received by the individual who trades the higher-valued property for the property of lower value. In this exchange, the cash payment or the value of the personal property received by the investor who is trading to a lower-valued property is subject to taxation if a capital gain is realized. The other investor defers all capital gains. The IRS refers to this situation as a **partially nontaxable exchange.**

In a nontaxable exchange, both investors must calculate the basis of the properties that they own after the exchange. They retain the adjusted basis that they originally had before the exchange, and they use the cash payment or the value of the personal property as an adjustment to the basis after the exchange. The investor who receives the cash payment or personal property subtracts its value from the adjusted basis. Through this process, each investor takes on the tax basis held by the other investor. Each investor's basis in the new property is the basis in the old property less any funds (the "boot") received plus the gain recognized. The important point is that both of the investors who entered into the tax-free exchange are able to defer capital gains tax and depreciation recapture. One investor defers all capital gains tax and depreciation recapture, and other investor is required to pay on the cash or personal property received on the day of the trade if a capital gain occurred.

DEFERRED EXCHANGE

A **deferred exchange** occurs when the taxpayer transfers investment property to another person and at a later point in time receives a like-kind investment property, which is known as the **replacement property.** The replacement property must be identified within 45 days of the date the original property was given up in the transfer. The identification of the replacement property must be a written document that contains pertinent information about the property. For real property, the IRS considers a legal description or at least a street address necessary. If the taxpayer receives a property within the 45-day identification period, the IRS considers it the replacement property.

If, before the replacement property is received, the taxpayer receives cash or unlike property in full payment for the original property transferred, the IRS will treat the transaction as a sale rather than a deferred exchange.

The taxpayer can transfer the original property for multiple properties under the following condition. Regardless of the number of properties the taxpayer transfers, the maximum number of replacement properties the taxpayer can receive is the larger of (1) three, or (2) any number of properties whose total fair market value at the end of the 45-day identification period is not more than double the total fair market value on the date of the transfer of the property or properties the taxpayer gave up.

The replacement property can be a property that is still being developed or constructed, but it must still be a like-kind, qualifying property. The fair market value of this property can be estimated as of the day the taxpayer expects to receive it.

The taxpayer must receive the replacement property by the earlier of the two following time periods:

1. The 180th day after the date on which the original property was transferred in the exchange, or
2. The due date, including extensions, for the taxpayer's tax return for the tax year in which the transfer of the property occurred.

LIKE-KIND EXCHANGES USING QUALIFIED INTERMEDIARIES

The nontaxable and deferred exchanges can be handled for the taxpayer by a qualified intermediary who enters into a written exchange agreement with the taxpayer to acquire and transfer the taxpayer's property and to acquire and transfer the replacement property. The written agreement must expressly limit the taxpayer's rights to receive, pledge, borrow, or otherwise obtain the benefits of money or other property held by the qualified intermediary.

The qualified intermediary cannot be (1) the taxpayer's agent at the time of the transaction (This includes any person who has been the taxpayer's employee, attorney, accountant, investment banker or broker, real estate agent or broker within the two-year period before the transfer of the property) or (2) a person related to the taxpayer or the taxpayer's agent. A very specific list of relationships is provided by the IRS to evaluate the concept of "relationship" in this case. The list includes both family ties and various business relationships.

What Is an Installment Sale?

The Internal Revenue Code also contains a procedure known as the **installment sale,** by which capital gains can be partially deferred in the year the property is sold. The deferral of capital gains taxes arises in this case because the full capital earned through the sale is not received in total in the year of the sale. The capital gain is spread over the years of the installment plan that is created by the taxpayer, the seller of the property, and the buyer at the time of the sale. Therefore, the taxpayer pays capital gains taxes over a multiyear period instead of having to pay the full capital gains tax in the year of the sale.

To calculate the taxable portion for each year, the seller must first calculate *gross profit,* which is the selling price less the sum of the adjusted basis, selling expenses, and recaptured additional depreciation. The selling price includes all financial benefits the seller receives from the buyer. These benefits include cash, the fair market value of securities, the unpaid balance of a mortgage that the buyer assumes, and the value of the installment note that the buyer signs as part of the deal. Once the gross profit is calculated, the *contract price* is determined by subtracting the mortgage balance that the buyer assumed from the selling price. Then, gross profit is divided by contract price to obtain the *gross profit percentage.*

The gross profit percentage is applied to the payments received in all years to obtain the capital gain in that year. This capital gain is treated in the usual manner—that is, it is added to ordinary income and taxed at the seller's effective tax rate in that year. For example, the taxpayer sells a parcel of land for $100,000. The adjusted basis of the land is $40,000. The gross profit is $60,000, making the gross profit percentage equal to 60 percent. (The gross profit is the capital gain from the sale.) The buyer pays $20,000 at the time of purchase and agrees to pay four more annual installments of $20,000 for a contract price of $100,000. The capital gain that has to be reported for each of the five installments of $20,000 is $20,000 times 60 percent, or $12,000 per installment.

If all of the other factors remained the same but the installment plan called for a total of 10 installments of $10,000 each, then the capital gain to report in each year would be $6,000.

The seller's purchase money mortgage to the buyer can be considered an installment plan. Consider the following situation. The taxpayer sells a parcel of land for $100,000. The adjusted basis of the land is $40,000. The gross profit is $60,000, making the gross profit percentage equal to 60 percent. The buyer pays $80,000 at the time of purchase and agrees to pay five annual installments of $4,000 for a contract price of $100,000. The capital gain that has to be reported for the year of sale is $80,000 times 60 percent, which equals $48,000, and for each of the five installments the capital gain to report is $4,000 times 60 percent, which equals $2,400 per installment.

More information can be obtained on the installment sale provisions from IRS Publication #537, *Installment Sales*.

Chapter Summary

Both the homeowner and the equity investor are affected by the Internal Revenue Code both during the time the property is owned and at the time the property is sold. The homeowner is allowed to make annual deductions for mortgage interest payments and real property taxes. When the single-family residence is sold and a capital gain is made, a capital gain exclusion is available to homeowners who meet the ownership and use tests established by the tax code.

For the real estate equity investor, the tax effects are more complicated. During the ownership period, the investor must establish the useful life and a depreciation technique for the property. The depreciation charge is an additional annual deduction allowed by the Internal Revenue Code. Upon the sale of the property, the equity investor must calculate the capital gain, the excess depreciation to be recaptured, and the minimum tax that must be paid. If a capital gain is made, and if excess depreciation was claimed, a tax liability must be paid unless the investor makes use of tax-deferral techniques known as the tax-free exchange or the installment sales plan.

The investor now can begin to make a rational judgment. The initial period profitability ratios may indicate that the investment is a good opportunity, but the analysis is still not complete. The tax impact at the time of sale of the property must be analyzed. Thus, all of the following factors must be considered in the process of analyzing an investment opportunity.

1. The amount, the timing, and the pattern of the BTCFs that arise from the property over its entire holding period.
2. All tax effects, both tax shelter and tax liability, that arise during the holding period.
3. The cash proceeds (or obligations, as the case may be) from the sale after analyzing all tax factors, including capital gains tax and the ordinary income tax liability on the recapture of the excess of accelerated depreciation over straight-line depreciation.
4. Recognition of the time value of money. A dollar received today has more value than a dollar received tomorrow. Money has a time value because when its payment is deferred, the ultimate recipient must sacrifice the regular savings rate of interest that could be earned at the bank and must forego special opportunities that may be available.

The present-value calculation gives information on more of these factors than the initial period rates of performance do. The present-value example used in this chapter enables the investor to consider cash flows from operations over the holding period, tax shelter effects over the holding period, and the time value of money. The after-tax equity dividend rate gives no information on cash flows after the initial period nor on the time value of money.

A website has been established for this chapter at http://epley.swcollege.com.

Review Questions

1. What expenditures associated with home ownership does the Internal Revenue Code allow as annual deductions? Which expenditures are not allowed?
2. Define adjusted basis and discuss the components of adjusted basis for both the single-family homeowner and the real estate equity investor.
3. Define long-term capital gain and explain how it is calculated for both the single-family homeowner and the real estate equity investor.
4. Discuss the methods by which long-term capital gain can be deferred by both the single-family homeowner and the real estate equity investor.
5. Explain how the equity investor calculates a 200-percent declining balance.
6. Explain the nature and purpose of the modified accelerated cost recovery system.
7. What are the Internal Revenue Code guidelines for the use of depreciation techniques for various categories of real estate?
8. Explain the process by which taxable income is calculated and how it is used by the equity investor to calculate the tax impact and consequently the level of after-tax cash flow (ATCF).

Discussion Questions

1. Explain how the decision to purchase a home might be affected if the federal government eliminated the homeowner's right to deduct annual expenditures that directly pertain to the physical asset.
2. Explain what the effect would be on an equity investment if all of the capital gain on the property were taxed as ordinary income.

Problems

1. Calculate the annual depreciation charges shown in Exhibit 12.5 on the assumption that depreciable real estate is 75 percent of the acquisition price.
2. For the investment decision portrayed in Exhibits 12.5 through 12.12, analyze the impact on the investment of each of the following changes that take place independently of one another.
   a. The investor's expected rate of return drops to 13 percent.
   b. The rent for two-bedroom units increases to $550.
   c. The investor's effective tax rate on income increases to 36 percent.
   d. Capital gains are taxed at 60 percent instead of 20 percent.
   e. The appreciation rate increases to 1.5 percent.

1. The issue of landscaping is a special situation in the rules governing deprecia-
    tion. An example used in "How to Depreciate Property" (Publication 946 for
    2000, p. 4) clarifies the issue. To paraphrase the information of page 4, the tax-
    payer cannot depreciate the land or the cost of land including the costs of
    clearing, grading, planting, and landscaping. But, the taxpayer can depreciate cer-
    tain landscaping costs incurred in preparing the land for business use. These
    landscaping costs must be closely associated with other depreciable property for
    which a recovery period can be specified. The example used refers to trees and
    shrubs planted around the perimeter of a building and other trees and shrubs
    planted away from the building at the periphery of the lot. If the building is
    destroyed or demolished, the landscaping at its perimeter will also be destroyed;
    this landscaping can be depreciated. The landscaping at the edge of the lot cannot
    be depreciated.

2. The 20% capital gain tax rate used in this example is based on the assumption
    that the individual investor sold the section 1231 property (real property held for
    the production of rent income) and that his marginal tax rate was 28 percent or
    higher. This is explicit in Sales and Dispositions of Assets (Publication 544).
    Other assets can have capital gain tax rates of 28 or 25 percent. If the investor
    has a marginal tax rate of 15 percent, the applicable capital gains tax rate can be
    either 15 or 10 percent. At this point, the investor needs professional tax planning
    assistance from a tax accountant or tax attorney.

    An additional stipulation that exists in the tax code complicates the calcula-
    tion of the capital gain. Using the example on p. 354, the total depreciation taken
    of $174,946 is subtracted from the capital gain of $114,049, yielding a negative
    $60,897. Since the gain cannot be negative, the taxpayer must report as ordinary
    income 25 percent of the total depreciation taken. In this case, it is $43,737. A
    calculation procedure for this calculation appears below.

Net proceeds from the sale	$ 962,103
Less the Adjusted Basis	– $ 848,054
Capital Gain	$ 114,049
Less cost recovery taken (total depreciation taken)	– $ 174,946
Gain subject to tax	0
Plus 25% of cost recovery taken (total depreciation taken)	$ 43,737

The Decision to Buy or Sell the Property

Agency and the Real Estate Agent

1. What is a real estate agent, and why would one be needed?

2. What are the types of agent relationships with the client?

3. How does misrepresentation and fraud occur?

4. What is a listing, and what are the types of contracts?

5. What is the difference between a REALTOR® and a real estate agent?

6. What are the typical clauses in a listing contract?

7. How does federal law and state regulation influence the listing contract?

When finished with this chapter, the student should be able to:

1. Explain the types of agency relationships with the client.

2. Explain the difference between misrepresentation and fraud.

3. Discuss the important clauses in a sales contract.

4. Discuss the listing, its typical components, and the types of listing contracts.

5. Explain how federal law and state regulations can affect the listing contract.

affirmative marketing agreement

agency

agent

broker

buyer's agency

client

commission

commission split

cooperating broker

customers

disclosed agency

dual agency

exclusive agency listing

exclusive right-to-sell listing

express agency

facilitator

fiduciary

fraud

implied agency

leasing agent

listing

listing agent

listing contract

misrepresentation

multiple listing

multiple listing service (MLS)

net listing

open listing

oral agency

principal

procuring cause

puffing

ratification

recovery fund

representation

sales agents

selling agent

single agency

special agency

specific performance

subagency

subagent

tenant's agent

INTRODUCTION

Anyone who owns real property or wants to buy or lease has the option of performing each step in searching, negotiating, and financing with his own knowledge, time, and expense. Many people, however, may elect to employ the services of a specialist—often a licensed real estate agent—to perform these steps as their representative. The potential consumer of these services should understand the agency–principal relationship to make an informed decision about whether to approach an agent for assistance.

Why Is the Decision to
Employ an Agent Important?

Several types of parties involved with real property may have the desire to employ an agent to satisfy a particular need. For example, an owner of property may ask an agent to locate a buyer. A tenant may need to relocate and rent more suitable space. An owner or property manager may desire to locate tenants to rent space in an office building, a shopping center, or an apartment.

The party in need of help must invest the time, expertise, and money to satisfy the need without any help. The client must ask, Can I do this by myself, and do I want to spend the time? If the answer is no, an agent is needed.

WHAT IS AN AGENT?

An **agent** represents the interests of another. Agents are regarded as specialists who give professional advice and charge either a percentage of the transaction price, called a **commission,** or a fee for time and expenses. In the real estate business, agents are regarded as *special agents* who create a **special agency** with the **client** (also known as the **principal**), who gives the agent specific instructions. Agents represent clients to the general public, who are the **customers.**

HOW IS THE AGENCY CREATED?

An agency should be created with a written agreement between the agent and the client. This document creates the agency, identifies the assignment with instructions for the agent, establishes the payment agreement, and announces this agency to the world. The agent provides **representation,** which is more than a service. The most critical proof of the creation of the agency is (1) the written agreement between the parties involved and (2) its disclosure. An agency is not necessarily created by the party who pays the fee.

EXPRESS AGENCY. An **express agency** is an agreement between the agent and the client, preferably in writing. This is the best and most frequent type of agency.

IMPLIED AGENCY. A customer could view an agent as a representative of her interests by the agent's words, actions, and conduct. All agents must avoid this impression (known as **implied agency**) by disclosing any prior express agency with a client to a potential customer at first contact. Agents must be extremely careful to ensure that their words and actions do not create an unintended or implied agency in the minds of the customers.

ORAL AGENCY. An **oral agency** may be created between the agent and the client, but this is not recommended. Further, the state licensing authority and the statute of frauds may require that an agency agreement be written to be enforceable in a court of law. A written agreement ensures that the agent is paid his commission or fee upon completion of the assignment.

RATIFICATION. A special set of circumstances could exist in which a principal is asked to condone and approve, or ratify, the actions of an agent even though the action was done without a formal agreement with the principal. This process is known as **ratification.** If the principal elects this option, the agency is "ratified." Should the principal not ratify the actions, no agency agreement exists.

PROCURING CAUSE. The fee is paid to the agent who was the procuring cause, or who was the cause of the transaction to be completed.

TYPES OF AGENTS AND AGENCY IN REAL ESTATE

Real estate agents are licensed by the state. All 50 states have relied on the concept of a **broker** to be the agent who represents the legal entity called the **agency** in a transaction. The broker has the authority to (1) establish the agency and (2) assemble **sales agents** who are responsible to the broker.

The IRS distinguishes between sales personnel who are associated with the firm as *employees* as opposed to *independent contractors*. Employees have job requirements such as regular hours, direction and supervision, a company retirement plan, and income tax withholding. Independent contractors have none of these characteristics. They are associated with the firm for the quality and volume of their work. The IRS should be consulted for a list of criteria.

Several types of agency may be created to satisfy the needs of the client.

Owner/Seller Agency

This agency is the oldest type and has dominated the real estate profession for many years. The agent represents the owner/seller with specific instructions to locate a customer or buyer who is "ready, willing, and able" to purchase the property at an announced price. The customer must be informed early in the transaction whom the agent represents.

This type of agency is known as the **listing,** which means that an owner selects a broker to employ as an agent and list the property for sale. The **listing contract** is the agency agreement that contains the instructions to the broker, property features, and payment terms.

Subagency

The owner/client and the broker must make a decision if any other **cooperating brokers** in competing firms will be offered **subagency.** A **subagent** is a cooperating broker who agrees to take instruction from the owner's broker, represent the client, and follow the terms in the agency agreement. A subagent who locates a customer will receive a portion of the negotiated fee. The owner's broker agrees to split the fee in exchange for a successful transaction. In sum, if the offer of subagency is accepted by a cooperating broker, one client has two agents. Of course, all of the sales agents in both firms now represent the same client.

Buyer's Agency

In a **buyer's agency,** the buyer/client employs an agent to represent his interests only, which typically means to locate a specific property that satisfies the buyer's criteria and to assist in the negotiation of the offer. The agent typically is paid by the buyer, although other forms of compensation are available.

Single Agency

A **single agency** is an agent who represents only one client in a transaction, such as the seller, buyer, lessor, or lessee.

Dual Agency

A broker who contracts with a seller and a buyer simultaneously is in a **dual agency.** An agency agreement is signed by both clients, and both must be informed early in the transaction about the other client. In sum, one agent represents two clients.

Tenant's Agent and Leasing Agent

A tenant desiring office, industrial, or retail space might employ a **tenant's agent** to search the market and negotiate the contract. The agent typically is a specialist in leasing arrangements. The negotiations might be with the **leasing agent,** who is employed by the owner to locate suitable tenants for the space that is for rent.

Facilitator

One concept that has been discussed by real estate agents is to allow the agency to function as a **facilitator** who simply brings the parties together for a fee. The agency's fiduciary responsibility (defined below) is eliminated, which means that liability is minimized. This concept is not yet popular among the state legislatures because it allows the agent to accept a state license to function as an agent while eliminating the responsibility of an agent in certain transactions.

Disclosed Agency

A recent trend among state legislatures is to require the real estate broker to disclose the agency relationship to a potential customer. Early in the discussion with a future buyer or seller, the agent must inform all parties about the nature of the agency relationship. This is done to assure that every party is well informed on the proper role of the agent. **Disclosed agency** is needed prior to the disclosure of any confidential information on the facts and details of the property, parties involved, and the transaction.

THE RESPONSIBILITIES OF THE AGENT

The agent has a **fiduciary** relationship to the client, which is considered to be a position of trust to administer the client's affairs and assets in the client's best interests. The agent's responsibilities include the following actions:

- *Accountability:* The receipt of all monies should be documented and held in trust to conform with the regulations of state licensing boards.
- *Confidentiality:* Relevant facts that could harm the client's position should not be made known.
- *Disclosure:* All known relevant facts must be made known.
- *Obedience:* The client's legal instructions must be followed.
- *Skill, care, and obedience:* Reasonable due diligence must be practiced in gathering facts and negotiating the contracts.

How Is Agency Ended?

Both the agent and the principal should understand the typical reasons for terminating an agency relationship. Reasons exist for an automatic cancellation by certain actions of either party. These reasons include the following:

ACTIONS BY AGENT
Completion of the purpose of the agency
Mutual agreement by both parties
Unprofessional actions

Loss of license
Bankruptcy
Conviction of a felony
Death

ACTIONS BY PRINCIPAL
Death
Breech of agency by principal
Bankruptcy
Mutual agreement by other parties

OTHERS
Expiration of agency agreement
Condemnation of property
Destruction of property

When Does Misrepresentation by the Agent Occur?

All agents must represent the material facts about the property in a clear and accurate manner. **Misrepresentation** of facts can be *intentional* or *unintentional*.

INTENTIONAL MISREPRESENTATION

Intentional misrepresentation is **fraud** if the affected party can (1) show intent, (2) prove that the information was used as the basis for making a decision, and (3) provide evidence that she suffered a dollar loss from the transaction. Several remedies may be available. First, the affected party may file a complaint with the state real estate commission. After an investigation and hearing, the commission may revoke or suspend the agent's license. Second, in some states the damaged party can ask the real estate commission to award actual damages. Third, the damaged party can sue the agent in civil court for additional damages or for the total amount.

UNINTENTIONAL MISREPRESENTATION

In most cases, misrepresentation is unintentional. For example, the potential buyer may ask the agent, "Does this farm have a good water supply?" The agent might reply that it does without bothering to check. This response could be viewed as misrepresentation to the buyer if the farm does not have a good supply of water. An agent *should not provide unverified facts to the potential buyer.* An alternative is to refer the buyer's questions to the owner. The agent could have responded, "I don't know," or "Let's ask the owner."

To protect real estate firms against unintentional misrepresentation, some states have established a special fund, called a **recovery fund,** that can be used to pay damaged consumers. In addition, the sales agent and the broker could still lose their licenses for grossly flagrant disregard of pertinent facts. Many firms carry "errors and omission insurance" to cover damages caused by their erroneous information or omission of information.

PUFFING

Agents must carefully distinguish between *opinions* and *facts*. Opinions, which must be identified as opinions, are offered to provide helpful information without intention to misrepresent. Statements of fact must be accurate. An exaggeration of a property's features is called **puffing.**

Property described as "the best investment that you've ever seen!" or "the most wonderful view in town!" is puffing. A description that includes the statement that the "property contains 4,575 square feet" or "a septic tank is not present" is a material fact and must be correct to avoid misrepresentation.

THE DISTINCTION BETWEEN A REAL ESTATE AGENT AND A REALTOR®

A real estate agent may elect to join the national trade group, which is called the National Association of REALTORS® (the NAR). NAR members abide by the NAR Code of Ethics, may use the symbol "R" in their advertising, and may be correctly described as a "REALTOR®," which is a trademarked term. Real estate agents who do not join do not enjoy these characteristics.

Thus, all REALTORS® must be real estate agents, but not all real estate agents are REALTORS®.

What Is the Listing?

The listing is discussed in additional detail here for two reasons. First, it has formed the largest volume of real estate business for many years. Second, members of the general public typically will encounter it first as they consider the purchase of a home.

The term *listing* is used to describe the contractual relationship between the agent and the owner of property. The owner typically instructs the agent to find a buyer who is ready, willing, and able to purchase the property. The agent expects to be compensated for accomplishing this task by being paid a commission, which is usually calculated as a percentage of the selling price.

AGENT–PRINCIPAL RELATIONSHIP

In a typical listing between the owner of property and an agent, the firm is viewed as the *agent* and the owner as the *principal*. The agency relationship must be created for the firm by the principal broker in the firm. Although a firm could have several brokers, only one could have the authority to contract. Thus, this agent–principal relationship can be described as being between the authorized listing broker representing the firm and the principal (the owner of the property).

PAYMENT OF THE COMMISSION

The commission or fee is not paid until the closing. At that time, all parties are certain the buyer can acquire the needed funds and will proceed with the transaction. Also, the buyer has either reviewed the abstract or has obtained a title insurance policy from the seller to confirm that the seller can convey all rights of ownership for the property. If the fee is paid when the sales contract is accepted by the seller, legal problems such as recovering the fee from the agent can arise if the buyer defaults before the closing. Thus, bills on the transaction are paid at the settlement.

Why Are Listings Important to the Agent?

A real estate firm has an incentive to establish as many agency relationships with as many principals as possible for two reasons. First, the firm's salespeople need an inventory to show prospective buyers. If the firm does not have an inventory of properties of various price ranges and types, the salespeople cannot satisfy the needs and desires of a prospective buyer. If the inventory is insufficient, the firm must rely on the listings of competitors, and consequently the commissions must be shared. A shared fee is not the maximum fee. Second, the firm will always receive a part of the fee from its own listings regardless of who sells the property. For these two reasons, listing is sometimes described as the "bread and butter" of a traditional brokerage office.

A PROPERLY LISTED PROPERTY

A cliché used in the real estate business is that "a properly listed property is a sold property." A proper listing typically has the following characteristics:

1. *The list price is close to the market value.* The seller should list the property for a price that is comparable to the prices of recently sold similar properties. A price that is too high will discourage prospective buyers.

2. *The agent has explained the meaning of the listing contract to the seller.* The agent should always spend whatever time is necessary in explaining to the seller the clauses and terms of the employment relationship. The seller should be told that the agent is working for the seller, the terms of that employment contained within the contract, and that a commission is to be paid when the agent's duty is accomplished.

3. *The agent has made a reasonable effort to uncover all pertinent facts about the property.* The agent needs to inquire about the condition of the property to determine whether it has any unfavorable features, such as sewer or septic tank problems, termite infestation, and water drainage problems.

Other characteristics of a listing depend on individual preferences. For example, a proper listing might also include the following features:

4. *A request by the agent to the seller to remove all personal property that does not remain with the real property.* If a buyer does not actually view these items, no confusion will arise later about whether they are included in the purchase price. Fixtures remain with the property.

5. *A request by the agent to the seller to provide a survey of the property boundaries.* The buyer who is informed in advance of the precise boundary of the property knows exactly what is being purchased.

6. *A request by the agent to the seller to provide an up-to-date abstract.* By accepting this provision when the property is listed, the seller agrees to provide the abstract and pay the expense. If the buyer later requests title insurance, the abstract can be used as the basis for the insurance policy.

7. *A request by the agent to the seller to give the buyer possession of the property on the day of closing.* A buyer who completes the closing but does not take possession has little control over damages to the property or a later failure by the seller to vacate the premises.

In a normal market, the proper listing of a property should eliminate many of the potential problems involved in its sale.

LISTING AGENT

The **listing agent** is legally bound to the needs and desires of the seller. The seller must be convinced that the agent's firm employs salespersons who are professional and competent, and that the property will be represented to the maximum number of potential buyers. In addition, the agent can counsel the seller on the firm's ability to help transfer to another property after the sale.

SELLING AGENT

The sales agent counsels the buyer, shows the available inventory, helps arrange financing, helps to prepare the offer, and in some circumstances presents the contract to the seller. The **selling agent** attempts to sell the buyer a property from the firm's own inventory. If the firm is both the listing agent *and* the selling agent, it retains all of the fee.

What Are the Types of Listing Contracts?

EXCLUSIVE RIGHT-TO-SELL LISTING CONTRACT

The distinguishing characteristic of an **exclusive right-to-sell listing** contract is that the listing broker is entitled to a fee regardless of who sells the property. The primary advantage to the broker is that the money and effort expended on advertising and showing the property will be to her benefit. The advantage to the owner is that a broker who holds an exclusive right-to-sell listing contract will usually put the most effort into selling the property. Even if the owner sells the property during the listing period, the broker is entitled to a commission. Moreover, a real estate firm may have prearranged agreements to show and sell property listed by other firms; a predetermined commission split is paid if the property is sold. Brokers prefer exclusive right-to-sell listings because of the protection of fee feature.

Exhibit 13.1 shows the terms of a typical right-to-sell listing contract. The provisions of the contract are described hereafter.

Agency

The first section of the contract establishes the agent–client relationship and sets forth several points of agreement between the broker and the client.

TIME PERIOD. The listing runs for a specific time period with a definite beginning and ending date. The state real estate license law may prohibit an automatic extension period. The broker is given the exclusive right-to-sell agency within this period.

MULTIPLE LISTING SERVICE. A **multiple listing service (MLS)** advertises the property among participating brokers, giving the property maximum exposure. The broker must pay the advertising expenses and agrees to cooperate with other brokers.

December 1, 2002

AGENCY

Time Period. For the services of the following named real estate broker, I list with this broker, from ___December 1___ ___2002___ to ___March 1___ ___2002___, inclusive, the property described below. I give this broker the exclusive right to sell this property within the time period.

MLS. I ☒ authorize ☐ do not authorize this broker to list the property with any multiple listing service in which he or she is a member, at the broker's expense, and to accept the cooperation and assistance of other brokers.

Right to Cancel. I may cancel this contract within the listing period by giving ___15___ days notice and paying a fee to the broker of ___$2,000.00___.

Referrals. I agree to refer to this broker all parties expressing an interest in purchasing this property.

PRICE

List Price. The broker will advertise this property at a price of ___$252,500___. The broker agrees to present all offers to purchase at a lower price to me for my consideration.

Deposits. The broker may accept deposits on offers to purchase and retain them until closing or my rejection of the offer.

Fixtures and Personal Property Included. The above list price includes all household fixtures normally considered to be included in a comparable property. Exceptions include the following: _The pool table does not remain, the master bath drapes should be removed, the storage shed in the backyard does not remain._

Encumbrances. I authorize the holder of any note secured by this property to disclose to the broker the precise terms of the note.

COMMISSION

Amount. I agree to pay the broker ___7___% of the selling price for (a) the sale or exchange of the property within the listing period by any person, OR (b) the sale or exchange of the property within 120 days after the listing expiration to any potential buyer shown the property by the broker during the listing period. I UNDERSTAND THAT THIS COMMISSION IS NEGOTIABLE.

Capable Buyer. The buyer must be ready, willing, and able to purchase the property as evidenced by the successful completion of the closing.

Default. If I default on an accepted contract of sale, I agree to pay the broker the commission.

REPRESENTATION

The real estate agency in this listing represents ONLY THE OWNER of the property.

(continued)

TITLE

Evidence of Good Title. In the event of sale or exchange, I agree to furnish at my option, an abstract of title or a commitment for title insurance in an amount equal to the purchase price. I will pay either expense.

Title. In the event of sale or exchange, I agree to furnish a ___general___ warranty deed conveying a marketable title in which my wife or husband will join, free and clear of all taxes and liens.

POSSESSION

Delivery of Keys. I agree to deliver possession and the keys no later than the closing.

APPORTIONMENTS

Real Property Taxes and Special Assessments. Delinquent property taxes shall be paid before closing. Current taxes and special assessment taxes shall be prorated through the day of closing.

Rents, Interest, Premiums. Prepaid rents, water rents, sewer rents, and mortgage interest shall be prorated through the day of closing.

MAINTENANCE AND DAMAGES

The broker shall not be responsible for maintenance of the premises nor damages unless such damage is caused by the broker's negligence.

DISCRIMINATION

The broker or owner shall not discriminate against any potential buyer because of race, creed, or national origin.

_____ Agent	_____ James D. Dunn Owner
by: _____ Broker	_____ Mary R. Dunn Owner

RIGHT TO CANCEL. The terms of breaking the contract with the agent are identified. A specific number of days of notice must be given, and a penalty must be paid.

REFERRALS. The owner agrees to refer to the broker all requests for information about the sale.

Price

The next section of the listing contract contains provisions related to the price of the property.

LIST PRICE. The broker and the seller agree on the *list price*. Once this price is stated on the contract, the agent cannot advertise the property for sale at any price higher or lower.

The list price is the *asking price*. Common practice is to ask the appraised value plus 5 to 10 percent. A property appraised for $50,000 would be listed at $50,000 plus, say, the maximum of 10 percent or $5,000, for a total of $55,000. This price enables the seller to negotiate in response to conditions offered by a buyer. In addition, prospective buyers typically offer less than the list price. Thus, the *list price* is equal to the *asking price,* which may or may not equal the *sales price* negotiated between the buyer and the seller.

DEPOSITS. The broker agrees to accept and hold all deposits attached to offers on the property. These funds are placed in the firm's *earnest money account,* a trust account that is separate from all personal funds.

FIXTURES AND PERSONAL PROPERTY INCLUDED. The list price includes all fixtures that are normally considered to be attached. Any exceptions—such as draperies, shelving, curtain rods, a refrigerator, or a pool table—should be identified.

ENCUMBRANCES. The owner authorizes the holder of any note on the property to disclose the terms.

Commission or Fee

Several stipulations pertaining to the agent's fee are agreed upon in the listing contract.

AMOUNT. The agent's fee is stated as a percentage of the sales price. It is paid for a successful sale during the listing period or during the 120 days after the listing period if the agent's efforts were the procuring cause or primary cause of the buyer's purchase of the property. The latter provision protects the agent if a potential buyer who is shown the property by the agent during the listing period does not decide to buy until after the listing has expired.

A competent real estate firm maintains records of its showings. Any attempt by the seller and the buyer to withhold a fee and sell at a lower price after the listing has expired will be met by a demand from the firm for the fee if the transaction occurs within 120 days of the listing contract's expiration date.

The fee between the agent and the seller must be negotiable. Requiring a "going rate" or "recommended rate" may be an antitrust violation, such as price fixing and collusion.

CAPABLE BUYER. The seller agrees to pay the fee when the agent presents a buyer who is ready, willing, and able to purchase the property as evidenced by a successful closing.

DEFAULT. The condition for default by the seller on an accepted sales contract does not require that notice be given to the agent, but the seller must pay the stipulated commission.

Representation

The agent is required by many state regulatory agencies to disclose clearly the parties represented. In this example, only the owner of the property is represented by this contract.

Title

The seller agrees to furnish *evidence of good title* in the form of an abstract or title insurance. The seller agrees to pay the required expense of such evidence. The seller has the option of indicating the *type of deed* that will be provided. Writing in the type of deed serves to remind the agent to verify the warranty on the deed.

Possession

The seller will not remain in possession of the property after the closing, as evidenced by the *delivery of keys* at the closing. The seller can negotiate possession before or after closing if the buyer is willing. The seller should be asked to pay the buyer a competitive level of rent and post a deposit against physical damage to the property.

Apportionments

The allocation of certain expenses between the buyer and seller is stipulated.

REAL PROPERTY TAXES AND SPECIAL ASSESSMENTS. The seller must pay delinquent property taxes before the closing. Real property taxes and special assessments are prorated between the buyer and seller through the day of closing. (Prorations are explained in detail in Chapter 17.)

RENTS, INTEREST, PREMIUMS. Prepaid rents, water rents, sewer rents, and mortgage interest are to be prorated between the buyer and seller through the day of closing.

Maintenance and Damages

The broker is not responsible for maintenance of the premises or for damages unless they are caused by the broker's negligence.

Discrimination

The owner and broker agree not to discriminate against any potential buyer on the basis of race, religion, ethnic origin, or gender.

Signatures

The listing contract should be signed by all of the owners of the property. The presence of all signatures indicates a willingness of all owners to sign the deed later. The signature of a wife indicates her desire to release her dower and homestead rights (not all states have these rights). In addition, the contract should be accepted by the principal broker of the firm because the firm is the agent.

MULTIPLE LISTING CONTRACT

A **multiple listing** contract is an exclusive-right-to-sell listing contract with one exception: the principal asks the agent to place the property in the MLS so that it can be offered by other cooperating brokers. Thus, others may sell this property, and the agent agrees to a fee split.

The MLS is composed of cooperating real estate firms who agree to share their listings to give the principal's property the maximum exposure. The **commission split** between the listing agent and the selling firm is governed by the MLS bylaws. Typically, the listing firm receives more than 50 percent of the total commission.

The owner benefits by placing the property in MLS because it provides the maximum amount of advertising among local firms. In addition, the principal still has an exclusive agent to represent his needs.

EXCLUSIVE AGENCY LISTING CONTRACT

The **exclusive agency listing** contract is identical to the exclusive right-to-sell listing contract with one exception: the owner may sell the property and pays no fee unless the agent can prove that the firm was the driving force (or **procuring cause**) of the sale. The firm, however, is guaranteed that it is the only agent representing the owner.

For an owner, this arrangement may appear to be the best—to have one agent attempting to sell the property and still maintain the right to sell without paying a fee if the opportunity arises. However, the agent may not invest much time or money in selling the property because she might not collect a commission to cover expenses and time. Consequently, an unethical agent may write the listing contract to prevent the property from being listed by a competing firm but may not do much to find a suitable buyer.

OPEN LISTING CONTRACT

An **open listing** contract carries no exclusive rights. An owner can give an open listing to any number of brokers at the same time and can still find a buyer without paying a fee. This arrangement gives the owner the greatest freedom of any listing form, but an agent has little incentive to expend time and money showing the property because someone else may be compensated if the property is sold. A firm's only protection is that it is entitled to a fee if it does find a buyer at the listing price and terms. Because of the agent's reluctance to develop a sales effort, few if any offers will be received, and the result may be no sale or a sale below market price. If a broker does find a buyer, however, the fee charged will be the same as with an exclusive right-to-sell listing contract.

A broker who has an open listing or an exclusive agency listing contract is entitled to a fee if he can prove that the property's sale was due primarily to his efforts. Suppose a broker shows an open listing property to a client and, during the listing period or during an extension, the client goes directly to the owner and concludes a deal. Even though the owner negotiates the transaction and prepares the sales contract, the broker is entitled to a full commission for finding the buyer. The same would be true if the owner and the buyer used a third person to purchase the property to avoid paying a fee. State laws protect the broker who in good faith has found a buyer at the request of an owner.

When an open listing is given to two or more brokers, the one who first produces a buyer is entitled to the commission. For example, Broker 1 shows the property to Client C, but no sale is made. Later, Client C goes to Broker 2 and makes an offer, which is accepted by the owner. Although two brokers have attempted to sell the property, only one has succeeded and she is the one entitled to a commission. The fact that Broker 1 received nothing, even after expending considerable effort, illustrates why brokers dislike open listings.

NET LISTING CONTRACT

A **net listing** contract is created when an owner states the price wanted for the property and then agrees to pay a fee equal to any amount the broker obtains over that price. The state real estate commission or commissioner should be consulted to assure that this type of fee is legal.

When Does a Breach of the Listing Happen?

A breach of the listing contract can occur in several ways, and it can affect the seller and the buyer as well as the agent.

BREACH BY THE BUYER

Consider a situation in which the agent has found a buyer who is ready, willing, and able to purchase the property, and the seller has accepted the buyer by signing the sales contract. The buyer suddenly changes his mind and will not appear at the closing although the seller has satisfied the terms of the listing and sales contract. The agent has fulfilled the terms of the listing contract, but the property is not sold. In this case the buyer *forfeits* the earnest money that was paid when the sales contract was signed. The money is divided between the agent and the principal according to the terms in the listing contract. Typically, the terms of the listing contract will reimburse the agent first for expenses, and any remainder is divided evenly between the agent and the principal. The agent may not receive more than the amount she would have received if the transaction had been completed.

BREACH BY THE SELLER

The seller can breach a listing contract in two ways. One is simply by telling the agent that he wants to break the listing. Typically, the listing contract requires a specific number of days' notice be given with a payment of funds to the agent to compensate for the time and expenses invested in the property. Second, the seller can breach the contract by refusing to accept an offer for the asking price by a buyer who is ready, willing, and able to purchase the property. In this case, the agent may have legitimate grounds to claim a fee because the instructions given by the seller were satisfied successfully.

CANCELLATION OF THE LISTING

The agency is ended and the listing contract typically is considered to be canceled when the principal dies, the agent or the principal files for bankruptcy, the property is destroyed, or the agent fails to retain a valid real estate license.

REMEDIES TO BREACH

The legal remedy for a breach is for the injured party to sue for either (1) specific performance or (2) damages. **Specific performance** requires the defaulting party to execute the contract.

How Are Fees Negotiated and Collected?

The amount of commission that the owner will pay the broker for services is a matter of negotiation between the seller and broker. The usual arrangement is to express the amount on the listing contract as a percentage of the sale or exchange price, although a stated dollar amount could be used if the owner and broker agreed. The broker recognizes that if the fee is too low, the firm will not spend time and effort finding a buyer. Typically, a commission or fee ranges from 5 to 8 percent of the selling price for houses, condominiums, and small apartment buildings, and from 6 to 10 percent for farms, ranches, and vacant land. On multimillion-dollar improved properties, fees may drop to 2 to 4 percent.

Several points of law affect the listing contract and the agent's collection of a fee. The agent is entitled to collect a fee under the following conditions:

1. The agent must hold a valid real estate license at the time of the sale. This point is contained in many state license laws.
2. A valid agency contract must be in effect at the time of the sale. A seller's agent cannot expect to collect a fee unless the property is listed. Thus, an agent should verify the validity of the listing contract before presenting a sales contract to the seller for acceptance.
3. The agent must be able to prove that he was the *procuring cause* of the sale. This requirement typically is met by the broker who is the first to present to the principal an offer that is accepted.

Does State Regulation of Listings Occur?

The state real estate commission (or commissioner) typically enforces regulations covering the procurement of listings and the use of advertising and signs. Typically, state regulations stipulate that the listing agent:

1. Must accept the responsibility of ascertaining all of the pertinent facts about adverse factors influencing the value.
2. Cannot collect a fee unless a valid listing contract is in effect.
3. Can offer to purchase the property for personal reasons only if the interest of the firm is disclosed in advance to the principal.
4. Can collect a fee from the buyer and the seller on the same property only if both are informed in advance.
5. Can place a sign on the property with the owner's permission (the sign must be removed promptly when the transaction is complete).
6. Must provide the principal with a copy of the listing contract.
7. Must include the name of the firm, the name of the broker, or both in all advertising.

8. Must include a definite expiration date on all listing contracts. An automatic extension date typically is not allowed.

What Is the Affirmative Marketing Agreement?

The **affirmative marketing agreement** is a document signed by the U.S. Department of Housing and Urban Development and members of the local real estate board who agree to cooperate to support equal opportunity in housing. Among other commitments, certain advertising requirements are imposed on real estate firms that sign the agreement. These requirements are listed below.

1. A periodic notice that advertises the agreement must be placed in the local newspaper.
2. The local newspaper shall print a "publisher's notice" on each page containing real estate advertising. One alternative is to print the Fair Housing and Equal Opportunity sign in every ad larger than six column inches.
3. The Fair Housing and Equal Opportunity sign must be displayed in a prominent location by each board member who signs the agreement.

Chapter Summary

All real estate transactions typically involve a contractual arrangement of some type. It is very important to all parties involved that the contract always be valid and enforceable. All five components of a legal contract should be present to make it valid. Valid contracts comply with the statute of frauds and are enforceable in a court of law.

The parties involved should be aware of misrepresentation, fraud, and breach. Misrepresentation lacks an intent to deceive while fraud includes it. Because either can occur with any party to a contract, all individuals must be aware of their comments, answers to questions, and actions. Breach occurs when one party cannot perform its role in executing the contract.

The oldest and most typical arrangement between a real estate agent and a client is when a seller employs an agent to find a buyer. Done through a contract called a listing, the seller outlines the terms of the sale, including the asking price.

One of the contracts used frequently is the sales contract, which outlines the terms of the purchase or sale. This document determines the terms that must take place either prior to or at the settlement.

Internet Applications

A website has been established for this chapter at http://epley.swcollege.com.

1. Define the types of agents. What is a special agency? Contrast the following:

special agency	tenant's agent
single agent	facilitator
dual agent	client
seller's agent	customer
buyer's agent	disclosed agency

2. How does an agent commit misrepresentation? Fraud?

3. What is a listing contract? What are several of its important clauses?

4. What are the types of listing contracts that may be used with agents? Contrast the following:

exclusive right-to-sell	net listing
exclusive agency	multiple listing
open listing	

5. What are the agent's fiduciary responsibilities?

6. How can a listing contract be ended by the agent? By the client? For other reasons?

7. Describe the more important components of a typical exclusive right-to-sell listing contract.

8. How does the state regulatory agency influence the listing contract?

9. Describe the meaning and impact of an affirmative marketing agreement.

10. Identify and discuss any information on listing contracts that is available using the Internet addresses.

1. When would an agent want to be a dual agent? A single agent? Would any potential conflict of interest exist between the interests of the two clients in a dual agency? Describe.

2. Describe the circumstances in which a client would want each of the following listing contracts:

   exclusive right-to-sell

   exclusive agency

   open

   net

3. Under which type of agency does the buyer have representation?

4. Describe any circumstances that would cause a client not to use an agent.

5. How easily can misrepresentation occur? Explain. How should an agent avoid these situations?

6. Discuss the information found in the various Internet assignments.

CHAPTER 14

Contracts and the Sales Contract

QUESTIONS TO BE ANSWERED

1. What are the types of contracts used in real estate?
2. What are the essential features of a real estate sales contract?

OBJECTIVES

When finished with this chapter, the student should be able to:

1. Identify and explain the legal classifications used to describe contracts.
2. Identify and describe the essential features of a valid contract.
3. Analyze the real estate sales contract on a clause-by-clause basis.
4. Identify and explain the difference between misrepresentation and fraud.
5. Identify the legal remedies available to the aggrieved party when a breach of contract occurs.

acceptance

accord and satisfaction

agreement

bilateral contract

binder

breach of contract

cancellation

competent parties

complete performance

contingency provisions

contract for deed

conveyance clause

counteroffer

discharge of contract

duress

duty to speak

enforceable contract

express contract

implied contract

installment contract

land contract

legality of purpose

liquidated damages

material fact

mistake of fact

mistake of law

necessity of writing

nominal damages

nonperformance

novation

offer

option

real estate sales contract

reality of consent

remedies

rescission

risk of loss clause

undue influence

unenforceable contract

unilateral contract

valid contract

void agreement

voidable contract

INTRODUCTION

A real estate transaction such as a common purchase, sale, or lease involves a contract between the parties involved. This chapter concentrates on the components of the contract and gives special attention to the document called the "contract of sale" that is used in a purchase and sale.

How Are Contracts Classified?

Contracts can be classified according to their legal characteristics—as valid, voidable, or void; enforceable or unenforceable; as bilateral or unilateral; and as express or implied. The ability to distinguish among these contract categories and the underlying legal characteristics is important in real estate decision making. The purpose of this chapter is to describe the general characteristics of all contracts, as well as the terms and provisions of the real estate sales contract and it provisions.

VALID, VOIDABLE, VOID, AND UNENFORCEABLE CONTRACTS

A **valid contract** fulfills all the legal requirements imposed by the body of law known as contract law and can therefore be *enforced* by the courts of law. A **voidable contract** is a valid contract, but one party to the contract can exercise the right to avoid or to set aside the contractual obligations incurred. The best-known example of a voidable contract is one between an adult and a minor. Under the law, the minor has the right to avoid or rescind a valid contract at his own discretion. Consequently, this contract is classified as "voidable" because the minor has the right of avoidance.

A **void agreement** is not a valid contract. It is an attempt to enter into a contract that does not fulfill the requirements imposed by contract law and therefore has no legal effect and is not recognized by the courts.

An **unenforceable contract** is a valid contract, but it is not recognized by the courts if any legal action is brought before the courts to enforce it. Many types of contracts, including the real estate sales contract, must be in writing in order for the courts to hear cases involving their enforcement. If such a contract were made orally, and if one of the parties failed to meet the obligations imposed in the contract, this oral contract could not be brought to the courts. The contract is valid, but the courts will not enforce it. The distinction between the unenforceable contract and the void agreement is that the unenforceable contract is a valid contract and the void agreement is not a valid contract.

BILATERAL AND UNILATERAL CONTRACTS

A **bilateral contract** is an agreement reached between two or more people. One person makes an offer or a promise to the other(s); if the other person (or people) accepts the offer, a bilateral contract is formed. As part of this process, each of the two parties to the contract makes a promise or performs an act and simultaneously receives a promise from the other party. A **unilateral contract** contains a promise or offer by only one of the parties to the contract. In other words, one person makes a promise or extends an offer, and the other person receives the benefit of the promise or offer contingent upon the performance of some act. A listing agreement is a unilateral contract that is used in the real estate business.

The real estate sales contract is a bilateral contract. When two individuals enter into an agreement to exchange property, one individual offers cash or other financial assets (or both) in order to receive the property. The second individual gives up the property in order to receive the cash. Each of the two parties gives up an asset and receives another asset in return.

EXPRESS AND IMPLIED CONTRACTS

An **express contract** is an explicit agreement. It can be either oral or written. The fundamental requirement is that the individuals discuss and then agree to the terms and conditions. A contract can also result from inferences about facts and circumstances. Such a contract is referred to as a contract "implied in fact," known as an **implied contract.** The agreement between the parties is derived from the presumed intent of the individuals as indicated by their conduct and their acts. A contract may be implied in fact whenever one person knowingly accepts a benefit from another person and the circumstances make it clear that the benefit was not intended as a gift. The person who accepts the benefit implicitly promises to pay the fair value of the benefit that is received.

The real estate sales contract can be characterized as a valid, bilateral, express, enforceable contract. It contains all of the legally essential features of a valid contract. The next section presents the legal requirements for valid contracts in greater detail.

What Are the Essential Features of a Valid and Enforceable Contract?

A valid contract is defined simply as a legally binding agreement—one that is enforceable by law. This agreement results from an exchange of acts, or of promises to do or not to do certain things. A full understanding of a contract, however, requires more than just an understanding of this simple definition. A contract must have the following essential legal features in order to be valid and enforceable in a court of law:

1. An agreement
2. A consideration
3. Competent parties
4. Reality of consent
5. Legality of purpose
6. Necessity of writing in certain instances

An **enforceable, valid contract** (including a real estate sales contract) must contain each of these features (see Exhibit 14.1).

THE AGREEMENT

Two acts constitute an **agreement**—the offer and the acceptance. The **offer** is the initial step undertaken in the formation of a contract between two individuals. In a real estate transaction, the offer is made by the potential buyer or an agent who is working for the

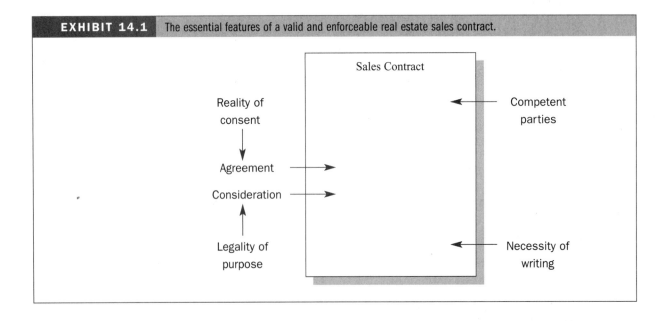

| EXHIBIT 14.1 | The essential features of a valid and enforceable real estate sales contract. |

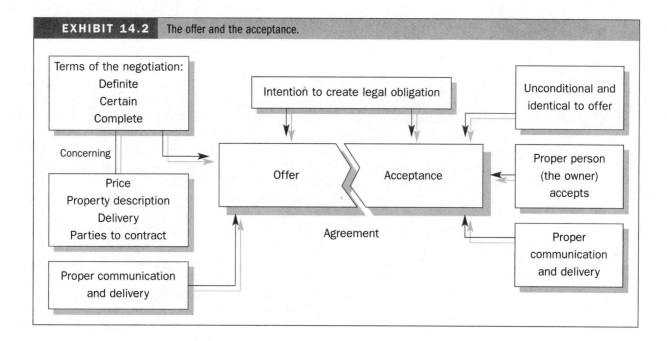

EXHIBIT 14.2 The offer and the acceptance.

Terms of the negotiation:
Definite
Certain
Complete

Concerning

Price
Property description
Delivery
Parties to contract

Proper communication
and delivery

Intention to create legal obligation

Offer

Acceptance

Agreement

Unconditional and
identical to offer

Proper person
(the owner)
accepts

Proper
communication
and delivery

buyer. The offer is a conditional promise made by the potential buyer to the seller of the property. The promise is viewed as being conditional because the potential buyer is not bound by the promise unless the seller responds to the offer in an appropriate and proper fashion. The seller's appropriate and proper response is the **acceptance** of the offer. An acceptance is thus an indication by the seller of a willingness to be bound by the terms of the offer. These two actions—the offer and the acceptance—constitute the agreement that is essential to a valid contract (see Exhibit 14.2).

Offer

An offer must be all of the following:

- Definite and certain   *specific on what they're offering*
- Complete
- Communicated to the seller
- Intended to create a legal obligation between the two parties

To be definite and certain, the offer must be clearly intelligible to a reasonable person and must be made under such circumstances that the person receiving it has reason to believe that the other party (offeror) is willing to deal on the terms indicated. Definiteness and certainty are required because the courts may have to determine whether or not the parties to the contract performed in compliance with the specified terms. If the terms of the transaction are vague, left out, or impossible to measure, there is no contract. The price to be paid by the buyer, the condition of the property, and the time of delivery are important terms of the sale that should be specified clearly. If for some reason these terms are not clearly specified, the contract is still enforceable if the court is convinced from the existing evidence that both the buyer and seller intended to be bound by the terms specified within the contract. If a time of performance is not stated or if a price is not specified, the court will imply a "reasonable time" for performance and a "reasonable price" for the commodity.

The offer must also be complete if the contract is to be enforceable in a court of law. All of the terms of the contract must be settled; none can be left to be determined by future negotiation. The offer cannot contain a statement that calls for future discussion of a term or condition of sale. A statement such as "price to be negotiated at the time of the exchange" is not sufficient. The courts have ruled that they cannot complete an unfinished contract, and thus the incomplete contract would be unenforceable, even though it could still be valid.

An offer must be communicated and delivered by the buyer to the seller in order for the contract to be effective. The communication can be made directly by the buyer or by an agent of the buyer. The offer can be made directly to the seller or to an agent of the seller, the real estate broker or salesperson, if the seller has given the agent the power to accept an offer. Communication and the delivery of the offer are necessary because the seller cannot act upon the offer until it has been communicated and delivered.

An offer can be effective even though a delay occurs in reaching the seller. When an offer is made, a delay is normally viewed as resulting from the negligence of the buyer or trouble with the means of communication chosen by the buyer. For example, the buyer may choose to communicate and deliver the offer by means of a telegraph company or the U.S. Postal Service. If either of these agents of the buyer causes a delay, the court feels that the seller should not bear the loss resulting from that delay. Therefore, the seller can take a reasonable amount of time to respond even if the effective time of the offer has expired. If the delay is apparent to the seller, however, the seller's acceptance of the offer must be communicated to the prospective buyer within a reasonable time after the offer would normally have been received. If he knows that there has been a delay in communicating the offer, he cannot take advantage of the delay.

The last characteristic of the offer, and of a contract in general, is the intention by both the prospective buyer and the seller to create a legal obligation. The two parties to the contract must agree about the specified terms. Consequently, a distinction must be made between a serious offer and a statement that is made in either jest or anger. The courts will not hold a person legally responsible for a statement made in jest or anger. A person is not considered to be making an offer when exasperation over a disabled automobile results in a statement such as "I'd sell this piece of junk for a nickel!"

In addition, a distinction is made between a serious offer and what the courts consider "invitations to bid." Individuals can make oral statements about general terms they might consider in a transaction. These statements may be made to open a discussion about specific terms of the sale. The courts generally understand that the detailed terms of the sale will be discussed, communicated, reduced to writing, and signed before any agreement between buyer and seller is held to be legally binding. A statement such as "Make me a serious offer for the car and I'll sell it" is considered an invitation to bid that can start a discussion that may or may not end in a contractual agreement.

Acceptance

The other half of the agreement is the acceptance. An acceptance occurs when the party to whom the offer has been made agrees to the proposal or does what is proposed. If the acceptance is to result in an enforceable agreement, it too must meet certain requirements. An acceptance must be all of the following:

- Made only by the person or persons to whom the offer was made
- Unconditional and identical to the terms of the offer
- Communicated to the offeror (prospective buyer)

The first of these points needs very little explanation. For a contract to be valid, the person accepting the offer must be the person to whom the offer was made. If the seller has given the authority to a lawyer or broker to accept an offer, the buyer can deliver the offer to the seller's agent.

The acceptance must occur without any conditions added to the offer and without any exceptions deleted from the offer. In other words, the seller must either accept or reject the offer as it is stated without changing the offer in any way. Any change in the terms required by either the seller or the buyer is made through a process of negotiation. During this negotiation process, the buyer and seller can enter into a series of offers and counteroffers. The original offer is made by the buyer. If the seller does not like all the terms, the seller can express a **counteroffer,** in which some of the original offer appears unchanged and some portion is deleted, added, or changed. The buyer can accept, reject, or amend the counteroffer. If the buyer accepts the counteroffer, the contract is created. Notice that the buyer and seller have changed roles—the buyer is the acceptor (offeree) and the seller is the offeror.

By amending the counteroffer, the buyer can establish a second counteroffer. The seller can accept, reject, or amend this amended counteroffer. If the seller accepts this version of the original offer, the contract is created. At this stage, the buyer is once again the offeror and the seller is the acceptor. This negotiation process can continue until a final offer is extended and accepted by the appropriate party. This final offer is the legal offer that must be accepted unconditionally.

Finally, the acceptance must be communicated and delivered to the buyer. As part of the acceptance process, the prospective buyer may require the acceptance to be delivered in a certain way. For example, the buyer may stipulate that an acceptance will not be effective until the offer is actually or physically received. If the acceptance is transmitted by mail or by fax, custom and tradition indicate when the acceptance is received. Acceptances sent by mail generally take effect when properly posted, with correct address and sufficient postage.

An agreement is legally enforceable only when actions occur on the part of the buyer and the seller. A person is not legally responsible to reply to an offer that is made by another individual. In other words, an offer cannot be stated in such a way that silence is considered an acceptance. Suppose an agreement in a contract contains statements made by the buyer to the effect that the offer is considered as accepted if a reply to the contrary is not forthcoming. This would not result in a contract coming into existence because of the silence of the offeree (except for certain unusual situations not necessary to this discussion).

Termination of the Offer

The offer stays in effect until one of four actions occurs:

1. The seller rejects the offer.
2. The seller makes a counteroffer.
3. The buyer revokes the offer.
4. Unforeseen circumstances invalidate the offer.

The first two actions should be clear from the previous discussion. The other two actions require elaboration. The buyer can revoke the offer by direct action or by terms stated in the offer. The buyer can call upon the seller by telephone or by personal visit and withdraw the offer prior to its acceptance; this is the direct action. The buyer can state a definite period of time in the contract for which the offer lasts. He can say, "This offer will be in effect until 6:00 P.M. on the 9th of March 2001," or the buyer can say, "This offer will be in effect for three days." Typically, offers for residential property last for three to five days. A longer period of time is stipulated for commercial and income-producing residential property.

If the time period for the offer passes, the offer has lapsed or expired. If a definite time period for the offer is not stated in the contract, the offer is assumed to be in effect for a "reasonable period of time." It is best to avoid any such interpretation by stating an expiration date for the offer.

Unforseen circumstances also can invalidate the offer. The buyer can die while the offer is in effect. If this occurs before the acceptance, the offer is terminated. If the buyer dies after the offer is accepted, the state law may require a signed contract as binding on the deceased person's estate and heirs. Destruction of the property prior to the acceptance also terminates the offer. However, if destruction occurs after the acceptance (that is, after the contract is signed), legal problems can arise. See the discussion about the "risk of loss" clause in the contract later in this chapter.

CONSIDERATION

In addition to the agreement, a valid contract requires that each party to the bargain actually give something to the other. In a sales contract for real estate, the *consideration* is the exchange of valuable assets. Typically, the buyer gives a financial asset and receives the parcel of real estate, and the seller receives cash or some other valuable asset and gives the real property.

If the consideration is an exchange of assets other than cash, the value of those assets should be approximately equal in order for the contract to be valid. However, if the consideration on each side of an agreement involves money, the consideration must be equal.

COMPETENT PARTIES

The individuals who enter into a contract must each have the legal capacity to make a contract. In other words, both individuals must have the ability to make legally binding agreements. Such people are known as **competent parties.** People who do not have the legal capacity to contract are those who are under the legal age, those who are considered insane, and those who are seriously intoxicated by liquor or drugs. Moreover, in certain states, convicts and enemy aliens from countries at war with the United States are also considered "incompetent" to enter into a contract.

Because of the basic tenet that the parties to a contract must understand the nature of the transaction and its consequences, individuals who signed a contract under the influence of alcohol or drugs are assumed to be incompetent. These individuals have a reasonable time after they attain sobriety to reconsider. Finally, because of the need to understand, contracts are not enforceable against insane people who are legally defined as "mentally deranged."

REALITY OF CONSENT

For a contract to be recognized as valid, it must be free of mistakes, misrepresentations, fraud, undue influence, and duress. The consent of each individual party to the contract must be real and intentional. Without this **reality of consent,** the contract is either void or voidable (see Exhibit 14.3).

EXHIBIT 14.3   The reality of consent.

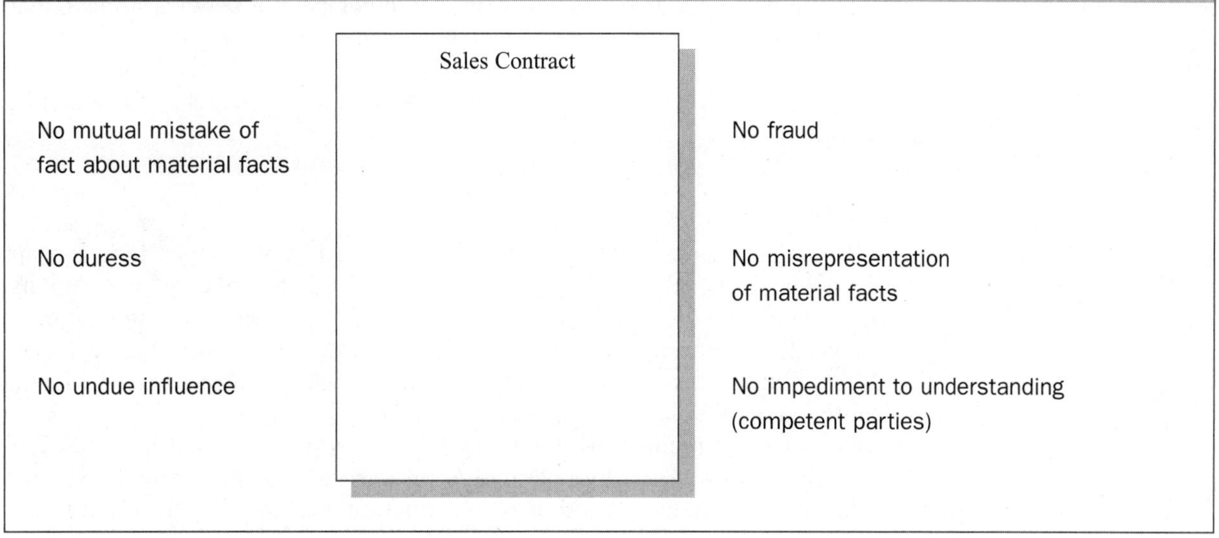

Sales Contract

No mutual mistake of
fact about material facts

No fraud

No duress

No misrepresentation
of material facts

No undue influence

No impediment to understanding
(competent parties)

Mistakes

Two types of mistakes are recognized in the law. One type is a **mistake of fact.** This mistake occurs when certain pieces of information or conditions in the contract are not true—for example, when the identity of a party to the contract is mistaken, when the identity of the subject property is mistaken, or when the true nature of the agreement is mistaken. These mistakes generally do not void a contract but could make it voidable. The second type of mistake is a **mistake of law,** which occurs when a person who has full knowledge of the facts makes an erroneous conclusion about the legal effect of those facts. Currently, this mistake cannot be the grounds for avoiding a contract.

Misrepresentation and Fraud

A mistake must be distinguished from a misrepresentation. A *mistake* is a misunderstanding or misconception that a person has about a fact. In contrast, a *misrepresentation* is an incorrect or improper statement about a fact that is made by an individual. A misrepresentation makes a contract voidable by the party to whom the misrepresentation was made. However, the contract is voidable only if the misrepresentation refers to a material fact. By law, a **material fact** is defined as information or evidence that a reasonable person would consider important when determining a course of action or reaching a decision.

A contract is voidable if a misrepresentation of a material fact was part of the basis for reaching the agreement. The misrepresentation can be intentional or unintentional. If it was intentional, the misrepresentation is classified as *fraud*. In either case, the victim of the misrepresentation may rescind the contract because the loss is the same whether the false statements were made innocently or intentionally. In the case of fraudulent misrepresentation, the victim is given a choice of the additional remedy of a suit for dollar damages.

If the courts are to judge whether a misrepresentation or a fraud occurred, a distinction must be made between a statement of fact and an opinion. The ultimate decision as to whether a statement is fact or opinion is a matter for the jury in a court trial. However, as a general guideline, *a fact is that which actually exists or actually occurred.* It is reality. In the case of a proven false statement of fact, the contract is voidable. In contrast, *opinion is a belief, a view, or a judgment.* A belief is stronger than an impression but is not positive or absolute knowledge. As a general rule, erroneous or uninformed opinions are not viewed as a basis for voiding a contract. However, if an individual states an opinion as one thing but in fact it is just the reverse, the individual has misstated a fact.

Duty to Speak

Historically, the laws governing the formation of contracts have followed the concept of caveat emptor (let the buyer beware), especially in relation to real estate transactions. The parties to a contract are required to exercise ordinary business sense in their dealings. As a result, the general rule is that silence in the absence of a **duty to speak** does not constitute fraud. Where there is a duty to speak, concealment of a material fact is equivalent to a fraudulent misrepresentation.

However, the law recognizes three situations in which a person has a duty to speak the truth. In these situations, failure to make true statements about a material fact constitutes fraudulent action. One situation pertains to the relationship between the seller of the property and the real estate broker. In this fiduciary relationship, both parties have the duty to speak the truth and to make a full disclosure of all the facts.

The second situation in which a person has a duty to speak reflects the courts' interpretation of justice, equity, and fair play. If an important material fact is known by one person but not by the other, the courts could rule that the contract is voidable.

The third situation arises when a person misstates or unintentionally misrepresents an important material fact. Upon discovering this misrepresentation, the person is obligated to correct the mistake immediately or when negotiations are renewed.

Duress and Undue Influence

Undue influence is the unfair advantage that one person has over another because of a relationship between the parties. If undue influence is proven, the contract is voidable by the individual who was unfairly or unduly influenced. **Duress** is the use of force to make a contract against the free will of the individual. Contracts entered under duress are voidable by the party who was forced into the agreement.

LEGALITY OF PURPOSE

Contracts must involve legal promises, actions, and objects, collectively known as **legality of purpose.** If illegal acts or objects form the basis of a contract, the law considers the contract to be illegal and consequently unenforceable in courts of law. An interpretation of unlawful or illegal purposes is based on activities or objects that are specifically prohibited by law, contrary to the rules established under common law, or contrary to stated public policy. Any contract that violates a statute or an ordinance is illegal and consequently is considered to be a void agreement.

NECESSITY OF WRITING

In general, contracts can be initiated by means of a written agreement. Oral agreements, however, are subject to failure of memory, misrepresentation, and possibly even fraud. To overcome these problems, the British Parliament passed the Statute of Frauds in 1677. Still in effect in the United States today, this statute requires that certain contractual agreements be evidenced by some written form of agreement, a requirement known as the **necessity of writing.** A contract to buy and sell real property or any partial interest in real property is governed by the Statute of Frauds and consequently must be evidenced in writing.

The Statute of Frauds does not require that all terms in the contract be reduced to writing. What is required is that some signed, written piece of evidence exist that gives the court a reason to believe that an agreement was made. The written evidence can be the contract itself or a memorandum, a written document that outlines the nature of the agreement and gives a judge reason to believe the two parties wanted to enter into a legally binding contractual agreement. To satisfy the Statute of Frauds, the memorandum of the contract must contain the names of the seller and the buyer, a sufficient description of the land, the contract price, the terms of sale, if other than cash, and the signature of the party against whom the suit is brought on the contract. A few states require both parties to sign the contract, and there appears to be a trend in this direction.

What Are Discharge, Nonperformance, and Breach of Contract?

After the real estate sales contract is negotiated and signed by the buyer and seller, the rights and duties created by that contract remain in force until one of three actions occurs: (1) the contract is discharged, which means that the rights and duties created by that contract are fulfilled in some manner; (2) one of the individuals who entered into the contract receives legal permission for nonperformance of the duties incurred in the contract; or (3) one individual party to the contract fails to perform according to the terms and provisions established in the contract.

DISCHARGE OR PERFORMANCE OF THE CONTRACT

The legal system fully intends that the usual method of **discharge of contract** is the **complete performance** by both parties of the obligations that each party incurred under the contractual agreement. Each party to the contract must perform the actions or fulfill the promises that were made, and each party expects the other party to do the same.

In addition to complete performance of the obligations stipulated in the contract, other means can be used to discharge a contract legally. One of the individuals involved in the contract can find a substitute. In other words, a party to the contract who becomes unwilling to meet the terms of the contract may find another person who is willing to assume those duties and obligations. This new party must agree to assume all of the responsibilities and duties of the original party who is seeking to be freed from the obligations of the contract. Moreover, both parties to the original contract must agree to the substitution. This process of finding an acceptable, willing substitute for one of the original parties is called **novation.** It is a way of fully and legally discharging the obligations of a contract.

The obligations incurred in the contract also can be legally discharged by the process of **accord and satisfaction.** An *accord* is a reformation of the agreement made between the two parties to the contract. One of the individuals undertakes to give an asset or to perform an action that is different from the one specified in the contract. Simultaneously, the other party to the contract must accept this asset or action. The term *satisfaction* denotes that the substitution was made with the agreement of all parties to the contract. The legal doctrine of accord and satisfaction requires that there be a dispute or uncertainty about the consideration specified in the contract. A compromise agreement is reached between the parties to the contract, their differences are reconciled (this is the accord), and the mutual obligations are satisfactorily discharged (this is the satisfaction). Exhibit 14.4 depicts the full contract process.

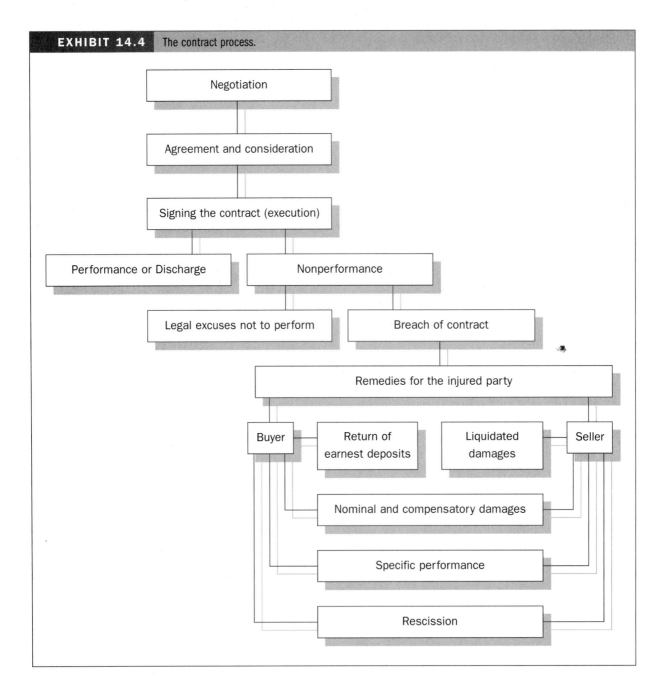

EXHIBIT 14.4 The contract process.

NONPERFORMANCE

Even though the contract binds two individuals to a certain agreement, one of the individuals can be relieved of the responsibilities of performing a contract by a legal excuse for nonperformance. Since competent parties are required for a valid contract, a legal incompetent, such as a minor, can be excused from having to perform the obligations specified in a contract (**nonperformance**). Also, if reality of consent is lacking, the party who did not give his or her true consent can be legally excused from the contract.

BREACH OF CONTRACT

A **breach of contract** is the failure to perform the acts or promises stipulated as the terms of the contract. Breach of contract is nonperformance of a contract as shown in Exhibit 14.4, but without a legally acceptable excuse. If one party to the contract does not perform according to the terms and agreements of that contract, the other party may be financially injured as a result of nonperformance. The injured party has legal recourse in this event. The courts may require that the contract be fulfilled, or they may provide that the injured party receive compensation for the injury or damages incurred because of the breach of contract.

The legal actions that the injured party can undertake are known as **remedies.** The law provides for three general classes of remedies:

1. Rescission or cancellation
2. Lawsuit to obtain financial compensation for the damages suffered
3. Lawsuit to obtain specific performance of the contract

The party to the contract who did not breach the agreement should be restored to the position she was in before signing the contract. This remedy—known as **rescission**— is shown in Exhibit 14.4. In this situation, both parties return any consideration they may have received, and the entire contract is rescinded. The rescission process can be accomplished voluntarily by agreement between the parties, or it can be instituted by court order at the request of the injured party. **Cancellation** is the same as rescission with the exception that the injured party retains the right to sue for damages.

In certain situations, the parties to the contract may foresee the possibility that a breach of contract may occur. Consequently, they may agree on an amount of money that would be paid to the injured party in case the default does take place. In this situation, the predetermined sum of money is known as **liquidated damages.** Common when actual damages would be difficult to prove, this arrangement is enforceable if the amount is reasonable. If damages are not reasonable, the court will deem them to be a penalty and will not enforce the agreement. The earnest money deposit can be viewed as liquidated damages in case of a breach of the sales contract, yet the aggrieved party also usually receives the right to sue for additional damages.

The courts also award damages on the basis that a breach of contract is an illegal action. If no fraud is intended, the courts may award **nominal damages** to the injured party, as shown in Exhibit 14.4. These nominal damages are granted in recognition that the rights of one of the parties, the injured party, have been violated. Typically, nominal damages are in the neighborhood of one dollar. They are awarded only when no financial loss is suffered by the aggrieved party to the contract.

The third remedy for breach of contract is *specific performance* (previously discussed in Chapter 13). Often, money damages are not an adequate remedy. In this event, the courts may grant the injured party a court order requiring that the defaulting party perform the contract according to the specific terms included in the agreement.

Is Misrepresentation Related to Contract Performance?

Misrepresentations can occur and pass unnoticed even if the material facts are available in sources of information that are readily and equally available to both parties to a contract. In these situations, the misrepresentation of a material fact would not always entitle the other party to cancel the contract. For example, some courts say that a buyer has no right to rely on a misrepresentation when the sources of information are equally available to both parties.

One such situation involves the zoning ordinance. The seller could misrepresent the nature of the land use restriction that affects the property. In this situation, an unintentional misrepresentation of existing state or local law affords no basis for rescission, because the law is presumably a matter of common knowledge, open and available to all who desire to explore its mysteries. The important phrase in this statement is "no basis for rescission."

The parties to the contract should make use of all readily available public information and take every opportunity to inspect the property. In certain situations, a misrepresentation will not be grounds to void a contract even though the misrepresentation can be the basis for filing a suit to obtain damages. The body of law relating to misrepresentation in contracts is slowly changing to eliminate any possibility that a person could profit from anther person's gullibility or ignorance. However, change is slow, and the buyer should not assume that his interests are totally protected in the law.

Finally, a misrepresentation, either intentional or unintentional, may not be discovered until the contract has actually been performed. After the closing date when the agreement has been fulfilled and the consideration exchanged, the buyer may discover that a misrepresentation was made. It is important to remember that the buyer is seldom in a position to discover the seller's misrepresentations until he has taken possession of the property. Some of the more common grounds for misrepresentation in such cases include the following:

- Magnitude and sources of the property's income, profits, and volume of business
- Location of the property's boundary lines
- Exact frontage of the property or the age of the improvements on the property
- Soil's drainage capacity and characteristics
- Existence or nonexistence of encumbrances, such as easements and liens

Both the buyer and the seller should be careful about their statements and understanding of these factors pertaining to the property being exchanged.

What Is the Real Estate Sales Contract?

The purpose of the **real estate sales contract** is to bind two individuals to the sale and the purchase of a property under certain specified, mutually agreeable terms and provisions. The real estate sales contract is the required written evidence of the offer and the acceptance of the consideration between two competent parties to the contract. This legal instrument does not convey any ownership rights to the property. It does not pass the rights of ownership from one individual to the other. It is merely written evidence of a mutual agreement to undertake the transfer of ownership rights to the physical commodity known as real estate.

No standard real estate contract is in use throughout the country. However, certain basic features are found in most real estate sales contracts. The features are explained here in reference to the sample contract in Exhibit 14.5. It is one of many forms that can be used as a real estate sales contract.

AGREEMENT AND THE CONSIDERATION

The first part of a real estate sales contract pertains to the agreement reached by the parties and the consideration that will be exchanged by those individuals. An examination of the sales contract in Exhibit 14.5 reveals that the buyer "agrees to buy" the property under the terms established in the document. Clause 1 of the contract is the offer. The seller's acceptance appears at the end of the contract in a clause that precedes the seller's signature and contains the phrase "the above offer is accepted." These two clauses, and the inferences therein, form the agreement required for a contract. The buyer offers to purchase under the conditions stated in the contract, and the seller accepts that offer as stated in the contract.

In Clause 3, the property is identified. The description of the property can take two forms. The full legal description of the property can be given in the clause, or it can be attached to the document if the attachment is identified in Clause 3. Alternatively, as in this document, the mailing address can be specified with the understanding that the buyer and seller both realize that the mailing address is not the legal description and that the legal description will be provided on the document that actually passes ownership rights. The legal implication of Clause 3 is that the seller will give the buyer the property contingent upon a simultaneous action in which the buyer gives the seller an asset of equivalent value.

The consideration is identified in Clause 4 of the contract. The second part of the consideration is specified in Clauses 5 and 6. These three clauses are the financial section of the real estate sales contract. In Clause 4, the buyer identifies the price she is willing to pay for the property when the exchange is made. At this point, both the buyer and the seller have promised to give something and simultaneously receive something.

The financial transaction, however, can be accomplished in a number of ways. Notice that Clauses 4 and 6 provide several options. The buyer can make a down payment and attempt to obtain a mortgage loan. These two components make up the financial asset that the buyer will give to the seller. When the buyer receives the funds from the lender, those funds will be used to pay off the seller's obligation under her mortgage.

In addition, Clause 4 mentions "earnest money"—the funds that the buyer places on deposit with the real estate broker or closing agent to serve as both an indication of intent to honor the contract and a guarantee that the broker and the seller will receive compensation if the buyer does not honor the contract. These funds are not an additional cash payment, because the earnest money is applied to the down payment at the time the property is traded. The seller wants an earnest money deposit that is large enough to cover any expenses that might have been incurred plus compensation for the contract not being fulfilled.

In addition to earnest money, the down payment, and the possibility of obtaining a new loan, other options can be stipulated in the financial section of the real estate sales contract. The potential buyer could assume the seller's loan. In this situation, most typically with the lending institution's approval, the buyer accepts the seller's

CONTRACT FOR THE SALE AND PURCHASE OF REAL ESTATE (OFFER AND ACCEPTANCE)

THIS CONTRACT IS DESIGNED TO BE USED PRIMARILY WITH SINGLE-FAMILY RESIDENTIAL PROPERTY.

THIS IS A LEGALLY BINDING CONTRACT! IF NOT FULLY UNDERSTOOD, ALWAYS SEEK ADVICE FROM YOUR ATTORNEY PRIOR TO SIGNING!

Time _____ AM/PM   Date _____ 20 _____,   State of _____

1. BUYER _____ agrees to buy, and
    SELLER _____ agrees to sell, the
    herein described property.

2. DISCLOSURE OF AGENCY: Buyer and seller above acknowledge that Broker _____ (sales
    agent or broker) and any subagents represent the Seller and this fact was fully disclosed.

3. PROPERTY LEGAL DESCRIPTION AND ADDRESS: _____
    _____
    _____
    _____
    City of _____, County _____, State _____
    and all improvements, known as _____.
    A legal description may be attached.

4. PURCHASE PRICE: The Buyer will pay a total of $ _____
        EARNEST MONEY: A sum attached to contract $ _____
            has been deposited with _____
            who shall hold it in trust, presuming clearance of the check.
        ADDITIONAL DOWN PAYMENT: Paid at closing and subject to $ _____
            adjustments and prorations
        BALANCE: Balance of price, is payable as: $ _____
        A. CASH: _____
        B. LOAN ASSUMPTION: Buyer is able to assume the existing loan in the approximate balance of
            $_____, with interest not to exceed _____% the first year, and payable over a period not
            less than _____ years.
        C. NEW LOAN: _____ FHA _____ VA _____ CONV _____ FmHA _____ FLB _____ Adjustable _____ Fixed
            Buyer is able to quality for a new loan with this property as a security interest in an amount not less
            than $_____, with interest not to exceed _____% the first year, and payable over a period
            not less than _____ years.
        D. OTHER: _____

5. LOAN AND CLOSING COSTS: Paid by S, Seller; B, Buyer;
    _____ Appraisal   _____ Survey
    _____ Attorney, closing   _____ Prepaid interest
    _____ Attorney documents   _____ PMI/FHA-MIP

(continued)

____ Credit report	____ Tax underwrit. service fee
____ Discount points	____ Title insurance, mortgagor
____ Hazard insurance	____ Title insurance, mortgagee
____ Heat/air. cond. inspect.	____ VA funding
____ Home warranty	____ Other _____
____ Loan origination	_____
____ Recording	_____
____ Septic tank inspect.	_____

The total cost paid by the BUYER shall not exceed $ _____

and total cost paid by SELLER shall not exceed $ _____

6. APPLICATION FOR FINANCING: If applicable, BUYER agrees to make application for a new loan or loan assumption within _____ days from the date of acceptance of this contract.

7. PRORATIONS AND LIENS: Property insurance, current real property taxes, special assessment taxes, rental payments, and unpaid interest on assumed loans shall be prorated as of the closing date unless otherwise specified therein. All property taxes due on or before the closing and all special assessments shall be paid by the SELLER. All security deposits, if applicable, shall be transferred to BUYER at closing. SELLER agrees to pay prior to closing any escrow shortage based upon an audit by the lender.

8. EARNEST MONEY AND DEFAULT: The earnest money shall be applied to the purchase price or closing costs. Specific performance is the essence of this contract.
   A. In the event of breach by the BUYER, the SELLER at his option may (a) accept the earnest money as liquidated damages. One-half shall be paid to the Broker, provided that the broker's portion shall not be larger than the total compensation under this contract, or (b) enter suit for damages in any court of jurisdiction, or (c) enter suit for specific performance in any court of jurisdiction.
   B. In the event of breach by the SELLER, the BUYER at his option may (a) accept the return of the earnest money and cancel the offer, or (b) enter a suit for damages in any court of jurisdiction, or (c) enter a suit for specific performance in any court of jurisdiction. Broker shall be paid the full compensation under this contract.
   C. If it becomes necessary to enter litigation to ensure the performance of this contract, the losing party agrees to pay all attorney fees and court costs.

9. CONVEYANCE: The SELLER is to furnish a GENERAL WARRANTY DEED. Reasonable time shall be allowed for preparation of and examination of title. Should examination of title reveal defects which can be cured, the SELLER hereby obligates himself to cure same as expeditiously as reasonably possible and to execute and tender a general warranty deed conveying title that can be insured (by a title company qualified to do and doing business in _____ (State)) EXCEPT for the following terms recorded in the county of _____: protective covenants, zoning ordinances, prior mineral reservations, and easements for public utilities.

If said title defects cannot be cured within 30 days after the closing date, then BUYER shall have the option of having his earnest money returned and being released from further liability hereon, or having SELLER

(continued)

complete the same as expeditiously as possible. SELLER represents that the property may be legally used for residential purposes and that no government agency has served any notice requiring repairs, alterations, or corrections of any existing conditions except as stated herein.

10. CLOSING: The closing date is estimated to be on or before _____. Parties may extend the date by mutual agreement.

11. POSSESSION: Possession shall be delivered to BUYER:

     A. _____ Upon closing date.

     B. _____ After closing date, but no later than _____ days after closing. SELLER agrees to pay BUYER at the closing $ _____ per day from closing to date possession is delivered.

12. RISK OF LOSS: Risk of loss or damage to the property by fire or other casualty occurring up to the time of closing is assumed by the SELLER. In the event of material damage by fire or otherwise before the closing, BUYER may declare this contract void and shall be entitled to the return of his earnest money, or the BUYER may elect to complete the transaction in accordance with this contract, provided the property is restored by the SELLER at SELLER's expense prior to the closing.

13. TERMITE CONTROL REQUIREMENTS:

     A. _____ None

     B. _____ Purchase price to include a current termite control policy issued by a licensed operator that subject property shows no evidence of termite or other wood destroying insect infestation, and if such infestation now exists, furnish warranty of approved treatment, and correct any structural damage caused by infestation.

     C. _____ Purchase price to include termite control policy and inspection report as required by HUD, VA, or lender.

14. FIXTURES AND ATTACHED EQUIPMENT: Unless specifically excluded herein, all fixtures and attached equipment, if any, are included in the purchase price. Such fixtures and attached equipment shall include, but not be limited to the following: carpeting, permanently attached mirrors, indoor and outdoor light fixtures, trees and shrubs, window air conditioners, window and door coverings, gas or electric grills, ceiling and attic fans, mail boxes, awnings, fencing, garage door openers and remote units, water softeners, propane and butane tanks, and antennas attached to the real property in a permanent manner. Other: _____
_____
_____

15. INSPECTIONS AND REPAIRS: BUYER certifies that he has inspected the property and all improvements thereon and accepts the property in its present condition. BUYER is not relying upon warranties, representations, or statements of agent or SELLER as to the age or condition of improvements, other than those specified therein. These provisions apply to and bind the heirs, executors, administrators, successors, and assignees of their respective parties.

     A. BUYER accepts the property in its present condition, subject only to the following: _____
_____
_____
_____

(continued)

B. The following items, if any, shall be in normal working order at closing: dishwasher, disposals, trash compactor, ranges, exhaust fans, electrical systems, heating and air conditioning systems, plumbing systems, and _____. BUYER shall have the right at his expense to inspect the above items prior to closing. If any of the above items are found not to be in normal working order, BUYER shall notify SELLER in writing 1-day prior to closing. After such notice as provided therein, SELLER agrees to pay the cost of repair of such items including FHA, VA, or other lender requirements, up to but not exceeding $ _____. If cost of such repairs will exceed the above amount, and SELLER refuses to pay the additional cost, BUYER may declare this contract null and void. If BUYER does not give notice of defects in writing prior to closing, subsequent repairs shall be at BUYER's expense.

16. SURVIVAL OF CONTRACT: Except as otherwise provided herein, all express representations and covenants set forth in this contract shall survive delivery of the deed and closing. All other contractual obligations shall terminate with closing.

17. EQUAL HOUSING OPPORTUNITY: This agency does business in accordance with the Federal Housing Law of the Civil Rights Acts. This agency does not discriminate against any person n the sale or rental of housing, in the financing of housing, and the provision of real estate brokerage services.

18. ALIENATION CLAUSE (DUE ON SALE): If the note and/or deed of trust or mortgage for any existing loan contains an alienation clause, the lender may demand full payment of the entire loan balance as a result of the transfer. Both parties acknowledge that they are not relying on any representation of the other party or broker with respect to the enforceability of such a provision in existing notes and/or deeds of trust of mortgages executed in accordance with this agreement. Both parties have been advised by the Broker to seek legal advice with respect to alienation.

19. LEGALLY BINDING CONTRACT: The undersigned parties understand that this is a legally binding contract and agree and accept all of the above items and terms. IF NOT UNDERSTOOD, SEEK COMPETENT LEGAL ADVICE!

20. FHA RESCIND CLAUSE: (Required only on FHA applications): The BUYER shall not be obligated to complete the purchase of the property described herein or to incur any penalty by forfeiture of earnest money unless the SELLER has delivered to the BUYER a written statement issued by the Federal Housing Commissioner setting forth the appraised value of $ _____, which the SELLER agrees to deliver to the BUYER promptly. The BUYER shall have the option of proceeding with the execution of this contract without regard to the amount of the appraised value in the statement.

21. SQUARE FOOTAGE: Buyer and Seller acknowledge that square footage is approximate. BUYER may have dwelling measured by independent and qualified third party, and the BUYER agrees to pay the cost.

22. SOIL CONDITION: BUYER and SELLER acknowledge that soil conditions are unknown. BUYER may have soil conditions tested by an independent and qualified third party, and BUYER agrees to pay the cost.

23. OTHER CONDITIONS: _____
_____
_____

24. EXPIRATION OF OFFER: This offer shall expire unless written acceptance is received by the Broker before _____ AM/PM on _____ 20____.

(continued)

ALL PARTIES ARE AWARE AND ACKNOWLEDGE THAT THE UNDERSIGNED AGENT(S), AND THE COMPANIES AFFILIATED WITH THE AGENTS, HAVE REPRESENTED THE INTERESTS OF THE SELLER THROUGHOUT.

OFFER

_____	_____	_____
Buyer	Sales agent	Broker

_____   _____
Buyer   Sales agent

_____
Phone:

_____
SS#:

ACCEPTANCE

The above offer is ACCEPTED on _____ 20____ at _____ AM/PM. I/We acknowledge that the below named agent is the procuring cause in securing this offer and agree to pay a fee of _____ for professional services rendered.

_____	_____	_____
Seller	Sales agent	Broker

_____
Seller

_____
Phone

_____
SS#/Tax ID #:

Note: This contract was assembled by the authors to represent typical clauses. The contract used in one locale will vary from jurisdiction to jurisdiction.

responsibility to pay off a mortgage. If this option is taken, the buyer would pay the difference between the value of the unpaid mortgage and the sales price to the seller at the closing.

Another option that could be exercised in the financial section is the issuance of a loan by the seller to the buyer. In this situation, a mortgage instrument of some form is drafted and signed by the buyer and seller. The buyer promises to pay the seller a certain mutually agreeable interest rate and also agrees to a predetermined repayment scheme.

In sum, the financial section of the real estate sales contract describes the financial asset that the buyer will give the seller in exchange for the property. The three components in the financial section are:

1. The earnest money deposit,
2. The cash that will be paid by the buyer at the time the property is traded, and
3. The mortgage provision, which can take three possible forms:
   (a) The buyer can obtain a new loan.
   (b) The buyer can assume the loan that was originally issued to the seller.
   (c) The buyer can obtain a loan directly from the seller (purchase money mortgage).

Various combinations of these financial arrangements can be used. For example, the property identified in Exhibit 14.5 could have sold under the following alternative conditions:

	CASE 1	CASE 2	CASE 3
Earnest money deposit	$ 10,000	$ 10,000	$ 10,000
Cash at closing from buyer	15,000	15,000	15,000
Mortgage assumption	0	100,000	0
New first loan	225,000	0	0
Loan from the seller to the buyer	0	125,000	225,000
	$ 250,000	$ 250,000	$ 250,000

All three cases contain $25,000 in equity and $225,000 in various forms of debt that the buyer will give the seller in exchange for the property.

CONTINGENCY PROVISIONS

The buyer may choose to incorporate several **contingency provisions** into the real estate sales contract. The sections of Clause 4 relating to a new loan and a loan assumption start with the phrases "the buyer is able to qualify for a new loan" and "the buyer is able to assume the existing loan." These statements provide a contingency by which the buyer can escape or avoid the contract. However, the contingency arises only if the buyer is unable to obtain a new mortgage or to assume the existing mortgage. As protection for her own interests, the seller should make sure that the mortgage terms the buyer is seeking are reasonable given the current market. If current interest rates are 11 percent per year and loan maturity is 25 years, the seller would be foolish to sign a contract in which the buyer is asking for a 5-percent mortgage for 50 years.

A second contingency clause commonly used in a sales contract provides that the offer is contingent upon the buyer's ability to sell the residential unit that is currently owned. In this situation, the buyer makes an offer on a replacement residence before an offer is received on the residence that he currently owns. Because the buyer would need the equity from the current home to purchase the new home, the contract could not be fulfilled if the current residence were not sold. These terms would be written in Clause 23.

The third contingency clause that the buyer can add to the sales contract provides that the offer will be contingent upon inspection of the property on the day of the closing. The buyer may insist on this clause to ensure that the seller will not be negligent in repairs and ordinary maintenance between the date the contract is signed and the date on which the property changes ownership, which may be two or three months later. The clause implies that the buyer reserves the right to void the contract if the property is not in the same condition as it was on the day the contract was signed. This contingency clause is used in addition to (and should not be confused with) Clause 15, which is entitled "Inspections and Repairs." This clause is a statement made by the buyer that the property was inspected and found to be satisfactory with regard to its age and the condition of improvements at the time the contract was signed.

The contingency provisions are placed in the contract by the buyer as protection against certain possible occurrences. The first contingency clause protects the buyer from a financial obligation that could not be discharged if a loan were not available. The second contingency clause protects the buyer from a financial obligation that could not be discharged unless the current dwelling in which the household lives is sold. Finally, the third contingency clause protects the buyer from taking possession of property that is not in the same physical condition as the property that was the basis for the contract.

MISCELLANEOUS PROVISIONS

The miscellaneous provisions are stated in other clauses of the real estate sales contract in Exhibit 14.5. Clause 9, the **conveyance clause,** is a statement describing the type and form of the deed that the seller will give to the buyer as indication of ownership. The deed is a legal instrument that passes ownership of the property. The conveyance clause specifically names a "general warranty deed" as the instrument that the buyer and seller agree to exchange as evidence of ownership.

Even though the buyer and seller have agreed to exchange a general warranty deed as evidence of title, the buyer wants proof that the seller does have the full rights of ownership that she is selling to the buyer. The buyer, therefore, requires that the seller furnish an abstract of title that is satisfactory to the buyer's attorney. The abstract of title is a legal document showing the property's history of ownership. By checking through the chain of ownership, the buyer's attorney can determine whether the current seller is in possession of the full rights of ownership that the buyer is expecting to receive.

The seller has the option of providing a paid title insurance policy in the amount of the purchase price instead of a title abstract. Title insurance offers the owner protection against loss of the property due to some defect in the title or ownership rights that the seller passes to the buyer. The seller could offer title insurance only if the title were good, as shown by an abstract and title search that was done when the seller purchased the property. If a title insurance policy is cheaper than the cost to obtain a new abstract, use of the title insurance option would be to the seller's financial benefit.

Clause 7 contains an agreement that the buyer will compensate the seller for any payments that the seller made for property taxes and any insurance payments applicable to the period of time after the property changes ownership.

Clause 10 is the closing clause that establishes a date and a time at which the buyer and seller and interested third parties, such as the buyer's attorney and the broker, will meet to consummate the transaction. This is the day and time when the property changes ownership.

Clause 11 accompanies Clause 10 because it is a statement of possession. The buyer owns the property immediately after the closing procedure is completed. However, the buyer and seller must agree on when the buyer takes possession of the property.

Clause 12, the **risk of loss clause,** identifies the responsibility for any casualty loss caused by fire, flood, windstorm, vandalism, and so forth that might occur between the time the sales contract is signed and the time of closing. The clause in Exhibit 14.5 specifically states that any loss or damage that may occur up to the time of the closing is assumed by the seller.

Clause 13 specifies the termite and pest control requirements typically stipulated by the buyer. As shown in Exhibit 14.5, the buyer requires that the seller provide a letter of clearance stating that there is no termite damage and that termites were not found on the property. The need for this letter of clearance generally arises in the southern and western states. This letter should be issued by a company that specializes in pest control and insect extermination.

Clause 14 is the fixtures and attached equipment clause. The purpose of this clause in the sales contract is to identify the items of personal property that are considered part of the real estate. The clause makes specific reference to such items as window air conditioners, carpeting, garage door openers and their remote units, and antennae that are to be viewed by both parties as transferring with the real estate. The clause defines a fixture on the basis of attachment. Those items that are "bolted, nailed, screwed, buried, or otherwise attached to the real property in a permanent manner" are fixtures.

However, the clause allows the parties to the contract to define some fixtures as personal property. The phrase "unless specifically excluded" means that the seller should make a list of specific items that are not to be traded with the property. The buyer also may include a list of personal property items that he would like to have traded with the property.

Clause 15 is the inspections and repair clause. It identifies the buyer's right to inspect the property and the seller's responsibility to keep the property in good repair until the closing. An important part of the clause is the statement that the buyer expects all appliances and mechanical equipment to be in normal working order at the time of the closing. If they are not, an agreement is made between the buyer and the seller about the extent of the repair expenditure that the seller wishes to incur.

The second part of Clause 15 is the inspection clause. The buyer should arrange for some formal inspection before the contract is signed. The inspection should be no sooner than the day of the closing, or it could be the day after the property is vacated by the seller if the seller vacates before the closing. An inspection is common but not mandatory. At the inspection, the buyer makes certain that all fixtures to remain with the property are in place and that all appliances and mechanical systems are in working order.

Clause 23 provides space to specify matters not discussed in preceding clauses or to raise issues not covered in the preprinted clauses. This clause can be used to clarify the issue of fixtures and attached equipment.

Clause 24 identifies the expiration date of the offer. The buyer should state an exact number of days during which the offer is outstanding. However, the buyer should realize that he must deliver the offer and communicate it to the seller without unreasonable delay.

The execution section of the contract follows Clause 24. The important signatures are the buyer's and the seller's because these signatures give evidence of the offer and acceptance. Furthermore, any interested parties, such as the brokers, should sign the contract so that they will also be bound by its terms and conditions. The very last section appearing on the sample contract is an agreement between the seller and the brokers about the brokers' commissions.

A question may arise about the need for signatures of witnesses, the need for an acknowledgment, and the necessity of recording the document. Generally, witnesses are not essential to the validity of a sales contract. Sales contracts are generally not acknowledged (that is, witnessed by a public official such as a notary public), and because they are short-term contracts they are generally not recorded.

What Other Types of Sales Contracts May be Used?

Three other types of sales contracts may be used:

OPTION

The **option** is a written contract that gives a potential buyer a right to buy the property prior to a specified date. The potential buyer pays the seller an agreed-upon sum of money to hold the property off the market until the option either is exercised or expires. Both the option payment and the holding period are part of the negotiation process. The written contract must contain the option payment, holding period, valid agreement, and consideration.

BINDER

The **binder** is shorter in length and contains only the essential terms, deposit, and intent of the parties involved to employ an attorney to prepare a formal longer contract. The formal contract may be so detailed that additional legal language is required.

CONTRACT FOR DEED

A **contract for deed,** also known as an **installment contract** or **land contract,** gives the buyer possession with all or part of the purchase price offered as credit to the buyer. The deed is held by the seller until the last payment is made. This type of purchase can present legal difficulties should the buyer default on payments, or should the seller default in delivering the deed.

Chapter Summary

The real estate sales contract is a valid, bilateral, express, and enforceable contract. As a valid contract, it contains all of the essential features required by the body of law known as contract law. It is a stated agreement negotiated between the two parties through the offer and acceptance process about an exchange of assets that are approximately equal; this exchange is the consideration that is satisfactory to the two parties to the contract. The contract is initiated and executed with the full and real consent of all parties to that contract. In addition, the object or action involved in the contract is legal. Finally, the real estate sales contract is expressed in written form.

The real estate sales contract contains many clauses and provisions. The two most important are the agreement and the consideration. The potential buyer and the seller reach a mutually acceptable decision about the exchange of assets that will take place. The buyer offers a certain financial package that consists of an earnest money deposit, cash at closing, and debt financing in exchange for the parcel of real estate. The seller accepts this financial package in exchange for the real property asset. After this financial agreement is reached, the buyer and the seller focus their attention on a series of other issues. Depending on the situation, these other issues can be of primary or secondary importance.

The body of contract law presupposes that all contracts will be honored by the parties involved. In this sense, the expectation is that all contracts will be discharged according to the conditions and terms specified within the document. However, in certain situations contracts are not discharged. There may be a legal excuse for this nonperformance, or one of the parties may breach the contract. Both the buyer and the seller should be fully aware of the legal excuses for nonperformance as well as the legal remedies available to them in the event of a breach of contract by the other party.

Internet Applications

A website has been established for this chapter at http://epley.swcollege.com.

Review Questions

1. Explain the differences among valid, void, voidable, enforceable, and unenforceable contracts.

2. Identify and explain the essential features of the offer and the acceptance.

3. In a real estate sales contract, what is the consideration?

4. Who are competent parties?

5. Distinguish between mistakes in fact and mistakes in law.

6. Distinguish between a material fact and an immaterial fact.

7. Define misrepresentation. When does it become fraud?

8. Under what circumstances do parties to a real estate sales contract have the duty to speak?

9. What four items can be discussed in the financial section of the real estate sales contract?

10. What are the three most common contingency provisions in a real estate sales contract?

11. Briefly discuss as many provisions of the sales contract as you can.

12. There are three ways of discharging a contract. One is to have both parties to the contract comply with all of the terms and obligations incurred in that contract. The other two ways are novation and accord and satisfaction. Explain the concept of novation and the concept of accord and satisfaction.

13. What are the legal excuses for nonperformance of a contract?

14. Describe the remedies available to the injured party when a breach of contract occurs.

Discussion Questions

1. Besides the legal requirement stipulated under the regulations of the Statute of Frauds, discuss the conceptual reasons why a real estate contract should be in written form.

2. Choose a friend or another student in the class and assign the role of buyer to one of you and the role of seller to the other. Then draft a real estate sales contract for an imaginary piece of property using simple, declarative statements, such as "The buyer will . . ." Compare the agreement and provisions of your contract with those in the contract shown in Exhibit 14.5.

3. Explain the meaning of the term *specific performance.*

4. Discuss the material found at the Internet addresses for this chapter on the website for this text.

## PART VI

The Decision to Manage the Property and Seek Information About the Lease

## CHAPTER 15

Real Estate Management and the Lease

1. What is the difference among the fee, the leased fee, and the leasehold, and how is each valued?

2. What must I know about the property management service in order to make a decision about managing the property?

3. What must I know about the typical clauses found in a lease?

4. What must I know about the typical clauses found in a commercial lease?

5. How can a lease be terminated?

6. What are the consequences when a lease is breached?

7. Are any consumer issues important? If yes, what are they?

8. What are the various types of rents that can be paid?

OBJECTIVES

When finished with this chapter, the student should be able to:

1. Discuss the differences among the fee, the leased fee, and the leasehold.

2. Discuss the services offered by a property manager.

3. Explain the typical parts of a lease.

4. State the rights and responsibilities of both the landlord and the tenant.

5. Discuss the types of clauses that may be found in a commercial lease.

actual possession	licensee
constructive eviction	nonfreehold
dispossession proceedings	overage rent
distraint	property management
distress	residential lease
eviction	right of possession
excess rent	right of redemption
fee	sandwich tenant
freehold	security deposit
implied warranty of habitability	subletting
invitee	summary proceedings
landlord's attachment	tenant
lease	trade fixtures
leased fee	trespasser

INTRODUCTION

When the investor decides to purchase a property, a collateral decision must also be made. Should the investor/property owner manage and operate the property or find a competent property manager to perform the task? In order to answer this question, the investor must know the full scope of administrative responsibilities that an investment property might require. Then, the investor has to decide which of these services a property manager will be contracted to perform. Consequently, an understanding of the property management function is important. To achieve this understanding, this chapter identifies the nature of the various management services that a property manager can provide and discusses the duties and responsibilities of a professional property manager.

What Is the Purpose of the Lease?

Chapter 2 discussed the four basic rights in real property: disposition, use, exclusion, and possession. Ownership of all four is called the *fee,* which is held *freehold,* or free of calendar time, which means it is held for a lifetime. The fee ownership rights are always valued by the appraiser using the current market rent and prices from comparable properties.

The fee owner has the right at any time to allow another party, the **tenant,** to use part of these rights for a definite period of time in exchange for money, or *contract rent.* The usual rights given to the tenant include use, exclusion, and possession, which are held **nonfreehold,** or for calendar time with a definite beginning and ending date.

Once this contractual arrangement is formalized in a **lease,** the value of the **leased fee** is now determined by the contract rent for the remaining term of the lease. Thus, the fee owner has a motivation to charge a contract rent that is at least equal to the current market rent on similar properties. In the strictest interpretation, the lease is both a conveyance and a contract. The owner of the rights, the landlord, gives or conveys certain rights to the property to the tenant. The tenant who receives these rights contracts with the landlord to pay money and perhaps perform certain other duties such as maintenance.

The fee is always valued at current market rents and prices. Once the fee is leased, it is valued at the contract rent negotiated between the two parties. Should the tenant negotiate a rent below the market rate, the lease rights held by the current tenant, the *leasehold,* has an economic value for **subletting.** Presuming the lease allows it, the current tenant could vacate the premises, set a rent slightly below the market rent, and re-lease to a second tenant. Thus, the first tenant would be a **sandwich tenant** between the fee owner and the second tenant and would pocket the difference between the two parties until the lease terminates.

Exhibit 15.1 shows the relationship among these terms and their value. A typical real estate assignment could involve any party, such as the fee owner, the first tenant,

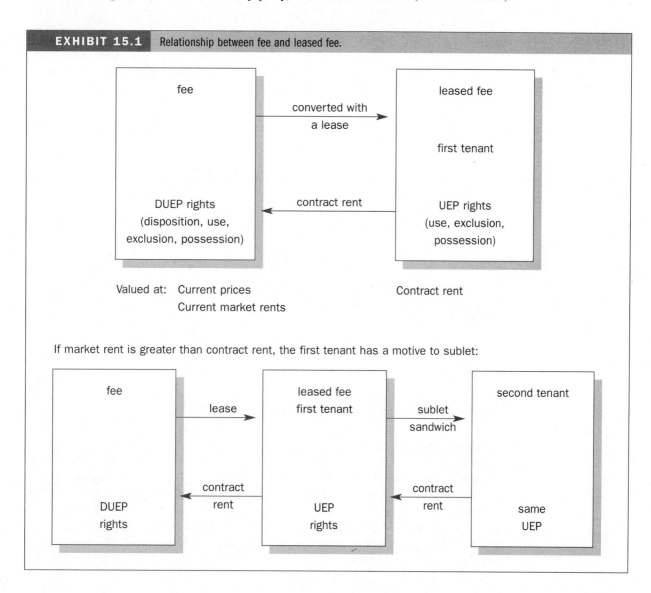

EXHIBIT 15.1   Relationship between fee and leased fee.

or the second tenant. An appraiser could be asked to establish a market value on the fee, the contract fee, the value of the sandwich lease, and the value of the leasehold. A real estate agent could be asked to represent the interests of any of the parties involved.

For example, examine the following office building in downtown that contains 20,000 rentable square feet. The market rent per square foot is $15, which is projected to increase by 4 percent annually by mutual agreement for the five-year term. After some negotiations, the tenant signs a gross lease for $215,000 contract rent annually that remains constant.

1. *What type of lease exists?* This is a gross lease with contract rent.
2. *How is the market value of the future rents claimed by the fee interest determined?* The market value of the market rent would be estimated by calculating the total income for each of the five years:

   $300,000   (20,000 × $15)
   $312,000   (20,000 × $15.60)
   $324,480   (20,000 × $16.224)
   $337,459   (20,000 × $16.873)
   $350,960   (20,000 × $17.548)

   These figures would be discounted to present value by a discount rate for the fee ownership. If that rate were equal to 10 percent, the value of the future rents claimed by the fee interest would be $1,222,771.
3. *Does the leasehold have value?* Yes, because the contract rent is less than the market rent.
4. *How is the leasehold valued?* The leasehold is valued by determining the present value of the difference between the two rent figures.

   $300,000 − $215,000 = $85,000
   $312,000 − $215,000 = $97,000
   $324,480 − $215,000 = $109,480
   $337,459 − $215,000 = $122,459
   $350,960 − $215,000 = $135,960

   These figures would be discounted to present value at a discount rate for the leasehold. If that rate were equal to 13 percent, the leasehold value would be equal to $375,961.

What Is the Property Management Function?

Property **management** is a professional activity that assists property owners in achieving their investment objectives. Depending on the individual and on the market circumstances, these investment objectives can vary. However, for the most part, the investor will probably seek to maximize the total return on the investment over the holding period. Obtaining this objective would require a combination of maximizing after-tax cash flow (ATCF) and maximizing equity increase through mortgage reduction and price appreciation. The property manager can provide many different services to help the investor achieve this goal. These property management services are discussed in the following subsections.

MANAGEMENT OF THE PHYSICAL ASSET

The professional property manager should be able to establish an adequate and well-defined maintenance program for the property. In order to perform this service, the property manager must understand the nature of physical deterioration. He must be able to make a physical inspection of the property and determine which items require immediate repair and which items can have maintenance and repair deferred. In addition, he must be able to estimate both the amount of funds that should be budgeted for repairs and maintenance in any given year and the amount of funds necessary to be set aside as a replacement reserve.

MANAGEMENT OF FINANCIAL RECORDS

The property manager should be able to perform the necessary financial accounting functions that are required for the property. This includes the generation of an owner's income and operating expense statement on both a monthly and an annual basis. An example of such a statement on an annual basis is provided in Chapter 6 as Exhibit 6.6. The property owner may choose to buy this service separately from the management of the physical asset or even from the rent collection service (to be discussed later in this chapter). In essence, the property owner would be buying the property manager's skills as an accountant.

MANAGEMENT OF THE TENANT ACQUISITION PROCESSES

In the very simplest terms, the property manager should be able to merchandise the rental space in her control. In order to fulfill this function, she should understand the various aspects of merchandising that will attract potential tenants. The property manager should know the effectiveness of advertising in newspapers, of mailing individualized brochures, and of placing "for rent" signs on the property itself. The property manager should know which of these techniques is currently most successful in the community.

MANAGEMENT OF THE RENT COLLECTION AND LEASE NEGOTIATION PROCESSES

The property manager can also provide rent collection and lease negotiation services. In this sense, the property management firm would be the depository for rent payments that are made by the tenants. The property manager would also provide a procedure by which delinquent rents could be collected. For example, if the rent is due on the first of the month but no later than the fifth of the month, the property manager could send out a late notice on the sixth of the month reminding the tenant of the late payment. Then, if the payment is not received by the 10th or the 15th of the month, the property manager could send out a second notification informing the tenant of both the lateness of the payment and legal action that will be undertaken if the payment is not made by the 15th of the month. In this way, the property manager removes one of the more distasteful aspects of rental property from the shoulders of the property owner.

MANAGEMENT OF THE FINANCIAL ASSET

In addition to the responsibilities of managing the physical asset and maintaining the financial records, the property manager can also provide the following investment counseling services:

1. Analyze the variables that enter into the property owner's decision to purchase the income-earning property. For this reason, it is important for the property manager to understand the basics of investment analysis.
2. Determine the level of market rent for the property and use this estimate to establish contract rents when the lease is signed.
3. Advise the owner on the nature and magnitude of operating expenses.
4. Advise the owner on the tax aspects of the investment decision by analyzing the quantity and quality of maintenance and repair expenditures versus improvement expenditures and establishing a useful life and salvage value for the property, which can be used in the permissible depreciation scheme.
5. Advise the owner on alternative ways to maximize equity increase through price appreciation by identifying several improvement alternatives and specifying the possible impact on rent receipts.
6. Advise on refinancing and the use of those funds to achieve specified investor objectives, such as tax shelter and pyramiding.
7. Advise on the lease provisions, including the rent agreement that will help to fulfill the property owner's investment objectives.

In summary, the property manager can serve as an investment analyst if the property manager has these skills and if the property owner is certain that the manager is capable and competent to give such advice.

GENERAL ASPECTS OF THE PROPERTY MANAGEMENT FUNCTION

The full scope of the property manager's responsibilities often extends beyond the day-to-day operations of the property and the economic performance of the property. In addition to the services discussed above, the property manager is also responsible for the supervision and evaluation of personnel who work in and on the subject property. If the property manager is an efficient and effective employee supervisor, operating expenditures can be reduced because of increased labor productivity.

How Is a Property Manager Selected?

The investor/property owner should realize that there are individual differences among people who identify themselves as property managers. An understanding of the differences that can arise among individuals is important in the selection process of a property manager. Most practitioners in the field of real estate management are property supervisors. The difference between a property supervisor and a property manager lies in the manner in which each views the job, the way in which each discharges responsibilities, the manner in which each makes decisions, and the criteria by which each measures success. The exact title that these individuals use is less important than the way that they relate to the scope of the assigned responsibilities that are given them by the property owner in the management agreement. In order to reach an understanding of the difference between a property manager and a property supervisor, the property owner must determine (1) whether the individuals are effective as well as efficient in discharging their responsibilities, and (2) whether they are given the authority as well as the responsibility to carry out their assigned tasks.

What Are the Selection Criteria
for Residential Tenants?

It is not possible for the property manager to make a complete analysis of every member of a family or household who applies for residential space in the subject property. However, the property manager should obtain information about certain characteristics of the tenant. The purpose of the discussion in this section is to identify criteria that can be used as a basis for tenant selection. Some of these criteria cannot be supported by the tenant information that is gathered. In this latter event, the property manager must operate subjectively and realize that there is a degree of uncertainty about any conclusions.

THE OCCUPANCY PERIOD

The property manager should attempt to find tenants whose tenancy will be long-term or medium-term, but definitely not short-term, in nature. Frequent turnover in occupancy generally creates greater than normal expenditures for advertising and turnkey operations.

HOUSEKEEPING ABILITY

A large portion of building maintenance is a matter of housekeeping. Cleanliness of the tenants' quarters and of the public or common space has a significant impact on the desirability of the property to prospective tenants. Consequently, tenants who are good housekeepers are preferred to tenants who are untidy. Moreover, the maintenance expenditures are lower in a building with good, clean tenants than it would be under other circumstances. However, the level of a prospective tenant's housekeeping ability is difficult to discern. A rough approximation could be the person's general appearance, but this would not be an accurate or exact measure of the household's attitude toward cleanliness.

COMPATIBILITY

The property manager should realize that to a degree the personal happiness of each tenant is dependent upon the compatibility of all tenants in the building. In residential property, the tenants could have some important common characteristics, such as income, age, and social background.

   The search for tenant compatibility in residential units should *not* lead the property manager to make unwarranted assumptions about the need for any type of discrimination. Racial, ethnic, religious, and sexual discrimination in housing is forbidden by law.

CREDIT RATING

The ability to pay rent remains one of the more important, if not the most important, tenant selection criteria. The property manager knows this fact and utilizes her judgment regarding necessary credit information about prospective tenants. In the analysis of the prospective tenant's credit rating, the property manager should ascertain the tenant's ability to pay the stipulated rent and the tenant's stability of employment. A credit check provides information with a greater degree of accuracy about rent-paying ability than about stability of employment.

What Is the Residential Lease?

Knowledge of the use and structure of the real estate lease is important in real estate decision making because many situations require an individual to enter into a **residential lease.** The individual may be subject to a lease as a tenant in an apartment or as a tenant in commercial space. As a commercial tenant, the individual may require retail space in a shopping center or office space in an office building. The individual who decides to purchase income-producing real estate will be subject to a lease as the owner or landlord of either residential units or commercial space. Consequently, an individual should be informed of all legal and financial aspects of the lease.

AGREEMENT AND CONSIDERATION

The terms *agreement* and *consideration* were discussed in Chapter 14 in relation to the offer and acceptance process in the sales contract. In the execution of a lease for residential space, the offer and acceptance components of the agreement usually take place at the same time. The landlord and the prospective tenant reach an agreement within a few minutes. The landlord usually indicates an asking price for the property, the potential tenant makes an offer to the landlord that is equal to the asking price, and the landlord accepts the offer. However, the tenant's offer need not be equal to the landlord's asking price. In this situation, the landlord and the prospective tenant may enter into a series of counteroffers until an agreement is reached.

THE RIGHTS AND RESPONSIBILITIES OF LANDLORD AND TENANT

The body of law pertaining to landlord–tenant relationships identifies certain rights and responsibilities of the two parties to the lease. If possible, the exact nature and extent of these rights and responsibilities should be defined and specified within the lease. However, if they are not specified in the lease, the body of law governing landlord–tenant relationships has established precedents that can be used to arbitrate any disagreement between the landlord and the tenant. Six of these major rights and responsibilities are described below.

Delivery of Possession

The first responsibility of the landlord is to deliver possession of the space to the tenant. Each lease must state the period of time during which the landlord promises possession of the space to the tenant. The provision may be stated as "January 1, 2000, through and including December 31, 2000." With such a statement, the landlord promises possession to the tenant beginning with the first day of January. The laws of the states are not in unanimous agreement about the nature of the landlord's promise. In some states, the landlord is held responsible for giving the tenant **actual possession** of the premises, whereas in other states the landlord is only responsible for giving the tenant the **right of possession.** The difference between actual possession and the right of possession is important. In states where the tenant is granted actual possession, the landlord is responsible for taking whatever action is necessary to put the tenant into the property on the first of January.

Use of the Property

Unless the lease restricts the tenant's use of the property, the tenant can use the property for any legal purpose. However, the landlord can place a clause in the lease that restricts the tenant's right to use. A landlord may, for example, restrict the premises to residential use only, to occupancy by no more than a certain number of persons, to the provision or selling of certain services or goods only, or to any other lawful purpose.

Tenant's Right to Exclude vs. Landlord's Right of Entry

The lease transfers the rights to possess and to use the property from the landlord to the tenant. In general, the tenant's right to use and to possess the property gives the tenant complete control of that property. Anyone who enters the property, including the landlord, without the tenant's consent is considered to be trespassing. This rule, however, is subject to two important exceptions:

1. The law recognizes the landlord's right to enter the property in order to collect rent.
2. The landlord can enter the property in order to prevent waste—that is, anything that is causing, or could cause, damage to the property—and to stop any nuisance.

Repairs and Maintenance

In general, the landlord has not been responsible under common law to maintain and repair the property that was leased to the tenant. This basic rule is expressed by the phrase *caveat lessee,* which translates "let the tenant beware." In essence, the landlord had no duty to maintain or repair the leased premises either before or after its occupancy. The same general principle was applicable to the tenant. The tenant's only responsibility was to preserve what he originally received—that is, to prevent deterioration of the leasehold subject to ordinary wear and tear. However, this basic rule is currently under question in the body of legal knowledge regarding landlord–tenant relationships. This legal view, as expressed in many legal cases and the statutes of most states, now imposes an expressed or implied obligation on the landlord to maintain and repair the property that is leased to the tenant. In other words, the current legal view is that the landlord makes an implied warranty of habitability in a lease.

Liability to Third Parties

When a third party is injured on the property, the law can hold either the tenant or the landlord liable for the injury depending on the circumstances created by the lease. There are three categories of third parties—invitees, licensees, and trespassers. An **invitee** is an individual who enters the property with either the express or implied consent of the tenant. The invitee enters the property to conduct business with the tenant. In the case of residential property, delivery persons, mail carriers, and meter readers would be considered invitees. The tenant has a responsibility to keep the property in a reasonably safe condition and to warn the individual of any condition that might be considered harmful. A **licensee** also is a person who enters the property with either the expressed or implied consent of the tenant. In the case of residential property, a licensee would be a guest of the tenant. A licensee must be warned of dangerous conditions, and the tenant must refrain from any conduct that might injure the visitor.

Finally, the **trespasser** is an individual who enters the property without the consent of the tenant. A trespasser takes the property as it is.

Right to Assign and Sublet

Unless a clause in the lease limits this right, the tenant can assign or sublet her rights in the property without the landlord's permission. An *assignment* (introduced in Chapter 8) is a process by which the original tenant transfers her *entire* unexpired rights in the leased property to a new tenant. The new tenant steps into the role of the original tenant. *Subletting* is the process by which the original tenant enters into a separate and distinct lease arrangement with a new tenant. This arrangement between the original tenant and the new tenant does not involve the landlord. Subletting is a transfer of a *portion,* but not all, of the original tenant's rights in the leased property. In other words, a sublet presupposes that the original tenant maintains some portion of the property. This portion can be either physical or temporal. The original tenant subleases some part of the space that was originally leased, or the original tenant subleases some portion of the time remaining in the original lease.

LEASE CLAUSES RELATING TO COMMON POINTS OF CONCERN BETWEEN THE LANDLORD AND THE TENANT

In addition to the major rights and responsibilities of the landlord and the tenant, the residential lease addresses other matters of concern to the parties to the lease. This section describes the clauses that typically appear in a residential lease to resolve matters of common concern.

FIXTURES. As defined previously in Chapter 1, fixtures are items of personal property attached to the structure so as to become part of the realty. When property is leased, the tenant may choose to attach his personal property to the improvement owned by the landlord. Once these items are attached, they are known by the generic name of fixtures. The disposition of these fixtures must be identified in the lease.

LANDLORD'S RIGHT TO ENTER TO SHOW THE PROPERTY. The landlord does not have the right to enter the property unless it is specified in the lease or unless the landlord is entering to collect the rent or to stop waste against the property. Due to this prohibition on their right to enter, landlords typically insert a clause into the lease that gives them some rights to show the property to a new tenant before the original lease expires. This clause generally comes into effect only after the original tenant has indicated that the lease will not be renewed.

HAZARD INSURANCE. The owner or landlord must have adequate insurance coverage against hazards such as fire and windstorms. The landlord who rents an entire structure to a single tenant can insert a lease clause requiring the tenant to carry such insurance and to provide adequate proof of the coverage. In the case of an apartment building, the landlord should always carry hazard insurance to cover the entire property.

SECURITY DEPOSITS. Although most states have enacted the landlord's lien or the landlord's attachment on the tenant's personal property as a security measure to guarantee payment of the rent as specified in the lease, both of these processes are subject to inconvenience, delay, and the cost of enforcing the legal action. Because of this inconvenience and cost, the practice arose of requiring the tenant to deposit money with the landlord to secure the payment of rent. The **security deposit** is intended to protect the landlord against default in rent payment as well as losses caused by the tenant's negligent behavior in relation to the landlord's property. Security deposits are not intended for the landlord's use to repair damages to the property that result from normal wear and tear.

UTILITY PAYMENTS. Responsibility for utility payments must be settled in the lease. In some instances, the landlord pays all utilities, such as electricity, natural gas, water, and trash collection. In other situations, the landlord provides trash collection and water but requires the tenant to pay for electricity and heating of the apartment. The arrangement should be specified clearly in the lease.

NOTIFICATION OF RENEWAL. A lease provision commonly included by the landlord requires the tenant to provide written notice of the intention to renew the lease. The clause typically states that the tenant must inform the landlord 60 or 30 days before the expiration of the current lease of an intention to renew the lease. In addition, the clause could state that the landlord has the right to change the conditions of the new lease. This provision enables the landlord to either increase rent or change the utility payment plans or some other aspect of the lease when the lease is renewed.

TRANSFER CLAUSE. The tenant is responsible for fulfilling the provisions of the lease even if she is transferred to a new job in a new locality. To avoid this jeopardy, the tenant should insist on a clause providing a release of the lease obligations if a relocation takes place. The transfer clause usually stipulates that the tenant's responsibilities terminate if a new job is taken that is 50, 75, or some other reasonable number of miles away from the residential unit for which the lease is written.

MISCELLANEOUS RULES AND REGULATIONS. In addition to the preceding specific clauses, the typical lease contains a section stating various rules and regulations that the landlord wishes to impose.

CONSUMER ISSUES IN THE LANDLORD–TENANT RELATIONSHIP

The residential lease agreement is affected by many consumer-oriented matters. One is the issue of the **implied warranty of habitability.** As explained in the earlier section on the rights and responsibilities of landlord and tenant, the courts currently hold that the landlord makes an implied warranty that the residential property will conform to minimum acceptable standards of livability. This section examines other consumer-oriented issues that affect the landlord–tenant relationship.

LIMITS IMPOSED ON THE LANDLORD'S RIGHT TO SELECT TENANTS. Under common law, the landlord has the right to rent property to whomever he pleases. This rule implies the right to refuse to rent to specific individuals and to refuse lease renewals to specific tenants. Currently, court decisions and statutes are beginning to impose limits on these rights. The federal and state fair housing acts expressly forbid the landlord to use race, ethnic origin, creed, or gender as a basis for a decision to issue a lease or renew a lease on property. However, the landlord still retains the right to make decisions based on creditworthiness, which can reflect employment history, promptness of discharging financial responsibilities, and adequacy of the prospective tenant's income level to meet the rent obligation.

LANDLORD'S DUTY TO PROTECT THE TENANT FROM CRIMINAL ACTS. Traditionally, the landlord did not have a responsibility or duty to protect the tenant from criminal acts committed by third parties. However, the courts are now beginning to place the responsibility on the lessor.

TENANT'S RIGHT TO WITHHOLD RENT. Traditionally, the landlord had the right to evict the tenant for nonpayment of rent. However, the courts are recognizing that a lease contains an implied warranty of habitability. In general, this means that the property is free from building and housing code violations. Some states allow the tenant to withhold all or part of the rent on the premise that the building or apartment is not habitable.

TENANT'S PROMISE TO COMPLY WITH LEGAL REQUIREMENTS AFFECTING THE PROPERTY. A lease typically requires that the tenant comply with all statutes, ordinances, and rules that are applicable to the property. In addition, the lease holds the tenant responsible for the correction and elimination of any nuisances and hazards that might be created by direct or indirect actions of the tenant. The legal interpretation of this requirement does not relate directly to the physical structure. The law does not hold the tenant responsible for structural changes to comply with statutes and ordinances; such compliance is viewed as the landlord's responsibility.

TENANT UNIONS. The single tenant in a multiunit apartment building has very little bargaining power with the landlord. To establish countervailing power, tenants have organized into unions for the purpose of bargaining with landlords.

How Can a Lease Be Terminated?

Leases can be terminated in many ways. Both the tenant and the landlord should understand the types of lease terminations and their effects.

EXPIRATION OF THE LEASE TERM. The most usual way for a lease to terminate is by the expiration of the mutually agreed period of tenancy. At that time, the tenant surrenders possession and use of the property to the landlord, and the landlord regains the leasehold estate and consequently has all of the rights of ownership in the property.

MUTUAL AGREEMENT TO TERMINATE. The lease may terminate before its expiration date if the landlord and tenant agree to its termination. For example, the tenant may hold a lease on the property for a definite period of time (a tenancy for years) and may find during the term of the lease that it would be better if the full lease term were not enforced. In this event, the tenant approaches the landlord and asks to be relieved of the responsibilities and obligations specified in the lease.

MERGER OF THE FREEHOLD AND LEASEHOLD ESTATES. A lease can terminate if the tenant purchases the property. In this case, the owner of the leasehold estate becomes the owner of the freehold estate, thereby canceling the lease.

BREACH OF CONTRACT. A breach of the conditions of the lease by either party can bring about its termination. When a tenant breaches the conditions of the lease, the landlord has many alternatives.

If the breach of contract involves nonpayment of rent or retaining possession of the property at the end of the term (tenancy at sufferance), the landlord is allowed in most states to undertake an action known as **summary proceedings** or **dispossession proceedings.** The landlord petitions the court in the local jurisdiction to regain possession of the property.

A landlord may breach the contract by depriving the tenant of use or possession of the entire leased property or a substantial portion of that property by either a positive act or a default. This action or default, which must be intentional and permanent, is known as **constructive eviction** by the landlord. It occurs when the tenant's use of the property is restricted or disturbed, either by the landlord's direct action or by his failure to act when there is a duty to act.

What Special-Purpose Clauses Can Appear in a Residential Lease?

Neither the landlord nor the tenant expects an apartment building to be damaged, destroyed, or condemned under eminent domain proceedings. The typical assumption is that if such events occur, the tenant will meet the obligations of the lease and neither default nor abandon the leased property. However, clauses can be placed in the lease to identify the tenant's responsibilities in such cases. Other clauses can be used to cover situations in which a landlord intends to use the property as collateral for a loan or to sell the property.

DAMAGE OR DESTRUCTION OF THE STRUCTURE. The residential lease can make provisions for the possibility that the structure can be damaged or destroyed. In common law, when land and a building are leased by the landlord to the tenant, the tenant is not freed of the responsibility to pay rent if the improvement is destroyed. However, a large number of states have abolished this unrealistic rule. In such states, if the building is destroyed or is damaged to such an extent that it is not usable by the tenant, the tenant is relieved of liability to pay the rent.

CONDEMNATION PROCEEDINGS AGAINST THE PROPERTY. The landlord could include a clause in the residential lease that would automatically terminate the lease on the day the property is taken by eminent domain proceedings. If this termination clause does not appear in the lease, the tenant may have a legal claim to some portion of the proceeds that the landlord obtains from the condemnation.

ABANDONMENT OF THE PROPERTY BY THE TENANT. Residential leases can provide for the contingency of abandonment of the premises by the tenant before the expiration date of the lease. The lease can state that the tenant continues to be liable for the rent until expiration of the lease. In this situation, if the landlord is able to find a new tenant, the original tenant is relieved of responsibility when the new lease is signed.

THE LANDLORD'S RIGHT TO MORTGAGE THE PROPERTY. When a lease is signed, the tenant's rights in the property are subordinated to any mortgages or other liens currently recorded against the property. However, once the lease is executed, a new mortgage with the property as collateral would be subordinate to the lease. To avoid this situation, the landlord could put a clause in the lease that would make the tenant's rights subordinate to a new mortgage.

DEFAULT BY THE TENANT. If a tenant fails to pay the mutually agreed upon rent, the tenant is in default of the lease provisions. In this case, the landlord has several remedies against the tenant. First, the statutes may create a lien on the tenant's personal property and financial assets. Second, a provision in common law known as **distraint** or **distress** allows the landlord to seize the tenant's property as security for the payment of rent. The landlord's right of distraint applies only when the tenant is in default, and it can be exercised only against the tenant's personal property that is on the leased property. The third remedy is typically known as the **landlord's attachment.** It enables the landlord legally to obtain the tenant's property as security against the eventual repayment of the rent while the courts are evaluating the merits of the landlord's claim.

SALE OF THE PROPERTY. If the landlord sells or gives away the property, the new owner accepts that property subject to the rights of the tenant. The new landlord remains responsible for fulfilling all the landlord's obligations as stipulated in the lease, unless the lease specifically includes a clause relieving the new landlord of such liability. This requirement is legally binding in the majority of states; however, the tenant should either insist on a clause to this effect in the lease or obtain legal opinion as to whether this stipulation is enforceable in the state in which the property is located.

How Important Are Tenant Selection Criteria for Commercial Properties?

The selection of tenants for commercial property focuses both on criteria that are comparable to those discussed in relationship to residential tenants and on criteria that are unique to a commercial tenant. A discussion of these criteria is presented in the following subsections.

CREDIT AND FINANCIAL RATING (PROFITABILITY)

The commercial tenant should be able to fulfill the financial obligations stipulated in the lease. In other words, the tenant should be able to pay the rent. If the prospective tenant is an established business, the property owner or property manager could check the tenant's credit rating and ask to see the audited financial records of the business or its published annual report. In this way, the financial capacity to pay rent can be determined.

TENANT REPUTATION

The value of commercial space is related to the prestige or reputation of the tenants who are located in the structure. The property owner/manager should recognize that the reputation of existing commercial tenants affects the desirability of the property to prospective tenants. If the property provides space to a group of prestigious tenants, the close physical proximity of these tenants will be desirable to prospective tenants and will allow the property owner/manager to command a higher rent level. Consequently, the property owner/manager should do everything in her power to obtain highly regarded tenants.

UNIQUE SPACE REQUIREMENTS

A commercial tenant may be perfectly acceptable from the point of view of reputation, credit, and profitability and yet be unsatisfactory because of unique requirements regarding space. Two examples of this should prove helpful. For instance, the location of a late-night restaurant on the top floor of a high-rise office building might be inappropriate if there is no way to provide security to the portions of the building not being used by the patrons of the restaurant. Most structures solve this problem by having direct access, by elevator, from the lobby to the restaurant, while all other portions of the structure are secured from intrusion by the restaurant's patrons. Another example might be the location of a bicycle repair shop or a roller skate rental store in the middle of a shopping mall. In this situation, a problem could arise between the needs of the shoppers in the mall and the patrons of the bicycle shop or roller skate store.

EXPANSION REQUIREMENTS

In the process of selecting tenants, the manager must be aware of the likelihood that the tenant may require an increase of space in the future. Such expansion problems can be troublesome because if the building is not able to fulfill this need for increased space, the tenant's occupancy will be temporary.

COMPATIBILITY AND AFFINITY

Commercial tenants should be compatible in the sense that the activities of one tenant do not deter or interfere with the flow of customers to the other tenants. As noted earlier, the customers of a bicycle repair shop located in the middle of a shopping mall could cause such interference if they entered through the regular pedestrian area of the mall.

What Is the Commercial Lease?

A number of features from a commercial lease were discussed in Chapter 10. Selected additional common clauses are included here to provide additional depth and to serve as a comparison to similar clauses that may appear in the residential lease.

AGREEMENT AND CONSIDERATION

In a commercial lease, the landlord and the tenant must reach an agreement about the rent to be paid and the space to be provided. Unlike the residential lease, in which the rent payment is usually stated as a flat fee, the commercial lease can stipulate any of a variety of payment schemes. Moreover, the commercial lease includes special provisions about the space.

RENT PAYMENT SCHEMES

Rent payment schemes were discussed in Chapter 10. Two additional possible lease clauses pertaining to rent follow.

EXCESS RENT. **Excess rent** is the dollar amount by which the contract rent exceeds market rent. This could happen when the location is extremely desirable. Other situations, such as changes in the market, are not expected to last in the long run because the tenant will seek a rent reduction.

OVERAGE RENT. Overage rent is rent paid in addition to the fixed base rent. Typically, this occurs when the total rent is based on sales.

Consider the following example of four leases in a small strip shopping center. All stores occupy a similar amount of space.

Store A: Tenant pays $32,000 annually. The owner pays all operating expenses.

Store B: Tenant pays $20,000 annually plus 2 percent of all retail sales over $750,000. The store's gross sales were $980,000.

Store C: Tenant pays $10,000 annually plus the insurance, property taxes, and routine maintenance totaling $28,000 annually.

Store D: Tenant pays $24,000 annually for the first year, and the owner pays all operating expenses. In years 2 to 6, the rent increases by an amount equal to the consumer price index.

Store A is paying rent under a gross lease. Store B is paying under a percentage lease, which is equal to $20,000 + .02(980,000 − 750,000), or $24,600. The $4,600 is the overage rent. Store C has negotiated a triple-net lease, which amounts to $36,000 annually. Store D has an escalated or indexed lease. If the consumer price index in year 2 equals 3.5 percent, the lease increases to $24,000(1.035), or $24,840 annually.

CLAUSES RELATING TO COMMON POINTS OF CONCERN BETWEEN LANDLORD AND TENANT

Many of the clauses discussed in relation to residential leases are also important clauses in commercial leases. The purpose of this section is to explain the relevance of those clauses to commercial property and to introduce other clauses that are significant only in commercial leases.

FIXTURES CLAUSE. The tenant's fixtures include a subcategory known as **trade fixtures,** which are personal property that the tenant in commercial space installs on the property and that she fully intends to detach and remove when the lease expires. These trade fixtures should be clearly identified and specified in the lease to prevent confusion later. The tenant does not have the right to claim trade fixtures that were installed by the landlord. If trade fixtures are in place, these items of real property belonging to the landlord must be distinguished from the tenant's trade fixtures, which are her personal property.

IMPROVEMENTS BY THE TENANT. The probability of the tenant making improvements to the property is higher for commercial than for residential property. The lease should contain a clause that eliminates any and all confusion about the ownership of such improvements. Typically, any such improvements to the property become the property of the landlord.

LANDLORD'S RIGHT TO RELOCATE THE TENANT. When attempting to lease space in a commercial property, the landlord should realize that all the space will not be leased simultaneously. The leasing process takes time, and problems can arise as the landlord attempts to achieve a 100-percent occupancy level. Consider an example in which the commercial property is an office building. One of the first tenants to sign a lease could be a small business operation that requires a small area within the property. The landlord and this tenant reach an agreement about a portion of the property's ground floor, and the lease is signed by both parties. Then, another desirable prospect approaches the landlord for commercial space. This prospective tenant is much larger than the original tenant and therefore requires an entire floor in the four-story building. This tenant wishes to have the ground floor, part of which is already leased to the small tenant. The prospective tenant will not accept space on two floors and is adamant about these requirements. Consequently, the prospective tenant probably will not rent.

BREAKDOWN CLAUSE. In many commercial operations, the landlord supplies the tenant with services and facilities other than the space that is being rented directly. The landlord may promise to provide cleaning services, elevator/escalator service, and air conditioning and therefore needs protection against liability if these services are interrupted. In the case of mechanical equipment, such as the elevator, the escalator, and the air conditioner, the lease could include a clause that frees the landlord from liability if these services are discontinued for repair, inspection, or other reasons beyond the landlord's control. In case of the labor services or cleaning services, the clause may read that the landlord is not liable for interruption of services due to labor disputes, such as strikes and walkouts.

HOURS-OF-BUSINESS AND MERCHANDISE-INVENTORY CLAUSES. Shopping center leases typically contain a clause that defines the hours of business during which the stores are to stay open. In general, the hours of the anchor tenants—the major department stores—are imposed as the standard hours that all tenants are to maintain. This stipulation benefits the landlord because it keeps the shopping center in operation for the maximum number of reasonable hours. During this time, all stores are open so the customer does not see a patchwork of open and closed stores as he walks through the mall. Under these circumstances, the total sales of the shopping center should be increased and the landlord's revenues from a percentage lease should also be greater.

UTILITIES. The payment of utilities should be identified in the lease to the greatest extent possible. Typically, the landlord pays for the common areas and the tenants pay for their leased space. However, some utility payments cannot be divided neatly. For example, the owner of a shopping center with an enclosed mall and open storefronts will have to pay for some portion of heat and air conditioning because the total utility bill cannot be subdivided easily among the tenants. In this case, the owner should put a "stop clause" into the lease. This clause defines the extent to which the owner will pay for utilities. When the utility bill exceeds the predetermined maximum, the extra expense is divided among the tenants in a predetermined manner. The basis could be square footage under lease. The purpose of the clause is to limit the landlord's utility payment during the lease term.

SIGNS. The commercial lease should also contain a clause that describes the nature and placement of the tenant's identifying name and advertising. The landlord does not want a hodgepodge of different-sized signs, in dramatically gaudy and contrasting colors, in inconvenient places. Nor does the landlord want the store windows and mall areas covered with advertising and placards. Therefore, the nature and use of signs by the tenant and the display of advertising should be specified in the lease.

EVALUATING THE COMMERCIAL LEASE

An individual who either owns or requires the use of commercial space should understand the many provisions that can be included within a commercial lease. Furthermore, the individual should realize that the commercial lease, just like the residential lease, is not a standardized document. Printed forms of the commercial lease are available, but they cover only the most typical situations. Every commercial lease is unique in some important way. Therefore, neither the landlord nor the tenant should assume that a printed commercial lease addresses all of the matters of concern because the interests of these two parties do not coincide on most issues.

CONDEMNATION

As introduced in Chapter 2, condemnation proceedings, or the taking of property under eminent domain, terminate a lease because both the landlord and the tenant are deprived of their ownership rights. The landlord loses the right to dispose of the property, and the tenant loses the rights of use and possession. Consequently, condemnation frees the landlord of any responsibility to provide possession and simultaneously frees the tenant from liability to pay rent to the landlord.

Every lease should contain some provision for condemnation. In short-term residential leases, the clause merely states that the landlord's responsibility to provide space under the lease agreement terminates upon the seizure of the property under eminent domain. In longer-term commercial leases, the two parties should reach an agreement about the exact nature of the clause. In a commercial lease, the landlord and tenant may have agreed that the rent is paid in advance. The clause should contain some statement that if condemnation occurs, advance rent payments should be prorated over the time period during which the tenant held possession. The landlord may have to refund some of the advance rent to the tenant when the property is condemned.

THE RIGHT OF REDEMPTION

In many states, although a tenant may have defaulted on the obligation to pay rent when more than five years remain on the unexpired lease, the tenant has the right to pay the unpaid rent and thereby obtain possession of the property (known as the **right of redemption**). Because the landlord does not consider such a tenant to be a good tenant, the landlord would want to eliminate this tenant's right to regain the property. Therefore, the landlord insists on a clause in the lease that waives the tenant's right of redemption. If a waiver of the right of redemption does not appear in a long-term lease, the landlord faces the danger that a dispossessed tenant will claim the right to regain possession and use of the property, even after initially defaulting on the rent.

Chapter Summary

Knowledge of the scope of services that can be provided by the property manager is important information for the investor/property owner. It provides the basis for making a decision about the management of the subject property after it is purchased. The full scope of property management services consists of managing the physical asset, the financial records, the tenant selection process, the lease negotiation process, and the financial asset as an investment.

Knowledge of the real estate lease is important in real estate decision making, both to the tenant in residential space and to the equity investor in income-producing property. Each party to a lease has certain rights and responsibilities relating to the delivery of possession, the use of the leased property, responsibility for maintenance and repair, liability for personal injury, the right to enter the property, and the right to assign or sublet the lease. Both parties to the lease must be concerned and informed about their legal responsibilities and their rights in these matters.

In addition to these rights and responsibilities, the residential lease contains numerous clauses pertaining to matters of mutual concern to the landlord and the tenant. In a residential lease, the two parties must reach an agreement about the tenant's fixtures, the landlord's right to show the property, the necessity to maintain hazard and liability insurance, the disposition of security deposits, the notification of renewal, the payment of utilities, and the termination of the lease due to the tenant's transfer from the area. In a commercial lease, the parties must agree on provisions for commercial fixtures, improvements made by the tenant, the landlord's right to relocate the tenant after the lease is signed, and breakdowns of mechanical equipment.

Leases are terminated in a variety of ways. Typically, leases for residential property terminate on the expiration date for the estate for years. A lease can be terminated by mutual agreement between the landlord and the tenant. Also, the tenant may purchase the property and thereby eliminate the need for the lease agreement. The tenant or the landlord may fail to meet the legal obligations incurred in the lease document. In this case, either one of the parties may be in breach of the lease agreement and thus in breach of contract.

There are several criteria that a property owner or a property manager must examine when selecting a commercial tenant. The business's financial rating, profitability, reputation, space requirements, expansion potential, and compatibility should be analyzed before a commercial lease is executed with any tenant.

In a commercial lease, each party—the landlord and the tenant—has certain rights and responsibilities related to the delivery of possession, the use of the leased property, the responsibility for maintenance and repair, the liability for personal injury, the right to enter the property, and the right to assign or sublet the lease. Both parties to the lease must be concerned and informed about their legal responsibilities and their rights in these matters.

Internet Applications

A website has been established for this chapter at http://epley.swcollege.com.

Review Questions

1. Consider the following example of four leases in a small strip shopping center. All stores occupy a similar amount of space.

Store A: Tenant pays $30,000 annually. The owner pays all operating expenses.

Store B: Tenant pays $25,000 annually plus 2 percent of all retail sales over $750,000. The store's gross sales were $1 million.

Store C: Tenant pays $18,000 annually plus the insurance, property taxes, and routine maintenance totaling $30,000 annually.

Store D: Tenant pays $26,000 annually for the first year, and the owner pays all operating expenses. In year 2, the rent increases by an amount equal to the consumer price index, or 2.78 percent.

What is each type of lease called? Is any overage rent paid by any of the four stores? Any excess rent? Calculate the rent in Stores B, C, and D.

2. Examine the following office building in a downtown area that contains 25,000 rentable square feet. The market rent per square foot is $18 and is projected to increase by 3 percent annually for the five-year term. After some negotiations, the tenant signs a gross lease for $210,000 annually that remains constant.

   (a) What type of lease exists?

   (b) How is the market value of the future rents claimed by the fee interest determined? The market value of the market rent would be estimated by calculating the total income for each of the five years.

   (c) How is the market value of the leasehold calculated?

3. Discuss the several tenant selection criteria that should be analyzed by the property owner or the property manager before a commercial lease is executed.

4. Identify and describe the various rent payment schemes that can be established within a commercial lease.

5. Discuss the issues that surround the commercial tenant's fixtures (trade fixtures) and any improvements that are made by the tenant.

6. What services can a property manager provide to the client?

7. What criteria are used in the tenant selection process?

8. What is the consideration that is exchanged between the landlord and the tenant in a residential lease?

9. In general terms, describe the rights and responsibilities of both the landlord and the tenant in the following matters:

   - delivery of the leased property
   - the landlord's rights to enter
   - the tenant's right to assign and sublet the property
   - the tenant's use of the property
   - liability for personal injury to third parties

10. Explain the need for a fixtures clause in the residential lease.

11. Why are security deposits needed? What was the landlord's original or common law security against default? What is the current practice? What relationships can be established between the landlord and the tenant with regard to the security deposits?

12. What consumer issues are involved in landlord–tenant relationships? State the various ways in which a lease can be terminated. In a breach of the contract, what is the difference between dispossession proceedings and constructive eviction?

Discussion Questions

1. Compose a list of questions you might ask a property manager to identify what services you might wish to purchase.

2. Find another person in your class, identify yourselves as the two parties to a residential lease, and draft a two-page lease in everyday language. Then, ask a third member of the class to critique it for content.

3. Should the tenant's profit level be used as the basis for establishing a percentage lease agreement? Discuss the advantages and disadvantages of this issue in detail.

4. Discuss the information found at the various web addresses shown for this chapter on the website for this text.

## PART VII

The Decision to Acquire or Transfer the Property

CHAPTER 16

Deed, Title Insurance, and Settlement

QUESTIONS TO BE ANSWERED

1. What is homeowner's insurance and why is it needed? What is a homeowner's warranty?

2. Why should the parties worry about evidence of good title?

3. What is a settlement, and what is the amount owed by the buyer and paid to the seller?

OBJECTIVES

When finished with this chapter, the student should be able to:

1. Explain title insurance and why it is needed.

2. Describe what is covered and omitted in the policy.

3. Explain the homeowner's warranty.

4. Describe the nature and purpose of closing, title, and conveyance.

5. Explain the relationship between closing, the listing, and the sales contract.

6. Discuss the importance of good title.

7. Specify the components of a valid deed.

8. Explain the importance of the Real Estate Settlement Procedures Act and the Truth-in-Lending Act to the closing.

9. Explain the differences among title insurance, property insurance, and a homeowner's warranty.

10. Explain and illustrate the debits and credits that are used in the two-column settlement statement.

11. Explain and illustrate a typical settlement statement for the buyer, the seller, and the broker.

12. State the alternatives available when the buyer or the seller defaults at the closing.

abstractor

assumption statement

attorney's opinion

bargain and sale deed

certificate of title

conveyance

covenant against encumbrances

covenant of further assurance

covenant of quiet enjoyment

covenant of seizin

covenant of warranty

credits

debits

deed

deed in escrow

default

equity title

evidence of good title

good title

grant deed

grantee

granting clause

grantor

habendum clause

homeowner's warranty

legal title

merchantable title

mill levy

property insurance

prorating

quitclaim deed

recording

revenue stamps

settlement

settlement statement

sheriff's deed

special warranty deed

title

title insurance

Torrens certificate

warranty deed

INTRODUCTION

The last step of a buying or selling transaction is to prepare for the closing or settlement. This is a date that is set by both parties when all terms of the sales contract are ready to be satisfied and the ownership rights are exchanged for consideration.

A number of decisions and documents must be prepared for a successful closing to occur. For example, the exact loan terms must be arranged with the lender. Property and hazard insurance must be purchased or assumed. A title insurance policy can be requested. An abstract might be ordered, and an attorney employed to give a title opinion. The property might need an appraisal. A closing agent must be hired to calculate the figures in the final statement and coordinate the completion of the documents. A deed must be prepared. In sum, all terms in the sales contract must be satisfied.

This chapter covers all of these points. This information is essential to assure that the buyer and seller satisfy all terms required in the transaction.

What Are the Title, the Conveyance, and the Deed?

A **title** is the proof of ownership. A **conveyance** is any legal document that transfers the title. For example, a **deed** is the conveyance used to transfer the title in most transactions. The term *title* can be used separately from the term *conveyance*. A buyer can write in a contract of sale that he wants "free and clear title," which means that the buyer expects to receive a deed that conveys this type of title. Once the deed has been passed from the owner to the new buyer, the terms *title* and *conveyance* lose their distinction. The new owner possesses both the title *and* the deed, which is the document that can be used to transfer that title again. Thus, the two terms often are used interchangeably.

In many states, the last legal step in a title transfer is the delivery and acceptance of the deed by the new owner. The buyer must have the deed in her possession.

What Is the Deed?

The seller's attorney writes a new deed. It must be a **merchantable title,** and the evidence in the form of an abstract plus the opinion assures all parties that it is a marketable title.

REQUIREMENTS FOR VALIDITY

A deed is a written instrument used to convey some right, interest, or title in real estate from the owner **(grantor)** to the buyer **(grantee).** The precise form and the language used in deeds varies in individual states. A deed typically will be considered valid if it contains the following components.

DOCUMENT MUST BE IN WRITING. The Statute of Frauds enacted by all states requires that documents for the exchange or sale of real property be in writing.

PARTIES MUST BE CAPABLE OF CONTRACTING. The parties to the contract must be able to contract; this is called *competent parties.*

PARTIES TO THE CONTRACT MUST BE NAMED. Two points are important. First, the name of the grantors on the new deed must be identical to the names of the grantees on the current deed to establish a correct chain of title. Second, the grantee must be clearly named.

CONSIDERATION IS IDENTIFIED. The deed typically identifies the *consideration.* Usually the omission of this part does not invalidate the deed with the exception of a bargain and sale deed (explained later in this chapter). Consideration can be written in any of three ways:

1. The actual cash and debt, if applicable: "$_____ in cash and a first mortgage for $_____."
2. Other valuable consideration: "$1 and other good and valuable consideration."
3. Love and affection: "The sum of $10 and love and affection."

The phrase "other good and valuable consideration" is used to disguise the amount paid because deeds are public records. The "love and affection" phrase disguises the amount in a sale or gift between family members.

DESCRIPTION. Because the deed is conveying the title and will be used to give constructive notice of ownership by being recorded in the courthouse, it must contain a legal description discussed in an earlier chapter.

GRANTING CLAUSE. The **granting clause** (also known as *words of conveyance*) does not consist of any specific set of words but describes the intention of the owner to transfer interests, rights, or the property at the present time. Typical wording includes "grant, bargain, and sell," "convey and quitclaim," and "convey and warrant."

When it is used, the **habendum clause** typically follows the granting clause and describes the extent of the estate granted. It is not essential to the deed, however. It starts with the words, "To have and to hold . . ."

DELIVERY OF THE DEED TO THE GRANTEE. The deed must be delivered and accepted by the grantee before the transfer of title is complete. Because the deed is a conveyance of the title, it must be held by the grantee to give evidence that the title has been transferred and accepted.

CATEGORIES OF DEEDS

Deeds used in the United States can be classified into two categories on the basis of whether or not the grantor gives a warranty. A *warranty* is an assurance by the seller that the property is free of any liens and debts. Common examples of each type are explained below.

Deeds Containing a Warranty

WARRANTY DEED. In a **warranty deed,** the grantor gives all (full) covenants. These covenants differ among regions depending upon their breadth, but typically include the following:

1. *Seizin:* The grantor (seller) possesses good title and can give possession and the inherent rights to the property. Typically, a grantor who gives this **covenant of seizin** is also giving a covenant covering the *right to convey.* Essentially, this covenant states that the grantor owns the right to transfer the title.

2. *Quiet enjoyment:* The **covenant of quiet enjoyment** states that the grantee (buyer) will not be bothered by subsequent claims of ownership from superior title(s) that can be used later to interfere with the ownership and use of the property by the new grantee.

Some states identify separately the **covenant of further assurance.** By adding this latter covenant to the deed, the grantor assures the grantee that additional action will be taken by the grantor to correct a problem or mistake discovered at a later date.

3. *Against encumbrances:* The **covenant against encumbrances** states that no additional encumbrances exist other than the ones that are known and stated. This covenant is often interpreted by the courts to be identical to a **covenant of warranty.**

In general, the warranty deed carries the grantor's covenant that she will take legal action to defend her claim to the title during her period of ownership and any previous periods. This deed conveys the property.

SPECIAL WARRANTY. The only difference between a general warranty deed and a **special warranty deed** is that the warranty given here covers only the period *after* the grantor assumed the ownership. This deed conveys the property.

Deeds Not Giving a Warranty

QUITCLAIM DEED. The **quitclaim deed** has that name printed across the top to identify it. This type of deed does not convey the property. The grantor gives up the right to claim the rights, interests, and title held at the time of the transfer. A quitclaim deed is typically used to correct a defect in the title or when the grantor does not desire to make any claims about the ownership. It is important to remember that this deed contains no warranty by the grantor.

BARGAIN AND SALE DEED. A **bargain and sale deed** has two principal components: (1) it conveys the property to the grantee, and (2) it contains the consideration. A true bargain and sale deed conveys no warranties. However, some states have legislated a warranty by state law.

SHERIFF'S DEED. A **sheriff's deed** is given to the new owner after a sale of property to recover past-due taxes. The deed contains no warranty.

GRANT DEED. A **grant deed** does not contain any stated warranties from the grantor, but state law typically requires the grantor to imply a warranty by using the word *grant.* The warranty typically includes the grantor's covenant that (1) the property has not already been conveyed to another party, and (2) the property has no encumbrances made during the grantor's possession only.

THE WARRANTY DEED

Exhibit 16.1 is a warranty deed. The relevant components are described below:

DOCUMENT IN WRITING. The transaction is contained in a written document. The type of deed is printed at the top of the page to prevent confusion.

PARTIES MUST BE CAPABLE OF CONTRACTING. To the best of everyone's knowledge, all parties are capable of contracting. In addition, the abstract has shown no reason why any of these parties should not enter this contract.

PARTIES TO THE CONTRACT ARE NAMED. The names of the grantor and the grantee are specifically stated.

CONSIDERATION. The consideration is stated.

DESCRIPTION. The legal description is stated.

GRANTING CLAUSE. The words "has granted, bargained, and sold" are the granting clause. The habendum clause identifies the rights that are passed. The warranty is contained in several sentences that transfer title, state that the grantor is lawfully seized of the premises, that the same is unencumbered, and that the grantor will warrant and defend forever the title against all claims.

SIGNATURES OF THE GRANTORS. The grantors have signed the deed, and a notary public has witnessed the signatures.

EXHIBIT 16.1　Warranty deed.

STATE OF _____, County of _____.

This INDENTURE, Made this _____ day of _____ in the Year of Two Thousand and _____ between _____ of the State of _____ and County of _____ of the first part, and _____ of the State of _____ and County of _____ of the second part,

WITNESSETH: That the said part _____ of the first part, for and in consideration of the sum of _____ Dollars, in hand paid, at and before the sealing and delivery of these presents, the receipt of which is hereby acknowledged, has _____ granted, bargained, sold and conveyed, and by these presents do _____ grant, bargain, sell and convey unto the said part _____ of the second part, _____ heirs and assigns, all that tract or parcel of land lying and being in

TO HAVE AND TO HOLD the said tract or parcel of land, with all and singular the rights, members and appurtenances thereof, to the same being, belonging, or in anywise appertaining, to the only proper use, benefit and behoof of the said part _____of the second part, _____ heirs and assigns, forever, in Fee Simple.

AND THE SAID part _____ of the first part, for _____ heirs, executors and administrators, will warrant and forever defend the right and title to the above described property, unto the said part _____ of the second part, _____ heirs and assigns, against the claims of all persons whomsoever.

IN WITNESS WHEREOF, the said part _____ of the first part has _____ hereunto set _____ hand and seal _____, the day and year above written.

Signed, sealed and delivered in presence of:

_____　　_____ (Seal)

_____　　_____ (Seal)

_____　　_____ (Seal)

LEGAL VERSUS EQUITY TITLE

Legal title belongs to the party who has possession of the deed and is named in the document as the grantee. **Equity title** is claimed by the party who has a financial obligation to repay funds used for the purchase of the property. The two can be separated in a transaction whereby a deed is transferred to the new owner giving legal title, but the current mortgage is untouched. For example, the deed can be exchanged for money, but the commitment to repay the outstanding mortgage debt can still remain with the previous owner. One party holds the deed, and another party holds the obligation to repay the debt. This situation can arise in an equity buy when no assumption statement is filed with the lender to release the previous mortgagor from the debt and commit the new mortgagor. The lender has no way of knowing that the property has been sold. The new owner typically must make some arrangement with the previous owner to make the payments on the debt.

Separation of the two types of title is unwise unless the parties are attempting to accomplish a specific purpose that requires such a transaction. A buyer should always request that legal title and equity title be transferred in the sale.

REVENUE STAMPS AND RECORDING

In most states, all conveyances of title are taxed. In some states, the seller is required by law to purchase **revenue stamps** (also known as transfer or documentary stamps) from the State Revenue Department, which will be affixed in the upper right corner.

Recording is best for the new owner. If **recording** is desired, the deed must have the revenue stamps affixed or evidence of payment of the transfer tax must be obtained before the deed is presented to the proper government office. The new owner pays a filing fee set by the state. The time, date, and place of recording are printed in the box in the upper right corner. These facts establish a priority to the claim of the property value and represent *constructive notice of ownership*.

What Is Good Title?

ownership rights

A seller can sell any combination of rights to the property that he actually owns but can sell no rights that he does not own. The buyer must assume the responsibility of determining whether the seller actually owns all of the legal rights to the property that he purports to own. This section explains how the buyer can confirm that the seller owns the rights and that there are no outstanding claims on the property value (known as **good title**). **Evidence of good title** or ownership that is free of known claims to the value can be shown by an abstract and attorney's opinion, a certificate of title, and a Torrens certificate. If the parties to the transaction choose, one may purchase a title insurance policy that protects the new owner against a possible loss in value from errors in the public records. The type used is determined by state law and local custom.

THE ABSTRACT AND THE ATTORNEY'S OPINION

An *abstract* (first introduced in Chapter 1) is a chronological list of previous transfers of ownership and claims of value upon the property and the removal of these claims. It usually starts with a land description and summarizes all of the succeeding deeds, mortgages, judgments, liens, and other claims to the value. The abstractor's certificate identifies the records that have and have not been examined.

The **abstractor** prepares the abstract. Typically, abstractors are attorneys, title companies, or public officials. In some regions, the abstractor may be required to post a bond against careless workmanship. The abstractor is liable for any records stipulated to be included in the abstract that are omitted. The abstractor is not liable for an opinion of the title.

An attorney is typically employed by the buyer to render an opinion on the condition of the title. The attorney reviews the abstract to determine whether any previous transfers were incomplete or whether any claims to the value remain outstanding. This **attorney's opinion** tells the seller that a warranty, quitclaim, or special warranty deed may be issued. It also tells the seller whether title insurance must be purchased.

CERTIFICATE OF TITLE

An abstract may be disregarded and legally a **certificate of title** may be issued instead by an abstractor, usually an attorney, who simply examined the public records.

THE TORRENS CERTIFICATE

The Torrens system is a procedure for land registration that originated in Australia and is used in some metropolitan areas in the United States. A landowner brings the deed and abstract to a public office to apply for a registration of the title in her name. Any person identified in the abstract and application is given a length of time to contest the application. If the application is not successfully contested, the owner receives a certificate of title attesting to her ownership. The **Torrens certificate** lists all of the claims to the value of the property.

No subsequent transaction is valid until a new registration is received. Thus, the owner may not simply pass a deed to a buyer but must submit the new deed and the appropriate documents to the public office again and wait for a new registration in the name of the new owner. The defense of the claims of ownership is assumed by the previous owner rather than by the public official who issues the registration.

TITLE INSURANCE

Title insurance is sold by a title insurance agent to protect the new owner against any loss from undiscovered title defects within the records examined. The premium is a one-time charge usually paid by the seller. The policy is nontransferable.

ABSTRACT VERSUS TITLE INSURANCE

A buyer can request an abstract with an attorney's opinion, title insurance, or both, depending on the custom within the region. An abstract with an opinion may require more time to prepare, especially if the buyer requests an abstract that traces the history of the property over 40 years instead of 25. Further, for title insurance without an abstract, the title company prepares a *title record,* which covers the same records as an abstract but is not typed in final form. The title insurance agent must examine this record to determine the extent of the coverage. Also, the title record may not extend more than 25 years into the past.

For maximum protection, the buyer could request an abstract for 40 years with an opinion *and* title insurance. The abstract gives a detailed history of all transactions with respect to the property, and the legal opinion indicates the validity of the transfers. The title insurance gives liability coverage over any mistakes contained within records that were examined.

The seller's decision to provide both depends on the local custom of providing evidence of good title. The seller may have an option of providing an abstract *or* title insurance within the sales contract.

MERCHANTABLE TITLE

The contract of sale may require the seller to provide a deed that is merchantable. If the seller accepts the buyer's offer with this statement in the contract, the seller agrees to provide a deed that is free from any clouds or defects. It is a title under which the buyer may have quiet and peaceful enjoyment on the property, and one which could be sold to a reasonable and prudent purchaser familiar with all the facts relative to the title of the property. A merchantable title (also known as a marketable title) may also be defined as one that a court of law would require a new owner to accept in the transaction.

What Is Title Insurance?

The standard title insurance policy insures the new buyer-owner against any loss in value that could possibly result if the property purchased was subject to undisclosed claims by other parties, or if the insured did not actually own the property. The title company agrees to undertake legal action at its own expense to eliminate any subsequent claims upon the title. Title insurance differs from other types of insurance in that it is insurance against actions that have occurred in the *past* as opposed to, say, property insurance, which insures the owner against actions that might occur in the *future*.

WHY TITLE INSURANCE IS NEEDED

Several reasons for needing title insurance exist. First, the deed is drafted by the attorney selected by the seller who can be a different person through several sales of the same property. Different attorneys can insert different language, which can cause confusion or doubt. Second, the parties signing the documents typically are not subject to definite verification of their identity, marital status, and age. Third, the method of indexing and preserving the documents can vary from location to location.

In addition, the title search for an abstract can be conducted by the abstractor first and the results then given to an attorney. Another procedure is for the attorney to examine the public records and then render an opinion on her own abstract. Furthermore, the attorneys involved could conceivably disagree in their search of the documents.

The result of the above points is that the seller may issue a deed to the buyer that is given in good faith that the title is good and marketable. However, the deed may be defective, the seller may not own all of the rights that are covered in the deed, the previous owner's title may be in question, missing heirs may exist, or previous common-law spouses may have rights.

Several short examples illustrate the need for title insurance:

Sara Clark had lived in her house for two years when she was notified that the abstractor who produced the abstract has missed a sum of old taxes, which had to be paid.

Janet Weiss was required to move her carport when her neighbor learned that the surveyor made a mistake. The structure was built partly on the neighbor's property.

Bob and Sue Gree were surprised to learn that the single man from whom they purchased their house was secretly married. They paid legal expenses to defend their title and lost to the wife in court.

The man and woman who sold the McNews their house were actually a man who owned a one-half interest and his mistress. After accepting the money, they disappeared, and the man's wife made a claim on the property because she owned the other one-half interest.

Amy Kristen purchased a house from the estate of Joyce Rogers. Joyce had a daughter who was born after her will was drawn, which omitted her. This daughter made a claim on the property after Amy had purchased it.

TYPES OF TITLE INSURANCE

Several types of title insurance policies are issued in the marketplace. Each policy attempts to cover and defend the particular rights in question. For example, the most common is the *owner's standard policy,* which insures the rights of the new owner up to the value stated in the policy. A *mortgagee's title insurance policy* insures the rights of the new owner up to the amount of the existing debt, but the beneficiary of any loss and subsequent payment is the lender. A *leasehold title insurance policy* insures the lessee that he possesses a valid lease. A *certificate of sale title insurance policy* insures the rights in property that has been purchased from a court sale.

STANDARD TITLE INSURANCE COVERAGE

This section discusses the most common coverage in a homeowner's standard title insurance policy. A person desiring title insurance coverage makes an application to the abstractor, who is typically employed by the title insurance company. The applicant pays a fee, based upon the value of the property, which covers the search through the public records and the insurance. This fee is paid once, typically by the seller of the property, and covers the insurance that is written to include the period of the new owner's possession and the heirs. If the new owner ever resells the property, a new policy is required.

The applicant for title insurance may purchase the standard coverage policy, which usually insures against defects in the public documents and specific items such as forgeries, incorrect marital statements, and incorrect grantors. The applicant also may purchase an extended policy that includes the standard coverage and additional insurance against defects that may be uncovered only by physically inspecting the property, interviewing the people who actually possess the property, or reexamining an accurate survey.

TYPICAL DEFECTS. The following examples are common defects typically covered in a title insurance policy:

- Duress in the execution of the instruments
- Marital rights of the spouse reported incorrectly
- An undisclosed divorce
- False representation of the true owner
- Forged documents
- Deeds written by grantors who were minors, aliens, or of unsound mind

ITEMS NOT COVERED. If the abstractor discovers a serious defect, the title insurance company typically will issue a *binder.* The binder will state the company's desire to insure the property upon the proper actions taken by the parties involved to solve or remove the defect. If this defect is not removed, no insurance is written to cover this one risk, although it is probably written to cover the remainder of the known rights.

A potential applicant for title insurance should remember that the insurance covers only errors in the public documents. Unrecorded documents are not covered. Questions pertaining to the accuracy of the survey are not covered. Verification of the legal rights of the parties actually in possession of the property is not covered. Nor are any defects listed under the binder covered.

What Is Property Insurance?

Property insurance covers risks to the property value that may occur in the future. These risks, called *perils,* include the following:

riots	vandalism
explosion	objects falling from the sky
fire, lightning	leakage, or steam from plumbing or
aircraft damage	air conditioning
damage to property by vehicles not owned by occupants	weight or damage from ice and snow
	collapse of building structure
windstorm, hail	damage from hot water system
smoke damage	freezing damage
theft	damage from short circuits
glass breakage	

TYPES OF POLICIES AVAILABLE

The purchaser may select from several types of policies. The basic difference among them is the number of perils covered, the dollar amount of risk that is insured, and the premium the purchaser pays for the coverage.

For example, the purchaser may elect to buy the standard *homeowner's basic policy,* which typically includes the following coverage:

trees, shrubs, plants	5% of amount on house
detached structures	12% of amount on house
house and attached structure	minimum of $20,000 but based on value
personal property	one-half of the insurance
personal liability	$50,000 liability for persons injured while on the property
medial payments	$1,000 per person for injuries suffered while on the property

The purchaser may elect to cover the property with the *homeowner's broad form,* which covers common perils, and the insured amounts are higher in all categories. The most complete coverage is the *homeowner's comprehensive form,* which will cover the property against every peril except any that are specifically named.

What Is a Homeowner's Warranty?

Title insurance provides the new owner-buyer with protection against *past* defects in the title records that might create future claims to the title. A **homeowner's warranty policy** gives the owner-buyer protection against *future* defects in the electrical and plumbing features in the property. While a standard homeowner's property insurance policy covers against destruction and loss such as by fire, tornado, and hail, the homeowner's warranty is purchased by the seller to give the new buyer protection against the defectiveness of the property's major systems or built-in appliances within the foreseeable future. The existence of a warranty program and its exact coverage can vary among states and companies.

The warranty typically is purchased by the seller to assist in the sale of the property so that the potential buyer does not have to worry about defective electrical and plumbing features. Sellers hope for a quicker sale, typically do not pay a premium until the property is sold (expecting fewer legal problems after the sale), and anticipate easier financing for the buyer. The buyer is assured that large unforeseen repair bills are insured.

A typical warranty could include the following:

MAJOR HOME SYSTEMS
hot water heater
heating system
plumbing system
electrical system

APPLIANCES (BUILT-IN)
exhaust fans in the kitchen, attic, and bathroom
oven, dishwasher, range, trash compactor, garbage disposal, and microwave appliances

OPTIONAL IN SOME STATES
exterior well pump
central air conditioner or evaporative cooler
spa and swimming pool equipment

How Important Is the Need for Settlement Preparation?

The actual settlement is the last step in the real estate transaction. It will progress smoothly only if all of the conditions in the contract of sale are fulfilled. For example, if the seller agreed to provide an abstract or title insurance, the abstract (chain of title) must be ordered and examined and a decision reached about the need for title insurance. In addition, if a sales agent has agreed to find a buyer who is ready, willing, and able to purchase the property, the agent wants to be sure the buyer applies for a mortgage and raises the necessary cash because the commission most likely will not be paid until closing.

SETTING THE SETTLEMENT DATE

Settlement is the exchange of the deed for the agreed-upon price. It takes place at a date, time, and location agreed upon by the parties in the sales contract. If an agent is involved in the transaction, he or she will help arrange the settlement date at a convenient time when all documents will have been prepared and all parties can appear.

The contract of sale requires that a date be determined for settlement that is agreeable to the buyer and the seller. By affixing their names to this contract, both parties are stating their intention to complete the transaction.

THE ESCROW ACCOUNT

The contract of sale usually includes a provision that any escrow account be prorated and distributed to the rightful owner on the date of closing. (Prorating will be discussed later in this chapter.) Failure to follow this provision is a breach of the contract.

A rule of reason that can be applied in the proration is that the property tax payments in the escrow account awaiting disbursement on the tax payment date shall remain with the property. They become the property of the new owner. Insurance premium payments paid to the account remain with the seller.

THE SETTLEMENT AGENT

Settlement can be conducted by the lender, the title company, an attorney, or an escrow agent. One of these parties, such as the lender, may insist on the right to supervise the closing (serving as the settlement agent) to ensure that all documents are properly completed. In this manner, the lender minimizes the risk in granting the loan. The others may conduct the settlement for a fee. They can pay the necessary expenses, see that the necessary legal documents are prepared, and prepare the statements.

SETTLEMENT BY A DEED IN ESCROW

Settlement by a **deed in escrow** is the same as a contract for deed. This transaction is actually an assumption whereby the buyer agrees to take over the seller's mortgage. The assumption agreement, abstract, old mortgage, and the new deed are given to an escrow agent. The agent agrees to follow the terms of an escrow agreement that is drawn up between the two parties outlining the terms, such as the amortization schedule, right to foreclosure in the event of nonpayment, and passing of the deed. The deed does not normally pass to the buyer until the last payment of the loan is made. The escrow agent in this arrangement can only perform those duties assigned by the escrow agreement.

This type of closing is useful if one party wants to preserve the terms of the first mortgage, if current interest rates are high and the buyer does not want a new loan, or if the seller is reluctant to pass the title for some reason.

What Are the Requirements of the Real Estate Settlement Procedures Act?

The Real Estate Settlement Procedures Act (RESPA) (introduced in Chapter 9) was passed in 1974 and amended in 1975 to protect the potential homebuyer from harmful practices (such as kickbacks), to provide the home buyer with relevant cost information before the closing, and to gather national statistics on closing costs and procedures.

The U.S. Department of Housing and Urban Development (HUD) has the authority for administering the requirements.

RESPA applies to any loan secured by a first lien on residential real property designed for the occupancy of one to four families. All lenders who are regulated by, or whose deposits are insured by, the federal government are covered. Loans guaranteed by the Secretary of HUD or intended to be sold to the Federal National Mortgage Association are included. Under Section 103(f) of the Truth-in-Lending Act, any creditor who originates more than $1 million in mortgages must comply.

EXEMPTIONS FROM RESPA

The following loans are exempt from RESPA:

- home improvement loans
- refinancing home loans
- loans for the purchase of vacant lots, provided that a one- to four-family unit is not constructed
- loans for the purchase of more than 25 acres
- assumptions or an equity buyout of an existing mortgage
- loans for the construction of one- to four-family units provided that the lot is owned by the borrower
- land sales where the title has not passed
- loans to pay for property that will be resold

RESPA LENDER REQUIREMENTS

RESPA imposes a number of requirements on lenders and loans that qualify. Four of the best known are the following:

1. *Good faith estimate of settlement costs.* The lender must provide within three business days of the receipt of the application a good faith estimate of the range of the costs that the borrower will be expected to pay. These estimates must be reasonable ranges for the costs.

2. *HUD information booklet.* The lender must provide the prospective borrower with a copy of the HUD information booklet within three business days of receipt of the application. The booklet explains the nature of settlement costs and how to select an attorney, a lender, and a settlement agent.

3. *Completion of HUD Form 1.* The settlement agent must complete this form, which itemizes all settlement costs, and must make it available *one business day prior to the closing.* It must be given to the buyer and the seller prior to or during the closing.

4. *Retaining a copy of HUD Form 1 for two years.* The lender must retain a copy of the form for at least two years or can dispose of the form earlier if the lender has no further interest in the property.

SPECIAL PROVISIONS OF RESPA

Certain acts are specifically prohibited under the RESPA regulations:

1. *Kickbacks:* No special payment for the referral of settlement business is allowed.

2. *Fees:* The lender may not charge for the preparation of HUD Form 1 or the Truth-in-Lending statement.

3. *Title company:* The seller may not require that a specific title company be used.

4. *Escrow account:* The lender may not require more funds to be placed into escrow than would be required for a full payment after one year.

What Are the Requirements of the Truth-in-Lending Act?

The Truth-in-Lending Act (Regulation Z, which was introduced in Chapter 9) requires the lender to disclose the *finance charge* and the *annual percentage rate (APR)* to the potential borrower. Whenever the funds are received for the transaction, the borrower will sign a statement certifying that she has been given the appropriate information concerning these two pieces of information. This signed document becomes the lender's evidence that the requirements of the act have been met.

What Is Prorating?

Certain bills against the property, such as property taxes and insurance payments, are paid under different payment systems. General property taxes are said to be a *payment in arrears* because they are paid in the year after they are assessed. For example, a property owner will pay taxes in the current year on property owned and assessed in the prior year. Another bill that is normally paid in arrears is mortgage interest. The borrower pays interest on the mortgage balance that has already been used for the previous period. Insurance premiums are a *payment in advance* because the property owner must pay the premium before the policy is issued.

Special property taxes levied for special improvement are usually paid *in advance*—that is, they are paid within the same year that the property is owned and assessed. Some streams of income from the property, such as rental payments, also are commonly received in advance.

Because certain payments on the property are classified as payments in advance while others are payments in arrears, someone must decide who owes what to whom on the day of settlement. Determining this amount and informing the property person that it is owed or will be received is part of the process of **prorating.** Proration also includes the calculation to determine the amount that is paid in advance or in arrears and the amount of income that is received in advance or in arrears.

Prorating is typically applied to general property taxes and special property taxes, mortgage interest, insurance, and income generated from the property. Other items may need prorating, such as utility bills, accrued salaries that are unpaid by the closing, and special unpaid bills. The following sections explain how the items appearing in a typical transaction are prorated. The same principles apply to those items that may be in need of prorating in a transaction but are not explained here.

PROPERTY TAXES

TAX BILL. In many states, real property taxes are determined by multiplying the mill levy by the assessed valuation on the tax rolls. For example, a property assessed at $80,000 by the local tax assessor in a district where the government mill levy is $0.007

would owe a total tax bill of $560 ($80,000 × .007). The annual tax bill covers general public services benefiting all land parcels in the taxing district, such as police protection, sanitary services, water, and fire protection.

ASSESSED VALUE AND MILL LEVY. The *assessed value* (introduced in Chapter 4) is the property value that is placed on the tax rolls by the county tax assessor. State statutes and the state constitution tell the assessor what criteria to use in determining this value. Some states may require that the assessed value be a predetermined fraction of the market value. The **mill levy** is the tax rate that is established by the governmental units that have the authority to tax the site. Typically, it is expressed in either two decimals for every $100 in value, or three decimals for every $1,000 in value.

DATE OF ASSESSMENT. States require that the property owner declare all property owned on a certain date, typically January 1. The tax bill on the property is calculated and paid in the *following* fiscal year on payments determined by the state. Thus, property taxes are said to be paid in arrears.

PRORATING REAL PROPERTY TAXES. Prorating of real property taxes must be related to the conditions contained within the contract of sale. The property tax funds set aside to accumulate until the date of payment are usually transferred with the property. The seller gives them to the new owner. Thus, the seller owes the buyer the amount of tax funds that will have accumulated from the assessment date, say January 1, through the day of closing.

For example, assume that the contract of sale requires the property taxes to be prorated, the listing contract shows that the property taxes are $630 for the current tax year, and the date of assessment is January 1. The prior year's taxes assessed on January 1 will be paid in the current year. The person supervising the closing must be sure the money for the taxes remains with the property. The seller owes the buyer property taxes for the period from January 1 through the closing date of February 10, and the amount is determined as follows:

> *Days*
> January 1 through February 10 = (31 days + 10 days) = 41 days
>
> *Rate per Day*
> $630 tax bill/365 days = $1.726 per day
>
> *Amount*
> 41 days × $1.726 = $70.77 taxes

The seller is expected to pay this amount to the buyer at the settlement.

SPECIAL ASSESSMENTS

Special assessments (introduced in Chapter 2) are special levies for special improvements. Such improvements are usually initiated and requested by local residents, and the taxes are self-imposed. Examples include installation of curbs and gutters, paving, and special projects for flood and irrigation control. The total tax bill is usually divided by the number of years that the government officials will allow for payment, and that amount is imposed on the taxpayer each year. The principal difference between the real property tax payment and the special property tax payment is that states require the special property taxes to be paid on the payment dates within the same year as they are imposed. Thus, they are said to be paid in advance.

The seller pays special assessments in advance. If the buyer and seller agree to prorate a special assessment that has been paid prior to the closing, the buyer must reimburse the seller for an amount covering the period from the day after closing to the last day of the tax year.

For example, assume that the contract of sale requires special assessments to be prorated, the listing contract shows a special assessment of $225 on the property, and the date of the assessment and the payment dates are identical to those for the real property tax. The state requires special assessments to be paid within the year of the assessment. The closing agent must make sure the seller is reimbursed for the period from the day after closing to the last day of the tax year. The amount is calculated as follows:

Days
February 11 through December 31 = (18 days + 306 days) = 324 days

Rate per Day
$225 special assessment taxes/365 days = $0.616 per day

Amount
324 days × $0.616 = $199.58

The buyer is expected to reimburse the seller for this special assessment at the closing.

TAXES FOR THE PREVIOUS YEAR

The taxes for the previous year should have been paid or may need to be paid soon, depending on the payment dates. The closing agent can call the county tax collector to find out whether the taxes for the previous year have been paid, and if they have not been paid whether the amount that is due is delinquent. The buyer or the agent should ask the seller to pay these taxes before closing if they can be paid according to the state's payment date. If the closing occurs at a time when the previous year's taxes cannot be paid, the buyer or the agent should require the seller to compensate the buyer for the amount needed to pay them on the first payment date. Taxes for a previous year are not prorated. Typically, the amount is added to the prorated amount for the current year, and the total is expressed as a single figure that the seller owes.

For example, assume that the closing agent has called the county tax collector and discovered that the taxes for the previous two tax years have been paid. Thus, the buyer will not discover any delinquencies at a later date. The current tax bill of $630 was due on February 4 but has not been paid. The agent will ask the seller to pay the $630 to the buyer at closing or present a paid receipt. The buyer pays the money to the tax collector within the payment dates set by state law. Thus, the seller pays the buyer for the amount that has been prorated plus the taxes that are due.

MORTGAGE INTEREST

If the buyer assumes the seller's current mortgage debt at the closing, the seller pays the buyer a prorated amount of mortgage interest, which is shown on both settlement statements. If the buyer obtains a new first mortgage and the seller pays the lender the remaining mortgage balance, the seller pays a prorated amount of mortgage interest to the lender. The amount is entered on the seller's statement only.

The interest paid covers the use of the mortgage balance during the previous period, usually a month. The amount for one month can be approximated by multiplying the outstanding balance at the beginning of the year by the interest rate and dividing by 12. For example, a mortgage with an outstanding balance of $30,000 carrying an interest rate of 9 percent would require an annual interest payment of $2,700, or roughly $225 per month. The exact amount would be determined by a debiting factor (0.09/12) to compute the interest on the mortgage balance owed immediately after the last payment. This total can be computed or taken from a book of amortization tables. The seller owes the amount of interest from the date of the last payment through the date of closing because interest typically is paid in arrears. The seller owes the mortgage during this period and is not released from it until it is satisfied at the closing. For example, if the payment was made on February 1 and closing is on February 10, the seller would owe interest for 10 days.

Assume the listing contract shows that the last mortgage payment of $241.39 was made on February 1. Interest through February 10 is owed by the seller because the mortgage is still the seller's liability until closing. This amount can be approximated by the following calculation.

Days
February 1 through February 10 = 10 days

Rate per Day
$30,000 × 0.09 = $2,700 per year
$2,700/365 days = $7.397 per day

Amount
10 days × $7.397 = $73.97

The seller would be expected to pay this amount at the closing.

INSURANCE

In some states, the buyer is responsible for insurance on the property through the day of closing, and in others, the seller is responsible.

The buyer has two options in purchasing insurance. One is to buy a new policy, in which case the seller cancels the current policy at midnight on the day of closing. The new policy goes into effect the day after the title transfer. This type of transaction does not involve proration and does not enter the closing at all except that the buyer must present evidence that an insurance policy has been purchased. The seller notifies his insurance company of the cancellation and receives a refund directly from the company.

The buyer's second option is to assume the seller's policy. This procedure requires prorating. The seller has paid the policy premium in advance and expects to be reimbursed by the buyer from the day after closing to the date of the next premium payment.

For example, assume the contract of sale shows that the insurance annual premium of $720 was paid on December 1. Because the buyer is going to assume the coverage, he owes the seller an amount equal to the premium covering the period from the day after the closing to December 1 of the following year.

Days
February 11 through December 1 = (365 days total − 31 days in Jan. − 10 days in Feb. − 30 days in Dec.) = 294 days

Rate per Day
$720 premium/365 days = $1.973 per day

Amount
294 days × $1.973 = $580.06

The buyer is expected to reimburse the seller for this amount at the closing.

INCOME GENERATED FROM THE PROPERTY

Income from the property is determined from a rental agreement that typically requires rental payment in advance of usage. A payment required in advance can be considered to be in arrears if it is delinquent.

The seller has the right to receive the income from the date it is due through the closing. Thus, if the rent has been paid prior to the closing, the seller has the right to keep the amount covering the time period from the date it was due through the date of closing. The remaining amount is paid by the seller to the buyer.

For example, assume the listing contract shows that the property includes a rental unit above the detached garage. The rent is $1,175 per month, payable on the first of each month. The rent was paid on February 1. The seller retains the portion for February 1 through 10. The remainder of the payment is given to the buyer at the closing. The remainder is calculated as follows:

Days
February 11 through February 28 = 18 days

Rate per Day
$1,175 rent/28 days = $41.964 per day

Amount
18 days × $41.964 = $755.35

The seller is expected to give this amount to the buyer at the closing.

Payments due at the end of the time period are prorated the same way. The seller can retain the portion of the payment covering the period through the day of closing. The remainder is given to the buyer.

What Are Expenses?

Other expenses must be paid prior to or at closing. These items and the person paying them are identified within the sales contract. The expenses are typically divided between the seller and the buyer as follows.

TYPICAL SELLER EXPENSES

- *Abstract.* The seller may have agreed in the contract of sale to provide an updated abstract, which is commonly prepared by a title company.
- *Title insurance.* The seller may have agreed to provide title insurance if it was requested by the buyer.
- *New deed.* The seller will need to have a new deed prepared to transfer title to the buyer.

- *Survey.* The seller may have agreed to provide a recertification of the property boundaries by a professional surveyor.
- *Termite protection.* The seller may have agreed to pay for an inspection, correction of damage, or a permanent bond.
- *Revenue stamps.* If revenue stamps are required on the title transfers, the seller usually purchases them.
- *New mortgage fees.* The seller may have agreed to pay for a portion or all of the mortgage fees imposed on the buyer. A prepayment penalty may also be included.
- *Agency commission.* The seller may have agreed to pay a commission to an agency.
- *Loan points.* The seller may have paid loan points on a loan received by the buyer.

WHAT ARE TYPICAL BUYER EXPENSES?

- *Abstract examination.* The buyer should always have an attorney examine the abstract to ensure that the title is fee simple; the attorney can determine whether title insurance is necessary.
- *Appraisal.* The buyer may want the property appraised to be sure the offering price is appropriate; the lender may require an appraisal as a part of the loan application.
- *Assumption statement.* An **assumption statement** needs to be prepared by an attorney if the seller's mortgage is assumed.
- *Processing fee.* The lender will typically charge a fee to record the assumption statement.
- *Credit report.* The lender may require a credit report if a new mortgage is involved.
- *Origination fee.* The lender may charge a fee to process a new loan application amounting to 1 to 2 percent of the mortgage amount.
- *Loan points.* The borrower may need to pay points to receive the loan.
- *Recording fee.* The buyer should have the new deed recorded.

What Are the Contents of the Settlement Statement?

A **settlement statement** shows the money owed and money to be received at closing. Separate statements are prepared for the buyer and for the seller. An additional statement is prepared for the closing agent if one is involved. The closing agent sees all three. The seller sees only her own. The same is true for the buyer.

The statements are prepared by the party who is employed by the seller and responsible for conducting the closing. If the buyer is applying for a new mortgage, the lender may request that closing be conducted on its premises.

As a matter of procedure, settlement is always conducted with the buyer first. If the buyer does not have the necessary funds, the transaction stops.

DEBITS AND CREDITS

Each settlement statement includes a list of prorated items, expenses paid by the individual, and the amount of money owed or to be collected. The amounts corresponding to these items are shown as *debits* and *credits*. Rather than memorizing certain items as debits and others as credits, it is better to learn the concepts as they apply to the people in the closing so that each item can be shown under the appropriate heading.

The *buyer's* settlement statement shows the following debits and credits:

Debits equal all figures that the buyer owes at the closing from the view of the closing agent's trust account. Some examples follow:

purchase price	assumption statement filing fee
abstract examination fee	recording fee
special assessments	insurance proration if policy was assumed
assumption statement fee	

Appraisal fees, loan points, and credit report fees owed by the buyer may not enter the trust account; they may be paid directly to the lender.

Credits equal the following figures from the view of the closing agent's trust account. Prorated amounts, receipts, and expenses can be included.

- Accounts the buyer agrees to pay in the future because they fall due after the closing. Examples include all first and second mortgage balances.
- Accounts that the buyer has already paid. One example is the earnest money attached to the contract of sale.
- Accounts that the seller owes to the buyer. Examples include property taxes, mortgage interest, and rental payments that are paid in advance.

The *seller's* statement shows the following debits and credits:

Debits equal all figures that the seller *owes* at the closing from the view of the closing agent's trust account. Prorated amounts, receipts, and expenses can be included. Some examples follow:

remaining balances on all mortgages	loan points, if applicable
	a survey expense
mortgage interest	rent for the balance of the month after closing
property taxes	
abstract preparation	agency commission, if one was employed
termite control fees	

Credits equal all figures that are *owed to the seller* at the closing from the view of the closing agent's trust account. Prorated amounts, receipts, and expenses can be included. Some examples follow:

purchase price

balance of the insurance premium, if one was assumed

balance of the special assessment if it was paid prior to the closing

A SETTLEMENT EXAMPLE

The following example shows prorating, expenses for the buyer and seller, and the proper construction of the settlement statement:

Sam Seller wants to sell a vacant lot. On June 2, 2001, he signs a six-month exclusive right-to-sell listing with ABC Realty for $72,000 and agrees to pay a brokerage fee equal to 6.5 percent.

Sam's loan on the lot with First Federal has an outstanding balance of $8,400 at 8 percent with monthly payments of $200 due on the first of each month. The payment on June 1 was paid.

Ben Buyer offers $68,800 subject to approval of a 30-year loan for $55,000 at 12 percent annual interest (the loan was preapproved). Ben deposits $7,000 earnest money with the agent and gives Sam three days to accept the offer.

Ben agrees to assume a one-year hazard liability policy with an annual premium of $703, which expires August 31, the same year as the listing agreement. Sam agrees to pay for the two-page deed preparation. The tax bill for the current year is $584, and the prior year has been paid.

The transaction will be closed on June 20, the same year as the listing agreement, and possession given at that time.

The following expenses are known:

Title preparation (paid by seller)	$140
Attorney's opinion (paid by buyer)	$45
Loan origination (paid by buyer)	1%
Deed preparation fee (paid by seller)	$45
Recording fee (paid by buyer)	$6

The settlement statement for Ben Buyer is shown in Exhibit 16.2, and the statement for Sam Seller appears in Exhibit 16.3. Each entry is explained below.

Real estate taxes: January 1 through June 20 = 171 days on the calendar

$$\frac{\$584}{365 \text{ days}} = \$1.60 \text{ daily} \times 171 \text{ days} = \$273.60 \text{ debit seller, credit buyer}$$

Insurance: June 20 through August 31 = 72 days

EXHIBIT 16.2	Settlement statement for the buyer for June 20 closing.	
	Debit	Credit
Purchase Price	$ 68,800.00	
Earnest Money		$ 7,000.00
First Mortgage		55,000.00
Attorney's Opinion	45.00	
Loan Origination Fee	550.00	
Recording Fee	6.00	
Hazard Insurance	138.96	
Property Taxes		273.60
Subtotal	$ 69,539.96	$ 62,273.60
Net Owed by Buyer		$ 7,266.36

EXHIBIT 16.3 — Settlement statement for the seller for June 20 closing.

	Debit	Credit
Purchase Price		$ 68,800.00
Balance on Mortgage	$ 8,400.00	
Title Preparation	140.00	
Broker's Fee	4,472.00	
Deed Preparation	45.00	
Interest for 20 Days	37.33	
Hazard Insurance		138.96
Property Taxes	273.60	
Subtotal	$ 13,367.93	$ 68,938.96
Net Owed by Seller	$ 55,571.03	

$\dfrac{\$703}{365 \text{ days}}$ = $1.93 daily × 72 days = $138.96 debit buyer, credit seller

Brokerage fee: $68,800 x 0.065 = $4,472 debit seller

Interest: June 1 through June 20 = 25 days

$\dfrac{\$8400 \times 0.08 \times 1/12}{30 \text{ days}}$ = $1.866 daily × 20 days = $37.33 debit seller

Purchase price: $68,800 debit buyer, credit seller

Loan origination fee: $55,000 × 0.01 = $550 debit buyer

Earnest money: $7,000 credit buyer

First mortgage: $55,000 credit buyer

Balance due on mortgage: $8,400 debit seller

All other expenses: All other expenses are debits to the party that pays.

The difference between the debit and credit columns for the buyer is $7,266.36, which the buyer brings to closing. The difference between the debit and credit columns for the seller is $55,571.03 which is paid to the seller during the settlement.

When Is the Title Transfer Completed?

The title transfer is completed when the deed is accepted voluntarily by the new owner. It must be physically in the new owner's possession.

RECORDING

Recording of the deed is usually optional for the new owner. However, *all deeds should be recorded immediately to provide constructive notice of ownership*. In cases such as an installment sale, the seller may prefer not to record the deed, in order to facilitate foreclosure in the event of default by the buyer.

PROPERTY TAX ASSESSMENT

The new owner should have the property assessed in her name at the tax assessor's office. This action establishes the owner's intention of paying property taxes. It is not part of the title transfer but helps protect the new title against fraud once the new owner receives it.

When Does Default at Closing Happen?

Default at closing happens when one of the parties fails to complete the closing and indicates a desire not to exchange the deed for money.

DEFAULT BY THE BUYER

If the buyer defaults on an accepted contract, the agent and the seller will divide the earnest money deposit. The terms of this division in case of default by the buyer usually are printed on the contract. If not, the agent can request that his expenses be reimbursed, and the remainder is divided evenly.

DEFAULT BY THE SELLER

If the seller decides not to complete the closing, resulting in a default by the seller, the buyer has three alternatives: (1) The buyer can simply forget the transaction and destroy the offer, (2) the buyer can take legal action to sue the seller for damages if there are damages, or (3) the buyer can sue the seller for specific performance of the contract.

How Does RESPA Apply to the Settlement?

RESPA requires that the lender give the new mortgagor a settlement statement one day prior to the closing if the mortgagor requests it. If the mortgagor does not request the statement in advance, it will be provided usually when the mortgage is signed. The lender's settlement statement shows all the charges necessary to obtain the loan—the credit report, appraisal, and loan origination fees, and the points and prepayment penalty, if applicable. These amounts may not enter the closing agent's trust account because the buyer or seller pays them directly to the lender. In fact, they may have been paid prior to the closing conducted by the closing agent.

Chapter Summary

The property owner should be aware of two types of insurance that can protect the value of the property. The first is title insurance, which provides liability coverage against errors of title that have occurred in the past. The second type is property insurance, which provides protection against various perils on the premises that can occur in the future. A third type of coverage is the homeowner's warranty, which is purchased by the seller for the benefit of the new owner. It typically gives the buyer coverage against structural defaults, defective appliances, and a breakdown in the electrical and plumbing systems.

Settlement is the exchange of funds for the deed, which takes place at a date, time, and place agreed upon by the buyer and seller. The closing agent supervises the closing and reminds the buyer and the seller of the conditions within the listing contract and the sales contract that must be satisfied before the closing.

Prorating is used to allocate such accounts as taxes, insurance, rents, and mortgage interest between the buyer and seller. It is necessary because the payment dates on these accounts are not consistent with the closing date. The seller has already paid taxes or insurance, and the buyer refunds the unused premium or payment. These amounts are not actual cash expenses but represent adjustments to the totals paid by the buyer to the closing agent and by the agent in turn to the seller. The prorated amounts and cash expenses are shown in the settlement statements for the buyer and seller as debits and credits, defined in relation to the agent's trust account.

The title transfer is completed when the new owner voluntarily accepts the new deed. If the buyer should default at the closing and refuse to pay the funds in exchange for the deed, the seller and agent can divide the earnest money as outlined within the listing contract. Other alternatives are to sue for nonperformance of the contract, or to sell the property and sue the buyer for any damages. If the seller fails to perform by not delivering the deed, the buyer can sue for nonperformance.

One of the most important points in a real estate transaction is evidence of good title. The seller must be able to present a title acceptable to the buyer's attorney. No buyer wants to purchase property subject to title defects or later claims that can adversely affect its value.

Several types of deeds can be used in the transaction depending on the information uncovered in the abstract. The buyer should always insist upon a warranty deed unless special circumstances suggest that another type is acceptable. The warranty deed, in general, states that the grantor will take legal action to defend his claim of ownership during his period of ownership and any earlier or later periods. This type gives the new owner the maximum amount of ownership protection.

The buyer and seller need to be aware of the special requirements imposed on the lender and other participants in the settlement process. The Real Estate Settlement Procedures Act and the Truth-in-Lending Act require the lender to provide information to the borrower, give estimates of settlement costs, and allow a choice of persons to perform part of the settlement work. Truth-in-Lending also requires the lender to disclose the interest rate period.

Preparation for the closing is as important as the closing. Assuring that the terms within the listing and sales contracts are satisfied is essential to all parties involved.

Internet Applications

A website has been established for this chapter at http://epley.swcollege.com.

1. Why should a potential property owner consider buying title insurance? What is its purpose? What does it cover?

2. Explain the defects that are covered and those that are not in a standard and an extended coverage policy, respectively. Describe the types of title insurance policies that are issued in the market.

3. What is the difference in coverage between a title insurance policy and a property insurance policy? What are the typical perils covered in the property insurance policy? Why does a seller need to purchase a homeowner's warranty? A buyer?

4. What is the typical coverage in the warranty? What is the closing, and what is the role of a *title, deed,* and *conveyance* in the closing?

5. What is evidence of good title? Why should a buyer be interested in good title?

6. Outline the components of a valid deed. What are the three types of consideration? Give examples.

7. Describe accurately the meaning of a warranty. Contrast warranty, quitclaim, special, bargain and sale, and grant deeds.

8. How does the Real Estate Settlement Procedures Act influence the closing? How does the Truth-in-Lending Act influence the closing?

9. John Smith is selling his lake cabin for $65,000 and the closing is set for February 1, 2002. Answer each of the following questions.

   (a) The property taxes for the prior year have been paid in the amount of $720. The taxes for the current year are the same amount and may be paid anytime between the third Monday in February and October 10, 2002. What is the prorated amount to be collected from the seller on the date of closing? What is the total amount entered into the seller's settlement statement? Are property taxes shown as a debit or a credit?

   (b) The buyer is assuming John's insurance policy on the property. The annual premium of $640 was paid on December 15 the prior year. What is the prorated amount that the buyer owes the seller? How is it shown in the seller's and buyer's settlement statements? What amount is shown in the settlement statements if the buyer presents his own policy at the closing?

   (c) John's lake cabin was part of a special improvement district, which built curbs and gutters for the neighborhood. John owed $300 for the year 2002 in special property taxes. Does this figure enter the seller's settlement statement? How and in what amount? Does it enter the buyer's settlement state? How and in what amount?

   (d) John's lake cabin has an apartment in the basement, which John had rented to a student for $95 per month due on the first of the month. The rent has not been paid for February 1, 2002. Does this figure or the prorated amount enter the seller's or the buyer's settlement statement? How, and by what amount?

10. What is the relationship of the listing contract and contract of sale to the settlement statements?

11. Identify several accounts that are typically prorated. Define a debit and a credit in the buyer's, seller's, and closing agent's settlement statements. Which accounts

are typically paid in arrears? Why? Which accounts are typically paid in advance? Why?

12. What recommendations should be given to the buyer, seller, and agent for ensuring an uneventful closing? Explain the difference between determining whether property taxes are paid and prorating taxes.

13. What is the difference between the settlement statement provided by the lender to satisfy RESPA requirements and the one provided by the closing agent?

14. What alternatives are available to the buyer if the seller defaults prior to the closing? What alternatives are available to the seller if the buyer defaults?

Discussion Questions

1. What are some reasons a potential property owner would not want title insurance?

2. In your opinion, is evidence of good title in the form of an abstract and opinion ever as good as title insurance?

3. Is property insurance a necessary expense for the owner? Do any situations exist in the market where it is not needed? If so, what situations?

4. Can a seller sell the property without a warranty? If yes, why pay the added expense?

5. What are the advantages and disadvantages of title insurance, property insurance, and the homeowner's warranty?

6. Why must a seller be prepared to present evidence of good title? Why should a buyer always request this evidence?

7. Why must a buyer take steps to protect his or her rights of ownership when purchasing property? Why will the agent not perform these steps?

8. Why should the buyer always require the seller to eliminate existing liens prior to the closing? Should the buyer ever rely on the seller's promise to pay the liens after the closing?

9. Describe a situation in which the new owner would be satisfied with a quitclaim deed.

10. What is the advantage of describing the consideration as "$1 and other good and valuable consideration"?

11. Discuss the material found on the text website for this chapter on closing, title, and deed transfer.

The Decision to Develop the Property

Real Estate Development

## CHAPTER 17

1. Who are the real estate professionals involved in real estate development?
2. What function do these professionals perform in the development process?
3. What constitutes the real estate development process?

OBJECTIVES

When finished with this chapter, the student should be able to:

1. Discuss the rewards that a real estate developer enjoys.
2. Identify real estate professionals who are members of the development team.
3. Discuss the risk management aspects of real estate development.
4. Discuss the steps in the real estate development process.

IMPORTANT TERMS

absorption rate

development process

egress

exit strategy

hard costs

infrastructure

ingress

investment brokers

land development

leasing brokers

real estate development

risk management

soft costs

tenant finish costs

tenant improvements

INTRODUCTION

Real estate development is one of the most exciting and satisfying specialties within the real estate arena. A developer must identify market participants' needs for space then creatively yet economically solve their space requirements. The developer does this either by constructing new improvements or by renovating existing buildings or perhaps just a portion of the space within a building. Not only must a real estate developer find an economical way to accomplish this, but the project must satisfy both the user's demands and any community demands reflected through the permitting process. Further, the project must provide enough rent to pay the project's operating expenses and financing costs and still leave enough money left over to provide a satisfactory return for the developer.

A real estate developer, or in many instances a real estate development team, must have a good working knowledge of the material presented in the previous chapters.

- There must be an ability to study the market for the property type and to understand the marketability aspects of the developed or rehabilitated property.

- The relationship between construction cost and market value must be understood. It would not make sense to construct a million dollar building that is only worth eight hundred thousand when it opens and rents out space to tenants.

- The financial return measured by either the net present value or the internal rate of return needs to be analyzed to judge the quality of the investment.

- Development regulations in the form of the zoning ordinance, subdivision regulations, and construction codes need consideration in the planning process.

- Financing issues with regard to the promissory note and the type of loan need to be factored into the investment analysis.

What Is Meant by Real Estate Development?

Real estate development includes two separate operations. The more limited one is **land development.** A land developer takes raw, unimproved land and converts it into sites ready for a builder to erect an improvement. In the process, the land developer (1) identifies market needs for buildable sites and a large tract of land that can fulfill those needs; (2) secures the proper zoning and other entitlements necessary to erect improvements upon the sites; (3) decides how to divide the land into building sites and then files subdivision maps that reflect the division with the appropriate governmental body; (4) clears and grades the land, as appropriate, so that buildings can be erected on each site; (5) secures the installation of utilities so they are accessible to the sites; (6) installs the curbs, gutters, and paved streets necessary to access the sites; and (7) markets the sites to builders so that houses, offices, industrial facilities, and so forth can be built upon the sites. Land development is a risk endeavor because end users for the sites have not yet been identified when the development project is undertaken or, frequently, completed. The land developer must then accept the marketing risk of finding builders or users who wish to buy or lease the sites.

Real estate development, on the other hand, generally includes several of the land development functions listed above but only as part of a broader plan that also incorporates the improvements to the site. Rather than preparing several building sites to be marketed to builders for future construction, the real estate developer frequently deals with just one improved site, one owner, or one improvement at a time. For example, the real estate developer might be interested in a warehouse facility, shopping center, or office building that houses several tenants, but each development project focuses on a single improvement or an integrated set of improvements. The real estate developer first concentrates on quantifying end users' needs for space, ranging from conducting informal surveys to obtaining lease or purchase commitments from users of the to-be-constructed space. Based on this indicator of market demand, the real estate developer identifies land upon which improvements can be built that will satisfy the demand. Third, the developer secures the proper zoning and other government entitlements necessary to have the improvements built. The fourth step is locating the improvements' "footprint" on the site. Fifth, the real estate developer can then clear and grade the land as necessary. Sixth, utilities are installed so they are available at the appropriate locations on the parcel. Seventh, the real estate developer oversees the construction of the improvements, including any improvements to the site such as parking, sidewalks, fencing, and landscaping. Finally, the real estate developer must market any remaining space to end users.

What Rewards Does the Real Estate Developer Enjoy?

Real estate development frequently is a complex, challenging undertaking. The developer (this term will refer to the real estate developer throughout the rest of this chapter) must correctly forecast the market supply and demand conditions present at the completion of development. That may be six months to three years after development begins, or one to five years after the developer begins to explore an idea. Such long-term forecasting is very difficult. Even if the developer correctly identifies a market niche that will have excess demand when the development project is ready to be leased or sold, he still must successfully complete the remaining seven steps listed in the previous section. Typically, the developer is a master coordinator. After the developer envisions the completed project, other members of the development team are used to implement the vision. This involves a tremendous amount of coordination of the work these interdisciplinary professionals do. The developer must smoothly and effectively manage the development process, leading the team members to achieve the results he has in mind. This, too, is difficult to do well.

However, the developer reaps several rewards when the team performs well. These rewards are related to the difficulties identified above. When the developer completes a project that *successfully satisfies the user's needs,* the knowledge that she is contributing to the solution of that user's space requirements is a tremendous source of satisfaction. Not only has she correctly identified a need in the marketplace for her services, but she has fulfilled that need with a quality project that has met the test of the marketplace. Sometimes the user is a business that is looking for space to better conduct its dealings, perhaps a manufacturer looking for industrial space, a distributor seeking warehouse facilities, or a retailer needing commercial space. At other times, the user is an individual or family seeking housing in an attractive, safe, and well-located apartment complex.

The second reward is the developer's knowledge that he has *successfully coordinated the talents of a wide array of individuals* into a well-functioning development team. Although the functions of each team member will be detailed later in the chapter, the team frequently includes a market researcher, a real estate lawyer, the equity investor(s), a landscape architect or land planner (or both), an architect, the property manager, a leasing or investment broker, engineers, an appraiser, and the construction and permanent lenders. The development business is a people business, and developers must know how to motivate and reward people in order to have them produce at their highest levels.

The third reward for the successful developer is financial remuneration in the form of profit obtained from the project. Developers assume a substantial amount of risk in all instances. For some projects the risk is less than for others. Even with build-to-suit development projects, the developer must still make sure that the project is completed on time and within the allowed budget. Even greater risks are involved with securing the governmental approvals for a site because the developer typically must invest some of his own funds, and surely his own time, prior to obtaining the approvals (or perhaps not obtaining them!). As a reward for assuming these and other risks, the developer often receives a substantial return on his investment.

When the project does not have an owner occupant at the development period, the project becomes more speculative as in the case of a shopping center or an office building. Here the developer, the investor, and the lending institution focus on the process of *pre-leasing,* which involves signing tenants to the space before the project starts construction or at a minimum in advance of completion and its opening.

A fourth reward to the developer is the knowledge that she is *using all of her business education* as she successfully completes a project. She must (1) understand accounting concepts because she monitors and controls project costs, (2) develop financing strategies as she seeks the working capital necessary to operate her business and the project financing necessary to build and own the improvements, (3) use production tools as she schedules the work of the different members of the development team so that all project milestones are met, (4) possess marketing skills so that the space is leased at market rental rates or the project is sold at no less than market value as soon as possible, and (5) exercise managerial oversight so that she hires the best available individuals, motivates them to achieve lofty goals, coordinates their activities over time, and then rewards them appropriately.

Fifth, the development business appeals to those who desire jobs that take them *both indoors and outdoors.* A substantial amount of time must be spent performing the administrative functions, which are typically done indoors, but even more time is involved in the supervision and coordination of the various team members, which is often done either outdoors or at some other party's office. In addition, the successful developer has dozens of ideas that never come to fruition. He is constantly talking to members of the community, both to other real estate professionals and to end users of space, trying to see whether he can solve the users' space needs in a cost-effective manner. This frequently involves "kicking the dirt" as he searches the community for sites that might be used for a new real estate development. Usually, these ideas are rejected as economically infeasible, but the developer is always searching for another opportunity, and these searches generally take him outdoors.

As alluded to in the previous paragraph, the developer is rewarded for *creatively solving the client's space needs with an economical improvement.* It is difficult to find the solution that best fits the user's needs and still have it be an economically feasible one. Whether the developer, the client, or a third party owns the improvements, the owner must receive a satisfactory return on his investment. Hence, the developer has to construct those improvements so that she can make money after selling them for a price that will provide the investor with a satisfactory return on his investment. This is a difficult balancing task, but the successful developer takes pleasure at being able to handle it.

Who Are the Members of the Development Team?

An earlier section of this chapter identified those individuals often serving as members of the development team as a market researcher, a real estate lawyer, the equity investor(s), a landscape architect or land planner (or both), an architect, the property manager, a leasing or investment broker, engineers, an appraiser, and the construction and permanent lenders. Of course, the scale of the project plays a role in the actual makeup of the team. For smaller projects, the developer performs many of the members' jobs himself because, even if the development is small, the same *functions* must be performed regardless of size. This section examines each of the team members in greater detail.

PUBLIC SECTOR REGULATORS

A prominent member of the development team not mentioned earlier is the public sector lawmakers and regulators. Developers must operate within a system of laws. In fact, we would not have the many development opportunities available today without our private property laws. Not only do these laws provide a framework that guarantees certain freedoms for the private property owner, but they also specify that the need to provide for the general public's health, welfare, and safety can override the property owner's freedoms. Thus, we have building codes to ensure improvements are constructed to meet minimum safety standards, zoning laws to prevent developers from placing incompatible uses next to each other and from building too big a project on a given size lot, transportation rules that allow only so many "curb cuts" for a project so that cars entering or leaving a project do not interfere with the general traffic flow, historical preservation rules and environmental laws that are designed to protect the environment for future generations, subdivision regulations that specify what impact fees must be paid as well as what types of roads, parks, and other public improvements

EXHIBIT 17.1	The development team.

Public Sector Regulators
Market Researcher
Real Estate Lawyer
Equity Investors
Landscape Architect and Land Planner
Property Manager
Brokers
Engineers
Appraisers
Lenders

are necessary in order to prevent the project from being a burden on the existing tax-payers, sewer and other utility access rules and their associated fees again designed to keep the taxpayers from having to pay additional amounts to support the new development, and a whole host of additional laws and regulations.

Regardless of the developer's political persuasion, he must recognize that he is in a highly regulated industry. Furthermore, development projects undertaken outside of the United States often face much greater governmental participation in the development process. Because the government is ever present, not only at local levels as indicated above but also at state and federal levels through tax, labor, lending, and environmental laws and regulations, it is wise for the developer to recognize this presence and treat the government as his partner. Working with the regulators is often the more productive and successful route, rather than treating them as the enemy. The more enlightened developers accomplish their goals more quickly and efficiently by entering into de facto partnerships with their regulators.

MARKET RESEARCHER

One of the keys to a real estate developer's success is her identification of unfulfilled space needs by end users. She will most likely conduct informal surveys of end users and real estate professionals in the area to judge such needs, especially during the early stages of development when she is trying to decide whether to pursue a particular development idea. Later, when the developer is ready to commit her own money (rather than just time) to the project or when she seeks financing for the project, she may hire a market researcher to conduct such surveys. Furthermore, the lender and equity investors (including the developer if she continues to own a stake in the project) will want independent confirmation of the continued demand for the property's space during their lending and ownership time horizons. Often, the market researcher provides this information.

Two situations exist in which the motivation is different. Sometimes the developer owns or controls a site and is looking for the most profitable use for that site. This is often called "a site looking for a use." The market research must then be focused on a narrower scale as the site features become a key qualifier. For example, site size, shape, and topography become limiting factors in the project selection. Accessibility to and from that site, as well as neighborhood compatibility and site zoning, take on crucial importance. Each of these features can limit the ability of the site to solve particular users' needs. Second, there are occasional circumstances in which the developer's project creates its own demand. For example, prior to the development of Borders' and Barnes and Noble's "big-box" bookstores with their large footprints, people bought books at independent booksellers and at shopping center bookstores like Waldenbooks and B. Dalton Bookseller. Before the first of these big-box bookstores proved the concept to be successful, market research would not have indicated the demand for such an improvement. Because this type of example makes market research seem much less important, most developers would like to believe that this happens frequently with their projects due to the projects' high quality and the unique locations they have selected. In reality, it occurs only rarely.

REAL ESTATE LAWYER

Real estate lawyers are an integral and important part of the development team. Not only is the real estate lawyer there to make sure the developer complies with all legal requirements the public authorities set forth, but he is also charged with structuring contracts. It is this responsibility that is much more challenging and often more reward-ing to the developer. As the lawyer drafts or reviews legal agreements the developer will have to sign, his main concern is visualizing how the contractual terms might adversely affect the developer in the future. If the adverse consequences can be elimi-nated by redrafting the contract, he does it. If they cannot be eliminated, then they must be negotiated so as to control them. The lawyer is frequently responsible for these negotiations.

EQUITY INVESTORS

It is rarely possible for the developer to borrow all of the funds needed to complete the development project. That means she must either inject more of her own capital into the project or have equity investors contribute some of their capital prior to completion of construction. Even if she is unable to convince the investors to assume the addition-al risk of investing in a property prior to the beginning of its operating phase, she still must bring the investors (and their money) in later. What makes more sense is for the investors to be a part of the development team, staying informed about the project throughout the process. It is especially important to let them know early in the discus-sions when their equity contributions will be needed, which emphasizes the need for excellent planning, budgeting, and cost controlling skills on the developer's part.

LANDSCAPE ARCHITECT OR LAND PLANNER

Development is done not in a vacuum but on sites that frequently possess some exist-ing landscaping and almost always require additional landscaping upon completion. One of the jobs of the landscape architect or land planner is to design a master plan that locates the improvements on the tract of land so as to best take advantage of the exist-ing natural environment. Then other features of that environment, such as roads, pathways, landscaping, outdoor lighting, and so forth, must be designed to blend most harmoniously with the existing features and the newly added improvements. Involving the landscape architect early in the development process assures that costly, last-minute changes to accommodate the natural environment's features are not made to already prepared plans.

Landscape architects differ from land planners in that the latter concentrate on preparing master plans for developers while the former not only do that but also design a variety of outdoor settings, including landscaping appropriate for the improvements, roadways, walkways, play areas, walking trails, bike paths, and so forth. The term *land-scape architect* will be used here on to refer to professionals who perform both roles.

ARCHITECT

Just as the landscape architect is concerned with the design of the natural environment, the architect is concerned with the design of the built environment. The developer also brings the architect into the development decision early on because it is crucial that the project be designed so that it can be built at a cost that will allow the developer to earn a satisfactory return, either upon sale of the project or through its operation. Moreover, these latter two situations are related. The more economically a project can be operat-ed and still bring in the same amount of rental income, the greater is its worth. When the developer sells his interest in the project, the project well designed with an eye toward operating efficiency will thus command a higher price.

PROPERTY MANAGER

The property manager is the specialist concerned with the day-to-day management and operation of the completed development project. Because the property manager's compensation is often tied to how efficiently he operates the property, he not only has an interest in the efficient design of the improvements but also has the necessary expertise to make constructive suggestions early in the design phase. Second, the property manager is frequently the developer's best link to the potential tenants for the space. He deals with the tenants on a daily basis and is privy to their space needs, not only for the projects he is managing but for the tenants' other space requirements that are presently being filled by competitive projects. For both of these reasons, it is imperative to involve the property manager early in the development process.

BROKERS

Brokers play different roles with different types of development projects. For example, when referring to commercial development projects (office, retail, and industrial space), most brokers are **leasing brokers.** As such, commercial brokers are another link with end users and the improvement features most suited to their needs. If the project is going to be represented exclusively by one broker or brokerage firm, then involving this team member in the design phase will make it easier to lease the space later. Even if the owner chooses not to enter into an exclusive arrangement, she should include both outside brokers as well as any on her staff (many developers do their own in-house leasing and management of their development projects) among the many individuals from whom she seeks market information.

Other brokers who may specialize in listing or selling properties (or both) are frequently known as **investment brokers** when dealing with commercial properties. They, too, are an important link to the market, this time with those who might have an interest in purchasing the property. The need for close coordination with them is less obvious, but they specialize in providing the connection between the needs of investors and the developers of projects. As the developer seeks equity investors willing to contribute their capital in exchange for an ownership share, the investment broker often provides substantial assistance in locating interested investors.

ENGINEERS

The development team also needs civil and mechanical engineers, although they work most closely with the architect and landscape architect. Civil engineers are experts in the design of **infrastructure** improvements, such as roads, utility installations, and storm drainage systems. Geotechnical engineers, a specialty within civil engineering, analyze the soils to determine load-bearing capacities, wastewater runoffs, the presence of hazardous wastes, and the hydrology of the soils. Finally, civil engineers work with the architect to make sure the structural strength of the improvements meets local safety standards. Mechanical engineers also work with the architect to design the necessary mechanical systems, such as the plumbing systems and the heating, ventilation, and air conditioning (HVAC) systems, to have adequate capacity to serve the needs of the improvements' tenants.

APPRAISERS

Recall that appraisers specialize in estimating property values. An appraiser will be retained to estimate the market value of the improvements once construction is completed and the property is operating. This is a difficult task because there is no market test of the attractiveness of the property prior to its completion, unless substantial preleasing has been done, and there is no operating history to use to estimate how costly it will be to run. Using information from comparable properties that are operating in similar markets, the appraiser estimates the development's value. The appraiser uses the estimate in obtaining both debt and equity financing for the property. The more familiar the appraiser is with the location and the type of project the developer is having built, the better the job she is likely to do. It behooves the developer to share his estimates of rental income and future expenses, as well as his construction costs, so that the appraiser has as much information as possible so that she can provide an accurate value estimate.

LENDERS

The lenders, who are responsible for providing the debt financing, are the final members of the development team. There are both construction lenders and permanent lenders. Construction lenders provide most of the funds necessary to pay to have the site prepared and the improvements built. Most of the construction financing is provided by commercial banks, as is a substantial amount of the permanent financing. Other permanent lenders include life insurance companies and, increasingly, secondary mortgage market investors operating through the securities dealers, conduits, and mortgage companies discussed in Chapter 10. Frequently, construction lenders will refuse to make their loans until they are assured of a source of repayment. The developer then must first secure a "takeout" commitment from a permanent lender, who agrees to provide the permanent financing (and thus take the construction lender out of the process) once construction is completed and the property is leased. With the takeout commitment in hand, the developer is able to obtain construction financing.

Because the lenders are providing a very large portion of the total funds needed, they are informally kept apprised of the development plans as the developer becomes convinced that a particular development project is economically feasible. Once the decision is made to go ahead with the project, then the lenders will receive a formal loan application detailing the developer's rationale for pursuing the project along with substantial quantitative market information to back up the developer's decision.

How Is Economic Feasibility Determined?

Developers are continually testing the economic feasibility of their development ideas. When they first get an idea, they use rough tests to gauge whether it makes economic sense to pursue the idea any further. For example, if a developer is considering a 100,000-square-foot warehouse, his knowledge of the local market might lead him to estimate that he could rent it for $0.50 per square foot (psf) per month, that lenders and investors would demand a 5-percent vacancy and collection loss, and that annual operating expenses would be in the neighborhood of $1.20 psf (see Exhibit 17.2). The annual potential gross income would be $6 psf (0.50 × 12). Subtracting a 5-percent vacancy and collection loss of $.30 ($6 × 0.05) gives a $5.70 annual effective gross income. Deducting $1.20 psf operating expenses from the effective gross income leaves an annual net operating income (NOI) of $4.50 psf ($5.70 − $1.20). Because this would be a 100,000-square-foot warehouse, the NOI would total $450,000. From his market awareness, the developer also knows that local capitalization rates for this type of project are currently running right at 9 percent. Dividing the NOI by the capitalization gives the developer a rough estimate of the project's $5 million market value ($450,000/0.09).

EXHIBIT 17.2 Income and value estimates.

Potential Gross Income ($0.50/sqft/mo x 100,000 sqft x 12 mo/yr)	$ 600,000
Less Vacancy and Collection Losses (600,0000 x 0.05)	− 30,000
Effective Gross Income	570,000
Less Operating Expenses ($1.20 psf x 100,000 sqft)	− 120,000
Net Operating Income	450,000
Divide by Capitalization Rate	+ 0.09
Property Value	$ 5,000,000

The developer is experienced enough to know that sites in the area where he feels there is a market demand for warehouse space are available for $9 psf. Because about twice as much site area as building area would be required, he estimates the site would cost about $1.8 million (100,000 × 2 × $9). He knows that construction costs are roughly $41 psf, including a reasonable development profit, so that the improvement cost totals $4.1 million (100,000 × $41). Total project cost would be the sum of the site and improvement costs, or $5.9 million (see Exhibit 17.3). Because it would cost more to build the warehouse than what the completed project would be worth, the developer should either reject the warehouse idea or find a less expensive way to have it built. In many cases, the developer performs these rough calculations, then drops the idea and searches for another one.

For some developers, the economic feasibility calculations are never much more detailed than these rough estimates. For most, however, the use of *discounted cash flow (DCF) analysis* (introduced in Chapter 11) becomes an invaluable decision tool. As developers become more financially sophisticated and proficient with time-value-of-money calculations and as projects become larger, more complex, and more costly, thereby requiring greater attention to risk control techniques, developers increasingly turn to DCF analysis.

The developer uses DCF analysis in a number of ways, but in all cases she is trying to achieve the same type of "go or no go" answer to a development question as she was seeking when using the rough calculations described earlier. For example, she may be using DCF analysis on a monthly (or perhaps quarterly) basis to determine whether

EXHIBIT 17.3 Cost estimates.

Site Acquisition Cost ($9.00/sqft x 100,000 sqft x2)	$ 1,800,000
Plus Improvement Costs (100,000 sqft x 41.00)	4,100,000
Total Project Costs	$ 5,900,000

development is warranted. She would use as monthly cash flows the negative development costs (including a development fee paid to herself) less the positive construction loan draws, then include a contracted or presumed sale less repayment of the construction loan at the end of the development period. The appropriate discount rate would be the developer's cost of equity capital.

In order to come up with a sales price in the previous example, the developer would estimate the project's annual NOI for each year an investor would be expected to retain ownership of the project (the holding period), and use that income as the annual cash flows. At the end of the holding period, the cash flow would be the project's re-sale price less any sales expenses the investor would have to pay. Those cash flows would be discounted at the property's yield rate, derived as shown earlier in Chapter 6. Because there would be no cash outflow specified as the initial purchase price, the calculated net present value (NPV) would be the same as the value of the project when construction is completed. That value would then be used as the developer's presumed sales price at the conclusion of construction.

Another example would be if the developer expected to retain ownership of the project for a certain number of years. Then, not only would the cash flows during development need to be considered, but the cash flows that were expected when the construction loan was repaid (negative) and replaced by the permanent loan (positive) along with any accompanying injection of equity capital (negative). The periodic before-tax cash flows to the developer during the holding period would be entered, along with the sales price (positive) less any sales expenses, permanent loan repayment, and loan prepayment penalty (negatives) at the end of the holding period. As before, the appropriate discount rate would be the developer's cost of equity capital. Of course, this analysis could be done on an after-tax basis as well.

A fourth example of situations in which the successful developer would use DCF analysis is when the developer is trying to decide whether to include a particular project feature. For example, assume he is developing an apartment complex and trying to decide whether to include covered (as well as uncovered) parking. He would calculate the increased rental income, and possibly lower vacancies, each year during an investor's anticipated holding period due to the presence of the additional amenity. These figures would be the cash flows in the NPV equation. The initial negative cash flow (period zero) would be the extra cost of the covered parking. This would be an all-inclusive cost figure, not just the hard costs associated with the covered parking, so that it would also include the additional financing costs, any extra architectural or engineering costs, any greater costs for the site if a larger one would be needed, additional profits to the developer based on the higher project costs, and so forth. Using the property yield as the discount rate, he would calculate the NPV of the covered parking option. If it were positive, then adding covered parking would be desirable; if it were negative, it would not. This type of analysis would be used for a number of different incremental project features.

LAND DEVELOPMENT ILLUSTRATION

While each of the preceding four examples is a valid situation in which DCF analysis might be used, a simple illustration of the use of DCF analysis provides a concrete reminder of its importance. To make the situation realistic, yet easy to grasp, consider a land developer who would have to spend $15,000 per acre to acquire 500 acres of raw development land for a total land cost of $7,500,000. This raw land might be used for an office building, shopping center, warehouse space, or any of several other uses. In this case, assume the land developer has thoroughly investigated the marketplace and discovered that the market demand for the tract is strongest if the land can be used as a residential subdivision. The developer would then sell the resulting building lots to homebuilders who would build single-family residences on the lots.

As his detailed analysis unfolds, the developer first investigates the market participants' demand for residential building lots. He would have to ascertain how many lots would be needed per year, what size and price range those lots would have to be sold for, and—most importantly—what portion of the market demand for lots he could reasonable expect his subdivision to capture. Based on his estimate of the annual **absorption rate** for building lots, he concludes he can sell 1/4-acre, 1/3-acre, and 1/2-acre lots over a four-year period as shown in Exhibit 17.4. This estimate of the demand for his lots is a crucial first step that must be done with the utmost care as the validity of the remaining analysis depends on the accuracy of the market demand forecast.

After dividing the 500-acre tract into lots, the developer no longer has all 500 acres available to sell. Some of the land will be needed for roads, utility and drainage easements, and storm water runoff detention ponds. Some of the land may be unmarketable wetlands or used for lakes. In order to secure public sector approvals, the developer may have to contribute some of the land for community park use or for a school. Although it differs from project to project, we will assume for this example that only 425 of the original 500 acres remain available for sale.

The 500-acre land development project will incur most of its development costs during the first three years, and the bulk of those during the first year, but the developer's market study indicates it will take four years to sell all the building lots. During that period, the developer expects to incur the development expenses listed in Exhibit 17.5. Notice the timing and magnitude of the expenses. Land development is a risky business as the expenses are front-loaded while the sales revenues, which are derived from the market absorption study summarized in Exhibit 17.4, are not received until much later in the process. Exhibit 17.6 includes both the revenue estimates and the development costs, along with sales expenses of 10 percent of the lot sales prices, in order to calculate the developer's annual net income from this project.

EXHIBIT 17.4 Number and price of lots sold.

Lot Size	Year				Total Lots Sold	Total Acreage Sold
	One	Two	Three	Four		
1/4-Acre Lots	112 lots @ $29,000	238 lots @ $31,900	118 lots @ $34,250	12 lots @ $34,250	480	120
1/3-Acre Lots	64 lots @ $40,000	374 lots @ $44,000	181 lots @ $47,250	26 lots @ $49,500	645	215
1/2-Acre Lots	5 lots @ $57,500	50 lots @ $58,500	101 lots @ $64,500	24 lots @ $71,000	180	90
Total Lots Sold	181	662	400	62	1305	
Total Acreage Sold	51.83	209.17	140.33	23.67		425

EXHIBIT 17.5 Land development costs (in dollars).

Cost Category	Year				Total Costs
	One	Two	Three	Four	
Clearing and Grading	3,310,000	1,280,000	0	0	4,590,000
Storm Sewers	1,150,000	0	0	0	1,150,000
Sanitary Sewers	2,870,000	0	0	0	2,870,000
Water Lines	1,700,000	0	0	0	1,700,000
Curbs and Gutters	564,000	423,000	188,000	0	1,175,000
Paving	2,808,000	2,106,000	936,000	0	5,850,000
Contractor Profit and Overhead	1,697,000	458,000	145,000	6,000	2,306,000
Engineering	2,295,000	0	0	0	2,295,000
Property Taxes	21,000	93,000	82,000	17,000	213,000
Legal	75,000	89,000	54,000	32,000	250,000
Miscellaneous	232,000	63,000	20,000	2,000	316,000
Contingency	250,000	68,000	21,000	1,000	340,000
Total Development Costs	16,972,000	4,580,000	1,446,000	57,000	23,055,000

EXHIBIT 17.6 Development net income (in dollars).

Lot Category	Year				Total Revenues
	One	Two	Three	Four	
1/4-Acre Lots	3,248,000	7,592,200	4,041,500	411,000	15,292,700
1/3-Acre Lots	2,560,000	16,456,000	8,552,250	1,287,000	28,855,250
1/2-Acre Lots	287,500	2,925,000	6,514,500	1,704,000	11,431,000
Total Lot Sales Revenues	6,095,500	26,973,200	19,108,250	3,402,000	55,578,950
Less Development Costs	(16,972,000)	(4,580,000)	(1,446,000)	(57,000)	(23,055,000)
Less Sales Expenses @ 10%	(609,550)	(2,697,320)	(1,910,825)	(340,200)	(5,557,895)
Net Income	(11,486,050)	19,695,880	15,751,425	3,004,800	26,966,055

EXHIBIT 17.7   The cash flows into the NPV calculation.

Year	Land Acquisition and Development Costs Less Revenues	Net Revenues	Discount Factor @ 25%	Present Value
0	− $ 7,500,000		1.0000	$ 7,500,000
1	− $ 11,486,050		0.8000	− $ 9,188,840
2		$ 19,695,880	0.6400	+ $ 12,605,363
3		$ 15,751,425	0.5120	+ $ 8,064,729
4		$ 3,004,800	0.4096	+ $ 1,230,766
NPV @ 25 %				+ $ 5,212,018

The "net income" figures in the last row of Exhibit 17.6, along with the cost of the raw land, are the cash flow numbers we need to use in the NPV equation. First, however, we need an estimate of the development's discount rate. The developer's cost of capital, his experience with similar projects, the assistance of real estate appraisers, and a comparison of this project's risk profile with that of other investments available in the capital markets are all valid techniques to derive a discount rate. Presume that the developer's extensive experience leads him to choose a discount rate of 25 percent. This suggests a rather risky project, and a residential subdivision land development project likely would fit that description.

The NPV calculation is based on the revenue and cost figures in Exhibit 17.7.

Since the NPV is positive at the discount rate of 25 percent, which that reflects the developer's perceptions of risk, the land developer should proceed with the project. The developer's rate of return in fact exceeds 25 percent, as was discussed in the investment chapter.

What Is Risk Management?

When a developer begins a new project, she often follows a certain sequence of steps. Sometimes she has a formal checklist to make sure she covers everything that must be done, and at other times her approach is more intuitive. Nevertheless, several functions must be performed prior to completion of the project. Many of these need to be done in roughly the same sequence with each project. Still, development is nonlinear by nature, and later items will sometimes be completed first and sometimes in tandem with the earlier ones. We refer to these steps and their associated sequence as the **development process,** which will be discussed later in the chapter. One notion, risk management, transcends each of the steps in the development process and will be discussed first.

Real estate development is a risky undertaking. However, developers would not have it any other way. They are risk takers. They receive a great deal of satisfaction from seeing an opportunity to satisfy a user's space needs, often an opportunity that others have yet to see, then successfully developing a project that satisfies those needs.

When the developer begins to identify the needs and a corresponding solution, there is no guarantee that users will agree that his solution will best meet their needs.

Other developers may propose better solutions; tenant needs may change before they sign a lease for the space; economic conditions may worsen during construction; costs may escalate due to shortages of materials and labor; the market environment may change before the project is completed; unforeseen conditions, such as hidden problems underground, environmental conditions on the site, historical property redevelopment restrictions, delays in governmental approvals, and so forth, may conspire to cause costly delays. Yet, developers accept these risks because of their nature as well the rewards they receive for having surmounted them.

Although developers are risk takers, they do want to identify and *control* the risks that face them so as to minimize the ultimate risk: the risk of project failure and, perhaps, developer bankruptcy along with it. This process is known as **risk management.** Note that we said "control" and "minimize," not "eliminate" risks. Indeed, many developers have gone through bankruptcy, some several times. Still, developers have several techniques they use to control risks.

EVALUATE INTERNAL STRENGTHS AND WEAKNESSES

One of the more difficult items is for the developer to be brutally honest as she evaluates herself, her organization, and her development team members. What are the strengths, and weaknesses, of each of the parties? How can she best select development projects that build on her and her team's strengths? What types of projects should she avoid so as to minimize the risk that her firm pursues projects for which they are not suited? Because developers are optimistic, "can do" individuals, this is one of the most difficult risk control techniques for the developer to adopt.

KEEP INVESTMENT LOW

Just as the first technique was difficult for the developer, this one is easy—if only everyone else cooperates! The developer strives to invest as little money as possible throughout the development process. Ideally, that means others will provide the capital. However, the lenders providing the debt capital and the investors providing the remainder of the equity capital want to see the developer make a substantial equity contribution so that his interests are aligned with theirs. What the developer must show them is twofold: first, that he has already spent a significant amount of cash on the project, and second, that he has made an even greater noncash contribution by devoting a considerable amount of his time initially to identifying and then subsequently to bringing the project forward to the point where it needs the contribution of additional capital.

The developer can take other steps to minimize his cash investment. He can use an *option* to acquire an interest in the site. An option gives the developer the right to acquire the site at a later date for an agreed-upon price upon payment of a very small amount today. This would give the developer the opportunity to have the geotechnical engineer check the site for its physical characteristics, to obtain the proper zoning and other governmental approvals, to line up the tenants through preleases, to secure the financing by commitments obtained from both the permanent and the construction lenders, and to lock up the equity investors through presales. If the market happens to be in the developer's favor, then he might even convince the site owner to apply the option payment to the purchase price. Another step the developer can take is to try and obtain *nonrecourse financing* from both the construction and permanent lenders. This type of financing does not allow the lender to claim ownership of personal assets in case of default. Although permanent lenders may readily grant such a request, construction lenders often require the developer's personal (or firm) guarantee.

REPEATEDLY TEST ECONOMIC FEASIBILITY

Another way to control development risks is to repeatedly test the project for economic feasibility. As described earlier in the chapter, these tests may be either rough calculations or sophisticated DCF analyses. The important point is that the developer tests the project for economic feasibility not just once but over and over as new information becomes available. It may be information about a change in market demand, a competitor now preparing to develop a similar project, lower (or higher) interest rates, a change in construction costs and timing due to labor or material shortages, additional preleasing, or any of a number of similar instances in which new information affects future cash flows. The developer has the analysis redone with current information then tests the continued economic viability of the project.

INCLUDE TEAM MEMBERS

Developers are also able to better manage their risks when team members are consulted early in the development process. Recall that the public is always a member of the development team. When the developer consults with local *public sector officials* on an informal basis as his plans are taking shape, it is easier to tailor those plans to maximize the chances of governmental acceptance than to subsequently have to revise them substantially after much time and effort has been spent on them. Moreover, there is always a give-and-take involved in the discussions, especially when the plans are not presented as an already completed package but as ones in which the developer is seeking the local officials' input to assist in developing a better project.

The same can be said for the other public the developer must satisfy: the *local residents.* Because they must live with the project as their neighbor and because they vote for the government officials, their views rightfully carry substantial weight. The developer wants to inform them of what she plans to develop and why she has chosen to do it in a particular way. When she includes them early in the development process, she can readily make changes that will enhance the community's acceptance of her project. Of course, there are times that she will be unable to accommodate their views, but early and frequent meetings provide her an opportunity to share the reasons for her actions.

Two other team members that should be involved early in the development process, but many times are not, are the *leasing broker* and the *property manager.* The failure to include their input during the plan's formative stages is a crucial mistake. As discussed earlier, they provide a direct link with the end user community, the tenants who would be the developer's leasing targets. They understand what features the tenants want. More importantly, they understand what features the tenants are willing to pay for. Ignoring this source of information increases the risks that the developer will not produce something the market demands. Furthermore, the property manager fully understands the importance of operating efficiencies. He can provide guidance about ways to achieve economies that will make ownership more lucrative, thus increasing the value of the completed project.

Finally, *architects,* including the *landscape architect,* are team members frequently included in the development's formative stages. The landscape architect can best locate the proposed project on the available site, taking care to maximize the space available for the improvements while taking best advantage of the features of the natural environment. The architect then follows up by designing improvements that optimize the leaseable space, given the constraints that the market participants place on him. This is where the architect, leasing broker, and property manager work together most closely.

DEFINE EXIT STRATEGIES

Because developers are optimistic by nature, many will not consider how best to terminate a project, or even that they should terminate it once they seriously have begun considering it. Of course, they expect to sell it for a profit, either when construction is completed and tenancy is stabilized or after they have held it as an investment for a number of years. Smart developers, however, will also identify strategies to stop the development process prior to signing contracts committing them to complete a project. For example, the site option, rather than the acquisition, strategy mentioned earlier as a way to reduce the investment is also a good **exit strategy.** The developer must be prepared to walk away from what he initially considered to be an extraordinary idea if it turns out not to be economically feasible. Clearly, it is better to do that with an option than if he already owns the property. Another strategy is for the developer to have alternate development plans for the site in case his primary plan becomes economically infeasible.

USE ADDITIONAL RISK CONTROL TECHNIQUES

A number of additional techniques exist that the developer may use to manage the risks he faces, but usually they are not as significant as the preceding ones. First, the developer should recognize the importance of situs. The word *situs* refers to the cross-effects of the surrounding land uses on the value of the developer's site, as well as to his site's effect on the surrounding land values. If he has the financial wherewithal, he may be able to control the effects of situs, as well as reap the benefits of a successful project, by acquiring a buffer zone around his project. Second, in most cases, the developer can reduce his risks by *pre-leasing* as much of the space as possible. Of course, this also means forsaking higher rental payments if the market or project turns out to be more positive than originally envisioned. Third, financial risks can be reduced by negotiating *fixed-price construction contracts.* Fourth, the developer will use *formalized scheduling algorithms* to make sure all the pieces of the development project are completed by the necessary deadlines.

The fifth additional risk control technique is the adoption of *comprehensive cash, expense, and accounting controls* so that the developer not only knows where the funds are being spent, but whether she is above or below the budget that she has prepared prior to signing the contracts. Of course, this also means she must be willing to institute the necessary economies if she finds the project's costs are exceeding projected amounts. Sixth, the developer should obtain title, liability, fire and extended coverage *insurance* to protect against those risks. Coverage is even available to protect against environmental hazards that may be present. The seventh risk control area is *financing.* Lenders want personal guarantees, floating interest rates, low loan-to-value ratios, early equity contributions, and strong debt service coverage ratios, while developers and other equity investors want just the opposite. Negotiating favorable financing, which is much easier during rapid business cycle upswings, helps the developer to control these risks. Finally, the developer controls risk by *paying attention to details.* For many developers, this is difficult. They are frequently "big picture" people who dream the dreams as they conceive of projects, rather than detail-oriented individuals. Nevertheless, they must pay attention to the details if they are not to be surprised when everything does not go according to their plans.

What Are the Steps in the Development Process?

Although the amount of detail varies by project size, participants, and location, the following development steps are universal. As business firms become more global, U.S. development companies are following them worldwide to service their space needs. But the same steps are followed by local development firms in any country. What varies the most is the role of government. In many countries, the government plays a much larger role than it does in the United States. Often, the government permissions and exactions are more difficult and time-consuming to obtain. Frequently, the government is also a local developer, just as occasionally occurs in the United States, and a public-private partnership must be negotiated. Still, the development steps stay the same.

Developers themselves are not a uniform breed. Some developers are flamboyant, while others are retiring. Some act intuitively, while others are analytical. Some operate with large staffs, while others are one-man shops. They are the same in their attitudes, however. They are risk takers who see opportunities where others see problems. They are innovative in their pursuit of atypical solutions to problems. And, they have the drive to aggressively see their projects through to completion in spite of adversities.

PRECONSTRUCTION STAGE

The development process is divided into three stages: (1) the tasks that must be done prior to the beginning of construction, (2) those that must be accomplished during construction, and (3) those that follow the completion of construction. Do not forget that the developer is constantly seeking to identify and control the risks she faces during each of these stages.

Market Analysis

The initial step in the development process is market analysis, which was discussed in more detail in Chapter 7. Usually, the developer continually and informally performs this task as she searches for development ideas whenever she visits with people or even while she is driving around. Later, the task becomes more formalized as a specialist is hired to provide a detailed market analysis suitable for developing the income and absorption or capture rate forecasts necessary to conduct an economic feasibility analysis properly.

EXHIBIT 17.8	Steps in the development process.

Preconstruction stage	**Construction stage**
Market analysis	Construction
Economic feasibility analysis	Marketing and sales
Site selection and analysis	
Site control	**Postconstruction stage**
Plan preparation and permit approval	Marketing and sales
Marketing and sales	Property management
Financing	

Market analysis begins with an identification of the market area for a proposed development project. Often, it is within the area in which the developer is currently operating, which may be a small city or a section of a larger metropolitan area for a smaller developer, the entire metropolitan area or region for larger developers, and nationwide or even globally for the largest developers. Typically, developers specialize in one or two product types (industrial, office, retail, residential, and so forth) so as to build expertise and a reputation within that area. Consequently, their market analysis is limited to geographical and product subsets of the available development market. They will probably limit their analyses to areas where demand is rapidly increasing, as reflected by rising rents, or is expected to be growing strongly in the near future.

Once they have identified their market area, developers use the tools described in Chapter 7 to assess supply and demand. Early in the analysis, heavy emphasis is placed on data provided by commercial brokers, universities, lenders, and other sources of free information. At this stage, the developer is trying to get a rough handle on whether an idea is worth pursuing. If it is, then the market analysis is progressively refined to include quantitative information about current and future supply and demand conditions. In particular, the developer is interested in ascertaining what the current market rents and vacancy levels are for the property idea being considered.

The developer's market analysis also needs to give her a good estimate of what portion of the market she could expect to capture through sales or leases of the units she would be developing. For example, if the market is expected to grow by 400,000 square feet annually and she would be developing 200,000 square feet of product next year, could she reasonably expect to capture 50 percent of the available demand or would other developers be likely to enter the market and capture more than 50 percent of it so that she would be limited to less than 50 percent. If so, how much less could she capture? In addition to the overall capture rate, the developer needs to know how quickly she will capture her share. This is known as the absorption rate, and it is particularly important in the DCF analyses when she must specify the timing of the cash inflows that come from leasing or selling the space.

Finally, developers will evaluate the political and community factors in the market analysis. Do the community members welcome new development or see it only as a source of additional traffic and crowding? Do the elected and appointed officials have a broad view of the community benefits development brings or do they reflect narrow and parochial concerns? Are attractive local tax and financial packages available that encourage new development? Are utilities readily available and at reasonable tap rates? Does the community require the contribution of a portion of the development for community use? Are development fees, governmental approvals, and local exactions reasonable in amount, thus reflecting a welcome for new development? Is the approval process a reasonable one or does it take an extraordinarily long time with high costs?

Economic Feasibility Analysis

While the developer is performing his market analysis, he simultaneously analyzes the proposed project's economic feasibility. This analysis is repeated over and over as the developer continues with his other analyses, moving from a simplistic but timely analysis early in the process to more detailed and sophisticated analyses as his dollar and time commitments become greater. In fact, the developer likely begins to test the economic feasibility of a project early in the market analysis, discarding those ideas that do not appear to be able to provide satisfactory returns and only focusing on those ideas that appear to be most profitable. Thus, the economic feasibility analysis is a major risk control tool that keeps the developer from spending his resources on ideas that do not have the potential to produce satisfactory returns.

When performing an economic feasibility analysis, the developer uses gross cost figures in the preliminary stages of his analysis, as shown earlier in this chapter. When the project appears to be one that will prove to be economically feasible, then the developer performs sufficient due diligence to identify the costs more precisely. No longer are historical cost data and overall square foot costs satisfactory; contractors must now be consulted to determine more detailed cost estimates. Ultimately, the contractors submit guaranteed bids to the developer, based in part on bids they receive from their subcontractors. The more detailed cost figures are broken down into categories. A typical breakdown appears in Exhibit 17.9.

Land: The largest category in the land costs section is the land's purchase price, but it also includes the following:

1. Cost of the land appraisal
2. Other closing costs, such as legal fees and title insurance
3. Miscellaneous expenses, which might include demolition costs, land clearing costs, existing utility relocation costs, and environmental costs related to the land

HARD COSTS. **Hard costs** are monies that are spent to have the improvements built. The category is divided into several subcategories: costs for the site, building shell, tenant improvements, signage, construction utilities, and miscellaneous items.

EXHIBIT 17.9	Development cost categories.

Land	Soft Costs
Land acquisition	Architecture and building engineering
Appraisal	Civil engineering
Other closing costs	Geotechnical engineering
Miscellaneous	Landscape architecture
Hard Costs	Surveys
Site	Construction testing
Earthwork	Regulatory approvals
Utilities	Impact fees
Stormwater	Utility connection fees
Hardscaping	Legal expenses
Landscaping	Financing
Miscellaneous	Brokerage commissions
Building shell	Marketing and promotion
Improvements	Construction period taxes
General contractor expenses	Project contingency
Tenant improvements	Development fee
Signage	Operating deficits
Construction utilities	Miscellaneous
Miscellaneous	

Site costs include all new improvement costs outside the footprint of the buildings. This would include costs for the following:

1. Earthwork improvements, such as the cutting, filling, addition, removal, and grading necessary to prepare the site for building
2. Placement of new utility lines and structures overhead and underground on the property, including transformers and pumping stations
3. Construction of on-site storm water detention or retention ponds
4. Hardscaping improvements, including curbs and gutters, paving, walkways, retaining walls, and so forth
5. Landscaping, including sprinkler systems and plants and materials such as ground mulch, seeding, and sod
6. Miscellaneous items, such as fencing, gates, site lighting, and any on-site sewage treatment facilities

Building shell is the largest single category of development costs. The developer usually hires a general contractor to construct the improvements, and the general contractor subsequently hires subcontractors to augment his own staff. Within the building shell category, costs are broken down into

1. all building improvements, including foundations, slabs or flooring, wall enclosures, roof, and everything within the exterior structure except for the tenant finish, and
2. general contractor expenses, such as insurance coverage and payment and performance bonds, if any, on the general contractor and subcontractors, all project-related indirect costs of the general contractor, and the general contractor's fee covering his overhead and profit.

Tenant improvements is another important category of hard costs. When a portion of the space within the building shell has been leased to a tenant, the tenant receives an allowance of so many dollars per square foot to have the shell space completed according to his specifications. The amount allocated for **tenant finish costs** or **tenant improvements** is included separately from the building shell costs.

The *signage* category includes all interior and exterior signs. This would include both identity and directional signage, including a building directory. *Construction utilities* costs include the water and power used during the construction period. *Miscellaneous* hard costs include the cost of the building permit, any interior landscaping within the improvements, construction progress photography, any special telecommunications and data systems costs (such as an uninterruptible power supply generator or rooftop antennae), any renovations of existing improvements on the property, any on-site rail costs (such as track and switching, crossing, and safety devices) for industrial properties, and any off-site infrastructure (such as utilities extensions, traffic signals, highway improvements, and rail spurs).

SOFT COSTS. **Soft costs** are those that are not spent directly on the construction of physical improvements but are used to pay the professionals involved in the project, the regulatory costs, the construction financing expenses, and the developer's overhead and profit.

Architecture and building engineering costs include the professional services from the core design and engineering consulting team. The architect usually employs the structural and mechanical engineers. *Civil engineering* costs include the site earthwork, utilities, paving, and storm drainage design and documentation. *Geotechnical engineering* costs include the soils testing, reporting, and recommendations. *Landscape architecture* costs include the landscaping and irrigation design and documentation fees. *Surveys* not only includes the property survey but may also include a topographic survey and a tree survey. *Construction testing* involves safety tests during construction of the concrete, reinforcing steel, structural steel including welds and bolted connections, floor flatness, curtain wall installation, roof, and fire suppression systems.

The *regulatory approvals* category covers all the fees required by regulatory entities for filing, processing, reserving, reviewing, inspecting, and approving required governmental permits. It also includes the professional fees for environmental hazards assessments, archeological studies, environmental impact studies, and wetlands determinations. *Impact fees* are segregated from other regulatory approval fees because they are considered extraordinary project-specific assessments necessary to obtain concessions or project approvals. They may be cash public improvements fees or may take the form of contributions, special construction projects, land trades, dedicated space, and so forth. *Utility connection fees,* sometimes known as tap fees, are nonconstruction assessments by utility providers necessary to obtain service authorizations. *Legal expenses* include the costs of representation before the regulatory or public entities as well as the costs of document preparation and review for leases, development agreements, construction and consultant contracts, regulatory submittals and agreements, easements, promissory notes and mortgages (or deeds of trust), and leases.

Financing costs include not only the interest on the construction loan but also the loan negotiation, origination, and closing fees for the construction loan and, if paid by the developer, the permanent loan, sale leaseback transaction, and synthetic lease. *Brokerage commissions* are those commissions payable on the immediate sale of the project or to commercial brokers for lease transactions. *Marketing and promotion* includes the costs of any groundbreaking, topping out, or grand opening events, project advertising, press releases, marketing materials, and photography or computer-generated illustrations used in promoting the project. *Construction period taxes* are the properly apportioned property taxes due during the construction period. The *project contingency* is an amount set aside to cover any cost increases—whether due to improper estimation, inflation, material or labor shortages, higher interest rates, weather delays, or labor strife—during the construction period. It is usually calculated as a percentage of the sum of hard and soft costs, except for the financing costs and the developer's fee. The *development fee* covers the developer's overhead and profit. It is usually calculated as a percentage of the sum of all costs except the land acquisition cost and, of course, the development fee. *Operating deficits* is an amount that covers the anticipated property operating expenses in excess of rental income after construction but prior to full lease-up. It includes utilities, property taxes, fire and extended coverage insurance, maintenance, and a property management fee for the period until some agreed percentage (perhaps 85 to 95 percent) of the space is projected to be leased. *Miscellaneous* soft costs would include any reimbursable expenses of the architects, engineers, and other consultants (such as travel, printing, postage, long distance telephone, and so forth) and expenses for construction loss protection (builder's risk insurance) and the developer's liability insurance.

Site Selection and Analysis

If the developer's market analysis appears to offer support for one of his ideas and, at least on a preliminary basis, also appears to be economically feasible, then he begins to search for a site. He begins by looking for a good *location,* which usually means good accessibility. It must be convenient for those who will be using the space to get there. Location near a good transportation system, whether it be highway, rail, air, or mass transit, is often critical. Moreover, the site has to have good access to and from the transportation system, something called **ingress** when referring to moving from the transportation system into the site and called **egress** when referring to moving back into the transportation system. For example, for a retail idea, the developer will want a site to which shoppers will have ready access. For an industrial idea, he will want good access to highway, rail, or air transportation systems. For an office, he will want good access both for the people who will be visiting the office as well as for those who will be working there. For residential, he will want good access to a transportation system that will allow the people who live there to readily get to employment centers. Finally, a good location is one in which the developer has monopoly power. He wants a site in an area where it would be difficult for a competitor to locate a similar project.

Another important factor is the site's *natural features.* Is the site large enough (or too large) for its intended use? Is the site shaped properly to maximize the income that can be generated there? Does it have soils that will support the weight of whatever improvement he envisions for the site? Will the soils readily absorb stormwater, or will water retention or detention ponds have to be built? Is the topography of the site such that it will be economically feasible to build on it, or will substantial resculpting of the surface have to be done? What natural vegetation does the site have, and how much of that can be saved? Particularly if it is a retail site, will the improvements have good visibility from the transportation system?

In her site analysis, the developer also focuses on the availability of *public services* in the community. Such considerations as police and fire response times, schools, and hospitals (if it is a residential development), and frequent garbage collection are important factors. She is also concerned with how affordable these items are, as reflected in property taxes and usage fees. Of immediate concern is the community's regulatory offices. How quickly and inexpensively can the needed permits be obtained? What is the attitude of the local governmental bodies toward development? Are they supportive or seeking to frustrate it?

Utilities availability and cost also are addressed in the site selection and analysis. Water and sewer services, often provided as one of the public services by the community, may prove to be big stumbling blocks. A capacity shortage in either area is neither quickly nor easily remedied. Power supplies for industrial uses may also present a major problem for an industrial project, as periodic brownouts and rolling shutoffs may be the norm for the community. Other utilities are more readily available, but the developer always checks to make sure that electricity, gas, oil, and telephone supplies are adequate. With the growth of data communications, the need for adequate, high-speed data transmission capacity is essential, especially for office developments.

Because sites vary in their *legal restrictions,* the developer pays close attention to this factor, too. Most of the time, legal strictures refer to the zoning or deed restrictions that prohibit various uses of the site. In some communities, it is fairly easy to change zoning or at least to obtain a variance that will allow the developer's intended use, but in others it is almost impossible. Moreover, some similarly named zoning categories are much more restrictive than in other communities. Of course, the local developer will be aware of such restrictions. In addition, *environmental constraints* may prove prohibitive in some communities. The developer will need to evaluate his proposed use's impact on the environment to see if it will violate the community's regulations concerning air or water pollution. Increased traffic congestion or noise pollution from the site's new use may force him to rethink a particular site. Finally, environmental constraints that adversely affect his proposed use can be caused by the presence of historical districts, wildlife habitats, and open space requirements.

The last but by no means least important piece in the site analysis puzzle is the *price* of the site. Even if all of the preceding site selection factors are positive, it may be that the price of the site makes it unacceptable. On the other hand, if only a select few of the preceding factors are negative, a relatively low price for the site may enable the developer to spend more to remedy those problems. How does the developer determine whether the site is acceptable? The developer will again perform her economic feasibility analysis to determine whether the site's proposed use makes financial sense.

Site Control

Once the developer locates a site that appears to meet the market analysis, site selection, and economic feasibility tests, he must then obtain control of the site so that others cannot acquire it while he completes his analyses. Recall that the developer is striving to minimize his cash outflows as a risk control tool in case the eventual project decision is to reject it and search for another one. His preferred course is use an *option to purchase*. In return for a relatively small cash payment, perhaps as little as 1 percent of the purchase price, the developer receives the right to purchase the property from the owner at an agreed-upon price at any time within some agreed-upon period, say, within the next year. He might even get the option price to be applied to the purchase price should he choose to exercise the option.

Prior to the expiration of the option contract, the developer will assemble control of other parcels in a similar fashion, presuming that he cannot acquire all the land needed for the development with this one parcel. He will also confer with local governmental officials about obtaining the proper permits for the development, have the geotechnical engineer conduct soils tests on the optioned site, and address any environmental concerns to make sure they will not prohibit the completion of the development. During this period, the developer will assemble the development team so that he knows each of the team members will be ready when they are called upon to perform their job. Based on their expertise, he will complete a much more detailed economic feasibility analysis to assure himself that the project is indeed financially rewarding. Finally, he will enter into preliminary prelease or presale agreements for as much of the improved space as possible, gauge equity investor interest in the completed project, and make tentative arrangements with the construction and permanent lenders for financing of the project.

If the developer is unable to negotiate a purchase option from the seller, he still must obtain control of the site. Fortunately, there are other alternatives, although each is less attractive than an option. He could enter into a *lease with an option to purchase*. This instrument usually requires that he pay monthly rent to the property owner, with the rent rarely being applied to the purchase price. Because the lease would run for one year, to make this example consistent with the pure option example, that would commit the developer to paying rent for the year. The rent total generally exceeds the option payment by a substantial amount. Another alternative is a *joint venture* with a money partner in which the venture purchases the property. Although this limits the cash outflow for the developer, it does commit him to the site prior to its complete analysis and thus increases, rather than decreases, his risk.

Yet another alternative is a joint venture with a governmental entity. If there is some public purpose to the development project which enhances the community's general welfare, then the public sector partner can acquire the site through *eminent domain*. Not only does this solution have the early ownership disadvantages of the joint venture option, but it also means the developer must work with a public sector partner. While this can be extremely profitable and enable the developer to obtain a monopoly location, many developers find the increased scrutiny, slower response times, and broader goals of the public-private partnership to be very difficult to live with. Finally, the developer may have to use an *outright purchase* of the site as the only way to gain control. As described earlier, this is one of the more risky choices the developer can make and he usually resorts to it only if the earlier alternatives are unavailable.

Plan Preparation and Permit Approval

Another preconstruction task in the development process involves securing the requisite governmental approvals. Once the site has been selected, the developer supervises the team's preparation of preliminary project plans. Ideally, the project is the type of development allowed for that site "by right"—that is, it meets the current zoning requirement for the site. If so, then a member of the municipal staff is able to approve the proposed project without further ado. If the site must be rezoned or a variance granted, as is often the case, these plans are used to acquire the necessary approvals from the local zoning body. Often the rezoning decision is a highly politicized one in which having the technically correct information may not be nearly as important as the interpersonal relationships that the developer has built with the citizens who serve on the zoning panel, the planning professionals who work for the community, and the elected officials who ultimately must approve the rezoning request. If the developer cannot secure the proper zoning—and there are times when it is impossible to revise the plan sufficiently to gain approval and still have an economically viable project—then the developer cuts her losses, follows her exit strategy, and looks to other ideas.

Presuming the zoning change, or perhaps just a variance, can be obtained, the developer then has more detailed project plans prepared. These are used to secure the necessary subdivision and building permit approvals, as described in Chapter 2. Although subdivision plans and building permits still may be subject to some political concerns, typically this is less of an issue than with zoning changes. In some communities, the developer also must sign a development agreement in which she outlines the expected end product of her development project and identifies what contributions to the community she will make in return for being given the right to undertake the project. The idea behind the contributions is to keep the project from burdening the existing taxpayers, because the new development must "pay for itself." Negotiating such agreements often is a long and arduous process because professional staff, elected officials, and neighborhood or other special interest groups must be consulted. Although it is the public sector members who must ultimately approve the agreement, the citizens groups frequently make this a very public and political process. Sometimes the negotiated contributions take the form of cash donations, or impact fees or exactions, paid to the city, school district, a municipal utility district, and so forth, but at other times they are contributions in kind. The latter might include contributions of land by the developer for a new school or park, improvements to the public transportation system so that the additional traffic generated by the development has minimal adverse impacts, on-site wastewater treatment facilities so that the municipal system is not overburdened, or the extension of water or sewer trunk lines on public rights-of-way to the new development.

Marketing and Sales

Marketing and sales generally begin during the preconstruction period, occur during construction, and then extend to the postconstruction period. Although this area was emphasized as one of the savvy developer's risk control tools, for many developers the emphasis placed on it during the preconstruction period is due in large part to the lender. During times of excess supply, lenders become very conservative in their loan underwriting. For a loan request to be considered, the permanent lender requires the developer to have preleased at least 50 percent of the space, and up to 80 percent during certain market environments. The leases must be to tenants and on terms approved by the lender. If that is done and the project is otherwise satisfactory, the lender will issue a permanent loan commitment (sometimes called a takeout commitment). Without the commitment, developers find construction lenders unwilling to make loans to them. If the project, or units within the project, are intended to be sold upon completion of construction, the purchasers usually obtain their own permanent financing. Without a takeout commitment to guarantee the construction lender that her loan will be repaid, the lender will require that a similarly large percentage of the space be presold to acceptable purchasers at prices he has approved.

In directing the preparation of an overall marketing strategy, the developer and his team members first review the market analyses and the project plans. One of the reasons they do this is to identify which market groups they wish to target as likely tenants or purchasers of the space to be built. Another reason is that they want to identify the project features and benefits that best meet the needs of the target market. They will then emphasize these items as they prepare their marketing plan. The plan typically includes the development of an advertising campaign, perhaps conducted in newspapers, in trade or professional magazines, through brochures, on television, via personal contact, or through multiple media outlets. With some property types, the campaign may include the preparation of a model unit available for display to potential users, while other property types rely on scale models and artist renderings. Finally, the leasing, sales, or investment brokers—whether they be members of the brokerage community at large, specifically hired to represent the project on an exclusive basis (see Chapter 15), or are on the developer's property management staff—must aggressively market the improvements to prospective users and investors.

Financing

The financing task is the final step in the development process prior to construction. The developer is now almost certain that she is going to proceed with a particular development project. She finalizes her projections for development costs based on the money she has already spent, the money she has committed to spend in the near future, the bids she has received from potential general contractors, and her development team's estimates for the remaining costs. With assistance from her marketing team, she reexamines the marketplace to obtain the most current information on demand, supply, rental rates, and operating expenses. She recalculates expected cash flows from the project's operations upon completion and uses those numbers in an updated DCF analysis. If the NPV is still positive, she is ready to proceed with the financing.

Although she has thought about it earlier in the development process, she must now settle on the form of ownership that she will use. Some developers prefer outright ownership of the project as a sole proprietor, but most look to some sort of indirect ownership. Ownership might be through a general or, more likely, limited partnership arrangement, a C corporation, an S corporation, or a limited liability company (LLC). Today's favorite is the LLC because it combines many of the most attractive features of the other forms. The LLC would most likely be a single-purpose entity owning just this project.

As a risk reduction tool, the developer has already visited informally with several lenders as her development idea was taking shape in order to assess their potential interest in financing the completed project. After now having decided upon the ownership structure, the developer would approach some of the lenders she had contacted earlier seeking their informal commitment for permanent financing. She might talk to three or four mortgage companies and a like number of commercial banks. When she isolates what appears to be the firm offering the best combination of terms with the best service, she makes formal application for a loan from that lender. Using that lender's letter of commitment, she is able to approach the different commercial banks interested in making construction loans for this project and locate the one offering the best interim financing. She then makes formal application for that financing and obtains a construction loan commitment.

Finally, if she needs equity investors, either because she does not intend to hold the property after the completion of construction or because she does intend to remain an investor but wants to limit her exposure by bringing additional investors on board, she may try to secure their investment commitments. She will probably be able to raise more money by waiting until development is complete and the space has been fully leased because investors then will accept a lower rate of return because they do not have to accept the development risks. If she needs their funds now, however, not only will she likely have more trouble finding investors, but she will also have to give them a larger share of the income as a reward for providing the funds when the development risks are still substantial. This is where the investment brokers on the team become active players.

LAND DEVELOPMENT LOAN

Recall the land development example for the residential subdivision that was shown in Exhibits 17.4 through 17.7. In addition to a large cash outflow of $7.5 million to purchase the property at the beginning of the development, there was another major cash outflow of almost $11.5 million for development costs during the first year. This was offset by cash inflows during the remaining three years of the project's life. Although this is a positive NPV project earning more than the required 40 percent annual rate of return, many developers do not have the financial resources to invest the required $19 million. Moreover, those that do often choose not to do so in order to spread their risk capital among a variety of projects. Instead, a developer would likely secure a land development loan.

After being convinced of the strength of the market demand for the proposed subdivision lots, a lender—typically a commercial bank—would gladly make the developer a land acquisition and development loan. For this type of project, a lender would offer a maximum loan of 80 percent of total project costs, or $18,444,000 ($23,055,000 from Exhibit 17.5 times 0.80). The actual loan amount may differ from $18,444,000 for two reasons. First, since the developer is able to cover some of the costs through the sale of lots, as shown in Exhibit 17.4, he does not need to borrow the full amount. On the other hand, the $18,444,000 does not include development loan interest, and the lender would include the interest in the amount lent. Because this is a risky project, the lender would charge a high rate of interest, say 18 percent. The developer, or the equity investor(s) attracted to the project by the developer, would first invest $4,611,000 (20 percent of the total development costs of $23,055,000). The development lender would fund the remaining cash outflows, plus interest, in the manner shown in Exhibit 17.10.

Exhibit 17.10 indicates that the project's positive cash flow of $19,695,880 at the end of year 2 more than repays the loan balance, including interest, of $17,244,038. The remainder of the cash flow from year 2, plus all the cash flow from years 3 and 4, is returned to the developer or investor, as shown in Exhibits 17.10 and 17.11. Although

EXHIBIT 17.10 Land development loan (in dollars).

	Development Costs Less Sales Revenues	Equity Cash Flow	Development Loan Cash Advanced	Development Loan Interest	Development Loan Balance
Start Yr 1		(4,611,000)	2,889,000	0	2,889,000
End Yr 1	(11,486,050)	0	11,486,050	1,553,765	15,928,815
End Yr 2	19,695,880	2,451,842	(17,244,038)	1,315,223	0
End Yr 3	15,751,425	15,751,425	0	0	0
End Yr 4	3,004,800	3,004,800	(0)	(0)	0

Note: The calculations in the exhibit make the following assumptions: (1) initial equity requirement for the development of the land is 20% of the $23,055,000 total project development cost, which is $4,611,000; (2) an interest rate of 18% on the loan; and (3) an average of 50% of each year's cash advance being outstanding during that year. In the first year, the interest rate of 18% is applied to 50% of $11,486,050 ($11,486,050 x 50% x 18%) + ($2,889,000 x 18%) = $1,553,765).

EXHIBIT 17.11 After-financing development net income (in dollars).

	Year				Total Revenues
Lot Category	One	Two	Three	Four	
1/4-Acre Lots	3,248,000	7,592,200	4,041,500	411,000	15,292,700
1/3-Acre Lots	2,560,000	16,456,000	8,552,250	1,287,000	28,855,250
1/2-Acre Lots	287,500	2,925,000	6,514,500	1,704,000	11,431,000
Total Lot Sales Revenues	6,095,500	26,973,200	19,108,250	3,402,000	55,578,950
Less Development Costs	(16,972,000)	(4,580,000)	(1,446,000)	(57,000)	(23,055,000)
Less Sales Expenses @ 10%	(609,550)	(2,697,320)	(1,910,825)	(340,200)	(5,557,895)
Cash Flow Before Financing	(11,486,050)	19,695,880	15,751,425	3,004,800	26,966,055
Plus Loan Advances or Less Loan Repayments	11,486,050	(18,240,408)	0	0	(6,754,358)
Cash Flow After Financing	0	1,455,472	15,751,425	3,004,800	20,211,697

the developer has less cash invested with the development loan, the risk of receiving a return on that cash now increases because the development lender must be repaid before the developer and/or investor(s) receive anything. Accordingly, the required rate of return may increase above the 40 percent rate.

The developer and/or investor(s) still must invest over $4.6 million, but the project's NPV remains positive. In fact, the anticipated internal rate of return is now in excess of 60 percent in order to compensate them for the greater risk associated with repayment of the development loan.

Securing Equity Capital

As in this example, the developer may want to attract equity investors, either because he cannot afford to fund the equity requirement himself, because he wants to limit his financial exposure by bringing additional investors on board, or because he does not intend to hold the property after the completion of development and he best controls his risks by selling it now. Consequently, he may secure investment commitments from potential investors at this point. In a development project in which he is constructing space to be leased, rather than sold, he will probably be able to raise more equity money by waiting until development is complete and the space has been fully leased since investors then will accept a lower rate of return as they do not have to accept the development risks. If he needs their funds now, however, not only will he likely have more trouble finding investors, but he will also have to give them a larger share of the income as a reward for providing the funds when the development risks are still substantial. This is where the investment brokers on the team become active players.

CONSTRUCTION STAGE

This is the stage in which final decisions are made about a number of items prior to signing contracts. Signing contracts eliminates many of the developer's exit strategies and binds him to the project.

Construction

Assuming the developer still is convinced that the project will provide a satisfactory return, he must sign contracts with the architect, engineers, and other consultants in order to have the building design finalized, detailed plans drawn, and the site plan and landscape architecture completed. After the contracts are signed, the architect will prepare bid documents and publish a request for proposals (RFP) to which general contractors will respond with their bids. An alternative to the RFP is to enter into negotiations with one or more general contractors. The end result of either approach is a construction contract. As a risk control device, the developer and lenders would prefer a fixed-price contract. Of course, the contractor would like to have a cost-plus contract in which he is reimbursed for the costs of construction plus guaranteed a reasonable profit. Depending upon the degree of competition, the final construction contract will fall somewhere between the two extremes, frequently with a cost-plus arrangement limited by a guaranteed maximum price.

Another set of contracts to be signed is the financing package. Formal loan applications must be submitted to both construction and permanent lenders prior to their issuance of the loan commitment documents. The purchase option on the land must be exercised, resulting in a large cash outflow that is at least partially funded by the construction loan. If they have not already been obtained, the governmental permits must be secured. Of course, the preleases or presales that have already been executed are contracts, too. In fact, it should be easier for the marketing team to secure additional preleases or presales contracts now that construction has actually begun.

The developer will have already assembled a construction management team to supervise the contractors as they construct the improvements. As part of the construction management team's task, they will have developed a formalized time sequencing document that will specify when certain tasks must begin in order be completed by critical dates. This way, all of the contractors will know when they must do their jobs in order to have them completed on time. Because other contractors will not be able to do their part until an earlier job is done, tasks must be completed in a timely fashion.

Finally, prior to the commencement of construction, the developer must institute detailed accounting and budgeting controls. Without knowing how much is being spent and when it is being spent, it is impossible to tell whether the project is within the budget allowed for it. Such a system will automatically prepare budget variance reports on a weekly basis and can be programmed to produce them on demand, so that anytime a project goes over budget the developer will be able to take quick and decisive action while it is still possible to correct minor imbalances. If the developer is going to earn a satisfactory profit, he must keep close tabs on expenditures.

Marketing and Sales

More intensive marketing of the space in the project is undertaken during the construction stage. As the physical changes to the site become visible, it will be easier for the marketing team to secure the leases or sell the units that end users can now see being constructed. The marketing team's goal is to have all the space committed for, either through leases or sales contracts, by the time construction is complete.

POSTCONSTRUCTION STAGE

This is the stage during which the merchant developer attempts to make an immediate sale of the entire project. For the investment developer, this is the beginning of the several-year holding period, after which he expects to sell his share of the project. In either case, the developer attempts to retain a long-term property management contract, although that may be difficult if the property purchaser has its own in-house property management team or an exclusive contract with another property management firm.

Marketing and Sales

If the space has not all been leased or sold, as appropriate, then marketing becomes even more focused after construction has been completed. Moreover, the leasing function has to be repeated several times during the life of the property as tenants move, whether because they need additional space, are attracted to other space, merge with another firm, or go out of business. With commercial space, who the different parties are is sometimes confusing to the outsider. Typically, there are brokers who specialize in leasing space (leasing brokers) and different brokers who specialize in selling properties (investment brokers). Moreover, some leasing brokers solely represent tenants who are looking for space (tenant rep brokers) as opposed to the more traditional leasing brokers who represent the property owner. Finally, there are individuals who run the day-to-day operations of the project (property managers).

Property Management

Property managers are largely responsible for the ultimate success of the project. They are the ones who must approve the new tenants and the rental rates they are paying, then keep those tenants as satisfied occupants of the space they are renting. Because large tenant improvement expenditures, as well as the payment of higher leasing commissions, must be made each time a new tenant (as opposed to an existing tenant) is signed to a lease, the developer must structure his property manager compensation scheme to *keep existing tenants satisfied* with their space. Tenant improvement costs and brokerage commissions are much lower when the manager is able to roll over an existing tenant to a new lease.

As described in more detail in Chapter 16, the manager has additional duties other than keeping existing tenants satisfied with their space. His foremost task is to *control expenses*. He must maintain detailed and accurate accounts so that he constantly knows how much is being spent in different areas compared to how much was budgeted. A good developer will base part of the manager's compensation on the budget items within the manager's control, sharing a portion of the savings with him and reducing his pay by a portion of the operating cost overruns. The property manager is also responsible for *collecting the rent.* He must establish a procedure, preferably a direct withdrawal from a tenant's bank account, for the tenant to routinely pay the rent when it is due. If the rent is not paid within the grace period allowed in the lease, then he must aggressively pursue the tenant until the rent is paid. It is much easier to correct small delinquencies than to address major ones.

Another major function of the property manager is to *pay the property's bills* when they come due. All of the expenses of operating the property are funneled through the property manager. He must keep track of when they must be paid, then pay them in a timely fashion. He is also charged with *maintaining the property.* The manager must regularly visit with the tenants to identify any repairs they feel need to be made, inspect the property routinely to note any physical problems that have arisen but have not yet resulted in tenant complaints, and then make sure that all repairs and maintenance are completed in a timely fashion. When he does this, the property manager not only enhances the long-term value of the project but also encourages the current tenants to renew their leases upon expiration. Sometimes property managers also have the authority to *upgrade the property.* When the competitive situation dictates that renovations are necessary, the property manager may be able to order such renovations. On the other hand, if the owner has a large portfolio of properties, he may have an asset manager whose duties would include scheduling such renovations.

Finally, as alluded to earlier in the controlling expenses category, it is the property manager's responsibility to *account for all financial transactions.* At the end of each month (or quarter or year or whatever period the owner desires), the property manager has to furnish the owner with a record showing what monies were received and from whom, what monies were spent and for what, and how much money is available in various accounts.

Chapter Summary

The real estate development process consists of many elements and requires knowledge of many aspects of the real estate discipline. Because of the need for this wide range of knowledge, a developer typically relies on a development team that consists of professionals with varied educational and experiential backgrounds. The team members' various skills come into play in different phases of the development process.

Internet Applications

A website has been established for this chapter at http://epley.swcollege.com.

Review Questions

1. What are the differences between land development and property (or real estate) development?

2. What reward do people most often assume real estate developers are most interested in? What other rewards do developers reap? Which reward(s) may be more important than financial remuneration?

3. Why is the public sector always a member of the development team?

4. Who are the key members of the development team? What role does the real estate developer play?

5. Why is it important that the developer understand discounted cash flow (DCF) analysis?

6. The real estate development process is fraught with risks. What techniques does the developer use to identify and control these risks?

7. The real estate development process can be thought of as a series of sequential, nonlinear steps. Most of the steps are undertaken during which stage of the development process?

8. How does real estate market analysis differ from real estate economic feasibility analysis?

9. Prior to site acquisition, the developer analyzes various sites. What factors does he consider?

10. How can a developer gain control over a site?

11. Why do marketing and sales extend through the pre-construction, construction, and post-construction stages?

12. When is project financing obtained?

13. How long does property management last?

Discussion Questions

1. What analytical skills does the real estate developer require to undertake the development process?

2. If a developer has limited time to devote to the development process for a property, should this time be spent predominantly on the preconstruction phase, the construction phase, or the postconstruction phase of the process?

3. What actions can a developer take to minimize the risk involved in acquiring a site for development?

Problems

1. You are a real estate developer who is thinking about developing a 200,000 square foot (gross building area) shopping center. Your market analysis indicates you could lease the space at an average monthly rental rate of $1.50 per square foot of gross leasable area. You expect to lose 1 percent of the built space for non-leasable uses such as an exterior maintenance equipment shed. A reasonable vacancy and collection loss percentage for this type of space in your local market would be 7 percent. Operating expenses typically account for about 25 percent of the collected income. A reasonable capitalization rate today would be 9.5 percent for this type of property in your local market. You would need approximately 600,000 square feet of land for your development and suitable land currently costs $75,000 per acre. Construction costs are currently running about $125 per square foot of gross building area. Using the back-of-the-envelope approach, should you pursue this development idea further?

2. Suppose the appropriate before-financing discount rate for the chapter's land development illustrations were not 40 percent, but 50 percent. Using DCF analysis, would the developer reach the same conclusion as shown in the chapter? Why or why not? (*Hint:* You need to use the cash flows from Exhibit 17.5.)

3. Again use the land development illustration in the chapter, except now assume the developer was able to convince the lender to make a 90 percent loan-to-value ratio loan. In return for the larger loan, and the greater risk of default, the lender increases the interest rate to 24 percent. Instead of the number shown in Exhibit 17.8, the loan's cash flow profile now appears as in Exhibit 17.12. Assume the developer's discount rate is 60 percent. You must revise the last two lines of Exhibit 17.10 and recalculate the project's NPV. Should the developer pursue this project? Why or why not?

EXHIBIT 17.12	Cash flow profile.				
	Development Costs Less Sales Revenues	Equity Cash Flow	Development Loan Cash Advanced	Development Loan Interest	Development Loan Balance
Start Yr 1	(7,500,000)	(2,305,500)	5,194,500	0	5,194,500
End Yr 1	(11,486,050)	0	11,486,050	2,625,006	19,305,556
End Yr 2	19,695,880	0	(19,695,880)	2,269,828	1,879,504
End Yr 3	15,751,425	13,670,546	(2,080,879)	201,375	0
End Yr 4	3,004,800	3,004,800	0	0	0

Trends in the Real Estate Industry

In most of the discussion in this textbook, the perspective was the existing state of affairs in the real estate industry, focusing on information about the current methods of analysis and information needed to make a decision about real estate. The Conclusion, however, will analyze existing trends in the U.S. economy and the real estate industry and use these trends to attempt to forecast future events that can affect a real estate decision.

What Major Changes Are Currently Taking Place?

Rapid and pervasive changes in technology, communications, information availability, e-commerce, and globalization are affecting the U.S. economy in general and the real estate industry in particular. This section of the chapter examines these changes over the recent past and tries to point to possible changes in the near future.

THE IMPACT OF COMPUTER TECHNOLOGY

In the not too distant past, real estate appraisers, investors, and financial analysts used paper, pencil, and four-function calculators to generate their respective analyses. This was the post–World War II era extending into and through the 1950s and early 1960s. In the late 1960s, real estate academics started to use mainframe computers to do the calculations required for discounted cash flow analysis, the technique of choice for investment analysis and income property valuation. Even though the mainframe computer greatly shortened the time for computations, the process of using this technological improvement was still time-consuming. In the

1970s, technological advances brought the financial calculator and software for the earliest personal computers to the hands of these analysts. During the 1980s and the 1990s, technological progress made these tools cheaper, more accessible, and the state of the art.

As we look at the present, the portable personal computer (PC) is the standard tool for all real estate professionals. The PC operates software that greatly enhances individual productivity. It has word processing and spreadsheet software in addition to the "office organizer" functions such as an address book, appointment book, calendar, notebook, telephone/fax/email address book, and other such information storage and retrieval systems. Digital video and still picture cameras are linked to the software in the PC with ever increasing ease of use. New software is currently making great inroads into professional practice. This software is GIS (geographic information system), which allows the analyst to display information in the form of charts and graphs, like the spreadsheet software, but also to display information spatially on very easily generated computer maps.

Computer technology has also made the presentation of information in academia and business more sophisticated. In the past, a blackboard and white chalk evolved to a green board and colored chalk—low technological presentations by any standard. Then came the overhead projector and transparencies. This was a step up in the application of technology. Software advances such as Harvard Graphics brought the level of the graphics from the photocopied printed page to formalized outlines and designs. Now, the computer and the LCD projector coupled with software such as PowerPoint are the minimum standard for business presentations. Academic presentations in general still lag behind at the overhead projector stage. Today, PowerPoint presentations are linked to visual images from digital cameras and videos. Sound is also included in these presentations. Tomorrow, the sophistication of PowerPoint and any new competitor will increase, allowing more diversity in the nature and the form of the presentations. The Internet provides real-time data and images from remote sites that are importable into a presentation.

Technological advancement in general and computer technological advance in particular provide the ability for teleconferencing and distance learning. The computer and the television are linked so that a live presentation or discussion at one location is open to full participation by individuals at another local, national, or global location. This technology will continue to change the process and procedure of passing information among individuals, businesses, and postsecondary educational institutions. Currently, some students are able to earn college degrees over the Internet. Your children may take many of their college classes from different educational institutions while sitting at a computer in their room or by simply going to a technologically enhanced classroom at the local college or university. This technology will also trickle down to the high school level and allow students in one school to take a specialized class offered in another school either in the same district or in a different school district.

As this trickle down effect works its way through the traditional educational system, it will also affect the nature and form of professional education for appraisers, brokers, consultants, investment analysts, and all other professionals in the real estate industry. Real estate commissions will have to consider the offering of on-line license preparation and continuing education courses just as they considered the issue of correspondence courses years ago. Professional organizations that offer real estate designations will have to meet the demand for more than the traditional face-to-face training programs. The traditional professional conference may hold on for some time because people need the face-to-face contact to do business and to keep personal relationships current.

In the future, computers will affect the sophistication of real estate analysis. Computer technology will allow business people in general and real estate professionals in particular to gather data easier and more quickly, and to analyze that data with greater accuracy, precision, and speed. Computer technology will make data collection and storage easier and more sophisticated. It will make data analysis more flexible.

THE EFFECT OF WIRELESS COMMUNICATIONS

Prior to the advent of cellular telecommunications technology, telephone calls were mostly made from fixed locations in the office or at home. The only exception was the early car phone, which was very cumbersome and expensive, and the pay telephone, which required parking the car to make a call on your way to some location. Eventually, cellular beepers and especially cell phones allowed individuals to keep in touch even when they were away from the office.

Today, computer literate individuals are able to use cellular and digital technology to link their personal computers to their office network as well as to the Internet. Coupling the future development of computer technology with digital telecommunications technology, a commercial property broker is able to show a prospective client in another city or country a specific property in another market. The site selection team for a retail company sitting in conference in Chicago is able to see real-time photographs and videos of three available retail properties in Sydney, Australia. A real property asset manager for an insurance company or a real estate investment trust located in New York City is able to show a prospective buyer in Berlin the financial statements for a specific property along with photos and discuss the information over an audio and visual Internet link.

Where is this technology going? Technological advances sweep through the general population in two steps. First, the most recent advance in technology is acquired and used by a small group of technologically sophisticated individuals. Over relatively short periods of time, this technology is adapted for, and adopted by, the general population. While the use of the current technology is broadening, the new advances are acquired by the technologically sophisticated individuals, and the cycle repeats.

THE EFFECT OF CHANGE IN INFORMATION AVAILABILITY

Over the past two decades, the quality of information available to the real estate analyst has improved because of computer technology, which has improved data assembly, storage, and retrieval. The computer makes it possible to upgrade databases with greater ease and speed. The computer makes it possible to store the data with greater efficiency; a few floppy disks replace a file drawer. A hard disk replaces a file cabinet or two. The floppy disk and now the CD have made data distribution easier, faster, and cheaper.

Computerization has also allowed the development of new firms that specialize in the generation of data and its sale to real estate analysts. Prior to the 1980s, real estate analysts had to rely on census data published in book form. Then, the analyst had to update the data from the census year to the current date by using locally available information. Today, many companies sell updated demographic and economic data for various geographic areas. The real estate analysts can buy such data for a county, a zip code, a census tract, and even a census block. In major metropolitan areas, the real estate analyst can acquire data on all forms of property types and have rent rates, vacancy rates, new construction, and product absorption virtually at his fingertips.

The information provided by these new firms has improved the analytical aspects of narrative appraisal reports, market analyses, and feasibility studies. In the near future, there will be a massive expansion of data availability from all levels of government. This data will be readily accessible and useable by even the least computer sophisticated individuals.

FUTURE DIRECTION OF THE INTERNET

Initially, the Internet was a mode of communication developed by the U.S. government to facilitate communication and data transmission by the scientific community. Subsequent development and growth of the Internet was linked to the existence of the PC. About 1990, private companies, public agencies, and individuals began placing information on the World Wide Web through the use of web pages. Today, an enormous amount of information can be gathered from the Internet. Some of it is good and reliable; some of it is trash. Previously, this information could only be gathered by making a personal trip from one location to another. The individual had to go to the library to check the card catalog and the shelves. The individual had to visit the organization to pick up the information. The website for this text gives you website and email addresses related to each chapter to facilitate your use of this new technology.

Where will the Internet go in the future? The best answer we can give is that it will go onward and upward by improving what it currently is and what it currently does. The quantity and the quality of the data sources on the Internet will improve. The extent of digital commerce, e-commerce, and e-business transacted on the Internet will increase. We will be able to find and buy more goods and services on the Internet.

Specifically referencing the real estate industry, many brokerage firms are providing information about single-family houses online. Written information is enhanced by photographs and a video of the features of the house. This process will expand to encompass retail, office, multifamily, and industrial space and structures. Many sites also currently offer residential mortgage loans on the Internet.

GLOBALIZATION

Not long ago, foreign trade was a very small portion of total U.S. economic activity. Over recent years, the U.S. economy has become more dependent on global economic relationships. Our consumers desire and buy many products produced by plants under the control of foreign corporations. Some of these foreign-owned production plants are located in those countries, but many are now located in the United States. The most noticeable of these products are German and Japanese automobiles. Electronic, cellar communication, and photographic equipment production also is dominated by foreign firms. We buy cheese, wine, and watches from foreign sources. Much of the clothing we buy is produced in foreign factories.

As our imports of foreign-owned products have increased, our export of goods and services has also increased. U.S. corporations have production plants in other countries, and foreign corporations have production plants in the United States. So, the proportion of our gross domestic product related to international transactions has steadily grown through the 1980s and the 1990s. This trend should continue into the first decade of the next millennium. Companies that currently have international markets will expand this portion of their total business. Companies that currently do not buy or sell in the international market will enter the market in the next 10 years.

The real estate industry will continue to see mergers among U.S. and foreign firms. Even though real estate markets will continue to be local in nature, the ownership and management of real estate will become increasing globalized. The typical real estate firm will have assets that are globally dispersed. Geographic diversification will become increasingly global diversification.

THE U.S. ECONOMY IN THE NEAR FUTURE

Three significant trends have been taking place in the U.S. economy in the last two decades. First, the regional disparities in the United States have been narrowing. In the late 1800s and the early 1900s, the Northeast and the North Central states were the industrialized portions of the country, and the other regions were the agricultural states. In the 1960s and the 1970s, the firms in the Northeast and the North Central states began a migration to the Southeast, Southwest, and Pacific Coast regions of the country. These firms and their production plants were leaving obsolete plants in high-wage-cost areas to locate in areas of new emerging markets, new plants, and nonunion labor markets. National headquarters moved from high office space cost areas in the North to lower-cost office space in the new emerging metropolitan areas. Business climate and quality of life factors played a large role in the migration decisions of both the firms and the people. The result of this trend from 1970 through 2000 has been an increase in the similarity of the industrial mix among the states, according to the U.S. Bureau of Labor Statistics, which provides data on the industrial composition of the states.

The second significant trend is the change in the industrial structure of the U.S. economy as a whole. Over the past 50 years, the proportion of U.S. workers in the manufacturing sector has steadily declined while the proportion of workers in finance, insurance, business services, health services, legal services, and real estate professions has increased. The U.S. economy has become less blue-collar and more white-collar. Fewer workers are in factories, and more are in offices. This trend will continue into the future, but the rate of change will become smaller and smaller.

The third trend is occurring in the quantity and the quality of the supply of labor. As the baby boom population segment (35- to 55-year-olds) ages over the next 20 years, the number of retirements will exceed the number of new entrants from the native population. Foreign migration will counterbalance this trend, but the growth in the supply of labor will slow as we enter the second decade of the twenty-first century.

The issue of the quality of the labor force is, and will be, a national concern. Recent figures have shown that graduates from U.S. high schools are losing ground in math and science to the students of the other industrialized nations of Europe and the Pacific Rim. Our future expansion in high-tech industries depends on our ability to educate our population for these employment opportunities. For this reason alone, our current relative position as a leader in the high-tech industries will diminish over time. We must find a way to increase the quantity and the quality of students leaving the typical high school and college in the areas of math and science. As part of this problem, we are experiencing an increase in the mismatch between the skills our domestic industries require and the attributes that our unemployed workers have.

Our blue-collar industries need workers trained to use various sophisticated tools and to work on capital-intensive production lines. The proportion of skilled craftsman in the labor force is not growing to match the need. Our high-tech industries need workers that understand computerized and highly automated assembly processes. The proportion of skilled workers in this area is not growing fast enough to match the need.

Our white-collar industries require workers trained in language skills. Can Johnny read, write, and reason? We have been asking this question since early in the 1980s. The answer seems to be that Johnny is not doing as well as his parents did. In the future, success in the high-tech, office-based industries will require high levels of the four Rs—reading, writing, arithmetic, and reasoning. It will also require the ability to handle the new generation of office equipment, such as the computer and teleconferencing equipment, as well as the ability to handle general use software applications (such as word processing and database management) and selected use software applications (such as spreadsheets).

THE EFFECT OF E-COMMERCE

The Internet had a dramatic effect on business and society during the late 1990s. This initial impact will grow in importance over the next 10 to 15 years. Business-to-business (b2b) communications will continue to thrive on the Internet as more businesses begin to use this medium. Business-to-consumer (b2c) retail activity will continue to grow and spread across most of the retail product categories as more consumers become computer literate (e-literate) and as they become more comfortable using this technology. There will be a differential effect among these categories. There will also be an increase in the magnitude of buy-sell transactions between consumers (c2c) as auction houses expand their volume of activity and as consumers increase their level of direct interaction.

What Changes Are Taking Place in the Real Estate Industry?

In the previous section the discussion focused on changes affecting the U.S. economy and its population in general and the real estate industry in particular. The discussion focused on technology, communications, information availability, e-commerce, and globalization. In this section we focus more directly on the real estate industry. The discussion involves the topics of ownership patterns, globalization, innovations in lending, and changes in the markets for the various types of real property.

CHANGING REAL ESTATE OWNERSHIP PATTERNS

In the past, ownership of real estate by investors was hands-on. The investor bought the property and either operated it or hired another person, the property manager, to operate it. Today, the investor needs to make a choice about the form of ownership desired. In addition to the hands-on form of ownership, the investor can choose a hands-off form of ownership. The limited partnership and the real estate investment trust (the REIT) are available choices. In both of these situations, the individual investor is totally removed from the operation of the property; the investor does not even select the property manager. In the case of the REIT, the investor-owner may not even know what properties are in the property pool. The investor buys into the name of the company issuing the REIT.

GLOBALIZATION IN THE REAL ESTATE INDUSTRY

In years past, the real estate business was viewed as a local business venture. A real estate practitioner became an expert about a property type in a local market. So, a big town would have a person specializing in residential brokerage, and another person would handle retail space leasing. A real estate appraiser would also specialize in a product type by focusing on residential or income property in a local area. The real estate businesses were typically owned and operated by a citizen of the community.

The concepts of horizontal integration and franchising entered this picture during the 1980s, and many of these locally owned brokerage firms were acquired to form national companies with branch offices in the local community (known as horizontal integration). At the same time, companies with centralized operations and a brand name began selling these services to local real estate firms (known as franchising). Today, we have real estate companies that have branch operations across the nation. These same firms will next move out beyond our borders. In the future, we will see a U.S.-based residential brokerage firm with an office next to the McDonalds restaurant in London or Moscow offering local residential properties for sale.

The ownership of real property was also geographically concentrated in the past. A real estate investor would actively own and operate the property down the street or across town. During the past two decades, such ownership patterns have expanded geographically. This trend will continue in the next decade. Investors who would invest locally will buy property in another, possibly a nonadjacent, geographic area. Big investment firms will continue to acquire property across the country and expand the acquisition of properties across the globe. Insurance companies acquire different types of properties in different geographic areas (known as geographic diversification).

FINANCIAL INNOVATIONS IN REAL ESTATE LENDING

In the past 70 years, many important changes took place in the area of residential finance. In the 1920s, the principal form of residential and commercial loan was the five-year term loan agreement, in which the borrower paid interest on the principal each year and then had to repay the principal at the end of the five-year term. Custom and a stable economy allowed the borrower to roll over the debt into a new five-year term loan. However, in the depression of the early 1930s, the five-year term loan led to foreclosures and subsequent evictions as property owners were unable to pay back the principal and lenders were unwilling to roll the debt over to a new time period.

In this financial atmosphere, the U.S. government in the form of the Federal Housing Administration created the long-term, positively amortized loan, which is currently called the fixed-rate mortgage. This form of financing was the principal and almost exclusive form of financing until the late 1970s, when high rates of inflation caused the institutions in the primary mortgage market to face the asset–liability mismatch and first-time home buyers to be priced out of the housing market. To ease the crisis, the U.S. government sponsored the creation of two new financing arrangements. The adjustable rate mortgage was created to ease the asset–liability mismatch, and the graduated payment mortgage was created to allow first-time home buyers to acquire houses by not pricing them out of the housing market. Both of these financial arrangements were discussed in the financial section of this text. What can we expect in the future?

The Reverse Annuity Mortgage

The mechanics of the reverse annuity mortgage (RAM) appear in Chapter 9. Our focus here is its future use. The benefits of this loan agreement accrue to homeowners who own their property and have paid off all outstanding loans on that property—fee simple ownership without mortgage liens. Upon retirement, part of their financial planning could include a monthly receipt of funds from the financial institution upon a promise by the retired couple to repay the funds to the lender at some predetermined and fully specified time in the future. If the timing of the repayment matches the life expectancy of the couple, the payment from the financial institution can be used as part of the inflow of retirement funds, allowing the couple to maintain a higher standard of living.

The financial institution receives an annual rate of return for providing this service. The receipt of the financial return to the lender occurs at the predetermined time when the property is sold and the proceeds from the sale are distributed between the financial institution and the retired couple's estate.

The disadvantage of the RAM occurs when the life expectancy of the retired couple exceeds the future time period when the property is to be sold. If at age 65, the couple expects to live until 85 and they take out a 20-year plan, but one or both members of the couple live longer than 20 years, then the contract still calls for the property to be sold. The individual faces a major dislocation and a reduction in lifestyle as the home is sold and the monthly payment stops. The financial institution faces the very real prospect of appearing on the nightly news as a heartless capitalist entity that kicks a senior citizen out of her home.

Will the RAM gain general acceptance in the next 10 to 20 years? We think that it will be a viable retirement option in the future. The retirement benefits to the homeowner are important, especially for those retirees whose only asset, or their principal asset, is the home. The negative public relations aspects of the eventual sale of the property can be overcome by a public awareness campaign sponsored by the financial community.

The Price-Level Adjusted Mortgage

One probable arrangement is the price-level adjusted mortgage (the PLAM), which makes the loan agreement sensitive to the inflation rate measured by the consumer price index (CPI). Economists always consider the real value of commodities, services, and resources—the real value of an entity measures the ability to acquire other commodities, services, or resources. If yesterday you could buy a toaster for $60, but today you have to pay $70 for the identical toaster, the real value of your income declined as the price level increased. Interest rates on a loan are the price of borrowing funds, and the interest payments received by the lender are the nominal value of that investment. As the price of goods and services measured by the CPI level increases, the real value of the interest payment received by the lender declines. In order to protect against a decline in real income, the lender would like the contract interest rate on the loan to reflect changes in the CPI.

The ARM discussed in Chapter 9 transferred the risk of interest rate fluctuations at a given level of the CPI from the lender to the borrower. This transfer of risk allowed the lender to issue ARMs at a lower initial contract rate. The PLAM transfers the risk of changes in the CPI from the lender to the borrower, so the initial interest rate on the PLAM should also be lower than it is for a fixed-rate mortgage.

Will the PLAM gain general acceptance in the next 10 to 20 years? We think it will be a viable mortgage option. Its eventual presentation to the public will resemble the process that led to the wide adoption of the ARM. Caps will limit the impact of periods of high inflation on the contract interest rate. The contract rate will be determined by the CPI, which is public information and out of the lender's control. The major conceptual problem that needs to be resolved is the relationship between the ARM and the PLAM. Interest rates as represented in a financial index and inflation as measured by the CPI move together in the same direction. The issue involves the process of setting the loan's initial period contract interest rate.

FACTORS AFFECTING TRADITIONAL RETAIL REAL ESTATE

In the future, traditional retail real estate will be affected by two major factors. These are the changing demographics of the retail market and the effect of Internet retail operations.

Changing Demographics

In 2000, the baby boomer population bulge (children born between 1949 and 1964) was between the ages of 36 and 54. The older portion of this group is in its peak earnings years and in its prime saving years. The younger portion of this group is entering its peak earnings years and is in its prime saving years. In general, the rising income levels, which should spur an increase in retail sales, will be counterbalanced by the increase in saving for retirement and their childrens' education. Retail sales will grow but at a rate substantially less than the increase in income. Also, over the last 10 years and extending into the future, the distribution of household income has been shifting to higher levels. In 1996, approximately 49 percent of all households had incomes in the highest quintile (top 20 percent) of all incomes. If this trend continues, as it should into the near future, in 2006 about 54 percent of all households will be in the top 20 percent of the income distribution. These households will be saving more, and they will be buying more upscale goods. This should have a positive impact on specialty retailers and should favor purchases in regional malls as opposed to big box retailers.

The reason for the growth of this upper income group is its level of education and its skills. An important part of its skill attainment is its ability to adapt to the rapid technological change that has taken place in the last 20 years.

The households in the other four quintiles have been declining in number over the last 20 years and should continue to decline over the next 10 years. They have already shown that they have a tendency to increase their purchases at power centers and discount stores. The end result will see the higher income group curtailing its total retail expenditures and shifting to the specialty stores and regional malls while the lower income groups will reduce their expenditures at regional malls and shift them to discount stores. The implication for retail real estate is very modest growth in total sales, per square foot sales, and the demand for new retail space.

Internet Retail Activity

The effect of Internet sales on retail real estate is shrouded in mystery. Some analysts think the Internet will have an enormous negative effect on the demand for retail space, while others think the negative effect will be minor. No one perceives a positive effect of the Internet on retail sales in traditional stores and upon retail space needs.

To start the discussion, let us go back in time. Once upon a time, retail sales took place in outdoor markets in town centers or at the intersection of major roads. Over time, retail activity went indoors in stores located in town centers or at the intersection of major roads. Initially, the stores were "general stores." From these "general stores," department stores and specialty stores developed. They were found in commercial districts in town centers or at the intersection of major roads. At this time, around 1880 or so, the first catalog sales opportunities arose in the form of the Sears and Roebuck and the Montgomery Ward catalogs. These catalogs were a "technological innovation" because they provided an alternative way to shop. The catalogs had a great effect in the geographic areas that were not adequately served by retail stores but did not have any major effect on the sales of the traditional retailing activity. As time passed, other shopping alternatives arose. In order of their appearance, we had mail order sales, telephone sales, and TV shopping. None of these has shown a dramatic effect on traditional retail, even though they account for relatively large sums of money. If these alternative shopping vehicles did not exist, or suddenly disappeared, retail sales in traditional retail outlets would increase, but the existence of these alternatives has never substantially reduced the need or desire for traditional retailing.

What about Internet retailing, the most recently formed retailing alternative? What impact will it have? Internet retailing is a high-tech version of each of the previous shopping alternatives. The Internet shows us pictures of the product like the catalog, the mail order brochure, and the TV shopping channel do. It provides information in printed form rather than in the telephone's oral form. Internet shopping is an innovation because it is a new way to market existing goods. But, Internet retailing is no different than these other alternatives. The shopper cannot physically inspect the product. This has always been an important aspect of shopping for "shopping goods," which are those goods for which the consumer desires a wide selection to choose from and the ability to make personal comparisons—touch, smell, squeeze, and see the fine details.

Thus, any effect of Internet retailing should be directed to those products that are standardized and well understood by the customer. In this sense, you can tell a book by its cover. This textbook will be the same whether you buy it at the bookstore or over the Internet at amazon.com, borders.com, or barnesandnoble.com. The same can be said for CDs, DVDs, movie videos, computers, and many other products. We should expect that more of these sales would take place over the Internet, and they have. But one mitigating circumstance is that the typical consumer does not see a substantial price reduction on the Internet, and he is sensitive to the high shipping and handling cost for the product but not so sensitive to the travel cost to the shopping center or the mall.

Many Internet customers will use the Internet to gather comparative information, print it out (no saving of trees here), and take the information to the traditional retail store to make the purchase. They get out of the house for a while. They save the shipping and handling costs. They can accomplish other things while they are out and about.

Internet shopping will affect all of its competition: traditional retail stores and the other alternative forms of retail shopping. Internet retailing will reduce sales in traditional stores, but it should have more of a dramatic effect than the introduction of any of the other alternative retailing opportunities. Internet retailing should also negatively effect catalog sales, mail order sales, and TV shopping sales.

Because we believe that the negative effect on sales volume in traditional retail stores will occur, the primary effect will appear as a reduction in the sales per square foot of the traditional stores. This will reduce their potential for paying rents, so rent increases in those stores most affected by Internet retailing competition will be slower to come and smaller in size. For those retail activities that are most susceptible to Internet retailing competition, the size of the typical store will shrink.

Consumer attitudes will help determine the impact of e-commerce and the Internet on traditional retail space. As a larger portion of the population becomes comfortable with the use of computer technology, the impact will increase. As more consumers desire convenience and are willing to pay for it, the impact of Internet retailing will grow. If consumer attitudes about the traditional shopping experience change from "it's a form of entertainment" to "it's a chore," the impact of Internet retailing will grow. All three of these trends are occurring and we think they will continue to expand in the future.

Currently, the biggest aspect of Internet sales is the purchasing activity of products between businesses. This should continue to grow because the consumer is an industrial buyer, and the product is standardized and well-known by the buyer.

CHANGES AFFECTING THE NATIONAL HOUSING MARKET

The national housing market will be affected by issues involving the changing nature of the demographics in the United States.

National Multifamily Housing Market

As we enter the first decade of the twenty-first century, the 21 to 34 age bracket will grow in number. This is the principal age-group that desires apartment living. So, we should see a period where the national figures for apartment vacancies decline and stabilize at low levels if the annual construction of new apartment units is not excessive—closer to 300,000 units per year than to 400,000 per year. Migration into this country will continue at approximately the current level of 1 million people per year. In the early years of their residence in this country, these immigrants increase the demand for apartments. Even when they have been here for five years, they have a relatively high rate of living in apartments, which is close to 75 percent. There will be a rapid growth of households entering the retirement years. In the past, a high percentage of retirees would sell their single-family residence and move to an apartment. This trend should continue, but it has been abated by the desire and ability of these households to stay in their existing home or to buy a replacement home instead of making the move to an apartment. The net effect of these demographic factors should be an improvement in the national multifamily housing market if the developers keep new construction in the range of the growth in apartment demand.

Low interest rates allow those renters who are able to accumulate savings to make down payments on single-family homes. The savings rate among this younger age-group has been declining over time, but their ability to raise funds from their parents for the down payment has been very good. Interest rates react both to fundamental economic factors in the economy and to shocks to the economy. In the near future, the fundamental economic factors affecting the inflation rate should be as they have been in the recent past. This leads to the conclusion that mortgage interest rates should average approximately 8 to 8.5 percent in the first decade of the twenty-first century. However, this conclusion rests on fiscal and monetary responsibility by the executive and legislative branches of our government. It rests on an energy market that is stable at its current level, requiring no oil embargoes and no wars in the oil-rich countries. It rests on a world at peace even if there are regional wars, such as those in the former Yugoslavia and in several of the nations on the African continent.

National Single-Family Housing Market

The national single-family housing market over the next 10 to 15 years should be affected by demographic changes. Over this time period, the large bulge of people and households currently in the 35 to 55 age-group will have purchased a house if they so desired. The next group moving into the prime house-buying age bracket will be smaller than it was in the past. This signals that new single-family housing construction will have to remain at levels lower than those of the 1990s.

CHANGES AFFECTING THE NATIONAL OFFICE MARKET

Total office space will continue to grow in the future, but the average annual addition of new space will be smaller than in the past. This will occur because firms using office space will continue to economize on this resource. Teleworking and office-sharing practices will continue to expand at a very modest level, reducing the demand for additional space.

The national office market has experienced cyclical levels of occupancy and will face such cycles in the future. However, the magnitude of the cycles in the future should not be as severe as in the past. The cycles arise because developers anticipate a need for additional square footage of office space and they act on this anticipated need. Unfortunately, the economics of development generate a need to provide the space in large blocks. Ten buildings of 10,000 square feet cost more to build than one 100,000-square-foot building. Also, what one developer anticipates is also anticipated by a second and often a third developer, who all act on their anticipations. So, an anticipated need for 150,000 square feet generates construction of 200,000 to 300,000 square feet of new space. The cycles in occupancy levels will not be as severe because the current crop of office developers are more sensitive to the fact that the others will act, and the new buildings will be on average phased in better than they were in the past. The negative impact on occupancy rates for a 400,000-square-foot building is less than that for an 800,000-square-foot building.

POSSIBLE FUTURE PATTERNS OF URBAN DEVELOPMENT

In the middle to late 1950s, the U.S. government embarked on the construction of the interstate highway system. The original purpose of this system of roads was to make automobile and truck transportation between major urban areas easier. As an additional benefit, rural communities along the interstate would benefit from the increased access to the metropolitan areas. In the past 40 years, the interstate system did accomplish these objectives. However, the more recent expansion of the interstate system within metropolitan areas has permitted a reliance on the automobile as the principal mode of commuter transportation within these metropolitan areas. With this reliance on automobiles have come urban sprawl as a development pattern and traffic congestion as commuters crowded the interstates to avoid surface streets with their lower speed limits and traffic lights.

As a consequence of this automobile-centered growth and development pattern, most major metropolitan areas suffer from traffic congestion and air pollution. Urban sprawl increases the costs of providing infrastructure such as streets and utilities, causing the need for greater property tax revenues to construct and maintain this automobile-oriented infrastructure.

Most metropolitan areas exhibit the development pattern described by a blend of the sector and the multinuclei patterns. In the future, we think that economic forces will operate to decrease the rate of urban sprawl into new, undeveloped geographic areas as well as decrease its dominance over currently developed geographic areas. This will happen as public attitudes are swayed by conservationists and environmentalists away from an auto-centered development pattern with its reliance on highways to a mass transit orientation. This modification in outlook will take many decades to have a substantial impact. Mass transit is only financially feasible if it serves a mass market of individuals. It must be able to move people from one area of high concentration to another such area and back again. Urban sprawl by its very nature does not create these concentrations. However, the high concentrations of employees in office, industrial, and retail nodes is the start of the process at one end of the line. What needs to be accomplished is the development of residential concentrations at the other end of the line. This could be done by high-density, infill developments in the form of attached single-family housing, such as high-rise condominium buildings or multifamily apartment projects. High-density single-family detached housing areas would also help as would the encouragement of voluntary car pooling to the mass transit nodes.

Government action can help foster these changes. What we see as private sector changes are the changes in public attitudes discussed above as well as an eventual increase in gasoline prices to levels reflecting existing prices in other countries of the world. We cannot permanently maintain gas prices in the $1.25 to $1.50 per gallon range when the rest of the world is paying twice as much. As our gas prices rise, commuters will be willing to abandon their solo drive to work and use some form of mass transit. Another factor that will work to encourage commuter use of mass transit will be the eventual high cost of land in the office, industrial, and retail nodes. As land prices move up from their current levels in these areas, it will be too expensive for the developer to create multiacre surface parking areas and to build multistory parking decks to support an office building. As land use becomes more intensive due to a relative increase in land prices, the developer will have to economize by minimizing the least productive or least profitable aspects of land use. Parking areas will fall into this category as land prices rise.

Will teleworking have an impact on urban sprawl? Teleworking and urban sprawl seem to be compatible. Teleworking allows the worker to stay at home in a geographic area of low-density development away from the current office node and use the computer and telecommunications links to the office. Teleworking is occurring and will continue to occur, but it will not replace all need for workers to congregate at a given location. There will always be a need as well as a desire for face-to-face contact. In our opinion, teleworking will allow a small portion of the white-collar workforce to eliminate 20 to 40 percent of their commute to work. When these people do go to the office, they should have a reasonable alternative to the automobile and single-occupant driving. This should help reduce the degree of traffic congestion and air pollution in metropolitan areas.

THE EFFECT OF GOVERNMENT POLICY ON REAL ESTATE DEVELOPMENT AND INVESTMENT

In the future, local and state governments will work to stimulate development more in the direction of infill projects for new construction and adaptive reuse for functionally obsolete structures. The governments can do this by providing some forms of financial subsidies to the developers to accomplish these objectives. Or, the local governments might use financial disincentives to slow the development of projects that lead to more urban sprawl. The zoning ordinance, the subdivision regulations, impact fees, and land dedication requirements will be the tools to generate the disincentives.

In the future, the solution to urban sprawl, traffic congestion, and pollution will require the cooperation and coordination of various government agencies and local municipalities. Piecemeal solutions have not worked in the past and will not work in the future. The endeavor to eliminate these evils rests on policies and procedures and does not include "politics" in its more insidious form. Will we be able to do this? *We* think it will happen, but as is usual for humans, it will not happen until the eleventh hour, when changes can no longer be put off.

Significant changes have occurred and will continue to occur. Some changes have taken a longer time to work their way through the economy, society, and the real estate industry. Some of these changes have been rapid; they have been revolutionary instead of evolutionary. It is interesting to try to chronicle these changes and these trends. It is more interesting to try to forecast them into the future. Only one thing is certain: we live in interesting times and continuing changes will make the future even more interesting.

Glossary

The following list of terms is not intended to be exhaustive, nor to include each "key term" already discussed and defined in the text. If the term is included in the text, a parenthetical number following the definition indicates the chapter in which the concept is discussed.

absorption analysis An examination of the changes in the economic and demographic factors on the demand side of the market to determine the length of time required for the vacant units in the market to be purchased or rented.

abstract A chronological history of previous transfers of ownership and claims of value that is reviewed by an attorney, who renders an opinion on the rights in the estate. (1)

abstractor The person compiling information from the public records for use as evidence of good title. (16)

accelerated depreciation method Mathematical expressions used to represent a situation in which the value declines in the early years of the useful life period are greater than the value declines in the latter years of the useful life period. (12)

acceleration Moving the maturity date in a loan to the current date as the first step toward foreclosure.

acceptance A statement made by the offeree to accept the offeror's offer without change. (14)

accrued depreciation The value decline in a building from physical deterioration, functional obsolescence, and external obsolescence. (5)

actual gross income The total income received by an income-earning property when each rentable space receives the contract rent specified in the lease that the landlord and the tenant signed.

adjusted basis The value of real property for income tax purposes, which is the cost of the property plus any capital improvements minus any depreciation deducted. (12)

affirmative marketing agreement An agreement between members of the local board of REALTORS® and the Department of Housing and Urban Development to support equal opportunity in housing. (13)

after-tax cash flow (ATCF) The numerical value of net operating income minus mortgage debt service and income taxes. (12)

air rights The legal claim to use of the air space above the land that typically does not include the rights to the site below. (1)

adjustable rate mortgage (ARM) A loan in which the interest rate and the monthly payment may be adjusted periodically through maturity. (9)

amortization Periodic repayments of debt. (8)

annual percentage rate (APR) The total finance charge on a loan, including the interest and all charges related to the financing, such as points. (9)

appraisal An estimate of the value of real property. (4)

appraisal process An orderly, logical, and concise step-by-step process for estimating the value of a parcel of real property. (1)

appraiser An individual who estimates the value of property. (1)

area analysis The use of general data about the nation, the region, and the local community to determine the factors that can affect the market value of the subject property.

area regulations The section of a zoning ordinance that specifies how a site can be used. It covers setback and side yard requirements. (2)

assessed value The value of the property estimated by the tax assessor for property tax purposes. (4)

assignment A document that transfers the rights of ownership to another party. In a lease, it transfers the rights of ownership held by the original tenant to a new tenant, who becomes responsible to the landlord for all of the provisions and obligations specified in the lease issued to the original owner; in a commercial loan, it transfers the right to collect income from the property from the mortgagor to the mortgagee in the event of default. (8)

assumption A sale wherein the buyer agrees to purchase the equity in the property and take over the debt payments. (8)

assumption statement A document given to the lender by the buyer stating that the buyer is assuming the liability for the remaining debt in an equity buy. (16)

attorney's opinion A legal opinion on the rights in the estate that is given from a chronological history of previous ownership and claims of value. (16)

balloon loan An amortized loan schedule whereby the last payment is larger than the preceding payments. (9)

band-of-investment technique A technique used by an appraiser to generate the overall capitalization rate.

bargain and sale deed A type of deed that conveys the property and contains no warranties. (16)

basic rate of interest An interest rate that reflects conditions in the money market. (6)

before-tax cash flow (BTCF) The funds remaining after debt service is subtracted from net operating income. (11)

bilateral contract A contract in which the two parties make a promise or an offer and simultaneously receive a promise or an offer from each other (14)

blanket mortgage One mortgage that covers several parcels of real estate. (8)

breach of contract The failure to perform the acts or promises stipulated in a contract. (14)

building code Building requirements enforced by the local government for the health and safety of the public. (2)

business or income risk The risk that future levels of actual gross income are less than their forecasted or anticipated levels. (11)

capital gain The gain derived by a property owner when the sales price is greater than the adjusted basis of the property. (12)

capital improvement expenditures Expenses incurred by the owner to improve the value of the property, increase its rent-earning potential, or lengthen its economic life. (6)

capital recovery rate A rate that reflects the loss in value of an improvement over its life and represents a rate of return of the investment. (6)

capitalization rate A rate used to generate the value estimate composed of two interest rates known as the basic rate of interest and the capital recovery rate. (6)

certificate of eligibility A document given by the Department of Veteran Affairs to the lender that certifies the veteran is eligible for the loan and gives the amount of the guaranty that can be applied to the loan. (9)

certificate of reasonable value A document given by the Department of Veteran Affairs to the lender that contains the selling price or the appraised value, whichever is lower.

certificate of title A document issued by an abstractor after reviewing the public records to determine the rights in the estate. (16)

client Typically, the party who pays the agent to solve a problem; normally, the client employs an agent to find a customer who will solve a problem. (13)

close on the buyer Any technique used to obtain an offer from the buyer.

commercial financing Funds used to purchase property that generates an income flow. (10)

commission split The sharing of a total commission between agents. (13)

community property Part of a situation, descending from Spanish rule, in which property owned by a couple is either separate or community. Community property refers to all assets received after the marriage excluding inheritance; each spouse is considered to have a separate and equal ownership in the real estate. (1)

comparable market analysis The process of estimating the value of the property using recently sold comparable properties. (5)

comparable property A parcel of real estate that is similar to the subject property in physical features, neighborhood location, terms of the sale, ownership rights, and time of sale. (5)

comparative method A method for estimating reproduction costs based on the use of published data on construction costs for standard residential units. (5)

condemnation The legal process of taking property through eminent domain. (2)

consideration The value exchanged for the title. (8)

construction code A police power designed to establish minimum acceptable standards for construction of improvements within the local jurisdiction (same as building code). (2)

constructive eviction An intentional and permanent action or default by the landlord that renders the property uninhabitable or unusable by the tenant. (15)

construction loan A loan for a short term to allow construction. (10)

contract for deed A purchase arrangement in which the present debt is assumed, the assumption statement and the new deed are placed in escrow, and the seller may carry some financing; the deed is passed when predetermined conditions (such as the final payment) are satisfied. (14)

contract rent The rental income generated as a result of the contractual commitments in the lease. (5)

conventional mortgage loan A mortgage without any government insurance or guarantee against default. (9)

conveyance A document that transfers the title, such as a deed. (16)

cost approach An appraisal technique in which cost data, vacant site value, and accrued depreciation are used to estimate the current market value of the property. (4)

cost recovery The new label created by the 1987 U.S. Congress to be placed on previous deductions called "depreciation." (12)

cost of capital The rate of return or the interest payment that must be paid in to borrow money. (11)

covenant of further assurance A clause within the warranty wherein the grantor states that he will take legal action to defend his ownership rights. (16)

covenant of quiet enjoyment The grantor's statement in a deed that no better title or lien exists that can be used later to interfere with the ownership and use of property by the new grantee. (16)

customer Typically, a member of the public who does not have a contractual relationship with the agent; normally, the client employs an agent to find a customer who will solve a problem. (13)

debt financing The use of assets belonging to other parties to purchase property. (10)

debt service Interest and amortization payments made by the owner of property to repay the mortgage loan. (6)

debt service coverage ratio Net operating income divided by debt service. (10)

deed A document that conveys the title and represents proof of ownership. (16)

deed of trust An instrument used in lieu of a mortgage in some states because it provides faster foreclosure. (8)

default by the buyer A situation in which the seller accepts the buyer's offer in the contract of sale and the buyer later does not fulfill the commitment to appear at closing with the required funds. (16)

default by the seller A situation in which the seller accepts the buyer's offer in a contract of sale and later does not fulfill the commitment to appear at closing with a new deed. (16)

default in prior payment clause A clause within the second mortgage that allows the second lender to correct a default on the first mortgage by making the payment, adding this amount to the indebtedness of the second loan, and then foreclosing on the first loan. (9)

default ratio Loan payments plus operating expenses divided by potential or effective gross income. (10)

delayed closing date A situation in which the buyer agrees to purchase the property and close at a future date and to rent the property until that date.

delinquency A situation in which the mortgagor, or debtor, has missed a number of payments.

demand The inverse relationship between price and quantity that represents the ability and willingness of consumers to purchase a commodity. (4)

demand for credit The total level of credit desired by all users at a given interest rate.

Department of Veteran Affairs (VA) A government agency that administers benefits to qualified veterans under the G.I. Bill of Rights. (9)

depreciation A tax deduction for income-producing properties. The new label created by the 1987 U. S. Congress is "cost recovery." (12)

depreciation recapture The process by which the Internal Revenue Code requires the equity investor to calculate excess depreciation claimed and to add this figure to personal income in the year of sale. (12)

design study A type of feasibility study that examines the impact on revenues and operating costs of different building characteristics, such as floor plans, height, and so on. (7)

direct prospecting Soliciting potential buyers by contacting specific individuals.

direct regulations Local government regulations that affect development in a direct manner (i.e., zoning, subdivision regulation, construction codes).

discharge of contract The complete performance of contractual terms by the parties to a contract. (14)

discount point One point equals one percent of the mortgage. This amount is paid typically at closing to receive a desired mortgage rate. Considered by the IRS to be prepaid interest. (8)

disposable income The amount of current (nominal) income remaining after federal, state, and local income taxes are paid.

dual agency A situation in which one agent has contracted with a seller and a buyer concurrently; typically, the contract with the seller authorizes the agent to sell, and the contract with the buyer authorizes the agent to buy. (13)

due on sale clause One part of the uniform covenants in a mortgage that allows the lender to call the loan due or adjust the interest rate on the remaining debt to the current rate. (8)

dull market A market in which changes in the economic and demographic factors produce a decline in price, a reduction in number of sales, or a combination of the two.

easement The right of one person to use the real estate of another for a specific purpose and under certain conditions. (2)

easement appurtenant An easement that exists where there are at least two parcels of real estate and one of these parcels (the dominant estate) receives benefits derived from the use of the other parcel of real estate (the servient estate). (2)

easement in gross An easement involving only one parcel of property where an individual other than the owner has the right to use that parcel for a specified purpose in a specified manner. (2)

economic base model A descriptive model of a local economy that identifies major economic sectors, the interrelationships among these sectors, and the nature of the sectors and interrelationships; typically the economy is divided into the sectors that produce for export (called the base sector) and the sector that consumes (called the nonbase sector).

economic life The number of years over which an income-earning property will generate a competitive level of net operating income. (6)

economic obsolescence A reduction in value caused by economic, physical, social, and governmental factors that are external to the subject property.

effective age The actual age of the property adjusted for observed accrued depreciation. (6)

effective gross income The income earned by the subject property after vacancy and collection losses are subtracted from potential gross income. (6)

Ellwood method A sophisticated version of a band-of-investment technique to create a capitalization rate.

eminent domain The right vested in the state government and given to local government, and at times even to private agencies, to acquire possession of private property for public purposes after paying the owner a just compensation. (2)

Equal Credit Opportunity Act A federal act that prohibits the lender from denying credit on the basis of covered classes, such as gender, race, religion, country of national origin, marital status, and age. (9)

equity Personal assets of the buyer used to purchase the property, which are defined as the current market value of the property less the unpaid mortgage. (11)

equity buy The outstanding balance on a loan is assumed by assuming the debt and paying the owner the equity in the property.

equity dividend rate Periodic cash flow (before-tax cash flow) in year one divided by the down payment; sometimes called the equity capitalization rate.

equity funds Personal assets that are used to purchase property. (1)

equitable right of redemption The right of the mortgagor to stop foreclosure prior to the sale of the property by paying all late payments and costs. (8)

equity yield rate The discount rate that equates the present value of annual before-tax cash flows over the holding period plus the present value of any projected before-tax capital gain to the initial equity. (11)

escalated lease A lease in which the rent repayment is established as a fixed or flat amount plus a predetermined yearly change based on some specific price index or component of the property's operating expenses (same as indexed lease). (10)

escheat The right of a state government to claim ownership of land if its current owner dies without leaving a will and if legal heirs cannot be found. (2)

escrow account A fund kept by the lender that includes monthly payments by the mortgagor for property taxes and property insurance premium; escrow funds are accepted by the real estate agent with the offer and held until the loan closing. (16)

estate for years A leasehold that continues for a definite period of time, such as one year. (1)

estate from year to year A leasehold that comes into effect after an estate for years expires and the landlord agrees to the tenant's continued possession of the property. (1)

estate pur autre vie A freehold estate not-of-inheritance that lasts for the lifetime of a third party. (1)

estoppel certificate A document prepared and signed by the mortgagor-debtor that states the precise amount of the remaining debt owed and any outstanding claims on the property. (8)

eviction A term commonly used as a synonym for dispossession proceedings. (15)

evidence of good title Proof that the seller possesses those rights requested by the buyer. (16)

excess rent The excess of contract rent minus market rent. (15)

exchange A trade between sellers where "likes" are exchanged for "likes."

exclusive agency listing contract A contractual relationship between the agent and the client whereby no other real estate agency can be used by the owner, but no commission is paid if the owner sells the property. (13)

exclusive right-to-sell listing contract An employment contract between the principal and the agent in which the agent is paid a commission regardless of who sells the property. (13)

executed contract A contract in which all parties have signed and conveyed their intention of completing their agreements.

export base theory An economic theory that links the growth of a local economy to its ability to sell exports to nonlocal buyers. (3)

express contract A written or oral contract in which there is an explicit agreement between the two individuals. (14)

farm A term used by real estate agents to describe a range of property prices, particular location of properties, or a particular location of people from which listings frequently are obtained.

Farmers Home Administration (FmHA) The old name of an agency under the U.S. Department of Agriculture that sells default insurance to a lender or loans directly to the borrower.

feasibility study A technique used to examine all of the pertinent facts affecting an equity investment in order to decide whether the proposed investment enables the investor to accomplish or achieve investment objectives. (7)

Federal Home Loan Mortgage Corporation (FHLMC or Freddie Mac) An institution that participates in the secondary mortgage market. (9)

Federal Housing Administration (FHA) A quasi-public agency that sells default insurance.

Federal Land Bank An institution created as part of the Farm Credit System to provide credit for the highly specialized needs of farmers and their marketing, supply, and business service operations.

Federal National Mortgage Association (FNMA or Fannie Mae) An association that is publicly controlled and privately owned that participates in the secondary mortgage market. (9)

fee simple estate Full rights of ownership, which may be limited by known conditions. (1)

fiduciary relationship The agent's responsibility to be loyal to, and to act in, the best interests of the principal. (13)

financial ratio Calculations that illustrate levels of performance that collectively indicate success or failure.

financial risk The risk that future levels of net operating income (generated by the property) will not be sufficient to allow the owner to repay the mortgage loan. (11)

financial study A type of feasibility study that investigates whether the rate of return on a project is large enough to attract capital to the project or to meet an investor's needs. (7)

fixed-rate mortgage loan A loan for which the interest rate is fixed over the life of the loan. (8)

fixture An item of personal property that is legally considered to be real estate because it is attached either to the land or to an improvement that is itself permanently attached to the land. (1)

foreclosure A legal process by which the mortgagor is evicted, the deed is recovered, and the property is sold to pay the loan. (8)

fraud A misrepresentation of a material fact, made either with knowledge of its falsity (intentional) or in reckless ignorance of the truth (unintentional), that results in injury to the party who relies on the fact. (13)

freehold estate The rights of ownership in real estate that last for the duration of a lifetime. (1)

freehold estate of inheritance A freehold estate in which the owner has the right to dispose of the property in addition to the rights of use, possession, and exclusion. (1)

freehold estate not of inheritance A freehold estate in which the current owner cannot dispose of the property through a sale or gift but can lease the property to a third party. The owner of this estate has only the rights of use, possession, and exclusion. (1)

functional obsolescence A reduction in value caused either by inherent defects in the design of the structure or by the structure's inability to satisfy current consumer needs. (5)

futures market The buying and selling of future contracts.

general agent A licensed firm or individual who is authorized by a client to accomplish a given objective for compensation; the agent has the right to make decisions about the best methods to employ in accomplishing the objective. (1)

general contractor An individual who enters into a contract with a client to build a structure by supervising all of the individual suppliers of products and services. (1)

general data Economic, physical, social, and governmental factors in the local economy, its region, and the national economy.

general lien A lien that affects the asset holdings or the wealth of an individual without specific reference to certain pieces of property. (2)

general partnership A business owned by any number of partners that does not have the same tax treatment as a limited partnership. (10)

good faith estimate of closing costs A document prepared by the lender and required under RESPA, stating estimates of the range of all closing costs. (9)

Government National Mortgage Association (GNMA or Ginnie Mae) A department within the Department of Housing and Urban Development that participates in the secondary mortgage market. (9)

government rectangular survey system A legal description based on lines of latitude (baselines) and lines of longitude (principal meridians), as well as distances and directions away from these baselines and meridians, used to specify the dimensions of a parcel of land. (2)

graduated payment lease A lease in which the rent payment level increases in a predetermined manner as time passes. (10)

graduated payment mortgage (GPM) A loan for which the initial monthly payments are lower than those required for a conventional loan and that increase annually at a constant percentage over the first few years of the loan. (9)

grant deed A deed that contains no stated warranties from the grantor but, as typically required by state laws, implies a warranty that no encumbrances have been placed on the property during the grantor's ownership and that the property has not already been conveyed. (16)

granting clause (words of conveyance) A phraseology within the deed whereby the owner expresses his/her current intent to pass the title. (16)

grantor The owner who is transferring title. (16)

gross income multiplier (GIM) technique A technique that can be used to convert either monthly or annual gross income into an estimate of current market value for an income producing property; it is the purchase price divided by the annual gross income. (6)

gross lease A lease agreement in which the rent payment is established as a fixed or flat payment. (10)

ground lease A lease agreement for the site only in which the rent payment is established as a fixed or flat payment. (10)

habendum clause A clause in the deed that explains the extent of the rights transferred and contains the warranty. (16)

hedge A position taken in the futures market that will exactly offset a decision in the current market to protect interest earnings on a loan.

height regulations Section of the zoning ordinance specifying maximum building height. (2)

highest and best use The legally permissible use of real estate that yields the highest return to the owner over a reasonable period of time. (4)

holdback (retainage) An amount of the permanent loan that is withheld by the permanent lender to cover the risk of early default by the borrower. (10)

holding period The length of time that the investor retains ownership of the real estate equity investment.

housing code A police power designed to establish socially acceptable minimum standards for safety and health in both existing and newly constructed buildings (same as occupancy code). (2)

improvements Man-made additions or changes that make the land usable for some economic purpose. (1)

improvements-on-the-land Permanently erected man-made structures that are placed on the land. (1)

improvements-to-the-land Man-made additions or changes to the shape, slope, or substance of the land. (1)

income approach An appraisal technique in which the potential revenue and the operating expenses of the subject property and an appropriate capitalization rate are used to estimate current market value; it is based on the principle of anticipation. (4)

income tax depreciation techniques Mathematical techniques established to represent value decline of a physical asset for income tax purposes.

independent contractor An agent who works for a firm wherein no one can control his/her actions.

indexed lease A lease in which the rent repayment is established as a fixed or flat amount plus a predetermined yearly change based on some specified price index or component of the property's operating expenses (same as escalated lease). (10)

indirect prospecting The act of soliciting potential buyers by advertising the property in anticipation that interested parties will identify themselves.

interest or money market risk The risk that the future value of the investment will be less than forecasted because the capitalization rate in the future will be higher than it was at the time of the initial appraisal and investment decision. (11)

intermediate theory A concept applied in some states whereby the mortgage is interpreted as being under title or lien theory and the courts have interpreted the opposite. (8)

intermediation An inflow of deposits caused by deposit rates that are competitive with rates paid on competing investments.

internal rate of return (IRR) A rate of return that makes the initial cost equal to the present value of a stream of future benefits or cash flows. (8)

investment The purchase of an income-earning asset. (11)

joint ownership Ownership of property as joint tenants, tenants in common, and tenancy by the entirety. (10)

joint tenancy A form of co-ownership in which each joint owner has an equal and undivided interest in the real property, and upon the death of one joint owner the rights of ownership pass to the surviving joint owners. (1)

junior lien A claim to the value of the property that is second in priority in the event of buyer default; the junior lien is subordinated to other liens.

land The surface of the earth plus mineral rights and air rights. (1)

land-to-building ratio Square footage of the site divided by gross building area. (10)

land contract A transaction whereby the seller extends credit to the purchaser for part of the selling price; typically, the buyer receives possession and its benefits but does not receive the deed until the last payment is made. (14)

leasehold A synonym for less-than-freehold estate. (1)

legal description Legally accepted method for stating the physical dimensions of a parcel of land. (2)

less-than-freehold estate The rights of ownership in real estate that are possessed for less than a lifetime. (1)

leverage The use of borrowed money to purchase an asset (whose rate of return should be greater than the interest rate on the borrowed funds). (10)

lien The right of a creditor to petition to the courts to force the sale of a debtor's property in order to obtain payment. (2)

lien theory A concept applied in some states whereby the mortgage is viewed as leaving the deed and possession with the mortgagor while giving the mortgagee a lien on the property. (8)

lien waiver A statement signed by laborers and suppliers of materials that no bills owed by the owner are unpaid.

life estate A freehold estate not-of-inheritance that lasts for the duration of the current owner's lifetime. (1)

limited partnership A pooling of investment funds characterized by a general partner and one or more limited partners that is given special tax treatment. (10)

liquidated damages A sum of money, mutually determined at the time of the making of the contract by the parties to the contract, that will be paid to the injured party in case of nonperformance or breach of contract. (14)

liquidity The ability to convert an asset into cash within a relatively short time without a loss of value in the transaction. (11)

listing A term used to describe the contractual relationship between the agent and the principal. (13)

listing agent The firm representing the principal. (13)

loan per square foot Mortgage loan divided by gross leasable area.

loan-to-value (LTV) ratio Mortgage loan divided by property value. (8)

local board The community association of REALTORS® and REALTOR®-ASSOCIATES that is part of the State Association and the National Association of REALTORS®. (1)

location study A type of feasibility study that identifies sites that will satisfy the needs of a project or use. (7)

lot and block system A legal description based on the use of maps and showing the dimensions of a site and its relationship to adjoining sites. (2)

management by objectives Establishing definite goals and developing a day-to-day plan to accomplish those goals.

market The economic environment in which property is exchanged. (4)

marketability analysis Examination of the economic, legal, and physical factors that affect a specific property. (7)

market analysis Examination of the market for a specific type of real estate. It examines demand and supply factors that affect the disaggregated real estate. (7)

market data approach An appraisal technique in which the sales prices of comparable properties that have been sold in the very recent past are used to estimate the market value of the subject property; it relies on the principle of substitution. (5)

market disaggregation The process of subdividing real estate into standardized groupings based on physical characteristics and locational attributes. (7)

market price The price of the product established in the market by the interaction of demand and supply.

market rent The rental income that a unit of space would most probably command in the open market as indicated by the current rents being negotiated for comparable space. (5)

market segmentation The process of subdividing consumers into homogeneous groupings based on their demographic, economic, or psychographic characteristics (tastes, preferences, habits, and so forth). (7)

market value The market price established in a market that is characterized by several necessary conditions, such as rational, well-informed, and typically motivated buyers and sellers; reasonable time of exposure of the product on the market; normal circumstances surrounding financing of the purchase; and freedom from undue bargaining power by one of the parties in the transaction. (6)

material fact A piece of information or evidence that a reasonable person would consider important when determining a course of action or reaching a decision. (14)

mechanic's lien A state right given to laborers and suppliers of materials to attach a claim upon the value of property for the nonpayment of labor or supplies. (2)

merchantable or marketable title A title that a court of law would require the buyer to accept; one that is free from clouds or defects. (16)

metes and bounds system A legal description whereby distances, directions, and angles of change in direction are used to specify the dimensions of a parcel of land. (2)

mineral rights The legal claim to the minerals below the surface of the land. (1)

misrepresentation An incorrect or improper statement about a fact. (13)

mistake of fact A mistake that occurs when a certain piece of information or certain conditions are not true. (14)

mistake of law A mistake that arises when a person who has full knowledge of the facts makes an erroneous conclusion about the legal effect of those facts. (14)

modified accelerated cost recovery system (MACRS) The system initiated by the IRS that identifies the years during which different kinds of property (real and personal) can be depreciated. (12)

mortgage The security instrument for the debt where the property is pledged as collateral. (8)

mortgage-backed bonds Bonds that are issued by a lender and backed by a pool of residential mortgages; the lender guarantees the principal and interest payment.

mortgage-backed security (MBS) A security that is issued by a lender and backed by a pool of residential mortgages. (9)

mortgage banker A lender who attempts to find borrowers for money obtained from the secondary mortgage market or private investors. (9)

mortgage constant Annual debt service divided by the initial loan balance; one of the six functions of $1 that will amortize the loan to zero by maturity and pay interest on the declining balance.

mortgagee The giver of the debt, the party receiving the payments, the lender. (8)

mortgagor The maker of the debt, the debtor, the party expected to pay. (8)

most probable selling price The market price established under somewhat less rigid requirements than market value. Buyers and sellers need not be com-

pletely informed; their abilities to obtain financing and the time period for exposure of the property in the market need only approximate normal circumstances.

multiple listing service (MLS) An organization of local real estate firms that agree to share listings to give the property maximum exposure. (13)

National Association of REALTORS® A national trade association that provides education, supports a code of ethics, and represents the members' interest politically. (1)

neighborhood A portion of a larger community characterized by homogeneity, or at least a complementary group of inhabitants, buildings, and land uses. (4)

neighborhood analysis The use of general data about the immediate surroundings of the subject property to determine the factors that can affect the market value of subject property. (4)

net lease A lease in which the payment is established as a fixed or flat amount plus one or more of the operating expenses associated with the property. (10)

net listing contract A contractual agreement between the client and the agent whereby the client specifies a minimum price for the property and the agent keeps as the commission any amount obtained over the minimum. (13)

net operating income (NOI) Effective gross income minus operating expenses. (6)

nonconforming use A use of land that existed before the existing zoning ordinance was imposed, which does not conform to the existing, permissible use of land. (2)

obsolescence A decrease in the value of the property caused by physical deterioration, functional design, and external factors to the site.

occupancy code A police power designed to establish socially acceptable standards for safety and health in both existing and newly constructed buildings (same as housing code). (2)

offer A conditional promise made by the offeror to the offeree, typically by the buyer to the seller. (14)

open end mortgage A mortgage that covers a commitment by the lender to advance additional funds in the future; the advances can be automatic or reevaluated upon each request. (8)

open listing contract A contractual relationship enabling the owner to use as many agents as she desires; and a commission is paid to the agent who presents the first acceptable offer to the owner. (13)

operating cost study A type of feasibility study that examines whether operating costs can be reduced. (7)

operating expense ratio Total operating expenses divided by effective gross income. (6)

operating expenses The total of all expenses incurred by the landlord and directly associated with providing the services and space that generate the rent revenue. (6)

option A legal instrument that allows a potential buyer to control a piece of property while a contingency (zoning change, financing, and so forth) is being investigated and removed. The right to control is purchased. (14)

origination Taking the application of a potential borrower.

overage rent Rent based on a minimum payment plus a percentage of sales. (15)

overall cap rate Net operating income divided by the sale price or market value. (10)

ownership costs The expenses that must be incurred by the owner of property to generate the benefits from the property and to maintain the property in the condition required to perpetuate the benefits.

package mortgage One debt that covers both real and personal property on a particular parcel. (8)

partial amortization Periodic repayment of the debt that does not reduce the debt to zero by the maturity date.

participation loan The lender claims a portion either of the equity in the property or of the future income in addition to an interest rate.

pass through certificates A certificate that is issued by a lender and backed by a pool of residential mortgages where the lender serves as a conduit and transmits principal and interest payments from the underlying loans to the investors.

payment in advance A liability on the real property that is paid the same year as the date of assessment and billing, such as special property taxes. (16)

payment in arrears A liability on the real property that is paid the year following the date of assessment and billing, such as real property taxes. (16)

percentage lease A lease in which the rent payment is established as a percentage of the commercial tenant's gross sales. (10)

periodic cash flow The funds that are derived from an investment and received on some date; periodic basis. (11)

permanent loan The long-term, first mortgage secured by the property. (10)

physical deterioration Structural disintegration or the wear-and-tear inherent in a structure. (5)

piggyback loan (split loan, joint loan) A financing arrangement between lenders to jointly advance the borrower a high percentage of the selling price.

plat map system A legal description based on the use of maps showing the dimensions of a site and its relationship to adjoining sites. (2)

points One point is an amount equal to 1 percent of the mortgage balance. Points are charged by the lender to increase the return on the mortgage and paid by the buyer to receive a desired mortgage rate. Points typically are paid at the closing. Considered by the IRS to be prepaid interest. (8)

police powers The powers granted to federal and state governments in their constitutions to protect the public by regulating factors that can affect the health, morals, safety, and general welfare of the community. (2)

potential gross income The total income generated by an income-producing property based on the assumption that the property receives market rent. (6)

present value technique A method used to discount to the present value a stream of benefits or cash flows that will be received in the future. (11)

price appreciation An increase in the sales price of real property. (11)

primary mortgage market The marketplace among the potential borrowers and the lenders who accept the mortgage applications. (9)

principal The client of the agent, the party that the agent represents. (13)

principal risk The risk that the future sales price of the property will be less than anticipated. (11)

priority of liens The order in which liens are honored in the case of actual sale; liens that are recorded first are given first priority. (2)

procuring cause Successful effort by an agent that leads to the buyer's purchase of a property. Proof of the agent's involvement is required if the agent is to collect a commission. (13)

promissory note A personal IOU or bond to repay. (8)

property manager An individual who specializes in the full-time administration of property for a fee. (1)

proprietary power A government's power to accept or refuse development action and plans under subdivision regulations and possible government problems and regulations.

prorating The process of dividing income and debits between the owner and the buyer. (16)

purchase money mortgage A mortgage commitment offered by the buyer to the seller in the purchase price whereby the seller extends credit for a portion of the total purchase price.

purchasing power risk The risk that the money an investor receives in the future will have less purchasing power than anticipated. (11)

pyramiding The practice of utilizing one property to obtain funds, or to collateralize the purchase of a second property. (11)

qualifying the buyer Part of the counseling process whereby the agent attempts to determine the buyer's financial assets to ensure that the property in question can be purchased using financing available to the buyer.

quantity survey method A method used to calculate reproduction costs based on establishing an inventory of all materials and labor required to reproduce the subject property. (5)

quitclaim deed A deed that contains no warranties. (16)

ratio technique A population updating technique that uses a known, current value for a large region to derive an unknown, current value for a subarea of that region. (3)

real estate A physical entity that consists of land and the man-made improvements permanently attached to it. (1)

real estate agent An individual licensed by the state to represent a client in a real estate transaction for compensation. Also, a firm that may be represented by licensed salespeople. (1)

real estate business All individuals and organizations receiving compensation for providing services. (1)

real estate commission The brokerage fee paid to the real estate agent. Also, a state board authorized to enforce the state license law by granting, revoking, and suspending licenses and by enacting rules and regulations that govern the conduct of the business; in some states, a commissioner serves in lieu of a commission. (1)

real estate counselor Any individual who offers advice about real estate for a fee. (1)

real estate developer Any person or firm that transforms property from one stage of use to another. (1)

real estate equity investment The use of accumulated savings to purchase income-earning real property.

real estate investment trust (REIT) A trust or association that has invested primarily in real estate and has applied for special tax treatment. (10)

real estate lender An individual or institution that loans funds for the purchase of real estate. (1)

Real Estate Settlement Procedures Act (RESPA) A federal act designed to protect the buyer from harmful loan practices, to provide relevant cost information prior to the closing, and to gather information statistics on closing costs and procedures. (9)

real income The income of the household measured in terms of the goods and services that the actual or nominal income can purchase.

real property The land, the improvements, and the rights of ownership. (1)

real property taxes Annual tax bill paid by the property owner for the general public services that benefit all land parcels in the taxing district, such as police protection, sanitary services, water, and fire protection.

REALTOR® A principal, partner, or officer who is actively engaged in the real estate business and a member of the local real estate board, State Association, and National Association of REALTORS®. (1)

REALTOR®-ASSOCIATE A salesperson, independent contractor, or certain affiliate members who are affiliated with a member firm of which the principal, partner, or officer is a REALTOR®. (1)

refinancing The act of replacing the current first mortgage by a new first mortgage. (8)

remaining economic life Economic life minus effective age. (6)

rent with option to buy A situation in which the renter agrees to rent the property for a specified period of time with the right to purchase the property at a predetermined date.

replacement cost The current cost incurred to construct a substitute property that is not necessarily similar to the subject property but provides the owner with the same level of benefits and satisfaction. (5)

reproduction cost The current cost that would be incurred to construct an exact replica or a perfect substitute for the subject property. (5)

restrictive covenant A statement placed in the deed by the seller that limits the buyer's use of the property. (2)

reversion The projected value of the property at the end of the holding period.

rights of ownership The rights to use, to possess, to exclude other people from, and to dispose of real estate. (1)

role playing Simulating an actual situation in which the agent is asked to respond as if on the job to enable outsiders to view the technique and provide constructive criticism.

sale and leaseback agreement A lease agreement in which the current owner offers to sell the property to a prospective buyer under the condition that a lease is executed at the time of sale giving the current owner the leasehold estate after the freehold estate is sold. (10)

salvage value The value of the improvement on the property at the end of the useful life. (12)

sandwich lease The lease signed by the second investor in a situation wherein an owner becomes a lessee by selling the new lease to a second investor, subleases from that person, and continues to operate the property.

savings and loan association A private company that accepts savings deposits and loans them in real estate mortgages. (9)

secondary mortgage market A group of quasi-public, public, and private institutions that buy mortgages from originators and that also buy and sell among themselves. (9)

second mortgage A debt on real property that has a claim to the value of the property that is second in priority to the first mortgage. (8)

security deposit Funds paid by the tenant to the landlord at the time the lease is executed as security against undue wear and tear or damage to the property. (15)

seller financing A process whereby the seller becomes a lender for all, or a portion, of the sales price. (8)

sensitivity analysis A technique used to determine the impact of changes in revenues, operating, financing, and tax expenses and other factors (such as holding period, etc.) on the present value or on the internal rate of return. (11)

settlement agent The person responsible for the closing and the preparation of the settlement (closing) statements. (16)

settlement statement A listing of income, expenses, and prorated amounts (if applicable) prepared typically by the settlement agent to account for all monies in the transaction; separate statements are prepared for the seller, the buyer, and the agent. (16)

sheriff's deed A type of deed given to the new owner after a sale of property to recover past-due taxes; it contains no warranty. (16)

sinking fund The amount per period that will grow to $1 at a given rate in a given period of time.

site development standards Sections of a zoning ordinance that affect the manner in which a site can be developed by setting minimum standards for square footage of the lot, setback, frontage and width, and maximum standards for height or the structure and land coverage. (See also area regulations and height regulations.)

special agency with the buyer A contractual relationship between the firm and the principal (the buyer) whereby the agent is given instructions to accomplish a certain task, such as locating and purchasing a special type of property. (13)

special agency with the seller A contractual relationship between the firm and the principal (the seller) whereby the agent is given authority to "find a buyer who is ready, willing, and able to purchase the property." (13)

special agent A licensed firm or individual authorized by a client to accomplish a given objective for compensation; typically, the special agent's right to make decisions about methods to accomplish the objective is limited. Listing contracts are typically viewed as special agency contracts. (1)

special assessments A separate tax bill paid by the owner of real property for special improvements that the neighborhood has requested from the taxing government, such as curbs and gutters, paving, and irrigation controls. (2)

special warranty deed A deed containing a warranty that covers only the grantor's period of ownership. (16)

specific data Physical and legal factors that characterize the site, the improvements, and the rights of ownership inherent in a particular piece of real property.

specific performance A legal remedy for breach of contract whereby the courts grant the injured party a court order requiring that the defaulting party perform the contract according to the specific terms of the contract entered into by the parties. (13)

spending power Use of a government's spending to affect development. Examples are land purchases for roads, schools, parks, and utilities.

stabilized vacancy ratio A percentage of gross income. (10)

standby permanent financing A commitment for a first mortgage that allows a developer to seek construction financing to initiate construction.

stock of housing The number of housing units of a certain type in existence at a given point in time.

straight-line depreciation A mathematical relationship stating that the value of property declines by an equal percentage in each year of its useful life. (12)

subchapter S corporation A corporation that may qualify for some of the same tax benefits as a limited partnership. (10)

subject property The property that is being considered or the property being appraised. (5)

subletting The process by which the original tenant enters into a separate and distinct lease with a new tenant to transfer a portion, but not all, of the original tenant's rights in the leased property. (15)

subordinated ground lease An owner sells the land to a third party on the condition that the owner's claim to ownership will be second in priority to any financing offered by a future lender.

subordination clause A clause within the second mortgage that places the second lender in second priority to the first lender. (8)

supply The direct relationship between price and quantity that represents the sellers' or producers' ability and willingness to produce and offer for sale units of commodity during a given period of time. (4)

supply of credit The total level of credit provided at a particular interest rate.

survey of the competition A component of a marketability study that investigates the competition faced by the subject property. (7)

syndicate A pooling of investors and their investment funds with a real estate professional to purchase property.

takeout commitment A promise by the permanent lender to pay off the construction (interim) lender when the construction is complete. (10)

taxable income The numerical value of net operating income minus mortgage interest payments and depreciation charges. (12)

tax bill The amount owed on the property for real property taxes.

tax deferral techniques Procedures whereby the Internal Revenue Code allows the investor to defer the payment of capital gains and depreciation recapture until some point in the future.

taxing power Use of a government's ability to collect taxes in order to affect development; examples are the modified accelerated cost recovery system (MACRS), investment credits by the federal government, and property tax exemptions, differential tax rates, and assessments by a local government.

tax shelter A means by which some portion of an individual investor's gross income can be protected from tax liability under the Internal Revenue Code. (11)

tenancy at will A leasehold for which the duration is not definitely specified; the duration continues as long as both the landlord and the tenant agree to its continuation. (1)

tenancy by sufferance A leasehold that comes into existence when a tenant's rights under one of the other leaseholds expires and the tenant retains possession against the landlord's wishes. (1)

tenancy by the entirety A type of ownership for married couples by which they own property as a sole owner if married at the time of accepting a deed. (1)

tenancy in common A form of co-ownership in which each owner owns a separate and identifiable interest in the property. (1)

term amortization A type of loan repayment where the debt is repaid in one final payment at maturity.

termite bond An insurance policy against future termite damage issued to the property owner after an inspection of the premises by a reputable pest control company, elimination of any infestation, and application of permanent chemicals around the foundation.

termite inspection An inspection of the premises by a reputable pest control company and a verbal statement concerning infestation and damage.

termite inspection receipt A document from a reputable pest control company stating that the property has no infestation and is free of damage.

title The proof of ownership; a deed is used to transfer the title. (16)

title company A private company that prepares real estate title abstracts and usually sells title insurance. (1)

title insurance Protection sold by an insurance company to cover any loss from undiscovered title defects within the records. (16)

title search An investigation of the history of the ownership of the property in the public records.

title theory A concept applied in some states whereby the mortgage is viewed as leaving the deed with the mortgagee and leaving possession with the mortgagor. (8)

Torrens certificate A certificate of title issued by a public official who reviews the deed and other appropriate documents to determine proper ownership; part of a system of land registration. (16)

trustee The escrow agent for a deed of trust.

Truth-in-Lending Act (Consumer Protection Act, Regulation Z) A federal law that requires the lender to disclose the finance charge and the annual percentage rate to the borrower in order that the cost of credit is known by the borrower in advance. (9)

underwriting The act of making a decision to approve or disapprove the loan based on credit scoring factors learned on the loan application.

unenforceable contract A valid contract that is not recognized by the courts in the event that any legal action is brought before the court to enforce it. (14)

unilateral contract A contract in which one person makes a promise or extends an offer and the other person receives the benefit of that promise or offer contingent upon the performance of some act. (14)

unit-in-place method A method for calculating reproduction cost based on the cost of assembling major components of the subject property. (5)

useful life The time period over which real property may be useful to the investor in the operation of a business or the production of income. (6)

use regulation Section of a zoning ordinance that specifies the extent to which land can be put to good use (also known as land use regulation).

vacancy analysis An examination of the number of vacant housing units in the market at the prevailing price in the market; consideration is given to the economic and demographic factors on both the demand and the supply sides of the market.

VA-guaranteed loan A loan obtained through a local lender that carries a Department of Veteran Affairs (VA) commitment to guarantee a predetermined amount of the loan in the event of default. (9)

valid contract A contract that fulfills all the legal requirements imposed by the body of law known as contract law. (14)

value-in-exchange The ability of one product to be exchanged for other products or commodities. (4)

value-in-use The satisfaction derived by the owner from use or consumption of a product or real estate. (4)

verification of deposit A form that the lender may ask the loan applicant to complete to allow the lender to verify the source of the necessary funds for the down payment.

verification of employment A form that the lender may ask the loan applicant to complete to identify the employer, the type of work, and the length of service.

voidable contract A contract in which one party can exercise the right to avoid, or to rescind, the contractual obligations incurred. (14)

void agreement An agreement that does not fulfill the legal requirements imposed by contract law; a contract that is not valid. (14)

warranty In general terms, the grantor's (owner's) statement that he or she will take legal action to defend his or her claims to the ownership during his or her period of ownership and possibly earlier or later periods. (16)

wraparound mortgage A situation in which a lender loans funds to a buyer who uses the money to purchase property by assuming an existing mortgage; the new lender writes the wraparound mortgage for the total of the assumption plus the amount loaned and charges the interest rate on this amount.

zoning ordinance A local ordinance whereby the local jurisdiction regulates the use of individual parcels of property. (2)

Index